PRAISE FOR *FIRE IN THE SKY*...

"This massive work is a notable achievement in the fields of WW II and aviation history."

—*Kradeg Book Review*

"Bergerud explores the battles and tactics involved and recreates vividly the fabric and texture of the struggle for air superiority over the South Pacific."

—*Kettering Oakwood Times*

"*Fire in the Sky* is possibly the very best analysis of a major air campaign ever placed in print. Bergerud's consummate writing style is very entertaining, his skillful use of personal anecdote combined with the detachment of a historian, blend into compelling reading and a truly enjoyable experience. . . . Destined to be the definitive history of the air war in the South Pacific, no serious student of World War Two or aviation can afford not to have this book in their personal library."

—**C. C. Jordan**
Planes and Pilots of World War II Internet Magazine

"Eric Bergerud's ability to balance narrative, anecdote, and analysis while maintaining his objectivity sets him apart from his contemporaries. *Fire in the Sky* is a true pleasure to read."

—**Jake Stub**
fighter pilot, VMF 121 and 115

FIRE
IN THE SKY

The Air War in the South Pacific

ERIC M. BERGERUD

Westview
PRESS
A Member of the Perseus Books Group

Copyright © 2000 by Westview Press, A Member of the Perseus Books Group

Published in 2001 in the United States of America by Westview Press, 5500 Central Avenue, Boulder, Colorado 80301–2877, and in the United Kingdom by Westview Press, 12 Hid's Copse Road, Cumnor Hill, Oxford OX2 9JJ

Find us on the World Wide Web at www.westviewpress.com

A CIP catalog record for this book is available from the Library of Congress.

ISBN 0-8133-3869-7 (pb)

Designed by Jeff Williams

The paper used in this publication meets the requirements of the American National Standard for Permanence of Paper for Printed Library Materials Z39.48–1984.

10   9   8   7   6   5   4

To

Lieutenant Earl Sanford Bergerud,
Southwest theater of operations; Luzon;
1943–1946

June Patricia Bergerud,
Tower, Kansas City Municipal Airport;
Fairfax Field, Kansas City, Missouri,
1943–1945

CONTENTS

MAPS

IMPORTANT MILITARY TERMS, ACRONYMS, AND PLACE-NAMES

For purposes of clarity I'd like to establish how I make reference to Japanese and Allied forces. Using official titles at first instance is standard, but it can become cumbersome thereafter. Thus for subsequent references in the text I will use acronyms as well as shorthand references (e.g., the "imperial navy," the "U.S. Army," etc.). Any generic reference (e.g., to "the navy" or "the army") will be clear from the context in which it appears.

ANGAU Australian New Guinea Administrative Unit. ANGAU was a wartime institution run by the Australian military and was responsible for organizing the native inhabitants of New Guinea in support of the war effort.

Anzac Originating in World War I, this acronym stood for Australian and New Zealand Army corps. During the period of this work, Australia and New Zealand did not have a unified command structure. I have used the phrase to refer to matters faced and weapons used by both nations, America's major allies in the South Pacific.

Bofors A 40mm automatic cannon most often employed for antiaircraft use. Originally a Swedish design, Bofors variations were found in most forces during World War II and continue in use today.

ComAirSopac Commander, Air, South Pacific. This was the office that commanded all land-based aircraft in SOPAC whether under U.S. Army, Marine, or U.S. Navy operational control. Several officers held this command. After Guadalcanal was occupied a subcommand was established (Commander, Air Forces, Solomons, or ComAirSol) to coordinate the air offensive in the Solomons. Both offices answered to Admiral Halsey and SOPAC.

Combined Fleet The combat command of the Imperial Japanese Navy and under the control of the navy General Staff; responsible for implementing naval operations. During much of 1942–1943 Combined Fleet was based at Truk in the Central Pacific. It was commanded by Admiral Yamamoto until his death in April 1943. The American equivalent was the U.S. Pacific Fleet at Pearl Harbor under Admiral Chester Nimitz.

Element The two-plane unit that was the foundation of all larger fighter units in Allied service. The element consisted of a leader and a wingman, or wing. Normally at least two elements would fly together, thereby creating a flight. The Japanese equivalent was the three-plane *shotai*.

Fifth Air Force (or 5th USAAF) The U.S. Army Air Force operating in New Guinea. In June 1944 it combined with Thirteenth Air Force to become the Far Eastern Air Force (FEAF).

IJA Imperial Japanese Army

IJN Imperial Japanese Navy

Imperial General Headquarters A standing organization in Tokyo that, when it met with the emperor, included the army and navy Chiefs of Staff. In theory, although rarely in practice, it coordinated the war effort and carried out the wishes of the emperor.

JAAF Japanese Army Air Force

JNAF Japanese Navy Air Force

Joint Chiefs of Staff (JCS) A standing committee including Army Chief of Staff General George C. Marshall, United States Navy Commander Ernest J. King, and General Henry "Hap" Arnold of the Army Air Force. The JCS was presided over by Admiral William Leahy, President Franklin Roosevelt's chief of staff. The JCS was responsible for coordinating U.S. military strategy.

LCI Landing Craft, Infantry. A large, seagoing, shallow-draft landing craft. LCIs were 160 feet long and could carry 200 men; they began arriving in the South Pacific in early 1943.

LST Landing Ship, Tank. One of the largest shallow-draft landing craft, the LST was 316 feet long and could transport tanks, men, and large quantities of supplies to a beachhead. LSTs arrived in the South Pacific in early 1943.

MAW Marine air wing. The rough equivalent to a U.S. Army air force; 1st and 2d MAWs operated in the Solomons.

New Guinea At the start of World War II the massive island was divided into three sections. The western half was Dutch New Guinea and long controlled by Holland; Northeast New Guinea and Papua were situated in the eastern half of the island. Great

Britain had transferred Papua to Australian control in the early twentieth century. After World War I the League of Nations allocated the German-controlled territories in the South Pacific to Australia as a mandate. Northeast New Guinea was the largest portion. However, the mandate also included the Bismarck Archipelago, a group of islands off the coast of Northeast New Guinea. The largest island in the archipelago was New Britain, which possessed a fine harbor at the small settlement of Rabaul. To complicate things further, the Germans had also possessed Bougainville, which was geographically and ethnically a part of the British-controlled Solomon Islands. Bougainville, therefore, was also a part of the Australian Mandate. (At present Indonesia controls the former Dutch holdings on New Guinea. All of the areas formerly administered by Australia make up the independent country of Papua New Guinea. The Solomon Islands, minus Bougainville, are now an independent republic.) In practice, the simple term "New Guinea" was often used to describe any portion of the island. Most of the military activity on New Guinea described in this book took place in Papua. The difference between Papua and Northeast New Guinea was purely administrative and corresponded to no geographic feature. Most soldiers did not know, or care, which part of New Guinea they were in.

Oerlikon   An automatic 20mm cannon. A Swiss design, the Oerlikon was found on some Axis aircraft. It was widely used by most countries during World War II in an antiaircraft role.

Pacific Theater of Operations   This formal military designation included the North and South Pacific Oceans. The U.S. military subdivided the Pacific Theater into several smaller areas: the South Pacific Area and the Southwest Pacific Area, divided along a north-south axis through the Solomon Islands. In the administrative atlas of an American general, then, Guadalcanal was in the former, whereas New Guinea was in the latter (it was all the Southeastern Area to the Japanese). The term "South Pacific" refers to the South and Southwest Areas.

RAAF   Royal Australian Air Force (usually pronounced "*are double-a ef*")

Rabaul   Located on the island of New Britain, Rabaul was the main Japanese air and naval base in the South Pacific.

RNZAF   Royal New Zealand Air Force

Shotai   A three-plane combat unit that was the building block of larger Japanese fighter formations. The Allied equivalent was the two-plane element.

SOPAC South Pacific Area of Operations. An area of command that included the Solomons and islands south. From October 1942 until late 1944 the commander of SOPAC was Admiral William Halsey, who reported directly to Admiral Nimitz, Commander of Pacific Fleet.

South Pacific See **Pacific Theater of Operations.**

Squadron Probably the most important operational unit on both sides in the war. Squadron sizes varied greatly depending upon the type of aircraft being deployed. A bomber squadron might have twelve, whereas a fighter squadron might field twenty-four. Three or four squadrons made up an air group.

Strategic Bombing Survey (Pacific) (SBS) A large study conducted immediately after hostilities intended to assess the impact of strategic bombing on the course of World War II. Employing hundreds of military and civilian specialists, the SBS had European and Pacific branches, both of which produced dozens of volumes of data and analysis. Although rich with invaluable information, the SBS was undoubtedly influenced by interservice rivalries made acute by the Armed Forces Reorganization Act passed in 1947. All data in this study comes from the Pacific series.

Thirteenth Air Force (or 13th USAAF) The United States Army Air Force that operated in the Solomons.

USAAF United States Army Air Force

USN United States Navy

PREFACE

This book analyzes in depth the air war between Japan and the Allies in the South Pacific during World War II. The struggle took place on an immense battlefield that included New Guinea, New Britain, and the Solomon Islands. The period I examine begins in early 1942, when both sides almost simultaneously mounted serious military operations in the area. Initially both operations were relatively small. However, when the Japanese decided to undertake a land invasion of Port Moresby, New Guinea, in July 1942 and the Americans counterattacked at Guadalcanal in August, this triggered a conflict that quickly grew larger, more important, and brazenly violent. I end the analysis in early 1944, when the Allies crushed Japanese land-based airpower at the great base at Rabaul, a process completed by May 1944. Their defensive line shattered and their forces greatly weakened by the debacle in the South Pacific, the Japanese were unable to resist the coming onslaught that put the Allies on Tokyo's doorstep just more than a year later.

Three years ago I wrote *Touched with Fire: The Land War in the South Pacific*, which analyzes the brutal ground struggle in the same theater. It was soon obvious I could not create a comprehensive view of the crucial campaign in the South Pacific without either greatly simplifying a complex and fascinating subject or subdividing it into multiple volumes. The latter approach had much to recommend it, because no theater of the war was so dependent upon a combination of land, air, and sea forces than was the South Pacific. Strategically the various forces were intimately related at every step. Yet the type of war fought, and the experiences confronted by those who were there, were profoundly different depending upon whether one faced the war in a foxhole, in a bomber, or from the deck of a warship. Although this volume can be read independently with no loss of comprehension, it is in a sense the second chapter in a larger work. In the future I hope to finish it with a volume on naval operations.

I chose the period (early 1942–early 1944) and location (the Solomon Islands and New Guinea, both near Australia) for four reasons. First, because the Japanese wanted to isolate Australia and the Allies wanted to defend it, the Pacific war was fought almost exclusively in this area for a year and a half after the June 1942 Battle of Midway. Indeed the struggle for dominance in the South Pacific began when Japan seized Rabaul northeast of Australia in January 1942. This simple fact is rarely appreciated in accounts of the war. Many authors have written in detail about Pearl Harbor, Bataan, and Midway, as well as the bloody island encounters at places like Saipan, Iwo Jima, and Okinawa. However, except for the fight on Guadalcanal (only one part of a much larger drama), few outside the narrow field of military history have paid attention to the complex, vital events in New Guinea and the Solomons. Consequently the general public has largely forgotten a critical piece of the Pacific war.

Second, unlike the concluding year and a half of war when Allied material strength overwhelmed Japan, the two sides fought on roughly equal terms much of the time. This is important, for it allows me to illustrate the unique type of war fought by each side before the Allies were able to dictate events completely due to quantitative and qualitative superiorities. As the contest began with Japan possessing an advantage in air strength and ended in a complete rout of the imperial air arm, I can also analyze the complex process that led to the unraveling of Japan's ability to wage air war effectively. This book thus looks at an entire campaign, not a single battle. The stage is large enough and the time frame long enough to illustrate and analyze the turning of the tide in the Pacific war. In itself this is an interesting, important, and, I believe, poorly understood subject.

Third, the nature of air combat in the South Pacific was unique in the war. In no theater was airpower more central to operations than in the South Pacific. Indeed the objective of every major strategic move during the campaign was to seize an air base. At the same time, the Japanese and Allied armies confronted each other on terrain that was brutal, primitive, and largely unknown. Airpower employed some of the most complex technology available to the combatants of the era. Yet it was employed in an unimaginably hostile environment for man and machine alike. The juxtaposition of these two factors leads to fascinating human chemistry. It also serves to emphasize the razor-thin edge between survival and oblivion for World War II airmen, as well as the innumerable directions from which threats could come.

Last, I think the scale of the campaign in the South Pacific is conducive to an examination of modern warfare. In retrospect one today can analyze a particular battle or engagement, or perhaps study an individual unit, and learn much. However, World War II was fought on a tremendous scale and always within strategic context. Similarly authors have done fine works on the far larger campaigns in Europe. There the immensity of scale makes it more difficult to find the juxtaposition between the individual and larger events. Only by the standards of World War II would the South Pacific campaign be considered small, as thousands of aircraft were involved. Yet relative to the massive air armadas found over Germany and Russia, the forces in the South Pacific were small. Moreover the battlefield did not move far once established. Most combat took place inside or very close to a triangle with Port Moresby at the western point, Guadalcanal at the eastern point, and Rabaul at the northern apex. Therefore the course of the campaign is clear, and I can show how it developed through the actions of many of the same units. Because the enemy was the same and the portions of the battlefield similar, the reflections of the veterans who I interviewed, and which I draw upon heavily, lend a good amount of coherence. This is, in other words, a good stage upon which to examine a complex phenomenon: twentieth-century warfare.

This book is not a standard narrative history. Because the stakes were so high, and Japan's ultimate defeat in the theater so important, specialists in the field have written much about the subject since the war. Both the U.S. and Australian governments commissioned large, detailed, and excellent multivolume official histories of the war. Controversies over the plans made and policies followed by various leaders punctuated the war itself and have become part of its historiography. In particular, I think it is safe to say, anything done by General Douglas MacArthur and his staff has become fair game for historical scrutiny.

Because the narrative groundwork has been done, I have not tried to create another account of the war in the South Pacific as viewed by important military commanders. Instead, aided by dozens of original interviews with American and Anzac veterans of the conflict, I have tried to examine and explain the war's texture and tempo. War has a grim purpose and is extremely complex. Sophisticated planning and doctrine are present at every level. Yet at the point of fire battle is the essence of chaos and violence. I have tried to find the point where the coherence of war meets the brutal experience that confronts those who fight it. In other words, rather than treating the struggle as a chess match between rival leaders, I have tried to reconstruct and cast light upon the flow of battle. Strategic considerations enter the story at several points, but the core of my book concerns the men who fought the war, the weapons they used, how they viewed events, and the nature of the battlefield where they tended to their forbidding task.

I have employed a topical, rather than chronological, structure in this book. Throughout the text frequent mention is made to fierce battles in faraway places. Some of the personalities and place-names might be familiar to modern readers; most are probably not. Consequently in Part I, concerning the construction of the air-base networks that defined the geographic limits of the battlefield, there is a summary of larger events. Enthusiasts of military history will find nothing novel there. However, those new to the subject, I believe, may profit from the context provided. I have also included a basic chronology of events (contained in the rear matter of the book) as well as a full set of maps (see the List of Maps, page ix). Once acquainted with the basic course of the campaign the reader can better see beyond the war of the generals and look directly at the dynamics that shaped the struggle for the South Pacific skies.

The core of the text is divided into three parts. In Part I, I examine the battlefield. This includes the seizure and construction of air-base networks that defined the strategic parameters of the campaign. It also includes an examination of the beastly terrain and climate that plagued every aspect of the campaign and made service in the theater dangerous for every person regardless of service.

In Part II I examine the aircraft employed by both sides. Technology is an indispensable part of any sound account of air warfare. My chronicle is not highly specialized, but I hope to show how technical matters limited and influenced operations on both sides of the battle line. I wish also to show to what degree technical changes that benefited the Allies and a more developed industrial base on the part of the United States helped to bring the proud Japanese air arm to its knees. I also look at the men who conducted the air war. I examine their training, their preparation for battle, and the complicated but fascinating subject of morale.

In Part III I analyze the dynamics of air combat from the points of view of fighter pilots as well as the aircrews who projected power in bombers. I examine tactics, maneuver, types of missions, and any attempt—usually futile—to prevent battle from sliding into chaos. Throughout I attempt to identify patterns of operations that make more comprehensible the short and intensely violent moments when enemy aircraft met at the point of fire.

I think my approach offers much to the general reader. Rather than recapitulate operational maneuvers I attempt to show how and why the conflict took the form it did. I hope my book helps the reader better understand events of great import to modern history. Although my work analyzes a particular time and place, the currents I describe run deep. Many of the matters I address are central to the core of battles, campaigns, and warfare. It is an extraordinary story.

Although my account is comprehensive and probes many areas not often viewed, it is impossible to tell the whole story. There is an obvious problem in doing that: aircraft carriers. Carriers were at the center of three major fleet engagements in the South Pacific. To depict how a carrier battle took place would have taken me deep into the realm of naval operations. Thus, although I have tried to put the carrier battles in a strategic context, I have not examined them in detail. Yet warplanes operated from carriers. So at a tactical, or technical, level I have used several accounts from carrier pilots to illustrate the flow of combat once in the air. In this sense I can also make a virtue out of necessity. Because the carrier battles were so dramatic they have dominated many accounts of the conflict in the South Pacific. Yet in terms of sorties flown, aircraft shot down, bombs dropped—indeed by any reasonable measure—the air war in the South Pacific was fought, won, and lost by land-based air forces. I might point out that between October 1942 and June 1944 there were no carrier engagements at all during the Pacific war. After October 1942 carriers did make their mark on rare, often notable, occasions, yet it was always in conjunction with the larger struggle for land bases.

Similarly I did not give as much space as is due to fleet reconnaissance, even though that was usually accomplished by using aircraft. The subject deserves a closer look within the context of naval operations. Likewise I do not deeply treat the fascinating subjects of codebreaking, signal intelligence, and the Coast Watchers; all receive mention but not detailed coverage. There are several excellent books on those subjects, and I decided instead to concentrate on the areas not yet well examined.

There is no question that this book is written from the Allied perspective. Although the "Allies" in the South Pacific were a part of the massive coalition aligned against Germany and Japan during World War II, in this context the term refers to the United States, Australia, and New Zealand. Readers of my work on the land war will probably notice that matters pertaining to the Australian war effort are not as prominent in this volume. This reflects Australia's role in the air war as compared to the ground conflict. On land the Australian army was central to the Allied effort in New Guinea. The Royal Australian Air Force never played a role as important. Much of that force was understandably deployed to defend the Australian mainland from possible Japanese attack. Australia also put much of its resources into what was essentially a separate air campaign against Japanese air units in the East Indies. The Australian contingent allocated to New Guinea understandably emphasized ground support of the army. Still, I think I do justice to the important role played by Anzac air units in the theater.

Naturally I take care to examine Japan and its role. There are several fine secondary works concerning the Japanese war effort. In addition, the U.S. government accumulated much information on all facets of the Japanese war effort for the United States Strategic Bombing Survey compiled immediately after the war. In addition, after the war General MacArthur's headquarters in Tokyo authorized a detailed account of Japanese operations written by former Japanese officers, which provides an indispensable account of the Pacific war from Tokyo's viewpoint. Unfortunately linguistic and geographic barriers face anyone who wishes to interview Japanese veterans, which means that fewer Japanese reflections are included as I would have liked. In any event I believe I cover the Japanese war effort accurately and fairly. Nevertheless it will become obvious that I believe that the unique ferocity of the war in the Pacific stemmed primarily from Japanese policy. I think it is self-evident that something went very wrong in Japan during the 1930s and that the war in Asia was due to Tokyo's overaggressive nature. I also believe that the foul political atmospheres in many countries during the interwar years were unique to that period of history. Nothing I have written detracts from the great respect I hold for Japan and its people.

There is much interest today in historical issues that relate to race and gender. Indeed many specialists in these fields are examining the experiences of racial minorities and women during World War II. I do not join them. My book focuses on war at the point of fire. Air combat in the South Pacific was the domain of fighting men. Because U.S. combat units were racially segregated during the period I examine, black airmen were not there. In short the important contributions of blacks and women in the Pacific war were mostly in rear areas and after the period I examine. The issues deserve more detailed treatment than I can offer here.

I have kept footnotes to a minimum but include my sources (see Sources and Bibliography, in the rear matter). I list all the veterans who helped me for this volume; the bibliography of selected sources should prove helpful. The Glossary of Military Terms, Acronyms, and Place-names, page xi, will help readers keep track of the various forces, commands, and the like—a complicated task at best. Some details within the interviews and other extracts will require a brief explanation, perhaps an outright definition. In those cases I inserted an editorial comment, set off by brackets and my initials [—EB]. The maps will guide readers through what is most likely an unfamiliar part of the world. Any errors in the book are mine alone.

I have many people to thank. Rob Williams and others affiliated with Westview Press have helped from the first day. The administration at Lincoln University has given me important support. The fine staff at Air University at Maxwell Air Force Base performed "above and beyond" during my stay there. Thanks also to Lex McAulay and Geoff Waters for help on the Australian effort, Henry Sakaida and Mark Peattie for insights on the Japanese air arm, Jack McCall for sharing information about anti-aircraft, and Jim O'Neil for invaluable data concerning bombs and weaponry.

Most of all I deeply appreciate the help given by dozens of World War II veterans from the American and Australian and New Zealand armed forces. I personally interviewed most of the veterans who contributed their time. Others sent me audiotapes or written accounts describing their experiences and reflections. Although I learned something from every veteran who assisted me, I would like to offer particular thanks to J.A.O. Stub and Robert DeHaven for their help and insight.

I did edit the interview material to make context obvious. However, I tried my utmost to preserve the actual words used. If a phrase is emphasized in a quotation, it is because the contributor wanted it so. Although a half-century has passed since the events the veterans so eloquently describe, their accounts correspond well with the official histories and other contemporary sources. More importantly they provide details of larger events that have not been recorded. They lived through a hard but crucial time in history, and their thoughts and perspectives have proved invaluable to every facet of my research.

Eric M. Bergerud

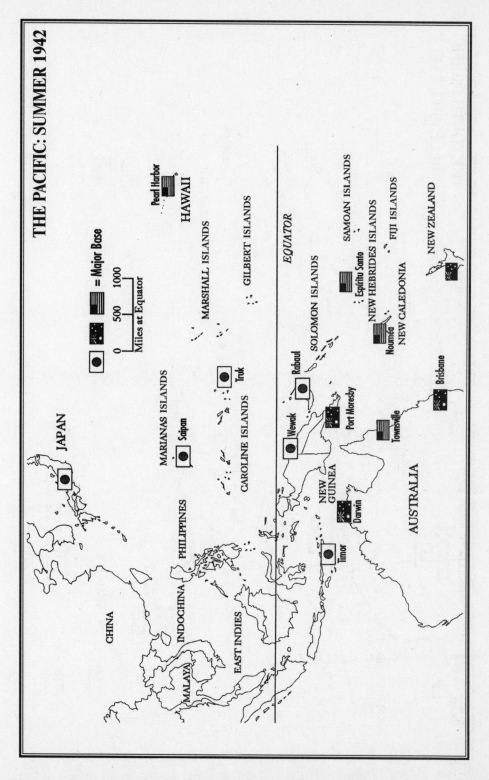

THE PACIFIC: SUMMER 1942

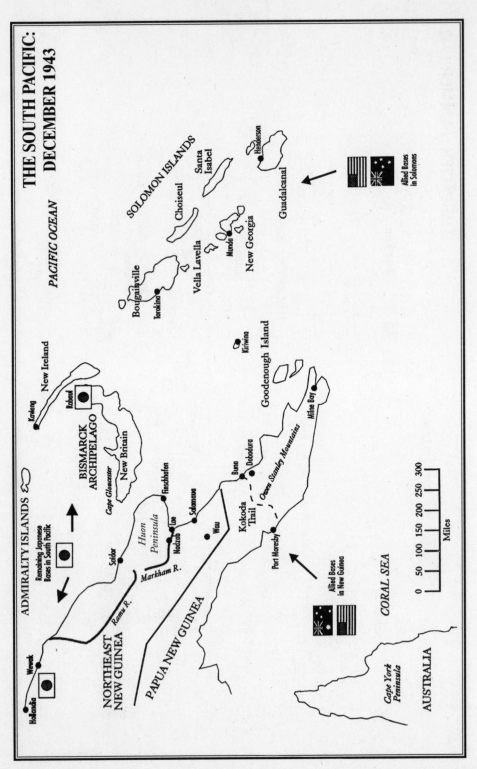

THE SOUTH PACIFIC: DECEMBER 1943

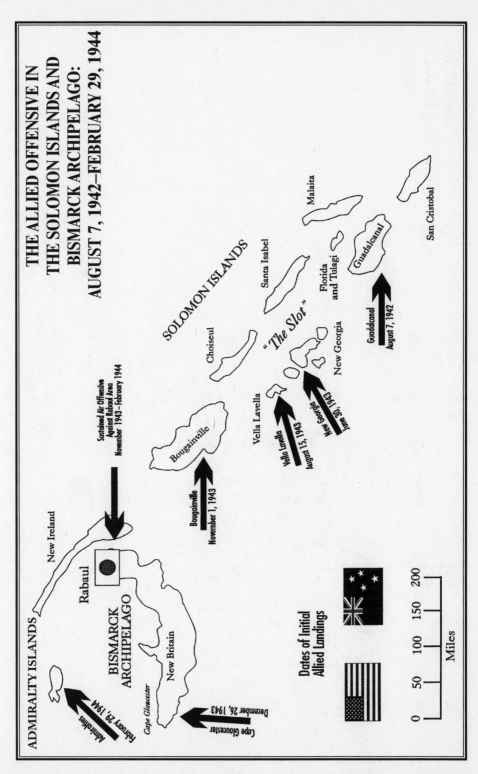

THE ALLIED OFFENSIVE IN
THE SOLOMON ISLANDS AND
BISMARCK ARCHIPELAGO:
AUGUST 7, 1942–FEBRUARY 29, 1944

ADMIRALTY ISLANDS

New Ireland

Rabaul

BISMARCK ARCHIPELAGO

Cape Gloucester

New Britain

Admiralties
February 29, 1944

Cape Gloucester
December 26, 1943

Sustained Air Offensive
Against Rabaul Area
November 1943–February 1944

Bougainville
November 1, 1943

Bougainville

SOLOMON ISLANDS

Choiseul

Vella Lavella

"The Slot"

Vella Lavella
August 15, 1943

New Georgia
June 30, 1943

New Georgia

Santa Isabel

Malaita

Florida
and Tulagi

Guadalcanal

Guadalcanal
August 7, 1942

San Cristobal

Dates of Initial
Allied Landings

0   50   100   150   200

Miles

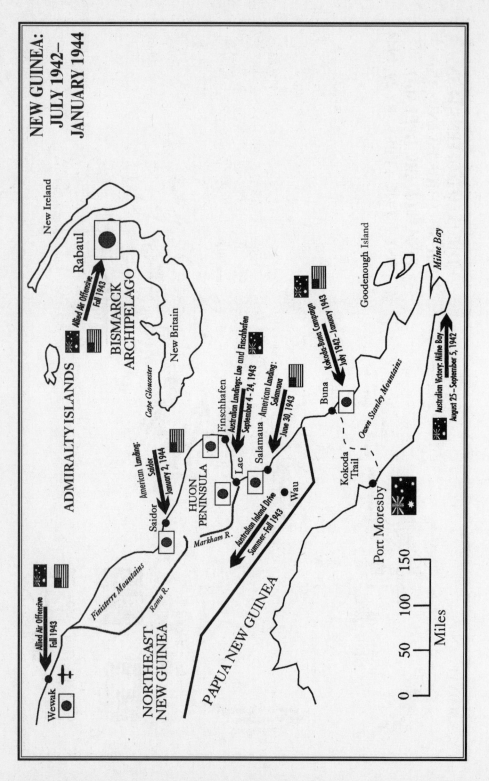

NEW GUINEA:
JULY 1942–
JANUARY 1944

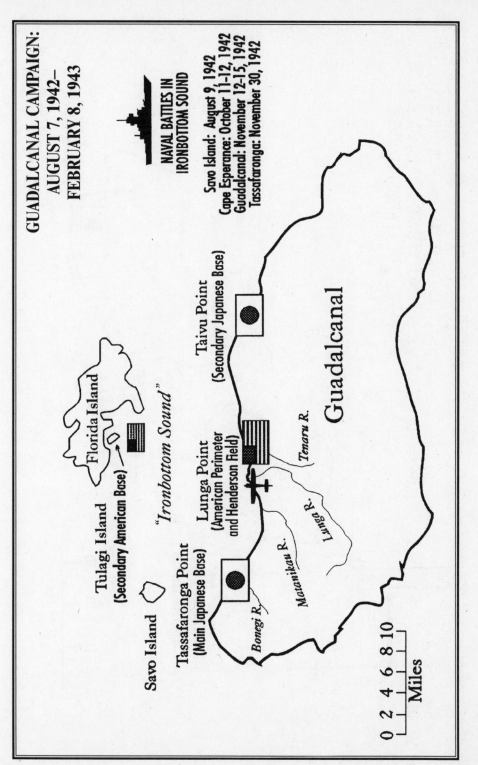

GUADALCANAL CAMPAIGN:
AUGUST 7, 1942–
FEBRUARY 8, 1943

NAVAL BATTLES IN
IRONBOTTOM SOUND

Savo Island: August 9, 1942
Cape Esperance: October 11–12, 1942
Guadalcanal: November 12–15, 1942
Tassafaronga: November 30, 1942

Florida Island

Tulagi Island
(Secondary American Base)

"Ironbottom Sound"

Savo Island

Tassafaronga Point
(Main Japanese Base)

Taivu Point
(Secondary Japanese Base)

Lunga Point
(American Perimeter
and Henderson Field)

Guadalcanal

Tenaru R.

Lunga R.

Matanikau R.

Bonegi R.

0 2 4 6 8 10
Miles

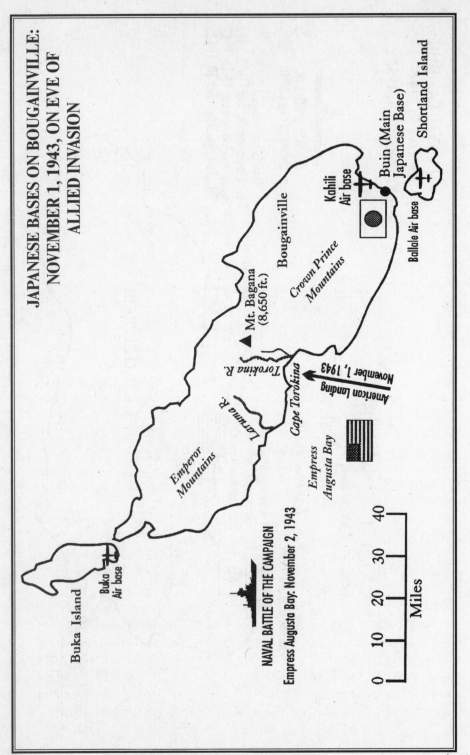

JAPANESE BASES ON BOUGAINVILLE:
NOVEMBER 1, 1943, ON EVE OF
ALLIED INVASION

Shortland Island

Buin (Main
Japanese Base)

Ballale Air base

Kahili
Air base

Bougainville

Crown Prince
Mountains

Mt. Bagana
(8,650 ft.)

Torokina R.

Laruma R.

Emperor
Mountains

American Landing
November 1, 1943

Cape Torokina

Empress
Augusta Bay

Buka Island

Buka
Air base

NAVAL BATTLE OF THE CAMPAIGN
Empress Augusta Bay, November 2, 1943

0   10   20   30   40

Miles

PART ONE

THE THREE-DIMENSIONAL BATTLEFIELD

Geography and terrain define the nature of the battlefield and are major factors shaping the outcome and duration of hostilities. As illustrated by countless historic examples, the shape and location of the battlefield can be decisive on both the tactical and strategic levels. The Union troops charging the stone wall at Fredericksburg discovered, like so many armies before them, the importance of high ground. At a grander level the Wehrmacht was treated to a wicked lesson in military geography as German tanks bogged down in the Russian mud and weeks later its supply-starved army skirted doom in the face of a massive winter Soviet counterblow.

Yet many commentators have underemphasized the role geography and terrain play in air warfare. It is true, after all, that the innate qualities of aircraft often give pilots an ability to choose and create their own tactical positions. Indeed seeking an advantage in the air is key to success in an air engagement. However, to understand the dynamics of a sustained air campaign, an analysis of the larger battlefield is a good place to start.

At the strategic level the availability and relative location of air bases limit what targets the attacker is able to strike and how well defending forces can rise to oppose. At the operational level the location and sophistication of the air base have a great impact on the number of planes that can fly on any given day and be supported in the long run. Furthermore the base is the shelter for the men who fly and maintain the aircraft. Any warplane spends far more time on the ground than in

1

the air. Thus the base is "home" for the men, and its makeup has great influence on morale.

The terrain that surrounds the base is also vitally important. How quickly a base can be built, repaired, and resupplied will largely be a function of where the base is located. This was particularly true in the South Pacific, where the brutal physical terrain and extreme geographic isolation of the theater shaped every facet of air operations and imposed extreme hardships on all that served there. Allied pilots in every theater flew aircraft and faced great risks, yet it is almost impossible to compare the experience of Allied airmen in Western Europe to their counterparts in the South Pacific, as they inhabited different worlds on the ground. Even the runways themselves were important. A good air base could not only support more aircraft but was also much safer to fly from. Yet the influence of terrain did not end at the runway. Because pilots in World War II, particularly those isolated by nature and politics to the South Pacific, lacked the communications and navigational aids taken for granted today, the ground below was never far from the airman's mind. This is very much true whether a pilot is flying over great stretches of ocean or over primeval and intensely hostile jungle.

Even the sky above—the atmosphere—became an important part of the terrain. As we shall see, altitude would tremendously influence aircraft performance and combat tactics in World War II. However, here we are considering the very nature of air itself. To pilots the air through which they fly is never a neutral environment. It can be "thick" or "thin" depending upon the altitude. More importantly it is the home of weather, a subject close to the heart of all good airmen. Different parts of the world have startlingly different weather patterns and thus radically different aerial terrain. These differences will permeate operations. On occasion nature could lend a hand to a military pilot—the sun could hide an attack, or a conveniently placed cloud could serve as a lifesaving refuge. Clear days, particularly in the bright air along the equator, allow an airman to see tremendous distances. Nevertheless pilots and aircrews respect and fear weather. Even today a very high percentage of accidents are due directly or indirectly to bad weather. During World War II treacherous storms, often appearing unexpectedly with great speed, could put an aircraft through a grueling test of structural strength and test the pilot's skill to the utmost. Probably worse, foul weather could blind an aircraft. At best that meant a mission would fail. At worst it could cause the airmen to get lost and possibly crash. This was a vital matter during World War II: More than half of all losses of aircraft in most theaters were due to accidents ranging from small to catastrophic.

At the heart of war is a unique combination of chaos and deadly purpose. At the point of fire organized activity, no matter how well prepared the warriors are, will eventually break down into disorder. However, the preparation of battle requires complex planning on the part of a large number of highly trained professional military men. The disposition of forces, the creation of a logistical network, and the gathering of supplies are all prerequisites to battle in the modern world. A great campaign also requires the leadership of governments and the support of nations. Therefore it is fitting that we begin our examination of the air war in the South Pacific with an analysis of the strategic framework created and imposed by the seizure and creation of air bases in the theater.

1

Defining the Battlefield: Air-Base Networks

War in an Unlikely Place: Japanese Air-Base Networks in the South Pacific

To understand the air-base networks that developed in the South Pacific and the war that was fought from them, it is important to make some basic observations concerning factors that made the theater unique. First, in the South and Southwest Pacific—in practice, eastern New Guinea and the Solomon Islands—there were no strategic objectives that had inherent value. There were no cities, no raw materials, no foodstuffs, nothing else that could have been of direct profit to the war effort of either side. Coconuts, the only item exported from the area before the war, were very far down the list of strategic materials and were readily available from other markets. Consequently had one side or the other occupied every square inch of this huge area, it would have helped itself not one iota and done no harm to the foe. The strategic importance of the theater lay entirely in its geographic relationship to other areas. A key by itself is of no value, but what lies behind the locked doorway might be precious indeed. The South Pacific was a strategic key to important doorways. For Japan control of the area would either help secure its conquests in Southeast Asia or serve as a stepping-stone toward the expansion of its perimeter. Conversely if the Allies gained control of the area, they would be in position to threaten the resources of the East Indies upon which Japan's war economy depended.

Second, because there was nothing of inherent importance to attack or defend, the air bases themselves became the only strategic objects of importance. Almost all air, ground, and naval action that took place in the greater South Pacific area was directed at seizing air bases and places where air bases could be built. Only in a handful of cases in the New Guinea campaign was a port the primary goal, and even in these instances an air base was always part of the bargain.

No area in the South Pacific was capable of supporting military operations employing its own resources. The area was remarkably hostile to twentieth-century man and possessed no basic physical infrastructure worthy of the name. In the entire area there was not one city. Inside the sleepy coastal settlements there were a few roads, but there was nothing resembling a road network in the theater. The crudest track that could allow passage by jeep was considered a good line of communication, and it probably did not go far. Although it is difficult to generalize on the subject, the widely dispersed indigenous population had no political stake in the war and, beyond providing manual labor, played a very small role in operations. (The peoples assisting the famous Australian Coast Watchers were notable exceptions, but in numbers they were few.) In short, this was one of the most primitive places on earth. However, airpower required some of the most sophisticated machines and support available to the combatant nations. Consequently everything required to fight had to be brought in from the outside. The aircraft themselves, all of the personnel, almost all food, all vehicles, all weapons, all communications, and all medical supplies had to be transported into the theater.

In addition, the South Pacific was an island war. In practice, the war was over islands within islands and the lines of communication between them. Because there was nothing of value beyond military bases, and because the terrain was so hostile, there was neither the need nor possibility of occupying a large portion of any major island. Guadalcanal is a good example. It was above average in size for the Solomons, being some eighty miles long and twenty-five miles wide. Had an island of that size in the Mediterranean been considered worth taking, an army would have exerted a strong presence throughout the territory. However, during the South Pacific campaign the Americans occupied a small perimeter near Lunga Point, where they built an airfield complex and held a narrow stretch of beach a few miles up and down the northern shoreline. When the climactic battle was raging on Guadalcanal between August and November 1942, the American perimeter around the crucial airstrips was not much larger than two miles by four miles. Most of Guadalcanal, during and after the battle, was left as it had always been. Many other islands in the Solomons had only token garrisons, and neither side exerted any meaningful control outside some small outposts. Although New Guinea is one of the largest islands in the world, bases there were even more separated than those in the Solomon Islands. One could go from island to island by sea, but bases and outposts in New Guinea were often linked only by a tortuous land or coastal route. In either case, any base in the South Pacific was extremely vulnerable to siege. If one side was dominant in the air over the ocean or the little ports sustaining its jungle bases, it could prevent amphibious invasion and allow friendly supply to sustain power. If it lost that dominance, its own bases would be cut off and rendered useless and the garrison doomed to gross hardship and possible starvation. Also, if air dominance was lost, it proved impossible to prevent an enemy force from taking an unoccupied or poorly defended area of the coast or moving overland for short distances. In either case, the object was the seizure of an enemy air base or the construction of a new one. Both sides learned the process quickly, and each attempted to strangle the other when possessing superior strength. The Japanese failed when they had their chance, but the Allies, once the initiative was theirs, annihilated Japan's air forces, isolated huge armies, and turned the entire theater into history's largest prisoner-of-war (POW) camp.

Obviously a symbiotic relationship existed between the forces of sea, land, and air. Despite the tremendous importance of air transport in the South Pacific, most supplies and all amphibious assaults were seaborne. Bases, because they would occupy land, had to be seized and defended by ground forces. Because Japan's central harbor and air base were at the same place (Rabaul), it proved possible for fast Japanese warships to slip through the reach of the Allied air forces and engage in ferocious surface battles at night. Yet ultimately if one side held air superiority over any patch of water during daylight, it was the warship that was on the defensive. The aircraft carrier engagements are fine illustrations of this point, but in the South Pacific land bases provided more decisive evidence. The cover of night was never total, and both navies paid a heavy price when attacked from the air. Thus without land forces there would have been no air bases to begin with. Without sea power it was not possible to sustain the flow of supplies required to keep aircraft fighting and the garrisons supported. Without air cover, warships were in deadly peril, merchant ships could not operate, and armies could not survive. It is impossible to say that one type of war—land, sea, or air— was the most important. Trying to a make judgment would be like arguing whether the heart is more important than the lungs to the human

body. Yet in other theaters during World War II it was possible to fight
a tenacious campaign in the face of enemy air superiority and without
the aid of sea power. In the postwar era, a few nations have triumphed
in war without any offensive airpower or naval forces. However, in the
South Pacific yielding air superiority for an extended time led inevitably
to calamity. In no theater of war in any conflict has airpower been more
important than in the South and Southwest Pacific.

It was also extremely difficult to find suitable locations for an air
base. In this regard, a comparison with World War II Europe in the
West illustrates the point well. Prior to combat Northern Europe was
strewn with airfields of all kinds, all connected to road networks. Expanding these bases was simple enough because the roads were there,
construction machinery was available, and local skilled labor was on
call. Constructing a new base was a matter of assembling assets already available. Experts knew the geography and geology. There were
no serious diseases lurking. The land had long been cleared, so engineers could choose between a variety of possible sites. Commanders
mandated an appropriate position and ordered the necessary men to
the job, and the field appeared.

In the South Pacific the Western European environment was turned
on its head. Almost nothing was known about the basic geography of
the area, much less its geology. Intense rainfall throughout the theater
greatly limited the terrain that was firm enough to handle extensive air
operations. Such areas existed, but no one knew where most of them
were situated. To make matters worse, although the entire area was
ridden with disease, some points were particularly rife with malaria.
Because nobody knew which areas had insufficient drainage or were
especially poisonous, the only way to find out was to try to build a
field and then fail. These factors placed a great premium on discovering a place for a good new air base or seizing one that was already
proven. A good base was not only a strategic necessity; it was a gift
from Mars, the ancient god of war.

Moreover, air bases in the South Pacific were useful only if commanders located them within an operational radius fitting their function. As noted, the main targets of air and amphibious attacks were
other air bases. Therefore the single most important geographic characteristic of a potential air base was the combat radius it would allow
aircraft to employ. The most meaningful scale was thus what airmen
called "fighter range." By early 1942 the tremendous importance of
fighter aircraft was recognized by both sides in the Pacific, and its
standing only increased throughout the war. Simply put, bombers
could not safely operate within range of enemy fighters unless they had

escort from their own fighters. The strategic problem that arose from this simple fact was serious. Fighters had inherently less range than bombers. Even when the range was extended with drop tanks and more efficient flying techniques, a fighter could use up its fuel during combat (as opposed to cruising) at a startling rate. Also, a fighter was much more vulnerable to disaster if it got lost, because it lacked the time required to find its position.

The definition of fighter range varied. Early Japanese fighters had extraordinary range and were able to operate up to 600 miles from base. For a brief period Japanese Zero pilots escorted bombers well over 500 miles on their strikes from Rabaul against Henderson Field on Guadalcanal. The price was high, however, and the Japanese never tried to sustain operations at such a range again. Thus phrases like "combat radius" should be viewed with great caution. In practice both air forces learned that it was extremely wise to allow for a large margin of error. Fuel consumption doubled during combat, and it was always good for pilot morale to believe that you had enough "juice" to return home. Also, heavier and more robust U.S. fighters (also flown by Anzac pilots) had a lesser range than did Japanese craft. Ironically the fighter range of Japanese aircraft decreased over time as more weight was allocated to a larger engine that would generate slightly greater speeds. The opposite occurred with U.S. aircraft. The second-generation fighters that appeared after early 1943 flew farther because they had larger fuel tanks. As a rule of thumb, fighter range for the Allies meant between 150 and 250 miles; for the Japanese it was 250–350 miles. For special missions, planes of either side could operate considerably farther. Nevertheless operational plans were made with the average mission in mind, and both sides learned to be conservative if they wished to preserve aircraft. As it was, hundreds of fighters throughout the theater had to ditch as they ran out of fuel before reaching home. Many of the same factors limited bomber range. A medium bomber rarely attacked a target more than 500 miles from home. (Again, there were exceptions, particularly with the Japanese Betty.) When they stretched their range beyond the more conservative fighter range, medium bombers would lessen their load of bombs to keep it safe. Heavy bombers likewise preferred a longer range to a heavier bomb load. Thus heavy bombers could make sporadic attacks, particularly at night, from extremely long range. Medium bombers could strike farther out than fighters, and often did, but preferred staying under the umbrella.

The differences in range also led naturally to differences in bases. Heavy bombers could fly a longer range but also needed the longest and best fields. Consequently bomber bases were often the most distant from the front. This situation paid a double dividend because bombers were more valuable and more vulnerable to air attack, so they were best kept out of harm's way. Medium bombers might well share a base with either heavies or fighters. Smaller attack aircraft like dive-bombers and land-based torpedo-bombers (which usually dropped conventional bombs) were normally glued to the fighters. Overall this meant that although air attack might begin from a great distance, a continuous and coordinated assault including all types of planes would not be launched until the respective bases were very close. This fact had two obvious results. First, it meant that the air war in the South Pacific, which took place over a vast area, would be a slow, step-by-step affair. Second, it meant that the air war in the South Pacific lasted for two years and developed into a merciless battle of attrition that would cost the lives of thousands of airmen.

One final distinction must be made before examining the beginning of air warfare in the South Pacific. Air bases varied greatly in sophistication and size. Both sides developed large base complexes that included several runways that could handle any aircraft, repair and maintenance facilities, relatively complex communications, substantial antiaircraft defenses, and a major garrison. The fields in these great complexes were near one another and probably connected by road; command was centralized. The Japanese had two such complexes: Rabaul in New Britain and Wewak in New Guinea. The Allies began with a major complex in the New Hebrides Islands and in the Townsville area of northern Australia. Thanks to good fortune, the Allies quickly added Port Moresby on southeastern Papua to the list of major complexes. After final victory, Guadalcanal joined the list, along with Dobodura in New Guinea. Acting as satellites from these major complexes were major bases that could handle and maintain a substantial number of aircraft but relied on the home base for more substantial support. For the Japanese, their major bases were in and near Bougainville (Buka, Buin, Kahili, and Shortlands), Gasmata on New Britain, Kavieng on New Ireland, and Lae on New Guinea. As the tide turned for the Allies, they created major bases at Munda on New Georgia, Torokina on Bougainville in the Solomons, and at Nadzab, Gusap, and Tsili Tsili on New Guinea, to name some of the most prominent. Last, there were the small bases. Although not major components in the air war, small outposts were invaluable as emergency fields. Often they were nothing more than mowed grass or flattened coral. In sum, a base complex like Rabaul had several fields, one over 5,000 feet long, and could potentially operate 450 planes of all types.

At the other end of the ladder were small emergency strips like Hood Point that did well if any aircraft that landed was able to take off again. Rabaul was defended by more than 70,000 men with supporting artillery of all kinds. Hood Point was manned by six men with a jeep. Clearly scale and function varied greatly.

A quick geographic tour of the South and Southwest Pacific will help make events more comprehensible. Although Australians are quick to point out that their country is the size of the United States, it is more properly compared to Canada. This was particularly true during World War II, when Australia's population was much smaller than at present. Like Canada, most of the people live in the southeastern portion of the nation. The small city of Perth and its nearby port, Freemantle, lay in the southwest opposite the Indian Ocean, serving as a nice comparison to Vancouver. Like Canada the central and northern sectors of the country had very small populations. The small port of Darwin, which lay very close to the midpoint of the northern Australian seaboard, was the major settlement in the area and was not linked to any major settlement in the northeastern state of Queensland by road. Distances are great in the South Pacific. Darwin is 2,000 miles from Sydney, almost exactly the same distance that separates it from Manila. To the north and northeast of Darwin lie the Philippine Islands and the former Dutch East Indies. Northeast of Darwin, and due north of Queensland, lies the great island of New Guinea and the Bismarck Archipelago.

In 1941 New Guinea was divided into three parts. The western half was part of the Dutch East Indies. The eastern half was divided between Papua New Guinea, an area originally controlled by Britain but ceded to Australian control early in the twentieth century. Until 1914 Germany had found its place in the sun in the Pacific, controlling northeastern New Guinea as well as three large islands slightly to the east. The islands known as New Britain and New Ireland made up the bulk of the Bismarck Archipelago. Rounding out the kaiser's tropical empire was the large island of Bougainville, which was geographically and ethnically a part of the Solomon Islands directly southeast of the Bismarcks. During World War I Australians quickly seized the German territories, and after the peace the Bismarcks, Bougainville, and Northeast New Guinea together formed the Australian Mandated Territories. The Solomons, an old British colony, was administered by a handful of British officials and a few dozen constabularies.

What developed into a fierce two-year battle of attrition between the Allies and Japan in the skies over the South Pacific began as a small component of Tokyo's stunning Pacific blitzkrieg in the five months after Pearl Harbor. In the months leading up to December 1941 the Japanese government and the Imperial High Command dealt with a multitude of issues that had great potential for unforeseen consequences. The Japanese knew this and fully realized that their decision to make war on the United States, the British Commonwealth, and the Netherlands was a historic gamble. It was impossible for Tokyo to envision the ramifications of each decision made within one of the broadest and most ambitious military campaigns in history.

In outline Japan's political and military quandaries were essentially quite simple. The war initiated by Japan against China had developed into a costly stalemate with no obvious end in sight. When Hitler crushed France and put Britain into mortal peril, a tremendous power vacuum appeared in mineral-rich Southeast Asia, still controlled, with the exception of Thailand, by Western powers. When Hitler attacked the Soviet Union in the summer of 1941, Japan's traditional enemy in the modern era also appeared to be headed for doom. Japan, that same summer, possessed a freedom of action undreamed of by previous governments in Tokyo. Whether a member of the Japanese elite sincerely believed that Japan had a mission to free Asia of European and American imperialism or simply found the argument a convenient justification for the creation of a greater Japanese empire was irrelevant. The fact remained that with France gone, and both Britain and the Soviet Union facing defeat, the opportunity presented itself to destroy the European empires in Southeast Asia and bring the fabulous geopolitical riches available there under Tokyo's control.

At the heart of Japanese policy in the late 1930s was an ingrained belief, among government elites, in Japan's cultural superiority combined with the acute awareness of the roadblocks preventing it from becoming a fully developed industrial power. Japan's population was large and young. This was a military advantage in the short run but made the country dependent on food imports. Except for the basic minerals that are commonly found in landmasses, Japan lacked the natural resources required for economic development. At the top of the list of resources not present, naturally, was oil.

So Japan, in the eyes of its leadership and much of its intelligentsia, was overpopulated and lacking in physical resources. This left the country dependent upon imports from other nations. Many nationalists argued that this situation was both dangerous and humiliating. Although the public was carefully shielded from the events, Japan's industrial weakness in the military realm was shockingly illustrated in 1939 when the tanks and artillery of the Red Army administered a brutal defeat to the light infantry army fielded by Japan in Manchuria.

Generals with foresight, many of whom were very influential in Tokyo, argued that a much larger defeat might await Japan unless its industrial base was brought up to a level to match that of the USSR or the United States.

Military expansion offered a tantalizing solution to all of Japan's problems. Manchuria, in addition to the Japanese homeland and Korea, would serve as the industrial heartland of a great power. The oil and minerals of Southeast Asia would allow the development of a fully mature industrial economy that would ultimately match (or surpass) any on earth. Prior to Hitler's triumphs such an expansion would require a suicidal war with at least the West and probably the USSR as well. When the Nazi juggernaut smashed the world's power relationships, a unique moment appeared that many in Tokyo were determined to take advantage of. Simultaneously in Washington, which had long been sympathetic to China's plight, there was a growing belief that Japan and Hitler were working in concert. When Japan occupied Indochina in July 1941, Washington retaliated with a trade embargo. Although the details are complex, Washington demanded that Japan cease its aggression in China and withdraw. Japan demanded something close to a free hand in Asia. Dependent on American oil and other commodities, Japan decided in September, a decision reaffirmed in November, to attack the West. (Although we shall never know what would have happened had the United States given in to Japanese demands after July 1941, it is my opinion that Japan would have attacked Southeast Asia under any circumstances. The time to profit from Nazi victories, as many Japanese expansionists argued, would not last forever.)

Ultimately Japan's decision to strike proved folly. However, given the fact that a German victory appeared extremely likely, it was a brutal but rational decision if judged by the circumstances of the moment. Japan was not unprepared for its great wager. Japanese agents had gathered information on potential targets and enemy forces throughout the Pacific. Japan's military forces, as events were to prove, lacked numerical and technological depth, but in terms of both quality and quantity Japan had a distinct edge in the Pacific in late 1941 in every area considered important by Imperial Headquarters. (Tokyo, by definition, did not know how badly it lagged in the crucial field of cryptography and overall intelligence, nor did the Japanese realize the full import of radar and sonar.) Already seasoned by several years of war in China, the naval, air, and land forces that would spearhead Japan's opening offensive were vigorously trained during the weeks before hostilities. Japan's power relative to its potential enemies was no doubt at the maximum point in December 1941.

Although Imperial Headquarters, which was inefficiently organized and always deeply divided by the miserable relationship that existed between the Imperial Japanese Navy (IJN) and Imperial Japanese Army (IJA), proved defective in the long run, the midranking officers who developed initial operational plans did a splendid job overall. Japanese planners assumed that they faced a long war. This was not out of preference but reflected the well-founded belief that neither the United States nor Britain would abandon Asia unless convinced by the imperial sword that further hostilities would be futile. No Japanese leader proposed the occupation of the United States, much less Britain, nor could planners count on the proposed Pearl Harbor raid to succeed. As Admiral Matome Ugaki, chief of staff to Commander of Combined Fleet Isoroku Yamamoto, noted in his diary not long after the war began, "Though a prolonged war is taken for granted, nobody is so foolish as to wish it upon himself." Consequently the Japanese decided to strike hard and fast and develop a defensible perimeter that would prove too costly for the Allies to overcome. Ultimately Tokyo believed that the Allies would see reason and sign a compromise peace highly favorable to Japan. In essence Japanese leaders hoped to repeat the success of their limited war against Russia in 1905 on a vastly larger scale.

Therefore Japanese planners were faced with two serious problems. The first was to develop a sophisticated plan of attack that would lead to the rapid defeat of enemy forces that on paper were powerful. The second problem was to decide how far the defensive barrier should extend. If planners were too timid, the Allies might catch their breath and be emboldened to make a strong counterblow. If the perimeter were allowed to grow too large, Japanese forces might become overextended and leave the Allies tempting targets to seize. Japan expected a war of attrition. However, for the attrition to be in Japan's favor, battle had to be conducted in proper conjunction with bases seized. It would do Japan no good to possess locations that the Allies could attack with a substantial superiority of force. With one glaring exception (clear only in hindsight) the Japanese solved their first problem brilliantly, using a large number of military operations that left the Allies reeling. Ultimately, however, because of the failure of the Imperial High Command to move decisively, Japan failed utterly to solve the second. The result was a strategic calamity for Tokyo. The result also led to two years of bloody air warfare in places no one seriously contemplated as future battlefields.

Overall the Japanese onslaught between December 1941 and May 1942 in the Pacific was a textbook example of how to employ almost every major military virtue: surprise, economy of force, momentum, and shock effect. The Japanese plan, finalized in November, developed almost without a hitch. The Pearl Harbor raid, which began the tidal wave, paralyzed the U.S. Pacific Fleet. The heart of Japan's carrier strike force carried out this task. Simultaneously air, naval, and ground operations began against the flanks of the overall Allied position to prevent any coordinated defense of Southeast Asia. In practice this meant immediate assault on Malaya, air attack on the Philippines, the dramatic destruction of two British battleships off Malaya, landings in Borneo, the conquest of Hong Kong, and the occupation of Guam. In the first six weeks, operations in Malaya had broken British resistance north of Singapore, the U.S. garrison on Luzon was trapped on Bataan, Wake Island had fallen (after delivering the invaders a rare slap), and the Japanese moved into the Bismarcks and launched a heavy carrier raid against Darwin on February 19. In late February the Japanese moved against Java, demolished a joint U.S.-British-Dutch fleet, and completed the conquest of the East Indies on March 9.

During most of these assaults naval and ground attacks had been supported by land-based Japanese airpower. The destruction of the British Force Z, based on the battleships *Prince of Wales* and *Repulse*, was the most dramatic example of Japanese land-based air prowess. Strategically the near destruction of U.S. airpower in the first few days of the Philippine campaign was also important. Where the land-based planes could not reach, the Japanese carrier strike force, soon back from Hawaii, delivered heavy blows. In early April the invincible carrier strike force under Vice Admiral Chuichi Nagumo began a massive raid against British shipping near Ceylon. The take was substantial: one British light aircraft carrier, two heavy cruisers, a destroyer, and two dozen merchantmen sunk. As we shall see, however, the British did not fight in vain and had inadvertently saved the Allied position in the Southwest Pacific. Naturally at the time the Ceylon raid was considered another in a long string of victories. The Japanese blitzkrieg finally paused in early May when the Americans surrendered the Philippines and the Japanese halted their advance into Burma after handing stinging defeats to both British and Chinese forces.

During these events a relatively small Japanese expedition seized the area around the town of Rabaul on the northeastern tip of New Britain in late January 1942. In physical terms, Rabaul was an ideal place to create a major base complex. The capital of the Australian Mandates, Rabaul, in South Pacific terms, was a metropolis with a population of approximately 1,000 Australians and Europeans prior to Pearl Harbor. (About half left after war broke out.) In addition,

Rabaul had become a center of the Chinese diaspora of the nineteenth century, and two or three thousand lived in Rabaul proper or villages nearby. In addition, approximately 20,000 indigenous peoples inhabited the northeastern corner of the island.

The center of the area was Rabaul Town. In the South Pacific this was a genuine asset. It provided headquarters buildings, a good place for communications gear, a good water supply, a crude telephone and electricity grid, and a multitude of smaller advantages that helped base development and made life, considering the theater, relatively comfortable. Later in 1942 three or four hundred prostitutes were imported from Korea to keep the Japanese servicemen happy. Also important was the existence of an agricultural economy, however small. Relations between the Japanese and the civilians were tense, but trade naturally took place. Fresh fruits and vegetables, so sorely lacking to most servicemen in the theater, existed in unusual plenty until the Japanese garrison later grew so large that it overwhelmed the supply. This helped the health of the aircrews and garrison. The relatively dense population also provided an unusually large number of laborers needed for base development.

The only disadvantage, barring the malarial conditions common to the theater, were a number of dormant and semiactive volcanic formations that ringed Rabaul. It gave the territory a sulphurous smell. When volcanic dust periodically appeared it irritated the throats of people nearby. Later in the war these small mountains proved invaluable antiaircraft positions and made life hellish for Allied low-level attack aircraft. In the early months, when the Allies were on the run everywhere, the Japanese found the volcanoes a nuisance and worried about a major eruption at any time. As was true in many parts of the Bismarcks and upper Solomons, small earthquakes were common, helping to keep the men on their toes. However, everything taken together, Rabaul was a good place to serve in the upside-down world found in the South Pacific.

More important than Rabaul Town, however, were the lovely Blanche Bay and Simpson Harbor. Simpson adjoined Rabaul Town and was one of the best natural anchorages in the Pacific, capable of sheltering 300,000 tons of shipping. The wharf facilities at Rabaul were crude, but Japanese engineers soon improved them greatly. As long as the sea-lanes were secure and the shipping available, Rabaul could sustain a major air, ground, and naval base. In addition, the Australian government, once it decided to garrison Rabaul in February 1941, had improved the small civilian airstrip at Rabaul Town (known as Lakunai) into a modest fighter field. Soon thereafter the Australians constructed a light-bomber field at Vunakanau, approximately nine miles southwest of town. Four days after the initial landings Zero fighters landed at Vunakanau, and the Japanese possessed a splendid forward base. By April Vunakanau was home to the IJN 4th Air Group of forty-eight fighters, forty-eight medium bombers, and twelve seaplanes—the approximate strength employed later during the opening days of the Guadalcanal campaign. At this point, however, no one had yet to realize that the Japanese had thereby established the centerpiece for two major military campaigns, in New Guinea and the Solomons. Thousands of Allied fliers would learn to respect the names of Lakunai, Vunakanau, and additional bases constructed later. For two years, Rabaul was the center of the storm in the Pacific war.

The Australian force had consisted of fewer than twenty obsolescent aircraft, not one of which should have been protecting a major objective. Necessarily the facilities the Japanese seized at Rabaul needed substantial expansion for serious operations. After the war the Japanese were criticized by Western authors and many of their own officers for lacking advanced and modern military engineer units. As we shall see, they were weak in this field, and the flaw cost Japan dearly. Perhaps the Japanese economy, still with one foot in the nineteenth century, could not support units resembling the U.S. Army Corps of Engineers or the famous Seabees (a play on *c*onstruction *b*attalions) of the United States Navy (USN). Perhaps also noncombatant forces suffered from Japan's aggressive military ethos and emphasis on attack. Both factors were undoubtedly at work, and many unforeseen weaknesses in technical services crippled Japan in a long war. I think, however, that the war in China also hurt Japan in this regard as it did in so many others. The Chinese Air Force was not able to launch a sophisticated bomber offensive on Japanese airfields. As the Japanese air forces of both IJA and IJN had long found it possible to dispense with the luxuries found at a great American base like Wright Field, they took a very utilitarian view toward the subject and saw no need for speedy work. Eventually Rabaul was by far the best-developed Japanese base complex in the theater. It may have been the best complex outside the homeland. (Clark Field in the Philippines was a likely exception—but it was constructed by the Americans.) The leisurely pace shown in airfield construction and expansion was almost certainly a function of experience as well as doctrine and technology. As in many other fields in air warfare against the Americans, lessons drawn from China proved wrong.

Japan was also harmed by the interaction of overconfidence, what the Japanese later called "victory disease," and the inefficiency that flourished in such an atmosphere. Interesting testimony on this subject was given right after the war by Vice Admiral Paul Weneker, the German naval attaché in Tokyo throughout hostilities. Weneker gave a scathing description of conditions at the front and at home in the wake of Japan's great victories:

> Early in the war I made a trip through the South Sea Islands to see conditions with my own eyes. I was astounded in the South Seas. The Japanese were thoroughly enjoying the lush life. They had parties continually and were drinking all the liquor they had captured. I asked them why they did not prepare fortifications and do something to make these places stronger, but they said that the Americans would never come, that they could not fight in the jungle and that they were not the kind of people who stand warfare in the south. As far as I know all those people in those places, both Army and Navy, once they got into a place where there was no fighting, would do nothing more about the war.
>
> Obviously in such time the war effort must be the maximum of the country, but here in Japan it was very difficult because of the corruption on every hand and the continual fighting for position. Anything would be done to get power during the war. Sometimes very good men were kept at their work only a few weeks or months because someone else would get the job through corruption. You cannot be efficient with key positions constantly changing.

It is not clear that Weneker visited Rabaul. It was closer to the front than other areas taken, yet the lassitude he described was probably present everywhere to some degree. Imperial forces worked from the outset to improve the position, although at a leisurely pace. The Japanese in their own way were excellent field engineers, a fact to which many a U.S. soldier and Marine could attest. When it first came to Rabaul, the South Seas Detachment was reinforced with an engineer unit. Shortly thereafter Fourth Fleet, which momentarily took over Rabaul, brought in its "base force" unit, or naval garrison. The garrison included a "pioneer unit," a poor substitute for a modern construction battalion. However, there was a great difference between field engineers and combat engineers, the latter being considered elite troops. Combat engineers were at the center of the modern battlefield, among the most important and highly skilled troops available. They were deadly in battle and often performed tasks of great peril. Japan's combat engineers were very formidable: They created marvelous field fortifications with crude materials and often fought to the death. Field engineers might find themselves under fire; approximately 400 USN Seabees died during the war. Indeed U.S. engineers took pride in working close to the front lines. Yet the job of field engineers was to build things and build them fast, not to fight. Japan's army engineers considered standard construction work undignified, although they were often called upon to do it. In addition, no soldier, engineers included, likes to dig or do serious manual labor.

Consequently field construction was left largely to the pioneer units. Ironically it appears that Admiral Yamamoto saw the need for superior base-construction capabilities. In 1936 he wrote, "As I see it, naval operations in the future will consist of capturing an island, then building an airfield in as short a time as possible—within a week or so, moving up air units, and using them to gain air and surface control over the next stretch of ocean." In this instance Yamamoto's thoughts were not matched by action. In November 1941 the Japanese began to organize pioneer battalions of 900–1,300 men. Approximately 60–75 percent of the men were draftees from Taiwan and Korea. A small number of Japanese personnel kept discipline and defended the pioneers. Others ran the small number of light bulldozers, concrete mixers, and other simple construction machinery used by the pioneers. Much of the work, however, was manual, and pioneers did not possess any heavy equipment. Compared to Allied counterparts, Japanese pioneer units were decidedly second-class. In addition, the Japanese employed labor battalions of about 800 men who were 90 percent non-Japanese. Labor battalions lacked even light equipment, and the Japanese component merely kept discipline. One wonders whether the morale in either type of unit would have been good considering the tense relations that existed between the Japanese and subject peoples. It is not clear how many labor battalions were used in the theater, but several pioneer units appeared.

As long as Combined Fleet viewed the situation favorably, there was no haste to develop Rabaul. Tokyo had just conquered a great empire, and much had to be done throughout Asia. Events in Rabaul were very low on the priority list. When American night air raids based in Australia began much sooner than most Japanese leaders anticipated, the need to improve and expand Rabaul became painfully obvious. The early raids did little damage, but military leaders are trained to allow for the worst. A well-dropped pattern of U.S. bombs could have destroyed or damaged many precious aircraft. In addition, the brutal New Guinea climate required more sophisticated installations. Furthermore, as the aircraft at Rabaul were often called upon to attack and defend as quickly as possible, they

could not function well unless the initial runway complex was substantially changed and rebuilt.

As the U.S. night raids increased, Japan increased its strength at
Rabaul. When Guadalcanal began in August 1942, even more work
was done to prepare the base for additional aircraft. When Japan lost
the Guadalcanal campaign in February 1943, Rabaul was transformed
into a fortress. Although Tokyo was well aware that the initiative had
been seized by the Allies, it determined to slow Allied advance, even if
it required the sacrifice of air and land units. Japanese army leaders
could read a map well and knew that if the Allies got past Rabaul the
road into the East Indies was wide open. Consequently an unusual pattern developed. Rabaul was a good base early in the war; for months
it continued to grow stronger. Its air units varied greatly in numbers,
but in general they increased in quantity, if not in quality, as the strategic situation declined. It was a foolish strategy in the long run, and by
the time Japan had built Rabaul into the Gibraltar of the Pacific the
situation had grown desperate.

Because Rabaul was the target of Allied efforts in two campaigns, it
is worthwhile to examine the base itself. Initially the two airfields and
excellent harbor made it a naturally good base. Eventually, however, as
Rabaul became central to two interlocking campaigns, the Japanese
developed a major air and naval base and a sizable land fortress as
well. In 1942 operations centered on the fields at Lakunai and Vunakanau. In Japanese terms, both were sophisticated affairs. Lakunai
was a fighter field, 4,300 feet long and 630 feet wide. Pioneer units
constructed two and a half miles of taxiways from the runway to
ninety fighter and ten bomber revetments. Revetments were simple
structures but important, and in the South Pacific they were the first
sign of a serious air base. Simply, a revetment was a pair or trio of
earthen walls higher than the aircraft that would shelter them during
attacks. Compared to a simple airstrip where aircraft were left sitting
near the field in the open, revetments were a great advance. If solidly
constructed with earth and/or coconut logs, a revetment could withstand blasts from nearby explosions and protect aircraft from bomb
fragments. The walls also restricted the size of the target and made the
job much more difficult for fighter-bombers on strafing runs. All important Allied air bases had revetments as soon as they could be built.
The revetment served both sides well. Finally brutal U.S. low-level attack techniques defeated the revetments and were key in destroying
Japan's air forces in the Pacific.

The taxiway is not one of the twentieth century's great technological
advances. However, in the South Pacific they were an important fea-

ture of air bases, particularly those, like Rabaul, that had to launch many planes at a moment's notice. Taxiways were small, thin roadways between the landing strip and the revetments. At Rabaul they were unpaved, which caused trouble. Combat aircraft of this era were extremely powerful and usually taxied from the revetment to the field. Most World War II aircraft, and all Japanese types, were tail-draggers, that is, they lacked tricycle landing gear, landing and taking off on two wheels and resting on a small tail wheel when stopped. It was no simple matter trying to control a heavy aircraft with at least a 1,000-horsepower engine using a rudder and brakes. During the taxi, the pilot could see very little from his tail-dragger. He was at least ten feet off of the ground and confined within the cockpit and canopy, a space usually designed to provide completely different sight angles. It was hard to see in front and impossible to see directly under the wings. When taxiing, pilots received aid from the ground crew's hand signals, sometimes with someone sitting directly on the wing and talking to the pilot. At best this was complex. If a heavy fighter—and all World War II fighters were heavy—went off the taxiway, it could sink into the mud and miss a mission. Often, depending on the weather, the dust was so heavy the pilot could see almost nothing in front, creating conditions for a rare but catastrophic collision. In either condition a good taxiway was one that was meticulously maintained and lacked soft spots from erosion and bomb damage. If a soft spot existed and was not discovered, the aircraft would very likely damage its landing gear and be out of action for a day, a week, perhaps the entire war. In addition, getting the aircraft from revetment to taxiway often had to be done very quickly. If the mission was an attack, it was important to gain attack formation as fast as possible; in defending the airfield, getting off the ground quickly might well make the difference between a successful defense and destruction. This was no time to hit a soft spot, yet such things plagued Japanese forces from the beginning to the end of the war. The effect was fewer aircraft in combat and a less favorable ratio of numbers, one that at some point meant the difference between stalemate and crushing defeat. Much of Japan's war effort foundered on the mundane issue of poor engineering that led to bad taxiways and slowly constructed airfields.

Vunakanau was the bomber field at Rabaul until most bombers were withdrawn in early 1944. It had a graded surface of 5,200 feet by 720 feet. However, as an illustration of the Japanese tendency to cut corners, the concrete portion of the strip measured 4,200 feet by 135 feet. There were ninety fighter and sixty larger bomber revetments connected by 6.5 miles of taxiway; the issues concerning revetments and taxiways were even more prominent at Vunakanau. For one a bomber was more valuable and expensive than a fighter, its loss felt more keenly. Bombers were also bigger and much more inviting targets to attacking aircraft, so they had to be well protected lest their life expectancy be short on the ground. Add to the equation the extra time bombers needed to get off the ground, as well as the greater dangers posed by a defective field or taxiway due to the bombers' immense weight, and it should be obvious why the Japanese ultimately put so much effort into Rabaul.

In summer 1942 the war began to get much hotter in the theater. Hoping for more offensive aircraft and also fearing more concentrated air attack (both of which took place) the Japanese decided to build more fields at Rabaul. In late December 1942 the Japanese built another bomber strip at Rapopo, about fourteen miles southeast of Rabaul. It was 4,600 feet by 630 feet and surfaced with concrete. Taxiways, as usual, were rolled dirt. It had revetments for ninety-four bombers and ten fighters. As part of a failed effort to involve the Japanese Army Air Force (JAAF), another field was built at Keravat to the southwest of Rabaul. Bungling engineers and drainage problems prevented it from being a decent strip. Eventually the IJN pioneers created an unpaved 4,200-foot strip that was used for emergency purposes only. In this regard the IJA's efforts were not entirely in vain. It was not at all unusual for pilots of damaged aircraft to want to land *now*, particularly if an alternate field was covered by the enemy. No doubt several dozen Japanese aircraft were saved by the tainted base. Yet one less field made the attack on Rabaul that much simpler when the mass Allied assault began in October 1943. Last the imperial navy built its last strip at Rabaul at Tobera, several miles south of the other major fields. It was a fighter base covered by interlocking steel plates (rare for the Japanese) and provided revetments for seventy-five fighters.

A sophisticated base required far more than airfields. The various strips at Rabaul had dozens of buildings housing fuel, ammunition, spare parts, and food, also serving as barracks for the 10,000-man Japanese ground crew. Officers who served in 1943 claimed that except for occasional shortfalls of ammunition, there was no lack of spare parts at Rabaul. This would have been important, because the smaller, cruder satellite strips had only basic maintenance facilities, sending aircraft to Rabaul for any major repairs. It is not clear, however, whether Rabaul had the complex repair and overhaul facilities that would have allowed mechanics to undertake periodic rebuilds, required by every World War II aircraft. A well-made World War II aircraft was reasonably reliable, but none was durable in the civilian sense of the term. Both sides routinely pushed aircraft far beyond the hours recommended for overhaul, but regardless of military necessity there came a time when the plane had to be rebuilt from the ground up. This meant the installation of a completely reconditioned or, better yet, new engine. Major components, such as a wing or landing gear assembly, might need replacement. It was vital that an aircraft not only perform as near as possible to specification (many exhausted planes were almost different aircraft because performance was so degraded) but also keep the stability required for the immense stress put on them. This advanced maintenance required top-grade facilities and extremely skilled technicians. The Japanese proved extremely weak in both areas.

It is difficult to say how many aircraft failed in the Rabaul area out of simple exhaustion. When the Australians occupied it after war's end, the installations had been pounded by air attack for nearly two solid years, and little was left of the many wrecks around the airfields. However, whenever U.S. troops occupied Japanese air bases, they invariably found aircraft scattered about, often with no obvious serious battle damage. A dramatic example of this is described by Fred Hitchcock, a ground crewman in the U.S. Fifth Air Force:

In 1945 we flew into Clark Field in the Philippines. One of our work details was to help clear the hundreds of Jap planes that were scattered all over the base. They told us there were 1,100 planes and I believe it; the number was staggering. . . . I'd say most of them had something like a spark plug missing, or a wheel was off. But the Japanese didn't seem to have a coordinated salvage effort. I was on the detail that tried to reorganize the mess. One plane might be lacking a carburetor when another one, a hundred yards away, had a carburetor. But they never had the coordinated effort to pool the parts and get the maximum number of planes up. When we raided the place their planes were so dispersed they couldn't get their flights in the air fast enough to do serious damage. Some were a mile or so from the runway. It was an unbelievable sight.

The actual air strength at Rabaul varied greatly. At the time of Guadalcanal it possessed something over 100 aircraft. Soon a buildup began and it was rare that strength went beneath 200. However, contrary to Allied intelligence reports at the time, it is also likely that Rabaul's strength never surpassed 350 aircraft, and if it did it was only for a very short period in late 1943. (Often the satellite fields handled many aircraft, so overall Japanese strength was formidable.) Also, in the South Pacific no base was able to put in the air the number of aircraft theoretically situated therein. Mechanical difficulties, minor accidents, and temporary combat damage always sliced the actual numbers in the air. The South Pacific heat, humidity, mud, and dust only made things worse.

Yet measuring the strength of Japanese forces at Rabaul does not tell us much about the balance of forces in the South Pacific. Although the commanders at Rabaul would have been doing a good job to get 250 aircraft off the ground, the entire theater, like all centers of air operations, was a sinkhole for planes and pilots. Both the imperial army and navy averaged 50 replacement aircraft per month for a year and a half; add to this the "temporary" reinforcement on the part of several hundred carrier-based aircraft in 1943, many of which never left the theater. We shall try to estimate losses later, but suffice it to note that Rabaul was a field that handled and lost 150 planes about ten times over. In the end about seventy survived the ordeal, leaving Japan's naval air arm in ruins.

By the time that Japanese air forces gave up the struggle at Rabaul in late February 1944, it had grown into an immense fortress. The IJA South Seas Detachment had seized Rabaul with some 5,000 men; the naval garrison that slowly increased in size took over the job when the army contingent marched off to grim destiny over the Kokoda Trail. When the Guadalcanal campaign was lost in early 1943 the IJA decided that it was imperative to build up the Japanese position in the South and Southwest Pacific, and Rabaul became the central bastion. Although Rabaul's position grew more precarious every month, the Japanese, desperate for time to build defenses elsewhere, continued to reinforce the island. By November 1943 there were 76,000 army troops and 21,000 navy personnel on New Britain, most in the Rabaul area. Since 1942 the Japanese had dramatically increased antiaircraft defenses. In November 1943 the IJN operated eight 12.7cm antiaircraft guns and fifteen 12cm guns. Such calibers were found on destroyers and could reach aircraft at any altitude. The army added ninety-five powerful 8cm and 7cm guns. In addition, there were another 250 smaller caliber rapid-fire antiaircraft mounts designed to attack low-flying attack aircraft. Japanese antiaircraft suffered from serious defects, yet the sheer number of guns employed made Rabaul a very dangerous target. Land defenses were even more imposing. There were forty large coastal defense guns and howitzers. More important were some sixty prepared positions supported by hundreds of machine guns and scores of artillery pieces. It is doubtful that any position attacked in the Pacific war by Allied ground forces was as well armed. As events developed, however, ground attack proved pointless when the Japanese aircraft and warships were driven from the battlefield. It must be emphasized, however, that Rabaul played a unique role in the South Pacific hostilities; no other Japanese base was remotely as powerful.

Even before South Seas Detachment seized Rabaul, Japanese planners had decided that they should occupy nearby areas on New Ireland, New Guinea, and Bougainville to extend Rabaul's reach and aid against possible future attack. On the same day as the attack on Rabaul, Major General Tomitaro Horii, commander of South Seas Detachment, detached a company of Japanese infantry to seize the unoccupied village of Kavieng on the northwestern tip of New Ireland. On February 9 another small detachment landed at the little island of Gasmata on the southern coast of New Britain. Both Kavieng and Gasmata later served as major satellite fields for Rabaul and earned the respect of Allied fliers sent to observe and attack them. Kavieng, in addition, was a fine anchorage and served as an excellent secondary port.

A few weeks later another small expedition headed to Bougainville to further extend the Rabaul position. In late March small numbers of Japanese troops occupied Shortland Islands just southeast of Bougainville, Buin on Bougainville's southeastern coast, and Buka Island a few hundred yards north of the main isle. The Australians had built small observation strips at most of these locations; in time Japanese pioneers created true bases.

The Japanese experience at Buin is a splendid example of the serious penalty paid by Japan for inferior technical and engineering services. Unlike Rabaul and Clark Field, for instance, there were no decent facilities for the Japanese to seize at Bougainville, only tiny airstrips designed for light civilian aircraft. Consequently the Japanese had to build bases from scratch. When the Americans landed at Guadalcanal, it was immediately obvious to Japanese naval aviators that their Zero fighters, essential for escorting Japanese bombers, were fighting at their maximum range when based at Rabaul. A crash program was started to speed development of the Kahili airfield, already begun near Buin. Despite exhortations and a serious tactical situation, Kahili did not open for business until October 20. Somewhat sooner, Buka was ready for emergency purposes but could not well support serious operations. For Japanese pilots this situation was damaging. Nearly a third of the Zero fighters available in the Rabaul area were newer models mounting a larger engine that sacrificed range for slightly superior speed. These planes could not reach Guadalcanal at all, cutting the Japanese fighter force by a third at the decisive point in the battle.

The exhaustion of pilots flying more than 500 miles each way in a cramped fighter can only be imagined. Flying from Buin cut this trip by nearly 250 miles, and a Buin strip would have been a great advantage when the campaign was in doubt. By the time Kahili and nearby Buin were open for business, the Americans had passed through their worst moment (something that was not clear on Guadalcanal at the time, however).

The Japanese also tried to extend the military influence of Rabaul westward toward New Guinea. Their attempt to do so began a remarkable chain of events that can only be described as extraordinarily fortunate for the Allies. These events, for the first time in the war, showed that the Imperial High Command was seriously prone to muddle. Most certainly the defects that appeared had counterparts in other military organizations. Officers are fond of saying that unless forces are totally mismatched in power, victory goes to the side that makes the fewest errors. Yet when pressed the Japanese command did not just make errors; it wallowed in confusion and indecision. Japan's operational planners had done a splendid job designing the initial blitzkrieg. However, in retrospect, serious disagreements between the army and navy as well as between factions within the navy had been covered over by the press of events and the cavalcade of victories. Worse still, the Japanese had not evolved an effective mechanism for developing a coherent response to an unexpected situation. Allied leaders feuded continually, yet at some point a decision was made. When Japanese leaders disagreed they often made a series of ad hoc arrangements that only put off the day of reckoning. Worse, the oblique style of making decisions in Japan led to self-deception. It is very safe to say that many Japanese plans failed simply because commanders did not really know what was expected of them. Under the best of circumstances the Pacific war was going to be a long, harsh struggle for Japan; systematic failure by higher echelons only worsened its situation. The officers and men of the imperial forces were remarkably brave and frequently showed great skill. Rarely in modern history have such good fighting men been so poorly led at the top.

To understand the remarkable events of February-May 1942, we must look back at the impulse that initially brought Japanese forces to Rabaul. Officially South Seas Detachment and Fourth Fleet were dispatched to Rabaul to obtain a base able to protect Truk Atoll, Japan's major base in the Central Pacific. Nearly 800 miles distant, Rabaul was not well suited to the task, but no other island lay between Truk and Australia. Thus in the narrowest sense the party line among the top ranks was accurate; in reality the situation was far more complicated and clearly illustrated one of the major disputes existing inside the Japanese military.

Unless a situation exists where one side is far stronger than the other, it is extremely difficult to separate a defensive move from an offensive one. All good officers know this and search for geographic positions that possess good defensive characteristics but also offer an advantageous position from which to attack. This simple military reality explains why, if one examines most campaigns closely, that both sides must both attack and defend. The Rabaul situation, however, cloaked a profound disagreement inside the Imperial High Command as to how to handle an obvious and pressing strategic dilemma: Australia.

Japanese agents had been active throughout the Pacific for years prior to Pearl Harbor. One of the last detailed appreciations, dated March 1941 and forwarded in September to Southern Command (the armies involved with the attacks in the Pacific), laid forth one set of reasons that Japanese officers could use to justify the seizure of Rabaul. In this report, Rabaul was not a defensive position but an offensive strongpoint:

> Military Value of British New Guinea and Solomon Islands: These possessions, together with the Dutch East Indies Archipelago, form a natural barrier dividing the Pacific Ocean from north to south. . . . They are separated from the Australian Continent by the narrow Torres Strait. Consequently possession of this territory would make it easy to obtain command of the air and sea in the Southwest Pacific and to acquire "stepping stone" bases for operations against Australia. Control of the southern coast of New Guinea, in particular control of Torres Strait, would cut communications between the South Pacific Ocean and Dutch East Indies as well as the Indian Ocean Area and would force the enemy fleet to detour to the southern coast of Australia.

Allied commanders looked at the same geographic point exactly the same way. Their weakness at the time prevented a serious defense of Rabaul, but they were willing to take great risks for New Guinea. In the words of the official U.S. history for strategic planning in the theater:

> The strategic significance of the inaccessible and inhospitable region comprising the southeastern portion of New Guinea and the Solomons lay in the fact that the straits and seas and its isolated communities provided a double path to the important east coast of Australia. The second route extended from the Bismarck Archipelago in a

southeasterly direction through the Solomons to the New Hebrides,
New Caledonia, the Finis and the island chain stretching eastward to
Hawaii. . . . At the apex of these two routes, on the island of New
Britain, lay Rabaul.

All Japanese operations near Rabaul early in the war had a dual significance. Strategically they addressed the Australia question for the
Imperial High Command. Tactically they went to the heart of a military concept held by every country in the world in 1941: Given a
rough equality of force, land-based air forces would defeat carrier-
based forces. In a short period of the war at Rabaul both of these
problems faced Combined Fleet, and Tokyo managed to bungle operations in both spheres. Although not clear at the time, the Japanese
suffered a serious defeat in the weeks after their seizure of Rabaul.

The Japanese military inflicted incalculable injury to its own cause
early in the war. The heart of the strategic catastrophe that Japan suffered late in 1942, ironically, derived from German victories in 1941.
The Japanese army allowed eleven reinforced divisions, or 20 percent
of its total force, to participate in the southern offensive. This was no
small number. Nevertheless, when assessing decisions by the IJA in the
early stage of the war, it is almost impossible to distinguish between
what generals considered legitimate military factors and an assessment
of how the army believed the war would develop along broader political lines. In the first six months of the war, the major concentration of
Japan's fifty-one full infantry divisions was in Manchuria. Approximately fourteen divisions served in China, whereas eleven were dispatched to the Pacific front: The remainder, which included some of
the best-trained and -equipped troops, remained observing the Soviet
frontier. The war against Russia in 1904 had been the defining moment in modern Japanese history. In addition, the defeat of 1939 had
either angered or shocked those officers allowed to know the unpleasant details. The prospect of the Soviet Union collapsing under Nazi
pressure and the Japanese attacking into Siberia was too tempting to
resist. The intense anticommunism of the Tojo government naturally
increased the fixation on Russia, despite the fact that Japanese diplo-
mats had signed a Soviet-Japanese nonaggression pact that summer. In
the world inhabited by leaders like Hitler, Stalin, and Tojo, pieces of
paper meant little.

As always the Japanese were one step behind the game. When Vice
Admiral Nagumo's aircraft attacked Pearl Harbor, German forces
were in dire danger outside Moscow. Although the long and bitter
Siberian winter made major operations impossible, and Moscow was

no immediate threat, Manchuria remained the center of the imperial army's attention throughout 1942.

The fixation on Manchuria was ultimately a political and not a military decision. The problem, however, when dealing with Japanese decisionmaking is that the respective services routinely lied to each other and kept secret important decisions. The most important argument normally used by the Japanese army for limiting the forces allocated to the southern (i.e., Pacific) front was lack of shipping. It is certainly true that there was never enough transport to suit military commanders. Yet whatever difficulties found by the IJA in 1942 to prevent dispatching another division or two to the Pacific front evaporated when the Americans stopped the Japanese advance and began, with Anzac help, to throw it back. In 1943, when American submarines were first beginning to make themselves felt, the Japanese army began to strip Manchuria of its troops. More than 300,000 headed for oblivion in the South Pacific. Several other divisions faced destruction by the Americans in the Central Pacific. Eventually when war broke out in Manchuria between Japan and the Soviet Union, Japanese forces were a pitiful token crushed within days by the Red Army. Altogether, it was one of the worst uses of manpower in modern military history.

On one point, however, the Japanese army and navy agreed. Considering the scope, speed, and limited losses suffered during the Pacific blitzkrieg, the spring of 1942 was no time to stop all offensive action and revert to the defensive. The question was where to go next. As is almost always the case during a major war, neither service spoke with a single voice. Interservice relationships, never good, made an agreement between the army and navy a difficult accomplishment under the best of circumstances. In addition, as noted, Japan lacked a well-defined mechanism for setting strategic goals. In consequence, there was a welter of plans put forward for future operations.

Some IJN planners argued in favor of an attack into the Indian Ocean. At its most grandiose level, this attack called for the employment of the whole of Combined Fleet and included the occupation of Ceylon with two divisions. Soon thereafter further landings might take place on Madagascar, perhaps even the mouth of the Persian Gulf. In theory such ideas had great appeal. The alliance between Japan and Berlin had never been a working partnership in the military sphere. In a sense the relationship was almost parasitic. The Germans hoped that the Japanese would keep American, Australian, and British troops busy in Asia. The Japanese hoped that the Germans would keep the Allies tied down in Europe. Yet the idea of linking up with the Germans in Central Asia had an obvious appeal in principle. Prewar advocates in Japan of the Tripartite Pact between Germany and Italy were especially drawn to the idea of turning the Axis into an active military alliance instead of a relationship of convenience. So those in the imperial navy who favored or were interested in the scheme made their arguments, and the army listened.

The IJN leaders hoped that an invasion of Ceylon, hard on the heels of the occupation of Burma, would topple British rule in India. Although it is not possible to rule out such an outcome, it was unlikely. Although ideologues in Tokyo might not have realized it, leaders of the Indian independence movement knew that they had won their battle—only the end game had yet to be played. Moreover, the desire for independence did not equate with a sympathy for Japan. The fiery pro-Axis rhetoric of Indian leader Chandras Bose struck a chord in some ears. Yet in the end far more Indian troops fought for Britain than against it. In addition, a collapse of trade between India and Britain would have been an enormous blow to the Indian economy. Further, if Britain did lose the war, independence would fall into India's lap regardless. Also, there was precious little reason to replace the obviously retreating Raj with a closer and extremely powerful Asian economic and military bloc dominated by Japan. Also, Ceylon was well defended, and its occupation could certainly not be taken for granted and was something to give the Japanese pause.

A move into Madagascar would have caused serious trouble for Britain. Had Hitler committed to a serious offensive in North Africa and the conquest of Malta, Britain's supply line to Suez would have been difficult if a sizable Japanese force were at both Ceylon and Madagascar. Yet distances are great in the Pacific, and slowing supplies would not mean stopping them. And the Japanese would have had to move very quickly. The British were strong enough by summer to stop a supply-starved Afrika Korps at Alamein. (Rommel's offensive stage in the "first" Battle of Alamein lasted only one day.) Many of the supplies that allowed Montgomery to rebuild Eighth Army were either in or near Suez at this time. Furthermore Madagascar was very far from Tokyo but very close to Capetown. It is not unreasonable to assume that the British could have stayed on the defensive in the desert and diverted forces to Madagascar. Unless Japan was willing to cede the Pacific to the U.S. fleet, Combined Fleet would have to leave soon. Therefore any Japanese garrison guarding an air or submarine base would have been an obvious target for an Allied counterstroke with all the geographic advantages in Allied hands. A Japanese effort in this area would thus have had value only in conjunction with the closest coordination with Hitler. This was something that Hitler had no intention of delivering and something that many Japanese had no real interest in asking for. Ultimately Japan did not go to war to tie up its navy off the coast of Africa.

A Japanese move into the Persian Gulf, however elegant on paper, would almost certainly have been a debacle. In July 1941 Britain and the USSR had occupied Iran. Implicit in the Soviet nonaggression pact with Japan that same year, as in any such agreement, was the premise that one side would not take military action that would directly threaten the other. By the summer of 1942 Soviet and Allied engineers were working furiously to prepare the Persian Gulf as the major line of supply for Lend-Lease supplies to the USSR. There is no reason to think that Stalin had any care whatsoever for the fate of the British Empire in Asia. Nevertheless the Soviet Union had a powerful incentive to keep Britain and the United States active and committed to the Europe-first strategy. A Japanese landing at the mouth of the gulf or closer to the oil fields would have been viewed by Moscow, almost without question, as an intensely hostile act. One thing was crystal clear in 1939 and was later confirmed in several Pacific battlefields: The Imperial Japanese Army could not stand in open terrain in the face of modern firepower. A Japanese land unit, however formidable in prepared positions, would have been an easy lunch for a Red Army attack. There were also British forces in Syria and Palestine. In mid-1942 Japan was already feeling the pressure of a widened war. Open conflict with the USSR at the end of an immense supply line was not something many Japanese planners wished for at that juncture.

In the event, after IJN adherents of the Ceylon–Indian Ocean drive made their proposition, the army turned down the plan, claiming that a shortage of shipping prevented the dispatching of two divisions to Ceylon. As other historians have pointed out, the men and ships were in fact available for this offensive, so we are left in the dark concerning the army's refusal to attack Ceylon. In all likelihood its leaders were understandably growing apprehensive about overextension and could not see that the benefits of an attack on Ceylon—all hypothetical gains anyway—were worth the risk and the certain strain on the Japanese war machine.

The second possible plan was an assault on the Hawaiian Islands. Not long after Pearl Harbor, many Japanese officers had realized that they might have missed a golden opportunity not only to paralyze the U.S. Pacific Fleet but to seize Oahu itself. An attack on Oahu, without the benefit of surprise, would have required the services of at least three IJA divisions. Considering the risks, the IJN did not formally make the proposal. However, naval planners also looked at an attack toward Hawaii without an initial assault on Oahu. The aim here would be the systematic conquest of the poorly defended outlying islands and, more importantly, to force a great Mahanian decisive battle against the carriers of the Pacific Fleet. All admirals believed in the ultimate importance of the decisive battle. They did not agree on timing. Many, for instance, wished it to be a counterattack to an American move into imperial waters. In any case, no one in Tokyo at this stage of the war had any appreciation of how rapidly the United States was reacting to the Pacific crisis. The Japanese assumed they had time to maneuver as they wished. In fact, however, the Allies were beginning to recover before Japanese conquests were complete in the Philippines and Burma. Nevertheless Tokyo felt confident enough to delay the showdown with the U.S. Pacific fleet until it had dealt with more immediately lucrative operations.

The third possibility open to Japan, in the eyes of some admirals, was an invasion of Australia. A look at the map made it obvious that something had to be done about Australia. Unlike the conquered islands of the Pacific, it was home to an enemy population that was firmly at home in the modern world. Prewar assessments had warned that Australia was an obvious base for a future Allied counterblow aimed at the East Indies. In addition, Australia was far from defenseless. Two battle-tested divisions were heading back to the homeland from the Mideast. In addition, a large militia force was being brought up to strength and furiously trained. Also, a move against southeastern Australia, where most of the population resided, entailed operations over very long distances. The IJN argued that three divisions positioned at strategic positions could paralyze Australia. More realistically the army estimated that ten to twelve divisions would be required to seize the heart of Australia. The army could see the defensive advantage of controlling Australia. It could also see that it would be a valuable addition to the empire. However, the IJN was asking the IJA to gut the Kwantung Army in Manchuria and deploy a high percentage of Japan's merchant marine to a battle that might prove difficult. Many admirals likewise had doubts about attacking Australia proper. Regardless, the army slammed the door on the proposal, as well as more modest plans to attack Brisbane and Queensland.

To repeat, we should not view these strategic disagreements as simply between the Japanese army and navy. Indeed had the IJN spoken with one voice, the possibility existed that the IJA might have gone along. Yet the army had proven very good at saying no and very bad at presenting alternatives. Because the army had thwarted so many different plans, many in the IJN were incensed. The frustration in March

1942 was vividly expressed by Captain Yoshitake Miwa, a young staff officer at Combined Fleet who was favored by Yamamoto: "We want to invade Ceylon; we are not allowed to! We want to invade Australia; we cannot! We want to attack Hawaii; we cannot do that either! All because the army will not agree to release the necessary forces. Though it is understandable that the army has to retain troops to deal with the Soviet Union, is it that impossible to spare us just one or two divisions out of a million men in Manchuria and 400,000 in China?"

In defense of IJA leaders, they had good reason to refuse all of the IJN's plans just described. Furthermore the plan ultimately accepted by the army would have aided Japan's war effort greatly had it succeeded. The army's great mistake was not in strategic direction but in timing. Had army leaders shown more foresight in the initial planning stage, and coordinated operations more clearly with the navy, it is almost certain that Japan could have secured the entire South Pacific for an indefinite period with the employment of only a very small force.

The story of this missed opportunity is complex and does not follow a simple chronology. The expedition to Rabaul, although developed in the advanced planning stage, was not a major aim of the IJN and certainly not a place where the Japanese army wished to write a blank check. General war-planning for a conflict between Japan and the Allies had been pending among Japanese leaders for years (likewise true for the Allies). However, operational plans—those to be converted into reality—appeared quite late in the game. September and November 1941 were the key months inside Japanese headquarters for developing the plans that were intended to conquer a great empire in a very short time. It was during this period, for instance, that Tokyo yielded to Yamamoto and approved the assault on Pearl Harbor.

The army was cool to the Rabaul expedition and even less enthusiastic toward any plans made to expand Rabaul's position. Prewar planners were, however, already confronting the Australia question. Shortly before the war army and navy planners made a list of possible Allied options once war had begun. All hoped that the Allies would do what the Japanese wanted (move toward Southeast Asia and the Philippines and accept a large naval battle), but simple prudence required appreciation of the situation if the Allies followed a different path. As is often the case in contingency planning, imperial officers were given one option that had an uncanny fit to events as they transpired: "In the event that the United States and Great Britain elected to avoid decisive battle early in the war, they would probably limit themselves for the time being to submarine and air attacks on Japanese supply lines. At the same time they would endeavor to secure their communication lines with Australia and India with a view to the eventual use of these territories as bases for the start of a counteroffensive." As events were to prove, these were hardly idle fears. Japan's southern position collapsed from Australian bases, and its western flank disintegrated later when attacked from India.

The above was a joint army-navy assessment of the coming war. The report sanctified an army expedition to Rabaul. Yet the army was extremely conservative when it allocated manpower. The force allocated to seize Rabaul and its vicinity was a reinforced infantry regiment (144th Regiment of the 55th Division—the South Seas Detachment under General Horii) and some naval garrison units. Because Rabaul was not considered a top priority, South Seas Detachment was ordered to capture Guam first, which it did in a few hours on December 10, 1941.

In an odd contradiction of strategic terms, the Imperial High Command feared that South Seas Detachment might encounter serious resistance at Rabaul given the position's obvious importance to Australia. In early January a dozen long-range bombers began periodic attacks on the weak Australian air units on Rabaul, quickly neutralizing them. Once it was realized that local commanders also wished to seize nearby positions in New Guinea, the long-range attacks were then directed toward Lae and Salamaua in New Guinea, both essentially undefended.

Japanese intelligence analysts correctly anticipated meeting 1,500 badly equipped Australian troops on Rabaul. They believed, also correctly, that South Seas Detachment could make quick work of them. However, there did exist the possibility of an admiral's worst nightmare: enemy surface ships getting within firing range of troop transports. (This had taken place once at Balikpapan on Java a few weeks before when an American squadron of ancient destroyers had sneaked into a harbor and torpedoed several troop ships, one of the few setbacks suffered by imperial forces in the early stage of the conflict.) Naval intelligence believed there were several Allied cruisers in southern Australian waters. They also feared the possibility of the unexpected appearance of a U.S. aircraft carrier. Consequently South Seas Detachment, pried from the clutches of Japan's army with a pliers, was given lavish support at exactly the wrong time.

When the transports carrying General Horii's men left Truk Atoll in mid-January, they were soon covered by much of Combined Fleet. The covering force included no less than four fleet aircraft carriers, two battleships, and several cruisers and destroyers—more surface ships than available in the Pacific by the combined Allied navies in January

1942. The huge fleet was certainly not required to prevail over the small ground force on Rabaul and its insignificant air contingent. Considering the weakness of any possible opposition, one wonders if Combined Fleet was already concerned about attack from the U.S. carriers that they had lost track of, or perhaps feared the still untried attacks of land-based medium and heavy bombers on transports. In northern Australia there were already a handful of American B-17 Flying Fortresses. There were a larger number of Australian Hudsons—a very poor bomber under the best of circumstances—based in Rabaul, Port Moresby, and northern Australia. The numbers of aircraft involved were small indeed: Fewer than twenty Allied bombers could take to the air if luck was on their side. The surface fleet feared by Japan existed and would play a great role in events in early May. However, at the moment, South Seas Detachment was as safe as naval power could make it. Nearly 100 carrier-based aircraft attacked Rabaul prior to landing to finish off what was left of the Australian defenders. Japanese ground forces, possessing a heavy superiority in numbers, lavish air support, and the support of fire from warships, made quick work of the job and secured Rabaul in two days. The heavy support was unnecessary at the moment. No Allied cruisers sortied; no Australian aircraft proved a threat. One-third of the covering force would have been more than adequate. After victory, the bulk of the covering force returned for other duties.

One naval unit remained at Rabaul: the Japanese Fourth Fleet under the command of the brilliant Shigeyoshi Inoue. Between October 1940 and August 1941 Inoue was chief of the Naval Aviation Department and a close friend of Yamamoto. More than any leading Japanese admiral, Inoue was what Americans would have termed "air-minded." Although Yamamoto and his young staff had great faith in the aircraft carriers, the head of Combined Fleet still retained great faith in the power of battleships. Inoue denounced the Japanese "Gun Club," to use another American term, as a dangerous anachronism. Airpower, Inoue argued, would dominate naval warfare. In addition, Inoue had nothing but scorn for those militarists who dismissed America's will to fight. Knowing the industrial potential of the United States, Inoue had been a strong opponent of the Axis and argued against war. Although threatened with assassination by nationalist hotheads, Inoue was never one to hide his opinions. Only his outstanding credentials and distinguished service allowed Inoue to continue in a responsible position.

After his stint on staff Inoue was given combat command as head of Fourth Fleet based in Truk. Sometimes called the "Mandates Fleet," it was designed to patrol territories long held by Japan. It was also the least powerful Japanese fleet, based upon three light cruisers, two minesweepers, and a squadron of destroyers. The main task given Fourth Fleet was the close escort of South Seas Detachment to Rabaul. After the powerful elements of Combined Fleet left, Tokyo decided to station Fourth Fleet at Rabaul. The fact that the smallest of Japan's fleets was sent to Rabaul with the smallest of its assault forces is indicative of the initially low priority given this part of the overall offensive. Yet events throughout the Pacific had proceeded better than anyone in Tokyo had a right to expect. Consequently well before Fourth Fleet left Truk, IJN leaders were already beginning to think in more aggressive terms concerning possible action in the New Britain area.

Strongly encouraged by Inoue, naval planners proposed that as soon as practical South Seas Detachment and Fourth Fleet should add depth to the base at Rabaul by seizing the little Australian seaplane base at Tulagi, a small anchorage a few miles from the then unknown island of Guadalcanal in the Solomons. In addition, the Japanese would seize the rough civilian airstrips at Lae and Salamaua just west of New Britain on the coast of New Guinea. As soon as a small number of Zeros could operate from Lae and provide some air support against the tiny but slowly growing Allied air contingent in northern Australia, Fourth Fleet would embark for Port Moresby on the southeastern coast of New Guinea just west of Lae. With Moresby and Lae in Japan's pocket, all of New Guinea would have been in imperial hands. The defensive and offensive implications are indicated by a strategic appreciation that accompanied the orders to increase the perimeter in late January:

1. Acquisition of air bases in the Solomons and Papua areas would vitally strengthen Japan's strategic position, giving the Navy the advantage of expanded aerial reconnaissance over waters in which enemy naval forces must maneuver for a counteroffensive from the southeast.
2. Seizure of such bases would deprive the Allies of key positions for a counterattack, and could be effected at the cost of committing a relatively small number of troops.
3. Japanese control over these areas would intensify pressure on northeastern Australia and hinder its use as a base of Allied (particularly air) operations.

Unstated was the obvious conclusion that holding all of New Guinea, the Bismarcks, and the Solomons would be a tremendous advantage if Tokyo decided to turn its efforts toward either a direct attack on Australia or a more likely attempt to cut it off from U.S. support.

A few weeks later, opponents of the Midway operation proposed that operations toward the Australian lines of communication with the United States were a superior alternative. Midway opponents argued that the biggest danger of the operation was that the U.S. Pacific Fleet would decline battle and cede Midway. Midway, some Japanese planners argued, was of dubious strategic value and would constitute a serious drain on shipping required to supply the garrison. In defense of the operations deep into the South Pacific, Yamamoto's opponents contended that the U.S. fleet would fight to keep Australia an active part of the Allied war effort. If the U.S. fleet did not fight, then Japan would possess objectives of great value worth the drain on shipping and supplies. Yamamoto's prestige was far too great for opposition to prevail. In addition, Yamamoto promised the army and his opponents in the navy that after he gained a great victory over the Pacific Fleet his warships would join with a large concentration of transports gathering in Truk and move into the South Pacific in the summer of 1942. With the clarity of hindsight we can see that Yamamoto's critics had a very strong argument. There was little subtlety in Yamamoto's operation. With Japan confining operations to one small target, the task of the U.S. Pacific Fleet—forewarned by the code-breakers—was greatly simplified. How events would have played out in the much broader expanse of the South Pacific is an intriguing question. It is hard to imagine how things could have turned out worse for Japan in light of the events at Midway.

At this juncture Combined Fleet engaged in two carrier raids that inflicted short-term damage to the reeling Allies; in the long run, however, this proved to be a strategic error of the first magnitude. The first, on February 19, was a four-carrier raid on the small and rudimentary Australian port of Darwin on the northern coast. The Japanese made this attack to secure the eastern flank of ongoing actions against Java. The 180 aircraft involved leveled Darwin but achieved little of value. There was nothing at Darwin capable of hindering Japanese actions in Java in any way. Quite the contrary: The Allies were abandoning Java. Any men or materiel that had embarked to the Indies would have ended up in Japanese hands. As it proved, Japanese land-based aircraft and surface warships had more than enough strength to finish off Allied air and naval forces in the area. When done with Darwin, Combined Fleet's carriers rushed to refit for another raid into the Indian Ocean.

While the Japanese were sailing away from Darwin, a small U.S. task force based upon the fleet carrier USS *Lexington* under the command of Vice Admiral Wilson Brown was heading toward Rabaul to make a raid of its own. In the early weeks of the war, unable to engage Japanese forces in serious battle, Admiral Chester Nimitz, new head of Pacific Fleet at Pearl Harbor, authorized a series of hit-and-run raids by America's three fleet carriers then in the Pacific: *Lexington*, *Enterprise*, and *Yorktown*. (A Japanese submarine torpedoed USS *Saratoga* near Pearl Harbor and damaged it. Combined Fleet counted it as sunk. USS *Hornet* had not yet arrived in Hawaiian waters, although it soon did so in most dramatic fashion. USS *Wasp* spent the first few months of the war aiding the British defense of Malta. Americans employed a small number of light escort carriers to ferry aircraft, but they were not expected to fight.) Nimitz hoped that such tactics would unsettle the Japanese, make them cautious, and slow them down. Indeed for a short time Combined Fleet dispatched two Japanese fleet carriers to guard the approaches to the Home Islands. Yet the policy had its critics. Sending U.S. carriers within launch range of Japanese bases had inherent risks from air attacks and submarines. U.S. admirals did not anticipate inflicting major blows against Combined Fleet but nevertheless risked precious assets. Luck was kind to Nimitz, and no U.S. carrier suffered any damage. Indeed, although no one knew it at the time, Admiral Brown did the Allied cause a tremendous service.

The first *Lexington* raid was not, in an operational sense, a great success. When approaching Rabaul on February 20, *Lexington* was sighted by a long-range Japanese seaplane. The *Lexington* was outside of even the prodigious range of the Zero. There was no timidity among Japanese officers, still flush with victory, and they immediately launched an attack on the *Lexington* by seventeen new Betty bombers, their entire long-range strike force of 24th Air Flotilla (sometimes called 11th Air Fleet) newly established at Rabaul. Fortunately for the Americans the torpedoes, which made the Betty so deadly against British surface ships early in the war, had not yet arrived, so the Japanese loaded bombs instead.

It may have made no difference. American radar picked up the raiders, and *Lexington*'s Wildcat fighters made an accurate intercept. In the air battle that followed, the Japanese suffered one of their worst tactical reverses of the early Pacific war. As confirmed by postwar Japanese records, Wildcats shot down fifteen of the bombers at the cost of two defenders. *Lexington* was never in serious danger. The Americans proved they could risk an engagement inside the air perimeter of a major Japanese base. They had also shown that Japanese bombers—whatever their other virtues—were extremely flimsy, a flaw that would cost Japanese airmen dearly. One can only imagine the reaction at Combined Fleet when the news arrived, its leaders knowing that four of their carriers were at sea some 1,200 miles east. Had Combined Fleet divided its carrier task force and covered the operations planned out of Rabaul, it would have had ample aircraft to demolish Darwin and might well have caught *Lexington*. Port Moresby and Tulagi both would have fallen, almost certainly, in weeks.

Infuriated, Inoue called for replacement aircraft to be flown in. While waiting to reequip his shattered bomber force, Inoue also delayed the invasion of Lae and Salamaua from March 3 to March 8. Under normal circumstances, five days is not a long postponement. In this case, however, the situation could not have worked out worse for the Japanese. The *Lexington* task force joined up with USS *Yorktown*, and Nimitz granted Wilson's request to strike Rabaul again. While the task force was sailing toward Rabaul, Allied reconnaissance picked up the Japanese transports and escorts embarking from Rabaul toward Lae and Salamaua. Wilson immediately saw that hitting a landing in progress offered the opportunity to rattle the Japanese seriously. The Japanese put their troops ashore on March 9 and swept away the insignificant opposition. The next day they received a shock. Wilson's task force, for reasons of safety, maneuvered toward Port Moresby and launched from the west of Lae. This required the 100 American aircraft to cross the Owen Stanley Mountains, but this potentially perilous operation was carried out without loss. The surprise was complete. In the raid that followed, U.S. aircraft attacked the transports and their escorts and lost only a single plane. Within hours a strike of eight U.S. B-17s also joined the attack. Had the carrier pilots been more experienced, no doubt the Japanese losses would have been worse. As it stood, Inoue's force was rudely treated. American planes sunk a minesweeper, a merchant-cruiser, and a transport and damaged a light cruiser and two destroyers.

Although not crushing, Fourth Fleet's losses were serious enough to cause postponement of the planned move on Port Moresby and Tulagi. In March Port Moresby was nearly undefended, and Zeros based at Lae could have easily dealt with any Australian and American air defenders. Yet the possibility of U.S. carriers in the area, and the painful realization that the Allied buildup in northern Australia was taking place much faster than anticipated, altered the equation. A Japanese invasion fleet going from Rabaul (or Lae) to Port Moresby had to steam uncomfortably close to Australia. Prior to Admiral Brown's raid, Inoue and Tokyo believed that Fourth Fleet could handle things by themselves. After the raid, however, the transports appeared much more vulnerable. An expedition without air protection from Combined Fleet's carriers was judged too risky. Unfortunately for Tokyo, Combined Fleet, at a moment when the Allies were still desperately weak, had embarked on a major carrier raid against Ceylon on April 9, 1942. The Ceylon raid was another illustrious tactical victory. However, by the time Nagumo's carriers had returned to imperial waters the Allied positions in the Indies, the Philippines, and Burma were obviously hopeless. However, this meant that Tokyo could no longer put off a final decision concerning where next to concentrate the action. Tokyo had squandered an opportunity go grab Port Moresby on the cheap. Although no one on either side of the Pacific could have anticipated it, the Japanese juggernaut had reached high tide. Within weeks the slow slide toward defeat began. (One individual who did not participate in further events was Wilson Brown, relieved because of failing health.)

Many fine historians have covered in detail the rapidly moving and critical events of mid-April through early June 1942. Because they deal with the realm of naval grand strategy, I shall not address them in any length. With the return of Combined Fleet's strike force from Ceylon, Yamamoto began pressing for the Midway operation. When the Doolittle Raid struck Japan, opposition to the Midway attack faded quickly. Yet the army was growing more concerned with Australia. Consequently Combined Fleet detached two fleet carriers, one light carrier, and several other warships to escort a troop convoy to Port Moresby. Inoue—the strongest advocate of a move against Port Moresby and the Australian supply lines—was overall commander at Rabaul. The Japanese also dispatched a much smaller expedition to Tulagi in the lower Solomons. The Japanese expected that the Allies would fight for Port Moresby—and they were right. Nimitz dispatched a task force based on the *Lexington* and *Yorktown* to the South Pacific, where it would meet up with a force of Australian and American cruisers and destroyers. Although Tokyo did not know it, Nimitz based his decision partially on intelligence gained from his now famous code-breakers.

The confused Battle of the Coral Sea raged on the seas during May 5–8. After raiding the small Japanese force on Tulagi, the U.S. carriers attacked the invasion fleet's support forces, sinking a light carrier. The next day the fleet carriers engaged. The Japanese sunk *Lexington* and damaged *Yorktown*. American raiders damaged *Shokaku* and badly mangled sister ship *Zuikaku*'s air group. Students of the battle have argued for fifty years over lost opportunities. For purposes of our story, the most important result was that Inoue, lacking adequate air cover, recalled the Moresby invasion fleet and postponed the attack until early July.

Inoue never received another opportunity for an assault on Port Moresby. Yamamoto's gamble at Midway ended in catastrophic failure. At Truk the imperial army and navy assembled a sizable force of transports and warships and troops intended to strike at New Caledonia, the Fijis, and Samoa. When news of Midway slowly filtered throughout the Japanese military, Combined Fleet postponed the great offensive into the South Pacific. Although the Allied counterattacks at Guadalcanal and Buna were months off, neither would have been possible without Combined Fleet's bitter defeats in the summer of 1942.

Some historians have argued that Japan's failure to capture Port Moresby and become well established in the lower Solomons was irrelevant because the entire war revolved around the outcome of carrier battles. Island bases, so goes the argument, proved ineffective when one side or the other possessed carrier superiority. Although championed by fine analysts such as H. P. Wilmot, this retrospective assessment of the overall situation is erroneous. In the first place, although U.S. carrier fighters had made short work of one raid on April 20, the Japanese had not proven that their carriers could effectively engage an alert and well-armed Allied air base. As events of 1943 would show dramatically, Allied land bases were far too powerful to attack with Japanese carriers after Midway had cut their numbers and the Battle of Santa Cruz (October 1942) had damaged their remaining air groups. To a large degree this reflected the tremendous errors made in Japanese warplane designs, which showed up most quickly in carrier engagements.

More significantly the carriers proved their tremendous potential in a series of engagements in 1942. Consequently their targets were each other. Outside of Pearl Harbor, very little damage was done by either side's carriers except the destruction and damage wrought on other carriers. The result was a kind of suicide pact. By the end of 1942 both Japan and the United States had skeleton carrier forces left. However, both sides were so weak that for nearly a year carriers had little active impact on the air war in the South Pacific.

In addition, a far more important factor was at work that could hardly be appreciated by Tokyo. Although the United States had resigned itself to losing the Philippine Islands, Guam, and Wake, there was nothing in the book of plans concerning Australia. It was true, as Japanese admirals like Inoue had feared, that Australia was an obvious line of advance for an Allied counterattack into the Indies. It is also true that there was tremendous pressure inside Washington to move the maximum amount of resources possible to Europe or the invasion of North Africa. For months General of the Army George Marshall and his supporters did battle with Admiral Ernest J. King and MacArthur over the allocation of American resources in the first year of the war. Ironically, despite two years of planning that assumed a U.S. offensive in the Pacific would only begin when the new ships began to appear in late 1943 and that the attack's axis would be across the Central Pacific, the United States made its first major commitment of forces in World War II to Australia—never seriously contemplated as a battlefield.

Australia, as we shall see, was also linked to the loss of the Philippines. When the Japanese seized Rabaul, bringing great urgency to Canberra's decision to recall two veteran Australian divisions from Europe and encouraging the U.S. Navy and Marines to make commitments at places never heard of prior to Pearl Harbor, they opened a theater that the United States had never seriously considered prior to the war. The nexus of the war in 1942 lay on the decks of the carriers only as long as one side could obtain a decisive advantage. Considering the balance of carrier forces during this period the result was stalemate. In this environment, land bases grew tremendously in importance. Wilmot describes Rabaul as "irrelevant." It's true that ultimately Rabaul could not protect the southern flank of the empire. However, its presence forced the Allies to wage two separate campaigns, lasting more than a year and a half, to crack the Rabaul position, hardly an "irrelevant" course of events.

Instead it is clear, in retrospect, that Tokyo bungled badly by not taking Moresby in early 1942 when the operation would have been so easy. Without Moresby—particularly if Japanese moves into the South Pacific had forced reinforcement shipping far to the south—it is likely that Marshall and his supporters would have simply closed down the Southwest Pacific Theater completely. Air units based in northern Australia could only launch long-range attacks, with little benefit, and serve as reconnaissance. It was unacceptable and repugnant for the United States to allow Australia to follow the same road as Bataan and Singapore. However, if the Japanese had seen the connection between politics and strategy, they could have made moves meant to make Australia an unproductive offensive base without mounting attacks that appeared to threaten Australia itself. Had Tokyo done so, Japan might well have shut down the Southwest and South Pacific Theaters before they began. Certainly keeping Allied forces off of New Guinea would have made Washington and Canberra face a very hard decision. If the

Allies wished to engage in the long and costly crawl up the coast of New Guinea, they would be forced to either recapture Moresby or seize the Solomons. Unless they were able to gather the resources to do both in 1942—an almost impossible scenario—the rationale for launching an offensive from the South Pacific itself would have naturally come into question as U.S. forces grew in the Central Pacific in 1943.

In short, had the Japanese seized Tulagi and Moresby early in the war, there is good reason to believe that the large U.S. buildup that took place in both theaters would have been postponed indefinitely. If Australia were considered safe, the United States might well have concentrated on building its position in Hawaiian waters in preparation for a Central Pacific offensive and moving more men and equipment to Europe. If the Allies feared for the basic security of Australia, it was very likely that they would have deployed defensively. They might well have tried to keep heavy bomber bases in operation in the northern sector of the country, but U.S. ground forces would have most likely been deployed south of Brisbane until the Allies could increase their strength. It is also very possible that the large force rushed to the Pacific by President Franklin D. Roosevelt in the first weeks of war might well have been directed to Europe if a secure defensive Japanese position had been established. Had the Allies been required to fight a major battle against a solid land air base just to begin a long campaign, the strong advocates of alternate strategies would have probably won the day. At minimum, a Japanese seizure of Moresby would have slowed an Allied offensive in New Guinea by months.

As it was, Japan suffered from the worst of two worlds. MacArthur came to Australia at the same time that the crack Australian infantry division arrived from Europe. Rapidly forces moved into Moresby, and indeed the Australian Army had their first victory over Japan when South Seas Detachment left the comfort of Rabaul to a horrid destiny in New Guinea. This problem was made worse by another Japanese defeat at Milne Bay in September 1942. At the same time, Japan's easy seizure of Tulagi triggered the first great U.S. counteroffensive of the war, a move made more urgent when U.S. reconnaissance aircraft discovered Japanese pioneers slowly building an airfield on nearby Guadalcanal. All of these battles were unforeseen by the U.S. military. If Japan did not have the resources to take Moresby after Midway, it would have been far better not to have stirred the pot. Had the Japanese played their cards correctly, an excellent opportunity existed that the Americans would not have made a major theater in the South Pacific. Had the Americans not done so, the Japanese would have had the time they desperately wanted to rebuild their carrier air groups. They also would have had the time to greatly reinforce defenses in the Central Pacific.

On one hand, their actions appeared to present serious threats—a situation that caused a vigorous Allied counterresponse. On the other, the Japanese never really attempted to capitalize on their momentary strategic advantages in the South Pacific. Thus Allied forces were drawn like flies to the theater, and ultimately the Japanese did nothing to keep their opponents from going over to the attack. The Allied effort was initially defensive in nature, but because they answered the early war's alarm bell with speed it was inevitable that the Allies would go on the offensive. Japan should have secured the theater or left it alone. In the long run, Japanese forces were drawn up and cooked like a chicken on a spit.

The Port Moresby story was not over, however, and the next Japanese attempt to seize it accelerated an expansion of the war in the South Pacific and also led directly to the creation of Japan's second major base complex in the theater, at Wewak.

Frustrated and furious at the failures at Coral Sea and Midway, the Japanese army decided to take Port Moresby with its own resources before the Allies built it into a major base of their own. Consequently in July 1942 General Horii took South Seas Detachment from Rabaul to the coastal settlement of Buna, south of Lae, and began an audacious march over the Owen Stanley Mountains. Initially the Japanese infantry displayed its superiority at jungle warfare, and Horii's men advanced steadily toward Moresby. However, the time for such a move had passed. The battle-hardened Australian infantry back from Europe quickly reinforced Moresby and moved forward to meet the Japanese. In September an attempt by the Japanese navy to support the advance by taking Milne Bay was thwarted by Australian forces, delivering Japan its first ground defeat of the war. At the same time Horii's drive had stalled outside Moresby. Without supplies and hope of reinforcement, Horii watched the Australians continue their buildup. Ominously MacArthur dispatched U.S. 32d Division to positions south of Buna, threatening to cut off Horii. Worse still, the U.S. landing at Guadalcanal meant that both army and navy reinforcements would be sent to the Solomons. Afraid that the Allies would cut off Horii, Tokyo ordered a retreat. During the march back over the Owen Stanleys the Australians mauled South Seas Detachment badly. When the remnants returned to the Buna area they joined entrenched army and navy service troops and suffered a murderous siege by Australian and American ground forces from November 1942 to January 1943. General Horii had been killed during the retreat to Buna. What remained of South Seas Detachment perished in the Buna area. As the hideous fighting near Buna took place, the Japanese army was also suffering defeat on Guadalcanal.

In December Imperial Headquarters decided to abandon Guadalcanal and that a realignment of forces was essential in the South Pacific. Thereafter the garrisons in the upper Solomons were greatly increased in size. However, the real shift came in New Guinea. Until the summer of 1942, the crude Japanese air bases at Lae and Salamaua were lightly defended. When it dawned on the army that the impending fall of Buna gave MacArthur a straight road up the coast of New Guinea, it rushed to reinforce. Thousands of men were sent to the Lae-Salamaua area. As time went on tens of thousands more went to positions farther north. In December the Japanese army occupied several new bases north of Lae. Troops were sent to Finschhafen, Saidor, Madang, and, above all, Wewak. In January they attempted a surprise offensive toward Wau, hoping to distract the Australian offensive, but they were stopped again. It proved to be one of the last offensives launched by the imperial army in the South Pacific.

As the Japanese buildup in New Guinea increased, Imperial Headquarters decided that the Japanese Army Air Force should also receive major reinforcement. Planners always talked about stabilizing the situation and renewing the offensive in New Guinea. If they believed this, they were not watching the growth of Allied forces at the same time. However, with Japanese army aircraft coming into the theater in large numbers, Madang became a medium-sized base. Pioneers built small, 1,200-foot fields in several locations up the New Guinea coast.

The major effort, however, was made at Wewak on the New Guinea coast northwest of Lae. Wewak, like all base complexes, had several strips separated by a few miles: But, Borum, Dagua, and Wewak itself. Data on the Wewak complex are not as detailed as those on Rabaul. Wewak was under long-range Allied reconnaissance for months prior to its activation in August 1943, and one flight recorded the presence of seventy revetments at Wewak. Japanese aircraft were lighter and designed to operate on smaller fields than their American counterparts, so the fields were rarely large by American standards. One Australian report mentions that Wewak field was approximately 2,000 feet long, not much larger than some of the small Allied fighter and emergency strips that dotted New Guinea. The intelligence officer of a U.S. fighter squadron noted that all of Wewak's fields were dirt and each lay on an east-west axis along a coastal plain.

Unlike Rabaul there was no naval contingent at Wewak, and initially there was no major garrison. Indeed the idea of constructing

Wewak and moving the imperial army's Fourth Air Fleet there was to support Japanese divisions active in the field. In the spring of 1944 two of these divisions, isolated from Japan, garrisoned the general Wewak area after Fourth Air Fleet had been crushed. Until war's end, they waited for an air force that never returned. Instead they reverted to a brutal, semiagrarian existence, all the while enduring small Australian bombing raids. At least half of the garrison, if one can call it that, perished of disease and starvation.

Thus unlike Rabaul Wewak was no fortress. Nevertheless in the summer of 1943 some 250–300 aircraft gathered at the Wewak strips. Fourth Air Fleet was formed on Rabaul but did not grow in numbers until moved to Wewak. The Rabaul aircraft were met by reinforcements from Dutch New Guinea. On paper Fourth Air Fleet had just more than 500 planes; in practice, however, Japanese squadrons in 1943 almost never matched their assigned strength. (This was normally true with American units also.) As befitted a defensive force, most were fighters or light bombers. However, all of the difficulties that hampered the creation of strong Japanese air bases were amplified at Wewak. The war was growing old by mid-1943, with Japan clearly losing. Shipping and skilled manpower were ever harder to procure. After the war, Colonel Inusaka Kaneko of Fourth Air Fleet's Supply Staff detailed the woes that crippled Wewak and ultimately made it the scene of a smashing and lopsided Allied air victory: "Up until April 1943 about 50 percent of aircraft on hand were in normal operation; subsequent to that time only about 25 percent of the total aircraft on hand were in full operation. This figure was even lower as the war progressed." In answering the obvious question of why operational readiness had declined so seriously, Kaneko gave a revealing glimpse into the lack of depth that so harmed the Japanese war effort:

The two main reasons were: First, poor maintenance, which was due to the poor equipment and lack of maintenance personnel, which also resulted in high operational accident rates, and second, the lack of pilots due to illness. . . . There was a marked decline in the quality of engine parts and spare parts in general. Although we had an air depot, the Zero Mark 4 had many operational accidents due to bad quality of spare parts. During the period between May 1943 and April 1944 the losses were divided as follows: result of aerial combat, 30 percent; destroyed on ground, 50 percent; operational losses, 20 percent. . . . With the machinery and labor available, we were not able to provide an area large enough to disperse our planes and had to keep them all in a narrow confined area. Also, low availability made it impossible to withdraw aircraft from threatened fields after receipt of warning of a possible air attack.

The result of these circumstances was calamity:

I can remember occasions when entire flights failed to come back. The figure varies with operational conditions. For planning purposes it was estimated that during big operations 50 percent of the fighters, 40 percent of the bombers, and 20 percent of the transport planes would have to be replaced. However, due to low production and shipping and ferry losses this plan was not followed; and consequently the New Guinea Air Force was destroyed. From May 1943 until the "Hollandia Operation" in April 1944 I would estimate a loss of 800 planes.

The circumstances described by Colonel Kaneko are an excellent example of the catastrophe that awaited a Japanese garrison that lost its ability to receive substantial supplies. Fighter pilot Joel Paris of the U.S. 7th Squadron described the type of event that strangled Wewak and many other Japanese bases:

We hit a convoy off of Wewak in late 1943, I believe. We were escorting B-24s hitting Wewak and we were up over 20,000 feet. Way out I saw some ships on the horizon. Nobody said a word, and I thought I was the only sonofabitch that saw them. But everybody had seen them and not said a thing on the radio to maintain security. When we got back they started loading the bombers and picked up some extra B-25s for a quick return trip. It was a convoy laying out waiting for us to do our normal "high noon" raid and then come in behind us. And sure enough, when we got back there about four o'clock and there was the convoy about ten miles offshore. The B-25s started skip-bombing these transports and sinking them right and left. The water was absolutely full of soldiers and sailors. They looked like corn flakes in milk. The B-25s and B-24s flew across the water dropping 500- and 1,000-lb. bombs into the water, killing the men swimming. We strafed them, too. This was a resupply into Wewak and those supplies would be used to shoot us down. We didn't give any quarter and they didn't either.

The defects at Wewak were worse than those at Rabaul, yet each revealed in different ways the shallowness of the Japanese industrial base. The same lack of technological balance crippled Japanese aircraft and harmed Tokyo's ability to create a mass of well-trained pilots. It is

ironic that inferior bulldozers could cost an air force dearly, but that
was exactly the case in the South Pacific. The fields at Wewak, and no
doubt many other bases, had too few taxiways leading to too few
revetments. When the order to scramble came, some aircraft could
never clear the traffic jam. As soon as a few heavy American bombs
disabled the runway, they were trapped. Add those victims to other
aircraft that were grounded because of inferior parts, and the numbers
of aircraft able to rise in battle declined. In turn, the aircraft that did
make it airborne were increasingly outnumbered and at increasingly
larger ratios. Obviously this situation built combat losses. The result
was enough to break combat effectiveness of the most intrepid units.
Eventually it became more important to keep a combat presence to
prevent the enemy from moving on to more lucrative targets than to
fight. That circumstance arose at Rabaul, which possessed far better
facilities than Wewak. Commander Tomoyoshi Horii, assistant commander of IJN 705th Air Group on Rabaul, described what took place
when the attacks became so powerful that defense was pointless. After
the war Horii was asked by American interrogators what was the policy of Japanese fighters at Rabaul when under attack toward the end
of the Allied offensive in late 1943: "Our fighters were usually too outnumbered to risk combat. When a raid was picked [up] by radar all
fighter aircraft would take off as a precaution. However, consumption
of gasoline caused many of them to return to the field between raids or
before a raid was over. Some of these fighters were destroyed on the
various fields."

Japan always held the smallest margin of error among the major combatants in World War II. Although the Allies took many false steps,
they were able to recover. And what Japan required was more of
everything useful to modern warfare; unfortunately for Tokyo the
economy could not provide the needed punch. In the face of such materiel weakness the Japanese required a wise, purposeful, and well-
coordinated military-political leadership able to assess the strengths
and weaknesses not only of Japan but also its enemies. However,
Tokyo lacked clarity of judgment. Poorly led and fundamentally weak,
Japan could only rely upon the often prodigious skills and great bravery of its servicemen to face an inherently stronger foe. It was not
enough. While the Japanese military ran in circles after the initial victories in the Pacific War, their enemies were reacting with great speed
and extraordinary determination to salvage a grim situation and turn
the tables on Japan. Now it is time to look at the Allied side of the
strategic equation.

Sites for Victory: Allied Base Networks

Most accounts of the Guadalcanal campaign note that the battle was fought at a time and place that neither side wanted. The observation is true enough. However, exactly the same can be said as to the entire American effort in the South Pacific. Although the Guadalcanal and Solomon campaigns both grew into major efforts and helped shred Japanese military power, no U.S. officer serving in 1940 would have dreamed in his worst nightmare a major campaign in the South Pacific. The possibility would have been less remote to an Australian, but the Aussies, too, were remarkably sanguine.

I would like to make some general observations concerning America's strategic situation on the eve of Pearl Harbor. First, although this was painfully obvious at the moment, many accounts of the period do not fully emphasize how miserably prepared the U.S. military was for World War II. When considering the dreadful situation in Europe in 1941, and the obvious possibility of war with Japan, the government's rearmament plans in 1939, 1940, and 1941 were pitifully inadequate in every way. In addition, the basic strategic outline for the war—defeat Germany first—was already accepted policy. Washington intended that U.S. forces in the Pacific stand on the defensive and guard the Alaska-Hawaii-Panama "Strategic Triangle." Indeed until late fall 1941, U.S. planners were most concerned with the defense of the Western Hemisphere itself. It appeared virtually certain that the Soviet Union would collapse and that the United States—and hopefully Britain—would face Hitler's merciless assault alone. As we know now, these fears were well-founded. American weakness was very apparent after Pearl Harbor in Washington. U.S. leaders knew that the United States was desperately short of every military asset, from infantrymen to battleships. Naturally this triggered a serious debate over the allocation of finite resources that lasted in one way or another throughout the war.

What is remarkable in retrospect is the ability of the American people, government, and military to react to a somber situation with great resolve and tremendous speed. Americans cut corners, rationalized procedures, shortened training schedules, and created a serviceable military within nine months of Pearl Harbor. By mid-1943 the industrial floodgates were open and an awesome war machine began to appear.

It is not possible to explore the complex subject of U.S. industrial mobilization in this narrative, although its results ultimately dominated the struggle for the South Pacific. However, I believe it is important to recognize the tremendous importance of the rational command structure that was functioning before hostilities. American generals and admirals fought among each other as though they were on different sides of hostilities, displayed ego conflicts that ranged from childish to neurotic, and made mistakes in large numbers. Yet unlike their Japanese opponents, U.S. military leaders operated in an environment where argument had purpose and policy was clearly articulated and flexible. Those involved were intensely partisan, but they argued their case on the merits and respected decisions that cut against individual judgments. If events necessitated a change in plans, then the plans would be changed and the job done. I think, in this regard, the stability provided by Roosevelt and Marshall can hardly be overrated. By and large, the officers that came out of this environment proved to be good ones. Accustomed to collaboration within their services, Americans proved very good at coalition warfare. This was of great importance because America's relationship with Australia and New Zealand was central to successful operations against Japan in the South Pacific. Yet Allied supremacy was visible only later. On December 8, 1941, the situation in the Pacific appeared very bleak.

If the Allies worked under a fundamentally flawed assumption prior to war (other than the safety of Pearl Harbor), it was overconfidence in British strength. It was true that many American and Australian officers realized that the British were badly overextended and would suffer defeat at the hands of Japan, but not even pessimists expected Japan to smash the British position in Southeast Asia and drive the Royal Navy into hiding in the Indian Ocean in less than two months. Instead most American officers were looking at either Europe or the Philippines. The destruction of British power in the Pacific, upon which Australia in particular had counted, left an enormous vacuum. With London out of the picture, the vacuum could ultimately be filled only by either Japan or a combination of U.S. and Australian forces ably assisted by New Zealand. As the events of early 1942 unfolded, twenty years of American strategic planning concerning the Pacific went into the trash as the Philippines quickly yielded their central position to Australia in the allocation of American resources.

The battle for the South Pacific, to the extent that the Americans had a role in determining its location, began as an offshoot of the Philippines campaign. Throughout the interwar period the U.S. military had assumed that a war between the United States and Japan would take place on an axis between Pearl Harbor and Manila. Both sides created great battle fleets, preparing for a Pacific version of the Battle of Jutland, altering plans from year to year. When the war in Europe broke out and substantial U.S. naval resources were shifted to the Atlantic, the Europe-first strategy was agreed upon; the USN decided that the Philippines, Wake, and Guam could not be held. If war came the USN would wait for the new ships authorized by Congress and attack Japanese possessions in the Central Pacific. If the situation in Europe became desperate, most American resources would be shifted to the Atlantic, with the Pacific Theater being put into deep freeze. This was rational strategy given the situation after the fall of France. One cannot dismiss the possibility that Hitler would have decided on a pause and that the United States would have moved against Japan. Some Japanese feared such an occurrence. But in 1941 few in Tokyo feared that a German victory in Europe would mean a Japanese defeat in the Pacific.

However, giving up the Philippines proved more difficult in practice than in theory. U.S. General Douglas MacArthur, believing himself and the Philippines betrayed, promised an effective defense if he was given reinforcement, particularly aircraft. The U.S. government then began to practice a not very successful version of deterrence. President Roosevelt and some of his advisers believed that a buildup at Pearl Harbor and the Philippines might deter Japan from further aggression in the Pacific. If war could not be prevented it might be delayed for a few precious months, thereby enabling the United States to strengthen its defenses. First, the fleet was moved from San Diego to Pearl Harbor. MacArthur received some reinforcements, although in his eyes they were not enough. Many admirals feared we were throwing good money after bad, yet the Philippines became a prime recipient of the pitifully small amounts of serviceable equipment available for combat in 1941. Had the United States determined to surrender the Philippines, as war plans of 1941 assumed, MacArthur was badly informed.

A matter of military doctrine came strongly into play during the months leading up to the war. The United States Army Air Force (USAAF) had believed that its heavy B-17 bombers could serve as effective weapons to neutralize Japanese airpower on Formosa and to attack a Japanese invasion fleet at sea. Considering the USN's reluctance to charge toward the Philippines and the relative lack of expense of bombers, optimists in Manila and Washington put great faith in the power of the B-17 to deter a Japanese attack. As one War Department official put it, a large force centered on bombers in the Philippines would act "as a threat to keep the Japs in line." Thus despite a desperate shortage of aircraft across the board, in the late summer of 1941 the USAAF allocated four bombardment groups or 272 aircraft and 130 fighters to the Philippines. As events worked out, leaders were allocating aircraft that did not yet exist, and in reality only a tiny percentage of the promised force arrived. Considering the events of early December, this was no doubt a good thing.

An obvious problem existed, however. If one was going to deter or fight Japan with modern bombers, how could Washington deploy the new planes as quickly as possible? Because of the great distances involved and their small size, fighters had to go by ship. Unloaded bombers, however, could fly very far. USAAF leaders decided to fly their B-17s to the Philippines. However, there was no pioneered air route in this part of the Pacific. Long-distance aviation was in its infancy in 1941 (Charles Lindbergh's flight was in 1927, and Amelia Earhart died in the South Pacific in 1937), and finding an obvious route from Hawaii to Manila was difficult. One thing was obvious: U.S. planes would have to cross over Japanese territory. In August 1941, under utmost secrecy, a delegation of USAAF officers toured Australian air bases at Rabaul, Port Moresby, and Darwin. All of these unknown and exotic places were soon to become all too familiar to U.S. airmen.

On the morning of September 5, 1941, the first flight of B-17s to Manila departed Hawaii. The first stop was a reasonably short hop, the 1,100 miles to Midway. Next was a similar run to Wake Island. Port Moresby was the next destination, but the route required U.S. aircraft to fly over Japanese Mandated Territories in the Central Pacific. The B-17s took off at midnight, maintained total radio silence, flew at 27,000 feet through heavy rain, and finally arrived after a 2,200-mile flight. The next run was a 900-mile jaunt to Darwin. From there the bombers flew to their somber fate at Clark Field near Manila. The USAAF had proven that Clark Field could be reinforced by air. Shortly it was obvious that this was a pointless achievement. The airmen had, however, helped precipitate the events that would bring Japan and the Allies into merciless combat in the South Pacific just months later.

There were obvious military and diplomatic dangers to flying over a sovereign nation's airspace without permission. Therefore another route swinging farther south had to be found. Actually the idea was not new. Since 1940 some in the USAAF had argued that the United States should develop a chain of fields across the South Pacific to take advantage of long-range aircraft. Until February 1941 the War Department turned down these requests on the grounds that the United States had no intention of moving long-range air units to the Far East and that it would be folly to construct bases that might fall into enemy hands. (This may have been a very wise decision. Had a well-developed complex existed in the South Pacific when war began, it is very likely that the Japanese would have moved on it quickly rather than chase phantoms near Ceylon and Darwin.) By October the War Department had reversed its policy and ordered a joint War Department–State Department effort to chart the appropriate routes, gain the necessary permission from foreign governments, and construct the bases required to supply the Philippines. The War Department ordered the Army Corps of Engineers to construct at least one 5,000-foot runway capable of handling B-17s on Christmas Island, Canton Island, Suva in the Fijis, New Caledonia, and Townsville, Australia, by January 15. Washington ordered the navy to improve Samoa and Palmyra Islands. While the United States was quickly becoming enmeshed in distant waters, another two flights of U.S. bombers were made over Japanese territory, bringing MacArthur's force of doomed B-17s to thirty-five.

In early November 1941 MacArthur ordered his air chief, Lieutenant General Lewis Brereton, to make a survey of the budding ferry route. Authorized by the War Department to spare little expense improving facilities, Brereton did not like what he saw. Precious B-17s had been damaged during their earlier flights at both Darwin and Moresby: A wrecked Flying Fortress (not the first) lay at Batchelor Field near Darwin. Brereton also noted that construction at Moresby was proceeding at a very slow pace despite the approach of the rainy season. Nearby was Group Commodore William Garing, who later recalled Brereton's visit:

> Prior to Pearl Harbor there were no serious preparations to wage an air war in northern Australia or New Guinea. The first thing that happened of consequence was when General Brereton flew out from the Philippines and arrived in Darwin. I flew up to meet him. He told me, "Group Captain, I have five million dollars in my pocket and I want to find out where I can build aerodromes so we can bring squadrons from America, through Australia and back into the PI." I said, "I can tell you exactly where to build them." I flew him down to Townsville where we had a big conference that included Chief of the Air Staff Air Marshall Jones. The Americans agreed to pay for improvements at various dromes like Mareeba in Queensland, near Cairns, Charters Towers, Port Moresby and a large complex near Townsville. Milne Bay had not yet been considered. Brereton didn't want anything to do with Rabaul and he was dead right there. A few months later when we got a lot of earth moving equipment out from the States we really started building.

Although Brereton's ultimate mission had no chance of success, it emphasized the importance of northern Australia. When war broke out, the Australians and Americans were already planning for the further development of Townsville, Darwin, and Moresby. Thus Brereton's visit saved precious months.

In a conflict where air bases played a central role, the ability to construct and develop them was critical. Japan's rudimentary military construction capability proved a serious burden and crippled its forces during Guadalcanal. In contrast, the United States and its Allies showed an impressive ability to organize major construction projects both quickly and efficiently. Although no one guessed it at the time, with the possible exception of Admiral Inoue, the ability of the U.S. command to change its priorities overnight and implement a major base construction plan in an area where no one had previously thought to fight eventually brought Japan's position in the South Pacific to ruin. It is also ironic that much of this work was under way prior to Pearl Harbor.

Japanese construction engineering, based on a few light machines and much manual work (essentially coolie labor), was little more efficient than that done by General William Sherman's troops in the March to the Sea during the U.S. Civil War. As in so many areas, Japan had one foot squarely in the nineteenth century.

The American effort was on a different level of sophistication. Prior to Pearl Harbor U.S. efforts were based upon an old but proven relationship between the Army Corps of Engineers and private contractors. The Corps had its own construction battalions and throughout the war increased them greatly in size. However, before the bombs began falling they made use of well-established contractors—civilians—many of which had become closely linked with the military prior to hostilities. The advantage was obvious. U.S. civilian contractors had no coolie labor to call upon by 1941. The Corps had officers who were fine managers and very competent engineers. Thus Corps battalions were made up of men who had a very high level of technical skill, because they had worked with many machines of every size. Unlike weaponry, which was in desperately short supply, companies that built construction machinery were among the first to benefit from the easing of the Great Depression. When rearmament began in 1940, the U.S. government was one of their best customers, as the military infrastructure in the United States had to be expanded tremendously to accommodate the millions of men who would be called to the colors. In addition, the Corps had a small but growing number of units that specialized in airfield construction. They employed heavy rollers, large earthmovers, and specialized devices, not to mention officers who knew the trade well. In the early stage of the war, however, the standard engineer labor battalions carried most of the load.

The problem was not lack of machinery but rather the lack of shipping to get the machinery to the engineers. Early in the war valuable implements of all types collected in American, Australian, and South Pacific ports, where they sat waiting for shipment to men working closer to the front. Many American engineers toiled hours under a hot sun with pick and shovel. However, even the most poorly equipped units had trucks, bulldozers, and other useful gear. Anything that could be used from the civilian economy in the area was quickly bought, leased, and requisitioned. In this regard, the Americans had an advantage over the Japanese. Several of the first bases were constructed in areas considered extremely underdeveloped by American terms. Yet in many cases the rudiments of a modern economy existed, thereby allowing the Corps to exercise its skillful ability to innovate. On the other side, the Japanese found little to help them on Rabaul and nothing whatsoever to aid efforts elsewhere in the South Pacific.

The Allies also contributed greatly. The air bases that appeared—almost by magic from the Japanese point of view—were often the products of local enterprise. The New Zealand government not only provided engineers on Fiji but also paid for a substantial improvement of island facilities through "reverse" Lend-Lease. The Free French government in New Caledonia gathered all the resources available and worked hard to complete the Tontouta airfield on New Caledonia and began work on a second. As one might expect, the Australians were able to render the most aid. In response to the U.S. request to Canberra in October 1941 to assist in constructing an air link to the Philippines, Australian engineers expanded civil fields at Rabaul, Moresby, Darwin, and Townsville to handle a modest number of heavy bombers. Darwin, which suffered more than its share of warfare, remained primarily an Australian logistical responsibility throughout most of the war.

The results spoke volumes. By December 28, 1941, a rudimentary route for B-17s across the South Pacific was ready. A small flight of bombers made the transit in early January. By the end of January, after several delays in construction, Christmas Island was opened, and the theoretical link between Hawaii and Manila was ready. Considering the lack of shipping, chaos inherent in the period, and magnitude of the task, this was a prodigious achievement.

The construction of the ferry route to Australia proved to carry far greater strategic importance than General Marshall and his supporters in the Pentagon ever imagined. As the Japanese advance pushed forward with relentless force, Marshall's treasured Europe-first strategy came under serious attack. Fortunately for all concerned Pearl Harbor ended forever any serious thought of trying to reinforce the Philippines. This was a bitter pill to swallow, and nobody in Washington quite gathered the courage to tell MacArthur bluntly that he was on his own. (Indeed in the weeks after Pearl Harbor small and brave air and naval units attempted to supply forces in the outlying islands of the Philippines, but nothing could be done to help the major U.S. force at Bataan.) MacArthur bore a grudge against Marshall till his last breath, but there was no decision per se to abandon the Philippines. Only Roosevelt hoped something could be done, but the U.S. military saw that the situation was beyond repair. The Pentagon illustrated this realization most dramatically on December 9 when it rerouted to Hawaii a large convoy of men and supplies bound for the Philippines that had sailed just prior to the Japanese attack. Remarkably Roosevelt intervened and ordered the convoy sent to Australia instead of Hawaii, convinced that any possibility of taking pressure off MacArthur lay in directing U.S. resources into the South Pacific. Hawaii, the president decided, would be supplied from the mainland.

Roosevelt's decision delighted the Australians. It also brought to a head a very obvious problem: If the United States was going to give up the effort to defend the Philippines, what was the purpose of the ferry route and proposed buildup in northern Australia? For a brief period the United States and the other Allies vainly attempted to protect the East Indies. Fortunately for the United States the Japanese advance was so swift that it was not possible to send sizeable air and ground units into the maelstrom of the so-called Malay Barrier. (The U.S. Navy was not so lucky, and several brave ships went down in a vain battle against overwhelming odds. Yet as previously noted, resistance to the Japanese ultimately paid tremendous strategic dividends.) A more obvious answer arose: Australia itself, rather than the Philippines, would become the base of U.S. operations in the Pacific until U.S. industrial might gained substantial naval superiority. However, if Australia was to serve as a key to America's position in the Pacific, then Australia and the lines of communication must be protected.

As late as Christmas Day 1941, Marshall had cabled Lieutenant General George Brett, commander of U.S. air forces in Australia: "The purpose is to make your command predominantly air, with the other elements limited to those needed for efficient air operations and security of bases." He further warned Brett that there was no intention of transforming Australia into a "second England." Nevertheless within weeks the United States ordered the deployment to Australia of the 41st and 32d Infantry Divisions, an air force of four bomb groups, four fighter groups, a training group, and the most sophisticated ground facilities. That was only the beginning. Admiral King was convinced that Japan was going to strike into the South Pacific and break the communications chain so hastily constructed and, as of yet, almost undefended. Consequently three infantry regiments were ordered to New Caledonia and re-formed as the Americal Division (Americans in New Caledonia). A Marine regiment went to Fiji, where it was joined by the 37th Division. Several other small U.S. Army and Marine units took up garrison duties. In addition, the 27th Division went to Hawaii in May.

A serious argument developed between the American army and navy over the buildup in the South Pacific. The army believed there would be enough warning to redeploy air and perhaps ground forces in case the Japanese moved. Consequently it was folly, they argued, to heavily garrison every important island on the way to Australia. Roosevelt reaffirmed the Europe-first commitment, and the army managed to stop the flow of troops for the time being. Dwight Eisenhower, then on Marshall's staff, put the army's case very nicely: "The Navy wants to take all the islands in the Pacific—have them held by Army troops, to become bases for Army pursuit and bombers. Then the Navy will have a safe place to sail its vessels." For its part, the navy had serious doubts that there would be time to redeploy. More fundamentally, King was convinced, with reason, that Japan was far from finished with its conquests and that every Japanese victory made an ultimate Allied triumph in the Pacific more distant and more costly.

No more infantry divisions went to the Pacific for many months. However, Marshall could never underestimate the ability of Admiral King to gain additional equipment for the Pacific. When the redoubtable MacArthur moved from the Philippines to Australia in April to take command of the newly created Southwest Pacific Theater, another powerful voice was added in favor of reinforcing the Pacific. The Pacific Theater in the long run did remain a poor relation to Europe. However, despite all plans to the contrary prior to December 7, the United States deployed more manpower to the Pacific Theater in 1942 than it did to Europe. (This trend reversed dramatically in 1943.) And compared to what Marshall would have liked to see, the Pacific continued to receive a larger percentage of U.S. resources than theoretically necessary.

The Japanese had walked into a bear trap. When one adds two crack Australian infantry divisions to the balance, the Japanese army held a very small majority of forces in the Pacific Theater. The air gap in

Japan's favor was larger but closing weekly. It was absolutely essential that Japan keep the momentum going forward and crucial that Combined Fleet maintain its qualitative and quantitative superiority for as long as possible. As we have seen, Japan suffered a reverse in the Coral Sea and catastrophe at Midway. With Combined Fleet licking its wounds, the Allies' scattered garrisons and air units, fearful until June 1942 that they would be attacked, could serve as an offensive force in an area where Japan was weak. Both King and MacArthur were quick to see that they did so. Furthermore two of the humble ferry bases created for a hopeless campaign in the Philippines rapidly became elaborate rear complexes capable of sustaining offensive campaigns in the Solomons and New Guinea.

Two Allied base complexes were pivotal in crushing Japan in the South Pacific. Each served as a strategic terminal from which the forward combat bases could gain their strength to function. This was essential for the Allies because, unlike the Japanese, they lacked major supply bases in close proximity to their fighting airfields. Support for Rabaul came from the longtime Japanese base at Truk Atoll or Japan itself, the Japanese being able to take advantage of interior lines. Although the Allies had built airstrips with great speed during spring 1942, they still lacked a solid base of supply to sustain large-scale offensive or defensive operations. Pearl Harbor was much too far east to support a campaign in the South Pacific, and the developed portion of Australia was too far south. Needed desperately were major installations within bomber and transport range of the battle zone. These core bases required a suitable harbor, several good airfields, command facilities, and, perhaps most important, sophisticated maintenance facilities capable of complete overhauls and able to forward supplies of spare parts to forward fields. Marshall may not have wanted a "second England," but if there was to be war in the South Pacific the United States and its Allies were going to have to build small cities. Once these major complexes were in place, the use and seizure of forward combat bases could commence in earnest.

The first Allied central base was at Townsville, in sparsely populated Queensland, Australia. It was a small agricultural city of some 25,000 prior to the war, although the civilian population shrunk as many people left for the safer southern states after Pearl Harbor. It was connected to Brisbane by a single-track railroad, its gauge different than that used in the rest of the country. Townsville had a small, shallow harbor with poor docking facilities; the port could and was improved. It did have large pieces of flat, solid ground and some local resources to aid construction.

Townsville's ultimate preeminence was unplanned. General Brett and the Australian government originally were more concerned about Darwin. The Japanese attacked Darwin several times with long-range bombers, and it appeared a likely place for a Japanese landing. Furthermore, in theory, it was a good place to launch operations against the East Indies. In the event, Darwin was both too primitive and too remote to serve as a good offensive base. Any Allied amphibious operation launched out of it would have been well outside of fighter range and thus required aircraft carriers, unavailable for months. And no Allied admiral would have relished operations in the confined waters of the Indies, ringed by dozens of Japanese air bases and several good anchorages for Combined Fleet. Indeed it was the remoteness of Darwin that saved it from Japanese invasion in the early weeks of the war. In the event, there was sharp air combat at Darwin early in the war, and the first U.S. fighters deployed to Australia served there. Nevertheless by July 1942 it was obvious that the locus of operations was not to be west from Darwin but north from Townsville to Port Moresby. Darwin also remained primarily an Australian responsibility. The first U.S. engineer unit to arrive in the north went to Darwin, but soon the effort shifted to Townsville, nearby Queensland areas, and New Guinea.

In March 1942 U.S. engineers, still badly short of equipment, began building at Woodstock, twenty miles southwest of Townsville. With crews working eight-hour shifts around the clock, one runway received an aircraft four days after construction began. Another company of engineers constructed a 2,500-foot by 100-foot strip covered by pierced steel plank, often called Marston mat. This was not ideal surfacing but was quick to install and far better than nothing, particularly if there was mud. A third strip in more demanding terrain was operational in two weeks. At the same time, Australian contractors scraped together every available piece of machinery and began constructing a field at Charters Towers, about forty miles north of Townsville. Problems arose, however, when the Americans began pressing for fields in northern Queensland on Cape York Peninsula. The Australian government decided that civilian contractors should not work north of Townsville lest they suffer air attack or be captured and executed if an invasion took place. Fortunately the humble Queensland Roads Commission stepped in and provided invaluable help to the undersupplied American engineers, adding an important base at Mareeba near the small coastal town of Cairns. A joint group even built a small field at Horn Island, just north of Cape York Peninsula.

Initially the fields were crude affairs. They lacked revetments, drainage, and taxiways, and the all-important ground facilities were extremely primitive. Yet as machinery began to arrive (much of it "requisitioned"—stolen—for competing projects in southern Australia, which were delayed for months), the capabilities of the Queensland bases increased tremendously. By the end of 1943 there were twenty-eight fields in Queensland, most clustered around Townsville. Another nine operated in the Darwin area. Allied engineers constructed a similar number near Perth in case of a backdoor Japanese attack. Although Townsville was a harsh area, several of these fields were improved and became the best outside southern Australia. Engineers also constructed full-service facilities for maintenance and aircraft overhaul. The facilities in Townsville and Queensland became far better than those at Rabaul, and eventually the price was paid by the Japanese.

The buildup in Queensland was part of a strategic debate that is still sensitive in Australia. In early 1942 there was much talk of the so-called Brisbane Line. The idea, sensibly, was that the southeastern quadrant of Australia should receive priority for defense planning. This included the major cities of Melbourne, Sydney, and Canberra. Because Australia was so large, went the reasoning, the frontier areas could be liberated when Australian forces were properly trained. In addition, the militia forces mobilized early in the war were organized on a state basis. States had great power in the Australian political system, and they expected their units to defend their homes. In retrospect this argument was complex. Canberra early in the Pacific war had no idea where its two precious volunteer divisions would go. The 6th and 7th Australian Independent Force (AIF) Divisions had already distinguished themselves in the Mideast. Canberra agreed that they be moved from the Mideast to the Malay Barrier. Within days after Pearl Harbor it was obvious to Canberra that the precious 8th Division was going to die trying to preserve the British position in Singapore. Sensibly Australian Prime Minister John J. Curtin demanded the return of 7th and 6th Divisions to Australia. Showing a bit of madness that marred his career, British Prime Minister Winston Churchill supported General Sir Archibald Wavell in asking Canberra for the services of either one or both of the divisions to defend Burma. Although it is difficult to make such judgments, Wavell's request and Churchill's endorsement of it probably did much to reinforce the growing attitude in Canberra that the United States, and not Great Britain, would defend Australia. It was a relationship that surprised both countries.

Australia in early 1942 believed itself an obvious target of the Japanese juggernaut. The card held up the sleeve of the government was the use and placement of the two veteran divisions returning from the

Mideast. Their arrival in March 1942 corresponded with the arrival of General MacArthur. MacArthur had abandoned an army, albeit on the orders of President Roosevelt. Yet more than any Australian general, MacArthur knew the strengths and weaknesses of the enemy. He also realistically appreciated the strength of his own forces. Whether MacArthur was a strategic genius or required conquests to compensate for past failures I will let others judge. It is true, regardless, that when MacArthur was made Supreme Commander, Southwest Pacific Forces, in April 1942 he already had the plans and the will to annihilate Japan; I doubt whether there was a better way to do this grisly job than MacArthur's. Nevertheless the MacArthur debate began long before the confrontation on the Yalu during Korea.

Simply put MacArthur was determined to move the war effort away from southeastern Australia to the north and into New Guinea. Initially he received lukewarm support from a government that, unlike the United States, feared for its existence and had suffered desperate failures in Southeast Asia. Specifically MacArthur was determined to hold Port Moresby and use it as a base to attack the Japanese. In March 1942 the enterprise appeared to be a long shot and, as noted above, would have been impossible without the aid of Japanese blunders. Indeed the 3,000-man militia garrison, which suffered frequent Japanese air attack, suffered from low morale, fearing—with good reason—that they would either have to "go bush" when a Japanese invasion fleet appeared on the horizon or fall into captivity. Repeatedly promised air reinforcement that had not yet arrived, the garrison troops began referring to "Tomorrowhawks" or "Neverhawks," a play off of the "Kittyhawk" designation that Australians used for the American P-40 Warhawk fighter.

Port Moresby possesses a grand name, but the reality in early 1942 was very different. Instead of being a port and a town, Moresby was a miserable little colonial settlement that had received slight military reinforcement prior to the war. Prior to the summer of 1942 Moresby had two fields, including Seven Mile Drome, a 5,000-foot surfaced runway that had been constructed with U.S. funds prior to the war as part of the Philippines ferry project but had been badly maintained and bombed several times by the Japanese. (The nomenclature in naming airfields was unusual at Port Moresby, as all fields had names that reflected their distance from the port. Consequently there was Three Mile Drome, Seven Mile Drome, Twelve Mile Drome, and so forth. All of these fields had official names. Seven Mile was officially Jackson Field. Most pilots, however, continued to favor using the distance-names.) There was also Three Mile Drome, a converted civilian strip that was, in the words of one pilot, "a 3,000 foot roller coaster with 300 foot hills at its ends and grades to make your hair stand on end." Bill Eaton with the 43d Bomb Group saw Moresby early in the war:

> The great Port Moresby was a pier and a couple of tin-roofed buildings. Its only importance was its ability to project power. Port Moresby was a key point in the development or exploitation of New Guinea. It was one of the few points of contact with the outside world that existed in that area of New Guinea. Whether it was worth having any contact is another question. Maybe the Japanese were as dumb as anybody else: Maybe they thought there was something there worth taking. What we would have lost was a couple of docks and a tin shack. But the main thing was that it was the place where the supplies and eventually military power flowed through.

U.S. aircraft began to trickle into northern Australia beginning in February 1942. A few unfortunate pilots fought the Japanese over Java. Material losses were worse than pilot losses. Fifty-seven precious new P-40 fighters were shipped to Java on the old aircraft carrier USS *Langley* and a freighter. *Langley*, the first aircraft carrier in U.S. service but long past its useful life, was sunk in an air attack. The freighter landed and unloaded twenty-seven fighters still in crates. Because the Japanese progress was faster than anyone anticipated and time was not available to assemble the aircraft, American sailors dumped the crated machines into the ocean to prevent their capture. General Brett ordered the Java survivors and new fighter squadrons arriving to proceed to Darwin; he sent bombers to Townsville. Thus it was up to the Royal Australian Air Force (RAAF) to send No. 75 Squadron, one of the first three fighter squadrons founded on Australian soil since Pearl Harbor, to Port Moresby. During a valiant defense half of the squadron became casualties, but the Allied presence was established and the Japanese began taking losses. Two squadrons of the U.S. 8th Fighter Group relieved the Australians in May.

In February a handful of B-17s operating out of Townsville began occasional shuttle raids on Rabaul itself. Afraid that the Japanese would destroy any bombers based at Moresby, the B-17s would fly into Moresby, take on fuel, and then proceed to attack Rabaul. None of these raids did great damage, and Japan continued to have the initiative over the New Guinea skies, but it was exactly this Allied presence that so concerned Inoue and later led the Japanese army to take their desperate gamble over the Kokoda Trail.

One of the first American units to arrive was the 101st Anti-aircraft Battalion, an antiaircraft unit, in May 1942. Moresby had four anti-aircraft guns and five machine guns to serve as air defense. Initially the 101st could add little but its own complement of heavy .50-caliber machine guns. It was already obvious that machine guns were poor anti-aircraft weapons because of their seriously limited range. Many soldiers and sailors called them "revenge weapons" because they could only down or damage an enemy after the foe had dropped its bombs. Lindsay Henderson was a young sergeant at the time and reflected on the ugly situation at Moresby at the time of the Battle of the Coral Sea:

Moresby was bombed-out when got there and there were wrecks in the harbor. As I recall there were five working aircraft on the field: one Hudson, two Wirraways, two P-39s and the wreckage of a Ford Trimotor. A few more fighters came in and so did some Aussie antiaircraft. Our positions were around Seven Mile or Jackson drome. We called it "Death Valley." The problem was that our fighters had a poor rate of climb and our radar gave them very little warning when an air raid was on the way. However, if Coast Watchers got the word to us soon enough, our fighters would get up as high as they could, dive through the Japanese formation, keep right on going until they came into Death Valley with the Zeros on their tail. There we'd work over the Japs that followed them down. I can't say it was much of a killing zone but it did scare the hell out of the enemy and we did get a few. We claimed sixteen. Later we got some 40mm cannon, which were much more effective.

Slowly U.S. and Australian units deployed in Moresby—and none too soon. In July South Seas Detachment began the audacious march over the Owen Stanley Mountains to capture Port Moresby. By this time American and Australian engineers had completed five airfields at Moresby and were nearly done with two more. This was remarkable work considering the endemic shortages, miserable climate, and frequent air raids. Naturally construction work under threat of air raid was a difficult matter. Moresby was within easy range of Rabaul's heavy bombers. In addition, in mid-1942 Allied antiaircraft was still weak, and Japanese fighters commonly strafed positions. Sergeant Henderson was strafed himself:

I had a small radio and picked up a mayday from one of our planes coming in. It was on the edge of an airfield and there were about 150 engineers out there working on the field. This plane came over and I set

up a blocking position because I knew he'd have Zeros behind him.
And there were. We knocked down one and two went away hurting. I
directed the fire and I was under fire. It was stupid, really. There I was
standing up on the entrenchment giving the directions to my machine-
gun crews. There wasn't much I could tell them with three Zeros
coming right in. Let me say that getting strafed is very interesting. The
plane that came in on me was close enough that I could have spit on
him. One of the Zeros went down and we claimed hits on the other
two. I was decorated that day and so were several others. It was early
in the war and I think they were looking for some reason to give a
medal to somebody. We hadn't had much good news yet.

Like many bomber crewmen, Bill Eaton found himself on the receiving end of a raid in mid-1942. Eaton was at Milne Bay, just South of
Moresby:

We'd received orders to test a B-17 on the runway they made at Milne
Bay. A red alert sounded. At first nothing, but then we hear this noise.
Above us there's this vee of vees formation of enemy bombers at about
6,000 feet: ideal bombing altitude. Everyone got into a ditch because
we didn't know where they were on their bomb run. When we saw
them they are almost directly overhead. If they'd already dropped their
bombs, the path would move under the plane so it's very possible that
they've already dropped and the bombs are on the way. Pretty soon you
can pick the bombs up. You could see everything happening: There was
no fighter cover, no antiaircraft, they caught us napping. Just a clean
bombing run. The bombs went right across our cantonment area and
the airfield. We lost our aircraft, a couple of people killed and a few
wounded. These were small bombs and did their jobs. I once counted—
I'd been through about eighty bombing raids. That was the only one
that I could see everything perfectly and was right in the middle of the
bomb pattern.
   When we were in the middle of the pattern it was a crapshoot: You'd
keep down and hope for the best. The bombs dropping were an
extraordinary sight. Every single one looks like it's coming straight at
you. And it is. It misses you by about ten yards up range, down range,
off to the right, off to the left. But at the time you're looking, it's
coming right at you. There's a technique at looking at bombs and
knowing whether they're going over you or fall short. You look at them
with your finger: If the bomb path stays right on your finger they're
coming right at you. If it traverses on past your finger it's going over, if
it traverses short of your finger it's dropping short. If it looks like it's

coming right at you, you might have time to get to another hole. That's what we were taught. The time of flight of these things is several seconds. When these guys were over I didn't need to use my finger cause they were putting their bombs right in the barrel.

Despite Japanese pressure the Allied buildup continued. Well over 20,000 garrison and service troops were stationed at Moresby by the end of July. At that time MacArthur brought in two brigades of the crack Australian 7th Division to deal with South Seas Detachment. Although it took them some time to acclimate to the hideous conditions in New Guinea, the Australians stalled the Japanese. Simultaneously the Marines landed at Guadalcanal and Japanese air units shifted almost entirely to the furious battle there, leaving South Seas Detachment alone. MacArthur brought up a U.S. division and the Japanese retreated toward the coastal town of Buna, where they were demolished after a savage siege.

MacArthur's greatest hopes had come to fruition. With Moresby firmly in Allied hands an offensive campaign in New Guinea was possible. For a year and a half Moresby served as the most important base on New Guinea. By fall almost all American engineers had been moved up from Queensland to New Guinea. One of their most important jobs was to transform Moresby into a true port. Once this was accomplished, the "sinews of war" could come steadily into the New Guinea theater. In addition, bomb groups originally based at Townsville were free to move up to Moresby when Japan was forced to go on the defensive. It was chilling news for Tokyo and, even more than defeat at Guadalcanal, precipitated a massive Japanese reinforcement of the South Pacific Theater.

But in order to carry forth an offensive in New Guinea the Allies required more fields closer to the front. The biggest problem with Port Moresby was that it was south of the Owen Stanley Mountains and Buna, whereas subsequent battlefields were north of them. This posed little problem for bombers and transports, barring the danger posed by ferocious weather, but crawling through the major mountain pass through the Owen Stanleys seriously reduced fighter range, particularly for the first generation of U.S. aircraft.

It was no easy quest to find airfields in New Guinea. Many small fields suitable for civilian light planes proved unsuitable for military use. The tremendous rainfall caused a high water table almost everywhere, and enormous trees made things worse. The first stroke of good fortune took place in June 1942. MacArthur badly wanted an air base and port at Milne Bay at the tip of Papua New Guinea. He feared, correctly, that the Japanese would have designs on it. He also realized it would be very helpful as a supply base for operations up the coast of northeastern New Guinea. On June 8 a twelve-man party of Australians and Americans, commanded by Lieutenant Colonel Leverett G. Yoder of the Army Corps of Engineers, surveyed Milne Bay and found a Lever Brothers coconut plantation at the head of Milne Bay that would serve as the location for at least three strips and a good wharf. The American engineers went to work and had two basic fighter strips operating within a month. An Australian militia battalion soon followed, as did two RAAF fighter squadrons. When it was obvious in late August that the Japanese were going to try to seize Milne Bay, several battalions of the 7th Division reinforced. Days later elite Japanese naval assault troops landed. After some anxious moments the Japanese were soundly defeated, with Australian P-40s causing serious damage.

Yoder soon made a far more important geological find. In early July, two weeks prior to the Japanese landings, Yoder and another party flew to Buna in search of an area for a good strip. They decided that the small strip at Buna itself had no potential. However, they found a plain covered with ten-foot-high kunai grass near the village of Dobodura fifteen miles south of Buna. Yoder and his group enthusiastically reported that Dobodura would prove a perfect place for a major base complex. MacArthur's airmen were delighted with the news but soon learned that South Seas Detachment was headed for Buna. Ironically the timing could not have been better. Had U.S. engineers begun construction prior to the Japanese landing, it is very likely that the Japanese would have been sorely tempted to make use of it. As it was, the Japanese landing at Buna could not be stopped. There is no evidence that Japanese engineers found the strategic gold lying at Dobodura. However, when the Australians drove the Japanese back to Buna, American engineers knew exactly where to construct a badly needed field.

Dobodura was, in its way, every bit as important as Moresby. The Buna-Sanananda campaign developed into a horrible battle of attrition between entrenched Japanese infantry and engineers and Australian and American soldiers. In November 1942 there were no shallow-draft landing craft in the South Pacific. Uncertain waters meant small vessels. Therefore, the first Allied offensive relied upon a motley navy of barges, fishing boats, and yachts—almost anything that was small and could stay afloat. The supply situation was a nightmare. The 32d Division had no artillery and the Australians only a handful of tubes, to use the vernacular.

Dobodura was a godsend to the men fighting at Buna. Robert Rutherford was a young officer in an antiaircraft unit assigned to protect the engineers building Dobodura from air attack; he described its advantages:

That was the first strip at Dobodura and it was made of packed sand and clay. Eventually there were three strips. It was an excellent strip because it drained quickly and compacted very well. When the engineers got in and put the steel matting down, they just put it on top: They barely needed it the ground was so firm. The river flowed right down the side of the strip. It looked like a floodplain from past eons. If you found an area like that, all you had to do was cut down the kunai grass and you had an airstrip.

Soon Dobodura was not only home to Allied fighters but also the port of entry to a small swarm of priceless C-47 transport aircraft, which brought in every type of supply and evacuated the wounded. The Australians even figured out a way to dismantle artillery pieces and fly some of them in. The only hope that the Japanese had at Buna was that the siege, as in medieval times, would collapse due to disease and lack of supply. Dobodura ensured that that would not happen; Japanese in the Buna area were doomed.

The Japanese had been weakened at Guadalcanal, which was lost just after Buna, and their positions at Lae and Salamaua were likewise in peril. When Dobodura opened in November more Allied aircraft were appearing, including some more modern types. Backed by the facilities at Moresby and Townsville, the Allies were able to keep more of their limited supply of aircraft combat-ready than could the Japanese at Rabaul. For the time being, however, the Japanese still had teeth, as Robert Rutherford found out:

At Buna we were pinching the Japanese very badly. They started to react with fierce air attacks from Gasmata and Rabaul. We were sent in to protect Dobodura. The day I landed, I got strafed. I was caught out in a field by a Zero. It was damn fortunate their 20mm cannon were on the wings because one path of bullets passed one side of me, the other passed on the other side. I will never forget that. That plane was right on top of me before I saw it. He came over fishtailing right over the palm trees there. I think he was after the field kitchen we had just unloaded. Our stove was brand-new and silver: He saw those and I'm sure that was what he was shooting at. In any case, I looked down and

saw the pockmarks left by the twenty millimeters. They left a hole
when they exploded about the size of your spread-out hand.

The Japanese got wise pretty fast. They did the same thing that they
did at Moresby. Their bombers came in a long line, like a parade-
ground formation with fifteen to twenty-five aircraft lined up at about
20,000 feet. They would drop their bombs in a pattern, trying to
blanket a valuable area, not hit an individual target. Their favorite
bomb was a daisy-cutter. I never saw a whole one. We had shell for the
155mm artillery piece that did the same thing. It had a fuse that stuck
out nearly a foot in front. When it hit, the explosion was instantaneous.
The fragments just cleared the ground. The Jap bombs did the same
thing. If a fellow had a head or a hand up, there was a possibility he
might lose it. . . . And the swirling, spinning whistle they made was
unforgettable.

Establishing Dobodura and taking Buna was the beginning and not
the end of the Allied offensive in New Guinea. From that time onward
the Japanese tasted defeat after defeat. They were stopped trying to
take a strategic airfield inland at Wau. In March 1943 Allied aircraft
obliterated a large supply convoy in the Bismarck Sea, illustrating dramatically that Japanese ground forces could not be supplied from any
point near the front. As basic supplies and shipping slowly moved into
his theater of war, MacArthur had the air bases, aircraft, and manpower to move up the New Guinea coast, bypassing major Japanese
garrisons. Each step brought new bases like Nadzab, Gusap, and Tsili
Tsili and moved the Allies to a position where they could break out of
New Guinea and move toward the Philippines and East Indies. The
C-47 transports helped supply a major Australian land campaign up
the Markham Valley. Along the way, Allied air units helped crush
Rabaul and devastated Wewak, ruining two Japanese air forces. Admiral Inoue, relieved from fleet duty after the Coral Sea and made
head of the Japanese Naval Academy, must have watched with horror
and understanding.

Admiral Inoue would also have understood the extraordinary events
that transpired in the South Pacific in the aftermath of Midway. Prior
to the Battle of the Coral Sea the U.S. Navy and its confederates were
preparing feverishly for a series of defensive battles expected to take
place between Pearl Harbor and New Zealand and Australia.
Prospects certainly did not look good in the spring. The navy decided
that Auckland, New Zealand, would serve as its forward base of operations for the theater despite its distance from potential battlefields
such as New Caledonia and Samoa. There can be little question that

the U.S. Pacific Fleet would have defended its lines of communication with the South Pacific. However, although no one liked to speak in these terms, if a desperate situation arose the security of the U.S. fleet took precedence in Washington to the security of New Zealand or Australia. Auckland, despite its geographic disadvantages, was an ideal base in every other respect and, during the defensive stage of the war, served admirably.

When Midway brought the strategic scale close to even, Admiral King proved quick to move. Although MacArthur and King despised each other they agreed that more U.S. forces should be sent to the Pacific. The U.S. services and their allies agreed on an arbitrary command line between the South Pacific and Southwest Pacific Areas. MacArthur commanded the Southwest Area and Vice Admiral Robert Ghormley was made commander of the South Pacific Area, a subdivision of the Pacific Theater commanded by Chester Nimitz. An arbitrary administrative line ran through the geographic realities of the overall theater. There was, however, a tremendous difference. MacArthur was a theater commander, the rank being defined and deified by the British-American Combined Chiefs of Staff. In other words, MacArthur ranked with Britain's Harold Alexander, Eisenhower, Lord Mountbatten, and Nimitz among the high lords of Allied strategy. His naval counterparts—Ghormley and Admiral William Halsey—held subordinate commands under Nimitz, who was MacArthur's only equal in the Pacific. Through the auspices of the Joint Chiefs of Staff (JCS), both the United States Army and USN (the Marine Corps obviously included) agreed upon a general three-stage assault against Rabaul. King had been calling for a move against Tulagi for months, and that would constitute the navy's portion of the first stage. However, in practice, the staged assault was so much paper in the basket until either commander could bring home some bacon. MacArthur faced South Seas Detachment's attack on Moresby. King was ready for his great gamble and greatest strategic triumph. Before playing his hand, however, King needed some chips.

Prior to Midway the route between Hawaii and Australia was a desperate improvisation designed to defend communications between the two points. After the American victory at Midway changed the strategic balance, the route could be used for an Allied offensive buildup. However, like the Allies in Australia and New Guinea, Ghormley and King needed sophisticated advance bases to support the move against the Solomons. Although the attack was scheduled for August, the Americans did not have their rear in order once it was obvious that Auckland was too distant to serve as a good fleet and air base. Instead the USN had to rely on some of the areas it had occupied while constructing the Philippines ferry route.

Because of pure inertia, a logical start was made at New Caledonia, the largest island between New Zealand, New Guinea, and southeastern Australia. As noted, the USN was so worried that Japan would attack New Caledonia that it convinced the U.S. Army that an entire division was required for its defense. (There was nothing at all foolish about this request, as the Japanese planned to attack New Caledonia after a victory at Midway.) A Free French possession, New Caledonia was the largest and best-suited island in the South Pacific to serve as both an advanced air and naval base. The capital, Nouméa, with a population of 11,000, offered some assets that could help the war effort, especially Tontouta Airfield. Nouméa hosted a house of prostitution that, to put it mildly, thrived throughout the war. Although by mid-1943 there were three fields on New Caledonia and the island was developing into a massive supply depot, anyone hoping for a touch of the Riviera in the South Pacific was sorely disappointed. John Herbert, who was a pilot aboard the British carrier HMS *Victorious* that constituted, along with *Saratoga*, the USN's carrier reserve in the summer of 1943, described Tontouta as a "dump." New Caledonia was a French colony, and to Herbert Nouméa was a "dirty, scruffy little town." In truth New Caledonia was not a major air base because it was too distant from the Solomons. Yet it was considerably closer to the Solomons than was New Zealand. When operations began at Guadalcanal in August, a frantic effort began to develop the port and supply facilities at Nouméa. By early 1943 Nouméa was an important naval base and the central depot supplying operations in the Solomons.

When Midway allowed a more aggressive deployment the Allies were quick to move north of New Caledonia into the New Hebrides Islands. King had his eye on the island of Efate in the southern New Hebrides from a very early date. In March a small U.S. Army detachment moved up and occupied the little jungle island, and in April a Marine battalion followed. The initial expedition literally sneaked in. There was considerable fear that if Japanese reconnaissance spotted the Marines building an airstrip, they would move down and take it. (The New Hebrides were indeed on the Japanese hit list scheduled to start after a Japanese victory at Midway.) Marine engineer Captain John K. Little related his feelings about a year after their clandestine arrival: "We were right up there under Tojo's chin. If he only opened his mouth we'd fall in. A couple of Jap destroyers could have cleaned us out at any time. That's what it meant being a forward echelon. We were for war all right. We were right on the edge of the falling off place." The Marines hacked a fighter base out of the jungle. In the months that followed Seabees built another fighter field and small bomber field along with basic port facilities. Efate, however, was a very malarial island, worse than others in that part of the Pacific. It was a hardship post and never lived up to King's designs.

Fortunately the Allies did not need Efate. Two hundred miles north of Efate (four hundred miles north of Nouméa) and five hundred miles southeast of Guadalcanal was Espíritu Santo, the largest island in the New Hebrides and the best situated to aid the planned U.S. attack on Guadalcanal. Although the largest island in the New Hebrides and possessing a splendid anchorage, Espíritu had a tiny population and was occupied in late June by a small U.S. unit. In July the Americans knew that the Japanese were building an airstrip on Guadalcanal. American engineers rushed to beat the Japanese to the punch (a race the Japanese did not know about) and in less than a month B-17s began bombing Guadalcanal. The USN quickly followed up by bringing in specialized aviation Seabee units and constructed two full-fledged bomber bases and two fighter bases capable of ferrying fighters to Guadalcanal. The USN constructed extensive air facilities, including a full shop that could refurbish warplanes, a hospital, and housing for a large air contingent.

More importantly Espíritu developed into the primary forward naval base in the first stage of the Solomons campaign. Although port facilities were crude, a naval repair vessel was brought in, and a supply of naval ammunition began to grow. It was to Espíritu that the USN warships retreated after the bloody battles off Guadalcanal. In early 1943 the navy brought in LION-1, a base force ordered to create a full-blown naval base at Espíritu. Huge stocks of fuel were gathered there, making Espíritu one of the busiest places in the South Pacific. It was a perfect complement to the growing supply depot at Nouméa. Espíritu had another advantage: Like Nouméa there was very little malaria. Nevertheless as a rear area there was nothing to attract the average serviceman other than the fact that it was out of range of Japanese air attack. Tom Powell was an airman on the famous carrier *Enterprise* and he found no fond memories reflecting on his days at Espíritu:

> We were in port a good deal of the time. We'd stay over on the beach
> in Quonset huts or tents. If we weren't flying we'd go skin-diving or
> swimming out in the surf. We had movies at night. We were billeted
> near a bomber strip and the road took a curve right through our camp.

Every time a truck would go by there'd be more coral dust to settle
down on our cots. There wasn't much there and we all got bored. We'd
eat a bunch of mutton and take cold showers. As a matter of fact for a
while we were allowed to go to the ship once a week for liberty. To
most sailors that sounds funny, but things were a lot better on board
ship. You could get a hot shower, an ice cream, watch a movie without
rain hitting your head, and sack out in a bunk without being attacked
by mosquitoes. So it wasn't bad for liberty. It was hot aboard ship, but
not that bad. If it got too hot, you'd go top side if you were in port and
look for some shade and sleep.

Yet the combination of Auckland, New Caledonia, and Espíritu
could not make up for the Allies' lack of ships and men: In almost any
rational quantification of men and materiel the Japanese still possessed
overall superiority in the South Pacific. However, this combination of
bases gave to the USN and the Allies the opportunity to concentrate
force and offer battle at a very early date. Admiral King had long had
his eye on Tulagi as the first location for a slow drive toward Rabaul.
Marshall and Nimitz agreed that this three-stage operation would ultimately lead to an attack on Rabaul itself. It is almost impossible to
determine what the respective commanders had in mind. King's heart
was never in the South Pacific. He believed that the fastest way to defeat Japan was to attack directly across the Central Pacific. The basic
logic was impeccable and was the Pacific version of the Europe-first
strategy. The most effective way to defeat Japan, so went the argument, was to neutralize Truk, seize Saipan and the Marianas, and
begin an assault on Japan by air directly.

The problem with the Central Pacific advance was that it did not
make sense to allocate large amounts of forces, particularly the fleet
units in existence after Midway, to a secondary campaign. Far better
to stand on the defensive and gather the attack force when it was ready
in late 1943, when the U.S. fleet would double in size in a few weeks
because of the building program. A timeout would have likewise aided
the Japanese. Indeed Combined Fleet wanted nothing more than to rebuild its carrier strike force after Midway.

King and his admirals faced a serious quandary. King very much
wanted to show that the USN and Marines could begin their arduous
task as soon as possible. In addition, they had genuine concerns that
the Japanese might still attempt to expand their zone of control deep
into the South Pacific. Yet a campaign in the South Pacific, now that
Australia and New Zealand were unquestionably safe, ran a serious
risk. Regardless of the losses at Midway, any major U.S. fleet action in

the fall of 1942 was a great gamble. King, Marshall, and every Japanese admiral in imperial intelligence realized that the *Essex*-class carriers, powerful light carriers, fast battleships, and a multitude of modern destroyers would be in action by late 1943. (This is not to mention the submarine fleet being constructed at a furious pace.) No one, particularly after a series of defeats going back to Pearl Harbor, could rule out a stinging blow to the USN. In addition, moving forward in the South Pacific engaged the navy with both the Australians and MacArthur. A "raid in force" was strategically pointless and politically dangerous. Furthermore MacArthur and the Australians were showing an ability to engage the Japanese Empire in a very serious manner by fall 1942. South Seas Detachment's attack over the Owen Stanleys guaranteed this.

These considerations never took place simultaneously during the early decision to invade Guadalcanal, but all came up during the Solomons campaign. MacArthur claimed that with one more division and the use of a major portion of the Pacific Fleet he could land on New Britain and quickly choke off Rabaul. The plan, in mid-1942, was not as mad as it might appear. The great land garrison on New Britain did not appear for months. MacArthur's plans did depend, however, on the ability of the USN to maintain naval supremacy over an area where his own air forces had not yet extended fighter range. MacArthur was not beyond a flight of fancy, but in this case an early attack on New Britain would have been audacious and promised huge gains compared to the risks. Whether the Pacific Fleet wanted it or not, Combined Fleet, still reeling from Midway, would have had to come out and fight a great action. The idea interested many admirals, but an older and seemingly more conservative idea won out.

That idea represented Admiral King's greatest moment: Operation Watchtower. The genesis of the operation came early. The Solomon Islands were never "occupied" the same way a European target was. Beyond that, there was always the matter of distance. Tulagi, the traditional British administrative center of the Solomons, also gave the owners the ability to launch long-range seaplanes across the area. After the Coral Sea victory Admiral King, with the full support of the Australian and New Zealand navies, decided that it was worth the effort to take Tulagi. Yet the Japanese had seized the anchorage during the Coral Sea campaign. Apparently by accident, a Japanese expedition from Tulagi found suitable ground upon which to build an airstrip on the neighboring island of Guadalcanal. The U.S. campaign, originally aimed at the small anchorage at Tulagi, quickly took on a frantic pace: They must take Guadalcanal before the Japanese airstrip was complete, or the entire operation would be unworthy of the risks imposed on Pacific Fleet. A moderate leader might well have delayed operations and hoped for the best in New Guinea. King, instead, went forward with little hesitation. Rarely if ever in American military history have ground troops and a fleet been assembled so quickly as the task force that struck Guadalcanal.

The Guadalcanal campaign revolved around the most famous air base of the Pacific War: Henderson Field. Several other battles were larger than Guadalcanal in the air (although not at sea), but none illustrated more clearly the tempo and flow of air combat in the South Pacific. Guadalcanal also proved that the Japanese had no idea how to wage war in the air. Misled by cheap victories in China and unable to accommodate lessons from the border conflict with Russia, the Japanese Navy Air Force (JNAF) gave itself a mission that it could not possibly accomplish. Once the Americans seized the airfield on Guadalcanal, the Japanese had only two choices: either withdraw and fight the Allies much nearer Rabaul, or commit Combined Fleet to a sustained engagement with nothing held back. As was so typical of the Japanese, Combined Fleet decided on a middle course that preserved the fleet for a battle that it must lose in the long run but also engaged enough imperial forces that the losses cut the nerve-endings out of both the IJN and the JNAF. The damage done to Combined Fleet was so severe that naval war likewise strategically ended in the Solomons.

The story itself it simple enough. The Marines landed on Guadalcanal on August 7, 1942. At the same time a smaller group destroyed the garrison at Tulagi. Surprised, the Japanese had only pioneers on Guadalcanal and few combat troops. On the second day the Marines completed the occupation of the airfield being constructed by the Japanese. The Guadalcanal effort included the largest group of Allied ships engaged for any effort up until that time. Leading the force were three fleet aircraft carriers that bombed every target imaginable during the landing. Inside the air range of Rabaul's bombers, the U.S. carriers were extremely eager to leave the area. Although the decision to do so has been defended by many and despised by the Marines, who felt abandoned by the USN strike force, the Americans were reacting to the same fear showed by the Japanese of land-based air attack. Combined Fleet, however, showed a weapon neglected until that time: the surface warships of the empire. Outside Savo Island, just off Guadalcanal, IJN warships wounded the Allied force badly just as the carriers were sailing to presumed safety. Four Allied cruisers went down as compared to one Japanese. Furthermore the possibility that the Japanese warships could have run amok among Allied transports was not lost on American commanders. As it was, the gruff but brilliant U.S. Admiral Kelly Turner began his illustrious career by keeping his transports in harbor for an entire day and sailing off with a huge grudge against the American strike force that should have been protecting the fleet. In fact, however, the victory won by Japan was utterly hollow. Four cruisers sunk was a good score, but the Japanese effort to stop the invasion had failed. On August 21 the Americans completed the airstrip already begun by the Japanese, and the first Marine fighters landed. Henderson Field, named to honor a Marine hero killed at Midway, immediately became the most important piece of real estate in the Pacific war.

What Yamamoto was learning would become common knowledge during World War II. If the invasion fleet arrived it was probably too late to do anything. This did not necessarily prove that carrier-based aircraft were superior to land-based defenders. Indeed the saga of Henderson Field proved the superiority of land-based aircraft—if they could keep within range of the targets. Guadalcanal would show that allowing an enemy land-based air force within one's strategic perimeter was remarkably similar to allowing an enemy to cross a river and establish a bridgehead. Once a bridgehead is established on land, it will either be destroyed or the attackers will ultimately break out. In aerial warfare the problem was exactly the same. If an air base became established there were only two ways to knock it out: a sustained and brutal air offensive, or a naval blockade and bombardment. Although the beginnings were humble, the lessons of Henderson Field illustrated the tremendous advantage held by the defense, as well as the great danger posed by even a small air base against shipping (both naval and transport). Although it would not have been any secret in Yamamoto's headquarters, most commentators since the war have missed the obvious: The Japanese at Rabaul were too far away to smother Henderson Field by air. Combined Fleet, for reasons that must always remain a mystery, refused to take the risk that could have led to victory: a sustained naval blockade and systematic and repeated bombardment of Henderson.

Henderson Field and the airfield complex developed at Guadalcanal are linked in history with the famous USN Seabees. At the outset of war, the USN's equivalent of the Army Corps of Engineers was the Civil Engineer Corps. Although working for the navy, the personnel were mostly civilians. Showing the fast action and improvisation that Tokyo did not expect, the USN immediately discerned the necessity for construction engineers working within the military framework. Rear Admiral Ben Moreell pushed for organization of USN construction units. On January 5, 1942, he gained authority to recruit men from the construction trades for assignment to a naval construction regiment composed of three naval construction battalions. This is the actual beginning of the Seabees. Admiral Moreell personally furnished the official motto: *Construimus, Batuimus*—"We Build, We Fight."

Admiral Moreell also won an administrative battle of great importance. Navy regulations required that command of naval personal go to line officers. Moreell, despite opposition from the navy's formidable bureaucracy, was granted his request that his Seabees be commanded by men who were commissioned from the Civil Engineer Corps. At the outset the navy substantially lowered recruitment standards for the Seabees. Although more than 200 Seabees were killed in action and nearly 2,000 wounded, their task—unlike the army's combat engineers or the Marines' pioneer battalions—was construction, not battle. Therefore the USN sensibly looked for men with experience in the building trades, not seamen. The age range was initially eighteen to fifty, and early in the war the USN found sixty-year-old men in the ranks. As a navy monograph on the subject noted:

> The first recruits were the men who had helped to build Boulder Dam, the national highways, and New York's skyscrapers; who had worked in the mines and quarries and dug the subway tunnels; who had worked in shipyards and built docks and wharfs and even ocean liners and aircraft carriers. By the end of the war, 325,000 such men had enlisted in the Seabees. They knew more than 60 skilled trades, not to mention the unofficial ones of souvenir making and "moonlight procurement."

At the end of 1942 the special status of the Seabees ended (other than their command by engineers). The labor shortage of skilled men at home was growing acute, and some of the older men were not up to the physical punishment sustained at places like Guadalcanal and the Aleutians. After December 1942 the Seabees gained their men from the Selective Service pool, and the average age and level of skill dropped. The men proved quick learners, however, and in the Pacific Theater the Seabees constructed 111 airfields and housing for 1.5 million men among other things. The Seabees often worked in close proximity with the Corps of Engineers. (On Okinawa a Seabee officer commanded 100,000 Seabees and army engineers in the largest construction command of the war.)

The actual construction of Henderson Field was largely done by the two Japanese pioneer units dispatched several weeks before. Because the Marines anticipated combat, of which there was luckily little, they did not immediately employ Seabees. Instead the job of completing the strip was left to the 1st Marine Division's combat engineers. The landing had been a logistical nightmare, and thanks to Japanese air attack and the defeat at Savo the original force of U.S. transports sailed away partially loaded. Only one U.S. bulldozer was ashore. Fortunately the Marines did capture the light Japanese construction equipment. Working feverishly they extended the strip to 3,800 feet in length and 150 in width.

The fact that Japanese soldiers made no effort to destroy their supplies—without which the Marines would have been in deadly peril—is testimony to the total surprise achieved by the Americans at Guadalcanal. Ironically Vice Admiral Gunichi Mikawa, the brilliant victor at Savo, had advised his superiors in previous weeks that a U.S. attack on Guadalcanal was possible. Inoue, too, prior to his reassignment in October, had expressed concern. Imperial Headquarters, however, was convinced that no U.S. offensive could take place before 1943. Japanese intelligence had not even identified the existence of the new command arrangement creating the South Pacific Area under Vice Admiral Robert Ghormley. The drift and disorganization noticed by German attaché Weneker was appearing at Rabaul. As the strip on Guadalcanal neared completion, it was still not clear where the Japanese were going to find the aircraft to operate. In the event, the Americans solved that problem for them.

By any definition Henderson was a very crude place in the early weeks of the struggle. It lacked taxiways, revetments, drainage, steel matting, and proper fuel tanks. Its rolled dirt surface was adequate but proved hazardous and vulnerable to temporary damage. Guadalcanal itself had nothing resembling workable dock facilities. The Marines, in short, needed the Seabees. They also needed the sailors of CUB-1, the first twelve naval units set up to help create and then operate small naval bases on islands like Guadalcanal where facilities did not exist. In mid-1942, however, neither CUBs or LIONs were even close to fully operational. The sailors of CUB-1 joined their Seabee comrades to help keep Henderson in action.

Keeping Henderson Field in operation and building a second and smaller fighter field nearby (immediately dubbed Fighter One) was a task that transcended anything in the realm of construction, engineering, and ground service. Instead Henderson itself was the center of an air, naval, and ground battle and became one of the great epics in American military history. Initially the 1st Marine Division had their way. The remains of the Japanese pioneers fled into the dense jungle.

(Several Koreans found the means to surrender.) Probably wisely General Archer Vandegrift, with his supply situation precarious and fearing a Japanese invasion over the same beach he had just seized at Lunga Point, decided to use his infantry to create a perimeter around Henderson Field. Not realizing the strength of the U.S. force on the island, 900 Japanese assault troops made a vain assault on the Marine perimeter on August 20 and suffered near annihilation. From that point on both the Americans and Japanese tried to reinforce their land forces on Guadalcanal. The Japanese seized beaches west of Lunga Point and of Henderson Field. Because of U.S. dive-bombers at Henderson, the Japanese did not feel that it was secure to bring in standard troop transports. Therefore—with some spectacular exceptions that triggered major naval engagements—the Japanese used destroyers and small barges to make the journey up the Solomons. Because there were islands on both sides of the line between Japanese-held Bougainville and the Marines at Henderson, the Americans called this Japanese line of approach the "Slot" and the ships that traveled it the "Tokyo Express."

So both sides attempted to build ground forces on the same island, their major positions separated only by about fifteen miles. The Japanese proved able to move a large force of infantry to Guadalcanal but were always short of supplies and materiel. The Americans moved in fewer men at first, but after the first hungry weeks they did a far better job of keeping the U.S. garrison supplied with food, medicine, and heavy weaponry. However, for more than four months the small perimeter around Henderson and Fighter One was under siege. Japanese infantry maintained observation posts, allowing them to detect everything at the airstrips; Japanese warships knew exactly where to make night bombardments. Also the JNAF at Rabaul, employing aircraft with great range, were able to strike at Henderson without fear of serious reprisal at their own base. Consequently the pilots, ground crews, and service personnel were under fire of one sort or another for weeks on end.

The most persistent threat came from a steady stream of Japanese air attacks. Tony Betchik was a crew chief for Marine Wildcat fighters and recalled the deadly routine:

Air attacks were almost every day during October. Sometimes several. You'd lose track of how many attacks there were. . . . When the Japs came in, the Zeros would come in and try to engage our fighters and try to draw them away from the bombers. The bombers would come in from in these vee formations—I'd count usually, about twenty-five planes. . . . They would come and believe me they had their bombs sighted right down the center of the field. The Zeros would try to keep the fighters away, and the bombers would drop their bombs. . . . After they dropped they'd continue on eastward. In the meantime our remaining fighters would try to engage. That October was especially bad because we often had few planes in the air. I tried to keep a record of all the strafings, bombings, and shellings and counted close to 200.

David Galvan was a rear gunner on a Marine dive-bomber. His description makes clear how crude and vulnerable Henderson Field was. As he also pointed out, attack did not always come from high level:

Henderson looked like a very small pasture with a whole lot of holes in it when I first arrived. I mean a narrow one too. When you come into Guadalcanal there was a grove of coconut trees, maybe three-quarters of a mile, then you go into an opening: a little kind of meadow that extended from Tenaru River running east by southeast. On the opposite side was jungle—thick jungle: a solid mass of trees and brush. There was no transition zone. . . . For a while in late August we only had about ten aircraft. We'd work in the open or in the jungle, which was a few feet away: gave us a lot of shade. . . . Sometimes those Bettys would come in awfully low, well under 5,000 feet. You could see right into the belly of the ship. It was incredible.

The Japanese also employed almost nightly harassment attacks by lone bombers, a tactic later employed by the Allies. Often the night intruder unsynchronized the propeller to make more noise. It's not clear whether this technique was done to add harassment value or to throw off the crude audio devices that were used to help direct night antiaircraft fire. In either case, the troops dubbed these planes "Washing Machine Charlie." The Charlie character became a fixture over every Pacific battlefield, but he is best known for his flights at Guadalcanal. Soldier Robert Ballantine, like everyone in perimeter, had to put up with Charlie:

You never knew where Charlie would drop a bomb. We would get into our big bunkers. After a while we got used to it. You'd sit there and watch him. The searchlight beams from the antiaircraft units would catch the plane. He was not very high, and he would fly in and out of the beam. Of course, they couldn't hit him, but it was quite a sight. Sometimes you could hear the bomb-bay door kind of click open. You sure could hear the bombs coming down. If it makes a kind of

swooshing, whirling noise the bomb is by you and will miss. If it's
hissing it's going to be close, and you might have to change your
underwear. Once a Betty bomber came down near our position on the
line. We went over to the wreck and checked it out. The crew couldn't
get out I guess and they were spread out all over. I've never seen so
many vertebrae: They looked like hambones.

As one might imagine, the Americans on Guadalcanal grew very
weary of being bombed and strafed with slight letup. When the enemy
took a blow, those lucky to see it were delighted. Marine Clifford Fox
describes an exceptional incident:

The Jap fighters would come down and strafe us. I was strafed several
times, especially when we were on the ridgelines. They'd came in at
treetop level or lower if there weren't any trees. If you looked up you
could see the pilot's face. One day in November on Bloody Ridge some
Zeros strafed us. It was a bad day for one of them. The Army flew P-39
Airacobras for low-altitude ground attack. They couldn't compete with
the Zeros at high altitude. But at ground level, they could get the jump
on a Zero. Anyway, this Jap came over and we ducked into our hole
and started shooting our rifles at him. That was futile really, but made
us feel good. Over the trees a P-39 came in. He caught the Jap plane
with his cannon and the Zero disintegrated in the air. It floated right
down into this ravine in the jungle in front of us. You could see the
pilot and the engine of this Zero coming down together. They were the
heaviest objects and going forward the fastest. The rest of the plane was
sort of floating earthward, shot to smithereens. We were all cheering.
But it didn't always go our way. A few times we saw our own planes
coming back from dogfights. Sometimes they couldn't make it to
Henderson and we would watch them crash into the jungle.

Another potential hazard presented itself from the air. When
bombers came over, antiaircraft opened fire. Shell fragments would
come raining down. (This was a very serious problem in cities that
underwent major air raids and were protected by hundreds of high-
caliber guns.) When the massed machine-gun fire of a large dogfight
took place right over the field, there was also potentially lethal debris
falling to earth.

Worse yet for the U.S. garrison, because the perimeter was so close to
the front lines, Japanese snipers could infiltrate and fire at the men
working on American aircraft in the open. Increasing the tension still
further was periodic artillery fire. All Japanese infantry units carried

small, 75mm pack howitzers that were poor artillery but could make life hazardous for aircraft ground crews. Later in the campaign the Japanese brought in some batteries of more-powerful guns. Lacking shells to make a sustained attack on the dug-in Marines, the Japanese gunners fired quick barrages (nicknamed "Pistol Pete" by the Americans) into Henderson. Such harassment led to self-imposed battlefield informality, where one did not sport one's rank and there was no saluting.

Twice during the siege of Henderson Field the Japanese made serious attacks on the perimeter. The brutal terrain gave them an unusual chance for success considering the respective size and firepower of the units involved. The first major attack, in September, came closer than any other to breaking the perimeter and allowing the Japanese to devastate Henderson, even if they lacked the men to hold it. Because the perimeter was so small the airmen of the Cactus Air Force became involved in these attacks. (Cactus Air Force comprised the air units on Guadalcanal; "Cactus" was the code name for the island.) David Galvan helped create a final line with the powerful machine guns of the Cactus Air Force during the Battle of Bloody Ridge, the closest the Japanese came to breaking the Marine line:

> In September we lined up our eight or so SBDs wing to wing with the rear guns facing the treelines so afraid we were that the Japs would break through. They also had two F4Fs with the tails jacked up so someone could fire the six .50-caliber machine guns. That night was hell: savagery on both sides. That night everything was firing; nothing was held back. Shells went flying over our head. We were very close to the battle and could hear the artillery, the gunfire, the screaming. The Marines on the Ridge were heroic. We knew it was make or break. It was very hard to see into the jungle, but if anyone had attacked the field, we would have fired with everything we had. The next morning everybody was worn out and exhausted but elated. Nobody was saying anything, nobody talking because it was so terrible. But you're also excited. In my case my ribs were hurting. I was chilled and shivering. The next morning my ribs felt so badly I just had to rejuvenate. We were quiet, we had our private thoughts. Everybody had a cigarette. I didn't smoke, but even I had one to calm down.

Although Guadalcanal is viewed today as a heroic struggle by the Marines and Cactus Air Force, the campaign was above all the place of suffering for the United States Navy. It was a battle that allowed no failure by any service, and the 150-year history of the USN propelled Pacific Fleet to Ironbottom Sound, the area between Guadalcanal and

Tulagi. Within fifty miles of Henderson field the USN and IJN fought
a series of vicious service battles at night, the outcomes of which potentially meant the difference between winning and losing the campaign. In between Pearl Harbor and the onset of the 1943 building
program, much of the USN's proud 1930s legacy perished off Guadalcanal. Fortunately for the United States the U.S. warships lost off
Lunga Point were joined at the bottom by many Japanese counterparts. The battles off Guadalcanal devastated the pre–Pearl Harbor
carrier force, severely damaged the first-generation "fast" battleships,
wreaked havoc on U.S. cruisers of all types, and left Ironbottom Sound
littered with dead destroyers. Yet the victims that sank with them, including two Japanese battleships, ultimately provided what Combined
Fleet feared most. The USN was badly hurt, but it had hurt the IJN in
turn. If the Japanese were not able to collect on their superior prewar
training and doctrine in 1942, the prospects for 1943, when the USN
would gain a superior force, were very gloomy.

At the time of the Battle of Guadalcanal, however, such considerations were abstract. Many men on the island, seeing only Japanese
bombers and suffering Japanese surface attack, feared another Allied
blunder. Considering the Allied record in the Philippines and East Indies, such pessimism was warranted. (Indeed Ghormley's indication
that the commander at Guadalcanal could consider surrender if necessary was his death sentence as commander.) Crew chief Betchik recalled the feeling on Guadalcanal during the period of crisis:

> We all feared defeat and capture, I think. We were afraid they were
> going to leave us there. We believed that Halsey and Roosevelt saved
> us. For a while we were almost cut off. I remember when they tried to
> bring in some gasoline on a barge and there were five naval personnel
> on the barge with a tug: The Japs blew up the barge and the tug. But
> we never got the gas. We were draining every drop possible out of
> gasoline drums we thought were already empty. Nothing was wasted.
> . . . Everything was desperately short in October, everything. When the
> army came in everything was better.

The airmen and ground crew at Guadalcanal suffered bombardment from Japanese destroyers on a regular basis. At night both sides
would send in their "cans" and bombard respective positions. However, the Americans, holding Henderson and Fighter One, possessed
a target that was good for any attack. Twice during the campaign
Combined Fleet sent capital ships to bombard Henderson, the first
coming on October, 17, 1942. On that evening Combined Fleet

risked two battleships and accompanying cruisers on an attack against Henderson that was to correspond with a breakthrough by Japanese infantry of the Marine perimeter. They also hoped to demolish Henderson totally. In practice the attack failed in both regards but gave the Marines the worst time of the campaign. Tony Betchik was there:

The "bombardment" was terrible almost beyond belief. They had battlewagons, cruisers and destroyers. After the big stuff pulled out a sub surfaced and shelled us. The fields were the main target all the time. This bothers me about accounts of Guadalcanal. Ground personnel like myself never get much credit because we weren't on the front—even though the front was a few hundred yards away. Those battles on the front were intense and fierce but few and lasted only a few hours. The men by the strip, however, were under constant shelling, bombing, strafing, sniper fire and artillery fire from the hills and then Washing Machine Charlie: We were under fire continuously. It never let up until the day I left. . . .

The bombardment started out with Charlie, a plane from a cruiser or battleship: a couple of them. Just prior to shelling they dropped parachute flares that lit up the terrain. It was a clear night and they dropped them right on the field. It was a very eerie sight: The flares were very bright, like an arc light and lit up a good bit of ground with a single flare. The planes dropped several of course. We could see the first salvo fired from the ship very clearly, but after the first shell hit we all headed for our holes and kept our head down. . . . We were all in there praying and swearing: just terrifying. It lasted about ninety minutes of constant fire. The time dragged, like it would never end. The sound was deafening: You could hear the shells come in making this freight train–like noise. We could see the flashes and light and glare would come into the hole: It wasn't that deep. I was watching the other guys in the hole myself and was terrified, and so were they. Bombardment wears you down psychologically; it's just draining. There's nothing to do but sit there.

During the Battle of Guadalcanal in November, perhaps the last decisive surface battle in naval history, the Japanese again tried to silence Henderson with a major bombardment from heavy cruisers but failed. By necessity the men on Guadalcanal, all huddled in a very small place, witnessed the great naval battles that decided their fate. They saw both the battles and the aftermath. Thomas Furlow was one of the young Marine fighter pilots sent to Henderson:

In November they had that big naval battle. Those night battles were
astounding. You'd see the guns firing like lightning, see those
explosions. All night long. . . . The next morning USS *Atlanta* [an
American light cruiser and flagship of the dead American Admiral
Norman Scott; it was scuttled later that day—EB] was sitting there
dead in the water and it looked like someone had taken a knife and
scraped the ship from one end to the others. The turrets were bent, the
damage was terrible. I remember sailors hanging on to all sorts of
things offshore. They brought in dozens to the canal: guys with legs
missing and everything. I flew escort on the remnants of our fleet. . . .

Perhaps 10,000 sailors from two navies drowned off the shoreline of
Guadalcanal. The tides and currents prevented them all from disap-
pearing into the deep waters of Ironbottom Sound. Instead, the battles
witnessed by thousands on the shore left a physical remnant, as Tony
Betchik recalls:

There were huge naval battles at night. We could see the flashes and see
the ships hit. The ships between Tulagi and Guadalcanal were
numerous: We couldn't miss it. There were many prayers on my lips for
those poor guys. I can see those flashes of red lighting the sky as they
fired, as they hit, and as the ships blew up. It was an astounding sight.
The time seemed to stand still you were so engulfed by the spectacle, a
spectator. You knew what was happening and that it affected you. But
it was spectacular.

The remains of the battles, even though far from shore, were not entirely hidden from those on the ground:

The coast of Guadalcanal was heavily infested with sharks. We were
told that the natives before the missionaries would shove the bodies of
their dead into canoes off Koli Point and the sharks would dispose of
the remains. The bodies of naval personnel after the bodies would wash
up on shore days after the battles, Japanese and American, often were
mutilated by sharks. Any aviator in the water was in trouble.
Ironbottom sound was filled with them.

Despite the extraordinary obstacles, the Seabees succeeded in slowly
improving the air base. Henderson Field had grown to 5,400 feet,
3,500 feet of which had steel matting. Fighter One was 4,600 feet of
rolled grass. In addition, they constructed Fighter Two, a graded,
3,200-foot dirt airstrip. Fighter Two was constructed on coral, which

gave it a strength that pilots liked. All of these fields were within a few hundred yards of one another.

There were Allied aircraft at Espíritu, Nouméa, and on the carriers. However, it is unlikely that more than seventy-five operational planes ever flew from Guadalcanal while the battle was in progress. Although the exact victory and loss figures of the respective sides are in some doubt, it was obvious that the trend of effective air actions was very much on the Allied side since October. This lesson was driven home with great force when the Japanese attempted to build an air base at Munda Point on the island of New Georgia, only 150 miles from Guadalcanal. The Japanese had suffered from the beginning by the great range their aircraft had to travel and the consequent difficulty they had escorting transport shipping.

Months too late, the Imperial High Command ordered two pioneer battalions and a naval base force secretly to land on New Georgia, where the Japanese had possessed an observation unit for months. They also faced one of the most effective and tenacious of the famous Coast Watchers (David Kennedy). The Japanese pioneers tried to construct a crude strip that could accommodate Zeros and serve as an emergency landing place for bombers. From the start of the campaign their formidable fighters had been crippled because they fought beyond the designed fighter range. Dozens of planes either dropped into the sea or were forced to use cruising techniques that were extremely hard on the engines. Therefore Imperial Headquarters ordered the dispatch of pioneer and naval base units to New Georgia. The Japanese tried in November with some success to build a field under the nose of Cactus Air Force. Japanese engineers bent the tips of high trees over the construction site to hide their activities.

Japanese efforts at Munda Point failed completely, and the reasons for this proved ill for Japan. Efforts at secrecy failed when Allied reconnaissance discovered the project. Long-range attacks began in early December. On December 23 twenty-four Zeros landed at Munda to protect the Japanese withdrawal from Guadalcanal and establish a base that could defend against Allied movements north up the Solomons. The stay was short, as the Japanese air base was soon annihilated by bombs dropped from tactical bombers flying for Cactus.

Yet the victory over a couple dozen aircraft at New Georgia was not what Guadalcanal signified. The Japanese lost air superiority over the Slot, and as a result Japan's ability to employ surface ships was drastically impeded. Genuine supply transports were last slaughtered near Guadalcanal in November. After that, although destroyers, barges, and submarines did their best, the 35,000-man imperial army created to crush the U.S. perimeter began to fall apart. In December the Americans broke out of the perimeter, yet during the weeks before the breakout Japanese land forces were being killed by the jungle itself. By December imperial forces were losing the ability to resist. On December 7 the Japanese commander of ground forces on Guadalcanal reported losing fifty men per day, mostly to illness. The Japanese reduced rations to one-sixth expected on the front line. The Japanese on Guadalcanal were starving to death.

It is very rare for a defeat to be considered a victory. The British evacuation at Dunkirk is an exception. If the British are to be honored for Dunkirk, the Imperial Japanese Navy should receive honor for its evacuation of Guadalcanal. At the very end, Japanese destroyers embarked fresh troops to slow the U.S. advance. Japanese air units from the Rabaul complex made attacks that succeeded in hiding the purpose of Combined Fleet. Fearing Japanese reinforcement, the Americans became cautious and lost the opportunity to demolish what remained of the Japanese land garrison on Guadalcanal. In the first two days of February Japanese destroyers carried away 10,000 men from Guadalcanal.

In retrospect, American commanders knew they had forfeited the chance to obliterate the Japanese garrison on Guadalcanal. Yet the numbers of men saved did not serve Japan well. The defeat at Guadalcanal, just as the defeat at Midway, was not objectively analyzed until well after the battle had taken place. By that time Imperial Headquarters had drawn every possible wrong lesson and put it into place. Guadalcanal was a victory of far greater magnitude than could have been hoped for by Admiral King.

One of the obvious fruits of victory was that Guadalcanal became a major base for further moves up the Solomons. It is not at all clear whether Admiral King genuinely welcomed this prospect or not. With the U.S. victory at Guadalcanal, there was no possibility of Japan pushing its boundaries farther. In addition, attrition had been serious on both sides, but the Americans knew that the ratio heavily favored them because of their greater ability to replace losses. Yet an agreement had been made with the U.S. Army to follow up the victory at Guadalcanal with an advance toward Rabaul. General MacArthur was allocating large numbers of men to what was to be a joint campaign; King had to comply. With the new fleet still building in early 1943 and actual reinforcements into the theater very limited, the USN also had incentive to keep the war alive in the South Pacific for the time being.

Guadalcanal itself became a major base for the move up the Solomons. It took months to repair a serious supply logjam at

Nouméa, but compared to its battle days Guadalcanal became a sophisticated base. There were three fighter fields and two bomber fields. In addition, Seabees built an underwater pipeline for the off-loading of aviation fuel directly into the storage tanks being built. Such a luxury was unthinkable on a Japanese base. There were eleven Seabee battalions on Guadalcanal, transforming it from a battlefield to a sophisticated forward base. These developments were good news for thousands of U.S. troops, a catastrophe for the Japanese. Because the Solomons were closely bunched, it never proved necessary—as when the Americans first invaded Guadalcanal—to have direct carrier support. This was important for Admiral Halsey because his carrier force was extremely weak. Combined Fleet's condition was no better. Therefore there were no carrier actions between October 1942 and June 1944. The Solomons, like New Guinea, proved a perfect arena for land-based aircraft of all types. The Marines' air groups, victorious at Guadalcanal, stayed in the theater and dealt even more heavy blows to the Japanese. The U.S. forces received better fighters and squeezed the Japanese even tighter.

Mistakes were made and the way was hard, but Halsey's technique of using ground-based fighters and bombers to protect a series of landings proved successful. As the U.S. air units gained undisputed air superiority, U.S. surface fleet units could operate with unprecedented aggressiveness. The Americans took over Guadalcanal in early February, and by early November they were attacking Bougainville and preparing for an attack on Rabaul. Yet many infantrymen and sailors, some of whom had *National Geographic* maps to guide them, could see little to cheer. Bougainville is a very long way from Japan. What U.S. servicemen did not understand was that a move past Rabaul put U.S. forces into the middle of the East Indies and the Philippines, allowing them to move huge distances. The only thing that stood between the Allies and complete victory was Combined Fleet. Allied victories in the South Pacific, however, had hurt Combined Fleet and its air arm very badly; its destruction in 1944 must be viewed with this factor in mind.

The most unusual and potentially most powerful air bases in the South Pacific were the aircraft carriers deployed by both navies. The interaction between naval power and the carriers was extremely complex in the South Pacific. There were five great carrier battles of the war, and three of them took place in the theater (Coral Sea, the battle over the eastern Solomons, and the violent encounter at Santa Cruz; Midway and the 1944 Battle of the Philippine Sea are outside this inquiry).

It is not my intention to explain fully the maneuvers of either fleets during South Pacific battles. Therefore I do not intend to enter the in-

tricate maneuvers that led to a carrier engagement. Yet to understand
the South Pacific campaign it is important to put the carriers into perspective. Carriers proved more powerful than even their strongest pro-
ponents believed prior to the war. The torpedo- and dive-bombers carried by the carriers quickly proved master, at least on a good day, to
anything afloat. This, at least, was the message of Pearl Harbor and
Midway.

There are three generalizations worth making concerning aircraft
carriers in the South Pacific during 1942. First, compared to land
bases, carriers were very large. In the early months of the war the serious shortages that plagued every ship and airstrip would have been
present on a U.S. carrier. When the U.S. carrier covering fleet lost
ten fighters in one day (the day after the landings at Guadalcanal),
Admiral "Black" Jack Fletcher used this as a justification to leave
the transports behind, knowing that replacing the fighters was no
easy matter. Yet each U.S. carrier could put some seventy to eighty
planes in the air during a full-scale strike; Japanese fleet carriers
could respond with between sixty and seventy. And the men flying
these planes were excellent pilots. The strenuous training undergone
by Japanese aviators became legendary. Their American opponents
were all well-prepared airmen at the beginning of the war, although
the ranks were quickly leavened with eager but inexperienced young
pilots. Probably the most skilled U.S. pilots were flying off the decks
of *Lexington, Yorktown, Hornet, Wasp, Saratoga*, and the legendary *Enterprise*. This was likewise true with Japan's great twins,
Shokaku and *Zuikaku*. One fleet carrier, if properly up to strength,
had more aircraft and better pilots than any but the most elaborate
land base.

Second, carriers by their nature were mobile. They were the striking
arm of the fleet, which increased the power of the fleet but greatly decreased the power of the carrier. For a carrier to operate in a task force
it required an escort comprising many vessels. Even with radio silence,
it was almost impossible for carrier forces to operate in complete secrecy. The IJN believed it solved that problem with complex codes,
only to be proved grossly wrong at Midway. In other words the great
carrier raids of Taranto and Pearl Harbor proved extremely difficult to
reproduce. What was far more likely was that both sides knew, on the
eve of an engagement, that the other side had carriers nearby. The trick
was to find them. The mutual mobility of the carriers after Midway established a most clear pattern. When a fleet engagement beckoned,
such as at the eastern Solomons and Santa Cruz, the carriers were
above all interested in killing each other. In this regard both sides were

successful. By the end of January 1943 the United States had lost fleet carriers *Yorktown, Lexington, Wasp,* and *Hornet.*

Some survived. *Saratoga,* the grandam of the carrier fleet, had been torpedoed twice and entered battle again in early 1943 as Halsey's only U.S. carrier for nine months. *Enterprise,* already the most distinguished ship in American naval history, was sent to Seattle for a complete overhaul to prepare for the second chapter in a combat career that lacks precedent among ships that have made war upon the seas. Admiral Nimitz very much wanted *Enterprise* overhauled and did not like the idea of *Saratoga* sailing alone for several months. Consequently the USN requested the service of HMS *Victorious,* a British carrier that operated with *Saratoga* during the summer months of 1943. The Japanese waited (largely in vain) for the rebuilding of their carrier fleet. The Americans awaited with certainty the arrival of *Essex*- and *Princeton*-class carriers that would give them a strike force that would change the basic mathematics of the Pacific war.

The third point, essential to understand, is that the pace of carrier engagements shaped the entire air campaign in the South Pacific. In the realm of carrier power, the two sides ended up with something that resembled a stalemate for a year and a half. Both sides squandered opportunities to smash the other at Coral Sea. Had Japan been victorious at Midway, I think it likely that the entire South Pacific Theater would have closed (beyond essential supplies for Australia) in the summer of 1942. As was suggested earlier, had Japan closed down the Solomons and New Guinea, MacArthur and King would have a had a much harder time mounting their counterattack into the South Pacific. But the dice did not always come down on the U.S. side. With a bit of good fortune perhaps both *Lexington* and *Yorktown* could have been saved. *Saratoga* was torpedoed twice. *I-19,* the Japanese submarine that made the most successful attack in the history of submarine warfare, sunk the newly arrived *Wasp* and damaged the fast battleship *North Carolina* in one attack. Thus the "miracle of Midway" was largely evened out by the deadly efforts of the Japanese submarine service.

By the time the battle for Guadalcanal began, the two navies were approximately equal in aircraft carriers. They risked their core fleets in two engagements, but both sides were content to cut their losses. In the carrier engagements almost all of the casualties were other carriers. When the dust settled, neither side had a powerful carrier force after Santa Cruz.

From the point of view of strategy the carriers in 1942, after Midway, were the dogs that did not bark. In other words if any side had gained solid carrier superiority the campaign in the South Pacific would have been unthinkable as it actually developed. If Japan had established clear superiority, the Americans would have never thought of attacking Guadalcanal. MacArthur would have done well to capture Buna and defend that line and points south. Had the Americans duplicated Midway at either fleet engagement at the Eastern Solomons or Santa Cruz, Japan would have had to abandon Guadalcanal immediately, and a powerful American task force, supported by Marines and soldiers, could have been expected at a number of targets, New Britain being at the top of the list.

For nearly a year a handful of carriers were available, but neither side wished an engagement. Of course this fact was not known with certitude by either side, and each watched the other for signs that it might commit its last carrier reserves. In the event, neither did. Consequently for a year the war in the South Pacific was fought between land-based aircraft.

As a keen naval analyst in 1939 might have predicted, the two sides had stopped each other. Because carriers became objects to employ against other carriers and, on occasion, other warships, a huge void opened for land-based aircraft. No one could predict the topsy-turvy world of World War II. Yet the people that argued that land-based airpower could dominate over carrier-based airpower had good arguments in the proof of war. However, when the U.S. carriers returned in strength they proved how carriers could demolish a land base. In retrospect this situation had nothing at all to do with doctrine. It had everything to do with forces. U.S. land bases proved impossible to destroy by any means because they had powerful defenses and good supply. Weaker Japanese land bases, despite formidable resistance, were ready victims to Allied airpower, whether land- or carrier-based.

It is interesting and important for this story to explain how aircraft carriers operated as air bases. (They were also central to fleet strategy, a subject I shall leave for another time.) A U.S. carrier in 1942 was a large air base and supply base for many smaller vessels. One of the important results of establishing bases like New Caledonia or Espíritu is that the carrier itself became a beast of burden. So a carrier on operations was never alone, and it supplied its fuel-hungry and most valuable escorts—the modern U.S. destroyers.

Also, U.S. fleet carriers emphasized techniques that would allow them to keep the maximum number of aircraft available for combat strike. Simply speaking, this meant that U.S. carriers kept most of their aircraft on the flight deck. In practice this meant that the planes lived on the flight deck and received service on the hanger deck. The disadvantage of the technique is that it left aircraft vulnerable to the elements. The advantage was that the Americans could get their planes off the deck in very short order. In addition, reserve aircraft were hung from the ceilings of the hanger deck if they were needed. Consequently U.S. carriers could launch more aircraft than the opponent.

A simple guide to a carrier is in order. The hull of the carrier itself, unlike most other warships, was covered by a functional superstructure called the flight deck. The flight deck was made of wood on U.S. carriers (easy to replace in action) and was large, perhaps 900 feet long. Underneath the flight deck was the hanger deck, where aircraft were repaired and fuel and ammunition were stored. The hanger deck was armored and an integral part of the ship. It was also where destructive fire was most likely to take place. Even late in the war *Bunker Hill* and *Franklin*, which possessed the most complex damage-control equipment, could not control bombs that set off explosions, part of life on hanger deck. Hanger deck and flight deck were connected by two large elevators. U.S. tactics were based on doing as much as possible on the flight deck. A damaged aircraft or one requiring the transfer of torpedoes and bombs might well go to the hanger deck. During battle, however, the action on a U.S. carrier took place on flight deck.

Carrier airmen had to deal with a new military choreography without precedent in warfare. Although the flight deck was somewhat over 800 feet long (extremely short for a land-based field) the actual "airfield" was much smaller. Whenever an aircraft carrier launched and landed its aircraft, it turned into the wind. In theory this was one of the great advantages that a carrier possessed. In practice, it proved far easier to launch into the wind than to recover planes if the ship was under attack. In either case, aircraft were expected to land and take off over extraordinarily small spaces.

The reasons were simple enough. When the carrier launched, most of the flight deck was occupied by aircraft ready to join the attack. When the carrier turned to accept aircraft, pilots were expected to snare one of several wires with a tailhook, lest they go over the side. The deck crews also established crash barriers, a type of temporary revetment to protect aircraft that had landed from being demolished by a misguided or wounded pilot. The crash barrier itself was made of cable and wire. In either case, the 800-foot runway shrank effectively to something less than 400.

Thus there was intense activity on any carrier deck. Although carrier battles were few, a carrier at sea kept a steady patrol of tactical bombers out in search of submarines. There was also a Combat Air Patrol of fighters over the carrier itself to guard against any possible

enemy air attack. This was no idle task, as Japanese bombers and flying boats, which could also drop bombs, had great range and could in
theory appear at almost any time.

When an engagement loomed or a large training exercise took place,
the deck crew put into action the crucial and well-drilled choreography required to launch and recover airplanes at maximum speed. Although the deck crew had small tractors, most of the work was manual. The flight-deck officer and the hanger-deck officer were in charge
of "spotting" the aircraft in just the right place. To aid in this task they
had a diagram of the flight and hanger decks called the "Ouija board,"
on which they moved cardboard cutouts of all the airplanes with
wings extended or folded. It was essential to make sure that one got
the maximum number of planes on deck and ready for launch without
overcrowding the deck. They also had to retrieve aircraft stored on the
hanger deck to the flight deck via the elevators (two or three depending upon the type). Considering the size of the deck, and the number
of planes involved, things were cramped and the margin of error low.
Upon landing pilots had two places to go: onto the deck or into the
ocean. And despite the obvious danger, exhilaration was part of the
experience for the deck crew.

Because of the extremely small size of a carrier deck, the elites of
both air forces congregated toward carrier action. During land-based
operations, in contrast, it was possible to send pilots into action with
very few hours of experience. Both sides in New Guinea and the South
Pacific employed fighter pilots who ideally would never have flown in
combat. But their bases were stationary and long. A carrier pilot had
to be able to set down his bird on a very short runway—if he could
find the carrier in the first place. Carriers were extremely fast vessels,
so for returning aircraft finding the ship was almost as much of an art
as finding the enemy.

Carriers also lost their share of aircraft due to accident. Very few aircraft went into the ocean on takeoff and landing, but the sheer quantity of activity guaranteed a certain percentage of accidents. A carrier
would always be followed by an aircraft recovery vessel, that is, a destroyer. Cans, which along with the carriers won the naval war against
Japan, had a certain rivalry. Perhaps this was on the part of the destroyers only, but a pilot who had mismanaged his landing or takeoff
would be traded for a few gallons of ice cream. A running joke was
that the navy believed its pilots were worth a gallon of ice cream but
not much more.

The carriers operated in a different world entirely.

Ultimately U.S. carrier pilots in mid-1944 were far better trained and flew in far greater numbers than did their counterparts. American pilots also flew superior aircraft. However, before the new ships could arrive, neither side could avoid a major confrontation in the South Pacific between mid-1942 and early 1944 that centered on land bases. Each side would pay for its decision, having to fight in an area considered among the worst on earth.

The Land and Air

New Guinea and the Solomon Islands lay between two great civilizations. For centuries peoples from the East Indies and Philippine Islands had steadily expanded the areas put under the plow or brought under the trading economy of classical Asia. South of New Guinea and the Solomons lay Australia, New Zealand, and the British—solid outposts of industrial revolution and Western political power.

Yet for centuries the peoples of the South Pacific mocked geography. Unlike the Amazon Basin, in the South Pacific the coast was open to penetration from all directions. Yet neither the ancient cultures of Southeast Asia nor the more-powerful empires of Europe paid measurable attention to any of the islands in the South and Southwest Pacific. When the British and French added the New Hebrides, or Solomon Islands, to their imperial list during the nineteenth century, neither side raised the slightest problem. This situation existed simply because neither country had anything to gain or lose in the South Pacific. Beyond matters of simple prestige, which never arose, France and England shared the meager wealth that appeared to exist for Europeans of the early twentieth century. Both countries established coconut plantations. Both countries brought missionaries. By 1920 the Solomon Islands were on most world maps, however small. None served as a diplomatic pretext for problems between France and Britain. After World War I the Australians and British agreed that Canberra should be brought more closely into the defense and decision-making in an area where no decisions were made. Beyond a few dozen British-owned coconut plantations, Australia defended nothing be-

yond an idea that British dominance could somehow be brought under
the Australian flag. Britain, which had not made a penny in the
Solomons, was more than glad to divest itself of a falling house. When
Pearl Harbor exploded, a small Australian garrison at Tulagi was there
to defend the world's greatest empire. The bitter contrast between
word and reality transformed the Pacific for a generation.

New Guinea, despite its proximity to the Indies, and for that matter
Australia, maintained a unique character until the 1930s. It must remain a great curiosity why New Guinea, or large parts of it, did not
follow the road of Java and Borneo. Certainly the Europeans coming
from the south were more than eager to grab anything worth taking.
Instead what happened was one of the world's great clashes of cultures. During the 1920s and 1930s, 400 years after discovery, Europeans found gold in the Markham and Ramu Valleys of northeastern
New Guinea. Considering the scale of the area, large numbers of Europeans came in to profit from the finds. In practice the number of fortunes made was small, mostly around Wau, an area that became an
odd and important battlefield during World War II. What was striking,
however, was that Western scholars, traders, and government officials
discovered, along with the deep Amazon, the last great area of cultures
unknown to the West. Those who braved the field in the 1920s were
more likely than Amazon expeditions to encounter tribes that had
never seen technically advanced civilization of any kind. The encounter stunned those who were inventing the field of anthropology. It
was possible to research the ways of humans prior to complex agricul-
ture and towns.

On the coast, New Guinea had much of the same qualities as the
Solomons or even the sleepy islands of the East Indies. Plantations existed in small numbers. Colonial officials were largely charged to see
that native labor was available to harvest coconuts. Psychological
force was employed in gathering the labor gangs, but at no time did
Australia or England have more than a few dozen men arranging work
contracts. The colonial powers did little more than elaborate on a type
of feudalism that already existed. The plantation owners paid the
chiefs, and the chiefs awarded the manpower. The pace of work was
very slow, the workers given small incentives. Structurally the world of
the South Pacific changed little, and external accommodation to the
Europeans was minimal where it took place at all.

Twenty miles inside the coastline were tribal groups that considered
war glorious and the death of any enemy a sign of heaven's grace. As
the gold miners and anthropologists found out in the 1920s and
1930s, there was a large, vigorous, and brutal society that existed as

though frozen in time for 10,000 years. Miners, explorers, and men of the cloth disappeared into this almost impenetrable vacuum of people and dense forest.

What Europeans ruled or examined is what moderns would call "triple-canopy rain forest." Back then it was simply called the "jungle," a term with a sinister connotation, for in the jungle nature ran riot. Wild animals killed men; the people who lived there were dangerous; nature itself was the greatest danger. In fact this was a good description of the jungle of New Guinea.

Modern War in a Primitive Place

The reason that Europeans and Southeast Asians had more or less ignored the Solomons and New Guinea for centuries was simple enough: Going to the South Pacific very likely meant death. The populations of the Solomons and New Guinea had accommodated to nature's killing machine, but most outsiders could not. The great rainfall and heat of the tropics made the area heaven for microbes of all types. Unlike areas north and south, there was no genuine dry season that forced microorganisms under some kind of natural cease-fire. Instead the barrier between Australia and Indonesia was malignant terrain for humans, being rife with malaria, dengue fever, typhus, and dysentery. Ironically armies and air forces could exist in this environment because of their numbers and the budding medical facilities behind them. Western settlements were far more precarious and lent surprisingly little to the war when it arrived. No blame can be given anyone, of course. There was no area in the world considered less likely to be a major battlefield than the malignant jungle of the South Pacific. No doubt, one of the reasons that the Allies prevailed when they did was simply that they proved better able to confront nature's onslaught than were the Japanese.

Although the South Pacific was not at all ready for a great war by industrial powers, that is what took place. By definition, war with large numbers of powerful weapons is a harsh challenge to human nature. The men from Japan, the United States, and the Anzac countries faced one another on a unique battlefield. The malignant terrain assaulted the men. Pilots had to fight debilitating illness as well as the enemy. The horrid climate pounded the machinery. The sinister obscurity encountered by every crewman of every plane who flew in the theater added to the problems posed by inherently poor morale. And because of the strategic alternatives set by the respective powers, none of the air forces fighting in the South Pacific received the supplies and replacements necessary to keep operations on an even keel.

The fighting men engaged in the air war in the South Pacific confronted every problem faced by those in secondary theaters like China
and Alaska. There was, however, a tremendous difference: The South
Pacific air war corresponded with a major commitment of land, sea,
and air forces against powerful enemy bastions. The Allied pilots had
it worse in the early stages of the war. Much was required of them and
little was given to them. Small consideration was given to the miserable conditions facing the Allied air forces by leaders like General
Henry "Hap" Arnold, whose heart lay in Europe. The Japanese, by necessity, attempted to maintain a superior force in the area. They were
not disturbed by a war in Europe. They knew where the Allies were
coming. Deficiencies in Japan's buildup resulted from overconfidence
and poor direction in Tokyo and from Combined Fleet.

Robert DeHaven was a fighter pilot for the 7th Squadron of the famous 49th Fighter Group. He recalls his theater with little fondness:
"It is impossible to describe New Guinea. No other theater was like it,
I don't think one will ever be like it. Bits and pieces you describe with
words and we have our photographs. But the totality is something that
those who weren't there can't possibly imagine. There was the heat,
rain, and mud. And there was a menace to the place."

Although the heat plagued everyone, the ground crews working the
flight line faced an unusually heavy burden. There was a great deal of
physical labor involved in many tasks undertaken during World War
II. The Army Corps of Engineers and navy Seabees both realized that
it was impossible to expect the same pace of work in the South Pacific
as in more congenial climates. The same was true for aircraft ground
crews. Frank Emmi was an armorer for the Fifth Air Force and found
the challenge of New Guinea's climate difficult to surmount: "On the
flight line, there was a lot of physical work involved in those days. For
instance, a lot of bombs put on fighters we loaded by hand. . . . And
the heat was so great that sometimes you could fry an egg on the skin
of an airplane. . . . But what could we do? There was no place to run
to." Lee Tipton was with Air Service Command in Thirteenth Air
Force. After one tour in the South Pacific, nostalgia did not call him
back for another visit: "I had no desire at all to return [for the fortieth
anniversary of the invasion]. The most terrible thing about my service
was the place itself. . . . Decay was in the air. And then there were the
mosquitoes and bugs of every description. It was not a very inhabit-
able place." Fighter pilot Robert Croft of 7th Squadron recalls the effect of the constant humidity: "It was never dry. They had a wet season and a rainy season. The moisture was either being sucked up by
evaporation or landing on your head. And it was extremely hot all the

time." C. L. Jones flew fighter aircraft for 39th Squadron, one of the first U.S. units dispatched to New Guinea. He points out that the oppressive climate added to the problem of fatigue, always a torture to men at war:

Fatigue starts to grind you down. We flew a lot of missions and the living conditions were so bad. In the early days Port Moresby was full of great American greenhorns. We had our tents and cots: some equipped with stolen air mattresses, but they didn't last long. Sleep was restless because of the heat, humidity, and Jap raids. When the Japs hit at night, you had to pile out and go into the slit trench and hope one of those daisy-cutters didn't shred something. So, you'd sleep during the day. I used to sleep on top of a recon tower because it was that much higher than the mosquitoes. When someone picked up an enemy attack, someone would fire a pistol or rifle shot. You'd rush out to your airplane. Now, it didn't matter if you'd just had a shower or were sitting under the shade, the heat got you. You climbed into your fighter, strapped on your parachute helped by the crew chief, and you fired up the engine and waited for your turn to take off. When sitting in that cockpit you were wringing wet with pure sweat. This is the jungle. You thunder off, get up there, and find your guys. When you get up to 8–9,000 feet you'd cool down because your air vents were opened. But you weren't air-conditioned like the later jets. Environmentally pure. There was sure no spit and polish in that theater. But heat or no heat, you couldn't expose all of your skin because of the mosquitoes and sunburn.

The South Pacific was no place for an officer who was a stickler for proper dress. Although medical personnel urged men to wear some kind of protection from mosquitoes during the day (everyone slept under netting), few listened. Pilots, who were officers, might well lounge around in cut-off fatigues, boots, T-shirt, and baseball cap. Military formality rarely stands up to field conditions. It was swamped in the South Pacific. Frank Champarty, a 5th USAAF medic, illustrates the point: "The heat was tough to take, simply terrible. My regular outfit was a pair of socks, a pair of bedroom slippers and a pair of pants cut off at the knees. Nothing above. That was it. I'd sit in the dispensary and the sweat was just rolling down. It was always 90 [degrees] or more. It might get chilly at night, but then it might rain. It really was wretched."

The sun itself could be an enemy. Most men would take some kind of defensive measures against the sunlight, but it was possible to let down one's defenses and pay a serious penalty. Fred Hitchcock was given tower duty on one of the small fields of the Gusap complex that supported the Australians in mid-1943. As Hitchcock points out, at this place and time, "200 kids" were running a major part of the air war with little interference from 5th USAAF Headquarters: "The sun is bearing down the whole time. . . . After two days in the sun . . . I checked a little mirror I had out and my lips were black from sunburn. They put salve all over myself. Then they put me back on the strip. Eventually I got used to it." J. W. Kennedy was the radio operator for one of the feared 5th USAAF B-25 Mitchell low-level strafers. For several months Kennedy's unit flew out of the major complex that the army developed at Dobodura, New Guinea. Long after the war Kennedy retained vivid memories of a land where nature ran riot:

Near Dobodura the jungle was typical rain forest. . . . When the sun went down it became pitch dark almost immediately. Soon after dark the bats would come out. We had these huge flying fox bats that lived in the trees behind us and the smell of the guano was terrible. They'd fly out and cover horizon to horizon. All you'd hear in the area were those squeaks they made. Shortly before dawn you'd hear them come back in. . . . Earlier when I was at Moresby and along the coast we'd see these big saltwater crocodiles in the marshes . . . a real danger to the coastal villagers. The snakes we'd hunt with machetes. At least the place didn't have tigers.

He continues with his description: "The thing that got you were the earthquakes. Every damn time there was a quake one of those trees would fall. . . . One morning we woke and the tent and the area was covered by what looked to be snow. Then we looked at it and figured a volcano had blown about 120 miles away and the ash had floated down our way. . . . We had tremendous rains constantly."

If anything, earthquakes were worse on Bougainville and Rabaul. (Contemporary Rabaul was devastated by a major volcanic eruption in 1994.) Leonard Owczarsak helped man a battery of powerful 90mm antiaircraft guns on Bougainville soon after the U.S. invasion in November 1943. He remembered a quake that would have no doubt flattened a city:

On Christmas morning of 1943 there was huge earthquake. The Japanese had launched air raids that night, so we were in our bunkers. About 5 A.M. our bunker . . . started shaking like crazy. We all dashed outside, afraid that it would cave in. It was almost impossible to stand because the earth was moving back and forth. What was really frightening were the huge trees that were shaking so bad we could hear the leaves ruffling. Nobody wanted one of those things coming down on their head. As it was, the quake shoved a two-and-a-half-ton truck 100 yards into the mess tent. There were aftershocks all day. You don't get accustomed to things like that.

One of the peculiarities of the tropics was the extremely rapid transformation of some types of land. Along the coast many areas were sunk in a permanent mangrove swamp. Other areas had red clay topsoil that turned into something like ice if trodden or driven upon. However, if drainage was good the intense heat could evaporate the mud between rains. Naturally airstrips were built on areas where drainage was good. Thus, even though serving in one of the wettest areas of the world, men serving at air bases were often plagued by dust. Melvin Levet was a weather officer for the army's Thirteenth Air Force in the Solomons. He describes this strange phenomenon: "Over any island mass it was typical to have thunderstorms almost any afternoon. When the sun goes down they clear up. It was so hot, however, that the water evaporated with tremendous speed. So it could be dusty one minute and then you'd drive down the road in a jeep and run into mud the next minute and five minutes later it was dry and dusty again—all depending on the drainage. This mud and dust was tough on operations."

The abuse suffered by the aircraft from the climate, made worse in some cases by enemy air attack, was a very serious matter. Although I shall examine the air forces and their fighting planes in greater detail, it is worthwhile to note here that throughout the period the operational bottleneck for both sides' operations was numbers of aircraft and spare parts, not a lack of pilots. Very simply, aircraft were precious commodities, and each loss hurt.

Early in the war aircraft on both sides were particularly vulnerable. Even the robust U.S. planes were not fully able to cope with mud and dust. From the point of view of the overall war, it meant very little that a plane was not flying because it had been shot down or because its pilot damaged the landing gear during a botched landing. Dust was a maintenance nightmare. Aircraft of the era were extremely complex and extremely vulnerable to erosion caused by dust simply because the planes' cooling apparatus sucked in air at all times and circulated the mud and dust into the inner workings. Likewise, dust was the bane of instruments. Many a flight was either canceled or ended in disappointment (or disaster) because dust had fouled an instrument.

As time progressed, the air forces began to adapt to the problem, the Allies better so than the Japanese. However, although maintenance procedures improved, and in 1943 superior aircraft arrived, another trend worked to worsen the situation. As the war progressed a greater percentage of Allied aircraft moved closer to the front. For instance, as late as January 1943, 51 percent of 5th USAAF personnel were still in Australia. By December 1943, 80 percent of the men had moved into New Guinea, and 60 percent were stationed north of the Owen Stanley Mountains. Although the men showed great tenacity in adapting to the punishing terrain, using any reasonable standard there was not any ideal air base north of the Owen Stanleys. Some were simply worse than others. A similar situation was taking place in the Solomons. Before Guadalcanal all of the Allied aircraft not on carriers were on the simple but adequate large island bases like Espíritu. As time went on, these bases, like their Australian counterparts near Townsville, became fine installations. However, Admiral Halsey's air commanders moved most of the combat aircraft closer to the front once the Americans took Guadalcanal. Simply put, as the air forces on both sides got larger it was more likely that they would fly from the worst fields because they were closest to the front lines. By the time the engineers improved the situation significantly it was time to move again. The Japanese position was somewhat different. With the exception of the later bases established near Wewak and Hollandia, they never successfully moved out of their Rabaul-Bougainville complex. Allied bombing attacks, however, eventually caused considerable damage to their fields. Japanese bases in New Guinea were considerably worse than their U.S. counterparts, and as we shall see Japan faced crippling maintenance problems. From beginning to end the South Pacific was a poor location for an air base.

World War II aircraft made great demands on the pilot. Under the best of circumstances there was a slight element of risk involved when an aircraft either took off or landed. The laws of physics made them vulnerable during both maneuvers. On a field that was covered with mud or clouded with dust, the danger was more acute. One of the most common mishaps was the ground loop. World War II aircraft were designed to fly. They had to land and take off reliably, but the pilot had to balance several forces. There was no steering wheel, in the automobile sense, for aircraft taxiing on the ground. The pilot controlled the plane with the rudder and the brakes. The engines, however, were tremendously powerful, and the aircraft very heavy. Single-engine planes faced the serious problem of torque—the centrifugal pull placed on the aircraft caused by the movement of the huge propellers.

Guiding an aircraft on the ground, whether taking off, landing, or on the taxiway, was an accident waiting for the unwary. On bad fields it happened more often than pilots wanted. Bud DeVere worked the tower at Henderson Field during the worst of the Japanese attacks and describes the ground loop: "One side of the plane drops, and it does a fast spin around. Like a pivot on that one dead spot. The wing would go down, stop it, and the other wing and the wheel that was up would swing right around. Sometimes half a circle, sometimes a whole circle. Damage [to the plane] was almost certain. Landing gear, props, it depended on the severity." DeVere believed that the Wildcat was initially vulnerable to ground loops because the hard tail wheel (carried in addition to a tailhook for ground landing) was designed for paved American runways, not the slippery conditions of Guadalcanal.

Tom Furlow was a Marine pilot at Guadalcanal during the peak of the battle. He confirms what DeVere saw from the tower:

> The Wildcat was a tough aircraft and got the job done, but it really wasn't well suited for land-based operations. The landing gear were very closely spaced. Aboard the carrier that wasn't a problem because you'd catch that wire and you'd stop. But on land you really had to be careful. The worst thing was take off, where the Wildcat was very prone to ground-looping because of that narrow gear. I almost got killed because of that. I was next to the field; a ground crewman was strapping me into my fighter. I saw this plane coming at me and it looked like it was going to hit me square. It kept on going okay but hit two aircraft past me on the same side of the strip. It killed the pilot and the crew chief that was with the plane. It was just one of many operational accidents. There were many of those. Most of those were caused by lack of experience and bad conditions.

Like Furlow, Roger Haberman was a fighter pilot flying for the illustrious Marine squadron VMF-121 on Guadalcanal. Haberman witnessed a catastrophic accident caused by inexperience made worse by a dangerous airfield: "On one occasion a kid took off and hit a line of planes and three planes and about four people were killed, including the pilot who caused the accident. He was in the dirt but didn't line up straight and he came off the left side. He couldn't see either and [crashed] right into some parked planes. He lined up but didn't come out straight. Those were not the conditions we trained for. But, what the hell, you go with what you have."

Problems at Guadalcanal continued after the crisis had passed in late 1942. Nuisance raids continued, and Seabees slowly improved the strips. However, more planes were pouring into the Canal, raising the possibility of accident. William Norris, a ground crewman of the army's 67th Squadron, witnessed the kind of near calamity that was extremely common in the theater: "It's hard to believe the damage that occurs when a plane comes in hard. Once on December 31 of 1942 we were on the new fighter strip. A P-39 was taking off, and a P-38 accidentally taxied too close on the runway and the '39 ran into it. The collision broke off part of the left wing of the P-38 and he went over into a bunker along the runway and collapsed his nose wheel. The '39 caught fire and burned to a cinder. The pilot got out luckily."

Problems with ground accidents were every bit as bad on New Guinea. There was probably no single Allied field complex in the Pacific Theater that was as miserable as that found on Guadalcanal during the battle. However, if anything the climate and ground were worse in New Guinea than in the Solomons, and rudimentary fields that would not have been considered for military use in peacetime sprouted throughout the miserable terrain. Although Rabaul developed into an adequate base, the Japanese fields in New Guinea, mostly seized from the retreating Australians, were among the worst in the theater. After the war famous Japanese ace Saburo Sakai described his first impression of the fighter base at Lae:

On April 8 I flew with eight other pilots from Rabaul to join our new base at Lae. I groaned when I circled the field. Where were the hangers, the maintenance shops and the control tower? Where was anything but a dirty small runway? I felt as though I were landing on a carrier deck. On three sides of the runway towered mountains of the rugged Papuan peninsula; the fourth side from which I approached was bordered by the ocean.

I could find little cause for humor in this forsaken mudhole. The runway was 3,000 feet at most and ran at a right angle from the mountain slope almost down to the water. Adjacent to the beach was a small aircraft hanger, riddled with shrapnel and bullet holes. Three shattered Australian transport planes lay in a heap and demolished equipment littered the area.

Seventh Squadron's Robert DeHaven was in the thick of the fighting in Papua during 1943–1944 and flew out of several airstrips. DeHaven spent much of his service flying the army's P-40, another aircraft known for its tendency to ground-loop:

You sat low in a P-40 and unlike the later P-38 it was a tail-dragger. [The Lockheed P-38 Lightning had tricycle landing gear, meaning it included a nosewheel; this afforded far better visibility and is standard on aircraft today.—EB] Visibility on the ground was far from ideal. Because of the mud on top of the steel planking, any airfield in New Guinea was conducive to a crash. Even a modest change of direction on mud could turn into ground loop. If you were lucky the wing didn't touch the ground. It was always a surprise when you'd feel the airplane starting to go. You try to apply the brakes and manipulate the rudder. However, if the surface was muddy the brakes were useless. It was very important to stay alert at all times. We lost a lot of planes that way.

Australian Air Commodore William Garing commanded the courageous and extremely effective fighter defense of Milne Bay during the failed Japanese invasion of August 1942. At a time when aircraft were precious, the elements often worked against the defenders. Like De-Haven, Garing's fighter pilots were flying Curtiss P-40 Kittyhawks.

When they took off you could hardly see the plane. A cascade of mud came up the sides and to the rear. Landing was the same, just a spray of mud. . . . Flying on mud amplified a nasty habit of the P-40. It was a terrific fighter-bomber but had a tendency to do a ground loop. If a pilot did one, he never did another. You had to be very cautious on use of rudder. That was the secret: A new pilot in a Beaufighter [Britain's excellent fighter-bomber much beloved by Australian pilots.—EB] came in and didn't understand this. He went into circles and ran into a Hudson bomber. You hated to see things like this, because at the time aircraft were far shorter than pilots.

No commander with any sense would tell his men that the airplanes were more valuable than pilots, but early in the war that was the harsh reality. So nobody said, "Save the airplane and hell with you." But in the long run we had to be as careful with planes as possible. That's why we continually improved the fields and built all of those revetments.

Bombers were also vulnerable to mishaps caused, at least to some degree, by wretched ground conditions. In some ways they were more vulnerable to calamity than were fighters. If a clogged engine quit during takeoff, serious trouble was very likely. Whether bomber or transport, multiengine aircraft were heavily laden on takeoff and required a sizeable strip. Unfortunately construction units were always short, and it was a rare field that lacked some type of hazard. A common danger for heavy aircraft was the treeline. The jungle adjoined most bases, and cutting down huge trees was no easy task. Frequently, therefore, the margin of error was uncomfortably thin.

How thin is best illustrated by the most catastrophic accident that took place in the South Pacific. Armies do not like to publicize these incidents, and the catastrophe to be described was kept secret for several years after the war: At 4:00 A.M. on September 7, 1943, five trucks containing the men and equipment for Company D of Australia's crack 2/33d Infantry Battalion were waiting to load onto transport aircraft at the end of a runway outside Port Moresby. An American B-24 heavy bomber, loaded with 500-pound bombs and 2,800 gallons of fuel, apparently suffered some kind of power loss on takeoff. Its wing hit a tree, sending the aircraft careening to the ground. Much of the burning fuel and bombs fell directly into the Australian trucks. Fifteen men were killed outright; forty-four later died of injuries, and ninety-two were injured but survived. The eleven-man bomber crew perished. Australian infantryman Bill Crooks was in one of the trucks and described the scene:

> The men had their ammo and their grenades including white phosphorous and explosives to distribute on the plane. Three of the 500-pound bombs exploded and the fourth was red-hot. I was blown into a tree with my kit on fire. I knifed the waist belt off and dropped to the ground and ran under a truck chassis. I knew what went up had to come down. I lay there and saw flaming petrol running down the track towards me. Then I saw one of my men stuck to this red-hot bomb and noticed his right leg partially gone. So I'm struggling and cutting, not even thinking about the bomb. I didn't realize it was a bomb until later. Anyway I got him off and then we were inundated by very brave U.S. airmen putting men on stretchers and giving morphine needles. I walked to the control tent to report to the adjutant that D Company was no more.

The casualty rate for bombers was very high. Good flying on the part of the pilot could save an aircraft in an emergency. An emergency could come on takeoff, landing, or somewhere in between. Under good conditions a skilled pilot could save the crew. When landing or ditching any combat plane, it was essential to keep the nose up. Although all pilots were taught this, the more powerful the aircraft the more difficult became the reaction. In a light trainer, students learned to bring their planes in at a slow speed with the nose up and make a three-point landing (two wheels beneath the wing and tail wheel simultaneously) by hitting the field at or near stall speed. For light aircraft stall speed was low. The faster and heavier the aircraft became, the stall speed increased greatly. What this meant in practice for all combat pilots, especially for bomber pilots, was they had to land at a speed that appeared at first to be much too fast. As we shall see, in the late 1930s it was possible to land large planes at high speeds. If unable to do so, the aircraft used during the war would have been unflyable. That said, pilots did not like fast landing speeds. Surprisingly few bomber pilots made mistakes on landing and takeoff in the theater, simply because so many of those not up to the job died during training. However, if anything went wrong, a bomber pilot had to keep his speed high at all costs so he could stay nose-up when it landed. There were few things predictable in the air war. However, if a warplane crashed nose-down, everyone died because of the tremendous kinetic energy involved. With the nose up, it might survive tremendous damage and the crew might survive. Undoubtedly the difference between a catastrophic crash and another damaged aircraft was often due to luck as well as pilot skill.

J. W. Kennedy served as a radioman on a B-25 in the 13th Squadron of Fifth Air Force. He arrived early and, as many aircrews did, stayed late. Kennedy described the slight difference between life and death in a disabled bomber:

> Who knows why some made it and others didn't? Sometimes a plane would hit the water and float for a couple of minutes, letting everyone get out. Sometimes it would break in half and immediately sink. How do you tell? It's the angle that the aircraft struck the ground. Standard procedure was full flaps, nose high, hit with the tail bumper on the water, or if you came in on land with your hydraulics shot out, the radio operator could crank down the flaps manually, the pilot would bring it in a little higher than stall speed, and then pull the throttles all the way back, mixture control full rich, throttle closed, and then reach up and grab the master electric switch, which was above the pilot on the left hand side, and let her ride down the dirt strip. . . . The airplane would stay in one piece but you bent the props. . . .
>
> On another mission our plane mushed back in on takeoff. An Australian staff officer was standing between the pilot and copilot on takeoff: You could tell he was a ground soldier because no airman would do that. The prop sheared off and the blade came through and decapitated the Australian. The other four walked away.

The proper ditching technique was an issue of tremendous importance to aircrews in the South Pacific. In general, the danger from enemy action, fighters, and antiaircraft was serious but not as great as that faced by pilots in the European theater. And the weather was not as hazardous as a European winter. However, maps and navigational aids were extremely unreliable in the Pacific. Worse, if battle damage, lack of fuel, or mechanical failure forced an aircraft down, there were only two places to go—into the ocean or into the jungle. An Allied pilot in distress over Europe could bail out with a parachute and stand an excellent chance of survival even if it meant a harsh incarceration in a German prisoner-of-war camp. (Obviously abandoning an aircraft was extremely risky under any circumstance. European-based airmen could also face extreme danger if forced down over the English Channel or North Sea.)

However, the possibility of going down in the South Pacific could only bring chills to the heart of any airman. Crewmen would take tremendous risks to return a badly damaged aircraft to base or at least find a stretch of shoreline where they could attempt a ditch. Of the two dangers—jungle and ocean—the jungle was the most feared. On its face, this seems an unlikely proposition. In most parts of the world, terra firma is the friend of a flier in distress. However, the jungles of New Guinea and the larger islands like Bougainville were so dense and brutal that to go down there was a virtual death sentence. For one thing the trees were very high. It is possible that the famous ace Neel Kearby was killed by parachuting into high trees, although he might have been killed by the Japanese. Regardless, someone parachuting into the jungle was in dreadful danger for this reason alone; obviously this condition made ditching into trees certain death. But even if someone made it to ground, the chance of returning was almost nil.

There was only a handful of paths made by native inhabitants and animals in the jungle. For the most part, the land was impenetrable vegetation. John Gallagher was a crewman on a B-25 of the 345th Bomb Group and reflects on the perils of the jungle: "Beyond our bases the jungle was awful. At the time it was terrible country. I mean terrible. There were headhunters, and lord knows what kinds of reptiles and insects and every germ on earth. If you went down in the jungle your chances of getting back were almost nonexistent." Fred Miller was a crewman on a B-25 of the 38th Bomb Group. He described the extraordinary difficulty of finding men within sight of the base itself:

> I'll give you an idea of how bad the jungle was. We had an engineer
> that flew with the pilot and copilot on testing an airplane after doing
> major maintenance on an engine—they don't take the unnecessary

crewmen for that duty. They were up there and the plane started acting up and the pilot ordered the three of them to bail. So the engineer bailed out seven miles from the airstrip. The copilot bailed out three miles away. It took them seven days to rescue the engineer who was seven miles away. I was in a light search airplane with an Aussie pilot and a native guide, and we flew over a native village probably less than a mile from where we could see the 'chute of the guy who'd gone down, the engineer. We dropped a gun and some food but he never got to them. They had to fly in one of their new amphibious jeeps or he'd have still been there. It took them three days to get the copilot. You just don't have any idea of what the jungle is like until you go back into it. Most U.S. soldiers never went inside the jungle because it was near suicide. . . . So if you went down it was curtains. Except for those men we saved near our base, we never had a single POW or a single survivor from any of our men that went down.

An aircraft over New Guinea would try to hug the coast. Going inland left them devoid of landmarks and vulnerable to the consequences of mechanical failure and a crash in the jungle. However, aircraft were frequently sent on missions that pushed their fuel supplies further than pilots would have liked. Or they might be sent on a ground attack or supply mission in support of Australian units inland. Consequently pilots often would fly either over open water or overland. Flying over open water was not generally an extremely dangerous operation for a bomber or reconnaissance aircraft, because they had great range and normally carried a navigator. Fighter pilots, however, had to do basic celestial navigation with simple charts. Normally it worked, but the consequence of error was obvious. To save fuel, aircraft also flew overland. The only real self-defense mechanism beyond the crude and very unreliable navigational aids provided by radio was the existence of the few emergency strips. The Allies and Japanese created such strips throughout the theater, and the concept was simple: If engineers discovered an area suitable for an airfield that was not in the strategic lines of attack and defense, they would build an extremely rudimentary field with no support facilities, simply to prevent aircraft from falling into the sea or jungle. Sometimes emergency fields were part of the simple civilian air-base system that existed before the war. On occasion in the Solomons some of the emergency strips also saw combat action, but that was not their reason for existence. They were manned by a handful of individuals, and it is difficult to estimate how many aircraft were saved thanks to these tiny fields. The nature of the job was different, however; emergency strips simply waited for a lost plane to drop in.

Hood Point was a good example of a New Guinea emergency strip. Situated southeast of Port Moresby, it had no strategic function whatsoever other than recovering aircraft that were lost or in danger. It was manned by a handful of Americans, all of whom found themselves in the middle of coastal, Australian-controlled Papua New Guinea. Robert White served several months at Hood Point and experienced a type of war that was extremely rare for an Allied serviceman in New Guinea:

Hood Point was . . . a grass strip with Marston matting on both ends and a thatched roof hut, quite large for the number of people assigned. . . . The beauty of it was that it was very close to the water and it was flat: nothing of height near. It was safe to come in. It couldn't take many planes, but it didn't have to. . . . There was some business. A couple of Australian P-40s landed. Another guy came in with a P-47 and turned over and couldn't get out. He was jammed down into the mud, so the natives helped dig him out. . . . Later a B-25 also came in. Day after day there would be nothing to do. It was interesting to talk with the pilots that dropped in. But even if Hood Point was no hotspot I liked it there, and so did most of the others.

Thomas Furlow, the Cactus fighter pilot, agreed with his comrades in New Guinea. As he put it after the war, "On a clear day you could look down in the water and see the sharks. But flying over the jungle was worse. If you had to ditch you wanted the water every time. In the jungle you probably were doomed." Pilots in the Solomons had some important advantages over their comrades in New Guinea. Often visibility was good or excellent in the area. The unusual geography of the Slot helped pilots of both sides. Although flying over water most of the time, pilots rarely were outside sight of land. This situation aided navigation, but it also helped Allied pilots to find help from the famous Australian and British Coast Watchers and their native comrades.

Before examining the issue of pilot rescue by the Coast Watchers, I believe it important to make some general points concerning the indigenous inhabitants of the South Pacific. Because there was so little of value in the area, the imperial hand of Australia and Britain was exercised with great restraint. Unlike larger colonies like India, where the British developed a native-born army of great size and proficiency backed by a professional civil service and ultimately supported by substantial numbers of British soldiers and officials, the Solomons was administered by a handful of civil servants and backed by a tiny and ill-equipped native constabulary. It is arguable that the missionary presence touched the lives of villagers more so than did the British and, later, the Australian government. As noted earlier, both missionary and government influence was confined to some areas along the coastline and in no case extended more than a few hundred yards inland. It is safe to say that there were tribesmen in central New Guinea, or perhaps even Bougainville, who were only vaguely aware that World War II was taking place.

Beyond lending scant support to the missionaries, the small number of Australian and British officials had very limited goals. In the Solomons the British negotiated short-term labor contracts with native chieftains to provide manpower for the coconut plantations that dotted the area. Over the years, a small trade network developed in the Solomons with small boats, sometimes run by men out of a Joseph Conrad novel, chugging throughout the islands exchanging simple consumer goods like cigarettes for various native wares. Larger boats might succeed in gaining a contract to ship coconuts to Tulagi where they were off-loaded to a small merchantman. There were also a sprinkling of Western amateur explorers, scholars, and a few hardy sightseers who made their way to the end of the world.

The Australians in New Guinea had a more formidable task. Like the British at Tulagi they also negotiated labor contracts for the coconut plantations found along the coast. The Australians also developed a somewhat larger native constabulary that helped stop, or at least slow, the often genocidal warfare that took place among hundreds of tribal groups that inhabited this sphere of New Guinea. This certainly does not imply that Australia "controlled" either Papua or the New Guinea Mandate. There were still huge areas that had never been in contact with Europeans, a situation that existed well into the postwar period. Some of the most warlike tribes had adopted an almost nihilistic view toward violence, and no doubt the Australians wished to stop the worst of the bloodshed, ongoing for thousands of years. Yet there was self-interest involved, too. The handful of Germans and Australians that braved an expedition into the interior early in the twentieth century found placer gold in the rivers of the Ramu and Markham Valleys. In the early 1930s prospectors made several gold strikes. The interior of New Guinea might harbor great riches, or so it seemed. Yet exploration and development could not take place without some simple harbors, roads, and basic peace between the prospectors and native populations.

When the Pacific war started, the situation in New Guinea changed dramatically. Because the handful of roads that existed were unable to handle serious traffic and because most of New Guinea had no roads at all, the Australian military required the services of large numbers of native porters. Canberra immediately put all of Australian-controlled New Guinea under martial law, administered by the Australian New Guinea Administrative Unit (ANGAU). ANGAU officials, many of whom had served in the previous civil administration, raised the booty paid to the village elites to get porters. By early 1942 more than 35,000 New Guinea natives were working for the Australian war effort. The work was hard and conditions harsh. However, the contracts were short-term, and few men would risk the anger of chiefs by avoiding impressment. In addition, the Australians found it wise to give those providing labor tiny sums of money and reward good work with simple consumer goods.

Later in the war Australian, British, and French officials in the theater (the French ran New Caledonia and were coadministrators of the New Hebrides) looked at the U.S. invasion of the area with growing horror. Americans, considering the local standards, were lavish with their payments for manual labor. Even worse, Americans were quick to employ natives in the Solomons for more complex work than colonial administers ever dreamed of. Frequently Americans hired native inhabitants individually, allowing men to bypass the village elites altogether. In addition, American GIs, once the supply pipeline allowed it, were generous with distributing canned foods, cigarettes, and other luxuries out of simple kindness. The Americans, simply put, were bringing the twentieth century to the Solomons, and the colonial nations rightly feared that in the postwar period the old power relationships would perish (as indeed they did).

In New Guinea, however, the U.S. presence was limited to the battlefields and air bases, and their impact on the local society was far less. This was also true of the Bismarcks and Bougainville. Americans never occupied any sizeable portion of New Britain. Bougainville may have surpassed New Guinea in the hostility of its population to the outside world. The U.S. presence there was restricted to the small perimeter around the Torokina air-base complex. Instead the contact that existed between the Allies and the inhabitants of New Guinea remained largely in the hands of ANGAU. Robert White ran into ANGAU at Hood Point:

> An ANGAU official used to visit us now and then. I looked forward to it because the guy was very interesting and we were always ready for a chat with a new face. . . . He was the head guy in that area of New Guinea. . . . He was only one man with a few native constables. We enjoyed his visits, but the natives were afraid of him. When the

Australian would come to visit, the natives would say "ANGAU's coming" and would run away. But the villagers got along fine once the young men took off. He'd visit with the chief and handle whatever they handled. The ANGAU official had them put on a dance at night, and it was an incredible thing to see. Only the men danced. I asked him, "How long do they dance?" He said, "until I tell them to stop." It's amazing how one man could have that much power. They did respect his authority. They could have easily killed the guy, but if he had any fear he sure hid it from me.

The village at Hood Point, directly on the coast, was large for the area and attracted a missionary. Robert White met him also, and the scene he described evokes very well the sleepy life one might have found in the Solomons or some of the coastal villages of New Guinea:

There was a missionary in the village who was very tall, but named Mr. Short. He was from England and had been there for twenty-five years by himself. He was a minister, doctor, and teacher. The natives loved him. Those people were as honest as could be. He taught them all the Christian virtues. The people seemed to us to be very happy. They didn't have a very long life span; maybe forty. The men hunted and fished and the women worked in the gardens; there was no shortage of food. They built their dwellings. I realize that what looked like to us as pleasure was their work, but they had things good. . . . We never had any trouble.

Once a week about twenty natives would come with machetes and cut the grass on the airstrip. . . . A few of them had been to Australia. But most of them seemed to like where they were. No crime, no pollution, no noise except the birds: a kind of paradise. . . . It was the same way it was a thousand years ago. . . .

I don't think the villagers near our strip were typical. I was told by the ANGAU official that the tribes were very different from each other. There were people not too far away from us inland from the coast that had the blowguns, bows and arrows, spears. I never ran into them and that's probably for the best. Our natives had one shotgun in the village. They also had a cricket team.

They knew we were going to chase the Japs out of their country, and they were happy about that. I met one native with five or six watches on his arm. I asked him where he got them. He said he'd hide up in a tree and when a Japanese soldier came by he'd jump him, kill him, and take his watch.

It is obviously not possible to verify the story told by the native to White, although Hood Point was not far from the battlefields near Port Moresby and Milne Bay in the fall of 1942. However, Australian intelligence received several reports that Japan's South Seas Detachment resorted to simple forced impressment of native porters during its march over the Owen Stanley Mountains in the summer of 1942. Ignorant of native customs, the Japanese mistreated some native women during their march. (Allied troops of all kinds were warned of dire consequences if they in any way harmed or harassed tribal women. I have heard no reports of Allied troops breaking the taboo on relations with the local female population. No doubt ANGAU's warnings on this subject were of help. Medical officials confirm these findings by noting that incidents of venereal disease were almost nonexistent in New Guinea, and the cases that did appear could be traced to a leave in Australia. When the army moved into the Philippines, incidents of venereal disease soared.) Worse yet, the Japanese apparently executed natives trying to escape forced labor. Some intelligence reports suggested that South Seas Detachment executed natives during the Japanese retreat because it feared the natives would report valuable military intelligence to the Australians. If any of these reports were true, imperial soldiers would have found themselves in the middle of a New Guinea blood feud—not a good place to be.

Judging by Japanese conduct in other parts of the empire, I think that it is reasonable to conclude that Japan was far better at making war than administering territories. Despite grand words—"Asia for the Asians"—the Japanese were quick to employ violence and cruelty at the slightest sign of disobedience on the part of subject peoples. No wonder there was an anti-Japanese guerilla movement in every occupied country. Interesting testimony on this issue comes from Father L. M. Mueller, head of the Sacred Heart Mission near Rabaul. A small number of German-speaking missionaries had heeded the call prior to World War I, and their presence continued during Australian administration. Although Father Mueller was Austrian, and consequently from a nation allied with Japan, he was imprisoned with a large number of Chinese, natives, and a handful of Europeans when Rabaul fell. After the war American interrogators asked Mueller about the Japanese treatment of the local inhabitants. He did not paint an attractive picture: "As far as I can say, they despised the Japs from the beginning. We were waiting at first to see what they were going to do, but after we saw what kind they were, we despised them. . . . All the natives were against them. All prisoners were treated alike; the whites, the Chinese and natives were mistreated terribly. Many of the natives were beheaded. Any little thing could be the cause. Men, women, and children alike were killed."

Nevertheless it would be fundamentally wrong to characterize most of the indigenous population as being pro-Allies or pro-Japanese. The coastal areas most affected by the war in the Solomons and New Guinea contained a small percentage of the population. Furthermore there was much coast and few foreigners. The actual size of the area controlled by either side was very small compared to the overall landmass. Therefore, particularly early in the war, it is safe to say that most people who lived in the South Pacific were utterly bewildered about the war. It was fought for causes they could not possibly understand with means that bordered on the magical. Many, because of the isolation, were unaffected totally by the great events taking place near them. The allegiance of many, perhaps most, of the islanders was heavily influenced by the possibility of reward. The Allies quickly understood this and began dropping basic supplies to native villages, and if a Coast Watcher was present an Allied submarine might drop off goods. This form of benign bribery could be most effective. The Japanese had small outposts throughout the Solomons and tried to convince the inhabitants that they would be paid if a Japanese flier was rescued or an Allied flier captured. In some cases the natives agreed, at least temporarily, to the terms and fulfilled their end of the bargain. The big disadvantage faced by Japan was the fact that the small number of Australian and British officials that served as an intelligence and rescue apparatus throughout the theater was based on relations made long before hostilities.

The story of the famous Coast Watchers is complicated and has been told elsewhere. For the moment it is important to recognize that the combination between the Coast Watchers and pro-Allied natives was responsible for saving dozens of Allied fliers from oblivion. The number of those helped by the natives is uncertain, but estimates of 500 aircrews do not seem at all off the mark. Some of the ordeals on the part of Allied fliers in the Solomons border on the epic.

Most experiences with the natives and Coast Watchers entailed tremendous risk. Crash landings and fortunate rendezvous with friendly forces were far more likely in the Solomons than in New Guinea because of the geographic factors outlined above. There was also an important technical element: Many of the Marine and USN aircraft that played such a prominent role in the Solomons campaign were designed to fly from carriers. Though for the most part they flew from land bases. However, carrier aircraft, to the extent such a thing is possible, were designed to ditch in the water. The navy was well aware that an unusual number of aircraft crashed on takeoff and landing from the tiny carrier decks. Furthermore designers believed that it was important that carrier aircraft be able to land at lower speeds than land-based cousins. A huge hazard continued to exist. Just like land-based aircraft, a carrier craft that ditched nose-down was probably a lost cause. Unless the pilot did things correctly, an aircraft ditching in the water issued a vicious jolt to everyone aboard. Undoubtedly many men died simply because they had been knocked unconscious and were unable to exit the plane during the few seconds before the aircraft sank. And no aircraft is a boat (although some seaplanes were dubbed "flying boats"). In theory a standard, unloaded aircraft might be able to stay afloat for a minute. In practice the time was normally less. Navy and Marine pilots at least had some type of training, however perfunctory, in ditching at sea. And there can be no doubt that planes designed for carrier operations, like the Wildcat, Dauntless, and Avenger, were far better to ditch at sea than were the land-based P-40, P-38, and B-25. Nevertheless, unless fire or drastic emergency forced a pilot to hit the silk, pilots of all services generally preferred to ditch. Fighter pilots had tiny rafts attached to their parachutes that were good for a few hours or days. But the little rafts were not controllable and almost impossible to see from the air. If a plane was in trouble it headed for shoreline.

There are numerous harrowing accounts of aircrew rescue by friendly peoples of the South Pacific. Although no two experiences were the same, Jesse Scott's adventure was representative. Scott was a radioman-gunner on an Avenger tactical bomber flying out of Guadalcanal in the spring of 1943. Scott was part of VT-21, one of the relatively rare land-based U.S. Navy squadrons. In April 1943 his aircraft was given the dangerous assignment of making a night attack on the well-defended Japanese base of Kahili in southern Bougainville. The Avenger was one of the first U.S. aircraft that sometimes carried radar. It was an imperfect instrument but helped save Scott's life:

We were badly damaged over Kahili and trying to get back south. Our radar was so crude that you couldn't tell the difference between ships, islands, and planes. You couldn't really tell the difference between a dog and a cat on our radar so it was pretty crude and not very effective. We had this blip. We had no contact with Coast Watchers in this area and could only hope the natives were friendly. But we knew we had to make it down somewhere soon. We were heading toward Mono Island, southwest of Bougainville, all the time but drifting around, disoriented. We were actually on the Coral Sea side of it. If we'd kept going it would have been death for all of us. But we kept following our blip and finally landed in the surf on Sterling Island, just across a channel from Mono. We thought it was Mono in the Treasuries, but it could have been one of a dozen islands. After, we got our raft pulled out of the surf, hid it, and started out looking. At daylight we saw some natives, and they turned and left. Pretty soon they came back with some Japs. We split up and crawled back in our hole by the raft. The next day I went out to find out where we were. I went out maybe half a mile. I sensed something or heard it, and hell, there were three Japs behind me. There was a big hole there about eighteen inches deep that I jumped into. I had heard some awfully bad things about the way Japs treated prisoners, so I was plenty scared. I had taken my own pistol overseas with me, a real nice Colt .38 Special. I had maybe thirty-five or forty cartridges in my web belt. I took them out and laid them on the edge of my hole. I sat there with my pistol cocked for maybe eight hours. I could hear them quite a while but later I couldn't hear anything, but I was afraid to lead anybody back to my crew. Remember, we didn't know anything about the damn Japs; we were fliers. The Marines filled us full of b.s. about them being invulnerable in the jungle and all this, almost superhuman. Fortunately that wasn't the case at all. The enemy on Sterling were bunglers from what I could see.

We went back to our raft but we had to find out where we were. So we crossed the channel onto Mono with our raft. We saw some native women working in a garden real soon, and we just followed their path. The natives were friendly: One spoke English very well, a teacher at a Methodist school near Munda before the war. Life there was interesting. I got pretty good at the local pidgin. I was on there for four months. . . . It was just plain fun, an adventure for a young man. The people were so kind to us. I don't know how many were on the island: Maybe 400 and every one of them knew we were there. The Japs would come over and sweep the island. The natives would guide them one way and take us the other. The Japs knew we were there too and sent more troops over. The natives were getting nervous about that and the Japs quit using them as guides. We were very careful not to have anything to do with the women there. Luckily the Japs weren't good to the natives. I didn't hear of any real atrocities but the Japs were definitely not popular. Some of the islands I hear were pretty friendly to the Japanese. The missionary activity had a lot to do with it I think. The Methodists had been active on Mono.

A month after we were shot down another TBF was downed and made the island. A day later a P-38 pilot ditched and spent six days in a

one-man raft before he made the island. He wasn't very coherent when
the natives found him. We had seven altogether. The other TBF crew
were very close friends: They had made plans to go into business or go
to college together after the war. But we didn't have that cohesion in
our crew. Different people, I guess. . . . The P-38 pilot was a good
fellow.

Finally a Coast Watcher, a New Zealand Army sergeant, and local
trader came in to make a recon because the troops were planning to
grab the Treasuries when they hit Bougainville. We went out with them
when they met their PT boats offshore. When we returned our
squadron had been rotated back to the States. I don't think anybody
knew we were alive. Everybody was in good health after our stay on
the island. The only thing wrong with me was that I was sick of the
sweet potatoes the natives ate all the time. The odd thing about Mono
was that it was nonmalarial, maybe the only island in the Solomons
that was. We were really fortunate that way. When we got back we
scavenged around for things we thought the natives could use and gave
them to six of the natives that had come out with us. They also were
trained in rifles and given guns. I don't think there were going to be any
stray Japs out there.

Emergencies and mishaps were common in aviation at the time.
However, during World War II calamities at the strip became an everyday affair. A "dead" plane nearby caused little remark. Marine fighter
pilot Joe Foss later remarked, "There wasn't a pilot or crewman in
World War II that didn't come within a hair's breadth of meeting their
Maker at some time. You just had to live with that." Bud DeVere, in
the tower at Henderson, recalls an incident that was all too common
throughout the theater. When an aircraft was mounted with a bomb,
the fuse was attached. No pilot would knowingly land an aircraft that
still carried an armed bomb. Instead, if a mission was not carried out,
the pilot would discharge the ordnance over a hopefully uninhabited
spot (easy enough to find in New Guinea or the Solomons) prior to
landing. However, a jammed bomb on a heavy bomber was common—and the cause of considerable anxiety. When a fighter or a dive-
bomber had a jammed bomb, it was stuck on the bottom of the aircraft's fuselage, causing an extremely dangerous situation. DeVere saw
wrecks of all kinds, but this one impressed him:

I did see an SBD come in that had not ejected his 500-pound bomb. His
plane was damaged, and when he hit the deck he thought his wheels
were down, but they weren't. He rode that bomb all the way down to

the end of the field like a T: Balancing the wings until he lost enough power. That bomb was armed. There was a rooster tail of sparks that looked like a pro water skier. We all thought it would go off. The pilot did a remarkable job. The meat wagon [ambulance] followed him all the way down the field with the siren on. What drama. The pilot and gunner jumped out of the plane mighty fast. Never saw a landing like that.

Another danger was jammed landing gear. Retractable landing gear, essential for high speed, was still a relatively recent innovation, and it often failed. Fred Hitchcock, who manned the tower at Gusap in New Guinea, described this type of incident and also suggested the almost blasé attitude cultivated by so many close shaves:

We had a crisis of some kind almost daily or at least it seems that way in retrospect. . . . Once in February 1944 we had our usual clear-blue sky. A P-47 was returning with one wheel up, one down, but the pilot didn't know which was down. We didn't do much talking over the radio in those days, but this was a time. We knew that a P-47 was the most rugged plane we had, so we told the guy to retract his gear and do a belly landing. By this time we had a metal strip. In comes the fighter and makes a beautiful landing, sliding right down the middle of the strip. I look up and see a spark and flame at the end of the runway. It's like the old-time movies, where a burning fuse heads toward a barrel of gunpowder. It was coming down toward him, not very fast, but steady as hell. He comes to a stop right in front of the tower. He gets out of his plane, takes off his earphones, and starts waving. While I'm trying to get him on the radio to warn him. What do you do? . . . So I went upside down, climbed outside the tower, took off my cap, and frantically started waving like a monkey. He saw me and saw the flame. He took off to a slit trench we'd dug near the runway. It wasn't two seconds until that plane blew up: gasoline, ammo, the whole works. He was okay. We just gave him a wave, and off he went to his outfit for lunch. Funny thing was that neither of us really thought anything about it. I didn't know who he was or vice versa. It was just another day at the office.

Hitchcock was not so blasé a little earlier, when a particularly hideous but not uncommon tragedy took place. Fighter pilots by and large loved their airplanes and frequently could not resist the impulse to push the envelope. Officially commanders discouraged unnecessary risk, but leaders knew that aggressiveness was an important ingredient for combat success. Consequently it was a rare pilot that did not break some regulation simply for the fun of it. Unfortunately the immense power and weight of a World War II fighter made it a very dangerous toy. Many pilots died learning this, and not all were inexperienced. Hitchcock had a ringside seat at the death of a fighter pilot:

The Japs used to hit Gusap now and then. We were very poorly defended, and the complaints got some reaction. We finally got some fighter cover. Four P-38s were given a patrol over the field to protect us when our boys were on a strike. The pilots probably got bored and started to zoom up and down. Obviously they shouldn't have done it. I don't know, but they might have been competing with each other. Sort of like playing chicken. Anyway, one of them didn't have the power to pull out. The plane crashed very hard and absolutely blew up. I rode past the crash a little later, and there was a blackened outline of a man in that plane. That really shook us.

The aerial battlefield of the South Pacific ranged over thousands of square miles. However, the grim flotsam of war was an everyday sight for pilots flying out of a field near the front. Wrecks caused by ditching, crashes, and fallen enemy aircraft collected rapidly around any important frontline air base. In many cases wrecks served as an invaluable source of spare parts. In other cases the men were simply not available to regularly tidy up the base. Obviously the ground crews would keep the field itself clear of debris if at all possible, but an aircraft was a large object, and there was often no obvious place to dispose of it. And if a wreck were towed out of sight it was not long before more would take its place.

Remarkably veterans of the air war rarely commented on this situation unless I asked them during interviews. A wreck at any commercial field would terrify passengers and be immediately removed. But in the upside-down world of war a demolished aircraft was nothing to comment upon because they were so common. Fighter pilot Joel Paris recalls, "There were crashed aircraft all over the place. Every strip. It was part of the landscape. You didn't even notice it, you lived with it. The reason was simple—airplanes crashed all the time." Paris's 7th Squadron comrade Robert DeHaven recalled things were no different at Japanese bases: "There were Japanese wrecks in huge numbers. Their supply service was obviously inadequate. Later in the war at Biak there were dozens of planes scattered about. We reconstructed an Oscar at Biak that was grounded for a twenty-five-cent part. Japanese ground control was poor, too. When our low-level bombers hit them they were sitting ducks, and wrecks littered the area."

Occasionally, however, even jaded servicemen witnessed the physics of war in a way that left an impression. In the summer of 1944 5th USAAF medic Frank Champarty was at Moratai, the scene of a brief but very fierce series of air battles, some of the last to take place in New Guinea:

One morning they came over strafing about 6 A.M. All our planes were lined up on the field. By luck we shot down a Japanese dive-bomber. When it went down it careened into the trees. We could see one Japanese crewman laying on the ground, one arm gone, one leg gone, and his head was all bashed in. But there was a crew of two, and we couldn't find the other one. He wasn't in the wreck. Around noon the outfit was going to take off in their B-24s, and one crew walked past their plane and saw a big hole in the side. There was the second Japanese. He had been shoved through the tail section when his plane crashed and thrown clean through this B-24.

The small but extremely important strip at Wau was singled out for its grim ornamentation by everyone that flew into it. It gained the attention because of its remarkable configuration, built on a 10-degree slope that allowed a very small size. Dave Vaughter, eventually one of Fifth Air Force's most experienced transport pilots, flew his C-47 into Wau several times and remembered its eccentricities:

Wau had a 10 percent grade with the lower end of the strip 240 feet lower than top end. You didn't learn this until you got there. Because of the mountain behind it, you didn't go around. Once you got on approach you landed. So in theory you never went around at Wau: If you touched down you landed. The Australians put barrels on the edge of the middle of the field. You aimed for the middle, not for the edge of the strip like you would on a normal strip, that's why they put the barrels there. You'd go in over the river at ninety mph with full flaps. The moment you're over river on the field side you pull the flaps up at once, put on full power, and landed full pulling up on the yoke, like you were going to take off. You had no problem whatsoever stopping because of the incline. It was a controlled crash, really. When you wanted to take off you'd turn the plane around and head down the hill. That was a little easier.

People that tried more finesse often ballooned it up the field a ways. There were two Junkers from mining days, a couple of B-17s, a P-38,

two C-47s, a B-24, and a few others. They'd all crashed trying to land
there. Wau was only really suitable for transports. It wasn't really
suitable for anything, but the Aussies needed it desperately as a supply
base. So these other aircraft should not have landed there logically. I'm
sure all were damaged, and the alternative was hitting the mountain. If
that was the case, Wau looked pretty good. So you were surrounded by
wrecks.

Wrecked aircraft and bomb damage at the base were not the only
signposts of violence. Engineers located some of the bases very near
old battlefields. On Guadalcanal the air base *was* the battlefield. Airmen stationed on Guadalcanal during the battle were within shouting
distance of the front and heard the monstrous din of artillery and the
yells of the Marines and the Japanese. Consequently the men on the
Canal had to confront carnage along with other deprivations. New
Zealand bomber pilot Ian Page reflected on this situation:

Having been raised on a large dairy farm in New Zealand I knew the
sight and smell of dead things. On Guadalcanal there were partial
skeletons and bones laying about everywhere, some covered by parts of
uniforms. They were Japanese, of course, as ours had been collected in
all the rear areas. One afternoon the daily deluge continued into the
evening, and by dark the bottom of our gully was covered by four to
five feet of water. It continued to rise until it entered our tent, which
was pitched on rising ground. We slept on canvas stretchers with
wooden supports. Mine was slightly higher at the rear of the tent. Each
of the four crewmen got out of bed as water contacted their canvas
while at the same time a terrible stench arose. By that time the water
had stopped rising, leaving my bed untouched. The others went up to
the ridge overlooking our camp to spend the night in the open. I put on
my gas mask and stayed in bed. In the morning the cause of the smell
was found to be the top half of a corpse which the heavy rain had
released from the hillside, and it had become lodged in bushes outside
our tent.

The Corps of Engineers began construction of the big base at Dobodura near Buna while battle raged there. Several miles from the action
there was no incentive for an airman to visit that grisly front while battle raged. After the Allies destroyed the Japanese garrison, however,
many of the men at Dobodura were drawn to visit the horrid and des-
olate battlefield. Howard Redmond, who served in the fighter control
for the 49th Fighter Group, made a trip to Buna mid-1943:

One of us went down to Buna soon after we arrived. The battle had been over for six months. But everything and I mean everything was shot to hell. You went around this corner and there was a huge army cemetery that was called "Eichelberger's Corner." [Informally named by bitter GIs after MG Robert Eichelberger, the American commander at Buna—EB] The palm trees were about six or eight feet tall, the tops just blown to hell. It was just a miserable dump, the worst hole anybody ever fought in. A damn swamp. A great big huge swamp. You could still smell the death. Or maybe it always smelled like that.

Carl Camp was a crewman on a B-24 for the well-known 90th Bomb Group. In late 1943 he visited the Australian portion of the Buna battlefield at Sanananda Point, the location of the most fierce fighting in a fierce encounter. Long after the battle it remained a menacing place:

A year after the battle I was walking up the Sanananda Trail and found a Jap skull. I took it because our group's nickname was the "Jolly Rogers" and the skull was our emblem. Someone stole it from me in Vietnam. That place was spooky. There were no birds. On this jeep trail near the coast it wasn't that bad. But the farther up the trail you went, we all got this creepy feeling, like there was something there. There was this old tree in a clearing that had been burned and sitting on top was a big black vulture. I tried going down the trail twice but I never made it to the coast. Others felt the same way, like it was haunted or cursed in some way. There were bones everywhere. I mean everywhere, and all cleaned by the insects. There was one little place that had a simple sign in English saying, "Japanese war cemetery," and there was a shovel there. There was an old Japanese hospital, and the dead were lying in rows, skeletons. Peaceful in a way: like they'd been put to death with a needle or something. I don't know. It was just terrible. It's almost impossible to explain.

It is ironic that the brutal conditions that pounded men and machines were accompanied, in some parts of the theater, by an astounding natural beauty. Ian Page, flying out of Guadalcanal, relished the view if not the location:

The heat and humidity were wretched on the ground, but from the air the islands were just idyllic. Simply idyllic. The water had a lovely deep-blue color. All of the trees and undergrowth, especially the trees on the coconut plantations, were all different hues of green. The mountains and active volcanoes rise to perhaps 4,000 feet. It was beautiful. The bigger islands had more open space and perhaps were less striking. But the smaller coral atolls were exactly what you would think a tropical island should look like. It was an astounding vista.

Like several soldiers I have spoken with in the past, Dan Harper, a ground crewman–gunner for a land-based USN Dauntless dive-bomber, was impressed with the small island in the Solomons called Vella Lavella:

Vella Lavella was great, a beautiful little island. Many of the natives had been to missionary school and spoke English well. Like all of the Solomons it was mountainous, but especially so. They actually filled in part of the Bay to make the airstrip down at the southeast corner of the island. I'm a little bit of a loner. I would go to the ordnance tent and draw out an .03 Springfield, some ammo, and go for a hike back into the mountains. It was idyllic. I remember those hikes like it was yesterday. Beautiful. I loved it. If I'd had another daughter, I'd probably have named her Vella. The real treat was, for some reason unknown to us, the malaria rate was considerably lower than the other Solomons. Possibly because it was so mountainous there was less area for swamps.

Although New Guinea treated men with a particularly heavy barrage of the worst nature can offer, many airmen found beauty there, too. Many commented about the sunsets. Supply officer James McDowell was one of the first Americans to arrive in the South Pacific and barely escaped the Japanese onslaught on Java. He ended his service when the Americans seized Leyte in late 1944, so McDowell saw much of the area. Long after the war McDowell recalled the natural light show found on the equator: "Conditions were bad at Port Moresby, but the most beautiful sunsets I've ever seen in my seventy-six years were there. Depending upon subtle changes in the atmosphere, one night the sunset would be red, another kind of blue, another green. Our HQ tent was right next to the shore, so we'd see the play of the light off the water. I've never seen anything like it." Fred Hitchcock of Fifth Air Force commented simply, "Gusap was the most beautiful place I've ever seen. You could look down the Markham Valley either way and the mountains seemed to converge far away in the distance. Later people told me that was good for my eyes looking at the horizon. I hope so, because I spent many an hour up in the tower admiring the beauty there."

Phil Caputo was a crewman on a B-25 when the war in New Guinea was reaching a climax in late 1943. Despite the danger, Caputo was struck by the exquisite sights of the South Seas he viewed from the air:

I loved flying, I miss it. It was beautiful, stupendous. When I came back myself and most of the crew became instructors, we'd get together and talk about how we missed the "old days" a few months before. There was nothing like it. Everything is clean, you see things that take your breath away. The air has a remarkable clarity near the equator. But when you'd fly over dense jungles you could smell it below you. The jungle had a very powerful, dense smell that was almost sweet.

Caputo's feelings were echoed with remarkable precision by Fred Cassidy, a pilot of one of Australia's powerful Beaufighter tactical attack planes:

The colors of the sea, the blues, the greens, the shades of whites and yellow were very lovely. And over the jungle you had this expanse of green. But it was hard to think of New Guinea as beautiful. The jungle had a smell that put you off. Even flying at low level you'd smell the jungle. Some of the islands were lovely, like the Treasuries. But in much of New Guinea the shoreline was rough mud and mangrove swamp: ghastly places to contemplate. So if there was a beauty to it, it was a deadly type, a menace.

The sweet smell that Caputo, Cassidy and many other jungle veterans remarked about was a natural result of the extraordinary fecundity of the tropics. The heat and moisture made the Solomons and New Guinea a splendid host for almost every microorganism known to the medical profession at the time—and some that were not. Indeed more than the harsh climate, bad airstrips, and forbidding terrain, it was disease that assaulted the air forces of both sides.

A Malignant Land

When I look at group pictures taken of airmen and ground crew who served in the South Pacific, I am struck by how gaunt the men appear. On photo they rarely appear despondent for the camera but exude a kind of sardonic confidence. But the men, with few exceptions, are very thin and carry the look of people who have lost weight and are not robust. The look of similar photos taken of Allied airmen in the European theater is very different. Although the fate of anyone serving on a combat aircraft in Europe was doubtful, physically the men are larger and appear healthier.

I make this comparison not to suggest that airmen who served in Europe lived well. The daily life of the European airmen was quite harsh. Rather it points out one of the central realities of the air and ground wars in the South Pacific: Most individuals on either side of war were, by normal civilian standards, suffering from serious illness. Although spared some of the brutal hardships that made the South Pacific one of the most foul places for infantry combat, the men flying the warplanes and those maintaining the aircraft were victim full measure of most of the illness that made the South Pacific a medical nightmare.

Before examining the disease problems faced in the South Pacific I would like to put the situation in perspective. Until World War I the most likely cause of death in most conflicts was disease. However, the lessons learned and taught by the great pioneers of public health in the late nineteenth and early twentieth centuries were not lost on military medicine. Until the 1930s this knowledge was almost entirely preventive. Armies understood the importance of basic sanitation, and the treatment of trauma was greatly improved.

The interwar period was a time of great advances in medicine. Vaccinations for diseases such as yellow fever were routine in the U.S. military and presumably for other services. The development of sulfa drugs gave doctors the ability, under certain circumstances, to face infection with a certain chance of success. A well-equipped hospital in an industrial nation in 1941 would be much closer to that of a half-century later than to that of a half-century before.

In addition, the medical structure had greatly matured in the decades before the war. Physicians were becoming more specialized. Nursing was a well-developed profession. The public, whether it truly understood matters or not, was beginning to understand that germs were real things and that many simple actions could cut down greatly one's chances of suffering from a disease. Still, many of the medical defenses built up since the beginning of the century wilted under the assault of the South Pacific jungle. Those that existed made possible a major campaign in an environment where no war would have been conceivable in earlier generations.

The worst threat faced by both sides was malaria. *Malaria* means "bad air" in Italian, reflecting the age-old belief that the disease was caused by rank-smelling air found in swamps. Since the late nineteenth century physicians have known it is not the swamp air that causes the malady but what flies in it. A protozoal disease, malaria infects numerous creatures. Some peoples living in tropical regions may have developed certain genetic defenses against malaria, although military surveys found many native peoples prime sufferers of the disease. Humans from temperate climates, which included almost everyone making war in the South Pacific, are genetically defenseless and easy prey to the disease.

Malaria has a pernicious cycle that makes it extremely tough to combat. It is caused by a tiny parasite transmitted through the bite of the female anopheles mosquito. Once in the blood the parasites travel to the liver and reproduce asexually. The cells that have reproduced burst and release parasites back into the bloodstream, where they enter the red blood cells. There they also reproduce asexually and feed on hemoglobin in the cells. The red blood cells burst, releasing both asexual and potential sexual forms of the parasite. When a female anopheles feeds on the infected blood, the sexual form of the parasite infects the mosquito, completing the life cycle. For reasons that are not understood well, the parasite either remains persistent in the liver, or infected red blood cells circulate for a very long time. In either case malaria usually recurs several times. An infected individual can suffer a recurrence years after initially contracting the disease. One obvious and fearful aspect of the disease is that both the victim and host infect each other. A mosquito not harboring the parasite that bites an infected human becomes infected. To make matters worse, a man stricken with malaria was more vulnerable to various maladies associated with fatigue. Obviously multiple attacks, which were extremely common, only amplified the problem. Within a short time a disease machine was created that had little to stop it early in 1942.

The anopheles thrives in the tidal swamps of the South Pacific. Guadalcanal, New Georgia, and Bougainville in the Solomons, as well as the Milne Bay and Buna areas of Papua, are among the most malarial places on earth. It is present in lesser degrees throughout the area's low-lying terrain. The air forces on both sides, in other words, were stationed in one of the most malarial areas on earth.

As one might imagine the situation was at its worst at the beginning of hostilities. In June 1942 the USAAF headquarters in Australia, soon to become Fifth Air Force, reported that of the 800 pilots in the theater, 10 percent were incapacitated by normal disease and that an additional 30 percent were out of action at any given time due to various tropical maladies. Later in the year 5th USAAF General George Kenney reported that in an average month 200 pilots were on the sick list due to disease, mostly malarial, and forty were killed or missing in action. For the period December 1942–June 1944 Fifth Air Force had a hospital admission rate per annum of 899 per 1,000 for all causes: Disease comprised 772. In other words in a given year 77 percent of personnel were admitted to hospital at least once for disease. This number is actually far worse than it appears. Because all of Fifth Air Force was included, it should be pointed out that many men served in low-disease-risk areas such as Australia. Had the figures included just the men in the frontline squadrons the numbers would have been far higher. In March 1943 the 5th USAAF surgeon reported: "In some areas of New Guinea, Milne Bay particularly, malaria has been widespread, in some units as many as 35 percent contracting it in one month. In this area it is a practical certainty that under present conditions a unit that remains there for a period of three or four months will become 100 percent infected with malaria." To underscore the point, in January 1943 Fifth Air Force withdrew one bomb squadron and two fighter groups from Milne Bay because of malaria.

Things were no better in the Solomons. During the early stages of Guadalcanal, air and ground crews suffered a staggering illness rate of 2,500 per 1,000 men per annum. In other words, each man was averaging 2.5 attacks of debilitating illness per year. (The valiant 1st Marine Division, when finally withdrawn in December, suffered an overall casualty rate approaching 80 percent, mostly from malaria and other diseases.) Frontline forces for newly formed Thirteenth Air Force reported fifty-five flying days lost per 100 officers each month due to illness.

The medical apparatus was very haphazard until well into 1944, and manpower and material shortages hampered the medical effort just as they did every other aspect of warmaking. Like the combat air units in general, there were very few survivors of the debacle in the Philippines, and very few well-trained flight surgeons made it out of the cauldron. Thus weakened, the army and navy did their best to assemble a medical apparatus on the run. In this regard, the navy's carrier air groups were in a better position, although hardly ideal. The army airmen had to start from scratch. After the war the USAAF composed a lengthy and expert official history. The authors commented on the South Pacific:

Medical personnel were always understaffed in the field. Many early units came without medical officers at all. Normal rotation of medical officers was disrupted throughout the entire war. Because ground crew were also badly under strength the flight officers were often doing their duty also. . . . In 1943 the officer carried as surgeon of 13th AF Air Force Service Command was actually the senior flight surgeon at the Rest Leave Area in New Zealand and was later carried in position of Air Force veterinary surgeon. Another carried as assistant surgeon, Air

Service Command, was actually working as neuropsychiatrist for the entire Air Forces.

One result of this shortage of medical personnel was an utter mystification when faced with tropical disease. One of the most common maladies treated in the South Pacific was the infamous Fever of Undetermined Origin, or FUO. Some doctors believed that FUO was a cover for men trying to get out of the theater, which no doubt was true in some cases. More often, however, the doctors and medics assisting them could not easily tell the difference between malaria, dengue fever, the common flu, or even severe dysentery. When overwhelmed by cases it was simple enough to mark "FUO" and put the stricken individual under observation for a few days and hope for the best. In addition a bout of malaria, particularly a relapse, could vary greatly in intensity. Many men with no particular desire for a short stay in the uncomfortable unit dispensaries might well decide to tough it out.

Dan Harper came down with malaria in early 1944 on Guadalcanal when the mosquito-control effort was beginning to decrease the incidence of the disease:

> Malaria wasn't a plague when I was there, but I managed to catch it. I didn't know what it was at first. I remember when I'd go out to work on my plane. The trailing edge of the wing where you'd get up to climb up to go take care of the nose guns is possibly eighteen to twenty inches off the ground. Here I was nineteen years old and I couldn't get my foot high enough without help to get up on the wings. I finally figured I had malaria. I never turned in with it, which might have been foolish, but everything seemed to turn out okay. When I'd feel it come on, I'd immediately climb in my bunk and try and scrounge some fruit juice and just try and sweat it out for twenty-four hours or a little longer.

B-25 radioman J. W. Kennedy spent a long tour in New Guinea with predictable results for his health:

> I had multiple attacks of malaria, several of dengue, and many what we called FUOs, "fever of undetermined origin," which was a medical way of saying they didn't know what was wrong. A malaria bout would last about three days. You took your atabrine every day but once in a while the malaria would overwhelm it. Then it's chills and fever, chill and fever. Then they give you quinine and you're all right. I had recurrences for about three years after the war. I was also pretty well covered by

jungle rot for almost fourteen months after I left the theater. I hope our next war is in southern France.

Even today malaria can be an extremely difficult disease to cure. During World War II no cure existed, and both sides employed suppressant drugs to ward off the scourge. I wish to stress that medication could only suppress symptoms, rather like aspirin relieves the pain of a headache, and did not cure the disease. The classic suppressant drug for malaria is quinine, one of the oldest known medications of proven clinical value. Quinine had serious drawbacks, however. It had a slight toxic effect on everyone that took it, leading to a ringing in the ears and sometimes nausea. In some instances, however, quinine was the best drug available, and the Allied doctors hoarded their small supply for particularly bad cases. From the Allied point of view the major drawback of quinine was that almost the entire world's supply came from Java, recently occupied by Japan. However, due to one of history's ironic turns, during World War I German chemists, cut off from their supply of quinine and facing malaria in the Balkans, brilliantly created a synthetic version called atabrine. After the war U.S. companies licensed atabrine. When hostilities commenced, and the military's supply of quinine was obviously not going to last long, U.S. pharmaceutical companies increased the production of atabrine a hundredfold. Despite the great efforts of U.S. drug companies (atabrine also became a prime commodity dispensed via Lend-Lease), the suppressant was in short supply until 1943. Early in the war it was often hand-delivered to flight surgeons by courier.

The major side effect of atabrine was that it caused those taking it to develop a yellowish hue on their skin. There were also rumors abounding that atabrine caused sterility. Consequently in the first months of war medical personnel had a difficult time getting men to take the only drug that promised to keep them more or less fit for duty. Marine fighter pilot Roger Haberman at Guadalcanal was one of those resisting treatment. He was also one of the lucky individuals who did not end up paying an immediate price:

Atabrine had no side effects for a flier, but it turned you a yellowish-brown. But you'd still get the damn malaria. I never took the damn pills. I told an officer to shove them. I got the hell stung out of me by mosquitoes and never came down with malaria. I'd wake up in the morning and have a welt the size of a baseball where my knee had struck the mosquito netting. Red as a beet. But I never got malaria. But most did. Joe Foss had an attack when we were coming back from New Zealand that was so bad we had to put a guard on him—he was so delirious he might have jumped overboard. And everybody had dysentery. I think it was because we were taking the water out of the Lunga River: They were washing stuff there too and soap would get into it and that would give you the runs.

Ultimately heavy command pressure and the obvious effectiveness of atabrine convinced most men it was worth the risk of taking it. However, the figures noted above indicate atabrine was frequently overwhelmed and malaria attacks were extremely common. Yet some studies done during the war strongly suggest that without atabrine the campaign in the South Pacific could not have taken place. Fifth Air Force conducted a study in early 1943 giving one group atabrine and a control group nothing. At the end of a month those taking atabrine had no malaria casualties, but the control group had a 60 percent rate of infection. On a more dramatic scale the U.S. Army conducted a grand medical experiment on the Americal Division. Deeply involved in the fighting for Guadalcanal, Americal was moved to Fiji to refit. While at Fiji the number of malaria cases rose from 1,000 cases per 1,000 men per annum to 14,000 cases per annum within three weeks of stopping the supply of atabrine.

The air forces and medical establishment reacted quickly to the grim situation caused by malaria. Prior to the war a pilot who suffered malaria was not allowed to fly again until he had shown no recurrence for two years. Malaria was always treated as a disease that required hospitalization. When the war began these safeguards went out the window almost immediately. Army pilots suffering from the disease were put in the squadron's dispensary. A severe case that entailed very high fever or multiple attacks was referred to the hospitals. Until mid-1942 and for several months later hospital treatment was provided by the Australians and New Zealanders. Ultimately the United States constructed modern hospitals throughout the theater and had hospital ships moving between them. However, for the period we are examining, most victims received treatment at a dispensary. The treatment was not long. Early in the war it was U.S. Army policy to give a malaria patient at least one month to recuperate prior to flying again. The command realized that this policy almost doomed the air forces, and permission to return to flight status was given to the flight surgeon. It is safe to assume that many flights in the theater were flown by extremely tired and perhaps semidelirious men. This policy was not changed until late 1944.

While air warfare raged in South Pacific skies, medical officers tried a number of vain efforts to lower the malaria rate by preventing the onset of the disease itself. Directives went out requiring men and women (a small number of female nurses began service in late 1942) to wear long-sleeved shirts and long pants and, at sunset, to tuck their pants inside socks or leggings. The men ignored these regulations universally. The officer heading the mosquito-control effort by Thirteenth Air Force in 1944 noted the "deplorable" example set by flight officers. The army began to dispense insect repellents in large quantities, but the men disliked the smell and the feel and doubted their efficacy. In some cases medics required that anyone wishing to see the night's movie (often in the rain) would have to douse themselves with repellent. This advice, too, was ignored.

Ultimately the cleverness and wealth of the Allied forces brought the scourge under some kind of control. By mid-1944 large-scale spraying of mosquito hatching areas was widespread near major bases. Small aircraft sprayed beaches or enemy territory prior to Allied invasion. However, the results of these efforts are difficult to assess with any accuracy. There is no doubt that large bases like Guadalcanal and Moresby were far safer in late 1944 than in earlier times. It is also true that when the front line moved into the Philippines, malaria decreased in importance because it was less common. Other diseases then began to vex the medical personnel of the South Pacific.

Malaria was not alone in claiming victims among those serving in the South Pacific. Another mosquito-borne disease, commonly known as dengue fever, was an ugly counterpart. Dengue was passed on by the aedes mosquito that bred on most surfaces and in small patches of water, a perfect description of any military camp. The aedes was a day-feeder, unlike the anopheles, which tended to come out after dark. Dengue was rarely fatal and was not recurrent. However, it was more painful to suffer and more likely to get out of hand than was malaria. Fighter pilot Joel Paris picked up a case of dengue while in New Guinea and did not enjoy it: "I got dengue fever. Our medical people considered it one of the minor diseases because it doesn't usually kill people. But it's tough, let me tell you. Your bones and joints hurt like hell. It makes your eyeballs hurt. Your eyelids hurt. I got malaria several times and yellow jaundice, too. I didn't miss many of them. New Guinea was a good place for germs and insects."

In certain areas scrub typhus was a serious problem. It was passed on by mites, and the fatality rate (3 percent) was unpleasantly high. Like all insect-related diseases, scrub typhus could cause epidemics. Small ones took place in New Guinea in late 1944, and they caused great concern. USAAF commanders decided that scrub typhus posed enough of a threat that they should ban the transportation of pets and mascots from one base to another. Every squadron in the Pacific had pets, and this order, like so many others, was simply ignored.

Outside of malaria, the malady that was most pernicious and costly to South Pacific airmen was dysentery in all its forms. Although the secret world of microorganisms was well understood by 1941, there were still many unexamined concepts accepted as truth. For instance, new soldiers appeared to be more vulnerable to dysentery than were veterans. Consequently medical personnel initially accepted attacks of dysentery as a natural reaction to a change in diet and climate. Later research proved that bad sanitation caused dysentery and related maladies. Many of the veterans had grown accustomed to the disease and simply learned to live with it. Indeed dysentery and food poisoning were so common that they may well have been the most underreported disease in the theater. This situation was not helped by the crude latrines, unsanitary mess halls, and unpoliced showers.

The worst type of intestinal disease was amoebic dysentery. Like all forms of dysentery it was underreported, but it had a nasty character. It was possible for someone to be infected by amoebic dysentery and not come down with symptoms. If one of these infected individuals handled food, he could spread the disease rapidly. Dysentery is probably the oldest and ugliest plague that armies have faced over the centuries. Amoebic dysentery turns the digestive tract into a corporeal battleground and caused serious, long-lasting suffering. One can imagine what happened if amoebic dysentery were added to malaria or dengue. Ground crewman Tony Betchik picked up both malaria and amoebic dysentery while servicing Wildcat fighters during the battle for Guadalcanal: "By the time I left Guadalcanal I had no solid bowel movements, constant diarrhea. Bloody as could be. So you lost a lot of weight. I was taken out of the Canal in one of those wire baskets: I couldn't even walk. They loaded me onto a transport plane. They had to carry me on. I had amoebic dysentery. . . . The dysentery caused ulcerated colitis; diarrhea on and off for forty years."

Poor sanitation also created fertile ground for a type of hepatitis, commonly known as camp jaundice. This malady was particularly common in the early days in both the Solomons and New Guinea. The best protection against jaundice was simple public health measures. However, until the Allied war machine began dispensing goods throughout the theater in mid-1943, the men were almost totally vulnerable. Initially latrines were simple trenches, the mess halls open tents. Lumber and screening for latrines and mess were in very short supply throughout the war. Ironically the airmen made things worse in this regard. As we shall see in greater detail, supply was either helped or hindered, depending upon one's perspective, by massive theft and large-scale barter. Air units, because they had a regular pipeline to Australia, were unusually well supplied with hard liquor, the most valuable commodity in the South Pacific. Much of the screening and lumber intended for sanitary facilities ended up in the hands of air units that used it to make their quarters more comfortable.

Perhaps the most widespread and despised malady was an affliction commonly known among military personnel as jungle rot. It is important to realize that men were almost never genuinely dry in the South Pacific. This meant that the slightest cut or chafing or injury of any kind was vulnerable to infection. A 13th USAAF meteorological unit veteran described daily life:

> You were wet anywhere in the Solomons. The first night I was there . . .
> in the middle of night I heard water running. It was raining outside. I
> turned on the flashlight and saw water running through the tent. You
> couldn't find anything high enough to get out of it, so it was always
> there. Everybody had this purple solution they put on your feet to stop
> jungle rot. I guess it was better than nothing, but not much. What we
> really needed was some nice, dry weather, and that was not to be
> found.

Rot could be far more than a simple annoyance. Hundreds of men proved so vulnerable to it that they had to be evacuated from the theater. Most had to simply endure. Lee Tipton of Thirteenth Air Force saw the results: "The area between people's toes became raw, absolutely raw. And between your fingers, your elbows and armpits, your groin. I knew people that went into hospital and lay in a tub of ginseng violet, the medication they used. But if there was any chance to rehabilitate a man in theater he was not sent home: You patched him up and back to work."

Poor diet was a major part of the mediocre morale found in many units. It could also have an impact on pilots that was probably completely unforeseen at the time. Australian Group Commodore Garing offered a good example:

> The air war in New Guinea was remarkable. It was fought with
> modern weapons and modern techniques in a Stone Age environment.
> The poor inhabitants had no idea what was going on, what modern
> war was like. Things were extremely primitive. The weather was

appalling. People were not prepared for the most simple of things. For instance, the army used to give our airmen beans for rations. Take gas in the stomach up to 20,000 feet it becomes a very big bubble. I had to get fresh bananas for them. The poor pilots couldn't stand the smell in the cockpit.

Although information concerning medical problems facing the Japanese is not as plentiful as data covering the Allied war effort, it indicates that if anything things were worse for imperial forces. To begin with the areas of the South Pacific occupied by the Japanese were no different than those held by the Allies. The Bismarcks and the coastal areas of New Guinea in Japanese possession were intensely malarial. The Japanese occupied some of the worst spots in the Solomons, such as Bougainville and New Georgia, for a year and a half. The Japanese army on Guadalcanal was devastated by disease and hunger. Very few of the survivors gallantly rescued by the Japanese navy at the end of battle ever fought again effectively.

Also, Japanese medicine and public health standards were below those found in Allied forces. When the Australian army finally occupied Rabaul after VJ-Day they were impressed by the number of doctors and medics that were still plying their trade. (It is worth noting that Rabaul received far more than the standard quota of supplies of all kinds because of its unique importance and size. More primitive outposts throughout the Solomons and New Guinea and Gasmata had no such luxury.) However, Allied physicians were far less impressed with the quality of Japanese care. For instance there was no obvious effort made to segregate patients by type of illness. Thus a man suffering an attack of malaria might be placed next to someone with tuberculosis—not a good idea. Apparently quinine was always in short supply. It is true that the Japanese controlled the source materials on Java, but the Japanese military was no more prepared than the Allies for a massive campaign in malarial areas. The empire dispatched more than 350,000 men to the South Pacific but also fought a major campaign in Burma, another medical disaster area. It is easy to imagine that production was far behind demand. As the war progressed, supply ships sent to Rabaul increasingly fell victim to U.S. submarines and aircraft. It is also safe to say that Japanese logistics, except in strict military items, was not up to Allied standards. Also, as previously noted, quinine caused some type of toxic side effects to many men, and atabrine was not produced by Japan. When the all-out siege of Rabaul began in November 1943, the supply service broke down quickly. By early 1944 suppressants and many basic medical supplies were no longer available at all.

Soon after the war General Hitoshi Imamura, commander in chief of Southeastern Forces, which controlled Japanese army troops in the Solomons, the Bismarcks, and a small part of New Guinea, estimated that 25,000 of his men died of disease, "mostly of malaria." (Imamura also estimated that 20,000 men were lost at sea while coming to or dispatching from Rabaul, the victims of Allied submarines and aircraft.) At Rabaul itself Allied figures showed that 4,400 men died of disease, just slightly less than the number of those killed by air raids and sporadic ground-fighting late in the war. These figures, reporting deaths and not simple hospital admissions, are far worse than any grim accounting on the Allied side.

The Allies did study the Japanese disease rates on Rabaul shortly after the war. The statistics are somber testimony to the Japanese ordeal: Between January and October 1943 the monthly percentage of "noneffectives" due to malaria ranged between 12.5 percent and 22.5 percent. Men stricken by "other illnesses" in the same period ranged between 8.7 percent and 12.3 percent. Total illness rates were at a low in August, with 21.8 percent of Rabaul forces stricken, to a high in May of 38.8 percent.

In November 1943 the figures for Rabaul took a very unusual turn. Although the men stricken by "other illnesses" remained static, those suffering from malaria plummeted. Those suffering from malaria went down in November to 10.7 percent, in December to 6.2 percent, January 1944 5.9 percent, February 6.9 percent, and March 8.3 percent. After March 1944 those rendered unfit due to malaria went back to the 1943 pattern. In 1945, as medical supplies became nonexistent, the rates for malaria alone reapproached 25 percent per month. The question is why did the malaria rates of Rabaul's garrison decline so drastically for the period between November 1943 and March 1944? No logical medical reason renders itself obvious. In the period in question the Allied air forces launched a crushing aerial offensive against Rabaul, forcing Japanese air units to abandon their bastion in late February. It is possible that with the battle raging, Tokyo redoubled its efforts to somehow get a sufficient supply of quinine to the embattled base. However, it was during exactly this period that the Japanese supply apparatus was suffering a smashing defeat. (The last Japanese supply vessel left Rabaul in March 1944.)

Logically it makes far more sense that medical supplies, like all other supplies—except for the massive stockpiles of ammunition—were growing more scarce, not more common. Although there is no direct corroborating evidence, I believe, considering the intensity of the Japanese battle ethos, that men simply refused to report sick with something as transient as malaria when the base was under siege. Those who did were probably suffering from severe attacks and were obviously of no military use. Allied combat aircrews noted a sharp decline in the skills of Japanese fighter pilots starting in mid-1943. This decline has usually been attributed, no doubt correctly, to lower training standards. However, I think that it is very possible that many of Rabaul's defenders in its hour of utmost peril were manning fighters and guns while suffering malarial attack. Any Japanese fighter pilot, regardless of his normal prowess, who was disoriented by disease would have been easy prey to the swarms of Allied fighters that covered every raid on Rabaul.

Over the past twenty years aviation author Henry Sakaida has cultivated good relations with many Japanese veteran aviators. His several books on the air war in the Pacific provide a wealth of information from the Japanese point of view. Sakaida described the medical situation at Rabaul:

> The harsh tropical environment added to the decline of the JNAF at Rabaul, for unlike their Allied counterparts, the Japanese failed to control the mosquito problem which devastated whole units with malaria. The Allies, on the other hand, sprayed and dusted their bases frequently with the insecticide DDT, which was unavailable to the Japanese. . . . So bad was the malaria problem that many veteran Zero pilots claimed that ill health was the leading cause of casualties at Rabaul.

A Dangerous Sky

The frustration and dangers faced by airmen in the South Pacific Theater did not end on the ground. Obviously the major threat facing aircrews was combat, a subject we will examine in detail. However, in such a large and primitive theater like the South Pacific, airmen were also vexed by difficulties in navigation. The men also had to face the unpredictable weather that could save or destroy a plane depending on what fate had in store.

The first problem faced by many pilots was getting aircraft into the theater. As mentioned, long-range flights of any kind were new to aviators in 1941. The development of powerful engines during the 1930s allowed a tremendous increase in range, but onboard instruments and ground-based navigational aids lagged behind the new capabilities of the aircraft. As it was prior to the war, most long-range flying was done over familiar ground and often followed roads and railroad tracks.

Although the airlines provided valuable instructors for combat transport, their experience at home ironically made them poorly suited for service at the front. Every safety standard known to aviation was thrown out the window in the South Pacific, and young pilots who knew no other environments proved quicker to take chances than did older pilots who were creating modern airlines and were understandably devoted to institutionalizing safe flying procedures. The importance of ignorance of standard procedure in the South Pacific was recalled by veteran C-47 pilot David Vaughter:

> On one occasion I had General Whitehead [Brigadier General Enis Whitehead, then 5th USAAF deputy commander; stationed in Moresby, he had greater control over operational decisions than did General Kenney, whose headquarters were at Brisbane.—EB] as copilot going to Wanigelia [a particularly nasty strip near Kokoda that was important before Dobodura was ready—EB], and I offered to let him land the plane. He said, "No, I don't dare. I'd rather have you young bucks handle that. I just wanted to see if it was as bad it's supposed to be." After we taxied around Whitehead complimented me and said if it was up to people as old as he was we wouldn't be going into places like this. It was a young man's game and I was twenty-one. Our ignorance was probably the primary factor that allowed us to get things done. We didn't realize what was hazardous or what was possible. After the war I spent my career with Eastern Airlines. Looking back I can see that much of what we did during the war was a little nuts.

However, even good conditions and great skill could not guarantee a happy landing. A number of celebrities and aviation pioneers died in crashes prior to the war. When war broke out safety standards eroded due to the sheer mass of new aircraft and rookie pilots. It is startling how many major figures of World War II died in aircraft accidents. Victims included Australian Chief of the General Staff Sir Brudenell White (along with Australia's ministers for air and army on the same plane), Canadian Minister of National Defence Norman Rogers, Vice Admiral Minechi Koga, who succeeded Yamamoto as head of Combined Fleet, and Fritz Todt, who was Albert Speer's predecessor as Germany's minister of armaments. U.S. officialdom was spared such losses, but bandleader Glenn Miller, one of the most famous men in the country, perished in Europe. Eddie Rickenbacker, America's most famous World War I war hero, escaped death by a whisker, surviving nearly a month on a raft in the South Pacific after his B-17 crashed. Simply put, aviation during World War II was a dangerous enterprise for anyone at any time, especially as young pilots took off to previously unthinkable destinations. The courage shown by leaders like Churchill and Roosevelt in making long trips by air should not be underrated.

Not expecting hostilities at the other end of earth, the USAAF had to develop a way to get their aircraft to their destination in the least possible time. As explained earlier, the skeleton of the great route from California to the South Pacific was created as a means to get B-17s to the Philippines. It was soon clear that most multiengine aircraft could employ the same route if ground crews made temporary modifications to the airplane. In the case of bombers, it was desirable to fly the aircraft to the front to save shipping rather than time. Generally only the pilot, copilot, and radioman made the trip, although if one was lucky the navigator was there, too. Gunners and flight engineers went by ship. Large aircraft are a major burden on shipping. They must be disassembled to save space—a time-consuming process on both sides of the journey—and their bulk hindered the shipment of supplies of all kinds, always short in the South Pacific. Bombers left people behind because the lesser weight carried increased their margin of error. Transport aircraft, for which there was an insatiable demand, flew with their entire three-man crew. In either case these aircraft were employing their maximum ferry ranges, and such flights carrying cargo or made round-trip would have been impossible.

Ed Stroebel was a flight engineer on a C-47 heading to Australia early in the war. As he noted, the route was long:

> The C-47 held 800 gallons of 100 octane, which would keep it in the air for about eight hours, maybe a little more. It took us fourteen hours to get from Fairfield, California, to Hawaii, and so we carried an additional 800 gallons in a special tank. Five planes went over and we only had one navigator on the command ship. You can bet we hoped that guy knew where he was going. It was tense. There was a "point of no return," and when we passed it Hawaii seemed awfully small. Later in the war flights like that became pretty common, but in 1942 that was a real accomplishment. After Hawaii we went to Christmas Island. The garrison at Christmas were great. They had a movie special for us, good food, and we stayed there all night. They gave us some old candy bars, which we hadn't seen for a long time. Little things like that lifted our spirits. Then to Canton, from there Fiji, next to New Caledonia, and finally Brisbane. It was a lot of flying, almost numbing. After

Christmas the only thing I remember was Canton. It's a tiny place and there's only one tree. What a hole.

At about the same time Ed Stroebel's unit was flying to Australia, the 405th Bomb Squadron embarked to the same destination in their B-25 Mitchells. Pilot Garrett Middlebrook noted after the war that seven of the thirty-two aircraft that left California were either lost or damaged, six due to pilot error. Although training improved, ferrying remained dangerous.

U.S. fighters naturally could not make a direct flight. The USN shipped the fighters to Hawaii or Espíritu. Carriers received air groups at Pearl Harbor. When possible the navy employed small escort carriers, later to become an indefensible part of the great U.S. Navy task forces that swept the Pacific during 1944–1945, to carry Marine fighters close to Guadalcanal to keep the time over water to a minimum. The small number of army fighters originally deployed at Guadalcanal could not take off from a carrier, so they had to brave a direct flight from Espíritu in aircraft that, unlike their naval cousins, were not designed to ditch in the water. Later U.S. fighters had greater range, and the trip from secondary bases to Guadalcanal lost much of its menace. During such missions a bomber with an experienced navigator would accompany fighters to act as a guide, as flying over open water was never taken lightly. Fighters bound for Australia were shipped to Brisbane, assembled and flown toward Townsville, and then taken to Moresby. Under normal circumstances this should have been a relatively safe flight, as fields were numerous and maps good. However, many of the pilots making this trip were poorly trained and got lost. A green pilot lost over Australia had a good chance of finding one field or another. As fighter pilot Robert DeHaven related it, the last leg from Australia to Moresby was hazardous for the unwary:

We had a ferry route from Cairns in Australia to Port Moresby. When you reached the coast of New Guinea there was a barrier reef of coral: If that was on your left when you passed to the shore you turned left and followed it to Moresby. If it was on your right you had to turn right or else you'd go up farther on the island of New Guinea, which a number of guys did—they simply turned the wrong way. This was dangerous for the new guys because they didn't know what the area looked like from the air. Much of navigation in New Guinea was by acquiring landmark. If you did get lost, you usually could find the coastline. But our P-40 had a limited range, and caution was advisable.

The situation was no better for the Japanese. Yet by the map the Japanese should have had a much easier time of it. The South Pacific Theater was far closer to the major Japanese bases at Truk, Formosa, and the Philippines, even Japan itself, than to California. Much of this advantage was lost, however, by the overextension of Japan's war effort. With an active front in the South Pacific, the possibility that the Americans might move toward the Central Pacific, the war in China, the Burma front, and the awful possibility that Russia might strike gave Japan very little in the way of strategic reserve. Consequently, after the initial deployment of units to the South Pacific, the Japanese had to struggle to keep their units up to strength. The IJN usually flew in fighters as well as bombers from Truk, although sometimes old carriers were utilized to ferry Zeros some of the distance. The army reinforced New Guinea via Formosa and the East Indies. With shipping badly organized and increasingly short, the army rarely was able to ship its aircraft into upper New Guinea.

After the war American interrogators asked several Japanese officers about losses due to accidents during ferry. Japanese naval aviators all estimated losses at 3–5 percent. Two commented that ground damage inflicted on new aircraft bound to Rabaul was not serious because the fields were in good repair. The situation in New Guinea, however, where fields were of much lower quality, was quite different. This figure is worse than it looks. I wish to examine this subject more closely, but for the moment it is important to understand that the Japanese did not usually rotate land-based air units. This stood in stark contrast to U.S. practice. Instead they attempted to keep their strength by constant reinforcement. The Japanese position steadily weakened despite an increase in aircraft production. Major C. Takahashi, a JAAF officer in the supply section, told interrogators after the war:

Of planes sent overseas [in early 1944—EB] we figured losses of 50 percent. Heaviest losses were between Kyushu and Formosa. Of those damaged, one half could be repaired. Losses from Japan to Formosa was heavy because of engine failure. Losses increased because run-in time for engines and flying tests were lowered from the early war and a lack of fuel. Weather also played a large part. Ferried planes guided by lead plane, and if anything happened to lead plane it put the others in difficulty. The 50 percent figure same for whole war. The early rates of mechanical failure were lower, but distance flown longer. There was also a decline in maintenance. The best maintenance men were sent forward and were stuck there.

Major Takahashi's comments must be kept in perspective. As suggested in his testimony, a "loss" was an airplane that did not arrive at the front when intended, not a plane destroyed. However, any plane delayed, because of the poor state of Japanese maintenance, might well never get to the front at all. In addition, Japanese combat pilots were more than busy after the spring of 1942. Therefore ferry pilots flew Japanese aircraft to their destinations. As imperial forces quickly adopted the best of their trainees into combat units, the ferry pilots were not the best available. Like the Americans, the Japanese tried to use guide aircraft for ferry use, but as time went on the odds increased that aircraft might get lost or become damaged when landing. The system of reinforcement was key to producing the most serious weakness on the part of imperial forces—a superiority in numbers of pilots over aircraft. Possessing more pilots than aircraft was a good thing if the number of aircraft was adequate. Allied air forces almost always maintained a surplus of pilots by design. However, the Allies rotated units more or less on a regular basis. When Japanese forces grew numerically inferior their experienced pilots continued to go to the well and inevitably dwindled in numbers. Japanese replacement pilots, instead of being eased into the combat environment, were thrust into the most difficult missions when more experienced comrades perished in action or fell ill. The result was a downward spiral in pilot quality. Naturally this situation was made much more serious as the Allies deployed superior aircraft.

The issue of quality and quantity is not always analyzed properly in accounts of the air war in the Pacific. Had the Japanese possessed more aircraft and been able to keep them operational, they would have had a much easier time converting neophyte pilots into competent combat pilots. Yet even though Japanese factories produced more aircraft as the war progressed, the numbers needed to slow the Allied onslaught did not arrive at the front. The Japanese retained a large number of excellent pilots until mid-1943 but lost them steadily just when a major increase of Allied strength took place. Many of the men who replaced the veterans were not up to the task and were flying aircraft increasingly in poor repair. The Japanese air forces were not so much shot out of the skies as worn down from many wounds.

In the early stage of the war both sides, particularly the Allies, were greatly hampered by gross ignorance of the basic terrain over which they were flying. The British, Dutch, and Australians had made naval charts during the decades prior to the war, and the general relative position of the major islands was clear enough, as was the coastline of New Guinea. Any area inland, however, was generally unknown territory. Obviously this made planning and executing operations extremely difficult. Navigation aids developed only slowly, and the enemy naturally made none available over hostile territory. So flying from one place to another was no easy prospect.

Rudimentary knowledge of the terrain and miserable maps combined with unpredictable weather to create very hazardous flying conditions. The 8th Photo Mapping Squadron was one of the first units deployed to New Guinea, an indication of the desperate need for better maps for both air and ground units. Fred Hargesheimer flew with the 8th early in the war and described the general ignorance: "Nobody knew anything about the South and Southwest Pacific. It was the last place we expected to fight a major campaign, so those of us sent there were on our own. When we got there the coordinates on the maps given us didn't agree with those on the maps given the Australians. The best thing we had were the German admiralty charts from pre–World War I. Even the best navigator will fail without decent maps. We were very busy."

Ignorance of the terrain and poor communications hindered airmen in their never-ending struggle against the dangers posed by poor weather. Any decent aviator has great respect for weather. In World War II flight officers, regardless of duty, learned basic aerial navigation. The weather facing men in the South Pacific was not extremely severe when compared with many other theaters. The air war in the South Pacific took place almost precisely on the equator. The South Pacific at the equator is an integral part of the meteorological geography that causes the fierce typhoons that occur both north and south of the line. However, along the equator itself, precipitation was intense, but titanic storms and dense haze were rare. The area fought over, however, whether in the Solomons or New Guinea, had scores of mountains big and small. New Guinea had large mountain ranges, most notably the Owen Stanleys, and all of the islands were volcanic in origin; peaks ranged from 1,500 feet to nearly 10,000 feet on Bougainville. Given the huge quantities of water and intense heat, combined with mountain peaks, huge cloud formations of many different varieties were common. The twin difficulties for World War II airmen were the unpredictable weather patterns and the deficient means available to deal with them. Consequently, even though spared the worst that nature theoretically could offer, in practice hundreds of aircraft were destroyed by dense cloud formations that caused planes to get hopelessly lost or by fierce storms that developed with startling speed and little warning. Naturally the steady stream of new pilots on both sides was most vulnerable to catastrophe, but even the most veteran pilots re-

mained cautious. It is safe to say that very few men finished a tour of
duty in the Pacific without having a brush with death due to weather
or navigation error.

Melvin Levet was a weather officer in the Solomons and described
the general meteorological problems:

Weather was an important subject for operations. But our verification
on forecast was about 55 percent. If you understand tropic weather you
can understand why. For the entire time I was there except at the end
we were within 10 degrees of the equator. You have very warm tropical
water that creates great masses of unstable clouds. A tropical front
where the northeast and southeast trade winds converge to form a
tropical front will meander back and forth from one side of the equator
to the other. That usually means a big buildup of clouds. You could see
the wavering of a tropical front from the insufficient information we
received, but beyond that it's pretty tough to pick up any major
changes. Thirteenth Air Force only canceled flights when the forecast
was that the home base would be socked in on return.

We were told by a general that 5th USAAF weather at Nadzab was
getting 85 percent successful predictions. He wanted to know why we
were getting less, not much over 50 percent. So we flew down to
Nadzab to visit the Fifth and find out their secrets. We found out they
forecast for systems: If it was rainy today they'd forecast thunderstorms
for tomorrow. If there were broken clouds today there will be broken
clouds tomorrow. We tried to employ instruments and sound principle
for prediction. Both of us employed the same instruments and charts.
Frankly nobody could predict that weather with precision, so
operations continued with that fact in mind. We simply couldn't
forecast very well over there.

Beyond the unpredictable conditions, the meteorological personnel
sent to the Pacific found that, like everyone else, they had to operate
on a shoestring. James Kubiak was a weather observer in the
Solomons in 1943 and described the situation:

I was a weather observer. The information I gathered went to
forecasters. When we plotted our weather map we were working on
information from about 100 stations in the entire Pacific at the time we
were on Guadalcanal. In the U.S. we had 700 stations plus 200–300 in
Canada and Alaska. When they did a map of the U.S. it took us three
hours to enter all the data on the map with little symbols and so forth.
There was a lot to work with there. You could pick out fronts and high

pressure areas. In the Pacific you just couldn't do that. You had to go more on what you saw than anything else.

I received training in Michigan. From the Indiana state line up to the Michigan Upper Peninsula there are probably twenty-five weather stations. That's about the distance from Guadalcanal up to Rabaul where they were bombing. In that area we only had four or five stations. So in the Pacific it was harder to get a good picture. They gave us good instruments, but we just didn't have enough weather stations. The stations were small, about a dozen men. It would have been a tough job no matter how many we had.

Meteorological stations struggled on as well as they could. They regularly sent up hydrogen balloons to measure wind velocity at several altitudes ranging from 2,000 feet to nearly 40,000 feet. Men also closely monitored barometric pressure with complex instruments, looking for rapid movements that indicated a storm in the making. They also employed special weather flights, as described by Dauntless pilot LeRoy Smith:

Each squadron provided two planes for a weather hop each morning. You took off predawn and climbed to the ceiling, maybe 18,000 feet. Then you'd come down in a giant circle at 500 feet a minute. In your wingtips they had the temperature and pressure readers, which they'd use to make the charts every day. They could tell what was moving through, what was changing. This duty rotated. If someone was in sick bay and not real sick or had mild dysentery they usually took the weather hop. It was interesting. By the time you got to 14,000 there was the sun coming up and by the time you got to 18,000 it looked like daytime. But you were high and when you descended the light disappeared. By the time you landed it's almost dark again because the rest of the world at ground level hadn't seen the sun yet. But you brought those charts back.

Weathermen were also eager to gain as much information as possible from pilots. As James Kubiak explained, this practice did not deliver the desired results.

We didn't feel what the pilots and aircrew were reporting about the weather was sufficient. . . . They were so starved for weather that we started sending a weatherman on bombing missions, just so we could gather more accurate data. It didn't help the mission you were on because when you're flying through a weather front it's a little late. But

we could relay information to people in the area so we had our
observers in the air. While I was in the Solomons as I recall we lost ten
weathermen shot down.

In fact in New Guinea some bomb groups began sending one aircraft in the squadron ahead of the others to radio back weather conditions every thirty minutes in code. It was a common-sense measure
and no doubt helped some formations avoid unexpected weather
fronts. Yet there was no real solution to the problem given the technology and terrain. Obviously these conditions led to some inaccurate
forecasting.

From a practical point of view bad weather posed two mortal dangers to pilots and crews. First, poor visibility might cause an aircraft to
get lost and run out of fuel over some of the world's most inhospitable
terrain. This hazard was particularly acute when, as often happened,
aircraft from either side conducted missions that forced pilots to expend most of their fuel, leaving them with little margin for error. Second, even if on course and possessing adequate fuel, all aircraft in the
theater were in danger of being destroyed by rapidly moving storms either directly by the storm itself or by crashing because of crippled visibility.

Pilots flying from Moresby to Dobodura or other sites went through
the "gap," a pass between peaks in the Stanleys that were 12,000 feet
or above. The distance for an aircraft was relatively short, so many
aircraft made the hop safely despite the almost daily cloud buildup.
No pilot liked going through the gap unless they were very high or
could see. The saying was that New Guinea was filled with "clouds
with rocks inside." Dozens of aircraft that made the trip through the
gap struck mountains of great size. They were listed among the many
"operational losses" that made up the majority of Allied losses in New
Guinea. No doubt many could have been prevented by pilots taking
longer and safer routes, but the war encouraged risk, and the number
of aircraft was many. Dozens of pilots who did not have the requisite
skills pushed the envelope for no genuine military reason and killed
themselves and crew because of bad judgment, trying to beat the
weather over the Owen Stanleys.

No pilot likes to get lost, and navigation errors, despite modern
technology, continue to pose hazards for private pilots. During an era
where navigational technology was unsophisticated, and in a theater
where everything was crude, it was easy enough to get lost even when
weather was good.

Fred Cassidy, who served as radioman and armorer on an Australian Beaufighter attack aircraft, witnessed the sort of confusion that nearly destroyed a pair of U.S. fighters in the summer of 1943:

War has no counterpart to civilian life. There is no similarity to the type of feelings you confront. You're young. You were frightened, very frightened, but very excited at the same time. You were well trained, but everything is happening fast and there is an exhilaration to things that are sweeping by you. I remember one day at Lae, which was one of the heaviest defended targets in the area late 1942 and early 1943. We'd been strafing up near Finschhafen and were coming home at about 4,000 feet, staying out over the water to give Lae and Salamaua some distance out of respect for their defenses. I saw two American Lightnings about a mile away with their wheels and flaps down heading the wrong direction. I thought that was strange. I had the frequencies of the day, knew what planes were supposed to be in the area, and quickly got on the air and said, "If you can hear me you two Lightnings near Lae, be careful because that strip is not one of ours." I told them who we were. We weren't supposed to break radio silence but the conditions demanded it. These two were so short of fuel; they were looking for any place and didn't know where they were. They saw a strip and were hoping for the best. We came in, they tagged along behind us, and they made Moresby. They came around and saw us; they were extremely grateful and believed we'd saved their lives, which I think we had.

Weather observer James Kubiak had ample opportunity to hear of reports of lost planes during his long tour. His reflections are of interest:

A lot of planes got lost and could not get back because of navigation errors. Bad weather would have a lot to do with that. Some of it was inexperience. The problem never ended when I was there. You'd lose contact with aircraft. Everyone would sit there waiting and waiting. Squadmates of the lost plane would come over to us every hour to see if the weather had changed. They were hoping their buddies had landed somewhere else and were going to come back. Sometimes they did. Pilots were known to land on other strips and not tell you for a day. Occasionally a Coast Watcher or sub would rescue someone. But usually an overdue plane was gone for good.

Although nature was the enemy in so many ways to men flying in the South Pacific, the remarkable clarity of the sky allowed hundreds of airmen to survive mistakes that might otherwise have proved fatal. Joel Paris flew fighters for the veteran 7th Squadron in New Guinea and commented on the subject:

In the Pacific you generally had tremendous visibility, up to approximately fifty miles. When we moved north toward the Philippines it began to get hazy. Later, when I went into China it really struck me how lucky we'd been over New Guinea because normal visibility over China was down to three or four miles. The lower you flew the worse it was, hazy and spooky. We weren't faced with that in the South Pacific because you could see so far. That's why so many people survived poor navigation. We had a lot of inexperienced men and we didn't have proper navigation facilities. There wasn't any radar in the aircraft; you depended strictly on time and distance. Without good visibility a lot of us wouldn't be around today. . . . The whole theater was very crude. We were just totally unprepared to fight a damn war down there.

Even if a pilot or navigator was on course, a storm or large cloud formation posed great danger. U.S. planes were extremely rugged, and pilots routinely flew through bad weather, as long as they thought the target might be clear enough to strike and home base visible enough for landing. It would have been rare for a U.S. aircraft to suffer fatal structural failure because of a storm, but it no doubt happened, particularly if a plane was tired or suffered from undiagnosed damage.

Lloyd Boren was a bombardier on a B-17—arguably the most rugged aircraft that flew in World War II—and flew several night missions against Rabaul early in the war. As he related it, even the Flying Fortress was not completely safe from the elements:

Coming back one night there was a terrific front, a real high one, in front of us. We tried to get over it at 20,000 feet and couldn't make it and running low on gas. So we had to fly through it and over the Owen Stanleys. Talk about rough. In a bad storm you're bouncing around like a tennis ball. There was St. Elmo's fire over the whole plane: really something to see. The pilot was new and had forgot to turn on his airspeed indicator. He refused to believe his needle and ball [a basic instrument that shows whether a plane is flying level—EB] and put the nose down to increase airspeed. At night in a cloud it's very hard to determine where the horizon is. I think vertigo caused a lot of accidents. You're supposed to trust your instruments, but a rookie pilot sometimes can't fight instinct, even though his instinct is usually wrong and the instruments usually are right. I think we went into an outside loop. Everybody was laying up on the ceiling during the loop. The bombsight flew up and hit me in the head on the ceiling. Robert Ripley even wrote this up: We did the only recorded loop in a B-17. That tore up that plane something terrible. The right wing was bent up and they never used the plane again: It was scavenged for parts. But we made it back and all of us kissed the ground. That was the only time I was really terrified while flying.

As Boren mentions, St. Elmo's fire was sometimes seen during storms. Jim Eaton was a gunner on a B-17 during a night raid early in the conflict and found beauty amid danger:

We'd get St. Elmo's sometimes. It's a spectacular sight. When certain atmospheric conditions get just so, you get a big sheet of flames coming off the props or between the guns and turret or anything out in the slipstream. You feel naked at night because good lord they can see you with that stuff. Once you learn to understand that it's not hazardous, you're not going to catch on fire, you don't worry. But it was an operational nuisance on a bombing mission: You're trying to be invisible and here's all this damn flame coming off the props. It's a glow, a bluish white. You just worry that the wrong people are going to see it.

The remedies available for an aircraft in trouble were few. If close to a base it was possible to exchange messages. The base had radar and could get a decent fix on a plane if within proper distance. In combat zones, however, radio silence was a strict policy, and sending a message to base was only done in unusual or very dangerous circumstances. But even if the base answered, the aircraft still possessed only an approximate idea of where to head. Consequently the normal response by pilots in a serious storm was to try to get below the clouds and obtain visual cues. This led to some very exciting flights, as one might imagine. LeRoy Smith took his Dauntless dive-bomber onto the deck to find home:

We had attacked Rabaul and were heading to base at Munda. The field at Green Island was being built then. In the Solomons it rains every day. Some days a little longer than others, but it always rains. When it does rain, it rains full-bore. You cannot believe the way it comes down. Me and another plane get caught in one of these downpours. So we're going as fast as we can go, belly on the water. I had my head sticking out the side of the cockpit trying to see. Both my wing and I saw the strip on Green Island at the same time. We both started talking at the same time. He wanted to get down, I wanted to get down. He peeled off and went one way around the island; I peeled off and went the other. We landed from the opposite ends of a runway that was not finished. That night the two of us slept on the mess hall table. It was still raining. If we were at altitude we were completely blind. There were no windshield wipers. A modern plane disperses water because of its high speed, but that wasn't true with an SBD at cruise speed. God we were scared.

When flying blind there was obviously the possibility of hitting a mountain or simply making a fatal error at low altitude and hitting the ocean. As Charles Kittell, a B-25 pilot with Thirteenth Air Force in the Solomons, points out, a formation flying blind also risked colliding with friendly aircraft: "We hit weather a number of times. Good luck was with us, but you always worried about collision. You'd break out of a weather front and sometimes see that you'd gone through the position of twelve different airplanes when you hit clear sky. Somewhere along the line you must have been very close to ending it all."

All of the nightmares that bad weather could produce occurred simultaneously on April 16, 1944, a mission the airmen of Fifth Air Force call "Black Sunday." In April 1944 General MacArthur was preparing for a series of landings up the coast of New Guinea, intending to bypass large Japanese garrisons. The centerpiece of the attack was the coastal settlement of Hollandia. At this stage of the war Fifth Air Force often sent up very large raids consisting of 150 bombers or more plus escorts. General Kenney's airmen pounded a number of targets in the Hollandia area in early April. On April 16 Kenney ordered a very high percentage of operational bombers under his command to soften up the area for MacArthur's landings, scheduled for April 22. The result was the worst day of the war for Fifth Air Force: Altogether the Americans lost thirty-one aircraft and thirty-two airmen. The airmen of the Fifth speak of Black Sunday in much the same terms of horror used by the men at Henderson Field who endured the bombardment by Japanese battleships a year and a half previously.

It is not possible here to reconstruct all that took place during the debacle on the return from Hollandia. Flights of bombers and fighters took off from several different strips and were aiming at several different targets. Apparently one large group went beyond the point at which they should turn and wasted half an hour of fuel prior to the strike. The Hollandia area itself was clear enough for a successful strike. However, as the aircraft were dropping their bombs a huge weather front built up between the raiders and their bases. Soon nearly every flight was socked in. As Hollandia was a long-range mission, there was very little margin of error for many of the planes. Against standard practice, radio beacons at Allied bases were turned on and radio silence was abandoned. Soon the airwaves were choked with distress signals. Fred Hitchcock was at the tower at Gusap and recalls, "On Black Sunday planes were coming back to Gusap frantically reporting they had wounded crewmen, were low on gas, and were lost because of the fog. At one point I had two wrecks on one runway and one on another. Guys were landing on the taxi strips. The priority system broke down and it was utter chaos."

As one might imagine it was worse inside the aircraft trapped in the prison of cloud and wind. B-24 navigator John Mullady nearly met death:

On Black Sunday a terrible weather front moved in and nobody knew where they were. We were struck by a very powerful downdraft that just pushed us down. Our pilot lost control at about 10,000 feet and told everybody to prepare to jump. Hell, we could hardly move, because the airplane was doing all kinds of gyrations, throwing us side to side and up and down. When we were shoved down we didn't know whether we were over water or land. It didn't matter anyway because we weren't going anywhere. It was hopeless to abandon the plane in those circumstances. . . . I remember seeing in my mind the local headlines—"LIEUTENANT MULLADY KILLED IN COMBAT." It was like a miracle. The pilot finally got control and came out at about 500 feet, just under the clouds and just above the ocean. So we made it back.

Carl Camp manned the top turret of a B-24 in the veteran 90th Bomb Group. Camp witnessed tragedy on Black Sunday:

We were lucky on Black Sunday because we had the fuel. When things started to come undone they told all "little boys" [fighters and small attack planes—EB] to head to "big brother" [bombers—EB]. Three fighters and an A-20 joined up with us to follow us in. There were people landing on the beach, bailing out over the water, and landing on unfinished strips. Men practiced every possible way to get killed that day. The A-20 I think made it, but I fear we lost all three of those fighters. We got over the Admiralties and the storm was still on, but they told us to expect a break in about an hour. But the fighters didn't have the fuel. They just dropped down one by one. They were P-47s.

You'd see them spit out some smoke and start slowing up, and down they went into the clouds. That damn near killed me, what could you do? We just sat and watched them die. It was so messed up that people didn't know whether a beach they could set down on was ours or Jap-held. The people over open water had to try to ditch in heavy seas or bail into it. That was curtains either way.

The issue of Japanese losses of any type is difficult and controversial. They flew over the same terrain using technology that was, if anything, less sophisticated. Furthermore no Japanese plane could remotely match the ruggedness of their Allied counterparts. During much of the struggle they had the advantage of defending their bases. Yet through-out the period the Japanese launched scores of major attacks, many over long distances. Indeed the Allies never sustained an offensive at a range as far as that which separated Rabaul from Guadalcanal. One must conclude that imperial airmen found the weather and terrain every bit as hazardous. I have no doubt that many Japanese pilots would have echoed the words of Zero pilot and ace Muasaaki Shi-makawa, who commented after the war, "The F4Fs at Guadalcanal were extremely tough fellows. We were confident in our skills and we were evenly matched. Our biggest enemies were long-range missions and bad weather. Many pilots lost their lives to stupid operational causes and not to enemy planes."

We will never know how many aircraft crashed and men died be-cause of the brutal terrain and unpredictable weather found in the South Pacific. It is very likely that more than half the aircraft lost in the theater fell foul of accident or simply disappeared. The exact percent-age will never be known with certainty. It is telling, I think, that we are still discovering wrecked aircraft in the New Guinea jungle. Perhaps this uncertainty is one of the most tragic aspects of this part of the war. One could train to fight the enemy. Superior aircraft were a great ad-vantage in combat. But when confronting nature, caprice played a role no airman could deny. Many American airmen recognized this. James Mullady reflects that "in my opinion the weather posed a bigger threat to the aircraft in my unit than the Japanese did." Veteran B-25 pilot Ben Fridge echoes the sentiment: "It is probably a fair statement to conclude the weather was as dangerous as the Japanese. Some days it was by far worse." Flight surgeon Victor Falk, who served valiantly on Guadalcanal, mourned the uncertain fate that befell many of his com-rades: "We had many losses that were unaccounted for. We simply didn't know what happened to them. Young men flew off and just never came back. Were they shot down? Did they collide in a cloud?

Did Japanese antiaircraft get them? Did they get lost and fly off over the ocean? Nobody knew. That was very hard on everyone."

Yet despite the tremendous obstacles posed by geography, climate, microbes run riot, poor facilities, and dangerous weather, two great air forces engaged in a two-year aerial slugfest over the South Pacific. To fight this war both sides required complex and powerful aircraft that appeared in a remarkably short period of technological advance in military aviation. They also needed thousands of young men trained to fight a complex and vicious war. Now it is time to examine the aircraft that fought in the South Pacific and the men who flew them.

PART TWO

MACHINES AND MEN IN
THE SOUTH PACIFIC

Throughout history war and technology have been intertwined at every level. The amount and type of destructive power that a military force can project at the point of fire is largely determined by the interaction between weapon type and numbers. The more complex the weaponry, the more important it is to understand its basic functions, dominant strengths, and fatal flaws. Although such generalizations are valid for all aspects of modern warfare, they are especially central to war in the air, a type of combat that presupposes complex weaponry. The central position played by the technical nature of the weapon must be investigated regardless of what level one wishes to analyze a campaign. Commanders plan campaigns under basic assumptions regarding the damage they can cause, the losses they will sustain, and the likely results of one plan of action as opposed to another. All these considerations are shaped by assumptions concerning the capabilities of the tools being employed by one's own forces as well as those of the enemy. Misjudgment of the technical balance of forces can harm commanders either way they jump. If they underestimate the power of their own side, they might well miss an opportunity to yield a telling blow. If they underestimate the power of the enemy, defeat awaits with near certainty. Indeed in the South Pacific the inability of Japanese commanders to temper their strategic goals with the limitations of their technology hastened the defeat of imperial forces in the area.

At the operational level, attackers and defenders attempted to maximize chances for success by tailoring tactical methods to the strengths and inevitable weaknesses of their craft. Early in the war this was no easy matter, as neither side really understood the best way to employ airpower, particularly in a theater as unusual as the South Pacific. In this regard the Allies proved also to have the advantage. By the summer of 1942—early in the game—Allied airmen were throwing away the book and developing tactical solutions to formidable problems when they were, at best, only equal in numbers and technology. Japanese forces, conversely, showed a marked inflexibility. This inflexibility, which proved so costly to the empire, was, I think, a combination of command paralysis and the flaws in Japanese weapon design.

It was also at the operational level that an interesting paradox concerning World War II aircraft became apparent. On one hand there was a general similarity in performance in both sides' aircraft, reflecting the international explosion of technical development that took place during the ten years leading up to Pearl Harbor. It is self-evident that had one side possessed a decisive superiority in technology, the long struggle in the skies over the South Pacific would have never taken place. To put it another way, early in the conflict, when a Japanese pilot was flying a superior fighter he was in deadly peril if he allowed a technically lesser Allied craft to gain a temporary advantage. When the technical balance shifted to the Allies, the same situation was true. Although Japanese fighters were inferior, well-flown machines proved deadly to the end.

On the other hand at the mission level the sometimes slight improvements made in one side's aircraft had immediate practical impact. Introducing a new type of plane did not allow one side to sweep the skies immediately, but it did change the overall ratio of attrition and the chances of successfully accomplishing a mission. If qualitative improvements were accompanied by quantitative superiority, all the better. Once again, the Allies proved to have the upper hand. Their aircraft evidenced a sounder design philosophy from the start. They were more versatile, allowing the development of deadly tactics, such as low-level strafing and skip-bombing attacks specifically tailored to the challenges of the theater. In early 1943 the Allies slowly gained an undisputed superiority in aircraft and had learned techniques necessary to gain the maximum advantage from their technical edge.

Last, it is essential to understand the basic qualities of the aircraft if one wishes to grasp anything of the experience faced by the thousands of men who engaged in the Pacific air war. Combat in the air is an intensely visceral experience. Whether or not the men understood the fine points of aerodynamic theory, in combat each of them came face-to-face with the laws of physics. Although amazingly young, the men who manned World War II combat aircraft had to master a wide array of skills and also had to use their skills with split-second notice. No one knew better than the aircrew that its plane was a powered, metallic bubble that was the only thing standing between it and mortal collision with the earth. Thus whenever I have the privilege to speak with the men who flew these planes it is no wonder that the subject so often centers around the various attributes of the aircraft flown. Although all airmen spent most of their time on the ground, they were closest to death while in the air. The purpose for their sacrifice and that of their comrades centered on how well they and their machines performed their missions. Furthermore I think it safe to say that many men grew attached to their aircraft. Many gained profound satisfaction in mastering deadly warplanes. Some simply learned to love flying aircraft of immense power and capable of extraordinary performance. Yet even in the hearts of the boldest airmen was the cold realization that due to their power and speed, World War II aircraft were hot, to use a phrase, and had to be treated with respect and caution. If ever there was a time when men and machine would meld as a single fighting unit, it was in aerial warfare. In this one regard I believe that the airmen of both sides would have found much in common.

Before examining the unique characteristics of various types of aircraft, as well as the operational impact that inevitably followed variations in design, it is wise to look at common attributes that existed in most or all World War II aircraft. Indeed if one steps back just a bit it becomes immediately obvious that basic similarities outweighed differences among individual models. Once we identify the quintessential features of the warplanes and understand why so many attributes were common, I think it will be much easier to analyze the patterns of combat as they existed in the South Pacific and World War II in general.

Technological advance does not proceed at an even rate. Bursts of tremendous change and creativity are often followed by extended periods of relative stagnation. Clever inventions are frequently ahead of their time and fail to have an impact when devised, only to reappear later when other developments make them practical. Sometimes such inventions are simply rediscovered. (Heaven knows how many are merely forgotten.) Obviously the perceived demand for a technology likewise plays a role. Paradoxically, however, there is also a great deal of serendipity involved. If many people are kicking rocks, individuals and small groups stumble on important things when no apparent demand exists for their discovery.

At present aircraft have existed for roughly a century. Although innovation has been ceaseless over the years, there have been three periods when events moved with startling speed: 1908–1915, 1930–1939, and 1945–1955. Although we can tip our hats to the Wright brothers, the period of creation in aviation history took place in Europe between 1908 and 1915. When the first Wright Flyer circled Kitty Hawk it was powered by twelve-horsepower twin engines and stayed aloft, in its last flights, for about forty minutes. Five years later, when the Flyer was first sold to the U.S. Army Signal Corps, it circled a field for one hour at 120 feet, traveling at forty miles per hour. Impressed by the Wrights' triumphal tour of the continent, European builders, particularly the French, quickly outdistanced the work done by the American pioneers. Rotary and inline engines exploded in power. Clever inventors inspired by brilliant theory dating from the mid-nineteenth century from a number of other fields helped develop ailerons, rudders, and elevators—the control surfaces that steer airplanes. Elementary moves toward streamlining appeared. European armies were quick to see the tremendous value of aircraft for reconnaissance and purchased several hundred. By 1914 engines with greater horsepower ratings (80–100) were standard, and, depending upon what attributes were desired, speeds of 70–110 miles per hour at altitudes up to 16,000 feet were reached. A few types achieved great size. The famous Sikorsky Mourometz of 1914 had four engines, boasted a 113-foot wingspan, and could fly for five hours with great reliability.

Some aviation histories point to World War I as a period of great technological progress. As more sophisticated accounts make clear, the opposite is the case. During hostilities the demand for better weapons is pressing and obvious. However, there is also a demand for something better *fast*. Also, weapon types are needed in huge numbers, so matters of production technique often become as important as weapon innovation itself. Wartime, therefore, is typically a period of refinement, not innovation. With the exception of the all-metal Junkers monoplanes (in prototype before 1914), planes developed during World War I became better weapons but broke little new ground. The basic rotary engine was more powerful but conceptually the same. The separate-cylinder inline engine, pioneered by the young Dr. Ferdinand Porsche for Austro-Daimler, produced 120 horsepower in 1913. The improved version (180 horsepower) produced by Mercedes powered most of the great German fighters. This basic configuration was retained until well after the war. (The famous U.S.-made Liberty was a Mercedes on steroids, producing 400 horsepower; it was also the end of the road for the separate-cylinder engine.) The only significant engine developed during the war was the famous Hispano-Suiza aluminum-cast block V-8, which appeared in 1915.

Thus despite the great many refinements performance itself improved very little during the conflict. One reason was the need to add weight and so-called parasitic drag to carry weapons. So although engines almost doubled in power, they increased speed by only twenty-five miles per hour or less. In an article published in 1923 prominent British designer Sir Leonard Bairstow commented, "Our war experience shows that, whilst we went forward as regard to horsepower, we went backwards with regard to aerodynamic efficiency." A colleague, Alec Ogilivie, commented the same year: "In coming to the consideration of the progress in aerodynamics during the period [World War I], it is accurate to state that substantially there was none."

By 1915, with the development of the Hispano-Suiza, the initial stage of creativity in aviation came to an end. Cumulative refinement took place during the war and continued at a slow but steady pace for ten years after the armistice. Among all types of aircraft, the fighter progressed the slowest. Initially there was little perceived need for more military aircraft, and wartime stocks served for several years. Just as importantly it proved difficult for airpower enthusiasts to demonstrate that the great expenditures for fighters during World War I had been worth the cost. During the interwar period there was virtually no doctrine in regard to obtaining and using air superiority. The civilian population was fascinated by racing and record-setting. Military planners increasingly looked at bombers as the logical area for development. Everywhere, thoughts of war were repugnant and funds short.

Another factor, often overlooked, was also at work. Military pilots of all nations have always loved airplanes. Interwar air forces could be remarkably selective in the men chosen because, unless one was a millionaire or a test pilot, there was no other place for pilots to play with aircraft as elaborate as military fighters. Because pilots loved flying, they cultivated an approach to flying that emphasized aerobatics. Although as aircraft grew faster it was obviously less and less possible to re-create the extraordinary dogfights of late World War I (an aircraft traveling 200 miles per hour requires a radius four times greater than one traveling 100 miles per hour to complete a circle), airmen clung to the techniques of the past. Few pilots by 1930 possessed combat experience, and I think it is fair to conclude that pilots preferred light and maneuverable aircraft because they were more fun to fly. It is noteworthy that every modern fighter produced during the immediate pre–World War II period was resisted initially by many pilots. Both Willy Messerschmitt and Mitsubishi's Jiro Horikoshi had to force their revolutionary designs (the Bf109 and Zero, respectively) down the throats of their own pilots. Similar experiences took place in other countries.

The result was predictable: Twenty years after the introduction of the Spad VII, fighters had improved very little. In 1936 probably the world's best fighter in active service was the Boeing P-26A Peashooter. Ironically Boeing's last fighter (though Boeing would eventually develop legendary strategic bombers like the B-17), the Peashooter was an all-metal monoplane. That capsule description sounds more elaborate than the actual aircraft. The P-26 had an open cockpit, braced wings, fixed landing gear, and a top speed of 234 miles per hour, very fast for the day; it carried an armament of two .30-caliber machine guns, the same as a World War I fighter. Note that the P-26 stayed in service until 1938. Four years before World War II began, fighters were inching forward in a direction obvious to no one. However, at exactly this period a combination of innovations transformed the situation completely almost overnight.

In 1936 the Peashooter and its foreign equivalents represented the state of the art for active-duty fighters. More serious advances had come in multiengine designs. By 1940 every combat aircraft that saw service in World War II was in production or prototype. Obviously much happened in a very short period. It is also obvious that the flurry of activity was fueled by the ugly international political climate that had even the most dedicated peace-lover mentally preparing for another crack at Armageddon. So the motivation for modernizing and expanding air forces existed on the part of both the predators and the potential prey. From a technical standpoint the revolutions in bomber and fighter designs became a matter of putting together several crucial innovations originally developed for multiengine aircraft. Yet it is important to realize that fighter development was not uppermost in any nation's thoughts until very late in the game. Bomber development shaped events. Aggressor states developed fighters as the limited wars in Spain and China illustrated the necessity of escort for bombing raids. Defensive nations developed their fighters out of a combined fear of the damage bombers could inflict on cities and the growing hope that bomber-inspired technology could be used to create fighters capable of thwarting the threat.

To help us better understand the breakneck speed of aviation development during the prewar period, a comparison with the modern situation is illuminating. The fighter planes of 1918 were a quantum leap from the frail craft flown by the Wright brothers just fifteen years earlier. The technology changed so quickly, particularly in the 1930s, that once a type was developed and produced its successor was already on the drawing board. A sophisticated fighter of 1918, like the Sopwith Snipe, had a maximum speed of approximately 120 miles per hour and carried two .30-caliber machine guns for armament. (The .30-caliber machine guns, as well as their 7.7mm equivalents, are often called "rifle caliber" because they employ the same caliber shell as a rifle.) Although a splendid weapon in its day, the Snipe would have been a hopeless anachronism on a battlefield in 1941, outclassed in every type of meaningful flight performance. In contrast a good aircraft of 1970 vintage (as distant from us as 1918 was from the pilots of 1941) such as the F-4 Phantom is still operational around the world. Change has continued in military aviation, but the pace and direction have transformed as well. If we look at the weapons carried the situation is reversed. The machine guns of a World War I fighter were fewer and smaller than those found on a World War II plane, but the difference was one of degree, not of kind. An advanced air-to-air missile found on today's best fighters, and the modern avionics to support it, are a tremendous leap from the weapon system found on the 1970 F-4. The emphasis, in other words, on a World War II fighter was on the aircraft itself, particularly the engine and airframe. The weapons it carried were powerful within a limited context but derivative of a much older technology.

One can think of an aircraft as a machine containing an engine, basic airframe (fuselage and wing), and subsystems. Designers argue among themselves which component is the most important to improve for overall progress. Because an aircraft is much more than the sum of its parts, this argument normally has no answer. Yet as to the interwar period the evidence is very strong that tremendous progress in engine design was the primary cause in advancing the capability of aircraft.

It is a good idea to provide a basic lexicon for aircraft engines. The inline engine was very similar in concept to the engines in most automobiles. There is a cast block of metal; inside it the cylinders, moving up and down by the detonation of fuel, drive a shaft that delivers power to the wheels or, in the case of airplanes, to the propeller. A radial engine has a very different configuration, as there is no large engine block. Instead the cylinders are arranged around the driveshaft in a circle (hence *radial*). Both inline and radial engines are internal-combustion engines and generate a great amount of heat. An inline engine overcomes heat with an elaborate liquid-cooling system. This allows the engineer to develop a long and relatively slender engine that receives most of the cooling via tubes that carry coolants. A radial engine, in contrast, is air-cooled. (Both engine types require oil lubricants.) The cylinders in a radial configuration are in direct contact with the airflow, and great efforts are taken to make the cylinders catch and retain the natural cooling effects of the inflowing air. Without good cooling, either type fails. A radial required very sophisticated metalwork to obtain cylinders that were both efficient and cool. An inline engine is in some ways more forgiving but requires an extremely robust structure to prevent oil and coolant leaks. Physically the two types are easy to identify. If a single engine aircraft, like the Japanese Zero and the U.S. Corsair, had a broad and blunt front end, it meant that the craft was powered by a radial engine that required as much air as possible. If a plane had a lean, long front end, like the U.S. P-40 and the famous British Spitfire, that was a sure sign that craft had an inline engine.

Both types had advantages. In theory an inline engine, long and thin, offered less drag and a more streamlined shape, which should lead to greater speed. Because of theoretically better cooling, engineers developed inline engines that had more power out of less displacement. In contrast radial engines were lighter because they dispensed with the engine block and the liquid-cooling systems. If designed and manufactured properly, radial engines achieved a well-deserved reputation for extreme reliability. Although less efficient relative to displacement, the radial was lighter. Designers simply made a less-efficient engine that was larger and consequently produced more power. This was a tremendously important factor in the Pacific war, as each side sought powerful aircraft that could operate from carrier decks. When taking off and landing—crucial to carrier operations—radial-engine aircraft excelled. They were more reliable and lighter than were inline-engine craft. Consequently both the Japanese and American navies concentrated almost exclusively on radials. The same characteristics made the radial the engine of choice for multiengine aircraft on both sides. A slight decrease in speed was more than compensated for by greater reliability and less weight. The slight disadvantage imposed by the additional drag of radial engines was compensated for by simply making the engines larger and more powerful.

Land-based fighters operated in a different environment. The USAAF, like its European counterparts, believed that the inline engine offered greater speed in relation to weight. This decision was made in the months before Pearl Harbor and may have been incorrect. In any case the first-generation U.S. Army fighters all had inline engines. Only the P-47 was powered by a radial. On the Japanese side, the Japanese army made a vain but very intelligent attempt to substitute an inline-engine fighter for the ubiquitous Zero.

In the field of engine development, as well as many other fields, the United States was a leader, which on its face makes no sense. Despite the boasts of American industrialists, the U.S. effort to produce a great air force during World War I was a debacle. Furthermore, although the U.S. military was determined to never again be caught without a more or less modern air force, military budgets in the United States were very small. To make matters worse, Congress enacted legislation that demanded open competition for both prototype and production contracts. In other words, a company could make a successful prototype but be undercut by another company for the contract to produce the aircraft. As time went on this was less likely to happen, but several firms, like Morse, were destroyed or harmed by this foolish policy. Yet the U.S. model had several hidden advantages. As aviation matured, industrial technique became increasingly important. World War I aircraft were, to a surprising degree, products of craftsmanship and very poorly suited to mass production. As canvas and wood gave way to metal, the core engineering technologies in which the United States led the world could be brought to bear in the field of aviation. The internal-combustion engine is an obvious case in point.

The first great U.S. aircraft engine was not the Liberty but the Curtis D-12 block inline introduced in 1922. Curtis racers powered by the D-12 were the first to crack the 200 miles-per-hour mark and traded speed records with French Hispano-Suiza–powered planes in the early 1920s. However, the D-12 was a much more reliable engine than was the Hispano-Suiza, and the U.S. Army purchased it to power all of their new fighters until 1927 (despite warehouses filled with unused Libertys). Clearly an excellent power plant, the D-12 was licensed to the Fairly Company in England, among others. Fairly was drawn to the commercial market and was more interested in the potential of the air-cooled radial. The Royal Air Force (RAF), however, like all European air forces, believed that the aerodynamic advantages deriving from the more slender inline engine made it superior to the radial for military use. Therefore the RAF prompted Rolls and Napier to build a domestic equivalent of the D-12.

The result was the splendid Rolls Royce Kestrel. The Kestrel's success set the RAF firmly in the inline camp. It also figured in one of the oddest episodes in aviation history. In 1933 the RAF purchased a low-wing Heinkel mailplane to test new radiators at high speed. The resultant hybrid flew at 260 miles per hour, fully thirty miles per hour faster than the original craft (powered by a bulky BMW inline). It was also fifty miles per hour faster than any RAF fighter then in service. The message to the RAF was clear: The biplane fighter was finished. The message to Germany was also clear: The Kestrel was a better engine than anything produced in Germany. In an era when budgets were tight and profits hard to come by, it was common to license a major invention to a foreign power. So it was that the Bf109 prototype flew (in front of a skeptical Luftwaffe audience) powered with a Kestrel.

Given a jump start by the clean and robust Kestrel, Rolls went on to develop the famous Merlin. From a design standpoint there were few major differences between the two except for displacement. The Kestrel produced 470 horsepower in 1927, the Merlin 1,050 horsepower in 1936. Despite its light weight and small displacement for an inline, the Merlin eventually proved a reliable power plant. (As one might expect there were teething troubles. The kinks were not ironed out of the Merlin until 1938, a longer time than it took foreign competitors to stabilize designs. Rolls Royce was working on a very innovative design: It is always challenging to milk power out of low displacement, and Rolls was a British company, which meant its engineers would seek difficult solutions to simple problems.) Like all good engines it was possible to increase the displacement and simple power. During the war the Merlin powered the Spitfire, Hurricane, Mosquito, Lancaster, Mustang, and P-40F, among others.

Although German engine design was retrograde well into the 1930s, German industrial technique (like that in the United States) was excellent. Hermann Göring, as well as heading the Luftwaffe, was responsible for overall German rearmament. The German aircraft industry, to put it mildly, did not lack for funds. As noted, German engineers could also examine foreign types at their leisure. In addition German designers were more closely connected to university aerodynamic theorists than was the case in other countries, and they became convinced from the start that the inline engine was the appropriate power plant for military use. It was German practice to develop robust and reliable engines even at the cost of higher displacement and weight. This tendency was well illustrated by the Junkers Motoren Jumo 210 and 211 engines that came out in 1936. The large-displacement Jumo 211 was a rugged model that powered the Stuka and most of Germany's twin-engine bombers. The Jumo 213 was a variation of the Jumo 211 that powered the Fw190D. In early 1938 Daimler Benz introduced the DB 600, the first of a series of engines that provided the backbone of the Reich's fighter arm. The DB, like the Jumo, was an inverted twelve-cylinder inline. It was the ingredient necessary to transform the Bf109 into a great aircraft. Also like the Jumo, there was nothing about the DB series that particularly distinguished it. The genius of German designers lay in their attention to detail. The DB was one of the first combat aircraft engines to employ fuel injection and had a very good version of the U.S.-inspired water-methanol injection system. Ultimately, however, the large displacement worked against the DB series. Later versions realized little increase in speed because of added weight from the engine and extra armament. (The last of the DB 601 series produced a healthy 1,475 horsepower. The DB 605, which went into the Bf109L, delivered 1,800 horsepower and great speed. It was very poorly mated to the Bf109 airframe, however, and was not considered a success. The DB, in other words, ran its course more quickly than did the Merlin, and there was no equivalent of the 1943 Rolls Royce Griffon to replace it.) The U.S. Allison inline, although a standard vee-configuration and not inverted, resembled the DB and Jumo engines in sacrificing efficiency for reliability. If anything, it was the toughest inline engine of World War II. The DB also showed up in the Pacific. The Japanese army licensed the DB 601 and put it into the Tony. (Because the Tony resembled the Me109, many U.S. pilots believed the Luftwaffe was active over the skies of New Guinea in early 1943.) Tokyo picked a good engine but lacked the production methods to create a reliable copy. Although the Tony was a decent plane when it flew (better than the Zero in fact), it proved more trouble to Japanese mechanics than did American pilots.

The United States gave a healthy shove toward the development of the inline engine. American designers, however, made the radial engine into the premier power plant for high-performance piston-driven aircraft. The radial was held back by the inherent complexity of connecting multiple cylinders to a single shaft. In addition, extremely fine tolerances were required to allow sufficient cooling.

Solving these problems was a matter of engineering as well as of industrial technique. European aeronautical engineering was always the equal to ours, but European industrial technique was not. Consequently mastering problems like the radial played directly into America's strong suit, and the results changed aviation forever. The demand for radials came from nascent commercial aviation because a good weight-to-power ratio promised by the radial had obvious attractions. More importantly, the U.S. Navy had suffered a series of difficulties due to poor cooling on its early aircraft. The development of the aircraft carrier made the radial even more attractive. An engine with a higher power-to-weight ratio promised lower landing speeds (crucial for carriers) and the ability for smaller planes to carry bombs and torpedoes. None of this was lost on Tokyo, and Japanese aviation was being dominated by the radial by the 1930s.

At the urging of the U.S. Navy a small company owned by the brilliant inventor Charles Lawrence was purchased by the Wright Corporation. Wright persuaded British pioneer Samuel Heron to team up with Lawrence. Together the two designed the Wright J-5 Whirlwind. In 1927 young Charles Lindbergh, with the approval of Ryan Corporation engineers, had a Whirlwind purchased for the *Spirit of Saint Louis*. We must remember that the transatlantic flight had claimed the lives of some of the world's great aviators, and engine malfunction was a likely cause. Lindbergh, and several men who followed him a few weeks later (Lindy was indeed lucky to get there first), had made it look easy. And they all flew aircraft powered by the Whirlwind, which had become, in one day, the most famous engine in aviation history. The radial was made.

Ironically success worked against Wright and its successor, Curtiss-Wright. Wright was a heavyweight for its day in the very small aviation community. (No firm anywhere involved with aviation ranked with major concerns like Ford.) Busy on a number of projects, and believing, like most companies, that the lucrative military market would be dominated by inline engines, Wright spread its efforts in all directions. Quietly encouraged by the navy, Wright president Frederic Rentschler, a firm believer in big radials, left his company with half of Wright's design team and founded Pratt and Whitney, arguably the builders of the greatest engines in aviation history. As Lindbergh was flying to Paris, Pratt and Whitney was testing the 22-L Wasp. Remarkably reliable and extremely efficient, the 450-horsepower Wasp was a tremendous success. (An improved version powered the U.S. Navy's first torpedo-bomber—a significant departure in retrospect.) The Wasp also shook the boardroom at Wright. Proven wrong by both the Wasp and its own Whirlwind, Wright quickly developed the splendid Cyclone.

It is important to realize that both the Wasp and Cyclone were extremely sound designs that allowed for a steady progression of very reliable engines, all based on the original models, that enabled designers to steadily increase power. The Whirlwind (tested in 1925) produced 220 horsepower; the PW Wasp (1926) put out 450; the original Cyclone (1927) raised the ante to 525. Radial development exploded during the 1930s. (Perhaps because Americans like baseball and statistics, the U.S. aviation industry began showing its love of numbers instead of names for identifying aircraft, engines, and subsystems in the late 1920s. For engines the displacement became, in effect, the name. The F4F Wildcat was powered by a Pratt and Whitney Double Wasp R-1830 with a 1,830cc displacement; the "R," of course, stood for "radial.")

A major advance was doubling the number of cylinders by aligning them in two banks. Engineers at the time argued over the advantage of doubling smaller-cylinder banks or increasing the size of the cylinders (usually nine) within a single bank. Originally the latter school had the upper hand. However, it was soon obvious that with better cooling techniques it was possible to increase the cylinder size of doubled banks. The argument thus concluded, the World War II radial was born. First off the mark in 1932 was the Pratt and Whitney Twin Wasp R-1830 (825 horsepower, later up to 1,200). The PW 1830 lacked the power to be a great fighter power plant, although the Wildcat did yeoman service. In multiengine work, however, the power plant proved ideal. It was mounted on the Douglas C-47 and Consolidated's B-24 and PBY Catalina. The PW R-2800 Double Wasp, introduced in 1939, was another story altogether. Without sacrificing reliability, Pratt and Whitney designers built an engine capable of producing 2,000 horsepower. The Double Wasp found a home on the P-47, the Corsair, Hellcat, Bearcat and, for good measure, the Martin B-26 Marauder, the best medium bomber of World War II. Simultaneously Curtiss-Wright beefed up its Cyclone series. The CW R-1820, introduced in 1933 at 600 horsepower, was producing 1,200 by the time it was mounted on the B-17G. (The CW 1820 was the last big-cylinder, single-row radial; Wright produced fine engines but was technically one step behind Pratt and Whitney, a fact that cost it dearly in the commercial market after World War II.) The 1820 also powered the marvelous Douglas Dauntless dive-bomber, arguably the most effective tactical bomber of the Pacific war, as well as the last Wildcats. Wright's first double-row, the R-2600, produced a robust 1,700 horsepower and was found on the B-25, A-20, Martin Mariner, Curtis Helldiver, and Grumman Avenger.

Although not obvious at the time, the Pratt and Whitney R-2800 and the Wright R-2600 represented the apogee of large piston–engine design. Both engines were splendid power plants, delivering fine performance, excellent reliability, and relative ease of production and maintenance. (The stress here is on the word "relative": All large aircraft engines were complex and required constant attention by ground crews and pilots.) The ease with which designers moved from the Whirlwind to the R-2800 could never be duplicated. Instead Wright and Pratt and Whitney designers ran into the brick wall of diminishing returns. Typically the two companies took different tacks when attempting to push the envelope. Wright developed a big-cylinder twin-bank, the famous (or infamous) CW R-3350. The 3350 kicked out a lusty 2,800 horsepower but at the cost of great complexity. The B-29, the most prominent customer of the 3350, was bedeviled, in early models, by engine fires upon takeoff. Postwar commercial applications fared better, but something radically different was needed.

Pratt and Whitney (which had started the war with 350 employees and ended with 40,000) contented itself with refining the R-2800 while a small team worked on the R-4360 Wasp Major. The 4360 was a quadruple-bank, twenty-eight-cylinder radial that produced 2,800 horsepower when tested in 1943 and well beyond 3,000 by 1945. Although it served well in commercial aircraft after the war, the huge Wasp Major almost made it into World War II fighter combat in the form of the Goodyear F2G, a type of Corsair on steroids. An ultra-Jug was also in the works at war's end. The Wasp Major, however, will always be associated with the huge B-36. The Wasp Major was also the end of the line. Turbos have kept propellers on many large aircraft since World War II. However, the real encore for the big radials was the jet.

German and Japanese radials illustrate the central importance of industrial technique. In the 1920s both countries were firmly behind inline engines. In 1930 BMW procured a license for a Pratt and Whitney Wasp derivative. Gaining a contract to place that engine into the Ju52 transport, BMW almost alone developed German radials. With the introduction of the fourteen-cylinder BMW 801 in 1940 the Luftwaffe possessed a splendid power plant for the feared Fw190. Although a BMW original design, the 801 showed the Pratt and Whitney philosophy. Fortunately for the Allies BMW never developed a good supercharger for the 801, a fact that had serious ramifications when the battle for Germany started in earnest in late 1943. There was nothing remarkable about the BMW design. However, it was rugged and took well to refinement throughout the war.

In contrast the Japanese followed a slope pointing downward. Until the early 1930s Japan's military aircraft were powered by license-built inlines from a variety of foreign sources. The Japanese navy, as noted, however, soon recognized the obvious advantages of radials. In 1936 Tokyo licensed a Gnome radial from France that became, with substantial variation, the Nakajima Sakae, the engine mounted in the Zero. A year later Mitsubishi picked up a Pratt and Whitney license that led to a variety of good engines that appeared in many aircraft. However, when Japanese engineers tried to advance the sophistication of their power plants they got into trouble the farther they strayed from the original foreign inspiration. This was not the fault of the designers. There was little mystery in the field of aircraft engines by World War II. On paper the power plants that went into the late-model Japanese fighters were excellent; in practice all were unreliable, hard to produce, and difficult to maintain. No wonder that both Zeros and Oscars were kept in production until VJ-Day.

The radical improvement of engine performance was not due merely to more complex designs. During the early 1920s technicians began to understand the concept of octane rating and the potential of fuel additives. The aviation fuel used in 1920, no different than that pumped into a Model T, had an octane rating of about 50. General Motors (no surprise there) discovered that lead additives increased combustion efficiency, and they were adopted by the U.S. military in the late 1920s. By 1936 the U.S. Army was the first to adopt a 100 octane–rated fuel. Racing aircraft used various concoctions (rather like racing cars in our era) to boost output, but these had little practical impact. During the war Allied aircraft had fuel with ratings over 120. This was one of the most important reasons that Allied aircraft had superior high-altitude performance over their Axis counterparts.

Superchargers completed the engine equation. Late-nineteenth-century European theorists, working without anything resembling a proper internal-combustion engine, had discussed the possibility of some type of blower arrangement for aircraft propulsion. The reason was simple enough. As known by anyone who lights a fire on a mountaintop, combustion is less efficient above sea level. In practice the difference is huge. An engine at 20,000 feet produces half the power of its sea-level rating; at 30,000 feet the percentage dips to less than a third. Prior to World War I aircraft were flying at altitudes above 10,000 feet, and designers were working on simple blower mechanisms to compress the fuel-air mixture sent into the cylinders to create an artificial "sea-level combustion" environment. The designers at Hispano-Suiza experimented, unsuccessfully, with a mechanism that would redirect engine exhaust into a simple turbine to power a blower, thus utilizing wasted exhaust to increase engine power at altitude. This research was picked up by General Motors and refined after World War I: The result was the turbosupercharger.

Early renditions of U.S. and French turbocharged aircraft set spectacular altitude records in the early 1920s, providing a tremendous boost to supercharger technology of all types. Turbos remained a U.S. technology because of the extremely delicate production problems and expensive alloys involved. Turbosupercharging was used in a number of U.S. aircraft during World War II, including most bombers as well as the P-47, P-38, and Northrop P-61 Black Widow. By World War II mechanical superchargers—gear-driven by the engine itself—were a part of every military engine in the world. Simple single-stage blowers, as found on the P-40 and P-39, functioned well enough up to about 10,000 feet, at which point performance began to suffer badly. (Bell and Curtis both claimed that the army's refusal to turbocharge the

P-40 and P-39 crippled the models. Evidence from the Merlin-powered P-40 does not support the contention. The excellent performance from the sophisticated mechanical supercharger given the P-63 Kingcobra indicates that Bell had a point. However, no supercharger would have solved the P-39's deficient range.) On paper the turbo system was superior and gave the highest "critical altitude" (the maximum-level performance) of over 30,000 feet.

Other manufacturers developed an array of gear-driven superchargers. By the mid-1930s the simple single-stage blower was common. The development of the modern engines like the Merlin, the DB 601, and the U.S. radials in the mid-1930s brought with them more complex types. Although heavier and lacking the technical elegance of the turbo, they were simpler to maintain and required little monitoring by the overworked fighter pilot. (Twin-engine aircraft, usually with a copilot, could better employ a variety of gauges than could a fighter.) The best of the lot was the two-stage double-speed supercharger developed for the Merlin-powered Spitfire IX, which gave the Spit a critical altitude of 30,000 feet. The U.S.-built model installed in the Mustang was lighter but less efficient, peaking at 25,000. The U.S. Navy's double-speeds, developed at the same time Rolls was creating theirs for the Merlin, were almost the equal of the Mustang's. German builders, hurt by their poor gasoline, had to increase the power of the engine to stay competitive at high altitudes. It was a race they slowly but inevitably lost. Japanese efforts, on paper, were excellent after 1941; in practice they proved grossly unreliable. The high altitude belonged to the Americans throughout most of the Pacific war, and thousands of Japanese aviators died as a result.

Complex technology always involves interaction, a fact that makes it difficult to explain and analyze. The supercharger, regardless of type, was a case in point. Although an airplane's engine is happy at sea level because it achieves maximum combustion, the airframe is better suited for the lighter air of higher altitude. If the power is sufficient, the lower drag found in lighter air allows the plane to fly faster. Depending upon its airframe, engine, and supercharger, various fighters found their maximum speed at altitudes ranging from 10,000 to 30,000 feet. The best example of this was the P-47. A huge aircraft for its type, Republic's Thunderbolt was perhaps the best fighter of the war above 25,000 feet. The twin-engine P-38 Lightning, another very large fighter, was also at its best at high altitude. Such considerations were of great importance, because supercharging allowed the single-engine fighter to maintain a speed advantage over multiengine types. In a world of crude superchargers the most effective way to handle speed at altitude was to increase power. By definition this favored multiengine aircraft. Indeed in 1935 it was not at all clear that fighters could catch bombers, and many doubted the future of the fighter altogether. Which bring us to our next topic: airframes.

Scientists have been fascinated for centuries by the movement of solids through fluids. Although they did not realize it, many of the great physicists of the past were developing the basic laws of aerodynamics. The next time you go camping, you can replicate a simple experiment that goes to the heart of both aeronautical and nautical design. (There is no coincidence that the words are close relatives: To a scientist both air and water are fluids. Finding the best way to move an object through the fluid is crucial whether one is designing a ship or an aircraft.) Push a stick into a slowly moving stream and observe the elliptic shape taken by the water as it passes around. The thicker the stick, the thicker and longer the ellipse. What you are observing is the best design for an object intending to pass through a fluid. The water passes evenly around both sides of the stick and joins at the rear with only a small eddy. (The eddy is important because it results from a vacuum inevitably caused, and because nature does not like vacuums it produces in its turn a counterflow that impedes forward movement. Anyone who has nearly choked to death riding in the bed of a pickup down an unpaved road knows firsthand the effect of eddies. There is no way to remove eddies entirely, but designers do everything within reason to decrease unnecessary ones.) The term for the ellipse caused by the stick in the water is "streamline." It is the shape for the hull of a ship. It is also the shape for the fuselage of an airplane (looking either from above or from the side), as well as the cross-section of any airfoil, including the propeller. As the Wright brothers proved, and as was shown many times during World War I, it is not necessary to design an aircraft in a streamline if you wish to fly. However, due to a quirk of physics, parasitic drag increases the faster any object moves through fluid. In other words if you want to design a fast aircraft (or ship), then it must be streamlined. Thus as long as power plants did not generate high speeds under any circumstances, there was little reason to stress streamlining. As power grew, however, it was necessary to rewrite the book on designing the airframe if one wished to translate the additional power into usable speed.

Aircraft historians argue over the impact made by air racing and the record-setting mania that so fascinated the general public during the interwar period. Some advances, for instance in wing design, no doubt resulted. The Supermarine seaplane that won the Schneider Cup (one of several racing competitions that awarded trophies) is usually considered the initial prototype of World War II's most illustrious fighter, the Spitfire. One could argue, however, that Reginald Mitchell used the prestige of the Schneider Cup to get the RAF to do what he wanted to do all along. It is more reasonable to conclude that commercial aviation had a much greater influence on the development of modern aircraft than did the racers and headline seekers. It should be noted, however, that the public love of such stunts found its reflection in the efforts of countless engineers and a small army of capitalists who invested huge amounts of time and money into aviation with little hard-nosed chance of return. Fortunes were made in aviation, but they came from World War II. Very few of the men involved in the business prior to wartime made a profit. The industry, particularly outside Germany and Japan, where rearmament was fully under way in the mid-1930s, was awash in red ink. Yet all had an unshakable faith that what they were doing would somehow change the world. They were right on that point. And thanks to World War II a few of them created industrial empires that endure until the present day.

It is important to appreciate that an unusually close relationship existed between civilian and military aviation, particularly in the United States. The aviation community in the interwar period was a very small one. Companies were tiny compared to, say, present-day Boeing. Many test pilots and some engineers were either former military pilots or in the active reserve. (Lindbergh was a good example.) Congress, heavily influenced by the strong reaction against World War I, took some ill-advised steps during the 1920s. However, along the way the lawmakers threw some very valuable bones to the industry. First was the National Advisory Committee for Aeronautics (NACA), founded in 1915. NACA developed into a small research facility and information clearinghouse on aviation matters. It would be difficult to find a major advance in the field in which NACA did not play some role. For a few nickels the U.S. government gave the domestic aviation industry a priceless instrument. Second, the United States had an unusually enlightened patent-sharing law (caused by vicious legal bloodletting between the early Wright and Curtis Corporations). An aviation patent registered in the United States could not be protected, although the holder, obviously, was owed a license from any who used it. This meant that a major invention could not be held as the exclusive property of any single company. To put it mildly, this made for a very competitive industry. But it also added an element of cooperative enterprise that likewise played a role. Add into this chemistry the fact that most of the major players were friends or acquaintances, and you have a close-knit community of friendly enemies. The military profited greatly from this arrangement and likewise fostered it. Army and navy engineers played an important role in aviation breakthroughs, and due to the nature of the fraternity, information moved quickly into the hands of private industry. All of this was most important because, as was the case in the radial engine, improvements in the United States played an unusually large role in the development of modern airframes and subsystems.

America's vital role in this grand industry was particularly remarkable because U.S. military budgets were smaller than those in Europe, European airlines received substantial subsidies during the interwar period (which probably hurt their technical development), and European (particularly German) theoretical knowledge at the university level was better than that found in the United States. (This situation changed in the late 1930s. During the war the very large university system in America was central to our ability to create a massive arms industry out of nothing in record time. As war trudged forward big thinkers played a crucial part in refining radar and communications. Early analog computing devices helped in the design of advanced projects like the B-29 and the laminar-flow airfoil that made the Mustang such a great fighter. Ultimately the atomic bomb was U.S. academia's greatest contribution to the air war.) In the interwar period aeronautics did not have the prestige found in Europe. Much of the work done in the United States was by the seat of the pants. Frequently this was the fastest and best way to get things done, yet the greatest single advance in fighter airframe design, the Me262 and its counterparts, derived from work done in German universities prior to the war. German rocketry came from the same source. It's the world's good fortune that Hitler was not keen on professors.

Although aviation saw a multitude of developments large and small during the interwar period, if I were going to pick a single point that led to the creation of the mature World War II fighter it would be the first flight of the Boeing Monomail in 1930. As the name implies, the single-engine plane was designed to carry mail, cargo, perhaps a few passengers. The Monomail had no single innovation to call its own, but it incorporated an unprecedented number of cutting-edge features. Its economic success was slight, but its technical success was sufficient to trigger a series of events that led directly to the B-17 and its foreign counterparts. Brutally efficient bombers—long talked about and feared within political circles—were a marvelous inducement to spend large sums of money on fighter development. There is nothing like fear (or the desire to produce it) to prod governments to open their checkbooks.

Let us look at what made the Monomail special. Because it carried a single 575-horsepower Pratt and Whitney radial, it had enough power to make a high degree of streamlining desirable. One must always appreciate interaction when assessing technology. The Monomail, for its time, had a large engine. A larger engine prompted designers to minimize parasitic drag to increase speed. In some areas it was worthwhile to increase weight if it also decreased drag. So it was with the Monomail. The Boeing plane employed retractable landing gear, which increased weight and added complexity. Yet the aerodynamic payoff proved worth it. Likewise the Monomail was one of the first planes to employ a development fostered in the late 1920s by the NACA: the engine cowl. The cowl was a simple enough concept, and French designers had used it with rotary engines early in World War I. However, large radials need reliable cooling. Despite much effort no one was able to design a cowl that did not impede engine cooling, that is, until the NACA breakthrough. The result was a significant decrease in parasitic drag caused by the wide radial engine.

The cowl and retractable gear increased weight but also increased performance. Yet the Monomail designers also took measures to decrease weight and increase strength. The first key to this trick is to use metal, common enough by 1930 in the civilian sector. However, Boeing designers employed a venerable design technique with unequaled success. Just as naval architects love streamlined objects, so do structural engineers admire the egg. The egg is remarkably strong for its weight and holds its shape without any internal or external support. Until the Monomail (and frequently after it) most airframes and wings had been held together by an intricate series of braces and supports. Great strength was possible but at the cost of both weight and, if braces were external, parasitic drag. This was the reason that canvas was used for most aircraft; the skin's role was to minimize eddies, not to hold the aircraft together. However, if one had good light alloys (aluminum is the obvious choice for much of the frame; thin tubular steel is another) and knew how to pull it off, it was possible to design a very spare frame and use the skin itself to support the stress placed on an aircraft during flight. In aeronautical terms this is called a "semimonocoque" construction (after the French word for "egg"). Boeing's rendition of the semimonocoque frame also employed stressed-skin construction, which allowed a smoother and stronger design. (The German Junkers firm had developed something close to a semimonocoque frame in 1915 and continued using it on its famous Ju52 transport throughout World War II. The skin that supported much of the weight, however, was corrugated sheetmetal. It worked for the Ju52 but, because of the tremendous drag caused, was unsuited for combat aircraft.) If properly executed the result is a lighter, stronger airframe. One immediate advantage of a superior frame that showed up on the Monomail (not, as usual, for the first time) was a cantilever wing, or an airfoil without external bracing. At lower speeds the elaborate bracing found on World War I aircraft had not caused serious difficulty. On a high-speed plane, however, bracing was anathema. Every combat aircraft of World II had cantilevered wings and tails. (Just to show that there is an exception to every rule, early models of the Bf109, otherwise a groundbreaker, used braces on the tail.)

The Monomail was converted to military use as the B-9, a very advanced bomber for its day (yet not good enough for adoption by the U.S. Army; Martin grabbed the contract with a slightly faster version that profited greatly from Boeing's research). More importantly a more advanced version, the Boeing 247, was offered as the world's best commercial airliner. In 1933 the claim was accurate, and United Airlines bought sixty models—a huge order for the time. This left TWA without anything better than Junkers and Ford Trimotors, solid aircraft but dead-end designs. During this period in aviation history it was still possible for a relatively new kid on the block to stir things up. In the early 1930s that new arrival was Douglas Aircraft, an experienced builder of military aircraft but a newcomer to the commercial multiengine market. A prototype, the DC-1, was soon followed by the sensational DC-2. Rewarded by a fat order from TWA, Douglas pushed on, and in 1936 TWA placed the first DC-3 into active service. As DC-3s were not replaced for short hauls until the early 1960s, and hundreds fly commercially today, it is obvious Douglas had done things right.

I find it ironic that the C-47, the military version of the DC-3, was given the nickname "Gooney Bird." In truth the Douglas aircraft have beautiful lines that for the period illustrate streamlining at its best. The DC-2 had all of the features of the Monomail and several others. First, it was a twin-engine aircraft. Prior to the DC-2 and Boeing 247, airlines insisted on three- and four-engine craft for longer flights. (Some hardy souls took their chances in single-engine transports.) The more-powerful radials put into the DC-2 convinced TWA that the plane could fly for a long distance and land with one engine. (The ramifications for bombers should be self-evident.) The well-cowled engines, protruding far from the wings, presented little drag and, because of their power, offered the potential of great speed. Douglas achieved this speed by decreasing the size of the wing relative to the weight of the aircraft. In aviation parlance, Douglas increased wing-loading. Not knowing anything about metal fatigue, Douglas built the DC-2 and DC-3 to specifications that made the aircraft unnecessarily strong, one of the reasons that some continue to fly. (This is a good example of designers intentionally expending some of the advantages gained from a good design on always unwelcome greater weight. In this case the goal was structural strength, which, to understate matters, Douglas achieved.)

There were two advances that appeared on the Douglas airliners that quickly found their way into all fields of aviation. First, the DC-2 was one of the first planes to use the variable-pitch propeller, one of the most important design developments of the interwar period. A propeller is an airfoil, just as a wing or a rudder. Quite simply the pitch (that is, the angle that the propeller's blades bite the air) on a variable-pitch prop can be adjusted depending upon the goals the pilot is seeking to achieve: good (i.e., fast) level speed, fast takeoff and climb rates, or altitude. At low speeds and altitudes the question is not vital, but at higher speeds and altitudes it becomes central. Although speculation concerning a variable-pitch prop began in the 1870s, British designers first interested the RAF in the concept shortly after World War I, but their execution did not match their ideas. American competitors were hot on the trail, however. In the late 1920s Curtiss-Wright began a crash program to mate their new radials with a variable-pitch prop. At the same time, an army engineer left the service, filed a patent on private work, and sold it to the Hamilton Standard Company. Both designs were similar in effect. Props, depending upon the situation, have an ideal RPM range (revolutions per minute). This prop's RPM range is usually lower than the RPM range of the engine's driveshaft. From the earliest days of design, some type of gear mechanism was necessary to rotate the prop slower than the driveshaft. With more complex gearing, and added weight, Curtiss-Wright and Hamilton Standard offered props that could change pitch upon the pilot's command during flight. Though not an ideal solution, it was far superior to any standard-pitch design. (Hamilton Standard helped Willy Messerschmitt convince Luftwaffe skeptics that his Bf109 could reach the promised speeds that the original prototype failed to reach using the single-pitch prop: a British engine and an American prop for the early 109—history laughs at us.) Naturally variable-pitch props appeared on the DC-2.

The increasing speed and weight of aircraft like the DC-2 and some of its U.S.-made contemporaries presented a huge quandary. The key to both speed and load-carrying was powerful engines, streamlined airframes, and wings with ever higher wing-loading. The problem, very simply, was how to land a fast and heavy aircraft without crashing. Heavy aircraft using conventional wing designs possessed higher stall speeds, which meant that developers were stymied unless they could figure out how to land planes at faster speeds or reduce their stall speeds. In practice they did both. The more important approach, by far, was the use of wing flaps. This was another World War I development that had no need at the time of original inspiration. In the 1920s German and British designers did much work on slotted wings and simple flap arrangements. The technology was nurtured and improved by the NACA and U.S. firms, and aircraft like the DC-2 were the among the first to employ them. The flap is a development that well illustrates chance and serendipity in technological innovation. It was a relatively simple concept, and early development did take place. (The slotted wing, of course, developed into the slatted wing, which we all have learned to love when landing on a jet airliner.) The concept, in retrospect, was key in allowing the higher wing-loading and faster speeds made possible by the more-powerful engines. There were dozens of models that could have made good use of reliable flaps by the early 1930s. But even the U.S. Navy, which could have used flaps to decrease takeoff and landing distances on carrier decks, showed little interest until Douglas, Boeing, and a few German makers demonstrated their value. Aviation designers in the 1930s, however, were quick learners. By 1937 every modern design—commercial and military—employed flaps. The other answer to the high-speed landing problem was to simply build airstrips longer and, if possible, to pave them. The modern airport was largely the result of wing flaps.

Douglas served notice to the world that a new era had arrived in aircraft design when in 1934 Boeing entered its 247 model into the famous London-to-Sydney air race. KLM Airlines countered with a brand-new DC-2. The normal run took two weeks. The race was won by a de Havilland Comet racer (later to appear as the Mosquito). The KLM DC-2 (which carried six passengers and 400 pounds of mail to illustrate the point), however, ran a close second in the spectacular time of ninety hours. Douglas had produced an aircraft capable of fast long-distance flight. Just as significantly it had produced a large aircraft capable of flying long distances carrying great weight. The DC-2, in addition, could match any fighter in the world in speed.

While Douglas executives celebrated their triumph (as well as the sizable orders that resulted for the DC-2 and DC-3), military airmen around the world knew that aviation technology had passed them by. If streamlined semimonocoque low-wing multiengine aircraft, powered by huge radials and fitted with flaps and retractable landing gear, could outrun a fighter, then it was obviously a matter of only months before someone started making bombers with the same attributes. Indeed every modern air force was developing advanced bombing types. Boeing soon drove that message home when it introduced the astounding B-17 in 1935. The B-17 was, from a technical point of view, a very well designed four-engine improvement of the DC-3. There was little new, but the performance envelope was raised in every category. As many grateful bomber crews later found out, the B-17, like the DC-3, was structurally stronger than was required for its task. In prototype form the B-17 could easily match or surpass the speed of any fighter, particularly at higher altitudes. When British Prime Minister Stanley Baldwin told his country at this time that "the bomber will always get through," technology was on his side. The B-15, developed by Boeing at the same time as the B-17, was a much larger aircraft and indicative of the type of weapon that gave peace-lovers nightmares. It was ahead of its time, but the technology showed up again in the B-29 and later in the B-36. As we shall see, the U.S. Army did not immediately adopt the B-17, but its very presence was an ominous portent of future developments. Around the world other nations were also developing bombers that were smaller than the B-17 but incorporated many of the same advances and could carry large bomb loads. Many could match or surpass the speed of the fighters that were in service during the mid-1930s. So-called appeasers, like Britain's Neville Chamberlain, who feared that aerial bombardment would lay Europe to waste and leave hollow any notion of victory were, on a certain level, correct.

There were, in essence, two ways a government could proceed. One was to build bombers in large numbers and perhaps keep a limited number of cheap pursuit aircraft (as fighters were called at the time) around for point defense. A great bomber fleet, so went the argument, would create a kind of deterrence, to employ a term from the nuclear age. However, the idea of leaving great cities and important targets open to attack and depending upon retaliation for protection was not appealing to any government. The alternative was to take the technology being developed principally by Americans for airliners and bombers and use it to make a fighter powerful and fast enough to establish a credible defense. It was a difficult choice. Fortunately for all concerned the group that got there first with the most was the last anyone in aviation expected: RAF Fighter Command.

Before looking at events in Britain and Germany in 1935, it is worth making the distinction between original and derivative fighter aircraft. (The distinction remains important today, as modern military forces frequently debate the merits of refining a proven weapon or designing an entirely new one.) A derivative design shows a direct lineage to an earlier model. The approach has the obvious merit of building upon a proven technology. Fewer teething troubles is one upside, and it proves possible to produce a decent aircraft fairly quickly. In addition—because a derivative design frequently requires only minor modifications of some essential components—it proves much easier to set up an assembly line, an important consideration if one needs to produce many units quickly. However, a derivative design carries a serious liability. The parent model, by definition, is in some way obsolescent, or there would be no need to replace it. Inevitably some of the obsolescence is passed on to the newer model. In practice this means that a derivative design reaches maturity quickly and finds an aeronautical dead end in a short period. By contrast an original aircraft derives from a new design. All aircraft are influenced to some degree by the designs that came before: The basic laws of flight that allowed the Wright Flyer to get off the ground operate on the modern F-16. Yet an original aircraft has progeny, not parents. The disadvantage of a new design is self-evident: It is more difficult and expensive to develop and inevitably suffers unforeseen problems because engineers are pushing technology into areas not well understood. Often original-design aircraft also are more complicated to produce and, at bare minimum, require new production facilities, thus increasing the lag time between prototype and guns in the air. However, a well-executed original had great potential for further development. In the long run the fiscal and psychological expense is usually worth it. This is particularly true if the odor of war is in the wind.

Britain developed the first great World War II fighter plane because its civilian government supported those in the RAF wise enough to see that Hugh Trenchard's bomber mania was ill-conceived and that defense was possible given the correct weapons. (Obviously simultaneous British developments in the infant field of radar added greatly to the arguments of Fighter Command.) Britain and France instituted the world's first independent air forces during World War I. After the war the RAF cultivated the so-called bomber cult. (The rarely read Italian theorist Giulio Douhet is frequently given credit for this dubious achievement, but his influence was slight in the real world. I am not sure which professor first convinced military historians that Douhet was aviation's Carl von Clausewitz, but whoever did so had no feel for the way military organizations work. Leaders like Trenchard of the RAF and Billy Mitchell in the U.S. Army Air Corps were a different matter.) The problem with the RAF doctrine was twofold. First, British defense budgets were much too small to develop bombers and the civilian market not mature enough to nurture the technology required. British bombers, simply put, were miserable machines. Had Britain put its money where its mouth was, the Lancaster would have been ready in 1939 instead of 1943.

More to the point, the doctrine of strategic bombing was, in the more innocent era of the 1930s, never properly developed. Generals grossly overrated the potential damage of a bombing raid and grossly underestimated the ability of an enemy's civilian population to stand up to the strain. A quick and painless victory, promised by so-called visionaries like Trenchard and Mitchell, was not remotely feasible. Instead what developed was a kind of deterrence. The RAF so inflated the power of strategic bombing that politicians, logically enough, grew terrified to use it. The massive series of air raids that all had predicted would come with the onset of another European general war did not take place at all in 1939. The harsh lessons of 1940, stupidly introduced by the Germans in Spain, Poland, and Holland, were required to shove a benign nation like Britain into the business of wholesale slaughter. As it was, few in the prewar era foresaw an aerial battle of attrition lasting six years.

If anything the fear of strategic bombing—in theory the guiding doctrine of the RAF—led to the first systematic efforts to defeat bombers by creating superior fighters. When the 1934 and 1935 specifications for a new British fighter were announced, it amounted to an admission that RAF Fighter Command was flying junk. At the time it was not alone. So embedded was the stupidity and rot that the Gloster Gladiator biplane was developed in the late 1930s as a hedge against the unproven monoplane. Other countries, including Germany, did the same—with predictable results in battle. Fortunately the United States entered the war later and had jettisoned the last of its biplanes, the Grumman F3F, before fighting began. However, the RAF asked its industry to re-create the fighter and do it as quickly as possible. We should note at the outset that none of this would have been possible without the concurrent development of the Merlin engine.

Also, the rebirth of Fighter Command illustrates wonderfully the advantages found in both derivative and original fighter designs. Although the development of the Spitfire actually began first, the fine designer Sydney Cram of Hawker proposed to modify his decent Fury biplane into a low-wing monoplane incorporating as much modern technology as possible. The resulting Hurricane was the most successful derivative-design fighter of World War II. Nimble and reasonably fast, the Hurricane was quick to develop (problems with the Merlin proved the biggest bottleneck) and relatively easy and cheap to produce. The Hurricane's problem was its old-style, braced-frame fuse-lage, which added unnecessary weight and limited the speed. As shown by the events of 1940 Fighter Command was very wise to order the Hurricane in large numbers. Nevertheless after the Battle of Britain the Hurricane was deployed to secondary theaters or converted to a ground attack plane. (A similar fate befell other yeoman derivative fighters such as the Wildcat and P-40.)

The Supermarine Spitfire was the quintessential original. I doubt any single designer in aviation history could match the brilliance of Reginald J. Mitchell of Supermarine. (Willy Messerschmitt, a fine designer in his own right, supervised a large and talented team once the Bf109 was accepted. Perhaps Jiro Horikoshi, designer of the Zero, rivals Mitchell in ingenuity, particularly given the paucity of technical resources Japan possessed. Yet when push came to shove the Zero proved to be based on a grossly flawed assumption of what was required in air combat; no one can say that about the Spitfire.) It was not necessary to convince Mitchell of the virtues of a low-wing monoplane: His Schneider Cup racers had done much to prove the innate superiority of the configuration. Yet Mitchell and his successors at Supermarine (Mitchell died shortly after the Spitfire prototype flew in 1936) did phenomenal work on the airframe. Although I do not share the view that the Spitfire was the war's most beautiful fighter (I'd tip my hat to the Zero or Fw190 in that regard), the streamlined fuselage stood out to the most casual onlooker. The cleverly placed radiators under the wings reduced a major cause of parasitic drag. Mitchell's great triumph, however, was the Spit's wing. The wing tip is the natural place for the formation of eddies as high-pressure air passing beneath the wing seeks to displace low-pressure air above it. (Difference in pressure—lift—is what allows aircraft to fly.) Consequently most of the lift in any wing comes from the root to the center. Likewise the center to the tip is tapered in the wing of any high-speed aircraft. In theory an elliptical shape is best able to minimize the drag caused by eddies at the tip. Recognizing this, Mitchell designed the famous elliptical wing found on the Spitfire. The Spit's wing was difficult and expensive to produce, but the RAF's decision to keep it was a very good one. The only better airframe to appear in World War II (outside Messerschmitt's brilliant and revolutionary swept-wing Me262 jet) was found on the P-51, with its laminar-flow wing and jetted exhaust. To give Mitchell his due, North American's engineers (who designed the Mustang) were working six years later and profited from two years of wartime experience.

The Spit's great opponent, of course, was the Bf109. Technically speaking, Messerschmitt put a 109 prototype into the air several

months before a Spitfire got off the ground. However, in stark contrast
to the RAF's conscious decision to move aggressively into uncharted
waters, the Luftwaffe ended up with the Bf109 almost by accident.
(The parallels with the development of the Mustang are extraordinary.) In 1934 Hitler, Göring, and their Nazi associates were planning
the construction of a massive air force. Göring and many of his followers were every bit as blind as Trenchard. Indeed early Luftwaffe
thought put much stock in the capability of bombers to win wars.
Willy Messerschmitt had the additional misfortune of producing a
faulty equivalent of the Monomail that had an unfortunate tendency
to crash (once with several Luftwaffe bigwigs aboard). Some of the
men killed were friends of Eduard Milch, Göring's right-hand man and
the Reich's commissioner for aviation. When the Luftwaffe—still "ille-
gal" under the terms of the armistice and the world's worst-kept secret—put forth specifications for a new fighter, Messerschmitt was allowed to produce a prototype (without government funding) and was
politely told that his aircraft, whatever it was, would never be chosen.
Having nothing to lose, Messerschmitt personally undertook to design
a state-of-the-art fighter. His design was so far in advance of German
contemporaries that he relied by necessity on key British and American
components to push events forward. The original prototype, although
greatly superior to its competitors in speed and climb rate, was disliked by the test pilots because it lacked maneuverability. There is little
doubt that Messerschmitt would have lost the fighter competition except that in 1936 Berlin received the startling news that the RAF had
ordered 310 Spitfires. By this time German test pilots were also beginning to see the wisdom in speed. Also Luftwaffe officials realized that
the DB 601 engine, still down the road, was obviously to the great
benefit of a plane like the Bf109. In 1936 Messerschmitt's team received an order to produce the aircraft in small numbers. A few
months later a handful was sent to Spain, where the planes shot the
rivets off of Soviet planes flown by the Republic. After Spain the Bf109
was made the Luftwaffe's top gun, and Willy Messerschmitt became
Göring's darling.

There were differences, of course, between the Spitfire and the
Bf109. Whereas Mitchell's Spitfire derived its greatness from a splen-
did airframe and superb wing, Messerschmitt developed the narrowest
possible fuselage to minimize drag. (The beautiful streamlining of the
Bf109, like other German aircraft of World War II, was influenced by
Germany's great tradition of glider design.) And yet both warplanes
had so much in common that together they defined the mature World
War II piston-engine fighter. Both were low-wing cantilevered mono-

planes of semimonocoque and stressed-skin construction. Because their airframes were light and strong, both fighters had a pronounced dihedral. (Dihedral is the upward angle between wing-root and fuselage when viewed from the front; it stabilizes flight. Because a wing achieves maximum lift when level, if a disturbance pushes one wing upward, the other levels out, increases lift, and reverses the effect of the disturbance. This illustrates the strength of the airframe required by a fighter expected to pull Gs, or the force exerted by gravity during maneuvers.) Both had retractable landing gear and fully enclosed canopies. The Spit was slightly larger, but the respective weights were remarkably similar. Both had good engines that started their life at approximately 1,000 horsepower and soon increased to the 1,400 range.

Furthermore both aircraft needed only one more piece to complete the puzzle, and it came, ironically, from the great fighter wasteland of the late 1930s—the United States. The device in question was the constant-speed prop. The variable-pitch prop greatly aided performance of multiengine aircraft, but the next step was to create a complex gearing mechanism (called a governor) to change prop pitch automatically depending upon the situation. (The pitch of the blade is the single most important factor in determining the speed a fighter travels.) The constant-speed prop led to a substantial increase in speed without an increase in engine power. The Germans eagerly picked the pockets of Hamilton Standard, and the VDM Company had a constant-speed prop in production by 1939. Although the British had done pioneering research on the technology, it was Supermarine's Mitchell himself who persuaded the RAF to fit a Hamilton variable-pitch prop to the early Spit. By 1939 de Havilland was building its own version of the Hamilton Standard constant-speed prop.

More-powerful engines and constant-speed props increased wing-loading and speed. It is interesting to note that both Messerschmitt and Supermarine decided to expend some of the excess power on devices that added weight but had combat virtues that made the trade-off worth the price; all of these features became standard on most World War II fighters. The first were short- and long-range radio sets. Short-range radios proved to be invaluable supplements to standard hand signals and became an integral part of the *schwarm*, or finger-four, formation adopted first by Germany and later copied by Britain and the United States. Long-range radios, when integrated with radar, allowed defenders to vector, or guide, fighters to an approaching foe. It also allowed attackers to utilize formations of unprecedented size and complexity. The second feature was simple pilot armor. Nothing could save a fighter caught in a full bullet stream, but incidental hits were very common, and protecting the pilot was good tactics and good for morale. More importantly both sides immediately before the war began installing crude self-sealing fuel tanks, a technology that was steadily improved although it cost both weight and range. It became increasingly difficult to down a fighter with a stray round or two. There were several variations on the general theme, but conceptually self-sealing tanks were similar. The fuel tank encased a second tank made of vulcanized rubber and other fabric. When a bullet struck the tank, escaping gasoline caused the rubber to melt and rebind, thereby creating its own patch. The rubber added weight and decreased the amount of fuel a tank could carry, but most air forces—Japan excepted—adopted the technology quickly and continued to refine it.

Also both the Spitfire and Bf109 received increasingly powerful armaments. Originally both mounted rifle-caliber machine guns. By the Battle of Britain the Bf109 carried a 20mm cannon; the Spitfire followed suit shortly thereafter. The .30-caliber twin machine gun, which had been standard armament on fighters as late as 1936, was an anachronism by Pearl Harbor. Lastly, early in the hostilities first the Luftwaffe and then the RAF discovered that fighters could carry bombs. This was an unthinkable concept as late as 1939. By 1944 swarms of fighters, most of them sporting Allied insignias, blanketed every theater of operation carrying a bomb load as substantial as that found in many bombers vintage 1935.

Above all the Spitfire and Bf109 had in common the three features that defined the core of the World War II fighter: high speed, high wing-loading, and enough structural strength to allow such aircraft to conduct aggressive combat maneuvers. Fighters that confronted each other in the years after the Battle of Britain improved in every category. Yet the essentials remained the same. As production demands outweighed the desire for innovation, World War II, like World War I, became a period of refinement, not fundamental creation. Yet these were machines of extraordinary beauty, great sophistication, and tremendous power. They required highly trained pilots and ground crews. Because of their unprecedented brute force, World War II fighters operated in a realm always shaped by the most draconian consequences of the laws of physics. In good hands they were capable of conducting maneuvers that pushed the human body to its physical limits. In good hands they were capable of destroying the largest aircraft in the world, not to mention each other. In good hands they could devastate an array of ground targets. Yet the power that allowed them to fill these roles made them merciless devices to the unwary and to anyone who asked one bit more than the plane was willing to give.

Prior to examining the aircraft flown by both sides during the struggle for the South Pacific, a few more general points should be made. First, many historians, even aviation writers, are quick to say that one type of plane was superior to another. Almost everyone writing about the first year of the Pacific war comments on the superiority of Japan's famous first-line fighter, the Mitsubishi A6M Zero, over its U.S. counterparts. It is wise to be wary of such generalizations. All aircraft are the products of design trade-offs. Assuming that high-quality technology is available, designers create an aircraft with certain combat characteristics in mind. When a designer seeks to optimize a certain combat trait, some other favorable characteristic might by necessity suffer. In general, for instance, no designer wants to waste weight. However, if engineers want to maximize speed they look to a powerful engine. Power and weight are closely related. Thus increasing the speed often means increasing the weight. It may also require a stronger, heavier airframe. Furthermore a plane designed to perform well at high altitudes will have different aeronautical characteristics than one designed to operate at medium or low altitudes. Defensive and offensive armament cause similar problems. Every pilot wanted armored protection around vulnerable areas (especially the cockpit) and self-sealing fuel tanks. Every pilot also wanted as much firepower as possible. However, armor and arms are very heavy. A light aircraft, particularly if designed with a large wing area, can be made to be extremely maneuverable. It can also generate good performance from a smaller engine. Yet such a plane inevitably sacrifices brute power, a strong airframe, and the ability to carry a substantial load of secondary weapons—like bombs. Aircraft development is therefore a sophisticated balancing act. Frequently the strengths and weaknesses of the resulting craft are subtle, clear only to the people close to operations.

Furthermore when judging an aircraft one must consider the environment in which it was flying. Operational realities may allow commanders and pilots to maximize the strengths and minimize the weaknesses of their aircraft. Yet just the opposite may take place. As we shall see this is exactly what took place in the Southwest Pacific in 1942. The mission and the aircraft, after all, must correspond. It is a great advantage, for instance, to fight over friendly territory. A pilot who can ditch or bail out successfully stands an excellent chance of fighting another day (in some cases, the same day). When over enemy ground, conversely, abandoning a stricken craft means imprisonment or a far greater chance of death due to exposure. Putting aside the obvious impact this situation has on pilot decisions and morale, it certainly influenced overall casualty rates among aircrews. This is not to mention that aircraft performance is also influenced by indirect factors. Good communications between ground and flight can be very important and can go a long way toward maximizing the assets at hand. But the opposite is also true. The quantity of spare parts and replacement aircraft is yet another factor.

One of the most difficult trade-offs engineers make concerns performance and safety. At a certain level the aircraft of this era were wonderfully built and extremely rugged. Several dozen fly today, thrilling great crowds at air shows, and thousands of skillful modern pilots lust to fly one. Yet they were warplanes. At the point of contact a warplane must be capable of extraordinary performance. Although all designers tried to build a level of redundancy into their designs and published specifications that were conservative, pilots pushed their craft to the maximum. This made all fighters inherently hard and dangerous to fly. If this was not so, they would have been poor fighters. In wartime conditions, of course, this factor is critical. No aircraft on the front line will ever receive the sort of maintenance that it would during peacetime. If something is a amiss during peacetime, the wise pilot (or his commander) will not allow the plane to fly. In combat—where sheer numbers are critical—pilots routinely flew craft that would have been grounded during better times. In addition basic flight controls were mechanical. A pilot performing combat maneuvers required strength and endurance. And World War II–era warplanes did not possess the self-diagnostics that exist in modern aircraft. Thus if pushed too far all fighters were very prone to mishap, which might lead to an aborted mission, a destroyed aircraft, or dead fliers.

The economic burdens placed on both the Allies and the Axis were great. Air forces are the most expensive of the armed services relative to size. Aircraft were expensive to produce, expensive to maintain, and, because of huge losses from all causes, in need of constant replacement. The combatants assigned thousands of their finest scientists and engineers to the task of designing better planes and production techniques. This task was never complete, as aircraft in operation received major and minor changes every few months. New types debuted regularly. Related technologies, such as communications and radar, merely contributed to the drain on intellectual resources.

The costs of operating air fleets were likewise great. Pilots were chosen from the best available military recruits. Training any pilot—even when done very poorly, as was the case in Japan late in the war—was a major undertaking. Aircraft consume fuel prodigiously whether in training, transit, or combat. Japan could never produce the oil required by its military forces, and as the war progressed officers of the

Imperial Japanese Navy had to decide whether to fly their aircraft or operate their warships. They chose the former in almost every case. Americans faced no shortages of oil, but they still had to bring it to the areas where it was needed, thousands of miles from the U.S. mainland. Countless merchant ships from both sides, operated in turn by thousands of crewmen, journeyed thousands of miles to far-flung bases to feed the tremendous appetites of air forces at war. Fuel and supplies went to storage at bases, which in turn were manned by large garrisons. The highly trained, and thus valuable, personnel who armed, fueled, and maintained warplanes far outnumbered pilots and aircrews. The rule of thumb was that every plane in the air required the efforts of ten people on the ground.

We can point to a major reason that the numbers of aircraft were so high: the devastating rate of attrition. When one accounts for combat, accidents, losses to weather, and simple aircraft fatigue, the target figure of 25 percent total force replacement per month (rarely obtained in the Pacific) was fully justified. Simply put, the men and machines on both sides were expendable. This grim fact reflected and shaped technology. At some levels aeronautical engineers were pushing the technological envelope when developing World War II–era warplanes. However, in all countries designers knew they were designing weapons that had to be produced in huge quantities. So before Pearl Harbor aeronautical engineers—many of whom were already looking ahead to the jet age and the era of civilian air travel—were hamstrung by that which was available, the skill levels one could expect from massive numbers of line workers, the skill levels one could expect from mass-trained pilots, and costs. Above all was the demand to get decent weapons to the fronts with as little delay as possible. Warplanes, then, were a kind of intermediate technology: Although the machines included some of the most advanced theories and were designed by brilliant men, the level of sophistication of the finished product was closer to a modern truck than to the infinitely complex, incredibly expensive military and civilian aircraft we see in the skies today.

The end product was a kind of war firmly rooted in time and place. The relentless aerial war of attrition that took place in the South Pacific during the first two years of war (a small theater by World War II standards) required aircraft that did not exist prior to 1940. Conversely in a later era the huge numbers of aircraft thrown into the military mincing machine would have been unfeasible economically and unnecessary militarily. For a brief period, however, thousands of brave, skilled, amazingly young men fought in the Pacific skies almost every day. Each knew he was playing for extraordinary stakes.

3

Japanese Warplanes

Military power was central to the development of the modern
Japanese state. Great victories over China and Russia at the beginning of the twentieth century gave the post-Meiji governments
tremendous prestige. They also answered a problem that bedeviled
military and civilian officials and thinkers alike. By itself, Japan
appeared to many contemporaries to be overpopulated and lacking
in natural resources. The shattering of Japanese isolation in the
mid-nineteenth century corresponded to the last surge of Western imperialism in Asia. It took little time for Japanese elites to understand that
military power based on modern principles was central to European and
U.S. power in the Pacific. It was thus natural for Tokyo to decide that it
should develop a powerful and complex military apparatus if it was to
avoid the same fate as China. Japanese leadership was painfully aware
that imperial military forces early in the twentieth century were very dependent upon foreign weapons, foreign advisers, and ultimately foreign
trade. The war against Russia and Japan's effective role on the side of
the West in World War I had proved that Tokyo's military machine was
formidable. Yet Tokyo understood that Japanese military triumphs had
been due largely to excellent use of purchased European equipment. It
also understood that Western weapons did not exist in a vacuum but
were the products of advanced industrialization. Victory in war had
shown that Japan could create a military organization effective enough
to achieve state aims. However, as long as Japan was dependent upon
foreign-bought weaponry, its position was tenuous. What would happen, military and civilian leaders alike wondered, if Japan had to fight

an advanced military power like Britain or the United States? The obvious answer was to develop a first-class, homegrown military apparatus.

Tokyo understood well that economic power and industrialization
were the basis of any modern state. The Japanese also understood that
their economic base was, by Western standards, extremely weak. Consequently in the early twentieth century the Japanese government
adopted a program sometimes referred to as "circumstantial adaptability." Simply put, this was a policy to develop as quickly as possible key
sectors of the industrial economy while making use of what was available from traditional agrarian Japan. Knowing that Western technology
was at the heart of power, the Japanese sent hundreds of top students
abroad for education. The government adopted an "export push"
economy to bring in foreign reserves necessary to purchase top-quality
technology from the West, which could then be studied and serve as an
inspiration for homegrown engineers. Unlike most countries in Asia,
Japan viewed the purchase of foreign technology as a building block for
future efforts rather than as machinery for immediate use.

On one level the policy was tremendously successful. In key areas of
the industrial economy the Japanese quickly adapted and even improved imported technology. We can see during this period the beginnings of Japan's modern economy. In the short run, however, there was
a very serious price to be paid. Japanese human, financial, and physical resources were limited. Concentrated in what Tokyo considered
vital areas, the industrial economy in the prewar period became seriously unbalanced. If the Japanese wished to concentrate efforts on a
limited goal, they were capable of impressive efforts. What was hidden, however, from their own leadership was Japan's inability to sustain a broadening base of high-quality construction and innovation.
Eventually both the quantity and quality of key weaponry suffered.

It was the curse of the era that for foreign and domestic reasons
Tokyo concentrated economic modernization on the creation of a
modern military. Although figures are difficult to analyze, it is likely
that Japan rivaled or surpassed the Soviet Union as the nation that
contributed the greatest percentage of its gross national product to
sustaining and developing its armed forces. As late as World War I
Tokyo purchased major warships from Britain. Twenty years later it
possessed a huge fleet built in Japanese yards. Much the same could be
said about the Japanese army.

As in all modern military forces, the Japanese leaders were very interested in aviation beginning very early. In 1909 Tokyo sent a small
delegation to France and Germany to obtain pilot training and buy a
small number of aircraft. By 1911 several aircraft were in the air over

Japan, and a Japanese pilot began modifying a French-made plane. In 1912 the IJN sent its own delegations to France and the United States to procure some seaplanes for evaluation. In the fall of 1914 four Japanese seaplanes bombed the German concession at Tsingtao and sank a German minelayer. Although the "victory" at Tsingtao, and symbolic service by a handful of Japanese airmen in France, constituted Japan's employment of military aviation during World War I, Japanese officers watched events in Europe with tremendous interest.

After the armistice in Europe events moved quickly in Japan. The army's air arm was transferred from the Transport Command in 1919 and elevated to the status of the Army Air Service. This reorganization coincided with the arrival of a large French military mission eager to sell aircraft and expertise. This delegation was one of many undertaken the world over by the French and British. Both countries had huge stockpiles of unneeded aircraft, thousands of trained personnel, and a very serious need for cash. The short-term results must have pleased Paris. The Japanese purchased a number of the famous SPAD XIII pursuit aircraft, thereby founding the army's fighter arm. The army also purchased the right to produce selected reconnaissance and training aircraft. In 1925 the Japanese Army Air Corps was founded with a status equal to that of the older and more prestigious branches, such as infantry and artillery. When founded, it already possessed 500 aircraft, a sizeable number for a service that had started from scratch less than a decade before.

The Japanese navy was quick to get into the action and eventually fielded the largest component of Japan's aerial arsenal. Ironically some Japanese leaders, naval officers among them, were frightened by the prospects of aerial attack on civilian targets that both sides in World War I had employed. In the early 1920s, when the world's great naval powers worked out a successful, if short-lived, naval limitation treaty, the Japanese suggested the abolition of or structural restrictions on the development of aircraft carriers. Considering in hindsight the fates of Japan's wooden cities during 1944–1945, such fears were fully justified. However, the navy was obviously of two minds on the subject. In 1921 the navy hosted a large British delegation that included some of Britain's top experts on naval aviation. (Some wise heads in the British Admiralty had misgivings about this venture, fearing already that Japan was a potential enemy in Asia.) Herbert Smith, one of the head designers during World War I at the famous British firm Sopwith, stayed on and helped design some of Japan's first modern naval aircraft. In addition, in 1922 the IJN launched *Hosho*, the world's first aircraft carrier built from the outset to serve the role. (Other nations had retrofitted various types of ships with a flight deck for experimental purposes.) In 1927 the Naval Air Division was established, and Japanese naval airpower was institutionalized.

Aircraft development in Japan, as in the United States, was largely left to private industry. Although several companies built aircraft throughout the interwar period, the industry was dominated by three giants. Prior to 1920 the great industrial combines of Mitsubishi and Kawasaki saw promise in aviation and established appropriate divisions. They were soon joined by the dynamic Nakajima Aeroplane Company, a dedicated aviation corporation. Although Nakajima was smaller than competitors, specialization had its advantages, and ultimately Nakajima became Japan's number-one supplier of aircraft. (Quantity did not equal quality in the skies: In the battles over the South Pacific Japanese pilots flying Mitsubishis presented the greatest challenge to the Allies.)

The Japanese picked the perfect time to begin developing its air arm. As noted earlier, the postwar period was not a particularly fertile ground for technical advances in the field, giving a newcomer a good chance to play catch-up. Also, much of aviation still depended upon labor-intensive work with wood and canvas and required the kind of workforce that Japan could develop quickly from preexisting traditions. Aircraft engines, a complex machine under any circumstance, posed a more difficult problem, one that Tokyo never properly solved. Simultaneously some of the brightest young engineers, trained abroad or in Japan by foreign instructors, gravitated to the wondrous new technology. To a degree the creation of an engineering elite was pushed by government policy. However, many of the best and brightest young engineers in Japan were every bit as captivated by the fascinating realm of aviation as were their counterparts in the West. Furthermore aviation was still very much a seat-of-the-pants affair. The basic theory of flight was well understood, or at least accurately observed, but many fine points were still awaiting refinement by bright and tenacious young men. When historians describe early developments in Japanese military aviation they emphasize, with good reason, the importance of foreign training and foreign influence. However, throughout most of the interwar period aviation technology was notably international, with each country learning from others. (At a different level this condition continued throughout the war. The United States and Britain profited greatly by sharing technology and tactical lessons.) In any case the Japanese apprentice period was extremely short.

In the early 1930s Tokyo decided to emphasize self-sufficiency in aircraft production. Although not alone in this desire, a driving force behind this initiative was Rear Admiral Isoroku Yamamoto, the head of the Technical Division of the Technical Aviation Department (1930–1933) who later became head of the department (1935–1936). The first batch of aircraft produced under the self-sufficiency program did not prove to be adequate fighting machines. Nevertheless the navy persevered and by 1935 was developing a series of world-class warplanes. The army's modernization lagged somewhat behind, but it was flying Japanese-made aircraft upon the outbreak of war with China in 1937.

The basic organizational structure of Japanese military aviation was likewise established early. Unlike Britain, France, and Germany, the Japanese did not establish an independent air force. Although the Japanese, like everyone else, believed in the power of terror-bombing to weaken enemy morale, the strategic position of Japan did not encourage the bomber cult. No doubt it was wise for the army and navy to develop their own air arms. Politically this outcome was inevitable. The army dominated the Japanese military and in the 1930s grew to dominate the Japanese government. Japanese generals were hardly ready to see the creation of a new rival—they had enough trouble intriguing against the navy. Conversely, no navy has ever voluntarily given up its air force. (Indeed, one of history's most bitter interservice disputes erupted in the United States immediately after World War II when the new U.S. Air Force tried to gain control of U.S. naval airpower.) Consequently there was no Japanese Billy Mitchell or Hugh Trenchard.

And there was no centralized command for Japanese air operations. Air fleets were delegated to various theaters or aircraft carriers and placed under the command of base or fleet commanders. Both the army and navy maintained separate "Air Headquarters" in Tokyo, but their authorities were administrative, not operational. In short there was no Japanese equivalent of USAAF General Hap Arnold. Ironically the U.S. Navy command structure was similar to that of Japan, with operational control given to commanders of carrier task forces. And so, for simplicity's sake I have followed the lead of many other historians and refer to the respective imperial air arms as the Japanese Army Air Force and the Japanese Navy Air Force.

As we shall examine presently, the United States also maintained independent army and navy air forces prior to and during World War II, although for different reasons. At the moment, however, I would like to point out one fundamental difference between the naval air arms of Japan and the United States: Although the Japanese pioneered the construction and development of aircraft carriers, they also developed a large and powerful land-based component to naval airpower. The IJN developed a fine collection of carrier-based aircraft but also purchased large numbers of multiengine bombers and believed it was fully prepared to fight extensive engagements from land bases. Indeed the first successful modern Japanese twin-engine bomber, the Mitsubishi G3M (Allied code name: Nell), was a project inspired and pushed by Yamamoto himself. Yamamoto wanted a long-range bomber that would aid Combined Fleet in a future showdown with Western nations in the Pacific. (His guess was a good one: A large force of Nells carrying torpedoes sank the British battleships *Repulse* and *Prince of Wales* in the first week of the war, dealing a wicked blow to British pride and crippling any hope that British forces could hold Malaya and Singapore.)

This policy was very much at variance with developments in the United States. American admirals saw the value of land-based reconnaissance aircraft. They also gave the Marine Corps a small land-based force (one that grew to significant size when war began). Nevertheless, due to both doctrine and agreement with the USAAF, the U.S. Navy concentrated its efforts on aircraft carriers and procured only warplanes that could operate from carrier decks. The implicit division between army and navy in Japan was geographic in the largest sense. When the Japanese developed their contingency plans for war with Western powers in the Pacific in the years prior to Pearl Harbor, the efforts in the Pacific were considered by Tokyo to be largely a "navy show." The army would face its traditional enemy, the USSR, and base its operations on the Asian mainland. Army strength delegated to Pacific operations would be kept to the minimum required. Therefore when the struggle began in the South Pacific, the Allies faced Japanese naval units almost exclusively, though most were in fact land-based. Only in 1943 did the Japanese army, alarmed at what it viewed as a catastrophe in the making, join the air battle in the South Pacific— with disastrous results.

The war with China accelerated development of the Japanese air arm, which by that time was modern and formidable. Unlike the Spanish Civil War, which the German Luftwaffe used as an extended proving ground, Japan's war with China required a major sustained effort. Events there did much to shape the nature of Japanese warplanes during World War II. During this period the Japanese accelerated efforts to construct a larger, more modern air arm, and a veil of secrecy descended on many aspects, no doubt leading Allied nations to underestimate the power of Japan's air strength. Hundreds of pilots also received a baptism of fire, and the lessons learned were circulated throughout the armed forces. Although it is difficult to underestimate the importance of combat experience, a strong argument can be made that the Japanese, unlike the Germans in Spain, drew many wrong conclusions from this brutal war that hurt them when facing more-powerful opposition.

In its initial stages the air war over China was fought by the Japanese navy. The army's modernization program was not yet complete, its forces concentrated in Manchuria opposite the Soviet border. The Nell achieved excellent range and respectable performance, yet because Japanese engine development was not up to world-class standards the Nell was very light for a bomber. In the first weeks of the war Chinese fighters, a collection of models from several countries, inflicted heavy losses on Japanese raiders. The assumption that bomber speed could allow attackers to avoid enemy fighters was proven terribly wrong. The small air war taking place over Spain simultaneously proved the same point. The JNAF can hardly be blamed for making this error, as it was duplicated by every combatant in World War II in the following years. The JNAF quickly arrived at a solution: Bombers needed fighter escort to be effective. Help was soon in coming. Mitsubishi engineers, headed by the young and brilliant Jiro Horikoshi, developed the A5M fighter (Allied code name: Claude), which proved able to disperse Chinese attacks and gain local air superiority. This victory, however, carried serious hidden liabilities.

Although praised in many publications since the war, the Claude was a good carrier-based aircraft but a second-class fighter. Until technology soon before Pearl Harbor changed the equation, navies around the world accepted the fact that fighters were by necessity an inferior breed. As they were required to operate on extremely small carrier decks, they had to be able to land at a slow speeds. This required—or so engineers thought—large wings relative to engine size. (In aviation parlance this is called "low wing loading," as the amount of lift provided by the wing area is low when divided by the power generated by the engine.) Also by the 1930s aircraft designed for carrier use required some kind of tailhook to grab an arrestor wire on the carrier deck to stop the plane in the shortest possible distance. This meant a carrier-based plane needed a strong undercarriage, which required extra weight. To gain decent performance Horikoshi, like the designers of the Nell, did everything possible to keep down weight. Like the Nell, the A5M was extremely vulnerable to any battle damage. The Claude was very nimble and Japanese pilots were extremely well trained. However, they were flying a decent escort fighter that was poor at anything else.

The fact that a light and nimble fighter could make the skies relatively safe for a light and fast bomber led the Japanese into a tactical trap of great consequence. In retrospect it is easy enough to see how these engagements ultimately helped dig the grave of the imperial air arm. Whenever a Japanese bombing raid, escorted by Claudes, was sent deep into China, the crude but effective network of observation posts would pick it up. If enough Chinese fighters were available, they might choose to take off and attack the bombers. Japanese pilots were tenacious and well trained and engaged Chinese interceptors when possible. At minimum this would very likely disrupt the Chinese attack. The Chinese mauled the raiders on several occasions, but in most fights Japanese pilots came home with the laurels (or, as military men would say in a tougher era, the Japanese "gained a favorable kill ratio"). The Japanese pilots were superior, and the Claude, although not up to European standards, was at least the equal of most planes faced over China until U.S. intervention after Pearl Harbor, and it usually enjoyed numerical superiority. Japanese successes in their nimble craft thus reinforced an existing predilection among Japanese fighter pilots to seek the air-to-air dogfight. After the war Horikoshi mentioned this point in his memoirs:

> Until this time [December 1937, when the Claude made its successful combat debut escorting large Japanese raids over Nanking—EB], it had been considered best to employ attack bombers against enemy bases so as to destroy planes on the ground. But the Sino-Japanese air battles taught us clearly it was more effective to down enemy airplanes in the sky with their pilots in them. The Japanese Navy decided to introduce, before any other country, the concept of using fighters to obtain air superiority. This tactic would later be carried out on a large scale by our fighters in the Pacific during World War II. Similar tactics were not used in the European theater until the last stages of the war. Hence there were no dogfighting aircraft in Europe similar to ours.

Horikoshi's description of the engagements in China might be correct as far as it goes. It is not a good assessment of European doctrine. By the time the Japanese were over Nanking, the Luftwaffe had developed escort techniques that emphasized engaging interceptors using superior altitude and speed instead of the World War I–style turning match. The British, for their part, were far more interested in developing techniques to attack bombers and considered fighter engagements only a means to that overriding end. By 1941 Americans had yet to learn the lessons being learned by the Luftwaffe concerning successful air combat, but they proved quick learners, as we shall see. In 1944, as Horikoshi alluded to, U.S. P-47 Thunderbolt and P-51

Mustang escorts forced the Luftwaffe to defend the Reich against B-17 bombing attacks and slowly ground the Germans into dust. The Americans used fighters that were heavy and very fast, employing high-speed hit-and-run tactics pioneered by the Luftwaffe, not the Japanese. (Luftwaffe air bases were also mercilessly attacked if in range of Allied medium bombers and fighter-bombers.) Moreover, the doctrine described by Horikoshi is not a good one. I want to examine tactics at length elsewhere (see Chapter 6), but it is worth noting here that in the South Pacific Allied air forces crushed Japanese opponents by hitting them with a blizzard of attacks of every type aimed at both airfields and airborne Japanese fighters. The Allies also learned that maneuverability was the least important attribute that a good fighter should have.

Yet Japan's trap, as described by Horikoshi, was more subtle. The bombers used by China were few and poor. Consequently the Claude proved a good escort, but the ability of a lightly built aircraft to serve as an interceptor of well-constructed bombers carrying decent defensive gunnery was completely unproven. When the answer came in during battles over the South Pacific, Tokyo learned that the lessons learned in China had no relevance. In addition, Chinese antiaircraft was neither numerous nor efficient. It was thus also unproven how well light Japanese aircraft would do when attacking targets (whether on land or at sea) that possessed powerful antiaircraft defenses. The light construction that gave Japanese bombers their long range and Japanese fighters their great maneuverability made them extremely vulnerable to the serious damage that usually accompanied a hit from modern antiaircraft guns of any caliber.

The last part of the tactical calamity the Japanese were constructing for themselves is the powerful voice given to fighter pilots in influencing fighter design. Near the city of Yokosuka a Japanese Naval arsenal served as the site for JNAF's first air base. Later the navy's first "Air Corps" [*Kokutai* in Japanese—the rough equivalent of a U.S. Naval Air Group, having squadrons of fighters and bombers supported by reconnaissance aircraft—EB] was formed at Yokosuka. The elite fighter squadron based there, commanded in 1934–1935 by Lieutenant Minoru Genda, later to gain great fame as a battle leader and tactician, served as an evaluation unit for new prototypes. Until shortly before the outbreak of war, Japanese contracts were open to competition from more than one firm, and the opinion of pilots at Yokosuka could make or break a design. Even when competitive bidding ceased for the sake of efficiency, Yokosuka's pilots continued to have great influence. Horikoshi described the importance of these pilots:

In those days, the Navy's Yokosuka Naval Air Corps was in charge of tests to determine combat characteristics. The group that handled fighters was their own fighter squadron, and during 1934–1935 it was nicknamed the "Genda Circus," as it was composed of Japan's best pilots and was commanded by Lt. Minoru Genda. The fate of our Prototype 9 single seater [the Claude—EB] depended entirely upon the critical eyes of these pilots. Their duties were to determine the aircraft's flying qualities, correct any weak points, and learn how best to handle or use the new machine. They also had an equally important duty: to determine future Navy fighter requirements for the defense of Japan.

As Horikoshi makes clear, the influence of Japanese pilots did not stop when the Claude was put into service. During the initial stages of designing the soon-to-be-famous Zero, Horikoshi's team had competitors from the prominent Nakajima. The Mitsubishi team believed the best fighter would result if they employed Mitsubishi's own Kinsei radial engine. However, in Japanese terms the Kinsei was a large engine that would require a larger airframe and more weight. Horikoshi bluntly admitted that he chose a lighter engine, not because it would deliver a better aircraft but because the pilots at Yokosuka would demand a light and nimble aircraft. Horikoshi describes his decision to choose a lighter engine against his own judgment: "Instead of pondering the future of the aircraft, our immediate job was to win the contract." There were pilots who believed that some maneuverability could be sacrificed to gain speed and range. The Mitsubishi team worked a minor miracle to satisfy both camps, but there is no question that Japanese pilots wanted a "super Claude" for their next fighter. And the Japanese pilots had clout far beyond their low rank.

I have already argued that fighter pilots of all air forces during the interwar period preferred light and maneuverable aircraft simply because they were more exhilarating to fly. In China nimble fighters seemed the correct tactical response. It is also possible that the dogfight fit well Japan's military ethos. Japanese fighter pilots during the war often made comparisons between their aircraft and the sword, which in Japan evoked images of the samurai and individual combat in service of the state. Japanese pilots, if one can draw general conclusions from doctrine and much evidence from diaries, considered themselves an elite. Pilots of other air forces thought much the same, but in Japan the warrior elite was also considered expendable. The attack was everything in the tactical arena, with little thought given to losses. Without a doubt, death in battle was given a position of honor that had no parallel in the West. If Japanese pilots thought of their fighters as a sword,

American pilots thought of theirs as flying machine guns that should be protected by designers to the extent possible. In a fight, or so it proved in World War II, a machine gun would vanquish a sword.

The next generation of aircraft designed by the Japanese evolved directly from the light planes and long-range planes deployed in China. The next bomber was the G4M (code name: Betty), which had better performance than the Nell but reflected the same design philosophy. The famous Zero was a far better plane than was the Claude, but it likewise retained light construction to gain the maneuverability demanded by pilots and range required for fleet use and to escort the Betty. The resulting Zero-Betty tandem was remarkably like the older Nell-Claude pairing. The escorts proved very good at protecting attack planes and gaining local air superiority, and the bombers functioned well when not under serious air or antiaircraft attack. However, Japan went to war against the United States using a bomber without proven ability to sustain the damage inevitable in a hard campaign and using a fighter without proven ability to shoot down modern bombers. If the Allies could break the link between the bomber and escort and devise tactics to compensate for the Zero's maneuverability, the whole Japanese edifice would collapse. In time, this is exactly what happened.

Japanese Navy Aircraft

Any description of the most important warplanes active in the Pacific war must begin with Japan's Mitsubishi A6M Zero. The Zero was the backbone of Japanese naval fighter forces from the beginning of the war to the end. Some Japanese army units also employed it. Japan produced approximately 11,000 Zeros during the war. The unique position held by the Zero, however, was due to more than numbers. The psychological impact of the Zero's spectacular entrance into the Pacific war was so great that all fighters were judged by the standards set by it. (American pilots, perhaps unwittingly, paid the Zero a unique honor: The American military assigned code names to Japanese aircraft. Male names, such as Oscar and Frank, designated fighters; female names, such as Betty and Val, designated bombers. However, few American pilots used the A6M's official code name, Zeke. Instead they used "Zero," a rough translation of *Rei-sen*, the Japanese name for the plane.) A dominant aircraft that justly deserved its great fame early in the war, the Zero also illustrates vividly the design trade-offs mentioned above. The development of the Zero and its successors also illuminates many of the strengths and weaknesses of the overall Japanese war effort.

In mid-1937 the JNAF established new specifications far in advance of those met by the Claude or any other fighter in the Japanese arsenal. The JNAF sought a plane that was fast, climbed well, had great range, carried cannons for punch, could maneuver as well as the Claude, and could operate from a carrier. Horikoshi and his colleagues at Mitsubishi, despite a brief effort from Nakajima, became the only group willing to attempt to match such challenging specifications. From the outset the Zero was designed to be as light as possible, unencumbered with unnecessary aerodynamic obstructions of any sort. To an extent, that design philosophy made virtue out of necessity. In the late 1930s, when the Zero was developed, the best Japanese engines generated approximately 800 horsepower, good enough for the time but soon greatly surpassed by other nations. The only way to meet the criteria was to minimize weight and dispense with anything that added unnecessary weight and needless drag.

The Zero's design team approached its formidable task imaginatively. The wing, built of advanced lightweight aluminum, was one piece and an integral part of the fuselage. This saved weight and made the plane easy to disassemble and maintain. The wing itself was long and wide, offering the light craft great lift. Because the large wing was matched by a very large tail and long fuselage, the Zero had exceptional stability. Although no fighter was easy to fly, the Zero was one of the few craft that largely lacked in-flight performance quirks that made the pilot's job harder and more dangerous. Mitsubishi designers also included a full bubble canopy and large cockpit, and Zero pilots enjoyed excellent visibility and room to move about during combat, factors highly rated in Japanese doctrine. The Zero's light weight also made it, for a fighter, fuel-efficient. Consequently it possessed a range of more than 1,100 miles. (As noted earlier, operational fighter range was much less than maximum range. Only the Zero could have sustained operations between Rabaul and Guadalcanal, but that distance—550 miles—was pushing the Zero past its limit. The theoretical range of an aircraft is often measured by its ability to fly from one point to another. This differs greatly from its flight radius, which assumes that the plane had to return to the point that it took off.) If necessary the plane could carry an external fuel tank, or drop tank, which extended the range to 1,900 miles, a tremendous advantage in widely dispersed Pacific combat. To complete the picture, the designers created an aircraft with unusual aerodynamic purity: The Zero was arguably the most beautiful piston-driven airplane ever built. Saburo Sakai, one of Japan's great aces, later described his initial impressions of the Zero: "The Zero excited me as nothing else had ever done. Even on the ground it had the cleanest lines I had ever seen in an aeroplane. It was a dream to fly. The aeroplane was the most sensitive I had ever flown, and even slight finger pressure brought instant response. We could hardly wait to meet enemy planes in this remarkable new aircraft."

In some respects the Zero was the greatest fighting aircraft of World War II. Because of its clean design, low weight relative to engine power, and high lift, the Zero was extremely nimble. At low speeds it could turn inside any U.S. plane with ease. A good pilot flying a Zero could perform complicated maneuvers in a split second. The plane's maneuverability was so exceptional that at the end of the war, long after its brief period of ascendancy, the Zero remained a deadly adversary if combat conditions were favorable.

Allied pilots who engaged the Zero early in the war were most impressed and, in some cases, shaken by what they encountered. By the time of the Guadalcanal campaign any illusions concerning Japanese technical inferiority had long vanished. Admiral Frank Fletcher, who commanded the three U.S. carriers that covered the Guadalcanal landings, commented after the war that "at that time the Japanese Zeros all wore Seven League Boots and our aviators gave them a lot of g.d. respect." Historian Robert Sherrod, author of the classic account of Marine Corps aviation in the Pacific war, wrote concerning the beginning of the Guadalcanal campaign: "It is necessary to remember that the Japanese Zero at this stage of the war was regarded with some of the awe in which the atomic bomb came to be held later. U.S. fighter pilots were apt to go into combat with a distinct inferiority complex. Tales from the Pacific had filtered back to the United States, which attributed to the Zero (and Japanese pilots) a sort of malevolent perfection."

Such tales filtering back were based on genuine calamity. Zeros had pounded Allied aircraft in the first weeks of the war. Zeros mauled U.S. fighters in the Philippines, Dutch fighters in the Indies, and Australian and British fighters in Malaya. The often decorated Australian ace, wing commander J. R. Kinninmont, saw the Zero in action over Singapore. Kinninmont was flying a distinctly mediocre U.S. Lend-Lease fighter, the Brewster Buffalo, and had been fortunate to live through the first few weeks of the war. Kinninmont and his comrades had already learned that it was extremely dangerous to engage a Zero in a low-speed dogfight. In January a few dozen vaunted British Hurricanes arrived in theater. As Kinninmont related it, morale soared for a moment until reality set in:

That evening at all the night spots the gay topic of conversation was "Hurricanes." The miracle had happened. The Hurricanes were here and their world was saved. "Boy! More stingers—long with ice. . . . The RAF [Royal Air Force] boys flying them began to mix it with the Zeros, which we knew was practically impossible. The Zero was just about the nippiest, most highly maneuverable fighter in the world. They buzzed around the Hurricanes like vicious bees. The RAF Hurricane pilots fought gallantly and courageously against overwhelming odds and during their brief period of operation in Malaya they scored several brilliant victories and shot down many Japs. But they too "took the knock."

Much of the initial Japanese advantage was due to superior numbers and psychological momentum. During the early stages of the New Guinea air war the Japanese advantage began to slow. It did not take long for American pilots to shed their inferiority complex at Guadalcanal, but all recognized that the Zero was a potentially lethal enemy. Long after the war, Cactus ace Joe Foss expressed his respect for the Zero and the pilots who flew them:

After my first kill a Zero shot me to pieces and I had to land with one on my tail. They were hungry that day. We were hit all the time. When you had so many Zeros around you expected to get hit. It wasn't a case of "if" but a case of "when." There was no way you could fly around and be clean. One day I landed and said I didn't get hit today. And one of my men said, "What's that?" One lone bullet had come through the canopy and hit the darn doughnut: That round pad you're supposed to lean against if you're launched from a catapult. I never knew that one. There wasn't a one of us that made it if the good Lord didn't want us to. There is no excuse for any of us to be around. If you weren't a believer before, a lot were when they left. I told my pilots that if you were alone and saw a Zero at the same altitude you were flying that you were outnumbered and should go for home. They were not a plane to tangle with unless you had an advantage.

The British in Malaya-Burma, Americans throughout the Pacific, and Australians stationed early at Moresby and Milne Bay learned the Zero's capabilities the hard way and respected them. In early 1943 the British agreed to transfer a fighter wing of Spitfire V fighters (three squadrons were Australian, one from RAF) to help defend Darwin, a target of incessant Japanese attacks from Timor. Eventually nearly 100 arrived. Many of the pilots had experience in the European theater and were confident of themselves and their famous fighter. Australian veterans of Darwin and New Guinea, however, warned the newcomers to avoid low-speed combat with Zeros. Some American pilots, including aces Joe Foss of Cactus and Jim Morehead of Fifth Air Force, echoed these warnings. Long after the war Morehead recalled his briefing to the newcomers, many of whom were already aces:

> We told them the basics. Don't think that because you could turn inside a German fighter that you could do the same with a Zero. I think the Aussies did listen to us. They were good pilots, and good pilots wanted to know what they were coming up against. But at first if they ran into a problem in an engagement, their gut reaction was to hark back to reactions formed by training and experience in Europe. So they tried Battle of Britain tactics almost as an instinct against the Japanese and paid a heavy price, including the lives of some very experienced pilots.

After some early engagements with Japanese raiders, during which the new Spitfire wing suffered serious losses (not all due to combat), the newcomers were given orders from RAAF command to avoid dog-fights with Japanese fighters. Soon the Spitfire wing adjusted to the new theater, and its performance improved, but not before being the last group of Allied pilots to be taught a hard lesson in Pacific war air combat.

In June 1942 a Japanese pilot was killed trying to crash-land his Zero in the Aleutians during a feint that was part of the Midway campaign. The Americans captured the aircraft almost intact. (In Burma the British had already captured a Ki43, JAAF's top-line fighter.) As the tide turned in the Allies' favor and they began to capture Japanese air bases, a number of operational Japanese aircraft fell into their hands. This was not at all unique. The Japanese captured several Allied planes early in the war. The British held several German aircraft. Because so much air combat took place over German lines, the Luftwaffe collected a small air force of flyable Allied aircraft. The information gleaned from investigating these prizes was of interest. However, because the various air forces fought each other daily, they quickly learned the practical capabilities of the opponents' planes. In truth combat observation was probably more helpful.

In October 1944 twelve U.S. test pilots were allowed to put a captured Zero through its paces and were impressed with many of its flight characteristics, even though the Zero was seriously obsolescent at that stage. Here are some of their remarks concerning the Zero: "Very little torque, easy to take off. . . . Very easy to land. Flies like a light trainer. Excellent visibility, good control but poor directional control after landing. . . . Excellent acceleration. . . . It is a dangerous airplane to dogfight at slow speeds. Excellent for low altitude offensive combat or any turning fight where radius of turn or maneuverability is required as prime."

A closer examination of the A6M, however, reveals several flaws. Some were a part of inevitable design trade-offs. Others, however, reflected the uneven and narrow base of Japan's war economy. One defect resulted from simple physics: Because the Zero was so light and the engine lacked brute power, it had poor diving characteristics. Simple kinetic energy allows a heavier aircraft, if powerful enough, to dive faster than a light one. Moreover, the high lift design of the Zero inevitably hurt it when it was trying to drop—a perfect example of a design trade-off. As we shall see, this had important ramifications in combat. A related issue was the Zero's high-altitude performance. It had a good flight ceiling (the maximum altitude at which it could fly) of 32,000 feet. However, the higher the altitude, the lower the density of the air. Aerodynamic lift generated by a large wing area, combined with light weight, is maximized at lower altitudes, whereas in thin air the lift dissipates. High-altitude performance rewards power and the low drag found on aircraft with smaller wings. (A plane like the P-51 Mustang had less wing area and far more power. In technical aviation terms, it possessed high wing loading, because a lot of power was devoted to keeping each square inch of the wing in the air.) In the Zero's case, it began to lose its exceptional maneuverability when flying above 15,000 feet. The closer the craft came to its maximum ceiling, the less it was able to maneuver. During the early stages of the war this did not matter, because U.S. fighters were underpowered and did not fight well at high altitude, either. When new U.S. types began appearing in early 1943, however, the Zero pilots faced a serious quandary: They could either yield the altitude advantage to the Americans, or engage at high altitudes, where the enemy aircraft had greatly superior performance. Either alternative was very dangerous.

Physics and economics intersected during the development of the Zero. Japan was a poor country, closer to Italy's level of economic development than to Germany's, much less that of the United States. Therefore the Mitsubishi design team worked its magic under serious economic constraints. A nimble, attack-oriented fighter fit Japanese military doctrine very nicely. However, at one level it also was less expensive to produce. The raw materials required were less than for an American fighter (which often weighed twice as much as the Zero), the fuel consumption was less, and items not directly related to flight performance were ignored. On another level the Zero's advanced design made it difficult to produce. There was much hand labor involved as well as work required from dozens of small workshops. Mitsubishi recognized this problem but believed that Japan's economy did not have a labor shortage, so the trade-off was worth it. However, it took Mitsubishi a very long time to produce the Zero in large numbers. During the period March 1939–March 1942, 837 Zeros were made. During April 1942–March 1943, when the JNAF needed planes desperately, only 1,689 were produced. During April 1943–March 1944 much progress was made, and 3,432 Zeros left the plants. The April 1944–March 1945 period saw production peak at 3,487 units. Altogether some 10,500 Zeros were made. (It is not clear how many were rejected for service, but the number would have been low; the Zero was a reliable airplane.) Considering the industrial resources available and the tremendous demands coming for military production of all kinds, Mitsubishi can be commended for its efforts. However, during the critical battles of the South Pacific Zeros were in short supply. There were enough to keep units up to strength but not enough to build many new units. In comparison, when U.S. production started to roll even the South Pacific Theater started receiving a suitable supply of planes. In mid-1943, when Mitsubishi was beginning to get the Zeros off the line in numbers, many new Allied units appeared in the theater, giving the Allies a quantitative superiority that would continue to increase throughout the war.

The Zero's light weight and innovative airframe was a good example of clever designers attempting to compensate for economic disadvantages. Because the A6M was so light, it could not also be structurally strong. Designers of the day created a strong airframe with heavier, denser parts, a more developed superstructure, and more welds and rivets. The Zero possessed two disadvantages because of its light airframe. First, although the craft had no peer in Allied forces at low-speed maneuver, a fast, abrupt flight maneuver near top speed threatened to cause structural damage. More importantly the light airframe made the Zero very vulnerable to battle damage. Blows that would do little harm to a heavier plane could put a Zero in jeopardy. There was little redundancy in construction, and so several points were vulnerable to damage that would cripple or collapse the frame. If surprised, Zero pilots were in mortal danger. Attacking U.S. bombers, a primary job of any Japanese fighter, was extremely dangerous. Moreover, the Zero's fragility amplified the inherent risks of ground attack missions. And because the Zero was so easily damaged it was more difficult to maintain in the field. Ironically the A6M, although designed to be easily fixed, was also designed in a way that ensured it would be easily damaged during combat. Given the rigors of the field, frailty greatly outweighed the maintenance issue. And even though the Zero was a forgiving plane to fly, it was the most dangerous plane imaginable in which one could fight. A careless or inexperienced pilot might not suffer seriously from an unexpected stall or spin; enemy fire, however, took a dreadful toll on any mediocre pilot.

This weakness was even more conspicuous because the Zero's cockpit, again to save weight, was not armored. (As the lessons of battle began to strike home, some Zero pilots had the ground crew at Rabaul install simple pieces of armor plate. They remained the minority.) The frail frame had a final disadvantage: It was not strong enough to support a large increase in weight, even when more-powerful engines became available, and so it became clear that the Zero badly needed additional firepower and armor. Therefore, although the Zero had several models, the last was not much better than the planes that went to war in December 1941. This contrasts markedly with other makes, such as the American Mustang and British Spitfire, which improved greatly as they were modified throughout the war.

Deficient fuel tanks compounded the problem. Most fighters that were developed immediately before World War II had some form of self-sealing fuel tank. American designers soon became leaders in this technology, and U.S. fighters were tough to flame. The Japanese, despite much effort after Pearl Harbor in this area, never developed a reliable self-sealing system. The fuel tanks on the first Zero models had no self-sealing mechanism and no armor protection. Machine guns on U.S. warplanes fired a mixture of armor-piercing, tracer, and incendiary bullets. (Solid lead shot appeared early in the war but seems to have been phased out in favor of armor-piercing and incendiary rounds.) If a Zero was hit in the fuel tank, the resulting fire might well destroy the plane and, if accompanied by an explosion, kill the pilot instantly. Structural failure could also easily start a fire, so it was never possible to tell whether a Zero's tanks blew or a catastrophic fire was caused by a collapsing airframe. In the end it did not matter: Already frail, the Zero was also a firetrap.

The Zero's vulnerability to fire was soon apparent to pilots on both sides. Roger Haberman, a Marine fighter pilot at Cactus during the height of the struggle for Guadalcanal, scored the first of his several victories, and just as for hundreds of later Allied pilots his victim was a flamer. As it turns out, Haberman's kill was one of the most unusual of that fierce campaign. In mid-October, soon after the battleship bombardment of Henderson Field, the Japanese attempted to exploit the weakness at Cactus to land troops and supplies from transports. The six transports, clearly visible from U.S. lines at Lunga Point, were carrying critical material for an imminent ground attack on the Marine perimeter and had Zero escorts above. Although badly weakened, the men at Cactus scraped together a small force to attack the transports. One of the raiders was the personal Consolidated PBY Catalina of General Roy Geiger, commander of Cactus Air Force. The PBY was a twin-engine amphibious patrol bomber ideal for reconnaissance but miserably suited for daylight attack against a target with fighter cover. Nevertheless Major Jack Cram, Geiger's pilot, received permission to strap two torpedoes to the PBY for an attempt to sneak through the escorts and slip a fish to one of the immobile transports while a handful of other U.S. planes occupied the Zeros by attacking from a different direction. A wild melee ensued (including a well-timed B-17 strike from Espíritu) during which three transports and much materiel were destroyed. Apparently one of Cram's torpedoes struck home and helped sink a precious transport. As one might imagine, the slow PBY, flying on the deck, immediately attracted several Zeros. Only miles from home, Cram ran for Fighter One as the Zeros peppered his PBY, slowly ripping it to shreds. Suffering from what later pilots would call "target fixation," the pursuing Zeros did not watch the skies as all closed on Fighter One. Roger Haberman was flying cover over the U.S. airfield. Employing his altitude advantage, Haberman dove to assist Cram's stricken PBY:

When I saw Cram coming in followed by these Zeros, I started firing about 2,000 feet above them, which you would never normally do. It's much better to wait till you are closer, but I sprayed this whole group knowing I couldn't do anything more than that under the circumstances. There were three or four of them shooting the hell out of this Catalina. I was firing away just to interrupt their attack and maybe let the PBY land. The planes were going at a right angle to me. One Zero pulled up and went out toward the ocean. I guess he was hit and wanted to get clear of our lines. I had a speed differential in my favor of about thirty-five knots. I pulled up right behind him, fired, and the Zero exploded. I was so damn close that I had to turn off because the flames from his gasoline were enveloping my plane.

Moments later both Cram and Haberman had their aircraft on the ground at Fighter One.

Japanese pilots knew better than anyone that a damaged Zero might turn into an instant inferno. One might imagine how the thought of burning to death affected some Japanese pilots. After the war, veteran Zero pilot Takao Tanimuzu laconically remarked that "you could always tell if it was a Zero or enemy plane that had crashed in the sea. The Zero left a fire on the surface, but the American plane just left an oil slick."

The list of weaknesses went beyond structural fragility. Because of its extraordinary maneuverability, the Zero was potentially a superb attack fighter. The armament carried, however, was not ideal. In this regard the Mitsubishi design team faced one of the most vexing problems in prewar fighter development: choosing between cannons and machine guns for the main armament. Since World War I the rifle-caliber machine gun had been the standard weapon on fighters. In the late 1930s, however, small-caliber cannons, usually 20mm, were available for aircraft use. A cannon round did more damage than a machine gun bullet. The round was heavier and carried an explosive charge. Very few hits from a cannon could destroy even a heavy bomber. There was a serious price to be paid, however: Cannon ammunition was heavy and bulky, and aircraft armed with cannons could carry few rounds. The rate of fire was also less than that of machine guns. In short it was harder to hit a target with a cannon because there were fewer pieces of lead in the air. A single hit, however, was much more damaging. A plane with rifle-caliber machine guns, in contrast, carried hundreds of rounds per gun, fired more quickly, and, because they were lighter, could be mounted in greater numbers. Many British fighters in the Battle of Britain carried eight .303-caliber light machine guns.

Because guns were the most important subsystem carried by any fighter and were very important on bombers, it is worthwhile to examine the subject. Ultimately, after all, a fighter plane was a flying gun platform. Regardless of performance, a plane without sound armament was of little value. The basic equation was complex, and no definitive answer arrived until the development of the incredibly destructive minigun rapid-fire cannons in the late 1950s (which continue in use on modern jet fighters). On the surface the trade-off appears simply one of bullets in the air, which would support machine-gun armament, as opposed to destructive effective, which favored the cannon. In reality things were more complicated. Rifle-caliber machine guns (.303-caliber or 7.7mm depending upon the nation) had a very high rate of fire, approximately 1,200 rounds per minute per gun. The guns themselves weighed about twenty-five pounds, which enabled an aircraft to carry more light machine guns, more ammunition, or both. However, caliber (usually diameter, sometimes length) can be deceptive. A .303 round weighed approximately half an ounce. A heavy machine-gun round—say, .50-caliber (13mm)—weighed 1.7 ounces. Consequently a heavy machine gun round had greater than three times the mass of a light round and could fire at about 700 rounds per minute. A 20mm (.80-caliber) cannon round weighed about 4.5 ounces and carried a small explosive charge to boot. Consequently the mass of the round increased dramatically with the caliber of the gun. These calculations led major European air forces and the Japanese to mount a combination of machine guns and cannons on their fighters.

The basic thrust of this argument gained many adherents in both the USAAF and the USN. However, the Americans soon decided on a different path that matched the demands placed on their aircraft. The Americans experimented extensively (often at British urging) with cannons and a cannon–machine gun combination on all major U.S. fighters. With the notable exception of the P-38 Lightning, the Americans decided that heavy machine guns were superior for fighters. The major reason American engineers decided so was because they conceived of fighters as being designed to shoot down other fighters. Unlike Germany, the United States never had to worry about strongly armed and armored heavy bombers. And as we shall see, no Japanese aircraft could stand up to a solid hit from a heavy machine gun. So the standard armament on most U.S. fighters was six .50-caliber machine guns. In theory (as the British tirelessly pointed out) this layout meant less weight (i.e., in lead) in the air during a sustained burst and sacrificed the extra benefit of an exploding bullet. However—the Americans would counter—it did mean more bullets in the air than did a mixed cannon–machine gun configuration. For the Americans, the crux of the matter was the destructive power of the .50-caliber round. Although a cannon round would do more damage, a heavy machine gun's armor-piercing bullet, at most angles, penetrated any pilot armor and bore a good hole in an engine block. And if it struck an enemy from any rear angle, it bore a hole through the aircraft or embedded into something very vital, such as the engine and cockpit. Therefore it did not make so much difference, if the target was a fighter, whether the round was 1.7 ounces or 4.5 ounces: Either would damage the enemy. If one accounts for the larger number of rounds—again, the Americans would argue—one stood a better chance of striking the enemy. It stood to reason that several bullets from a massed burst of six machine guns would be more effective than two cannons with a lesser rate of fire. In addition, because heavy machine-gun rounds were lighter than cannon rounds it was possible to carry far more of them, lessening the chance of running out of ammunition during a fight.

With the Zero, the Japanese again fell between two stools. It had two rifle-caliber machine guns and two 20mm cannons. Both had serious weaknesses. A rifle-caliber machine gun fired quickly, but the bullet's mass was inadequate to cause fatal damage to a heavily built U.S. fighter unless the Japanese pilot was an excellent shot or very lucky. Moreover, a rifle-caliber machine gun, unlike a .50-caliber gun, could not penetrate the pilot armor at most angles; it would rip much smaller holes in fuel tanks but not necessarily do fatal damage to an engine block. Furthermore the potential effective range of a light machine gun was about 600 yards, but in practice it proved hard to strike home unless closer. Cannons and heavy machine guns in theory offered better range, but considering the gunsight of the day most kills were made inside that range. Still, at most ranges cannons and heavy machine guns were more accurate. And so excellent marksmen, which Japan possessed initially, could overcome this problem by using the Zero's maneuverability to gain a very close shot and shred an enemy with light machine guns using a large burst. If they could strike home with the cannons, all the better.

However, in both cases the ballistic qualities of light machine guns and Japanese cannons were poor. Despite theoretical range, it was very important to get as close as possible with light machine guns, especially given that during a rear attack the bullet lost impact as the target moved farther away. In theory cannons should have compensated for this problem, yet in practice the Japanese 20mm cannon was a poor weapon. Its rate of fire was low, and the initial muzzle velocity (the speed at which bullet leaves barrel) was poor. To make matters worse, on early Zero models the cannon barrels—again, to save drag—were made as short as possible, further weakening ballistic properties. In short it was hard to hit a target with a Japanese 20mm cannon. It was easier to strike with the light machine guns, but they were not likely to gain a rapid kill. It did not help that early Zeros only carried sixty cannon rounds. Famous ace Saburo Sakai commented after the war: "Our 20 mm cannons were big, heavy and slow firing. It was extremely hard to hit a moving target. Shooting down an enemy aircraft was like hitting a dragonfly with a rifle! It was never easy to score . . . our opponents were tough."

Mitsubishi and other designers were quick to recognize the problem. Most, fearful of Allied bombers, began to develop new aircraft with multiple cannons. However, for the Zero, improvements in armaments were not dramatic throughout the war. It remained a fighter with mediocre armament and very poor defensive strength.

The technology known today as avionics (electronics designed for use in aircraft) was also poor on the Zero. Like all modern fighters, the Zero carried radio equipment for both short-range communications (e.g., between planes and between plane and tower) and long-range communications (between plane and base at a distance). Radios aboard World War II aircraft were always troublesome. The Japanese versions, however, were badly designed and extremely delicate, and the breakdown rate was very high. In the field where conditions were harsh, the failure rate was so high, and replacement parts so frequently unavailable, that many Zero pilots ordered their radios removed to save weight. Ground-based radar was rare and unreliable, but even when it functioned properly it could not aid aircraft unless good communications existed between ground and air. As we shall see, the Americans' mastery of radar technology was key to their destruction of Japanese airpower.

Despite all its shortcomings, the Zero was a splendid fighting machine for its day. Its strengths were real and apparent to friend and foe alike. Although loss figures will forever remain something of a mystery, the Zero gave as good as it got during 1942 and remained an excellent escort until 1943. It also was the world's premier carrier-based fighter until the introduction of the F6F Hellcat in late 1943. Because the Zero was so active, it should be no surprise that its weaknesses were soon diagnosed and exploited by Allied pilots.

In retrospect the greatest weakness of the Zero was not in the aircraft but back in Japan itself. As Mitsubishi team leader Jiro Horikoshi later conceded, "Even the best fighters become obsolete within two years during times of war and four years during times of peace." As early as 1938 the Japanese navy saw the need for a different and superior fighter for land-based combat. It went to Horikoshi and proposed a fast and rugged land-based fighter that would sacrifice range and maneuverability for speed and firepower. At the time, the Mitsubishi team was too small to allow all-out development of a new plane alongside the Zero. When the design team got down to work, however, it discovered that the proposed navy plane stretched Japanese technology beyond reasonable limits. Struggling under a new aircraft design carrying a new engine, the first prototype did not fly until March 1942. The JM2 (Allied code name: Jack; in Japanese, *Raiden*, or "Thunderbolt") was delayed by one problem after another. If constructed by U.S. standards, the Jack would have been in the air in early 1943, in time to battle second-generation Allied fighters. As it was, the Jack did not see serious action until late 1944, and fewer than 500 were produced overall. Similar JAAF efforts met a similar fate. Good designs on paper never became reliable weapons in significant numbers. Consequently the venerable Zero remained the mainstay of the JNAF until war's end. Already outclassed by mid-1943, the Zero by 1945 was a mockery of Japanese ambition and symbolized the empire's inability to fight a protracted conflict with a major power.

When operations developed according to plan, the Zero engaged Allied fighters to protect strikes by Japanese light and heavy bombers. When Mitsubishi was asked to replace the Claude with the more advanced fighter, the navy also requested a replacement for the Nell bomber. Specifications called for a twin-engine bomber with great range, capability to carry a heavy bomb load or single torpedo, excellent speed, and defensive firepower superior to the Nell's. The result was the Mitsubishi G4M (Allied code name: Betty), Japan's most famous bomber. With initial specifications made in 1937 and service tests beginning in January 1940, the Betty was an almost exact contemporary of the Zero and, like its comrade, stayed in action until VJ-Day. (Ominously for the long term, development of the Betty was slowed because Mitsubishi was also designing the Zero. U.S. companies during this period often suffered the same problem but could ultimately overcome it, as the pool of engineering talent to draw from was far larger. As illustrated by the development of the Jack, which coincided with work on the Zero and Betty, Mitsubishi never could do this.)

Just as the Claude and Nell were a tandem, so were the Zero and Betty. As long as Bettys could attack targets cleared by Zeros, or were accompanied by heavy escort against inferior enemy fighter defenses, the bomber proved able to strike targets from startling range. Some Bettys joined Nells in the destruction of Force Z. Others struck targets in the Philippines and Indonesia. Staging from Rabaul, Bettys joined Combined Fleet's massive strike on Darwin in February 1942. Betty attacks added greatly to the shock effect of the early Japanese blitzkrieg. Possessing medium-altitude performance that matched the vaunted U.S. B-17 Flying Fortress, the Betty was exactly the kind of plane Yamamoto had long wanted for his land-based strike forces. Yet the Betty proved a serious failure, and Yamamoto lost his life riding in one.

Crippling problems with the Betty appeared sooner than those later found in the Zero. On the surface both planes appeared to possess very similar strengths and weaknesses, and to a degree that was true. Like the Zero, the Betty's performance for the era was very good. It was a very fast bomber with a prodigious range. Like the Zero it achieved its great range and good performance thanks to very light construction. However, a crucial difference existed between the Betty and the Zero. When Horikoshi's team worked on the Zero (another team did the

Betty), they were seriously constrained by the size of the Sakae engine, the power plant that was ultimately chosen. Even if a slightly more powerful engine was chosen, the Zero would have been an underpowered aircraft by world standards; thus light weight was essential if Horikoshi wished to maintain speed, maneuverability, and range.

The designers of the Betty, in trying to please the navy, committed a terrible blunder duplicating the Zero formula. The first Betty model to see large-scale deployment was powered by two Mitsubishi Kasei radial engines, each putting out approximately 1,400 horsepower. This gave the Betty a good deal of power, not much less than the much heavier U.S. B-25 Mitchell. The question thus became what the design team would choose to do with the adequate power at its disposal. Maneuverability was not an issue. Even the lightest twin-engine bomber is not nimble in the sense that a fighter is nimble. And by 1941 multi-engine bombers were unable to outrun fighters as prewar bomber enthusiasts had predicted. Instead the power was employed to give the Betty astounding range: 3,700 miles in theory, more than the B-17. This fit nicely into Yamamoto's concept of a very long range land-based strike bomber that could project Japanese power far into the Pacific. Loaded and operating in real-world circumstances, however, the Betty could not fly that far.

However, in retrospect we can see that the Betty was a flying contradiction. To gain great range, the bomber was lightly built, poorly armed, and almost unarmored. We can excuse Mitsubishi for not putting adequate defensive armament on the early Betty, as that was a mistake committed by all the air forces early in the war. Trading structural strength for range, however, was a terrible bargain. Early on, Mitsubishi fitted a rubber seal under the large fuel tanks and even fitted the plane with fire extinguishers. Yet compared to U.S.-made self-sealing systems this was a pale effort. Indeed the size of the tanks themselves, which allowed the great range, simply made a bigger target for Allied fighters to deliver a fatal blow. Likewise the plane was unarmored and structurally weak, making it that much more vulnerable. Worse yet, the armament fitted was badly chosen. Early-model Bettys had five rifle-caliber machine guns fitted in blisters (windows with gun mounts through which gunners aimed their weapons manually—a bad system for accurate fire) and a single 20mm cannon mounted in a crude rear turret. Japanese crews knew how vulnerable their aircraft was. At first given the nickname the "Flying Cigar" because of its shape, the Betty was soon known among Japanese fliers as the "Flying Cigarette Lighter." Allied pilots, quickly learning the Betty's weakness, picked up on the same theme and called it the "Flying Zippo."

The Japanese command was all too aware of the Betty's shortcomings soon after the days of easy victories ended. As earlier noted, a flight of Bettys attacking USS *Lexington* was slaughtered in February 1942. That was only the beginning. Immediately after the war Lieutenant Commander Ohira, a top evaluator and test pilot at Yokosuka, after two years in combat, described the Betty's defects to American officers:

The Betty had weak defensive power and exploded easily when hit. It had a single cannon and was known as the "one shot fighter." [This was because of the 20mm's slow rate of fire.—EB] Although we improved the quality of our machine guns, our development of defense cannons for large bombers and of power gun mounts was very slow. Furthermore, because there was insufficient training in the sighting and firing of power gun mounts, the losses in heavy bombers were very great. [The Japanese considered the Betty a heavy bomber; they had no equivalent of the B-24.—EB] Due to poor Japanese production the equipment was poor and the aircraft difficult to maintain. Although the Japanese air force had great morale, namely a willingness to sacrifice their lives in defense, the performance of our planes was much poorer than those of the Allied forces.

Jim Morehead of 8th Squadron of the famous 49th Fighter Group was one of the earliest American pilots to participate in South Pacific combat. After being chased out of Java by the Japanese juggernaut, he was posted at Darwin, then under steady attack by bombers based on Timor. As described in his memoirs, on April 25, 1942, Morehead's flight scored one of the first, but far from last, Allied victories over a Betty:

The bombers looked shiny and new and I knew I had not seen this airplane in the skies over Java. The turrets in the tail of the planes were firing, and I realized they were 20mm guns because they were firing so slowly, one could have counted the rounds, or rather the puffs of smoke that came from each round. My tracers were going to the right of the gunner, whom I could see plainly. I kicked the left rudder, sawing my tracers across the turret, and the gunner stopped firing. . . . I pulled farther to the left, raking the left engine, which started burning, but my speed was overtaking the big ship and I dove beneath it as I sped past.

Now I was approaching the lead ship of this element, and his tail gunner was firing those slow shots at me. With my throttle back and directly in the prop wash of both bombers, I was slowing rapidly. I glided right up to the gunner, and, precisely as before, I sawed the tracers across the turret and he stopped firing. I figured I was a target of the nose gunner of the ship I had just passed, and of a bunch of Zeros too, but I could see no tracers going by, so I kept shooting while switching to the left engine. About that time a sluice of oil came from the right engine of this later bomber, covering my windshield. I then stalled out, as I had forgotten to add throttle. The P-40 dropped a hundred feet or so in the stall as two burning bombers heeled over above me.

Morehead was right about being a target, and his P-40 was a total wreck after landing. But it had been a rare good day for the USAAF early in the war, with eight Bettys shot down along with three escorts with no U.S. pilots lost.

Morehead's account points out the extreme vulnerability of the Betty to fighter attack. Obviously antiaircraft could also blow one to pieces. Morehead's attack was made successfully despite the presence of Zero escorts, a feat later replicated at Guadalcanal many times. As one can imagine, a Betty attack without escort, as illustrated during the *Lexington* assault, was almost suicide. This brings to the surface the extraordinary design flaw of the aircraft: Even the Zero, which could reach very far, could not begin to escort a flight of Bettys employing their maximum range; conversely without escorts the Bettys were flying death traps. Consequently the Betty's range was essentially irrelevant. The JNAF would have been far wiser to sacrifice range and speed for structural strength and armor. It is true that long-range Betty attacks, on a very few occasions, inflicted damage on U.S. warships. It is also true that if spotted at great distance a high-flying Betty had a good chance to avoid pursuit by Allied fighters. Nevertheless Japan needed the equivalent of a B-25, which was almost as fast as the Betty, carried an equal bomb load, and was extremely rugged. The B-25's range was less than half that of the Betty, but had the Japanese deployed their version of the Mitchell it still would have boasted range greater than the Zero's. As it was, B-25s preferred a fighter escort, despite their ruggedness. If alone, however, they had an excellent chance of surviving attack. This was even more true of U.S. heavy bombers such as the B-17 and B-24.

We have extraordinary testimony as to the experience of a Japanese Betty crew under U.S. fighter attack. The most famous fighter mission of World War II took place on April 18, 1943, when sixteen P-38 Lightnings intercepted two Bettys, along with six escorting Zeros, transporting Admiral Isoroku Yamamoto, commander of Combined

Fleet, and his staff during a visit to Bougainville. The details of the mission are controversial. However, Yamamoto's chief of staff, Admiral Matome Ugaki, kept an elegant diary throughout the war. (Although not a pilot, Ugaki, seeking an honorable death, perished during one of the last kamikaze missions of the war.) Through Ugaki's eyes, we can envision the deadly chaos that accompanied the last moments of a bomber:

The weather was fine, visibility good. From time to time three fighters each were seen escorting to the right and left in the rear above. I remember our altitude was about 1,500 meters. . . . The second plane was flying in tandem with the first aircraft at its side rear in perfect formation, so I feared our wingtips might touch. I could clearly see the profile of the commander in chief in the skipper's seat and the other people moving in the first plane. I enjoyed a pleasant flight as I followed the explanation of the topography down below with an aviation map. When we reached the west side of Bougainville and were passing straight over the jungle with altitude lowered to seven hundred or eight hundred meters, the skipper handed me a piece of paper on which was written, "Expect to arrive at 0745." I looked at my wrist watch and it was just 0730 and I thought it would be fifteen minutes more before we landed.

At this point the plane suddenly started to dive, following the first plane, and went down to fifty meters. We all wondered what happened! I asked the skipper, an air warrant officer, who was in the passage, "What's the matter?" "May be some mistake," he answered. But it was a great mistake to say so and he was most careless. . . . By the time we lowered altitude to treetop level, air combat had already been in progress between our escorting fighters and the enemy. Four times as many as our fighters [Ugaki understandably exaggerates: Only four P-38s attacked the bombers; the others flew high cover at 12,000 feet— EB], the enemy planes bore down mercilessly upon the bigger game of the two bombers. We made a quick turn of over 90 degrees to evade them. Watching the sky above and noticing an enemy plane charging in, the skipper tapped the chief pilot's shoulder and directed him to turn left or right.

The first plane turned to the right and the second to the left. The distance between them increased. After we evaded about twice, I turned to the right to see how the first plane was evading. What I saw then was astounding. Lo! The first plane was staggering southward, just brushing the jungle top with reduced speed, emitting black smoke and flame. It was about four thousand meters away from us. I just said to myself "My God!" I could think of nothing else. I grabbed the shoulder of Air Staff Officer Muroi, pointed to the first aircraft and said, "Look at the commander in chief's plane!" This became my parting with him forever. All this happened in only about twenty seconds.

In the meantime, my plane turned again sharply to evade another enemy attack, and we lost sight of the commander in chief's aircraft. . . . The next glance revealed that the plane was no more to be seen, only a pall of black smoke rising to the sky from the jungle. Oh! Everything was over now! . . . At that moment our plane was at full speed and soon came out over the sea. Enemy attacks were at first concentrated on the first plane. Looking back, I could see dogfights still going on.

Making a rising half turn and then a quick turn, a P-38 came upon us at last. Here he comes! Our machine gun opened fire upon him desperately. Although it worked well, it didn't seem to hit him. The enemy P-38 rapidly closed in, taking advantage of his superior speed. His gunfire caught us splendidly, and oncoming bullets were seen on both sides of our plane. I felt them hitting our aircraft from time to time. Now we were hopeless, and I thought my end was very near at hand.

The sound of our machine-gun fire was reduced by this time, and the skipper could not be heard any more. I thought quite a number must have been killed in the plane. Staff Officer Muroi was leaning on a table with his face down and arms outstretched. He must have already been killed. The chief pilot sitting in front of me felt bullets hitting the right wing and tried to get down to sea level with a down rudder in preparation for a crash landing. . . . When the bomber was near the sea surface, the pilot lost control. He pulled back all the throttles at once, but it was no use. The ship ditched into the sea at full speed and rolled over to the left by more than 90 degrees. . . . Everything went black and I felt the sea water rushing all over my body with fair pressure. I could do absolutely nothing. I told myself, "This is the end of Ugaki."
. . . Right after I gave it all up, all of a sudden it lightened. When I opened my eyes, incredibly, I found myself floating on the sea surface. What a miracle! The fuselage had already disappeared and the right wing was standing upside down in the sea right behind me and was still burning fiercely. I couldn't see any men around.

Counting Ugaki, there were three survivors in the second plane. All on the first plane, including Yamamoto, perished. A Japanese army patrol rushed to the scene and arrived the following morning. According to Ugaki, this is what they found:

The remains of the fleet surgeon were recognizable as his body was only half burned, but all the rest were difficult to identify as they were burned and decomposed. . . . The body of the commander in chief [i.e., Yamamoto—EB] was found on the seat outside of the plane, still gripping his sword. It hadn't decomposed yet and was said to be in a state of great dignity. He must really have been superhuman. . . . A postmortem made while his body was being carried on a sub-chaser found two piercing machine-gun bullet wounds in his lower jaw and shoulder. Most probably he was killed instantly while in the air.

As we shall see, the Betty's frailty led the Japanese to adopt tactics that made bombing raids nearly futile. And there was more bad news for Japan. For Japan's technology, the Betty, like the Zero, was an advanced aircraft. A multiengine aircraft is more difficult to build than a fighter under any circumstances. During the period January 1941–January 1944 only 1,200 Bettys were produced. Another 1,100 came off the line in the last year of the war. Thus when considering staggering combat losses, accidents, and inevitable wear and tear, Japan's supply of its best bomber was inadequate. So overall the Betty was an extremely poor weapon and proved very badly suited for the war that developed in the South Pacific. As the Americans later illustrated with dramatic effect, medium bombers could be devastating weapons. The Japanese could not counter with their own blistering assaults.

The JNAF did have two tactical bombers that for a short time played a very important role in the South Pacific. The first was the Nakajima B5N (code name: Kate). The Kate was designed as a modern torpedo-bomber to be escorted by the Zero. It was also capable of serving as a light tactical bomber. When carrier-based, the Kate delivered some terrible punishment to the U.S. Navy. It decimated battleship row at Pearl Harbor and sank three U.S. carriers in later battles. Reasonably fast with excellent manners typical of all early Japanese World War II carrier-based aircraft, the Kate was a good aircraft flown by extremely good pilots and carried the best aerial torpedo of the day. The Kate's stablemate on imperial carriers was the Aichi D3A1 dive-bomber (Allied code name: Val). The Val had decent speed but was underpowered and could not carry a 1,000-pound bomb, a factor that weakened its effectiveness. Like the Kate (and the Zero for that matter) its early-war pilots were extremely good, no doubt contributing more to the aircraft's success than any inherent qualities. Both the Val and the Kate were badly armed and desperately vulnerable to fighter attack. During carrier battles, which were one-shot affairs, that did not matter much. Yet after both plane types were shot up badly during the Battle of Santa Cruz, the sun clearly was setting for them. Several squadrons appeared at Rabaul for land-based combat but proved so vulnerable that their use was prohibited. As we shall see, even the far more rugged U.S. single-engine tactical bombers found the going very tough during sustained operations against land targets.

Japanese Army Aircraft

Shortly after the Japanese navy released the specifications that led ultimately to the A6M Zero, the Japanese army likewise authorized the development of a new fighter. Like many military forces before, during, and after World War II, the Japanese army prepared minimum specifications for its new fighter. Long engaged with the motley collection of planes that made up the Chinese Air Force and facing a large but crude Soviet fighter force, the JAAF put a high premium on flight performance. Light, very maneuverable fighters served well in China, and it was only natural that army airmen would request a similar plane when issuing their initial specifications to the designers. The Japanese army, consequently, built a fighter for the wrong war. This mistake reflected the nearly impenetrable gap that divided the Japanese army and navy. The army controlled events in China. Any drive into Southeast Asia, the army believed, would be the navy's responsibility. Resource allocation in the army was a particularly acute problem. Japanese ground forces, as clashes with the Soviet army had shown, were seriously deficient in artillery and armored vehicles. The army consequently settled for a light, inexpensive fighter that could rule the skies in China. Fighting the Americans, they believed, would be the navy's job. Events did not follow the script, however, and Japanese army pilots became deeply engaged against Americans in the Southwest Pacific.

The end product was the Nakajima Ki43 (Allied code name: Oscar; Peregrine Falcon to the Japanese). Although it followed the path of the successful Zero in many respects, the low-weight–high-maneuverability formula lost coherence in this design. Oscar was the lightest fighter used by any major combatant during World War II, weighing almost 800 pounds less than the delicate Zero. Like the Zero it was designed to maximize lift and maneuverability. Oscar was the most nimble fighter to serve in the war, superior to the Zero itself in this regard. Very maneuverable and possessing an excellent rate of steep climb, Oscar was a frustrating opponent. Like all fighters that served in the Pacific, the Ki43 was dangerous if the circumstances favored its pilot. While flying his powerful P-38 Lightning, American ace Perry Dahl had a confrontation with an Oscar in the fall of 1943 over New Guinea:

> There were four of us one day that caught one little lone Oscar, and that was the lightest, most maneuverable fighter they made—it only had two .30-caliber guns on it—but we made passes on that Oscar for over forty minutes. I came home with a hole in my prop—we never touched him. It was just remarkable. This guy was so sharp. When you'd line up and start to fire he could turn into you, he could dance on the rudders, and just turn around and fly back almost underneath itself. And all four of us just gave up and flew back home.

Robert DeHaven, one of the top 5th USAAF aces, recalled the almost phenomenal maneuverability of the Oscar. The maneuver he describes, the Immelmann turn (named after World War I German ace Max Immelmann), was a challenging maneuver for any World War II fighter. It required that the aircraft go into a steep climb, change direction, and level out going on a different course (essentially a half-loop upward followed by a half-roll). Because of the steep climb, the gain in altitude was paid for by a sharp decrease in speed. As DeHaven recounts, the Oscar was so light and nimble that it could complete an Immelmann and then quickly do a second, even followed by a hammerhead stall, which requires a pilot to raise the nose, kick the rudder, and descend downward in a stall. This maneuver, following a double Immelmann, is the sort of thing that thrills modern airshow crowds observing featherlight acrobatic aircraft. No military aircraft during World War II was capable of this complicated move except the Oscar:

> You'd be lucky to get one Immelmann out of a [Ki61] Tony starting from an initial flight attitude, whereas an Oscar, it really could do a double, and I saw it happen too many times. I'm not too sure that a Zero, unless he had proper conditions set up, maximum throttle, and all-out level flight, could do it. But I saw an Oscar do several double Immelmanns, even topped off by a hammerhead stall. That's pretty fancy to watch. It was an enormously maneuverable airplane. The Oscar was designed to be an army fighter for the Manchurian and Chinese theaters. It had great maneuverability but with its armament of two machine guns, it wasn't too far from the Sopwith Camel era in some ways.

Like Dahl, DeHaven led a flight of four U.S. aircraft (P-40s) against a well-flown Oscar and came away empty: "There were four of us against an Oscar. The pilot was a master. As I made a pass he'd turn straight into me. I spread my flight out, so there was no possible place for him to turn, but he was too good. I got a snapshot and that was it. After the fourth attempt I broke off the attack. We were getting low and were near the Japanese base. The possibility of being jumped by Japanese from above argued for prudence."

Oscar pilots paid a high price for their craft's single positive attribute. Although the engine was the same Sakae radial fitted to the Zero, the craft's configuration and ultralight frame restricted speed. Oscar was approximately forty miles per hour slower than the Zero and consequently also slower than all U.S. fighters. In addition the Oscar was inadequately armed. Early Oscars were armed with two 7.7mm machine guns, the same armament as a Sopwith Camel from World War I. Although sufficient in China, two small machine guns constituted a wretched weapon system in the South Pacific. Later the Japanese gave the Oscar twin 13mm (.50-caliber) machine guns, but its armament was almost pitifully inadequate for the theater it was thrust into. It was particularly unsuitable for the critical role of intercepting bombers. Lightly armed, the Oscar was also extremely fragile. Like the Zero it had no armor and no self-sealing fuel tanks. Its airframe was even less durable than its navy counterpart's. Battle damage that a Zero could survive might well destroy an Oscar. Unfortunately for Japanese pilots, when Oscars were sent against U.S. combat aircraft they found that damage was a common occurrence. Perry Dahl, so impressed with the Oscar at its best, also recognized its flaws: "It was really a fantastic, maneuverable little airplane. But they gave up something to get that, of course. They gave up armament. They gave up speed. They weren't stressed for it. When you hit one of those dudes it blew up. I mean right now. If you hit her right it really went." Sammy Pierce, an ace with the famous 49th Fighter Group in New Guinea, met Oscars often in his P-40. He described the Oscar's strengths and weaknesses succinctly: "The Oscar was probably the slowest Japanese fighter in the theater and had very light armament, but it was a performing fool. An experienced pilot in an Oscar was not that much of a threat to an experienced P-40 pilot, because of the Oscar's lack of guns and the P-40's ability to take it, but he could send you home talking to yourself."

In fairness to the JAAF, its leaders realized rapidly that the Ki43 was not competitive with more modern designs, and nothing could be done to transform it. Quicker than the navy, the JAAF began to develop entirely new models of fighters. The first was the Ki61 (Allied code name: Tony; to the Japanese it was the *Hien*, or "Swallow"). The Tony was unusual in two respects. First, it was the only inline-engine Japanese warplane fielded in substantial numbers in the war. Second, it was one of the rare cases of technical cooperation between Germany and Japan that led to results in the field. (As already noted, cooperation between Britain and the United States was deep at all technological levels and extremely fruitful.) The Tony also illustrates, probably better than any single aircraft, why Japan should not have been at war with the United States.

The Tony was a project of Kawasaki, a firm that dominated JAAF procurement throughout much of the interwar period until losing its position to upstarts from Nakajima. Kawasaki had, however, cultivated good relations in Germany and secured, in early 1940, blueprints for the Daimler Benz 601A engine that powered the Bf109E, the Luftwaffe's most advanced fighter, as well as a license to produce it. Along with the blueprints came two German-made versions so the Japanese could study the machine in the flesh. Messerschmitt cooperated by allowed investigation of the Bf109's airframe, and in March 1942 two Bf109Es were smuggled to Japan via submarine. Impressed by the prospect of a European-class fighter, the Japanese army awarded Kawasaki a contract for a new fighter in late 1940. After Kawasaki "improved" and adapted the DB 601A engine to Japanese industrial technique, it built a prototype that first flew a few weeks after Pearl Harbor. Despite having blueprints of a proven weapon, teething troubles were irksome, and actual production did not begin until August 1942.

In early 1943, after the stinging defeat at Guadalcanal and the Allied victory at Buna that clearly foreshadowed further moves by MacArthur in New Guinea, the Japanese army began to look at events in the Southern Theater with something resembling panic. It began stripping units from Manchuria and China and built up a major army in New Guinea. Seeing that the navy had its hands full at Rabaul, the army decided to send air units there to defend the Solomons. Although there were fewer than 200 Tonys in service at the time, the JAAF deployed them to Rabaul. Things did not start well. During one of the first ferry flights of twenty-seven Tonys from Truk to Rabaul, half got lost and ditched along a coral reef northeast of their destination. (The pilots were found and rescued two weeks later.) The Tony was a problem child from the start. As it proved, the stay in Rabaul was not long. The army and navy agreed to divide the theater: New Guinea would be army turf, whereas the JNAF would continue to defend the Solomons and Rabaul. As a consequence in the spring of 1943 the army began building up a base complex near Wewak in New Guinea, and it was in this area that the JAAF confronted U.S. and Australian aircraft.

When operating correctly the Tony proved a fine aircraft, much superior to the Zero. When it appeared in New Guinea in mid-1943 it proved a tough opponent for U.S. fighters. It was reasonably fast, had decent high-altitude performance, and could dive faster than a P-39 and very nearly as fast as a P-40. It was no longer an easy matter for an Allied fighter pilot to get out of Dodge with a high-speed dive, a most unwelcome discovery. Although not as tough as a U.S. fighter, the Tony carried armor for the pilot and self-sealing fuel tanks that were unreliable but far better than nothing. Its maximum range (650 miles) was far less than the Zero's, but as events were proving Japan needed defenders, not attackers. Armed with four .50-caliber machine guns, the Tony was undergunned for an interceptor but adequately armed for combat against fighters. When Americans captured a Tony during a landing at Cape Gloucester in western New Britain in December 1943, evaluators were impressed with its very well balanced performance. The Tony did not quite match the second-generation U.S. fighters like the F4U Corsair and P-38 Lightning in most categories of performance, but the differences were slight, and a good pilot could make the Tony a dangerous weapon indeed.

Unfortunately for the JAAF the development of the Tony illustrated vividly everything that was wrong with the Japanese aviation industry. Although Kawasaki had been given permission to prepare for production in 1941, the numbers of aircraft introduced proceeded at a sluggish pace. As we shall see, the JAAF soon confronted disaster in New Guinea and needed more planes desperately. However, from April to October 1943 production averaged barely fifty planes per month, nowhere near the number required to keep up strength in New Guinea, much less to replace Oscars with the more advanced plane. It was not until November that production reached 100 per month. By that time the JAAF in New Guinea was beginning to collapse. So it was that the Oscar fought and lost the battles in New Guinea.

Numbers were not the only problem. Despite having German blueprints and German aircraft to study, Japanese factories could not produce a reliable aircraft. A very high percentage of Tonys received from the plant failed inspection and had to be delivered to the large JAAF depot at Kagamigahara in Japan to be repaired. As mentioned, many Tonys were lost during deployment, and many others arrived suffering mechanical difficulties. There were, however, only a handful of well-trained Tony mechanics, and spare parts were always terribly short. Repair equipment was in short supply or nonexistent in New Guinea.

The closest Tony supply depot was 1,000 miles away in the Indies. An engine change required the plane to be shipped to Clark Field near Manila. Problems with engine-cooling and hydraulic systems plagued the warplane and frustrated the inexperienced ground crews in the field.

Still, Kawasaki continued to work on the Tony. Late in the war it became one of the most effective aircraft to defend Japan against bomber attack. Yet when the Tony was needed it was a failure. No wonder the Zero and Oscar remained in production until the end. Although obsolescent at the war's conclusion, they were far preferable to nothing.

The Japanese army had nothing to help beleaguered Betty crews in the bomber realm. Their twin-engine bombers proved easy meat for Allied fighters and were never produced in numbers large enough. Some lucky raids inflicted damage, and night attacks sometimes caused distress. But for the most part JAAF bombers were seriously overmatched in 1943. Richard Gallagher, a former 5th USAAF intelligence officer in the 7th Fighter Squadron, later became a keen student of Japanese aircraft. After the war he laconically portrayed the disrespect held by most Allied airmen for JAAF bombers they met in New Guinea. The plane Gallagher described was the Kawasaki Ki48 twin-engine bomber (Allied code name: Lily): "Based on intelligence reports that I did hear in those days, combined with my conversations with American and Australian air crews, and also photos seen during and after the war, I personally think that the Lily has a record that has never been cited before. I now propose that the following should be put on record: 'The Lily bomber was the plane most destroyed or damaged on the ground, by enemy air action, in World War II in the Pacific Theater.'"

To complete this dim picture, both the JNAF and the JAAF did not foresee the necessity for large numbers of transport aircraft. There was no technological reason for this defect. Japan had several serviceable twin-engine aircraft and could certainly have built a fine transport. The Germans soldiered on well enough with the ancient Ju52. Ironically, Japanese companies held licenses to produce the U.S. DC-3 (C-47 in its military guise). Considering the futility of most of Japan's multiengine bombing raids, it seems obvious that Tokyo would have been far better off to produce fewer Lilys and more transports. When the Allies came to fight they found C-47s worth their weight in gold. Indeed demand was insatiable and fights over allocations of this aircraft were probably more heated than over any of the combat models.

In retrospect the downward spiral that consumed Japan's war effort in the air was predictable. Japan lacked the technological depth to fight an aerial war of attrition where production numbers and quality were the equivalent of reserves in land battle. Once the psychological shock of the initial Japanese victories had worn off for the Allies, the Japanese soon discovered they had taken the wrong road technologically and did not have the ability to change course. Looking back it is very sobering that Japan's air effort, however bravely fought, began losing momentum months before the Americans began deploying their second-generation fighters and improved bombers. The Japanese leadership had staked everything on Germany's ability to destroy the USSR and then paralyze Britain and the United States. When that dream died in the Russian snow, the air war over South Pacific jungles died with it. Japan was no longer fighting China. After Pearl Harbor, it had decided to make war against the United States, Australia, and New Zealand. The leadership in Tokyo had committed a fatal blunder.

Allied Aircraft

Although it was not apparent early during hostilities, the men and women who produced, supported, and flew U.S. combat aircraft during World War II created the most effective killing machine in the history of aerial warfare. Because the crisis in the Southwest Pacific drew the limited U.S. air resources available like a magnet, the Japanese pilots flying in the Solomons and New Guinea were the first to discover this reality—and paid the consequences. During 1943 American pilots in the Pacific, splendidly assisted by many top-notch Australian and New Zealand units, launched a savage assault against Japanese airpower. Simultaneously the same brutally efficient process began in Europe. In very short order the Allies dealt a damaging blow to the qualitative edges held by the Japanese and German air units. With their good pilots dead, leaders in Tokyo and Berlin watched with horror as the Americans annihilated entire air forces and laid waste great cities. At war's end, U.S. airpower was supreme.

None of this is news to students of World War II. Unfortunately many writers have explained America's crushing victory in the air as being the result of huge numerical superiority in combat aircraft. This simple explanation does not correspond with the flow of aerial warfare in World War II. In both the Pacific and the Atlantic, U.S. warplanes dealt fierce blows to opponents long before any large superiority in numbers prevailed. Much of the early damage was done by warplanes that were, at best, equal to the opposition in combat capability. Furthermore emphasizing the numerical aspect obscures other essential factors in this deadly equation. American airmen did not crudely swamp the opposition with hordes of aircraft. Instead the United States fashioned a superbly balanced aerial combat arm characterized by an intelligent combination of design, production, doctrine, and support. The men and machines that were the end product proved in the field to be superior to their opponents in almost every way.

Forging the aerial killing machine that did so much to win World War II for the United States and the Allies was a difficult and extremely circuitous process. On one hand, as outlined earlier, advances in aviation technology during the interwar period increasingly played into the strong suit of U.S. industry: sophisticated production technique and technological depth. Yet before American and Allied airmen crushed Japan in the South Pacific, their predecessors of the interwar period had to overcome several serious obstacles. Some of the problems faced were predictable results of the political realities that existed during the period. Other quandaries were created by political blunders and one very serious error in doctrine.

Although far smaller than the European armies, the United States Army was interested in the infant aviation technology prior to World War I and procured a small number of aircraft. The obvious need was reconnaissance, and the tiny air arm was initially given to the Army Signal Corps. The navy was a couple years behind, but the senior service was prodded along by the brilliant aviation pioneer Glenn Martin, who in 1910 dropped some lead-pipe "bombs" on a mock battleship on an inland lake, thereby starting the warplane-versus-battleship debate that raged inside the navy until Pearl Harbor brought it to a screeching halt. At the same time, Martin arranged for one of his civilian pilots to land and take off an early-model plane from the deck of a cruiser. No doubt Martin's efforts were self-serving stunts, but they had already captured an interested audience. One of the navy's first air-minded officers was none other than Admiral George Dewey himself, the most famous naval leader between David Farragut and Halsey. In 1911 the navy allocated $25,000 to procure a handful of aircraft from Martin. As in the army, early naval aviators were interested in reconnaissance and showed a logical interest in seaplanes.

World War I changed everything. Although U.S. industry failed badly in producing a large air arm, the American Air Service fielded a large and vigorous force for fighting in the climactic battles that raged in 1918. Although some unfortunate aviators flew badly produced U.S. bombers, most piloted French and British warplanes. Ace Eddie Rickenbacker, a genuinely remarkable fighter pilot, was also one of America's greatest war heroes. Because the campaign of 1918 was much more fluid than the earlier trench warfare, attack aircraft on both sides wreaked havoc against infantry and horses on clogged road-ways. At the same time, Britain and France began a serious bombing campaign against some German cities in retribution for earlier German zeppelin and bomber raids on urban areas. None of this was lost on young American Air Service officers, particularly their tactical leader, William "Billy" Mitchell.

Mitchell and his zealous supporters caused an extraordinary political ruckus in the years after World War I among the U.S. Congress, the public, and the two services. As a prophet Mitchell was far more often wrong than right (unless one allows that he foresaw the development of nuclear weapons—most unlikely). For instance Mitchell predicted that in a future war aircraft carriers would be unable to function because long-range bombers would sink them. These same bombers would make it impossible to ferry large armies across oceans. This was not a good depiction of the war to come. In addition, Mitchell was extraordinarily unpolitic and richly deserved rebuke at his later court-martial.

Yet the fire lit by Mitchell forced the U.S. government and its armed forces to consider what type of air arm they should develop. This would have happened in any case, but it is very likely that the Mitchell debate, which engendered several congressional hearings and military boards, helped to quickly clarify the basic structure of the U.S. air arm along a very rational manner. Ironically Mitchell's slash-and-burn appeals to the public, which greatly inflated some genuinely interesting military exercises Mitchell had organized when his airmen sunk obsolete U.S. and German warships, alienated the entire military establishment (minus Mitchell's devoted band of junior officers). The army proved willing to slowly grant the Air Service greater autonomy but completely rejected an independent air force. The USN was appalled by Mitchell's demand that an independent air force control naval aviation as well. Consequently the navy created the Bureau of Aeronautics in 1921 and made the fateful decision that a navy flier was an officer first and a pilot second. Both decisions paid handsome dividends during World War II.

Indeed the army's autonomous but subordinate air force was perfectly designed for a world war. Because the airmen, whether they liked it or not, were forced to listen to the infantry and artillery officers who dominated the regular army, airmen were forced to allocate resources to the fighters, attack bombers, reconnaissance aircraft, and transports. Had a Mitchell-minded independent air force developed after World War I, all of these types of aircraft would have been neglected in favor of the heavy bomber. Yet ground commanders gave the airmen enough freedom in allocating development funds that fliers found the means to develop the world's best heavy bombers. The result, eventually, was the superbly balanced United States Army Air Force (the USAAF replaced the Air Service in the summer of 1941; its commander sat on the Joint Chiefs of Staff). Other nations created splendid aircraft, but none had the variety of first-class fighting machines possessed by the USAAF by mid-1943.

As for the USN, the decision to integrate aviation into the family was a stroke of brilliance. The RAF had control of the Royal Navy's aircraft for most of the interwar period and neglected them terribly. The result was that Britain had fine aircraft carriers and miserable aircraft. As it was, when the Fleet Air Arm was returned to Royal Navy control shortly before the war, pilots constituted an odd sort of caste. An American pilot, in contrast, might well expect to command a vessel or a task force. (Even before World War II pilots argued that carriers should be commanded by officers who held wings, and ultimately they got their wish.) It is true that aviators had a running battle within the navy between themselves and advocates of the big gun. Certainly the USN did not fully appreciate the potential of naval aviation until Pearl Harbor. Yet in that regard the USN was like every other navy, including that of Japan. For all of the power of the battleship admirals, the navy pioneered carrier-based aviation throughout the interwar period. In the crisis years prior to World War II the navy gave a very high priority to constructing excellent carriers. Even before the famous Vinson Bill, which authorized a huge expansion of the navy, the navy had laid the groundwork for the great carrier task forces that smashed the Japanese in 1944. And because the navy built and maintained carriers, it was interested in aircraft suitable for carrier operations. Although the pace of development proved not quite fast enough, the aircraft eventually deployed in mid-1942 through late 1943 were uniformly excellent.

In the fifteen years after World War I both the army and navy developed aircraft that were competitive with those from other nations. Without a war in sight, no government allocated funds required to push potential advances in aviation technology. As Japan showed, the 1920s and early 1930s were an excellent time to play catch-up. During this time the U.S. government purchased some fine aircraft. Military contracts proved essential to foster the development of a domestic aviation industry. Yet both the army and navy essentially encouraged the development of competitive prototypes. Often procurement orders for individual models were less than 100. Consequently by 1935 the United States possessed small numbers of modern aircraft. The orders given to the various companies helped keep many of them in business. Considering the political realities of the era this policy made the best of necessity. Both services attempted with some success to associate their efforts with the general fascination held by the general public for everything involved with aviation. Various long flights and record-breaking stunts served the services well in the public eye. Nevertheless it must be stressed that the army's air arm, and to a lesser extent the navy's, were not designed for immediate war. As noted already, many of the greatest advances in aviation came from the potentially promising civilian sector. The military departments were marking time, but they were also ensuring that if another crisis arose, the United States would not have to fly another nation's aircraft in war.

The United States possessed an absolutely unforeseen but extremely important advantage over most other nations. If either service purchased an aircraft, it might be called upon to serve in Alaska or the Panama Canal, and distances between bases were great. Therefore both services put a great premium on ruggedness and also required an adequate range for their planes. The dynamic of metal fatigue was not well known at the time, and when aircraft shifted from wood-and-canvas construction to metal the U.S. services were willing to pay for some extra metal to get a stout aircraft. Also the many engineers involved with civilian designs had learned to pay much attention to sturdiness and reliability, two traits essential for convincing passengers to fly instead of using the railways. In the event, all U.S. aircraft during World War II were very rugged compared to those of any other air force, especially Japan's. Interesting testimony on this comes from the memoirs of Brigadier General Ben Kelsey, chief of the USAAF Fighter Project from 1934 to 1943:

> Peacetime maneuvers for the United States involved deployment from Michigan to Florida, from one coast to the other, from arctic climate to deserts, and from sea level to the high plains and mountain areas. Sequential planes coming from a factory might be assigned to Alaska, or Panama, Florida or Arizona. When gathered for maneuvers, they might mass in Louisiana or New England in the winter. Cold weather testing was done on new articles in Fairbanks, but gunnery contests might be held on Muoc Dry Lake or Honey Lake north of Reno. The planes automatically included provisions for operating in any or all of these surroundings. That versatility was unique in this country.
>
> This inherent characteristic was brought home clearly when I had occasion to take a Spitfire Mark V [a midwar version of Britain's famous fighter—EB] from Wright Field in Ohio to Los Angeles and

back. Because of its limited range, it was necessary to land at a number of little-used intermediate fields. The cooling on the ground at some fields was inadequate to permit taxiing from landing to the service area or from the hangers to the takeoff end of the field. Long runways on high altitude desert fields involved crosswind taxiing where the brakes faded away and required readjusting. The marginal stability that added so much to the superb maneuvering of the plane for combat and short flights became tiring and uncomfortable on long flights in rough air. The plane that was superior in all respects in its own country would not have met our standards or been accepted unless modified, when evaluated by our acceptance and evaluating boards. The Spitfires going to Africa had an additional radiator. The other side of the picture has to be revealed too. Our planes were not considered desirable when evaluated abroad where adaptability bred into them had no real significance.

Weighed against the industrial and environmental advantages possessed by American airmen were two serious difficulties, one self-imposed. Officers at the Air Force Tactical School at Maxwell Air Force Base (the forerunner to Air University) were responsible for the development of air force doctrine. Followers of Mitchell were most prominent at Maxwell, and it is safe to say that many leading army airmen were devoted followers of the bomber cult. In 1933 the army announced it required a new heavy bomber. On its own initiative, knowing well the feelings inside the Army Air Corps, Boeing decided to develop prototypes of two bombers that possessed size beyond past precedent. The extremely large B-15 got the juices flowing at Maxwell, but eventually it proved underpowered and was a failure. (An even larger prototype, the XB-19, was later built, and it also failed; much of the technology appeared in Boeing's B-29 Superfortress and Convair's B-36 Peacemaker strategic bombers.) A scaled-down version of the B-15, however, was a very different affair: When first flown in 1935 the B-17 Flying Fortress was an astounding technical achievement. Unlike the superheavies the B-17 was clearly a solid design despite the crash of an early prototype. Prior to the appearance of the Flying Fortress Mitchell's followers worked in the field of theory. Possessing a powerful and remarkably beautiful aircraft that had long range and great speed, the bomber cult had a weapon to put its ideas into action. The future, or so it seemed, had arrived.

Fortunately for the United States the men at Maxwell did not run the army, and opposition to four-engine bombers appeared at once. Army leaders feared that expending precious funds on a fleet of heavy bombers would cause airmen to abandon the mission of tactical support for land armies. The navy saw the heavy bomber as a threat to its traditional position as guardian of American shores. (A compromise had been worked out with the army allowing the army to protect the coast out to a distance of 100 miles: Anything more distant was the navy's responsibility. Obviously this was excellent news for supporters of the aircraft carrier.) Both the army and navy feared that the huge expenditures involved would deprive them both of funds needed for overall force modernization. The army argued that there was no possible reason for a peaceful America to wish for long-range bombers and even characterized the concept as "aggressive." (It is difficult to believe this argument reflected army views. However, it was a good justification in the isolationist era to keep the Maxwell crowd quiet.) Consequently the army staff turned down the B-17 in favor of the Douglas B-18, a mediocre medium bomber that had the advantage of being cheap and quickly deployable. To keep options open, however, the army did allow the Air Corps to acquire a few more B-17 prototypes for experimental purposes. In September 1939 there were fourteen four-engine bombers in service in the Army Air Corps.

Although some ugly military politics were involved, the army had made exactly the right decision considering the time. I am not disputing in any way that the B-17 and other heavy bombers played a great role in eventual victory. There is no doubt that the country should have begun mass deployment of the B-17 at least a year before it did. However, had the officers in the Air Corps been given their way on procurement, there can be little doubt that a heavy bomber effort launched before the political climate allowed appropriate funding would have had a negative, perhaps disastrous, effect on the development of medium bombers and fighters. (It should be pointed out that the Air Corps recommended as early as 1935 that all future bomber procurement be for four-engine types. Fortunately a blunder of monumental proportions was avoided by the army chiefs of staff. It should also be pointed out that in the crisis prior to Pearl Harbor the enthusiasm for the B-17 spread into the civilian leadership and played no small role in encouraging false American hopes of deterring Japanese moves into Southeast Asia or even defending the Philippines with heavy bombers. This cruel mirage died quickly at Clark Field on December 8, 1941.) As it was, the navy progressed with carrier development, the army possessed a proven prototype for the best heavy bomber on earth, and funds were still available for work on medium bombers and advanced fighters. No thanks to the followers of Billy Mitchell, the United States ultimately fielded a remarkably well balanced air arm, on sea and land, when war opened the production floodgates.

Although the USAAF was ultimately given excellent weapons, the bomber cult did hamper the development of fighters. In Chapter 5 I will examine combat doctrine further, but I should note here that at Maxwell there was lively debate over all facets of airpower. Mitchell's supporters ruled the roost, but advocates for pursuit planes existed and argued their case well. The most famous was Claire Chennault, a controversial figure during the war but a far better prophet than Mitchell. Bomber advocates at Maxwell, as well as in other countries, argued that because fighters had so little speed advantage over bombers they would have an extremely difficult time intercepting a raid. This was obviously preradar doctrine and arguably reflected the World War I experience. (By 1918 bomber interceptions were by no means unusual; this precedent, as so often in war, was simply unclear.) Consequently many airmen envisioned fighters as weapons to defend the most obvious targets like air bases and great cities. It was Chennault's argument that a well-coordinated ground observation network could allow fighters to attack bombers prior to the raiders reaching their target—a doctrine he was able to implement in China with some success.

Yet bomber advocates wanted no competitors for funds and influence and sought to keep Chennault's followers in their place. The worst self-inflicted wound centered around fighter escort. Some bomber advocates (probably most) believed escort was unnecessary altogether. Others wanted heavily armed, twin-engine aircraft in small numbers to keep fighters at bay. The idea that fighters should be designed to possess great range of their own was considered a threat to the whole bomber doctrine, because if escort was required then the implication was that fighters were a threat and bombers not invincible. Therefore the Air Corps simply forbade the development of long-range fighters. Although auxiliary drop tanks were already in use in the 1920s, they were banned in the 1930s. Fortunately for all concerned the Air Corps did allow fittings installed on fighters' wings that would allow fitting of small bombs. On their own, designers made wings stronger than required to allow an external load to be carried. The navy never made such a mistake, and ultimately the army saw the error of its ways. Yet as we shall see it took mechanics working on their own in northern Australia to fit many army fighters with homemade drop tanks before the genuine article arrived. The tragic consequences of this blind policy for strategic bombers in Europe have been documented in hundreds of accounts.

However, the major reason that the United States fought the first year of the war with inadequate aircraft had little to do with USN or Air Corps doctrine. The real problem was the refusal of the U.S. government to see the mortal peril that was arising abroad. At the same time that the U.S. aviation industry was creating some of the best technology in the world, Washington was paralyzed by the Great Depression and isolationism. During the period 1935–1937 America's future allies and enemies were making a quantum leap in both bomber and fighter development, and so the United States fell badly behind in aircraft technology. This was no small matter. During this period many of the developments pioneered in the United States made their way into the arsenals of other nations. Unlike the 1920s, this was not a period during which a country could safely get behind the cutting edge, yet that is exactly what happened in the case of the United States. In short the Americans fell behind while Britain was developing the Hurricane and Spitfire, Germany was perfecting the excellent Bf109, and Japan was starting development of the Zero. And while U.S. enemies and Allied countries were developing aircraft for use in World War II, the United States fielded a series of planes that were obsolescent by the time of deployment.

War clouds prodded the army and navy to take more energetic measures. More importantly Congress grudgingly and very slowly began to open its wallet. Both services ordered better aircraft yet with a slowness and lack of numbers that greatly inhibited development. In January 1937 the army offered the first of many specifications for fighters that would match those being developed in Europe. The Lockheed Corporation responded with plans for an extremely innovative fighter that eventually became the P-38 Lightning, a legendary twin-engine, twin-boom warplane. The P-38 prototype did not fly until January 1939; delivery of production models did not begin until August 1941 and then in small numbers. In October 1937 the Bell Corporation received the order for a prototype that became the P-39 Airacobra. Delivery of the first few did not take place until January 1941, and only 600 had been produced by the time of Pearl Harbor. (Only a small percentage of this total was in squadron service, as we shall see.) In January 1939 a new army competition was held, and Curtiss won with the P-40, a greatly improved version of the P-36. Republic Aviation, the successor to Seversky, received an order for a prototype of what became the P-47 Thunderbolt in June 1940, but this barrel-chested model did not see serious production until early 1943.

The navy did a better job of preparing for war, but it, too, remained a step behind. In 1936 the navy issued specifications for a new carrier fighter. It ordered prototypes from Grumman for an improved version of the already standard F3F biplane (Grumman quickly decided to submit a monoplane instead), as well as from the smaller Brewster Company. In 1938 the navy decided that the Brewster Buffalo was the superior aircraft and placed an order for fifty units. By October wiser heads realized that Brewster's efforts might fail, and an order for fifty Grumman F4Fs was placed. Yet it took until December 1940 for the first F4F (which became the famous Wildcat) to arrive for fleet deployment. By Pearl Harbor approximately 300 Wildcats had left the assembly line and were hurriedly thrown into service.

As might be expected, the United States had far better fortune with multiengine aircraft. The Douglas Corporation, with the DC-3 and B-18 already under its belt, independently developed a twin-engine light bomber, first flown in October 1938. Although the Air Corps had little faith in light bombers, the French were very impressed and placed a large order. When France fell the United States Army, influenced by the Luftwaffe's deadly use of attack bombers, had a rapid change of heart and purchased Douglas's effort, which it designated the A-20 (which became the Havoc). At about the same time a remarkable newcomer, North American Aviation, which had previously built small utility aircraft, proposed a twin-engine bomber, designated the NA-41. With high speed and a good bomb load, the North American design had excellent prospects until a prototype crash. Now cured of any doubts concerning the value of attack aviation, the army also contracted with Martin for an extremely fast and sophisticated twin-engine medium bomber, which developed into the B-26 Marauder. Fortunately for Pacific airmen, Martin could not produce the B-26 in large enough numbers, so the army also procured the North American design, which was soon designated the B-25 Mitchell. (It is ironic that a medium tactical bomber bore Mitchell's name when it was the type of plane that Mitchell abhorred. Yet this aircraft proved devastating in the Pacific and Mediterranean; the Martin B-26 terrorized Germans in Western Europe.) In the cherished realm of heavy bombers, the B-17 was the world's best developed prototype, having flown in small numbers for almost four years prior to September 1939. All that was required was for the order to proceed. In August 1939 the army agreed to evaluate a prototype of an extremely advanced four-engine bomber, the Consolidated B-24 Liberator. However, the hard school of war had not yet taught American designers the absolute necessity of strong defensive armament even if it meant loss in airspeed. Consequently all U.S. bombers were poorly armed, though structurally strong. Worse yet, the numbers available for early use in the Pacific Theater were pitifully small.

There are three important points to make regarding this survey of U.S. aircraft procurement during the four years preceding Pearl Harbor. First, in the realm of fighter development Americans had fallen a year behind potential enemies. Germany and Japan issued advanced specifications for fighter aircraft months before the United States. More importantly both nations developed warplanes in a semiwar economy and were able to push development more briskly. For instance the first production-capable Zero was not flown until January 1940. Yet because the JNAF was so impressed, Mitsubishi produced nearly 900 Zeros by March 1942. Had the U.S. government authorized and demanded a similar effort from Lockheed, there is little doubt that the Zero would have encountered P-38s months earlier than was the case. During the same period only the Curtiss P-40 was produced in substantial quantity. However, the P-40 was scattered across the country, and most were not yet placed in regular squadron service. In December 1941 there were roughly seventy-five P-40s in the Philippines to withstand the Japanese onslaught. Other types of U.S. aircraft existed in much smaller numbers. When Japan attacked Pearl Harbor the navy possessed some 350 Wildcats, the Marines another sixty. There were 900 P-39s in existence, but only a few dozen were in regular service. In December 1941 they were all inferior to the Zero, and all were dispersed. Only a few were in active squadron service and ready for immediate combat. The second-generation fighters—the P-38, P-47, and F4U Corsair—were just entering production when war began and did not see serious service until 1943.

Second, much of U.S. air strength was siphoned off by foreign contracts and Lend-Lease. The liberal export policies favored by the Roosevelt administration raised many qualms inside both services, as they believed the aircraft they needed were going to foreign shores. (It is ironic that the first Wildcat and P-40 victories were scored by British pilots against German aircraft prior to Pearl Harbor.) In retrospect Lend Lease was a tremendous strategic success for the United States. In the short run, however, it restricted the growth of U.S. units. Also in the long run, foreign orders were tremendously advantageous for the U.S. aviation industry. Lacking steady government patronage, many companies had existed for years despite recurring financial losses. When a variety of nations approached them, willing to buy anything that could fly, it is not surprising that U.S. companies were willing to oblige. Pratt and Whitney, for instance, was in serious financial difficulty prior to the Munich crisis. Almost overnight the problem switched from a lack of orders to a lack of capacity for almost all U.S. companies. Obviously this spurred the development of plants and laid the groundwork for greater production to come. However, in this case, too, there was a price to be paid. Lockheed, for instance, was developing the P-38. It also was producing a poor light bomber based on Lockheed's successful civilian airliner, the Electra. The British needed a light bomber for reconnaissance and maritime patrol and ordered many. For a small company like Lockheed, the immediate opportunity for profit helped boost production of the Hudson (the name Britain gave the bomber) and slowed work on the promising P-38. Furthermore several hundred of the P-40s produced were shipped to the British, and later to the Russians, just when U.S. officers were crying for modern warplanes.

The third point is related to the second: Because the United States had followed a policy of procuring small orders while encouraging large numbers of prototypes, there were a large number of innovative aviation companies active. Most existed on a financial shoestring, and none were large. Again this situation contrasted dramatically with large manufacturers in Germany and Japan, companies that did not have to worry as much about the bottom line. When the wartime boom arrived, U.S. aviation was not in the least prepared for a quantum leap in orders. The necessary expansion—building plants, developing machine tools, and similar enterprises—fit the overall structure of the U.S. economy well in the long run. But even when companies are spurred into furious effort by war, creating production facilities takes time. By late 1943 the United States was matching the aircraft production of the entire world. However, during the months before and after Pearl Harbor the U.S. armed forces had to wait for production to meet demand. Shortages of all kinds of aircraft existed, and that was compounded by a serious lack of spare parts. For more than a year American officers watched helplessly as aircraft were allocated to them as if from misers. This was particularly true for secondary theaters—like the South Pacific.

One final remark is in order before proceeding to our examination of the major Allied warplanes that fought in the South Pacific. Each was extremely complex and very powerful. Each model was a challenge to fly, required good ground support, and was utterly unforgiving of carelessness. So in comparing one plane with another, it is important to remember that terms like "fast" and "slow" are meaningful only in reference to other warplanes.

Also there was no such thing as an all-purpose warplane. Aircrews are very opinionated concerning their aircraft in which they served.

For instance there is no clear consensus over which Allied fighter was the best in the theater: Veteran Corsair, Hellcat, and P-38 pilots today relish defending their respective mounts (some P-47 pilots will chime in, particularly if they were given frequent ground attack missions). There was and is good reason for this. Mission types varied greatly, and one type of plane might be better suited to a particular mission but inferior in different circumstances. Airmen also had different perspectives than do military and aviation historians. Most Allied airmen were brave and skilled young men and very willing to risk harm to perform their duty. They were, however, extremely interested in staying alive. So aircraft qualities such as ruggedness, good visibility, and forgiving flight characteristics rated just as highly as pure performance and firepower. Those writing about air warfare consider military airplanes as killing machines, which is true enough. To the men inside, however, these were living machines in a sense, and many a pilot who survived combat tours developed a soft spot in his heart for the machine that got him home in one piece, regardless of its fighting capabilities on paper. Lastly, these warplanes were flown by men. Pilot and crew skill would do much to compensate for technical inferiority. Each model had its rightful place in the war, and even though some were better than others, none was a failure. Like the Japanese inventory (see Chapter 3), any aircraft in good hands fighting over the South Pacific could inflict painful damage to the enemy.

Allied Fighters

The reader will notice that Chapter 3 (on Japanese warplanes) and this chapter (on Allied aircraft) are organized differently. In Japanese service the navy and army operated in largely different spheres. The division between the two was more geographic than functional, and both flew the same basic types of aircraft; the only real difference is that carrier planes were a navy exclusive. Thus I organized Chapter 3 according to the respective services (army and navy). The Allied equation requires a different analysis, as the very mix of aircraft was different. Both the USAAF and USN flew fighters, and the USN and Marine Corps specialized in carrier-style aircraft—fighters and tactical bombers. The USAAF was given the major role in medium and heavy bombardment, although later in the war the USN and Marines procured small numbers of bombers for armed reconnaissance. Furthermore the Allies did fight as a team. The Anzac forces were involved in both the Solomons and New Guinea early on. More importantly the USAAF was an important part of the Solomons drive dominated by the USN and Marines. The function of the various aircraft, therefore, was more important than the service they were attached to.

Throughout most of the great struggle for the South Pacific the most numerous fighter flown by U.S. Army and Anzac pilots was the Curtiss P-40 Warhawk. (British import versions of the P-40 flew as the Tomahawk and Kittyhawk. For some reason the name "Warhawk," although used in the popular press, never stuck with American pilots; to them the craft was simply the "P-40.") Yet the fact that this workhorse received major procurement was largely because the United States had neglected fighters. In April 1939, when Congress awarded Curtiss-Wright a contract to build 550 P-40s (the largest aviation contract in American history until that time), a storm of controversy erupted in aviation circles. Other corporations accused Curtiss of simply modifying an older plane (the P-36) and wedding it to a new Allison engine. The result, they charged, was an aircraft that would be inferior to foreign makes. Curtiss responded that the P-40 was a sound design and, because it was based on much proven technology, could be produced quickly, economically, and in large numbers. America, Curtiss argued, needed fighters quickly. Better aircraft, after all, were in the pipeline already. In the end both Curtiss and its critics were correct. Nevertheless Congress was wise. Whatever its faults the P-40 was there when the crunch came, and its more sophisticated competitors were not. It proved useful enough that production continued until 1944, with some 13,000 aircraft being churned out. This was a good run even by World War II standards, and when peace came pilots from every Allied nation were flying P-40s supplied by the United States.

Whatever its weaknesses the P-40 did possess the basic requisites of a modern fighter: It was a low-wing cantilevered monoplane with stressed skin over a semimonocoque airframe. Nevertheless the P-40 was almost the mirror image of the great Japanese Zero. The Allison engine in the P-40E model, which was the most numerous type of P-40 used in the Southwest Pacific, generated 1,300 horsepower, considerably more than the 950-horsepower output coming from the Zero's radial. The P-40, however, was much heavier. Having a much poorer power-to-weight ratio than the Zero, the P-40 was designed to maximize different attributes than its Japanese opponent. Whereas the Zero was given a huge wing and tail for lift and maneuverability, the P-40's wing was two feet shorter, with a smaller area, and set back much farther; all this in a plane two feet longer than the Zero. The P-40's designers attempted in this way to maximize speed on both a straight line and in a dive. Consequently the P-40 was much less maneuverable than was the Zero in most ways but its equal in speed and considerably faster in a dive. Nevertheless all P-40 models were underpowered considering their weights. The Allison engine, unless turbocharged, did not perform well at high altitudes. Unfortunately turbochargers were in short supply, and the army reserved them for bombers and more advanced fighters like the P-38 and P-47. The various Allison engines mounted on the P-40 required the "thick" air found at moderate altitudes to operate efficiently. Poor performance at high altitudes was a serious disadvantage, because it made it much more difficult to engage high-flying bombers and reconnaissance aircraft. The Zero, although also optimized for fighting at moderate altitudes, handled "thin" air somewhat better than did early-model P-40s, giving it yet another advantage.

There was no hiding the fact that the P-40 was not on the cutting edge of aviation technology when it went to war. Although the long, low fuselage gave the plane the look of a fighter, the airframe was not innovative in any way. This was not a disaster by any means. The Allison was very reliable for an inline engine and gave good performance up to 15,000 feet. When the Allies began to control the flow of battle they also were able to influence the altitude at which it took place. Consequently, with the Allies determined to press home daylight bombing attacks at much lower altitudes than found in Europe, combat at extreme altitudes was not common in the Pacific, which was good news for the P-40.

Although the Zero possessed many superior flight characteristics compared to the P-40, the U.S. fighter had better armament and was much more sturdy. The early-model P-40s that fought the Japanese advance in the Philippines and the East Indies had two .50-caliber and four .30-caliber machine guns. When U.S. squadrons deployed in strength in New Guinea they flew more advanced models that had six .50-caliber machine guns, more pilot armor, and much better self-sealing fuel tanks. The number of rounds carried per gun was low, and a pilot could exhaust his ammunition in not much more than ten seconds of continuous firing. And like all early war fighters the P-40 was prone to gun-jams. But if the guns fired correctly a huge number of lethal rounds filled the air—plenty to obliterate a Zero. Consequently the P-40 did not need the extra punch that came from a cannon.

In the early days of the war the P-40 was treated roughly by Japanese fighters and was crushed on the ground in the Philippines and thrown into action with great haste in the East Indies. American pilots fought disorganized actions against a numerically superior enemy. Although the Japanese usually had the advantage of altitude, many American pilots tried to dogfight the Zero—with disastrous results. Yet it did not take long for American and Australian pilots to accommodate the strengths of the P-40 to the tactical situation and soon gain an equality of terms.

One of the many advantages held by the Allies in the Pacific war was a remarkable quickness to alter tactics if those employed failed. Prior to Pearl Harbor General Chennault, then in China, was telling his former comrades in Washington that the P-40 was effective if used correctly. Australian squadrons based at Port Moresby in March-April 1942 learned the same lessons. By the time the USAAF deployed several P-40 squadrons in New Guinea the outlines of proper doctrine existed. The key was good group tactics (more of which later) and keeping up speed. If the Japanese had altitude advantage, which was often the case early in the war, a P-40 would turn into the attacker (a technique advocated by the famous German ace Oswald Boelcke in World War I) and offer to trade bursts in a head-to-head pass. Well-armed and tough, the P-40 had odds in its favor. After the completed pass the Allied pilot would dive out and head for safety. If the P-40 had equal or superior altitude the approved technique was to make a pass, fire, and hope for a hit. If the flight was still coherent, it would gain a small amount of altitude and repeat the performance. If a P-40 could achieve good attack position on a Betty or other Japanese bomber, the imperial raider faced likely destruction in the face of six heavy machine guns. These were conservative tactics but greatly lowered risk of death in combat, which was good news for both pilot and plane-starved commanders.

If the opportunity presented itself a skilled P-40 pilot could mix it up with a Zero at medium and low altitudes with better chances for success than men flying more advanced aircraft. Although the P-40 had many defects, it was quite nimble for a U.S. fighter at medium and low altitudes. Because the P-40 had a slight speed advantage over the Zero and could dive far better, it could take advantage of the Zero's poor high-speed handling. The Zero had large wings and large ailerons, which allowed it to make spectacular maneuvers if the speed was 200 knots or less. However, above that speed air pressure made it far more difficult for those large ailerons to move. Above 300 knots the Japanese aircraft maneuvered very badly. (Because the Oscar amplified the design philosophy of the Zero, this tendency was even more marked in that Japanese army fighter, often encountered by P-40 pilots.) The P-40, with its high wing-loading, reversed the equation. The wings and ailerons were smaller, offering far less drag at high speeds. The P-40 did not have a very tight turning radius, but it did have a very good roll rate (the ability to change direction, particularly at high speeds). In other words, physics worked precisely the opposite for the Zero (and

Oscar) and the P-40. At slow speeds a well-piloted Zero could gain position with ease. At fast speeds a P-40 actually had an edge—for a moment. The problem facing the P-40 pilot was to know when the edge left him. A maneuver of any type costs an aircraft either speed or altitude. Thus the advantage was real but transient. Nevertheless with the usual opportunity to break off (given by the P-40s superior dive speed), some good pilots engaged nimble Japanese fighters with very successful results.

Joel Paris was an ace with the famous 49th Fighter Group's 7th Squadron in New Guinea:

I never felt that I was a second-class citizen in a P-40. In many ways I thought the P-40 was better than the more modern fighters. I had a hell of a lot of time in a P-40, probably close to a thousand hours. I could make it sit up and talk. It was an unforgiving airplane. If you stalled it more than two feet upside down it was liable to land more than two feet off the ground. It had vicious stall characteristics. . . . If you knew what you were doing you could fight a Jap on even terms, but you had to make him fight your way. He could outturn you at slow speed. You could outturn him at high speed. When you got in a turning fight with him, you dropped your nose down so you kept your airspeed up, you could outturn him. At low speed he could outroll you because of those big ailerons: They looked like barn doors on the Zero. If your speed was up over 275, you could outroll it. His big ailerons didn't have the strength to make high-speed rolls; it was like they were set in concrete. The same thing happened at a high-speed climb. He could outclimb you at slow speed, say at 90 miles per hour, he could climb real steep. But if you kept it going up to 250 or more you could outclimb him. So you could make him fight your way. You could push things, too. Because you knew one thing: If you decided you wanted to go home, you could go home. He couldn't because you could outrun him. He couldn't leave the fight because you were faster. That left you in control of the fight. Mind you: The P-40 was a fine combat plane.

Paris described how this worked out when he destroyed an Oscar in early 1944:

The long nose of the P-40 hindered the aircraft as a gun platform. If the enemy was in any kind of a turn, and I'm talking about a gentle turn not a desperate evasive, and you were approaching in a 1- to 15-degree angle from his tail, you would have to pull your nose in front of him to be able to lead him. In a P-40 you had no way of seeing him; you had to lead him blind. But you could get your nose positioned quickly. I did that to an Oscar. I pulled the gunsight through him until I had what I hoped was the right point and then fired about a two-and-a-half-second burst. I ceased firing, eased off the stick, dropped the nose down to see what damage I'd done when the enemy came up from under my nose. It was a beautiful sight when that nose dropped down and the Oscar came up into sight burning. But unfortunately you couldn't get to actually see the hits strike home when in a situation like that. Kills like this were common in a P-40: a quick, well-aimed burst and a burning enemy.

The attribute praised by all P-40 pilots was its strength. Many P-40 pilots recalled owing their lives to the plane's ability to absorb punishment. Veteran Sammy Pierce of 49th Fighter Group testified to the great strength of the airframe. In early 1943, pursued closely by two Zeros and desperate to escape, Pierce put his aircraft into a maximum power dive that in theory could have destroyed his plane:

I dove Number 42 to the point where the airspeed indicator went all the way around, the manifold pressure went to the stop, and the RPM went 300 past normal maximum. Even using full left rudder trim, standing on the left rudder, and using left aileron, the torque caused the P-40 to want to roll to the right. But it stayed together and kept flying, even though the rudder had to be replaced. Several times we took some fairly good hits that didn't really affect the flying or performance.

Robert DeHaven of the 49th Fighter Group's 7th Squadron could speak with great authority concerning the P-40. At war's end DeHaven led the squadron in confirmed victories with fourteen, ten of them in a P-40. Thus DeHaven was one of the very few double-aces who flew a first-generation U.S. fighter. (His remaining four kills came after 7th Squadron received P-38s.) Like Paris, he had words of praise for the P-40:

After training I requested duty in the Pacific and I requested being posted to a P-40 squadron and both wishes were granted. This was early in 1943 and most pilots already desired more advanced types and some thought my decision a mistake. Yet I had been inspired by the deeds of the Flying Tigers [Chennault's China-based American Volunteer Group, which painted the noses of its P-40s with the legendary bared-fangs motif—EB]. We had also heard accounts that the P-38 was difficult to bail out of because of its twin-boom tail and that it was difficult when flying with one engine. I also knew that P-38s were still rare in the theater and I wanted to get into the war as soon as possible. That wish, too, was granted. I never regretted the choice. If you flew wisely, the P-40 was a very capable aircraft. In many conditions it could outturn a P-38, a fact that some pilots didn't realize when they made the transition between the two aircraft. The P-40 kept me alive and allowed me to accomplish my mission. The real problem with it was lack of range. As we pushed the Japanese back, P-40 pilots were slowly left out of the war. So when I moved to P-38s, an excellent aircraft, I did so not because I believed that the P-40 was an inferior fighter but that I knew the P-38 would allow us to reach the enemy. I was a fighter pilot and that was what I was supposed to do.

In December 1943 DeHaven scored his fifth kill and became an ace. It was almost his last victory. Yet thanks to some good flying, good luck, and the P-40's legendary ruggedness he was back in the air in two days. Note that DeHaven's adversaries were Tonys, one Japanese aircraft that could dive nearly as well as the P-40:

My fifth kill took place on a mission near Madang. We were on a fighter sweep to Hansa Bay with eight P-40s. At 0930 while our flight was at 13,000 we observed approximately fifteen to twenty enemy fighters, Oscars and Tonys, in no particular formation at about 13,000 feet and approaching from the southwest. The Japanese fighters were brown and grey-green and mottled camouflage in color. We dropped belly tanks and turned to attack. Some Tonys dived slightly and proceeded to head for our rear while others came from the side. We dived slightly to pick up speed and I prepared to turn into two Tonys that were closing on my tail. Suddenly two came from our left side, and I thought one was making a pass at my element leader, Captain Brinson. I rolled slightly and expended a two- or three-second burst. To be honest I have no clear recollection of really seeing the Tony take any hits at all. However, the captain had a better view and later stated that although no apparent damage was visible the pilot bailed out and the Tony crashed southwest of Alexishafen. Because of Brinson's report I was credited with the kill.

As I pulled up a Tony behind me shot away my rudder control. With no rudder control I was forced to aileron-roll straight down until my speed was well over 400 miles per hour. On the first or second roll I observed one enemy fighter strike the ground about fifteen miles west of Alexishafen—and later found out that it had been shot down by another one of our pilots. As I neared the ground the Tony was still on my tail. The Japanese pilot was very good at his job and he systematically shot out my hydraulics, radio, and left guns. I straightened out and headed for a low cloud formation against the foothills near our base at Gusap. The Tony was still on me, but he suddenly broke off to the right and pulled away. As I pulled up over the hill I observed four more Tonys passing about 1,000 feet above me. I obviously don't know why the Tony broke off. He was low and might have worried about being jumped by our fighters. But I actually think those four other Tonys saved me. The Tony and P-40 looked a lot alike, which caused a lot of trouble for us in other situations. But this time, it is very likely that the Japanese pilot on my tail thought the Tonys were P-40s and he was more intent on defending himself than finishing me off.

Whatever the case I returned to base. I couldn't get the gear down so I belly-landed. My plane was a total wreck. I have no idea whether that Tony pilot claimed me as a victory, but he certainly had a legitimate right to because my airplane was forced to crash-land and was totally wiped out. I survived, which was the main thing. They gave me some whiskey, which was most welcome, and I think I slept for about twenty-four hours. The Japanese were certainly shooting back that day.

As DeHaven remarks the transition from the P-40 to the much larger and more-powerful P-38 was not without difficulty. Ralph Easterling arrived at 49th Fighter Group in early 1944 and was present when 8th Squadron handed in its P-40s for Lightnings. As he described it, a little aerial culture shock took place:

The P-40 was quite maneuverable and quick on the controls. After we transitioned to P-38s there was some fierce fighting in October and November at Tacloban on Leyte. This Japanese fighter was closing on me in a head-on run. I'm thinking that I have five good guns in the nose and, "Ha, you're stupid, I've got you." Just as he got into range, he rolled over and did a split-S [a type of maneuver—EB]. I thought, "I still got you." Mentally I was back in my P-40. In my P-40 I would have been right on his tail. I followed him down in the '38 and when he pulled out I was still going down; the enemy got clean away. The P-40 was a little like a P-51. You were sitting right in your power plant and it went; you pointed it and it would go about anywhere. It was a nimble little aircraft.

The P-40 remained in a few American units well into 1944. Some Anzac squadrons flew it until war's end. One could argue that the P-40, overshadowed by more capable fighters, was one of the most under-rated aircraft of the war. Yet the plane had its detractors. Jim Morehead flew early-model P-40s in the first desperate months over Java and Darwin when he became one of the first American aces in the Pacific. In his memoirs he quoted Secretary of War Henry Stimson's description of the aircraft as "junk." Later in an interview Morehead moderated this view but made some very interesting observations about the P-40 and the government that produced it:

> If you had the right conditions the P-40 could get the job done. My boys proved that at Darwin. It was rugged and we could dive better than the Zero. And it was the only thing we had at the time. But that's what angers me. Before the war officers assured us that American pilots were flying some of the best planes in the world. Everyone underestimated the Japanese and the Zero was a real shock. A year and a half later we were flying the best planes. But I remain bitter that our government, backed by the most advanced economy in the world, would send their men to war in aircraft that were inferior to that of the enemy. Later P-40s were better but never great. There was no reason we should not have started the war with the best. A lot of good men died because of that.

• • •

A less successful fighter accompanied the P-40 in U.S. Army squadrons early in the war. On paper the Bell P-39 Airacobra was one of the most advanced aircraft in the world. The P-39 was originally designed to please those in the army who wanted a ground-support aircraft that carried some punch but also could defend itself against fighters. They decided that the 37mm cannon—in 1939 the standard caliber for many tanks and antitank guns—would be an ideal weapon. The question was how to get it into an aircraft. The result proposed by Bell was innovative, and the P-39 became the first fighter designed to fit a pre-determined weapon. Because the 37mm cannon and its ammunition were heavy, Bell designers decided that it must fire through the propeller hub. This meant that the cannon was placed where the engine should be. Bell surmounted this obvious difficulty by putting the P-39's engine behind the pilot. Also, it was the first plane equipped with tricycle landing gear. Very small for a U.S. fighter, the P-39 had high wing-loading that promised good speed. Indeed early prototypes of the P-39 were very fast at all altitudes and quite nimble. Much was expected from the new machine, but events dealt it several misfortunes.

By the time the Airacobra entered active service in early 1941, much of the plane's promise had evaporated. The operational P-39 bore little resemblance to the prototype. By the time all of the necessary combat gear, including weaponry, ammunition, self-sealing fuel tanks, and armor, were added, and the little plane's weight soared, it was all too clear that the Airacobra was seriously underpowered. It equaled the Zero in speed at low altitudes, but its performance dropped off quickly the higher it flew. Like the P-40 the Airacobra's Allison engine lacked a supercharger, making the plane extremely sluggish above 15,000 feet. It was less maneuverable than the P-40, much less the Zero, at any altitude. Many P-39 pilots watched helplessly as battles raged above them. By the time they had made a slow climb to the necessary altitude, the combatants were gone. Unless circumstances were very unusual a P-39 offered little threat to a high-flying bomber.

The P-39 suffered its first defeat before entering battle. Using the figures derived from its prototypes, Bell had interested the British in buying several hundred of the new craft. The British wanted a fighter, not a ground-support weapon, so they asked for a 20mm cannon and some other minor modifications. The export version of the P-39 was designated the P-400. (The British preferred names to numbers for their aircraft, so they dubbed the aircraft the "Airacobra," which stuck. The British also named the Mustang and convinced Lockheed that "Lightning" was a better name than "Atlanta" for the P-38.) Much to their disappointment the British found that the P-400 did not even come close to matching specifications, so they canceled the order. When Pearl Harbor came the army was glad to have anything with wings, so it dispatched P-400s and P-39s to the South Pacific.

P-39 pilots were not always pleased with the weapon. Some called it the "Iron Dog." C. L. Jones, a pilot with 39th Squadron, was one of those who arrived in February 1942. He found little to like about the Airacobra:

I always asked for a P-400 because it had a 20mm cannon. I didn't want that bloody 37mm because it jammed all the time. It had many faults, but in early 1942 we could use anything that had guns on it and could fly. We used to say we flew the "speedy, deadly Airacobra: deadly to its own pilot." The army brass ruined the plane when they took the supercharger off the Allison and decided to make it a tank-killer. When the war started it was obviously very quickly that the Zero would be flying higher than 10–12,000 and would get the jump on us. I don't know who made that decision, but whoever it was cost the lives of lots of guys. But we had to make do with what you had. The first thing . . .

absolutely critical with a P-39 was to make sure you saw the enemy first. If you did you could maneuver for a favorable attack or get out or you won't live long enough to do any good. That's not "running away," that was avoiding being outmaneuvered. If Zeros attacked P-39s with an 8,000–10,000 altitude advantage they were totally in the driver's seat.

When the first P-39 squadrons moved up to defend Port Moresby they also had to contend with bad geography. In the first months Allied radar and spotters were either nonexistent or ineffective north of the Owen Stanley Mountains. Japanese raids on Moresby, therefore, were masked by the Stanleys and picked up only during the last leg toward Moresby. It was usually impossible in the short time allowed to get interceptors high enough to contest incoming bombers. Those that tried were often caught by escorting Zeros flying well above the Allied interceptors. (This same problem hurt the Australian No. 75 Squadron of P-40s that first defended Moresby.) The result was one-sided attacks and serious P-39 losses. Edwards Park, a P-39 pilot for 41st Squadron, recalled that "we were so short of airplanes at first that when my squadron went up to New Guinea it had orders to go out to sea and not try to fight on a scramble. Just get off the ground to avoid bombing and strafing attack."

Although many P-39 pilots cursed the army's decision not to turbocharge the Airacobra, it is not clear that the USAAF bungled an opportunity to field a first-class fighter. One of the model's worst faults was a serious lack of range. The P-39 was a small aircraft, and the engine occupied the area that would normally contain the fuel tank. The small wings allowed little space for fuel, especially when fitted with self-sealing tanks. A small drop tank was fitted to the Airacobra, but even then it was dangerous to fly for much longer than two hours. In concept the P-39 was much closer to the short-range fighters of Europe and was poorly suited to Pacific service. In 1942, when Bell introduced the greatly improved P-63 Kingcobra, the USAAF declined to purchase it and sent it to the Soviet Union, where it was far better suited to the close combat of the Eastern Front.

Despite all of its faults the P-39 was a modern fighter and far better than nothing. At altitudes under 10,000 feet it was, on paper anyway, somewhat faster than the Zero. Like all U.S. fighters it was well built and could dive very well. The mixed armament scheme proved troublesome, but the plane could throw out a lot of lead if everything worked. Some of its pilots found things to like in the Airacobra. Edwards Park put it well:

Pilots had a love-hate relationship with the P-39. It depended upon what you going to try to do with it. Aside from being used wrong as an interceptor it wasn't very fast unless you put the nose straight down and then it could go like hell. It didn't have altitude. It also had poor range. Without the belly tank it couldn't make a mission over two hours and that was pushing things. We got an extra hour with a belly tank. When we were up high on scrambles as soon as the nose went down the plane really dropped. But it was a wonderful plane to learn to fly and to learn to turn with. You didn't ever move the controls much through your turns, so you thought about your acrobatics. But it could do some very weird things. If you actually moved the controls you had a very good chance of doing a high-speed stall and a snap roll. It was very delicate. Poorly trained pilots could get in trouble with a P-39. . . .

We were stuck with the P-39s and our job was to survive. . . . We didn't have many aces, but in many ways that's a healthy squadron. The squadrons that were hot on aces sometimes sacrificed things to get those ace figures up. We were businesslike: Get the job done with the tools available.

As the months wore on, P-39 units added to the attrition that was eating away at Japanese units. Furthermore ground support did prove important in New Guinea, and the P-39 proved well suited to that task if not beyond range. In time the 37mm cannon proved more reliable as ground crews learned its mysteries. After that the Airacobra was a good aircraft at attacking the multitude of small ships and barges that the Japanese grew increasingly to depend upon for supplies. The 67th Squadron, often fielding only four planes, on Guadalcanal inflicted serious damage on Japanese ground units opposing the Marines. The 67th Squadron's aircraft proved deadly during the battle for Bloody Ridge later in September and during the various attempts by the Japanese to resupply their forces during daylight. Similar missions with larger numbers of aircraft were flown against the dense cover that protected the Japanese at Buna. In addition, P-39s were available to cover C-47 flights into dangerous places like Dobodura and Wau.

Until August 1942, except for the Battle of the Coral Sea in May, USAAF and Australian pilots flying over Australia and New Guinea bore the brunt of the air war against Japan. When the Marines invaded Guadalcanal an entirely new front opened up in the Solomons. For six months Marine pilots flying from famous Henderson Field on Guadalcanal, as well as comrades in the U.S. Navy operating from Admiral Halsey's aircraft carriers, were in the center of the storm. Fortunately for the United States during late 1942, when the entire campaign was in the balance, navy and Marine pilots had an able fighter—the Grumman F4F Wildcat.

Grumman engineers designed the Wildcat for use on aircraft carriers, a Grumman specialty. Its F3F biplane was the standard navy fighter before the war and a design influence on the Wildcat. The Wildcat, like all carrier-based planes (including the Zero), had to be built in such a way that allowed carrier pilots to cope with the difficult challenges presented by takeoffs and landings on a tiny, tossing flight deck. Knowing this the Grumman designers, like their Japanese counterparts working on the Zero, gave the Wildcat great lift by situating the large wing very far forward on the fuselage. The high lift generated by the large wing area helped the pilot take off quickly and land slowly. It also made the Wildcat the most maneuverable aircraft flown by American pilots in 1942.

Like the Zero the Wildcat paid a penalty for its high lift: slower level speed. High lift, so necessary for low-speed performance, works against pure speed. The only way to compensate for this reality is to increase the power of the engine. Eventually this is what American designers did. When Grumman produced the Wildcat, however, the 1,200-horsepower Pratt and Whitney radial engine was the best available. Note that the Zero possessed even greater lift than did the Wildcat and mounted a somewhat smaller engine. The Zero, however, was nearly 1,600 pounds lighter, giving it a better power-to-weight ratio. Consequently at most altitudes the Zero was slightly faster than the Wildcat. The USN and Grumman, however, helped to even the odds somewhat by fitting the Pratt and Whitney engine with the first of what became the standard mechanically driven two-stage two-speed supercharger, thereby allowing the engine to keep its power up to a reasonable altitude. Like all the early-war fighters, however, the Wildcat was happier below 20,000 feet than above it. Although the Wildcat was nimble for a U.S. warplane, it could not match the Zero's outstanding flight characteristics in most spheres.

Marine and Navy pilots at the time did not, in general, hold the Wildcat in very high esteem. In the carrier engagements and early in the Guadalcanal campaign they felt outclassed when confronting the Zero. In August 1942 Lieutenant Commander John Thach, a hero at Midway and a famous tactician, told his superiors:

> In connection with the performance of the Zero fighter, any success we had against the Zero is not due to performance of the airplane we fly but is the result of the comparatively poor marksmanship on the part of

the Japanese, stupid mistakes made by a few of their pilots and superior marksmanship and teamwork on the part of some of our pilots. . . . This deficiency not only prevents our fighter [the F4F—EB] from properly carrying out its mission but it has had an alarming effect on the morale of the fighter pilots in the Fleet at this time and on those who are going to be sent to the Fleet.

J.A.O. Stub, a pilot with the Marine squadron VMF-121 on Guadalcanal, recalls a pep talk given by one the famous leaders of the Cactus Air Force, Lieutenant Colonel Joe Bauer: "Bauer was a splendid leader and pilot. When comparing the Zero with the F4F, Bauer said, 'A Zero can go faster than you can, it climbs faster than you can, and it can outmaneuver you. Aside from those things, you've got a better airplane.'" Yet in time the Wildcat showed some very formidable features. For carrier use the F4F was extremely stable, thus keeping down the accidental losses that plagued carrier operations. Interesting testimony on this comes from John Herbert, a British pilot who flew off of HMS *Victorious*. In early 1943 the Royal Navy agreed to lend *Victorious* to Admiral Halsey in the South Pacific so the battle-scarred *Enterprise* could receive a full refit on the West Coast. By this time Fleet Air Arm was largely equipped with F4Fs, which it called the "Martlet." Later Herbert flew ground-support missions from an escort carrier in the Mediterranean. Herbert was a fan of Grumman's fighter:

Concerning the Wildcat I echo the line of one of our best test pilots—it was probably the finest deck-landing naval aircraft ever built. It wasn't much good on land because the wheels were narrow, so if you had a slight crosswind and weren't that good you could ground-loop it very easily. But for deck landing visibility was superb. I once landed a Wildcat with a hole in one wing big enough to put my desk through. I've landed with most of the tail shot away and with holes all over it, and bits dripping out of the engine, and still the bloody thing flew. It was incredibly good. The Spitfire was the opposite. On land the Spitfire V was a splendid aircraft. When they tried to put it on board carrier, where it was called the Seafire, it just didn't have the strength. The Royal Navy employed many American aircraft and the pilots appreciated them greatly.

When the Marine aviators moved to Guadalcanal they brought Wildcats, and it was at Henderson Field and Fighter One that they gained their greatest fame. As VMF-121 veteran Roger Haberman recalled, the transition from carrier to land was not completely smooth:

The Wildcat was not well suited for the fight at Guadalcanal. It had a bunch of weight in the back that we could have dispensed with very nicely. It was beefed up for carrier landings in the rear and we didn't need it. But there wasn't anything to be done in that regard. So because of this weight we'd work like hell to climb to 23,000–24,000 feet. At that altitude when you make a turn you lose 1,000 feet, and it's very easy to stall out. In theory the F4F had a higher service ceiling but not in practice. You'd look up and there sit the Japs at 30,000 looking right down your gazoo. A real fun time. You couldn't get that bird much higher than 24,000: not you, not Jesus, nobody. The bird wouldn't go any higher.

Yet the Wildcat, when flown well, was the Zero's equal. Weight and horsepower both help in a dive. Although the P-40 was superior to all fighters flying in the Pacific during 1942 in that vital attribute, the Wildcat could outdive the Zero. The Wildcat, like the Zero, was also a very stable design, lacking particularly dangerous idiosyncrasies. Most Wildcats mounted six .50-caliber machine guns, an excellent weapon system against Japanese fighters. In sum the Wildcat was a very well balanced aircraft: Adequate in speed, nimble, and well armed, it could absorb great punishment.

Thomas Furlow, one of Haberman's squadronmates, offered measured praise to the fighter he flew at Guadalcanal:

The Wildcat was a simple plane. You didn't really have to monitor much. The air-cooled engine was a real advantage. I saw many planes that came in that had been hit, cylinders missing, shot off. And the plane got back. An inline engine went down fast if the coolant was damaged. And you had to crank the landing gear up by hand. It was hard to fly formation and crank the thing—you'd be looking down for the crank and looking around at other aircraft. And later you had to crank it down. The tail wheel stayed down all the time. But it was a reliable way to lower gear. I don't remember anyone coming in on their belly because the gear wouldn't go down. It was extremely forgiving except for the ground loops. And also extremely rugged. It had good armor plating and was beautifully put together. Grumman knew how to make tough planes. You couldn't pull the wings off it in maneuver or anything like that.

Furlow often flew wing for Joe Foss, who, flying the Wildcat, became the Marines' highest-scoring ace. Foss likewise praised the toughness of the F4F:

Even though the Japs had us outnumbered, they didn't want to mix it up close. They realized that we'd fight like a screeching cat in a dark bag with a snake in it. They knew they might get hit, so they'd hesitate—stay on the outside and try to make a jab at us. If I'd have been directing their activities I wouldn't have gotten into our group at all. I would have made high-speed runs to pick off U.S. planes from the outside. I'd be darned if I'd ever gotten tangled up close with our planes. We had six .50-caliber machine guns, and the enemy knew if they got caught and were clobbered that their machine was liable to blow up. Our pilots had the advantage of worrying a lot less about that. We'd take a lot of lead all the time. People have asked me, "Wouldn't you rather have had a P-51?" and I'd say, "No way." With the number of times that I got whacked, if I'd had something that leaked I'd have been out of action in a hurry with a frozen engine. The Wildcat came from what we called "Grumman Iron Works."

As J.A.O. Stub points out, one of the Wildcat's great strengths was its superior dive speed over the Zero, allowing many Allied pilots to escape destruction: "The F4F was slow and it had those mushy Grumman ailerons. But it was rugged and it could dive. In a hard dive the drag would build up, but a pilot could make an aileron turn. At very high speed, the Zero could barely maneuver. So, if you changed direction with your nose down, the Zero couldn't follow you." Additional testimony to the Wildcat's capabilities comes from Japanese ace Saburo Sakai. Sakai recalled his first encounter with a Wildcat, which took place near Guadalcanal:

I realized that the Grumman's fighting performance far exceeded that of any American, Dutch, or Chinese fighter planes, but I had full confidence in my ability. For some strange reason, even after I had poured about five or six hundred rounds of ammunition directly into the Grumman, the aeroplane did not fall, but kept on flying. I thought this very odd—it had never happened before—and closed the distance between the two aeroplanes until I could almost reach out and touch the Grumman. To my surprise, his rudder and tail were ripped to shreds, looking like an old torn piece of "rag." . . .

[A short while later] I saw them about 1,500 feet below me—a single Wildcat pursued by three Zeros, firing in short bursts at the frantic Japanese planes. All four planes were in a wild dogfight, flying tight left spirals. The Zeros should have been able to take the lone Grumman without any trouble, but every time a Zero caught the Wildcat before its guns the enemy plane flipped away wildly and came out again on the tail of the Zero. I had never seen such flying before.

Sakai came to the aid of his comrades, and a very rare event soon took place: a classic one-on-one dogfight. After fierce battle during which, according to Sakai, "my heart pounded wildly, my head felt as it if it weighed a ton," the Japanese ace gained the advantage:

> When I was only fifty yards away, the Wildcat broke out of his loop
> and astonished me by flying straight and level. At this distance I would
> not need the cannon: I pumped 200 rounds into the Grumman's
> cockpit, watching the bullets chewing the thin metal skin and shattering
> the glass. I could not believe what I saw: The Wildcat continued flying
> almost as if nothing had happened. A Zero which had taken that many
> bullets would have been a ball of fire by now.

•   •   •

At the end of 1942 the American command began deploying a second generation of fighters to units throughout the world. In Europe improved models of the P-51 Mustang and P-47 Thunderbolt started to arrive, slowly giving American pilots a qualitative edge over their German opponents. Yet it was in the Southwest Pacific cauldron where American pilots first employed their new aircraft with deadly effect.

It is fitting that the hard-pressed Marine pilots at Henderson Field on Guadalcanal were among the first to receive substantial shipments of one of the new models, the Vought F4U Corsair. (The navy used the letter *F* to designate "fighter." Although the army discarded the old term "pursuit" in favor of "fighter" early in 1941, it continued to designate fighters using the letter *P* for "pursuit"; the P-40 and P-38 are examples.)

American pilots first approached the Corsair with extremely mixed feelings. Such a reaction was most understandable, as the Corsair was a unique-looking aircraft with an unusual history. In 1939 the USN was eager to develop an airplane powered by a new, extremely powerful 2,000-horsepower radial engine being tested by Pratt and Whitney; naturally the craft had to be able to fly from a carrier. The navy favored lighter machines for carrier work, but the new engine was heavy. The answer to this quandary, developed by Vought, was to marry the massive new engine with an airframe that by U.S. standards was as light as possible. The resulting fighter, the F4U Corsair, possessed an unmistakable appearance. Vought designers fitted the Corsair with an angled gull wing to improve its landing characteristics and to allow ground clearance for its huge propeller. Because of the wing design there was not room enough to fit six machine guns as well as large fuel tanks inside the wing. Consequently designers repositioned the fuel tanks toward the front of the fuselage, and the cockpit was placed very far aft, almost behind the wing, giving the craft an extremely long nose. (Corsair pilots sometimes called their plane "Hose-nose"; for some reason this graceful machine also acquired the nickname "Hog.") The pilot sat almost on the floor and operated his rudder peddles with his legs outstretched. One pilot said he felt like a "chariot rider steering a team of horses." This factor in turn restricted the pilot's forward vision when approaching a carrier and made it hard to see the landing signal officer, the man who used signal flags to guide pilots on the final approach to the flight deck.

Pacific veterans badly wanted a new aircraft that would give them a decisive edge over the Zero. Most new pilots—who constituted the vast majority of the navy and Marine air arms early in the war—wanted to get into the war with a hot fighter. However, before large-scale deployment began for the Corsair, scuttlebutt had already tagged it as the "ensign eliminator." The rookies, having nothing to compare it to and somewhat bewildered by any fighter, probably did not single out the F4U for anxiety. Yet veteran pilots knew how many losses came from accidents and how important it was for a pilot to concentrate on the business at hand during combat instead of pondering potential operational failures. So all were delighted at the prospect of a very fast fighter with superior range to the Wildcat. Yet the news that the F4U was a problem child caused some heartburn among the knowledgeable. Veteran pilot Captain Tom Blackburn was given command of a new squadron, the soon-to-be-famous VF-17 "Jolly Rogers," in December 1942. VF-17 was intended for one of the new *Essex*-class carriers and was to employ the Corsair. As Blackburn wrote in his memoirs, "I quickly learned that the F4U was an airplane the navy's own flight-test activities regarded with much trepidation and whose characteristics were cloaked in mystery and, to some degree, misinformation."

Blackburn's information was not all wrong. Everything about the Corsair was new, including its monstrous 2,000-horsepower R-2800 Pratt and Whitney radial. Typical for the prewar and early-war periods, Corsair development was done by a tiny number of people, and disturbing problems of all sorts cropped up. A few crashes (not unusual for any new machine) and many near catastrophes kept the test pilots unusually alert. A particularly ominous feature of the F4U prototype, never to be totally solved, was difficult control and a tendency to stall at low speeds on landing approach. To say the least, this was not an attribute any carrier pilot would seek and was potentially dangerous anywhere. All Corsair pilots were taught to stay alert when flying "low and slow." Unlike the Wildcat the Corsair was not a forgiving warplane.

One problem had nothing to do with the Vought design. As test pilots in other very fast fighters around the world were discovering, the field of aerodynamics was confronting the phenomenon of compressibility. This potentially fatal challenge faced both test pilots and combat pilots alike, and it is worth some examination. As an aircraft approaches the speed of sound unusual things happen to the airflow over the plane's surfaces. This was no problem in level flight because no World War II aircraft could approach Mach speed. (Mach 1 is 725 miles per hour at sea level but only 663 miles per hour at 25,000 feet.) However, when an aircraft went into a power dive from high altitude all bets were off. The problem was not just that the new generation of airplanes was faster; these fighters also flew higher, and as air temperature decreases so does the speed of sound. This meant it was easier to experience compressibility at the higher altitudes in which the new generation was designed to operate. (Earlier fighters like the P-40 rarely suffered this problem because they so rarely began a nose-over dive at high altitude.)

Boone Guyton was a lead test pilot in the Corsair program at Vought and described the principle of compressibility:

> When an airplane flies through the air, there are regions where the local airstream velocity relative to the aircraft's surface is greater than the speed of the airplane. Like near the front of the fuselage, over the upper surfaces of the wings, over the front half of the tail surfaces. This local velocity is greatest over the leading edge of the wing when the wing is producing lift, as it must do in a dive recovery.
>
> As the airplane speed gets higher, and closer to the speed of sound, local sonic velocities—even supersonic velocities—can occur at those points. When this happens, the affected airplane part undergoes a change. Local shock waves form at the beginning of the supersonic region. Pressures from the rear cannot be transmitted forward through shock wave. Flow can separate from surface, become oscillatory, cause shaking and buffeting of that part of the airplane.

In practice this meant that during a high-speed power dive, particularly if started from high altitude, the pilot would encounter severe

buffeting and a near loss of control of the aircraft. Several test pilots
around the world had simply buried their aircraft into the earth, leaving designers wondering what had gone wrong. Other aircraft merely
disintegrated under the strain. The problem was that such calamities
could be the result of any number of causes. In any case the whitecoats
at Vought and other companies were beginning to catch on. The big
question was whether a given airplane was strong enough to take the
structural stress and whether the pilot could stand the tremendous effort required to regain stick control and then stay conscious as his
body was assaulted by heavy G-forces during pullout. Guyton had already survived one dangerous encounter with compressibility early in
the program without knowing its cause. With the navy putting pressure on Vought, its engineers guessed that the Corsair was stout
enough to handle the stress and that when the aircraft lost altitude the
increasing air temperature (which raised the speed of sound) would return control to the pilot. It was up to Guyton and others like him to
find out whether this was in fact true. Assured by Vought design wizard William Schoolfield that getting to lower altitude would do the
trick, Guyton began a series of dive tests. One began at 28,000 feet
and served as an excellent example of compressibility and the wisdom
of Vought's engineers:

> As the Corsair hurtled toward earth, I darted glances at the trembling
> instrument panel, watching for any clue of incipient failure.
> . . . Suddenly the stick was trembling in my hands, only this time the
> amplitude was larger. The airplane began shuddering hard as the
> buffeting about the tail increased. My alarm bell went off. Self-
> preservation took over. Immediately I pulled back on the stick with
> both hands, but it yielded little and the nose wasn't coming up. As I
> strained, pulling harder, the shuddering increased and it felt like the
> airplane was in a high speed stall. I wanted to release it from the
> punishment, but that would put us steeper. Tightening my grip on the
> stick, I held the shaking elevators where they were, and fought the
> apprehension arising within me. The wetness inside my tight oxygen
> mask gathered about my mouth. I thought, *God, Schoolfield, I hope
> you're right*. Then abruptly, all of the buffeting slackened as though by
> command. My bulging eyes caught the white needle spinning backward.
> Twelve thousand feet—or was it ten? Pure guesstimate. Like a gift from
> the sky I felt the controls smooth out as the elevator took hold. I pulled
> hard, the nose came up fast—and I began to swallow again. Bottoming
> out at 3,500 feet, the Corsair roared over the island and out across the
> water. Does one ever get used to abhorrent fear?

Engineers could alleviate the problem somewhat by smoothing out as many of the problem surfaces as possible. (This was one great advantage held by the Mustang's famous laminar-flow wing.) The P-38, with its great weight, suffered seriously from this difficulty, and Lockheed decided to install dive brakes to slow the fighter's descent. However, this was no real answer, because during an emergency speed was what every pilot needed to survive. No smart pilot went into a high-speed dive without reason. When one was required, any good pilot knew how much he could ask of the machine. Buffeting and temporary loss of control were inevitable, yet American pilots could be reasonably certain that their planes would hold together. Ultimately it was up to the pilot to complete the dive maneuver by pulling out. One can see why careful speed control and "smooth" flying were emphasized by instructors.

The Corsair was not ready for fleet deployment in late 1942, but the USN was desperate for a better fighter. For a long time rumors flew that the entire project would be scrapped in favor of Grumman's new fighter, the F6F Hellcat. Yet the F4U's potential was great, and the navy never carried out the threat. However, the heat was on, and Vought delivered a production model of the Corsair well before the bugs had been worked out. Blackburn's VF-17 was one of the Corsair squadrons assigned to *Bunker Hill*, one of the cherished *Essex*-class carriers. Blackburn's squadron, well enough trained in the navy way, largely comprised new pilots, who quickly learned that the F4U was prone to bouncing during landing. They did not like its performance at low speed and the poor visibility caused by the long nose. There was a very serious shortage of spare parts and an equally great shortage of ground crews that knew the idiosyncrasies of the new plane. Consequently the Corsair was often on the ground awaiting service of uneven quality. It also tended to leak oil, which would foul the windshield. A safety device intended to prevent the flaps from extending at high speed often failed on approach, causing the flaps to extend prematurely and a serious lack of lift when needed most. The storage battery, located behind the cockpit, had the nasty habit of boiling over. And an error in the tailhook design—a very small error in a simple piece of equipment—caused the type of accident that chilled the heart of any carrier skipper. Blackburn described the result:

> After touchdowns with not unreasonable bounces, several of our planes surged ahead undecelerated instead of being arrested. [In other words the tailhook did not hold firm on the arrestor wires.—EB] Hog after Hog, deployed in perfect three point attitude, pranged into the barrier

cables at around 60 knots. Almost every time, the runaway went up
and over in the barrier, strewing expensive debris in all directions, often
as not breaking in two at the engine mount. Miraculously, there were
no pilot injuries.

Blackburn and all concerned on *Bunker Hill* concluded the obvious:
The Corsair was, as Blackburn put it, "by no stretch of the imagination carrier ready." Blackburn also knew that the spare parts situation
was bleak, as Vought had rushed into production. However, the Corsair was already reaching Marine squadrons, and too much had been
invested to junk the project. Blackburn and his men had seen the
fighter at its best in most flights. He was offered the opportunity to
leave the carrier and operate his squadron from land. If he declined,
VF-17 would be reequipped with F6F Hellcats. Under normal circumstances, in the navy world, this was a demotion, but Blackburn believed that his men were flying a tremendous aircraft and accepted the
opportunity to stick with the Corsair—even if that meant flying from
land bases. With this decision Blackburn and his men entered history
as the famous Jolly Rogers, serving with great distinction in the
Solomons.

The Corsair's problems on carrier decks were conversely wonderful
tidings for the Marines. Whatever its difficulties—many of which were
ironed out quickly—the Corsair was the fastest aircraft in the Pacific,
capable of speeds well over 400 miles per hour. Vought had put great
work into its ailerons, and the plane had an excellent roll rate. It was
very tough and well armed. The Corps was accustomed to receiving
equipment that the navy did not want, and for once it was given a genuinely great weapon. Marine pilot J.A.O. Stub commented:

> I was a Marine and had little good to say about the navy. I am certain
> that had the admirals been given the opportunity they would have stuck
> us with Hellcats or something worse. But because they couldn't solve
> the relatively simple problems of getting the Corsair carrier-ready, we
> were given a tremendous airplane. The Corsair took some care, but it
> was a great fighter. It was the fastest plane in the theater, handled
> beautifully, and could outroll the Hellcat with ease. It was also a solid
> plane and could take punishment. It was a wonderful weapon and we
> were delighted to get it.

Like Stub, other Marine veterans of a tour at Guadalcanal with
Wildcats were particularly impressed with the Corsair when they returned to the South Pacific. Roger Haberman recalled:

When I came back from overseas several of us ran a training section at El Toro. We run about thirty-five guys through per class. Then to Mojave and affiliated with VMO-251, all trained in Grummans. We trained them in Corsairs and I know that from experience that everyone that went from a Wildcat to a Corsair just loved it. You had a 2,000-horsepower engine, and the thing handles like a baby buggy. . . . We taught these guys to land it nose-up, use their peripheral vision, and look straight ahead at the instrument panel. We had no problem at all. In the officers' club later the opinion was 1,000 percent that they loved the aircraft and looked forward to using it. Not a negative word at all.

By the time the Corsair was deployed to Guadalcanal, the great battle there was over and the Allies were preparing for an offensive. The first squadrons were still green and had not yet developed combat techniques appropriate for their aircraft. VMF-124 was deployed in late January, and the men were not acclimated to the theater gradually: On February 14 they escorted B-24 Liberator heavy bombers on a strike against the major Japanese base at Buin, near Bougainville. (Wildcats could not have escorted bombers this far, foreshadowing ominous events for the Japanese.) The U.S. formation was hit hard by defending Zeros and lost two Corsairs, four new P-38s, two P-40s, and two Liberators. The Japanese lost three defenders, one due to a collision with a Corsair. The pilots of VMF-124 remembered this engagement as the St. Valentine's Day Massacre.

This poor beginning was rarely repeated. Learning quickly that their altitude advantage multiplied their superiority in speed, Corsair units quickly began to shred Japanese opposition despite the fact that they faced the disadvantage of flying over enemy territory. A few years after the war Commander Masatake Okumiya, one of Japan's leading tactical leaders in the Solomon campaign, and Jiro Horikoshi assessed the impact of the Corsair: "In a short period the excellent qualities of the Corsair became only too evident, and the enemy rapidly increased Corsair fighter strength in the Solomons campaign. . . . Faster than the Zero in level flight and capable of infinitely greater diving speeds, the Corsairs soon proved to be a great nuisance to our fighters. . . . The Corsair was the first single-engine fighter which clearly surpassed the Zero in performance."

By mid-1944 the navy was having second thoughts about the Corsair. Later in the war the USN developed various techniques to overcome the Corsair's problems, and by 1945 the Corsair was flying from carriers throughout the Pacific (often in Marine squadrons). Naval commanders were most wise to reevaluate the situation, for the Corsair in many respects was the greatest fighter produced in World War II by any nation. Quickly it proved superior to the famous Hellcat in many ways and appeared increasingly on carriers. Because the Corsair proved capable of handling a stream of design modifications, it stayed in production for years, and hundreds of USN and Marine pilots flew it during the Korean War. The Corsair remained in reserve service through the early 1960s.

Unfortunately for Japan the Corsair did not arrive alone. While Corsairs began arriving at Guadalcanal the army started deploying one of its new fighters to the South Pacific—the Lockheed P-38 Lightning (actually a few P-38s had arrived in theater first, in December 1942). Six months later several squadrons were flying the Lightning. By the end of 1943 the P-38 was the backbone of the USAAF fighter arm in the Pacific. Unlike the Corsair, which enjoyed a long postwar career, the Lightning's tour of duty did not extend beyond hostilities. Yet rarely in the history of modern warfare has a weapon been better suited to its time and place than the Lightning in the Pacific. The P-38 was the weapon of choice for some of America's greatest aces during World War II. 5th USAAF P-38s swept the Japanese from New Guinea, and 13th USAAF Lightning pilots in the Solomons helped make that area a graveyard for the JNAF. Although it had drawbacks that hampered its effectiveness in Europe, its Pacific service helped make it one of America's most successful World War II fighters.

The Lightning's road from drafting table to battlefield was unusual, more so even than the Corsair. In 1937 the army issued specifications for an interceptor capable of high-speed flight at both sea level and at 20,000 feet. When radar was still in its infancy, reaching altitude quickly was critical. Therefore the fighter also had to reach 20,000 feet in six minutes. Many designers felt the army was asking them to break the laws of physics given the engines then available. A design team at Lockheed, however, proposed a solution to the problem that eventually proved as brilliant as it was unorthodox. Lockheed developed a prototype of a two-engine fighter with twin tails. The pilot flew in a small copula attached to the wing bridging between the two engines; it was as though the aircraft had two fuselages. The design doubled the engine power of the Allison power plant chosen without doubling the size of the aircraft. The twin tails allowed the large plane to maneuver very well at high speed. No aircraft in the world was configured in this manner, and the Lightning possessed an unmistakable silhouette.

Like the P-39 Airacobra the P-38 prototype performed very well. However, as the craft took on armament, avionics, and the essentials of an operational fighter its performance dropped off alarmingly. The Allison engine that appeared adequate in 1938 had become seriously underpowered by 1941 and threatened to cripple another promising design. The British canceled a large order for P-38s, finding them nearly worthless above 15,000 feet. The P-38 was saved by the addition of turbosuperchargers to the 1,225-horsepower Allison engines. However, as a scathing (and admirable, for its day) internal Lockheed report written early during the war revealed, many of the fighter's problems were due to serious errors in management. The top designers were among the best in the business, but a radical design like the P-38 required a large team of very good people. Unfortunately, as Lockheed admitted, many of its best personnel were shifted to lucrative export models like the Hudson. Their replacements were often green, and blunders in simple matters required continual reworking of components. The Lockheed report indicates that large-scale delivery of the P-38 was set back at least nine months simply due to bad management and elementary design failures. Implicit in the report is that the delay was even worse. Put another way, had Lockheed concentrated its best people on the P-38 and kept a tighter hand on the tiller, the Zeros over Darwin in early 1942 might well have met Lightnings instead of P-40s. Nevertheless, as Lockheed's management acknowledged, the army's need for a modern fighter was so great that the military had little choice but wait until the aircraft was ready.

The P-38F, the first model sent to the Pacific in quantity, ultimately proved a devastating fighter. Lockheed had performed brilliantly, creating the only successful twin-engine fighter of the war. It could attain roughly 400 miles per hour and possessed excellent performance above 20,000 feet. Large and heavy, the Lightning was not a nimble aircraft, yet considering its size it had a reasonably good turning radius and a decent overall rate of roll. However, the twin-engine design carried a subtle disadvantage while rolling. Because the ailerons had to move the weight of an engine as well as the wing, simple inertia made the initial rate of roll slow, which hurt the P-38 in Europe more than in the Pacific. Yet at high speeds, like other U.S. fighters the P-38 could turn inside a Zero, particularly at high altitudes. Because of brute power, the Lightning had an excellent rate of climb and could outdive the Zero. The propellers were set to turn in the opposite direction, negating the torque found in single-engine piston-driven machines. The Lightning, therefore, was unusually stable during normal flight. Unassisted the P-38's range (roughly 400 miles) was superior to other U.S. fighters but still less than desirable. However, because the aircraft had so much power it could carry a sizeable external load, including bombs (later rockets) or a drop tank. When engineers fitted large drop tanks to the P-38 it had excellent range indeed. In addition the strange configuration carried a unique advantage. Because the pilot's compartment was not burdened with an engine, Lockheed designers were able to mount all of the weapons in the nose: A pilot could almost point the aircraft and have a reasonable chance of scoring a hit. Mounting four .50-caliber machine guns and a 20mm cannon, the Lightning would strike with tremendous power. Every weakness of Japanese aircraft corresponded to a strong point possessed by the P-38. Overall the Lightning became an excellent weapon in its environment.

The P-38's graceful but unusual shape and great size impressed the airmen when they first gazed upon it. Even veteran combat pilots were struck by their new weapon. Robert DeHaven recalled meeting the P-38:

> The P-38 was very unusual. Imagine what I felt when first climbing on board that airplane. Sitting on that tricycle landing gear, it was very high off the ground. There was a stepladder that dropped out of the tail end of the fuselage pod, and you took two steps up this ladder and the third step was onto the wing next to the canopy. I remember doing that with a parachute on, nimbly going up that ladder. In the last few years I've been invited by the Confederate Air Force to sit in the cockpit of a '38. Even without a parachute I had to use two hands to get up that stupid ladder, and I'd probably still be struggling if somebody hadn't pushed me from behind. It was a good-sized airplane. In comparison the P-39 was a midget, almost like a toy.

The early examples deployed had some disadvantages, perhaps some imaginary but many real. Pilots worried that the twin booms would make a bailout more hazardous. Whether their fears were justified is difficult to document, but one can see why many pilots believed it. The twin engines proved good and bad. 5th USAAF commander General Kenney was a tremendous booster of the P-38 and found the two-engine configuration one of the aircraft's strong features. Please note that Kenney's observations concerning sharks were quite true:

> I wanted the P-38 in the Pacific because of the long distances, but not only long distances. You look down from the cockpit and you can see schools of sharks swimming around. They never look healthy to a man flying over them. Say we were going into a combat and you go in with a P-51, a 100-percent warplane: Give it a status of 100 for combat. The pilot starts out with a rating of 100. But by the time he gets four or five

hundred miles out over the ocean his morale has been going down steadily by looking at that water down there, and my guess was that he would arrive at combat about a 50-percent-efficient pilot. So the total score of pilot and plane is 150. Now the P-38 is not a bad combat airplane—I'd give it a rating of 75 as compared to the P-51, easily—maybe more than that—but give it 75. But the pilot arrives there 100 percent—he's just as good as when he took off because he knows one of those big fans can bring him home. He's got two engines. So his score—his fighting score is 175 against the other's 150. And you could hang gasoline on them. We put two 3,000-gallon tanks on those wings. One time we took off, flew 1,200 nautical miles, and fought over the target for forty minutes and then came home. Now some of them ran out of gas taxiing back on the runway, but still they all got back—we didn't lose a single airplane because of fuel. [General Kenney was noted for overstatement. He was correct that extra range increased safety, but many P–38s, like all models, were missing in action, some undoubtedly due to getting lost and running out of fuel.—EB]

In early summer 1943 Perry Dahl began his tour in the illustrious 475th Fighter Group, nicknamed "Satan's Angels." Interviewed thirty years later, after a varied flying career in the U.S. Air Force, Dahl had lost none of his respect for the Lightning. Although several nations tried to develop a twin-engine fighter, the P-38 was the only successful example to serve in the war. (Some of the most advanced modern warplanes now carry twin jet engines.) As Dahl recalls, the configuration added an extra level to the durability that characterized all American fighters: "The airplane was really good in the Pacific because of the twin engines. We flew over miles and miles of water. I had twelve-hour missions in the airplane, unrefueled, across the China Sea and back, over 1,000 miles each way. That's a long time to be sitting in an airplane, and in a single engine airplane if something happens with one engine..." As Dahl pointed out, a combat pilot might put his extra power plant to unusual use and limp home on one engine:

One day I was flying and I was watching a flight of Zeros and waiting for them to attack: They were trying to maneuver to get around to the sun. I was watching them intently when I saw this flash out of my peripheral vision. There was another Zero, twenty yards off my other wing pounding at me. I didn't have time to do anything so I just threw that engine up into him, and he just shot the bejeezus out of it. I just threw that engine up and let it take all the hits. I kept everything at full power and I just screamed for the deck and went home. After all of the cooling ran out of that right engine, I shut her down and went home on the other engine. In a single-engine airplane he would have had me. I got home with eighty-four holes in the airplane.

Yet the configuration had some disadvantages. With two engines instead of one, maintenance was more difficult. A 5th USAAF P-40 squadron was given twenty-four aircraft, although it was a rare day when all could fly. A P-38 squadron shrank to twenty because of the extra demands placed on the ground crew. In addition, its size made it a bigger target. No major matter during air combat, this became important during ground attack, which all fighters undertook as the months went on. Two engines doubled the chance that an enemy round could start a fire—almost always a disaster. Early-model P-38s had only one generator; if it failed the other engine would continue to operate, but all electoral systems failed, causing an emergency situation.

Perhaps the biggest problem with the twin engines arose during takeoff and landing. If things went well the P-38 had no problems on a good field, but the complex engines were most prone to shutdown during takeoff. With its counterrotating props, which made the P-38 such an excellent aircraft when operating properly, one can imagine the wicked torque and low power that confronted a pilot if an engine failed on takeoff. An experienced hand could handle the situation, a familiar enough event to bomber pilots. However, many fresh pilots were not at their best facing this problem, which would strike with extraordinary rapidity. Lockheed claimed the P-38 was ready to fly on one engine, but Robert DeHaven expressed reservations:

One of the great drawbacks of the early P-38s was that the aircraft was virtually unmanageable on a single engine in the hands of a young, low-flying-time, inexperienced pilot. This problem was bad enough that they actually grounded the plane in the Eighth Air Force because of one-engine fatalities. If an engine quit on takeoff there was great danger. I flew the '38 and I loved it. It was a marvelous gun platform. But if Mr. Lockheed had intended that airplane to fly on one engine he wouldn't have installed two. The company claimed it would fly as well on one engine as two, but that was a big hmmm ... maybe—especially on takeoff or landing.

Early P-38 pilots found that because of its great speed and weight (well over twice that of a Zero and, if fully loaded, nearly that of a Betty) it was extremely vulnerable to the compressibility problem that bedeviled all second-generation fighters. To make matters worse, the airflow surfaces were multiplied by the aircraft's configuration. In practice this meant that pilots had to be very careful with a P-38 in a high-speed dive. Like all U.S. aircraft it was well built and could out-dive a Zero. However, pilots soon learned that the simple tactic of putting the nose down, which worked so well in the P-40, could lead to catastrophe in a P-38. Lockheed eventually put dive brakes on the Lightning (rather like a dive-bomber) and gave the fighter hydrauli-cally boosted ailerons. The brakes might save a pilot if he got into an overly ambitious dive, but the Lightning would never dive as fast as other U.S. planes. The new ailerons improved the high-speed roll of the P-38, but some pilots believed it robbed the aircraft of "feel" on landing. The main lesson learned by wise Lightning pilots was to ac-cept the aircraft's failings and concentrate on its strengths. As was typ-ical it took some time before pilots realized that the P-38 was a differ-ent bird than those before it. Robert DeHaven commented on the subject:

> The P-38 was very fast and had good firepower. That gave a lot of people a lot of false confidence when they first went to P-38s. Their limitations on tactics were the same as those we were accustomed to in P-40s but even more so. You did not go looking for a close-in dogfight with an Oscar or Zero. At many altitudes you could outturn a P-38 in a P-40. Japanese fighters were quicker yet at slow speed. But new pilots did not always realize the consequences. If the speed bled off a P-38, which happened very easily, it could be in very serious trouble against a Japanese fighter. Many of our men found out the hard way, particularly when we first started receiving them.

Yet whatever its design trade-offs, the Lightning quickly proved deadly against Japanese targets in the Pacific. Those accustomed to the flawed P-39 found the transition something like magic. C. L. Jones em-braced the P-38 with no qualifications: "With the P-38 you found a target and fired." This was thanks to one of the P-38's best features: the great firepower mounted in the center of the cupola.

Thus with an advantage in altitude, speed, climb rate, and firepower, it is no wonder that the P-38 became the standard USAAF fighter; in experienced hands it became a dreadful foe to Japanese fighters and could destroy a Japanese bomber in quick order. After the war Lieu-tenant Commander Mitsugu Kofukuda, who commanded the Japanese Sixth Air Corps near Bougainville, commented on the vicious quandary faced by Japanese fighters when facing the P-38:

Soon after their introduction to combat, the big, heavy P-38 fighters learned to take advantage of their excellent high altitude speed and performance and of their superior diving speed. They adopted the tactics of diving from high altitude, slashing into the Zero formations with their heavy machine guns and cannon, and zooming upwards in a climb no Zero could hope to match. Taking every advantage of their superior high-altitude performance and high speed, they were rarely caught in a position in which they could be forced to engage in close-in fighting. . . . On some occasions P-38 formations would descend from their usual great altitude in high-speed formation dives; the initial attacking wave scattered the Zeros. Other formations would follow from their vantage points to rip through the disorganized Zero fighters, inflicting unexpectedly heavy losses.

Masatake Okumiya, another officer at Rabaul, described the P-38 as "an enemy of terrifying effectiveness."

The spring of 1943 was one of triumph for the Allies at New Guinea. Warplanes from Fifth Air Force, joined by a growing and effective Australian cohort, had slowly driven the Japanese over to the defensive. In March the Allies scored a stunning victory in the Battle of the Bismarck Sea. However, such favorable trends covered a serious problem: Although Allied ground crews were steadily improving their skills, a World War II fighter could stand only so much wear and tear before losing its effectiveness and becoming dangerous. Simply put the aircraft sent to Australia and New Guinea during 1942 were tiring out—and quickly. In addition offensive operations required aircraft with greater range than the P-39 and P-40 could provide, and the supply of P-38s headed for the theater was going to be limited for the immediate future. Yet General Kenney was desperate for more aircraft, particularly models that could outperform Japanese opponents. On a trip to Washington Kenney pressed his case with Hap Arnold and President Roosevelt; he was promised extra P-38s, but not in the numbers he wished. He was also offered a fighter group of new Republic P-47 Thunderbolts, which Kenney took without hesitation.

Many 5th USAAF officers, including Colonel Paul Wurtsmith, head of 5th USAAF Fighter Command, openly grumbled at the prospect. The P-47, along with the P-38, had been intended, in the prewar period, to serve as the USAAF's answer to modern European fighters. As with the Lightning, development proved more difficult than expected. Also like so many new fighters the initial debut in Europe disappointed everyone. By this time the remarkable Merlin-powered P-51, although still not recognized for the masterpiece it was, was in the pipeline, and the P-47 looked like a white elephant to some. This, of course, was the reason that Arnold was willing to part with some for operations in the Pacific.

If doubters of the F4U Corsair appear misguided in retrospect, this is even more true of officers who sold the Jug short (the nickname "Jug" stuck like glue among P-47 pilots). It is easy enough to see why the P-47 would have aroused skepticism. To begin the Jug did not look like a fighter, and no one would accuse the P-47 of possessing beauty. What struck one and all was its size—nearly twice that of the P-40. When the first Jugs arrived in Australia astonished RAAF ground crewman asked a U.S. pilot, "Where is the rest of the crew?" Even with the redoubtable Pratt and Whitney R-2800 radial power plant, it was difficult to believe that a craft so large and heavy could climb and maneuver like a fighter should. The doubters were correct on both scores: The Jug had a poor climb rate and was clumsy while traveling low and slow. To make matters worse, although the Jug carried considerably more fuel than a P-40, the weight and poor fuel economy meant the early P-47's range did not surpass even the P-40's. An overstuffed, clumsy aircraft with poor range was not what USAAF officers lusted after.

Closer examination, however, shows that the USAAF had a genuine diamond in the rough that required only a few field modifications, better pilots, and coherent doctrine to transform it into a powerful, versatile fighter. Kenney personally had much to do with that outcome. Because it was close to the bottom of the military food chain, Fifth Air Force was already experienced in performing field modifications at its northern Australian depots. Kenney's engineers quickly developed a 200-gallon drop tank for the P-47, and the Fifth contracted with Australian Ford for construction (thus moving much more quickly than was possible through channels at home). When P-47s were ready to move into theater in sizeable numbers in summer 1943, their range surpassed that of the P-40 (but never equaled that of the P-38).

Although the Jug always had critics, the fighter soon displayed unexpected advantages. The P-47 mated the large Pratt and Whitney radial with a turbosupercharger. This could do little to help climb, but it did wonders for high-altitude performance, pumping out its maximum power at 27,000 feet. And in thin air power was the single most important factor in maneuverability, and as many German fighters found out the hard way the P-47, however clumsy when low and slow, was fast and nimble at very high altitude. Indeed the Jug was the best high-altitude fighter used by American pilots during the war. (It is a reasonable assumption that had USAAF pilots in the Pacific confronted more high-flying Tonys, the Jug would have been more popular than it was in the theater.)

The P-47 was an American-style fighter written large just as the Oscar represented an extreme in Japanese design. In a country that made rugged aircraft, the P-47 was famous for strength. In a service that made good use of dive speed, only the late-model Mustang could match the Jug. One European theater pilot commented that "I have never seen a plane that could get rid of such appalling hunks of altitude in such a short time." Another European veteran commented that "our evasive action in combat was to dive until you saw 500 mph . . . and you could be sure there was no one behind you any longer." As the war progressed in both theaters ground support became an ever greater responsibility of heavily armed fighter-bombers. In this extremely dangerous role the Jug had no equal. One veteran of the Far Eastern Air Force (FEAF, the successor of 5th USAAF and 13th USAAF that was established just prior to the Philippine invasion) recalled the gloom that descended upon his squadron after receiving news in 1945 that it was to be rearmed with P-51D Mustangs, the master of European skies. Whatever the marvelous fighting qualities of the Mustang, the pilots in question, doing mostly ground attack, greatly appreciated the strength and power of the Jug. In their jargon the Mustang was the "Spamcan" and, because of its water-cooled Merlin, less likely to come home heavily damaged.

During the summer of 1943 Fifth Air Force received the 348th Fighter Group, made up of three Jug squadrons. After the initial break-in period the 348th compiled a distinguished record, led by leader Neel Kearby, who won the Congressional Medal of Honor for action over Wewak in fall 1943. The 348th compiled an excellent record that reflected the nature of the P-47. Japanese pilots were able to down only a handful the group's Jugs (ironically Kearby was shot down by an Oscar); as usual a good number were lost to antiaircraft fire, mishap, and navigational error.

Edwards Park of 41st Squadron transitioned from P-39s to P-47s in late 1943. Going from the smallest USAAF fighter to the largest was a major transition. Park also experienced firsthand the Jug's toughness:

"We flew like the P-38 pilots did. We would go into a shallow dive, make a pass, and then climb away. There was a lot to monitor and you had to watch speed. Once I pushed my Jug hard and blew a cylinder. I brought it back home and felt I had done something wrong. My crew chief told me 'this is a combat aircraft, it's made to take it. You can push it very hard.'" Like many P-39 pilots, particularly when the Japanese were principally busy over Guadalcanal, Park had been in few large engagements and had no confirmed victories. When flying a Jug Park had the advantage of a much more powerful aircraft, as well as eight .50-caliber machine guns: "I approached a Tony at a high deflection but got off a good burst. I could see the bullets rip into the Tony and they made him slide sideways, so great was the impact. For a Japanese plane the Tony was strong and the pilot was able to bail."

For a very brief period in early 1944 a majority of 5th USAAF fighter squadrons flew P-47s. Although it is difficult to identify the reasons behind fighter allocation among theaters, it does appear that in late 1943 Eighth Air Force, in reaction to the crippling losses suffered by unescorted B-17s over Schweinfurt, Germany, decided that it needed long-range escorts immediately. With the Mustang still strangely neglected, this meant pairing P-47s with longer-range P-38s. The result was a brief shortage of Lightnings. The famous 9th Squadron of 49th Fighter Group was given Jugs to replace worn-out Lightnings, a decision that caused a rebellion inside 5th USAAF Fighter Command. As Lockheed increased production of the Lightning and Eighth Air Force discovered the P-51, this problem solved itself in a few months. Although several squadrons flew Jugs until the end of the war, or until reequipped with Mustangs, most squadrons received Kenney's favored Lightning. The P-38's greater range made it ideal in the Pacific (assuming that no Mustangs were to appear until the European war was nearly over), so the decision was a good one. Yet like the P-38 a fast and high-flying P-47 posed a tactical problem the Japanese could not solve.

The last U.S. fighter to play a role in the South Pacific was less important for its numbers and enemy kills than for its symbolization of doom for Japanese aircraft at Rabaul. The last carrier battle fought in 1942 was at Santa Cruz in October. In that clash small numbers of Wildcats confronted small numbers of Zeros. For more than a year carriers on both sides, with the notable exception of the shuttle attack made by aircraft from *Enterprise* at Guadalcanal in November, played indirect roles in operations and never came to blows. During this period the United States launched several new heavy and light carriers. Knowing that the Wildcat had seen its day, the U.S. Navy equipped its new ships with the F6F Hellcat. (The Wildcat itself fought on from the decks of escort carriers until war's end.)

In concept the F6F was a much improved Wildcat; the Grumman look certainly existed. Yet the Hellcat was a completely new aircraft. As large as the P-47 and powered by the redoubtable Pratt and Whitney 2800, the Hellcat fit the combat conditions of 1944 perfectly. The Hellcat had a good rate of climb, was tough as nails, and, like all U.S. aircraft, could dive extremely well. Like the Wildcat it had excellent landing characteristics and, considering its size and power, was a forgiving fighter for the era. By late 1943 the navy was producing huge numbers of reasonably well trained pilots, and they were given an aircraft that was reasonably manageable to fly; the fit was perfect. The big, stubby fighter afforded excellent visibility. In combat it represented disaster to Japanese pilots still flying the Zero. The Hellcat lacked the speed of the Corsair, Lightning, and Jug, yet it was faster than the Zero. Like the Corsair it had good performance at 20,000–25,000 feet, so at altitude it could outperform any Japanese aircraft. It also had a tighter turning radius than the USAAF aircraft and Corsair and consequently could mix it up with a Zero for a longer period than any other U.S. fighter. With its heavy armor and well-made self-sealing tanks, the Hellcat was extremely tough. Its performance disadvantages against the Zero appeared only when a Hellcat pilot allowed himself to lose speed and enter airspace where a Zero could appear from nowhere. By the time the Hellcat appeared, most of the Japanese pilots who could maximize the Zero had been killed in action.

After the war Jiro Horikoshi maintained that the Hellcat had been designed specifically to destroy Zeros. This was not altogether true, but the effect was the same. Ace Sadamu Komachi, one of the few veterans to survive the Rabaul battles, had no fond memories of the Hellcat: "The Grummans would get on your tail and just shower you with bullets! It was just awful. I wish we had six .50s like the Grummans and Corsairs." Hellcats fought fiercely on the large carrier raids made against Rabaul and neighboring fields in December 1943. Yet it was not the damage that they did that was so destructive. The arrival of the Hellcat meant the return of the U.S. carriers. As Rabaul and Wewak withered, isolating the huge land garrisons sent to protect them, the USN was ready to up the ante in the Pacific air war. Land-based fighters and bombers played a central role until the end, but in 1944 and early 1945 the navy's enormous carrier-based task forces were able to push the Pacific war from Rabaul to Okinawa.

Allied Bombers

The superiority of U.S. aircraft over Japanese is better illustrated in bombers than fighters. This was no small matter in the South Pacific, because an ability to damage enemy air bases and destroy shipping was central to all operations. Until late-war operations illustrated the potential destructive power of the fighter-bomber, the ability to project airpower was largely in the hands of the bomber crewmen. Fighters could make the aerial battlefield much safer for bombers, but it was the heavier aircraft that did the damage. An amphibious force or a land campaign found enemy fighters by themselves to be a nuisance. A bombing attack, however, was a very serious matter. Bombers in sufficient numbers were very helpful to ground forces. Disproving completely the prewar Japanese doctrine that the best way to achieve air superiority was to kill enemy aircraft in flight, a steady bombing campaign proved able to smother the greatest of air bases, leaving an enemy air force a shambles on the ground. Probably most important in the South Pacific was the ability of bombers to destroy shipping. A warship operating in daylight without air cover was in desperate danger. Even more vulnerable were the merchant ships that delivered the supplies required to allow all arms—naval, ground, and air—to function properly. If bombers could roam freely, any garrison was as good as dead. The Allied advances up the Solomons and across New Guinea, as well as the isolation of the large Japanese garrison at Timor in the East Indies, were due to a hail of bombs coming from a variety of aircraft.

The first major land-based bomber fielded by the Allies was the Boeing B-17 Flying Fortress. This is not the place for a history of World War II's most famous strategic bomber. However, the aircraft played an unanticipated and successful part in the South Pacific. Aviation historians have not been kind to the B-17 as employed early in the Pacific war. The major sting to its reputation was in the role assigned by USAAF—sinking ships—which was unsuited to the big bomber at that stage of the war. Unfortunately, defending U.S. territory by destroying enemy fleets at sea was exactly the task that bomber enthusiasts pointed to as one of the primary reasons for developing long-range bombers in the first place. Billy Mitchell's early demonstrations that bombers could destroy stationary and unmanned warships proved, in the event, to be the wrong lesson. And there is much reason to conclude that followers of the bomber cult used the potential of flying coastal defense (read: sinking ships) as a political justification for building bombers meant to strike land targets. Whatever the case, the B-17s sent to the Philippines in the months before Pearl Harbor rarely got an opportunity to implement theory. Whatever chance they had was compromised by inexperienced crews, bad weather, and small numbers. Pummeled on the ground, harassed by fighters, and forced to withdraw from Manila early in the war, the Flying Fortress did not

perform as advertised. However, if one judges the B-17 by what it did
and not by what overzealous advocates promised prior to Pearl Harbor, a very different picture emerges. Once the Allies caught their
breath and began buildups in Australia and New Caledonia, as we
shall see, a small number of B-17s proved invaluable in reconnaissance, harassing attacks on major Japanese targets, and developing innovative techniques to strike the enemy in an unusual theater. And to
sweeten the bitter pill of burning bombers in December 1941, the
Fortress on certain important occasions did prove able to damage and
sink Japanese shipping.

The U.S. government transferred a few early-model B-17s to the
Royal Air Force in early 1941 for experimental operations. RAF officers were usually quick to assess the strengths and weaknesses of U.S.
aircraft, but in this instance they missed the formidable potential of the
Fortress. (RAF Bomber Command had been battered during its own
daylight raids and was already preparing for night offensives.) So it
was that history's most famous bomber made its debut in the Pacific
despite the fact that it took little time to illustrate that it was a poor
ship-killer and had to operate in an environment very badly suited to
an aircraft far more complex than any fighter.

The B-17 prototype flew in 1935. Aircraft flying that early saw little
war service, and fewer yet finished the conflict in huge numbers. In
truth the B-17 was in some ways obsolescent by 1942. Alone among
heavy bombers, the Fortress had a low-wing configuration, like the
C-47 and most fighters, which became the source of both strength and
weakness. The spar attaching the wings to the fuselage constricted the
area available for the bomb bay, thus inhibiting the bomb load. In addition Boeing's engineers gave the Fortress a very large wing and tail.
For a bomber the B-17 had extremely low wing-loading. With its four
turbocharged Curtiss-Wright radials, the Fortress had very good performance at high altitudes and, for a heavy bomber, maneuvered well.
The layout gave it good landing characteristics at low speeds, a trait
that saved many crewmen's lives when a damaged plane came in. Like
most fighters the Fortress was a tail-dragger, and its good manners
helped as well. No bomber is easy to land, especially on the crude
fields of World War II, so the extra lift of the big wing was a bonus. (It
is no coincidence, however, that the B-17 was the USAAF's last tail-
dragging bomber; the tricycle landing gear, valuable for smaller aircraft, was more helpful yet when taking off and landing a ten-ton aircraft.)

The very clean but conventional design also contributed to tremendous structural strength, the quality that most endeared the Fortress to

thousands of crewmen. The first B-17s to be deployed to the Philippines were early models. The Americans, like so many other air forces, believed that high speeds at high altitudes were the best defense against interception; some planes even lacked tailguns, and none had modern bottom turrets. After the bashing suffered on the ground in the Philippines and Java, USAAF assumptions did not prove so far off the mark. Early B-17s did not have effective defensive armament yet proved hard to catch and down because of structural integrity. Yet losses to fighters and antiaircraft quickly confirmed a lesson already proven in Europe: Sacrificing speed and range for more firepower and armor was a trade well worth making. By the summer of 1942 USAAF leaders were sending airmen in the Solomons and New Guinea a few squadrons of precious B-17Es, the first model that genuinely deserved the nickname "Fortress." Naturally nothing could change the malignant nature of the theater: Weather, bad fields, lack of navigation aids, inexperienced crews (both air and ground), and a constant shortage of spare parts did more damage than did Japanese interceptors. Still, the ultimate test of sturdiness came during combat.

In February 1943 a flight of four B-17 bombers with an escort of four P-40s attacked Shortland Harbor near Bougainville. At this stage of the war over the Solomons some Japanese units showed signs of operational decline. Others, however, still had the old magic: Obviously the American raiders confronted Japanese veterans. A large flight of Zeros jumped the Americans, destroyed three B-17s, and scattered the escorts. The remaining B-17 was pursued by several Zeros for half an hour. Major H. H. McCarroll, the squadron's flight surgeon, was a passenger on the flight and wrote an account soon after landing:

> The fight ended up at 1,200 feet with our pilot, Captain Thomas, flying full-bore. All of our machine-gun ammunition had been expended twenty minutes before the Zeros left. The Zeros used bold tactics. Some of the enemy planes approached to within ten yards of the wing tips of the B-17, then executed a half roll on the same level. Sometimes, the enemy would climb, and at others, he would dive. One Zero flew in upside down and came about ten feet above the bomber in a slight dive, firing down. Another one came in toward the nose, pulled straight up into a loop, and came back over upside down firing. Their tactics were different and bolder than those observed previously in this area. The Zeros pilots showed no fear of the B-17s guns. When they started a pass they completed it.
>
> The B-17 was riddled with 7.7 and 20mm bullets. One waist gunner and the bombardier had severe gunshot wounds. All gunners and the

co-pilot received shrapnel wounds. Number 1 and number 2 engines
were functioning about one third their normal efficiency. All twin cables
had been severed by gun fire and that together with the great amount of
torque made flying difficult and hazardous. It seemed impossible to get
the ship home and a water landing was contemplated. Because two
crew members were seriously wounded, Captain Thomas tried one
more thing. In order to keep the plane on an even keel, the pilot and
the copilot held the wheel control forward with their knees, and
maintained sufficient left rudder to compensate for the torque. After
manually cranking down the landing gear and flaps, a near-perfect
landing was made on Henderson Field even though both tires were flat.

Whether obvious or not at the time, this was one of the last bombing missions conducted by B-17s in the Pacific Theater. The Fortress
soldiered on as a reconnaissance aircraft and transport, but the
bombers were wearing out fast. At this stage of the war governments
rarely immediately replaced airplanes in the South Pacific with new
and superior models. Instead, with the exception of a few fighter
squadrons of Corsairs and P-38s, the air forces waited for planes to
wear out and only then brought in newer models. The life expectancy
of the few B-17s was particularly limited. Officers called upon
Fortresses in Australia and the Solomons to fly many missions of all
types, including long-range flights, which increased wear and tear on
aircraft and crew. Add to the equation improving but still mediocre
maintenance, and the Forts were beaten up by 1943. (The importance
of qualified ground crews for heavy bombers can hardly be overstressed. Far more complex than fighters, heavies did not prove as
amenable to the kind of patchwork maintenance that could keep a
fighter in the air. Obviously everyone involved realized that if a
bomber were lost due to mishap, ten men might lose their lives. There
were many individual exceptions, but I think that it's safe to say that
heavy bombers did not receive the high level of maintenance required
until well into 1943.)

When the time arrived to phase B-17s into less strenuous duties (some
finally ended up in the States for maintenance training), they were replaced by the Consolidated B-24 Liberator. In the late 1930s Consolidated Corporation had made its reputation on producing fine trainers
and flying boats. Just prior to World War II Consolidated hired the
young David Davis, a brilliant engineer with unorthodox ideas on
wing design. The resulting "Davis" wing showed tremendous promise
in wind-tunnel testing and was used on a successful flying boat. It was

General Douglas MacArthur, the most controversial military leader in American history. Whatever his personal flaws and missteps in other times in his career, MacArthur's campaign in New Guinea and the liberation of the Philippines showed strategic genius. (National Archives)

Admiral Isoroku Yamamoto, commander of Combined Fleet. He established the Imperial Japanese Navy's basic strategy until his death in 1943. After stunning successes early in the war, his strategic grasp faltered badly during the Guadalcanal campaign. (U.S. Navy)

Admiral Chester Nimitz (left), commander of U.S. Pacific Fleet, talks with Admiral William Halsey. Commander of the Allied effort in the Solomons after October 1942, Halsey showed great courage and strategic flair. Like MacArthur, Halsey based much of his planning on the range and capabilities of his air arm. (U.S. Navy)

Major General George Kenney. Kenney pushed his men and aircraft further than a more cautious commander would have. Yet Kenney was greatly admired by his men for his aggressiveness and willingness to "throw away the book." (U.S. Air Force)

Marine pilots of the famous "Black Sheep" (VMF 214) scramble for a mission over the Solomons in late 1943. (USMC)

Rabaul Town and the wharf area, struck by high-level Allied attackers in early 1944. By this period the harbor is empty of major shipping. (National Archives)

Tontouta Airfield on Nouméa, New Caledonia, in November 1943. Allied fields and facilities in the New Hebrides and New Caledonia were invaluable during the Solomons campaign, providing the construction of a complex and well-equipped rear area. (U.S. Navy)

USN Seabees and Marines repair bomb damage to Henderson during October. Catering to a damaged field proved laborious but quick to repair unless heavy bombs were used in huge numbers over sustained periods. Japanese bomb loads were much too light to cripple a field. Notice the steel Marston mat (or pierced steel planking), which enabled American engineers to create fields strong enough to handle bombers very quickly. The Japanese had no equivalent. (U.S. Air Force)

A Marine Wildcat takes off from Fighter One. Despite nearly daily rain, evaporation was so rapid that dust became a serious problem for safety and maintenance. As a group took off, those in the rear were nearly blinded. (U.S. Marine Corps)

Henderson Field just days before it began accepting fighters in August 1942. A year later Guadalcanal hosted a complex of four sophisticated airfields.
(U.S. Marine Corps)

Early-model B-17s on Port Moresby pioneering an air route from Hawaii to the Philippines. Although not realizing it, the Allies were setting the stage for the South Pacific air war months before Pearl Harbor. (Royal Australian Air Force)

The airfield at Munda Point in September 1943. Six weeks previously this area had been pulverized during the fierce battle for New Georgia. USN Seabees had Munda operational within two weeks of capture. Note that revetments and basic facilities are already under construction. The ability of the Americans to construct airfields far more quickly than could the Japanese was key to Allied victory. (U.S. Marine Corps)

A group of Japanese aircraft grounded for lack of simple parts or good maintenance. This unit was captured near Manila, but similar sights were common as Allied forces captured Japanese bases in the South Pacific. The frequent failure of Japan to support and maintain its aircraft in the field was devastating to the imperial war effort. (U.S. Navy)

An Australian Wirraway tactical bomber destroyed in a Japanese air raid against the Wau airfield in February 1943. Fighting was so close to Wau during this period that transports landed under fire to unload Australian combat troops, who then walked a few hundred yards to the front. (Australian War Memorial)

Two American ground crewmen take a rest on the gull wings of a Corsair. It is probably early, late, or after a rain. An aircraft sitting in the full South Pacific sun was as hot as a griddle. (National Archives)

The "bomb line" heads for unseen American aircraft. These appear to be 1,000-pound bombs. Any American bomber could accommodate this powerful weapon as could many fighters. As always, ground work in the South Pacific was arduous because of the intense heat and humidity. (National Archives)

A Bristol Beaufighter flying through the Owen Stanley Mountains in 1942. Carrying a massive load of 20mm cannons in the nose, the Beaufighter was a devastating ground-support aircraft and the most useful aircraft flown by the RAAF not provided by American Lend-Lease. (Royal Australian Air Force)

The B-17 was overadvertised as a ship-killer prior to the war. Nevertheless in the South Pacific it proved a versatile and valuable weapon. The plane's legendary ruggedness posed tremendous problems for Japanese interceptors. (National Archives)

A C-47 takes off. Although often called the "Gooney Bird," the C-47 was one of the most beautiful piston-engine aircraft made and encompassed revolutionary features when put into service. It proved so reliable and versatile that it became one of the most sought after aircraft in the Allied arsenal. This C-47 has a New Zealand crew but the aircraft was flown by every Allied combatant as well as, ironically, by the Japanese. (Royal New Zealand Air Force)

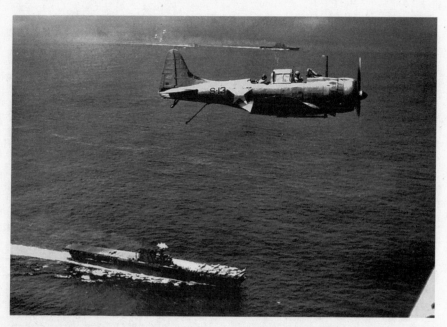

A U.S. Navy Dauntless, tailhook extended, is about to land on America's greatest warship, the USS *Enterprise*. In the distance is the *Saratoga*. This photo was taken during December 1943 when *Sara* rejoined the fleet. The Dauntless was the greatest big ship–killing aircraft in the Pacific war and proved tough enough for land operations. (U.S. Navy)

A Mitsubishi G4M1 bomber (Allied code name: "Betty"). Although having extraordinary range and great speed, the Betty was extremely fragile for a bomber. Because it could not safely operate outside fighter cover, the Betty's attributes were worthless. It was Japan's poorest design of the early war. (U.S. Air Force)

The cockpit of a P-38 Lightning. This photo shows most but not all of the instruments and switches that had to be monitored by a fighter pilot. (Like all bombers but unlike other fighters, the Lightning was fitted with a yoke instead of a stick for steering the plane.) Extremely complex and powerful, all World War II fighters were prone to mechanical mishap and vulnerable to pilot error. Half of all losses in combat theaters were traced to accidents or navigational error. (Air Force Museum)

New Zealand P-40s (Kittyhawks in Commonwealth parlance) make a long flight from Espíritu Santo to Guadalcanal. They are guided by a Hudson, a serviceable but mediocre patrol-bomber. Ferrying fighters across expanses of water was always hazardous and often ended in trouble. The Hudson had better communications and navigation capabilities than any fighter and served as guide. The Americans used similar techniques. (Royal New Zealand Air Force)

B-25 Mitchells on the New Guinea coast in 1944. In all of its different models, the B-25 proved to have good performance and excellent reliability. It was the perfect medium bomber for the rough climate and terrain found in the South Pacific. (U.S. Air Force)

The P-40 Warhawk was the U.S. Army's main fighter until well into 1943, when it was replaced by the P-38 Lightning and P-47 Thunderbolt. It had good performance below 20,000 feet and was extremely rugged. Along with the Wildcat, the P-40 fought the Zero to a standstill in the South Pacific. The aircraft gained its greatest fame with Fifth Air Force, but this New Zealand study of the plane is splendid. In addition, RNZAF P-40 squadrons were in great demand in the Solomons, because they provided excellent close support to U.S. bombing missions against Japanese bases. (Royal New Zealand Air Force)

Nose art was a fixture on almost every U.S. Army aircraft. Often, planes had nicknames and figures on both sides—one for the crew chief and another for the pilot. As might be expected, great aces had access to the best local artists. The most famous and elaborate nose art from the South Pacific was "Marge," a beautiful photo-image of his wife carried on almost all aircraft flown by ace Richard Bong. (U.S. Air Force)

The Mitsubishi A6M fighter, popularly known on both sides as the "Zero," was the most famous aircraft of the Pacific war. Its early-war performance, especially in range and maneuverability, surpassed anything in the Allied arsenal. The Zero's frailty and poor high-speed performance became obvious only as the war progressed. (U.S. Air Force)

Another view of the Zero shows the aerodynamic purity that made it one of the most beautiful piston-engine aircraft ever flown. What it does not show are structural stress points and unguarded fuel tanks, which made the aircraft vulnerable to even the lightest airborne weapons. Unable to take a shot, the Zero was a miserable interceptor because it had to face gunners in Allied bombers. (U.S. Air Force)

The Kawasaki Ki61 Hien (Swallow) army fighter (code name: "Tony"). When flying under optimal conditions the Tony challenged the P-38 in performance. Japan licensed the same engine used by the famous German Bf109, yet Japan lacked the technical expertise to create a reliable aircraft from a good design. Tonys were maintenance nightmares and spent most of their time on the ground, where they were destroyed by Allied aircraft. Other second-generation Japanese fighters suffered a similar fate. The Tony is the best illustration of Japan's basic immaturity in the crucial field of industrial technique. (U.S. Navy)

The F4U Corsair, arguably the best fighter to fly over the Pacific. Tough, well armed, and extremely fast, the Corsair had every advantage over the Zero. Trouble with carrier operations kept it land-based until 1944, much to the delight of the Marines, who received most of the early Corsairs. This aircraft, however, is flown by the famous USN ace Ira Kepford of VF-17, an illustrious land-based squadron in the Solomons. (National Archives)

The Grumman F4F-4 Wildcat, the mainstay of the U.S. Navy and Marine Corps air arms until early 1943. Although inferior to the Zero in categories of performance, a Wildcat could dive much faster, possessed better firepower, and was much more rugged than its Japanese opponent. Unlike Zeros, Wildcats proved excellent bomber-interceptors. By the end of the Guadalcanal campaign, Marine and USN Wildcat pilots were gaining ascendancy over the Japanese even before second-generation U.S. aircraft arrived. (National Archives)

The A-20 Havoc was the best light bomber in the Pacific, and General Kenney knew it. Unfortunately he had to wait his turn as hundreds went to the USSR via Lend-Lease. The Australians and British also liked the extremely fast and well-made bomber. It was a perfect strafer. (U.S. Air Force)

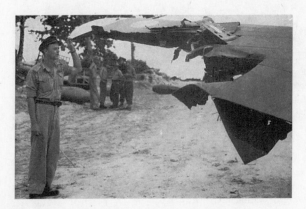

The ruggedness of U.S.-built aircraft was legendary. In this photo an amazed Australian pilot inspects the mauled wing of a P-40 that sustained a 200-mile flight home. Hundreds of Allied pilots had similar if less dramatic experiences. (Royal Australian Air Force)

the core of Consolidated's proposal to build a successor to the B-17. A cross section of the new wing was shaped something like a teardrop. It was thick at the wing root (engineers would say that it had a large "camber") but very narrow, long, and tapered in both cross section and width. In theory this meant efficient lift and great load-carrying capacity. With very high wing-loading, Davis incorporated an extensible Fowler flap to his wing to aid in providing lift for takeoff and lower stall speeds on landing. (More elaborate versions are found on large jets today.)

The B-24 prototype flew in December 1939, just six months after a contract was approved. Particularly when compared with the graceful B-17, the new bomber was not appealing to the eye. Many of its crewmen dubbed the plane the "Flying Boxcar," and rarely has a nickname been more apt. Although ungainly, the aircraft had many attractive features. It was powered by four fine Pratt and Whitney 1830 radials. Early in the war Consolidated fitted turbochargers to the engines. Because the Davis wing was set above the midpoint of the fuselage, nothing interfered with the bomb bay, giving the B-24 a large payload. Good airframe design and engines offered excellent range. Tricycle landing gear aided ground-handling and allowed takeoff from shorter strips. Much design effort was directed toward creating an aircraft that would be quicker and less expensive to build than its competitors. World War II aircraft were too complex to mass-produce in the typical sense, yet Consolidated saw to it that major components could be assembled with less labor and specialized skills than was the case with the B-17 (much less the B-29). When full-scale production began it proved possible to have several companies produce the aircraft. By war's end the United States produced 18,000 B-24s, more than any other U.S. warplane.

Although a very important weapon and an undeniably successful design, the B-24 had weaknesses that prevented it from replacing the B-17, but in practice they complemented one another. As usual the British received the first production models; they insisted on better self-sealing fuel tanks and more armament. Still, the RAF immediately saw great potential and eventually received approximately 1,500 B-24s. The bomber proved useful in the desert and over Sicily, but the main recipient was Coastal Command, which found the B-24 to be an ideal antisubmarine patrol bomber. The British thought enough of it to call it the "Liberator," a nickname that stuck in the press and was often used by crewmen.

Some of the Liberator's faults were more critical in Europe than in the Pacific. Even when turbocharged, the B-24 proved a very difficult aircraft to fly above 20,000 feet. Indeed the physical effort required to pilot the craft was substantial. Carl Camp was a B-24 crewman of the famous 5th USAAF 90th Bomb Group in 1943 and recalled that elbow grease came in handy when flying a Liberator:

Flying a B-24 took a lot of muscle power. . . . We were making a low altitude gunnery practice run and the copilot was manning a gun. The pilot had me sit in for the copilot and told me to help him out because when we had to pull up from low altitude he wanted the extra muscle power to raise the nose. We were flying fast, so that was a tough job. When he pulled back the yoke and started pushing on the rudder, I thought, "My god it was like pushing on lead bars or something." It was terribly hard. If ever there was an aircraft that needed hydraulic boost that dog was one of them. Yet some of them came back with both engines on one side off and both the pilot and copilot standing on the opposite rudder trying to keep the thing straight. They'd barely make it if they made it at all and on the ground they'd be suffering from muscle strains and pulls. Some went into a spin because they simply couldn't hold it any longer. A heavy bomber could be a beast if it was damaged.

Going from the ultrarugged and conventional B-17 to a B-24 was not always an easy experience for a crewman. Jim Eaton of 43d Bomb Group arrived in Australia in mid-1942 and flew B-17s during the darkest hours of the war in New Guinea. In early 1943 the 43d began to receive Liberators. Although Eaton had learned intimately the faults of the early-model B-17s, the Liberator was new territory. Eaton described his transition from doubter to supporter of the B-24:

Moving to the '24 was an interesting experience. You have to remember that attitudes are formed under the most unusual circumstances. I flew in an early model of the B-24 in May '42 for the first time. I was taking replacements to war in the South Pacific. We took off at night, sun came up, and I'm in the nose with two or three other guys. We were flying toward Fiji. I look out and the wings are flopping up and down. They didn't do that in a B-17. That was not a comfortable feeling seeing those wings flap. So right there I decide that I hope I never had to fly one of those things.

Now we made the transition to '24s in March 1943. We'd been bombed out of Milne Bay. We got bombed out there on 17 January and lost everything we had. So we borrowed an airplane and went on R&R

in Mareeba in northern Australia. While we were there we went through transition to B-24s. The first mission we flew we found that we could carry twice as many bombs twice as far as the B-17. Hey, that's pretty good. Instead of making your bomb run on the way home like in a B-17 you could fly around for a while looking things over. You didn't have to worry about fuel. As it turned out, the '24 was a hell of a good plane for operations in the Pacific. We didn't know it at first, but as time went on we grew much more comfortable in a '24 than in a B-17 from the standpoint of reserve fuel, bomb load, and gunnery. We had power turrets, just like the '17, and even had a nose turret. So our attitudes shifted radically, but in our specific mission with long flights it was the only airplane. The tricycle landing gear was an advantage, and we had ample clearance even when heavily loaded.

Most crewmen tried not to dwell on the prospect of being shot down, but the Liberator was not as robust as the B-17. The production techniques that saved time also undoubtedly compromised structural strength. The Davis wing, which helped give the B-24 its great range and large bomb bay, was weaker than that of the B-17. There were structural weak spots that could cause catastrophic failure if hit. (Anyone who has studied the bombing offensive over Germany has seen several photos of Liberators going down with a wing blown off; B-17 crewmen in Europe were known to comment that the best possible escort was a nearby formation of Liberators because the Luftwaffe would attack them first.)

Yet comparisons are relative by definition. Perhaps the Liberator was not as tough as the B-17, but it was still a U.S. aircraft, and none of those were weak. A Japanese Betty crewman would have been amazed by the armor and armament in the B-24. Ironically some of the most important armament was homegrown. Good Japanese pilots, like their Luftwaffe counterparts, quickly realized that the B-24 was weakly armed in the nose because that was where the bombardier was positioned. Consequently fighters began making head-on attacks, with sometimes disastrous results for the bomber. Therefore ground crews of the 90th Bomb Group took the small tail turret out of a wrecked B-24, repositioned the bombardier, and installed the extra turret in the front. (This was not the first or last time that Fifth Air Force took matters into its own hands and made unauthorized field modifications. Several, like the B-24 chin turret, were quickly adopted by authorized depots and influenced aircraft companies in the homeland.) In any case in the Pacific environment the Liberator was a difficult opponent for the Japanese. Carl Camp of 90th Bomb Group recalled a potentially hazardous situation (one that probably would have blown a Betty to pieces) that turned out well:

> We were attacked by fighters a few times but we had been lucky. Our plane was never hit by any of the attackers. That was rare, so we were called the "virgins." On our thirty-third mission our luck ran out. I was looking at the wing when one of the bullets hit, and then a Japanese shell. I saw this tiny bullet hole, then a few more, a little debris, and the jagged edges. I thought, "Oh hell, here it starts after thirty-three missions." I expected to see a fire any second. But the self-sealing fuel cells held. When we landed they just patched the hole and up we went a day or two later. Scared the hell out of me though. But that was it. I ended up flying fifty-six [missions]. I was lucky. All I ever had was malaria and dysentery at the same time.

The B-24 proved a very effective weapon in the South Pacific. With Eighth Air Force in Europe showing a preference for B-17s, the more easily produced B-24s began to appear throughout the world performing many roles. They were ideal long-range reconnaissance aircraft, VIP transports (Churchill had one), antisubmarine patrol planes, and, of course, fine bombers. In 1944 Australia received Liberators for their air offensive against the East Indies. Even the U.S. Navy (and through it the Marine Corps) received Liberators. It was very rare for the army and navy to share aircraft whether it made sense or not. However, in 1942 the USAAF was eager to begin production of the new B-29, but plant space was lacking. The navy owned a plant in Renton, Washington, that was producing an unsatisfactory patrol bomber. The USAAF offered to supply the navy with B-24s, B-25s, and some Lockheed Venturas in return for use of the Fenton plant, conveniently close to Boeing. In a rare moment of interservice amicability, the navy agreed quickly. Naturally the navy changed the designation (to PB4Y), but it served well throughout the war.

Although heavy bombers had great advantages, the prewar army's insistence that medium and light bombers receive serious attention paid tremendous dividends in all theaters, particularly the South Pacific. In the many arguments that raged over the potential value of strategic bombers during the 1930s, advocates of medium and light bombers conceded that such planes would lack extreme range, have smaller bomb loads, and be more vulnerable to enemy defenses. However, they argued that twin-engine bombers would be cheaper, easier to produce, easier to maintain, and faster. Also, within reasonable operational ranges a good medium or light bomber could carry an effective bomb load and still be stout. And not every target had equal value, so attacking a factory complex might require one type of weapon, whereas striking an airbase required another. Above all the ground-pounders who ran the prewar army wanted aircraft that could assist in direct tactical operations and attack enemy lines of communication close to the front ("interdiction" in army parlance). Given that the army did not yet possess fighters powerful enough to serve as deadly light attack planes, all these arguments favored twin-engine bombers. It was a genre that U.S. aviation completely dominated. In the strange environment of the South Pacific it was a type of aircraft that reinvented itself. By mid-1943, in addition to serving as capable bombers, USAAF mediums (frowned upon by the bomber cult) proved deadly antishipping weapons, a role in which heavy craft, despite prewar claims to the contrary, never excelled.

The first modern medium bomber employed by the USAAF was the controversial Martin B-26 Marauder. Unlike several other U.S. makes the B-26 was homegrown and not developed for the RAF. In a USAAF competition with the prototype of the North American B-25 the Marauder won easily. One can see why. When first delivered to the USAAF 22d Bomb Group in late 1941 the B-26 was the most innovative medium in the world. Externally the Marauder bore a superficial resemblance to the Japanese Betty. Both had a cigar-shaped fuselage and very large tail. In every other area the Martin marched to its own drummer.

When aircrews describe a plane or pilot as "hot," it can be a compliment or a caution—often the two are closely connected. The B-26, more than any other U.S. aircraft of World War II, was hot. Designed just as Pratt and Whitney was beginning production of its 2,000-horsepower R-2800 engine, Martin engineers designed the Marauder almost like a fighter. Able to call on tremendous power, the B-26 was fitted with very short, small wings mounted high on the fuselage, resulting in extremely high wing-loading for a bomber. The fuselage was intricately designed for a large bomb load, great speed, and unprecedented structural strength for a medium. Unlike every other bomber introduced by the USAAF the B-26 was reasonably well armed from the beginning, carrying five .50-caliber machine guns. The Marauder's Achilles' heel was takeoff and landing. With his lift coming less from the wing than from brute power, a pilot had to take off and land at extremely high speeds—more than 100 miles per hour. If one of the new Pratt and Whitney's failed or suffered a runaway prop during takeoff, the aircraft would careen off the field with little warning. Pilot error during landing meant a high-speed crash. As the aircraft grew heavier, which it inevitably did, such problems increased. In short the Marauder was a dangerous plane. Fred Miller trained at MacDill Field in Florida, where B-26 training took place:

> We lost a lot of our B-26s in Tampa. We lost them every way possible.
> We lost them on takeoff and landing. We'd practice dive-bombing
> from 15,000 feet and pull out at 1,000 feet. A lot of pilots didn't pull
> out. One was buried so deep they just pulled the tail section out and
> left the plane in there. We'd train for torpedoes and get right on the
> deck. But there were swells down there and you could look out both
> sides of the plane and see water on both sides. We lost some that way,
> too.

The pilots of 22d Bomb Group were the first to discover this problem and suffered several mishaps. However, they had long flown the twin-engine Douglas B-18 and were able to adjust to the new weapon. The real problem came when new pilots entered service under the rapid training programs of the early-war period. A series of fatal training accidents plagued the aircraft. Frightened new pilots soon started calling the B-26 the "Martin Murderer" or the "Flying Prostitute" because it had "no visible means of support." The worst saying of all was "one a day at Tampa Bay," a reference to the fatal accidents at MacDill. The problem was so serious that Congress investigated (Harry Truman was involved) and General Arnold ordered a review of the entire program. It looked for a short period as though the B-26 might be canceled or sent back to the drawing board. Ironically some good reports from the 22d, since sent to Australia, helped keep the B-26 program alive. Eventually General James Doolittle, with his tremendous prestige, helped persuade the government and USAAF doubters that the Marauder was a sound aircraft if training and ground service could be improved. Doolittle, to put it mildly, was correct. Although it was expensive to produce and always remained an unforgiving airplane, the B-26 developed into an outstanding bomber in the European theater. At home at medium and low altitudes the Marauder terrorized German ground forces (late models carried eleven .50-caliber machine guns and an excellent bomb load) and compiled an excellent record for accuracy during strategic missions. The Marauder's eventual triumph in Europe—where officers were given first choice of America's best weapons—relegated the competing B-25 to the Mediterranean Theater and, as one might expect, the Pacific. Everyone benefited as a result.

Despite its tremendous promise the B-26 ultimately did not prove a success in the South Pacific, however. B-26 squadrons were among the first bombers to operate from northern Australia. Because Moresby was too dangerous to fly from, bombers would fly up from Australia, refuel at Moresby, make the attack, and reverse course. With so few aircraft and so many targets it was rare for aircraft to concentrate for an attack and impossible to sustain any kind of offensive. Therefore many B-26 crews had the unenviable task of attacking Rabaul and Lae during daylight without fighter escort. Considering these circumstances combat losses were light indeed. The Marauder was very strong and, with the typical field alterations, very well armed and dangerous for Zeros to attack. Many pilots who learned the aircraft's quirks and crews who had confidence in their pilots developed a loyalty to the aircraft. Major Dill Ellis piloted a Marauder with the 22d early in the war. After his tour he was debriefed by USAAF intelligence, which was trying to assess the new bomber's safety and effectiveness. Ellis strongly defended his plane:

> In one case we got a pilot who had been an instructor in the States in a B-26 outfit. We flew with him and, as a result, kept him as a copilot for a month and a half, gave him 25 hours of transition, and finally checked him out. And he was an instructor and trained in the States before he came over! His main trouble, as well as that of some other pilots, was that they all seemed to be afraid of the ship. I cannot understand that. The B-26 is one of the best medium bombers that any has without a doubt! In a year of combat flying I have seen the B-25 and B-26 in action, and there is no question in my mind but that the B-26 is the best medium bomber. It is mainly because the B-26 will take a beating where the B-25 won't. I have seen instances where eight B-25s were hit by fifteen Japs, and only three of them came back. We could have the same number of B-26s and not lose a ship—or maybe one at most. That would be without pursuit escort.

Some of the aircrews of the 22d obviously agreed with Ellis. In January 1943 the group sent its tired Marauders to Townsville for refitting. By cannibalizing parts, 5th USAAF mechanics restored enough aircraft for one squadron. The men of 19th Squadron of the 22d agreed that they would prefer to stick with their stout and fast Marauders instead of moving to B-25s. The 19th also received permission to strip their aircraft of paint, which saved much weight and added about 10 miles per hour to top speed. They became known as the "Silver Squadron." (Soon USAAF bomber and fighter groups in Europe began stripping the paint. It also became standard practice for P-38 squadrons in the South Pacific, although most bombers kept their paint. This practice drew scorn from some Luftwaffe and British pilots because it made U.S. aircraft easier to see at a distance. One 8th USAAF Mustang pilot told me simply that the Americans wanted the Luftwaffe to find them so U.S. fighters could shoot down German interceptors and their pilots.)

Despite the fine record of some B-26 units, many other aircrews found that the Marauder's bad reputation was well earned, particularly on the poor airfields in the theater. Charles Kittell was a veteran B-25 pilot in the Solomons and had no desire to exchange his Mitchell for a Marauder in the South Pacific: "The B-26 was out there first. It was very fast and developed a fine combat record, but it required a lot of runway. It cost us a lot of people on landing and takeoff. You had to really know what you were doing with one. And most of us didn't. If you lost an engine on takeoff in a '25 you could probably get your rudder in and control it: In a '26 unless you were darn good you were dead." Furthermore the long-range missions assigned early Marauder units pushed range to the maximum. Jim Eaton was a gunner on a B-17 that was a very early arrival in New Guinea. As Eaton recalled, the Marauder was being asked to do too much:

> Before we really got cranked up the B-26s were hitting Rabaul. There was a B-26 about every ten minutes' flying time off the end of the runway. They just didn't have the range. On return flights in the '17s you could almost position yourself by the B-26 crashes: They just couldn't make it back. We were desperate, and those missions were something we could do. To us at the time it was a normal war; it was later that I could see how miserable things were. When you're young, whatever is taking place is normal, no matter how hideous.

General Kenney was far more in agreement with Kittell and Eaton than with Major Ellis. Furthermore Kenney was in no position to demand a particular type of aircraft. Much the same could be said about 13th USAAF leaders in the Solomons. Easier to produce and easier on rookie pilots than the Marauder, B-25s were available in growing numbers after mid-1942. Therefore by January 1944, when the last worn-out Marauder was retired from service in the South Pacific, the B-25 Mitchell had long become the medium bomber of choice (and necessity). After some false starts the Mitchell proved the best bomber in the theater.

It was one of the many ironies of prewar aviation that the holding company that eventually became North American Aviation got its start by acquiring the Fokker Corporation of America. Fokker was a Dutch firm run by the brilliant designer of Germany's greatest aircraft of World War I. During the interwar period, despite on-and-off connections with major aviation concerns, North American's creations had been modestly solid. It struck gold with the AT-6 trainer, flown as the Texan in the United States, the Harvard in Britain. (North American produced more than 17,000 Texans, and the docile aircraft proved so ideal that it stayed in service worldwide for twenty years. Several hundred remain airworthy today.) In 1940 North American, working with the RAF, began developing the P-51 Mustang, the war's best all-around fighter. And during the early jet age the company designed the famous F-86 Sabre, the main fighter for the new United States Air Force. Obviously North American did things right.

In addition to an omnipresent trainer and the marvelous Mustang, North American designed the most heavily produced U.S. medium bomber: the B-25 Mitchell. Although it was a modern design in every way and capable of fine overall performance, North American's designers did not try to push the envelope with the Mitchell like their counterparts working on the B-26. This proved a wise decision, as the United States badly needed aircraft that were reasonably uncomplicated to produce and suitable for hordes of imperfectly trained airmen.

A few early-model B-25s were among the first U.S. aircraft to arrive in the South Pacific. In a bizarre coincidence North American's Dutch connection appeared again after the original tie to Fokker. In summer 1941 the USAAF was pressuring Washington to slow Lend-Lease commitments to hasten the buildup of U.S. units. However, the Dutch government-in-exile—the Nazis had overrun Holland in May 1940—pled desperately for aircraft to defend holdings in the East Indies. As Washington wished to deter or slow a Japanese advance in that area, North American agreed to sell 160 B-25s to the Dutch. The governments agreed to arrange transfer in Australia. Thus in January 1942 sixty Mitchells took off from California bound for Brisbane and Dutch service.

With the Japanese cutting through Southeast Asia, U.S. commanders in Australia began screaming for aircraft. The Dutch eventually received enough aircraft to field a squadron, which was put under Aus-

tralian command and sent to the Darwin area. However, most of the
initial batch ended up in American hands where they were sorely
needed. Ten planes originally intended for Holland participated in one
of the most dramatic missions of the war. General MacArthur, just arrived in Australia from his flight from the Philippines, ordered ten
Mitchells and three B-17s to fly into Mindanao on April 12. After a
2,600-mile flight in two stages the small group arrived. For several
days they launched raids under the nose of the Japanese forces. Amazingly only one B-17 was lost and the rest of the force returned to Australia. Insulted by Mitchells in the Philippines, Japan was humiliated
by them days later. On April 18 sixteen B-25s took off from USS *Hornet* and bombed Tokyo, shaking the Japanese government and delivering an extraordinary boost to American morale. The audacious
Doolittle Raid proved a small taste of the tremendous damage that Allied B-25s were to inflict on imperial forces throughout the war.

Slowly B-25 squadrons began to arrive in Australia and later in the
Solomons. Few aircraft of the war engendered greater loyalty and affection on the part of its aircrew than did the B-25. Charles Kittell was
a 13th USAAF B-25 pilot and had high praise for his aircraft:

Anyone who flew the B-25 loved it. It was forgiving. You could make
all sorts of mistakes and live to tell about it. We didn't have a lot of
hours of training in World War II. It was a war run on numbers.
Someone with 500 hours was an old-timer. So you couldn't count on
experience. So it was a perfect plane for the kids they were sending out
to the Pacific. It was easy to land, easy to fly, and it got you back. If
you lost an engine you could come home on one with little problem. It
had another advantage. Because it was fast for its time the P-38s loved
to fly fighter escort for it because they didn't have to throttle back.
We'd go along at nearly two-fifty. B-24s were considerably slower and
the escorts got very impatient. The only thing we didn't like was that it
was so god-awful noisy. I have 80 percent loss of some of my hearing
range, and it is partially due to my service with B-25s. But it was a
fantastic aircraft for that time and place.

Although the Mitchell did not have the unusual structural integrity
of the B-26, it was a very tough bird nevertheless. Charles Kittell witnessed an incident that illustrated this vital quality:

After I came back from the Pacific they made me an instructor at
Mitchel Field. Hofstra College is right next to it. I saw this pilot who
had lost an engine come in too hot; as so many people do for some

reason, he tried to go around without pulling his gear and flaps up, which you can do with quarter flaps, but not full, and I watched him cartwheel that B-25 into Hofstra campus and tore it completely apart. The only injury was a broken nose to the copilot. They were lucky but that's how well a B-25 could put up with stuff like that.

Robert Larsen of the famous 5th USAAF 345th Bomb Group echoed Kittell's opinion:

I loved the B-25 as a pilot. It was very forgiving and perfect for young guys like ourselves. That saved a lot of our fannies. We didn't know much about flying, you know. We might have 200 hours total. And it took a lot of punishment. That's the most important thing you can ask of a warplane. From other people's point of view there are different considerations: how many bombs the plane will carry, its range, altitude. But it brought us back alive so the crews all loved it. Something like the B-26 was too much for kids right out of flying school.

Mitchells were designed originally to drop their bombs from above 20,000 feet against large enemy facilities. As happened so often in war, practice did not match theory. As events unfolded, Mitchells in the South Pacific, when used as standard bombers, learned to drop just above light antiaircraft fire, or 6,000–10,000 feet. Many such missions damaged the Japanese war effort. Nevertheless B-25 pilots and USAAF officers soon learned that there was a shortage of targets that medium bombers had been expected to assault. They thus aided land campaigns by carpet-bombing battlefields like Buna and Munda and attacked air base hangers. But targets that pilots found in Europe, such as rail yards, wharves, port facilities, factories, and possibly large troop concentrations, rarely existed in the jungles. As Robert Larsen of 345th Bomb Group puts it, early in the war B-25s "killed a lot of monkeys and knocked down a lot of trees" when operating as standard bombers. Like heavy bombers, the Mitchell did not prove an ideal weapon to attack ships from medium altitudes. They could raid air bases, but Japanese planes had usually scrambled by then (often to intercept the bombers) or were protected in revetments. The B-25 needed a facelift that would better suit it to the theater.

And thus the story of the Mitchell meets up with the last USAAF bomber employed in the South Pacific: the Douglas A-20 Havoc. (The "A" designation—for "attack"—indicates that the aircraft was smaller than a bomber.) The A-20 was another machine spawned by the European conflict, not any interest on the part of the U.S. officers. In the late 1930s ground-support aircraft, much desired by the army's line officers, were at or near the bottom of the Air Corps pecking order. Seeing war clouds, Douglas Corporation developed the DB-7, a light bomber with high speed and short range. France, by now in near panic, immediately placed a large order. Although a few saw combat in France, most ended up in British hands after France's capitulation. Initially the RAF was not sure what to do with the plane, which it flew as the Boston. Still, it was RAF doctrine—as was the case in the USAAF—that anything a light bomber could do a medium and heavy bomber could do better. But the extremely fast Boston could shoot down night-bombers, so the RAF modified some for night-fighting work, and the resulting Havoc lent yet another name to the stable of U.S. aircraft types nicknamed by the British. When it was given more armament and armor, the British warmed to the aircraft, and it gave fine service in the Western Desert.

By this time American officers also had a change of heart. Hoping to please ground commanders, the Air Corps placed a small order for A-20s (the DB-7 designation changed). More than 3,000 would enter U.S. service. (An even greater number went to the USSR via Lend-Lease.) The first lot of A-20s was deployed with 3d Bomb Group, the Air Corps premier attack group during the prewar period. As luck would have it 3d Bomb Group, with its A-20s and B-25s, was soon on its way to Australia.

The early A-20s demonstrated impressive performance. Like the B-25 the Havoc was powered by twin Wright Cyclone R-2600 engines. Not yet weighed down with extra armor and a rear turret, in theory the A-20 could reach 340 miles per hour—nearly a match for the Zero. (In practice the equation would have been much more complex, but the A-20 and B-25 could outrun a Zero that did not have a substantial altitude advantage if spotted at a great enough distance.) The handling of the aircraft was unusually clean, and it was a great favorite with pilots. The problems were its relatively limited range—not much greater than a fighter—a small bomb load, and poor armament.

Some of these problems were solved on the spot. Fifth Air Force, supported by its sophisticated base complex in northern Australia, developed a prodigious reputation for ingenious field modifications of warplanes. When the Third arrived in northern Australia it found that the A-20s lacked guns and bomb racks. So it was that the Havoc became the first plane to receive the 5th USAAF makeover. Much of the work was inspired and supervised by one of the war's genuinely unusual characters: Paul Gunn. One of the last Americans out of the Philippines, Gunn was a former USN flight instructor and official with Philippine Air Lines. In the chaos he was separated from his wife and children, who were interned by the Japanese. (All survived.) Gunn thus had no love for the Japanese. In an extremely young military organization Gunn was considered ancient when given the rank of captain at age forty, and he quickly picked up the nickname "Pappy." He was also a clever master of gadgets and do-it-yourself modification. Field modifications were nothing new in 1942—all armed forces make small improvements to meet field conditions. Major modifications that changed the nature of a weapon, however, were almost always left to the manufacturers, often based on reports from the field.

Gunn was lucky that he worked for Kenney. Kenney had worked with the Material Division of the Air Corps, had flown with attack squadrons, and was keen on technical innovation of all kinds. Furthermore, being near the bottom of the supply barrel, Kenney decided that altering his own aircraft would be far faster and more effective than waiting for deliveries from stateside. In addition Kenney could call on invaluable support from Australian industry. Kenney's airmen already had learned that poor frontal armament made bombers vulnerable to head-on fighter attacks. 5th USAAF pilots had also learned that air bases and ships were not productively attacked from high altitudes. For all these reasons Pappy Gunn, when given the chance, threw away the book on the A-20.

Originally the Havoc, like the B-25, had a clear nose for a bombardier. Gunn, however, decided the Havoc was made for treetop attack because of its great speed. Consequently he removed the clear nose, dispensed with the bombardier, and replaced both with four (later six) .50-caliber forward-firing machine guns; he also rigged it so the bomb release could be operated by the pilot. This gave a formation of A-20s formidable punch from the front and allowed it to drop an array of small bombs with delay-action fuses. The most famous of these was a Kenney invention from the 1920s, commonly known as the parafrag. It was a twenty-four-pound fragmentation bomb attached to a small parachute, dropped at less than 100 feet. Attacking low, strafing and bombing, the A-20 was a far greater threat to an air base. The chance for surprise—catching Japanese aircraft on the ground and shredding them—was much greater. This modified configuration also made the A-20 ideal for hunting the barges and small coastal vessels the Japanese often used to supply forces in New Guinea. Last, it made the A-20 a candidate for the new antishipping low-level tactic: skip-bombing, a topic we shall examine in Chapter 7.

Although the Havoc was constrained by its short range, Kenney would have been delighted to get more of them. However, USAAF officers in North Africa found the aircraft very useful, and Lend-Lease soaked up even more. After the initial shipment to 3d Bomb Group, Fifth Air Force had to wait until late 1943 before receiving a major reinforcement of factory-produced A-20 strafers. (The Australians also received a squadron.) In the meantime Fifth Air Force had to make do with machines on hand.

The success of the A-20 experiment encouraged Gunn and his associates to look at the B-25, which had similar problems. High-level missions were often unproductive, and the aircraft was vulnerable to frontal attacks. Despite the fact that the Mitchell weighed half again as much as the Havoc, Kenney encouraged Gunn to do his best. The Mitchell proved up to the ensuing abuse. In the words of Norm Avery, who worked on the B-25 project for North American: "The B-25 proved remarkably adaptable to numerous field and depot modifications and out in the Southwest Pacific became the object of more outright butchery, 'cut to fit, bend to suit, weld to match and scrap if necessary,' innovations than any other airplane."

After several weeks of work Gunn and his assistants had made the B-25 into an entirely different aircraft. The first thing was to correct a design error in the B-25 (it also existed in the B-24). The original lower turrets (often called "ball" or "ventral" turrets) were designed to be depressed during flight and operated by a gunner who aimed through a mirror. The result was often airsickness and vertigo. Harold Maul shared the universal dislike of the design: "The worst thing ever designed was the bottom turret on the B-25. It was the stupidest bit of equipment. My God, the operator is sitting in one place getting a reverse image through the mirror. He couldn't hit a thing. It slowed the damn plane down, and we weren't getting belly attacks anyway. What they really needed was a rear gun, which they eventually installed." As the ball turret was intended for low-level attack, Gunn simply removed it and hoped that the top turret would provide adequate defense for the rear. (Some pilots placed sticks on the rear of their bombers to mimic a rear gun. Ironically the first B-25s did carry a lone .30-caliber in the rear that was removed to save weight.) More importantly Gunn's crew removed the bombardier in favor of four forward-firing .50-calibers. On each side of the nose two more .50s were installed in pods. In addition the top (or dorsal) turret gunner could fire forward, giving the aircraft the capability of firing ten .50-caliber machine guns forward. The aircraft was also fitted with parafrag racks to complement the normal bomb load. Soon enough the modified Mitchell proved the perfect platform for skip-bombing. The result was the famous B-25 strafer.

Kenney was delighted with the results but feared that the guns and ammunition mounted in the front would throw off the center of gravity. He queried Gunn on the question, and according to Kenney Gunn replied that he had thrown it away to lighten the ship. In fact Gunn's modified planes were known to cause some problems, and the factory-produced strafer, greatly influenced by Gunn's work, that appeared in early 1944 was even more powerful and better made. In any form the weapon was devastating.

According to Rich Walker, a P-39 pilot in northern Australia awaiting shipment north who jumped at the chance to transition to B-25s: "We could strike antiaircraft, aircraft on the ground, shipping, against everything vital to the theater." Although massed .50-caliber machine guns would not penetrate heavy armor, almost anything else was desperately vulnerable to its withering fire. Phil Caputo was a gunner and flight engineer on a 345th Bomb Group strafer and sung the praise of the massed .50s:

> Barge-hunting was a common mission and we'd strafe them. After a while the Japanese cut that out because it got too dangerous to move by day. I never saw a barge fire back. The guys loved going after them because it was like shooting fish in the barrel. Our .50s could make a real mess out of a barge. You'd see guys go flying in the air when they got hit. When someone got hit by a .50-cal slug it slams them—it's a tremendous impact. Also the Japanese would be flying over into the water trying to dodge bullets. I once saw a motorcycle swept right off the runway by our .50s—picked into the air and thrown aside. Getting hit by twelve forward-firing .50s would be like hitting a brick wall traveling at a thousand miles an hour. A Zero would just explode in the air if you hit it right. It was a very powerful weapon. It would tear things to pieces.

Some of Gunn's work filtered into later B-25s. Even glass-nose models kept the four .50s in the forward pods and gave the bombardier an additional .50 of his own. Gunn and company were, however, involved in a less successful innovation. Small shipping was an important target. Consequently Gunn fitted a 75mm cannon to the nose of a B-25. Although Gunn got the aircraft to function, it was not a favorite among pilots because the recoil stressed the ship, and accuracy was poor.

Although 13th USAAF bombers rendered distinguished service in the Solomons, much of the aerial bombardment in that area was undertaken by Marine and USN squadrons equipped with tactical bombers procured by the latter. Although designed for carrier use, these single-engine attack planes proved well suited for land-based use if circumstances were right.

There were good reasons that naval aircraft—whether land-based or not—played an unusually large role in the Solomons whereas single-engine tactical aircraft were rejected by Fifth Air Force in New Guinea. First, the Marines flew what the navy gave them and had no direct role in aircraft procurement. Indeed light attack aircraft were frequently poorly suited for attacks against land targets (see Chapter 7). However, unlike in New Guinea the air war in the Solomons was fought in tandem with a naval struggle. The Guadalcanal campaign included some of the most violent and dramatic naval battles in history. Periodic clashes between fleet units took place throughout 1943. In addition there was always the possibility that the Japanese might decide to make an all-out commitment of Combined Fleet to the struggle for the Solomons, a move that would have precipitated a general naval engagement. Throughout the Guadalcanal campaign Marine and USN bombers based at Henderson had played a central role in the naval equation. In 1943 it was simple prudence to have large numbers of aircraft that were killers of warships, regardless of their weaknesses against land targets. In New Guinea waters it was rare to see Japanese warships larger than a destroyer, so aircraft were tailored to demolish air bases and destroy merchant vessels.

The two attack aircraft employed by the Marines and USN were the Douglas SBD dive-bomber and the Grumman TBF torpedo-bomber. (Unlike the army the USN liked to name its planes and needed no inspiration from the British; the SBD flew as the Dauntless, the TBF as the Avenger.) Although originally designed as a tandem for carrier engagements, the pair played very different roles during most of the South Pacific campaign.

The USN had been interested in dive-bombers and torpedo-bombers since the mid-1920s. Unlike Mitchell's bomber-cult followers, naval aviators were not convinced that level-bombing at medium and high altitudes was a good way to attack fast and nimble warships. Torpedo attack, until the navy refined techniques in 1944, required a slow and low approach, obviously dangerous. The payoff, however, could be substantial: Delivering explosives below the waterline could damage even the most powerful warship and possibly sink lesser breeds. The dive-bomber promised a fast and accurate attack that was less risky and more likely to strike home. Although a bomb was probably not as lethal as a torpedo (absent a direct hit on a vital point), it, too, promised serious damage. Furthermore, as USN fliers and Mitchell had shown in the early 1920s, a near-miss with a bomb would create a tremendous concussion; amplified by seawater, it could cause serious, perhaps crippling damage to a hull. Naturally any merchant ship was even more vulnerable. Just as eager as the Army Air Corps to exploit air shows and Hollywood, the dashing dive-bomber pilot became a glamour figure. (Germany was the only European power seriously interested in dive-bombers and observed USN developments closely.)

Although an older design, the Dauntless proved the superior ship-killer, giving it tremendous importance in the carrier engagements of 1942 and the Guadalcanal campaign. But the SBD was long in coming from drawing board to carrier deck. Originally designed by Northrop Corporation (owned by Douglas), it was intended to meet navy specifications issued in late 1934. The design was supervised by John Northrop himself, and early decisions did much to forge the aircraft's advantages and weaknesses. Northrop and the navy both wanted a low-wing monoplane with retractable landing gear and a powerful engine. Northrop believed that strong wings were essential, as this machine would have to dive faster with a heavier bomb load than any existing USN biplane. Taking a page from the development of the DC-3, Northrop employed a multicell wing that was very strong but not too heavy. When fitted with dive brakes (to slow the dive) the SBD could attack at a very respectable 70 degrees, promising a quick yet accurate attack. The disadvantage was that the wing could not be folded, common for all carrier-based machines. To partially offset that problem Northrop created a very small bomber, not much larger than a Wildcat and smaller and considerably lighter than the second-generation fighters.

The first were flown in 1935; the USN ordered fifty from Northrop as the BT-1 (as it was designated) and deployed them on its two fleet carriers: *Lexington* and *Saratoga*. Soon evidencing some vicious flight characteristics—many at low speed, which was so necessary to the navy—several BT-1s crashed, and the navy withdrew them from service. Knowing of problems, Northrop had already started a second model. During the money-lean prewar years, however, it was long before the navy appreciated the results. In the meantime Douglas took over the project and convinced the increasingly anxious USN to purchase 140 SBDs in early 1939 ("SB" stood for "scout-bomber" to distinguish it from bombers; the "D" designated "Douglas"). The first models showed far better improvement but lacked armor and self-sealing fuel tanks. Knowing better models were on the way, the navy solved the inventory problem by giving its castoffs to the Marine Corps.

When the USN began receiving large numbers of SBD-3s—the most common early-war Dauntless model—it was getting a solid machine. (Often derisively referred to as "slow but deadly" by its crews, the Dauntless was actually reasonably fast for an early-war aircraft.) Capable of 250 miles per hour, it was nearly as fast as its unarmored Japanese counterpart, the Val, and considerably faster than the much heavier German Stuka dive-bomber. Considering the type, it was well armed, mounting two forward-firing .50-caliber machine guns and a twin .30-caliber for the rear gunner. It could also carry a 1,000-pound bomb, which proved powerful enough to inflict dreadful damage to any ship. (The Val could carry only 800 pounds, a fact that may have saved some big U.S. warships, including *Enterprise*.) A variety of ordnance combinations were possible to fit the mission. Once the SBD had dropped its bomb load, it proved surprisingly maneuverable and accounted for several Japanese aircraft in duels. The range was not excellent yet exceeded the early fighters. And as fighters improved so did the SBD: It could normally operate effectively inside U.S. fighter range, which was much more important than the inherent range of the SBD itself. Yet the Dauntless was from a technical standpoint already showing its age prior to its moments of greatest glory. The low-wing configuration meant there could be no bomb bay, and ordnance had to be mounted externally, thus creating considerable drag. The Dauntless's static wing wasted precious space on carrier decks and was a constant irritant to officers. Its light weight and small size—required to keep the wingspan short—necessarily made the SBD vulnerable to battle damage. Still, it was strong, could handle a hard dive, and absorbed a good amount of damage. Whatever its drawbacks the SBD was popular among crewmen. The ugly handling difficulties that plagued early models were repaired, and the Dauntless became one of the war's most forgiving aircraft. LeRoy Smith flew a Marine Dauntless in many missions against heavily defended Japanese targets in the Solomons during 1943. Although shot down once, Smith was a fan of the SBD:

A military aircraft is built differently than a civilian plane. They're made to do very demanding maneuvers: an upside-down spin, barrel rolls, anything you can think of. You'd get up to 10,000 feet, dive out, and put stress on a military plane that no civilian pilot in a private plane would dream of—they'd simply come apart. When you're in that power dive you heard that Wright radial just a'hammering out there—

it's so noisy in the cockpit because it's being blown right back at you. After a bomb run it was very pleasant in the cockpit. When you pulled out of the dive and cleared the target my gunner and I would light a cigar. You were still alive and had no reason to take it home. It's warm and you're perspiring. In a very few seconds you're coming from about 1,500 to 2,500 feet and the temperature changes a lot. So the SBD was a workhorse. It would come home with huge holes in the wings and pieces shot off all over. She was a real workhorse, a gorgeous airplane, and I was very lucky to fly it.

A few SBDs were purchased by the army and designated the A-24; some saw action in the East Indies and were roughly treated by the Japanese. Others were flown by Fifth Air Force in New Guinea early in the war and likewise suffered badly (in July 1942 seven of eight A-24s were destroyed by Zeros during a single raid; after the debacle the machines was withdrawn from the front line in New Guinea). Marine and USN pilots, who knew little of the circumstances, tended to blame inexperienced flying on the part of their army comrades; no doubt there was truth in that. However, the army's failure with the SBD did point up a serious limitation in small tactical bombers. Navy SBDs performed splendidly in the great carrier battles, yet there was a fundamental difference between that type of engagement and a land campaign. Most carrier battles were over in a day and usually entailed a single sortie by attack planes. Even without escort, the odds favored dive-bombers in any single mission. And the stakes were so out of proportion—trading dive-bombers for warships—that any losses suffered were considered well worth the exchange in war's cruel math. Land attacks were a different matter altogether. A ground target required dozens of attacks. Over the Solomons SBDs received fighter escort for every raid. As it was, antiaircraft took a heavy toll on Dauntlesses. The stakes were also different. A hanger or antiaircraft facility might well not be worth the risk of losing an attack plane—they were small potatoes indeed when compared to a warship. Yet when it came time to attack a ship in the Solomons the Dauntless was usually nearby, and there was no more effective weapon for the task.

The SBD became a magnificent weapon during a magnificent moment in history, as no aircraft did more to bring Allied victory in the Pacific war. (The reliable Dauntless was preferred by many pilots to its successor, the very hot Curtiss Helldiver, on paper a much better aircraft.) But its moment of glory was brief, and indeed the entire dive-bomber concept was, we can see in retrospect, a dead end. As the war progressed Allied antiaircraft, when paired with radar control, became so deadly that even a dive-bomber formation was in peril. At the same time, Allied pilots found that fast fighter-bombers could dive-bomb and glide-bomb (a fast, low-angle attack) with great effectiveness. Indeed some fighters carried a larger bomb load than did the Dauntless. Soon after the war Douglas produced the AD Skyraider, which was a heavy, versatile, extremely powerful attack aircraft that served in Korea and Vietnam. Never employed against a ship and operating in U.S.-controlled airspace, the Skyraider was arguably closer in concept to the TBF Avenger than to the petit SBD Dauntless.

The TBF was a typical Grumman design. Honoring the unofficial Grumman motto—"build 'em tough, build 'em simple"—the Avenger was brought into production rapidly. Replying to USN specifications issued in 1939, Grumman had a TBF prototype flying in August 1941. Impressed, the navy had already given Grumman an order for 260 TBFs. Nearly 10,000 Avengers were produced by Grumman as well as Eastern (under license) throughout the war.

Although not a revolutionary design, the TBF had several useful features. The USN had anticipated that torpedo-bombers would be vulnerable to fighter attack during low-level approaches. Therefore the USN required that the new aircraft carry a rear turret fitted with a .50-caliber machine gun. With standard hydraulic bomber turrets being too heavy, Grumman engineers, with help from General Electric, created a lightweight, electrically powered turret that proved effective. Carrying the pilot, gunner, and radioman-bombardier, the TBF was a large plane. Although it was structurally sturdy (as expected from a Grumman product), designers stressed weight management. The result was a large body with a fifty-foot wingspan, still only slightly heavier than the Corsair and Hellcat. A TBF pilot would fold the aircraft's wings via a switch in the cockpit without aid from ground crews. With wings folded, the Avenger was economical with deck space. But unlike the SBD the TBF was not nimble. Like other Grumman machines the Avenger was docile at low speeds, offered good pilot vision, and was a good ride for green pilots.

Performance was adequate, slightly faster than the Dauntless. Possessing an internal bomb bay, an Avenger could carry a torpedo or 2,000 pounds of bombs, a good load for the type. With a sound design, and powered by the reliable Wright 2600 radial, the TBF proved one of the most versatile aircraft in the navy's arsenal. It was widely employed for reconnaissance, antisubmarine patrol in all theaters (several German U-boats fell to TBF depth-bombs), and attack. Avengers were popular among Lend-Lease partners. Its service life, in one form or another, lasted several years beyond World War II.

Aircrews liked the Avenger for the same reason they liked all modern naval aircraft: It could absorb heavy battle damage and survive. Jesse Scott served with a U.S. Navy "composite" squadron (including fighters, SBDs, and TBFs) that was deployed to Henderson in late January 1943. Scott was a radioman who was given a .30-caliber machine gun that could fire out of a small window at the aircraft's lower rear. On his first mission Scott found out that the TBF could take a pounding:

On our first mission we were supposed to attack some Jap destroyers that were going to reinforce their garrison. Later we found out they were trying to supply their rear guard and withdraw who they could. But we didn't know that. We went after these Japanese tin cans. We were supposed to wait at about 14,000 until the SBDs got one dead in the water and then we'd come down and put a fish in it. It wouldn't have made any difference because none of our torpedoes went off in the first year of the war anyway. The navy trained me pretty well as a radioman, although I rarely sent any messages. Gunnery was a different matter. One day they took us out to a range and they had some air-cooled .30-cal machine guns; the instructor told us to grab the grips, put our chins up to our thumbs, and look down the site then squeeze off as short a burst as you can, maybe five rounds. That was the total gunnery training. Before my first mission I had cleared the gun maybe half a dozen times and fired a quick burst as procedures demanded. That was it for my gunnery experience. A few minutes later I had shot down a Zero.

As it happened we never made our drop. Coordination was off, so we did not have fighter cover. I was looking out my window with my little machine gun and I saw this Zero come up behind us and below until he was about fifty yards away. He was so close I could almost smell him. Our machine-gun belts were loaded with one armor-piercing, one incendiary, one tracer round in sequence. One advantage of the .30-caliber was that the bullets were small and you could carry a lot of rounds. We wanted the tracers to scare off people, not really to hit anything. They weren't as effective as the other two. But it looks like you have a lot of firepower with tracers, even if you don't. With a steady stream of tracers it was like pointing a garden hose, and he was back there so close I couldn't have missed him anyway even though I barely knew how to use the gun. The plane started to smoke right away when the tracers hit it and it started heading down. My little gun didn't have much range or punch, but those Zeros didn't have any armor or self-sealing fuel tanks, so they were very vulnerable.

Now it wasn't all one-sided. This guy I shot down had us bore-sighted and was shooting us to ribbons. He had his two cannons and two light machine guns firing away. You could see them flashing as they fired. He just ruined our plane. I realized we were getting shot up okay. It's a pretty big area in the rear of a TBF—you could stand up. There's an aluminum seat that folds up against the bulkhead: That's where the radio operator sits when he's not at the tail gun. A cannon shell exploded against that seat and splattered all over. When we tried to make our torpedo run we couldn't release our torpedo. That's when we learned there was something wrong underneath. But that didn't stop us getting shot at by the destroyers down there. There was another Zero flying wing on us probably shooting at the plane right ahead of us. I looked out the little window on the side and saw him. He was so close that I started to draw my pistol to shoot through that plastic window. Kind of a funny reaction. After that I brought a tommy gun with us; thinking it if ever happened again I'd have something better than a pistol. We were real spooky about landing on those steel mats with the bomb-bay doors not closed. We didn't know for sure just how close that torpedo was to dropping: I don't know if it was armed, but with our luck it might have been the only time in the early war that exploded. We landed and ran very fast. Maybe the torpedo wasn't armed, maybe it was a dud. Either way, nothing exploded. But our plane was so damn badly shot up. They surveyed it when we got it back, and it was badly crippled and barely salvageable. We lost two TBFs that mission. All of this on our first flight.

But the biggest disappointment, at least for the navy before 1944, was poor performance as a torpedo-bomber despite some successful moments. The light Japanese carrier *Ryujo* took a torpedo from an Avenger at the Battle of the Eastern Solomons, which helped SBDs send the enemy ship to the bottom. (During the Battle of the Coral Sea in May 1942 obsolete U.S. Devastator torpedo-planes hit the light carrier *Shoho* several times and perhaps deserve credit for sinking it.) During the climactic naval Battle of Guadalcanal in November 1942 TBFs from *Enterprise* struck the crippled Japanese battleship *Hiei*, sealing its fate. Avengers also contributed to the slaughter of the merchant convoy the next day, which ended any hope Japan had of winning the land battle at Guadalcanal. Yet when compared to the devastating attacks made by Japanese torpedo-bombers in the same period against several U.S. capital ships (starting at Pearl Harbor) TBF successes were limited.

Torpedo attack is a complex operation, and no doubt inadequate execution was part of the story. However, as was clear by 1943, the Avenger was a victim of the U.S. torpedo debacle. This is not the place to examine this vexing problem in any detail. It is sufficient to note that torpedoes—the lone weapon carried by submarines, some aircraft, and surface warships—had the potential to destroy even the most powerful vessel. It is also sadly true that each modern torpedo type sent to war by the United States Navy was defective. (Naturally this increased the importance of the Dauntless; at least American bombs exploded properly.) The failure to test this crucial weapon prior to hostilities created the greatest technological failure in the history of the American military. As one might imagine, Avenger aircrews were bitter in retrospect. Jim Guyton was a TBF crewman flying off from *Enterprise*:

> There were serious troubles with the early torpedoes. It used to scare the hell out of you. We had planes in the hanger deck with bombs on them: All of a sudden they changed to torpedoes. That's when I started to worry. Because going in on a torpedo attack meant going low and slow. . . . Somebody finally said, wait a minute, why not keep flying straight ahead right over the ship . . . and that became our doctrine. . . . In the TBF there was a little door on the starboard side with a crank inside. You'd use it to set the depth of the torpedo run. . . . We suspected that a lot were not set right: If you set six it might run at twenty. But we could never prove anything. We did get torpedo hits on the transports on the canal and they were set at six. Later we got a torpex warhead and it put a good dent in a ship. In '42 the warhead was quite small. That's why sometimes a Japanese ship would take several hits and not sink right away—which is amazing when you think about what a torpedo is supposed to do. The Japanese models did more damage and you were in trouble if you got hit by one. You look at photos at the Japanese Kate bombers and you see that big torpedo of theirs sticking way out, like it's leading the plane along.

Until new torpedoes arrived later in the war and made the Avenger the best torpedo-bomber in the Pacific, the TBF performed most of its service in 1943 as a conventional bomber against land bases. Although no single-engine plane had the structural strength of a medium bomber, the Avenger was up to the task. According to pilot Jesse Scott, "TBFs had a tremendous carrying capacity and great versatility. Under certain configurations we could carry almost as much as a B-17.

... We lacked the crew and armor so we could carry a lot. We could carry four 500-pound bombs or depth charges; or a torpedo, which was close to a ton. It was really built. Of course any carrier plane had to be."

U.S. aircraft were not the only enemy encountered by the Japanese in the South Pacific: Australia and New Zealand proved formidable U.S. allies despite their size. When hostilities began in September 1939 Australia and New Zealand followed Britain into war, reflecting the countries' cultural, political, and military connections. When they did so both countries had only a skeletal air arm. The Royal Australian Air Force employed just more than 3,000 men and was flying a motley collection of obsolescent British types. The Royal New Zealand Air Force (RNZAF) had an even more meager force.

The Commonwealth nations moved quickly to resolve this question, but the road was not easy. Indeed, the RAF counted heavily on substantial numbers of personnel arriving from the Commonwealth. In the end most of the 170,000 men trained by 1945 (75,000 pilots) were integrated into the RAF, although some independent squadrons existed. As it was, Anzac pilots and aircrews proved an indispensable part of the RAF and provided splendid service throughout the war. (More than 4,000 Australian aircrewmen of RAF Bomber Command lost their lives—a painful percentage of Australia's overall 34,000 deaths in the war. Altogether 5,300 Australian airmen lost their lives in the war. New Zealand's proportional casualties were higher yet, with 4,300 airmen lost. Both countries lost approximately 75 percent of their men in Europe.) Certainly one of the manifest calamities from London's point of view inherent in Pearl Harbor and the loss of Singapore was an inevitable shift of Australian and New Zealand manpower away from Europe and toward the Pacific.

Implicit was the fundamental assumption that Britain would protect Australia and New Zealand in case of war with Japan. This was a vital matter, as both watched Japanese moves in the late 1930s with great anxiety. Although the Australians were as guilty as Britain and the United States in underestimating Japan's military power, their confidence in Britain's support was not total. The bulk of the Australian army was made up of a conscript militia specifically designed to protect Australia. In air matters this concern manifested in 1936 in the creation of the Commonwealth Aircraft Corporation (CAC), founded on the principle that Australia should be able to produce modern warplanes and not rely entirely on outside supply. The RAAF then expanded with remarkable speed. By mid-1942 there were 42,000 trained aircrew in Australia and half again that number in training. By April 1943 the RAAF fielded thirty-one squadrons; at this same time Fifth Air Force fielded thirty-three squadrons. When RAAF strength peaked in August 1944, 180,000 personnel were manning some 3,000 warplanes, giving Australia one of the largest air forces in the world in 1945.

One could argue that given the numerical size of the RAAF and undoubted quality of its personnel, the number of aircraft allocated to the most active combat front—New Guinea—was not high. The seven squadrons of 9th Operational Group, which were directly under the control of Fifth Air Force but commanded by Australian officers, were less than one-quarter of the RAAF. Furthermore one could argue that the RAAF was handicapped by a generally mediocre collection of aircraft. However, an examination of the overall force structure and mission of the RAAF provides a more balanced picture.

The American air units in the South Pacific made up only a small portion of overall U.S. air strength. As often noted, Europe had first call on men and aircraft. In addition, there were many squadrons protecting the Panama Canal and Alaska and conducting antisubmarine patrols off both coasts. The U.S. units sent to the South Pacific were not there to protect the United States but to wrest control of the skies from the Japanese. The RAAF was likewise resisting Japan directly and played no small role in eventually crushing the imperial air arm in the theater. However, RAAF units had to perform all of the duties that home-based squadrons did in the United States. These missions were far more important in Australia than in the United States. The long Australian coastline was uncomfortably close to several major Japanese naval bases and was an obvious hunting ground for submarines. Yet until the Allies successfully concluded the Buna and Guadalcanal campaigns in early 1943, the Australian government could not safely dismiss the possibility of invasion of the Australian mainland. The shocking raid on Darwin early in the war was a perilous moment for the Australian government, and there were fears that the Japanese might try a repeat against a target like Perth. In addition, the Japanese carrier raid on Darwin was only the beginning of a year-long offensive against the port by Japanese aircraft based in Timor in the Indies. Some of the earliest fighting in the South Pacific took place over Darwin. When the situation stabilized the RAAF began to trade blows with the Japanese. Darwin, in other words, was a separate and very active air front that required a major commitment of force. In April 1943 the RAAF commanders at Darwin had six Australian squadrons, one U.S. heavy bomber squadron, a Dutch squadron of B-25s, and the sole land-based RAF squadron in the South Pacific manning Spitfires. As the war progressed, so did the RAAF offensive against Japan in the Indies, ultimately leading to the isolation of a substantial Japanese army garrison on Timor and nearby islands. Moreover the RAAF had to join in the unending struggle to obtain supplies from the U.S. Army, which, far more than the USN, was committed to the Europe-first strategy. Australia continually requested more and better aircraft from the United States under Lend-Lease but did not see them arrive in sufficient numbers until the South Pacific campaign was effectively won. As an Allied nation, Australia took a backseat to U.S. forces in terms of supply. (One Australian mission succeeded in obtaining a large number of an aircraft called the Vultee Vengeance; soon enough the Australians knew that the Americans had unloaded junk.) Last, the RAAF was expected to support the large Australian army that carried the Allied ground effort until early 1944 in New Guinea. For all of these reasons the RAAF was made up of aircraft that were designed to protect Australia's coastline, make continual reconnaissance over vast areas, provide defense for Darwin, and support Australian ground forces. Regrettably from Canberra's point of view the RAAF did not get first crack at the best aircraft available in the theater.

Although never enough early in the war, the RAAF did benefit from Lend-Lease. The principal Australian fighter throughout the war was the P-40. Some A-20s (flown as the Boston by Australians) also filled Aussie squadrons. The USN's redoubtable PBY Catalina was the backbone of Australia's reconnaissance effort. As the war progressed, the RAAF received Liberators and Mitchells for an offensive against the East Indies.

One U.S. aircraft widely used by the RAAF and the RNZAF was the Lockheed Hudson. Like so many other aircraft that served in the South Pacific, the Hudson was a product of the European war. The RAF and Coastal Command were interested in procuring a light reconnaissance bomber. Lockheed quickly proposed a militarized version of its successful Electra airliner. Given a crew of four, two forward-firing light machine guns, and a top turret (a retractable ball turret was soon added), the Hudson had decent range and was reliable, easy to fly, and easy to maintain. Having a poor bomb load and lacking anything like the structural strength of a U.S. medium bomber, the Hudson was adequate for a number of roles, but winning the Pacific war was not one of them. Nevertheless both Australia and New Zealand fought with what was available.

The RAAF also manned a large number of home-built and imported British aircraft. The first CAC creation was the famous Wirraway. After setting up shop, CAC officials examined foreign aircraft, an initial effort into the unknown realm of constructing modern warplanes. Their choice, despite some sentiment for a British aircraft, was the North American AT-6 Texan. CAC officials chose the AT-6 because they believed it would be a relatively simple aircraft to produce and would give everyone involved at CAC valuable experience. They also believed that if given appropriate armament the docile Texan might serve as a light attack aircraft and, in a pinch, as a fighter. The CAC did give the Wirraway a more-powerful engine than the U.S. version, but nothing could make even that splendid aircraft become a modern fighting machine. As we shall see, the Wirraway's ability to fly low and slow made it a most welcome sight to Australian soldiers looking for ground support, at least for a time. However, when called on as a fighter the Wirraway was a catastrophe when matched against the Zero.

CAC soon began production of more serious aircraft. However, in early 1942, with the Wirraway experiment complete, CAC was left with 2,000 workers and a plant. Therefore the Australian government agreed to produce an Australian fighter to take advantage. The Boomerang was not a serious effort, employing many of the parts and design characteristics of the AT-6 Texan and being passed off as a fighter. The slowest fighter in the Pacific war, the Boomerang carried twin 20mm cannons and could defend a specific point effectively. Essentially a prewar fighter, it had good flight characteristics and a small turning radius. Its lack of speed and range sentenced the aircraft to a backwater of the Pacific war.

CAC was not in existence to produce the Boomerang, however. Instead Great Britain expected CAC to become a major producer of the Bristol Beaufort. Bristol was a highly regarded producer of warplanes for the prewar RAF. Its major contribution was the Blenheim medium bomber, which proved inadequate in every way. The Beaufort was a thinned-down version of the Blenheim and was likewise inferior. None of this was obvious when CAC began production just before the war. The Beaufort could carry a torpedo, which was very attractive to the Australian government. But it was slow, underarmed, and unreliable. CAC produced more than 700 Beauforts, and the RAF found the make usable in the desert; the Australian and British governments quarreled over who would receive the completed aircraft. In the end the Australians won out and supplied several squadrons with Beauforts. Like any modern warplane the Beaufort could be dangerous if conditions were correct. Nevertheless it required considerable ground attention and had mediocre performance; at best the Beaufort was a mediocre aircraft in the South Pacific.

Bristol's successor to the Beaufort was an excellent design, and RAAF profited greatly from it. Like all modern air forces in the prewar period Britain was interested in a twin-engine fighter that could carry substantial armament and have good range at the expense of maneuverability. The result was the Bristol Beaufighter. The Beaufighter relied upon many of the Beaufort's parts and design configurations and consequently was ready to fly in a short period. As the name suggests the Beaufighter was designed to be an interceptor and not a bomber. Unlike the Beaufort it had no bombardier and bomb bay. The aircraft's advantages were a good top speed (more than 300 miles per hour) and an extraordinarily destructive forward-firing armament, which included four 20mm cannons and six .30-caliber machine guns. In addition the radioman had, depending on the model, at least one .30-caliber machine gun to fire from the rear. About 100 British-made Beaufighters arrived for battle in the South Pacific. In early 1944 the Australians began producing their own version, which included six .50-caliber machine guns to complement the four cannons. No fighter in World War II (with the possible exception of the Me262 jet) had more firepower from the front than did the Beaufighter.

The Beaufighter in the Pacific was not a true fighter but a lighter and faster version of the A-20. It was also the only Allied aircraft that carried a British-made radial engine, the Hercules. Its targets were on the ground, not in the air. Like all of the 5th USAAF strafers the Beaufighters proved a scourge to Japanese shipping and airfields. Unless carrying bombs (made possible by ground modification) the Beaufighter could run even with a Zero on the deck. Fred Cassidy of 30th Squadron was one of the first to fly a Beaufighter; he recalled it as something of a turning point:

I was in 30th Squadron, which was formed in March '42 and first to get Beaufighters. . . . The Beaufighter was rather like a Mosquito. It was a British design: A plane called the Beaufort was the forerunner. The first Beaufighter was first up in 1939 powered by a pair of Hercules radials. They were very silent, that was the beauty of them. The engines were out in front of the nose. So you saw these two great big Hercules engines and a flying gun platform. We called them "flying artillery." We had four 20mm cannons and six 7.7mm machine guns all firing forward. When they fired forward you knew it: The whole plane took a step backward. The four cannons were in the nose and six machine guns in the wings. And nothing fired backward. There was no airplane in the world at that time that had as much firepower as a Beaufighter. Everything was rated at sea level because strafing was our major role.

We flew right on the deck most of the time. We often attacked shipping but did not often see fighters. However, when we hit airdromes Zeros would sometimes be waiting for you. You'd go over the strip, hit it, and the Zeros would dive on you: make one dive—we'd turn inside that—they'd go across you—and we'd come back again the other way—and so on. They could make about three passes if they jumped us with altitude advantage. But once we leveled out we were home-free. They could stay with us nearly even for a few miles, but they couldn't get any height on us. They used to come and sit on their wing about a hundred yards from you. We couldn't fire at them because we had nothing firing sideways and neither did they, so after a bit they'd peel off and go home. So we could hold them at deck level and fortunate for us.

The RAAF also commanded three squadrons of Spitfire Vs at Darwin. Eventually nearly 100 Spitfires were brought in and kept up to strength, on paper at least, for some months. Several of the pilots had seen extensive combat in the European theater and were among the best-prepared airmen in the South Pacific. Although the Spitfire squadrons landed some stinging blows to Japanese raiders from Timor, their overall performance was a disappointment. In theory the Spitfire V should have matched up well with the Zero. Carrying a mixed armament of 20mm cannons and rifle-caliber machine guns, the Spit had more than enough firepower to deal with any Japanese aircraft. Although no Allied aircraft was as maneuverable as the Zero under 15,000 feet, the Spitfire was considerably more nimble than any U.S. fighter.

The Spitfire fully deserved its sterling reputation in Europe, but several elements worked against it in the South Pacific. European designers were interested in combat performance above all and were willing to sacrifice both ruggedness and range to get it. (In 1944 this fact cost the Spit dearly. Although marvelous aircraft, the late-model Spitfires lacked the range to participate in the gigantic aerial melees that took place between U.S. fighter escorts and the Luftwaffe over Germany.) In the wicked environment found in the South Pacific the complex Spitfire was plagued by a series of mechanical difficulties made worse by the unreliable supply of spare parts. The percentage of aircraft grounded in the Spitfire squadrons was much worse than one would have found in a humble P-40 unit. Furthermore the British fighter had very limited range. In World War II getting ground radar to vector fighters to a point of interception was a complex enterprise and often failed. If Spitfires were not put in the right position they might well find that pursuit would put them in danger of running out of fuel.

When Japanese raids ceased in mid-1943 it was not because they had been defeated by Darwin's defenders. Rather it was because the catastrophe befalling imperial forces in the Solomons required an endless call for reinforcements for Rabaul. When the RAAF near Darwin went on the offensive in earnest against the Indies, Spitfires lacked anything like the range required to carry the war to the enemy.

New Zealand units operated across the arbitrary command line that divided the South Pacific Area from the Southwest Pacific Area. Although air command in the Solomons was very complicated, the area commander was Admiral William Halsey. The New Zealand government never attempted to produce its own aircraft (New Zealand was rural, to say the least). When Pearl Harbor came, several thousand New Zealand pilots were flying with the RAF, most manning British squadrons. (By war's end more than 10,000 were serving in the RAF and Fleet Air Arm.) New Zealand, like Australia, was directly in the Japanese line of fire after Pearl Harbor. The New Zealand government requested the recall of several hundred veteran pilots to serve as the nucleus of what grew into a surprisingly large air arm.

During the early period the Americans requested that New Zealand aircrews use their unspectacular but serviceable Hudson patrol bombers to watch the waters around New Zealand and Fiji. This was no small matter, as Fiji was high on the Japanese list for plucking until Midway. Soon RNZAF Hudsons were patrolling the crucial U.S. bases of Espíritu and New Caledonia. In November an RNZAF Hudson squadron moved to Henderson, thus initiating New Zealand's part in the battle over the Solomons. With an operational range of about 400 miles, the Hudson proved very useful in the Solomons, where submarines were a potential threat and sightings of Japanese warships a regular occurrence. In April 1943 No. 15 Squadron arrived on Guadalcanal with P-40s. RNZAF fighter squadrons took part in many of the fierce engagements triggered by each new U.S. landing farther up the Solomons. These engagements did much more than the Guadalcanal campaign to damage the JNAF, and by the time the JNAF abandoned Rabaul in April, New Zealand fighters had claimed ninety-nine kills.

When Japan left Rabaul the RNZAF reoriented itself to ground attack in support of New Zealand ground forces that fought a fitful campaign against the large Japanese garrisons on Bougainville and New Britain (which the Allies had bypassed). Beginning in April 1944 RNZAF fighter squadrons began to receive F4U Corsairs. No doubt many New Zealand fighter pilots wished that the U.S. Navy had been more prompt in upgrading their fighter arm. The Corsair was splendid both as fighter and fighter-bomber, so the transition was still well worth doing. Altogether the RNZAF fielded thirteen fighter squadrons (six of which did most of the air-fighting), nine patrol-bomber squadrons, and two flying-boat squadrons. For good measure RNZAF aircrews briefly manned SBDs and TBFs. Considering New Zealand's substantial contribution to the European war, and considering the fact that the population was smaller than Chicago's, the RNZAF's role in the Pacific was impressive. When Japanese officers pondered the opposition they faced from both Australia and New Zealand, they must have been painfully aware they lacked similar allies to aid them in the Pacific.

This is by no means a complete catalog of aircraft that fought in the South Pacific. It is clear, however, that in an air battle of attrition U.S. aviation technology proved in most ways superior to Japanese technology from beginning to end. As the Americans armed themselves with more modern types, and the Japanese Empire did not, Allied superiority grew to a yawning gap.

However, the aircraft required thousands of men to fly them and even more to keep them in the air. In many ways these men were among the best the combatants had to offer and required rigorous training. Furthermore at the beginning of the war both sides operated without a well-articulated doctrine of gaining and holding air superiority. The vital factor of tactics was likewise an area that the men had to refine on the spot. Indeed one reason that the South Pacific air war reached stalemate so quickly and shifted inexorably toward Allied superiority was the ability of U.S. airmen to solve the strategic and tactical problems posed by a unique theater, whereas the Japanese proved unable to adapt operations to the task at hand. Also, airmen and ground crews on both sides had to face the relentless assaults by nature, geography, and enemy violence that posed grave difficulties in maintaining morale to fight. It is time to examine the men who faced each other over South Pacific skies.

5

Airmen in
the South Pacific

W orld War II military aircraft represented highly advanced applied
technology for the era. Produced in huge numbers, these machines also became a staggering expense for all the combatant powers. Even before Pearl Harbor airpower had proven itself to be a key component of modern war. Complex, expensive, and vitally important, warplanes required many highly skilled men as pilots, aircrews, and maintenance workers. Some areas of military service, such as duty on submarines, required men with equally specialized skills. Air forces, however, demanded qualified men in huge numbers. In short, warring nations demanded the best and brightest of available personnel. In this arena, as in so many others, the Allies proved to possess resources far superior to Japan's. In retrospect it is possible that the Western Allies allocated too many men to the air war, for manpower shortages plagued the last nine months of the Allies' bloody ground war in Europe. (The USAAF by war's end enrolled 2.2 million men; the regular army fielded 5.8 million.) Such considerations, however, gave no solace to the Japanese during the war. Despite the low priority of the theater, Allied air forces slowly increased in quality and quantity until mid-1943, a point where they became powerful enough to send Japanese air units into a hopeless downward spiral to VJ-Day.

All aircrews and most ground crews were volunteers. Although I think it is important to discern patterns in the lives of the men who struggled for the South Pacific skies, any such attempt can only be imperfect. Although the missions involved and physical environments confronted were similar, the motivations of the individuals involved, the quality of their training, the level of morale, and a myriad of other factors varied from man to man. As one 5th USAAF veteran, in a fine display of dry GI wit, told author Susan Sheehan after the war, "Everyone's career in the Army Air Corps was like everyone else's, only different." Nevertheless the human factor in the air war was central to its course and demands examination.

Preparation for War

Men who serviced military aircraft for maintenance and armament—a seemingly unending duty—faced tasks that were physically and mentally grueling. Aircrews had privileges envied by millions of men in the Allied armed forces but faced extraordinary dangers. Yet no combatant nation suffered for lack of volunteers for service in its air force. Indeed the bottleneck was not willing men but a lack of serviceable combat aircraft and a shortage of training facilities.

Many motives impelled young men to service in the colossal air war that did much to define the nature of World War II. Ironically one of the most important influences was the astounding fame gained by World War I fighter aces, many of them German. (Perhaps because of the sheer size of the struggle, no World War II pilot gained the great renown earned by World War I veterans like Manfred von Richthofen, Paul-René Fonck, and Eddie Rickenbacker.) This was greatly amplified by the intrepid deeds of civilian air pioneers during the interwar period. With the possible exception of major political leaders and the most famous athletes, aviators like Charles Lindbergh and Amelia Earhart were the most famous people in the world. American pilots gathered much of the limelight, but every nation capable of supporting a basic aviation infrastructure had local heroes who set records of one sort or another. (Japan's government-supported "civilian" aviation sector posted several impressive feats to its credit during the 1930s.) And air services were quick to capitalize on the international mania, performing stunts that would hopefully gain public support and loosen governmental purse strings. Extremely popular air races only added to the public's fascination; impressionable youth were among the most dazzled. 5th USAAF fighter pilot Ralph Easterling's direction was influenced by the impressions of his youth:

> I wanted to serve in aviation because I'd always loved airplanes. I was putting together model airplanes when I was about eight. By the time I was eleven years old we lived about a mile from a small airport in the

mountains of North Carolina. I went down there and hung around hoping they'd need some help. I began to help out, learned some maintenance, and even did a little flying. This was about 1935. I was lucky. It was a kind of golden age of aviation before the war. So much was new. We were doing some night flights up in the mountains when that was very rare. We'd line the runway with oil cans with a mix of about 50 percent oil and gasoline, put wicks in them on both sides on the runway, and turn on some automobile lights and hope for the best. A lot of pilots pulled it off. Later a lot of the older pilots I passed time with became instructors when the military buildup began.

John Herbert, who flew a Wildcat off the deck of HMS *Victorious* in 1943, recalled that Easterling's sentiments were held by many across the Atlantic:

I'd wanted to fly since I was a child. I read books about aviation, I understood the theory of flight when I was about eight or nine. I could name every ace or every type of aircraft that flew in World War I. I was just mad keen on aviation and so were some of my friends. When I was young aircraft were still a kind of magical novelty—when you saw a plane you'd run outside and yell "Look!" I used to take my second-hand bicycle down to Croyton, the main airport, and sit there all day long watching the aircraft. And once a year the RAF put on an air display, which was heaven. I knew all the planes, the engines, everything. Now combine that with the extraordinary prestige of the Royal Navy and you can understand why I was so eager to join the Fleet Air Arm. I joined just before the fall of France. No one could foresee the extraordinary role the RAF would soon play.

Carl Camp, a flight engineer and gunner on a 5th USAAF B-24, was likewise bitten by the aviation bug early in life:

I had wanted to join the Air Corps since I was three years old when I saw one of those old army biplanes fly over my house in Beaumont, Texas. My dad took me up the first time when I was six. I can remember that first flight perfectly, especially coming down and all of those wires singing in the wind. It was a Travel Air with a great big cockpit up front. My dad was holding me in his lap because I couldn't see over the side of the cockpit. I looked back at the pilot behind us in his helmet and goggles and sure enough he gave me gave me a helmet and goggles. I almost went to heaven I was so happy. That did it for me and airplanes right there. I flew a couple times after that and was fascinated by the whole thing. So when I joined the army at age sixteen aviation was a simple choice. At age seventeen I was flying in an old B-18.

In some cases an interest in aviation intermingled with a desire to leave a home scarred by years of economic depression. Bomber crewman Jim Eaton was looking for a way out:

From the time I was five years old I'd thought about where I was going. I did this on an oil rig ninety feet in the air. I could see forever across the Texas Panhandle. Lindbergh flew the Atlantic that year. That sounded exciting and something I'd like to do. Anything to get out of where I was. We were living in an oil town, a boomtown, not a regular Texas town. There were two rows of ruts across the prairie with tin shacks on each side of them filled with a lot of people who were dropouts from every other place in the U.S. It wasn't an established community and I wanted out. That desire stayed with me all through school.

Although aviation mania played a role for many men to one degree or another, other motivations were at work. As many airmen admitted, a prime attraction of air service (no doubt such considerations helped the navy likewise) was that it removed the threat of draft and a stint in the infantry. I doubt that a fear of ground combat had much to do with such calculations; the future course of war was unknown for everyone involved. That said, only the most ignorant young men could not realize that serving on military aircraft would be very hazardous duty. In the event, casualty rates in the infantry were higher than in the Allied air forces, but death rates for many air units matched or surpassed those suffered by the most hard-pressed Allied ground units. The things men destined for air service wanted to avoid were marching, severe discipline, and bad living conditions. (As we shall see some airmen in the South Pacific might have questioned their decision on that last count.) Fighter pilot Perry Dahl learned the hard way that he had no wish to be a "ground-pounder":

In 1942 I was stationed at Fort Lewis, Washington, as an infantryman and as a medic. Gray Field was nearby. Pilots used to fly over, do mock strafings, and drop flour bags on us when we were on field maneuvers. So on many occasions I ended up in that wet climate being covered with flour, looking like a doughman. I would come sloshing back in after a three-day forced march and watch all those aviators sitting out sunning themselves on the wings of their airplanes. Aviation looked like pretty good duty.

John Herbert's love of airplanes was matched by a most understandable distaste for the expected war in the trenches. As is evident, Herbert was willing to stretch the truth in order to participate in World War II above the battlefield:

I certainly was not going to join the army. My father had been in World War I in the trenches, and the stories he told convinced me I should never hold a rifle and be up to my hips in mud somewhere. If I was going to die I'd do it in an airplane or submarine—fast and comfortable. And, to be honest, I didn't like loud bangs: I wasn't a bad shot with .50-caliber machine guns from a Wildcat but I didn't like firing a rifle or revolver.

I was a scholarship boy at public school and graduated with honors. I went through an interview to see if I was fit for service in the Fleet Air Arm. I entered a room where the occasion would take place. There was a commander in the middle, flanked by a pair of lieutenant commanders. You sat in a chair, rather like being in the dock. They asked some vital questions: Do you play football? I hated the sport but said, "Oh, yes sir, first eleven," which was an absolute lie. Cricket? I can't stand cricket, and still think its the most boring sport on earth, but I said, "Oh, yes sir, a good 'all-rounder' sir." These questions were considered adequate to admit me to the Royal Navy and I became a cadet. Most of the public school boys I knew could have answered those questions truthfully.

On some occasions the infinite mysteries of military organization combined with blind luck to put a man in the air. Tom Powell, who served as a gunner on an Avenger flying from the *Enterprise*, had his first taste of naval service on another aircraft carrier. Ill luck for one ship proved good news for Powell:

Before the war I was in 1st Division aboard the *Saratoga*. Most of the deck force on the *Sara* were trying to get into aviation. However, getting a transfer was almost impossible because the various divisions needed all the experienced people they could get. The *Sara* had some rough luck but it helped me. Shortly after Pearl Harbor the *Sara* got hit by a Japanese submarine. We went back to Pearl Harbor to repair this big hole in our side. When the war broke out the *Sara* carried some eight-inch guns. . . . The navy had already decided the guns were a

waste and removed them while we were under repair. My battle station
was range finder–operator for these guns. So I was out of a job and we
were out of the war for a few months. This boatswain's mate I knew
comes up to me and says, "Hey, Powell, I hear you're from San Diego. I
got a draft going out to Air Group 10 near there. Want to go?" That
was great news because I had relatives down there. I'd have taken duty
in Timbuktu for six months duty in San Diego at that moment. So
that's how I ended up in Air Group 10. First, I was a machinist mate.
Then they came around and asked for volunteers for combat
aircrewmen. I volunteered along with a bunch of other guys. Everybody
was hot and ready early in the war.

War between nations by definition creates circumstances that fit into
no usual category. Australia between the wars was divided on the need
and value of the great sacrifices rendered to the British during World
War I. Although some believed that the blood spilled for the British
Empire had been largely wasted, others believed that the Great War
had proved to be the defining moment in Australian history. In retrospect one can only admire the willingness on the part of the Australian
government to render many volunteers and huge amounts of funds to
the war against Hitler despite the enormous geographic distance separating Australia from the initial theater of war. For Beaufighter crewman Fred Cassidy the unique political chemistry found in Australia
shaped his military service:

We were all very patriotic; it was part of the culture of the time. My
father had been in the First World War and he got killed in the Second
at Damascus in November 1941 at age forty-two. He was a motor
mechanic and certainly didn't need to go. We joined together. I wanted
to join the army with him. He said, "No you won't because I lost two
brothers in the first war. You can join anything else but not the army."
They needed motor mechanics. He joined a headquarters unit out here
never expecting overseas service, but things got tough and they needed
mechanics in the Mideast. He was fit as can be, so he volunteered. But
he didn't have to go. It gives you an idea of how feelings were then.
   Following my father's wishes I joined the RAAF in March 1941. Out
here we have wide-open spaces: Australia is nearly as big as the U.S. In
1941 when we were training out in those country towns with miles and
miles of what we call in Australia "miles and miles": That's all you see.
We all flew these little old airplanes doing our exercises. There was no
thought about fighting a war on our own doorstep, far from it. We
were all concerned with Germany and Europe. We were hell-bent on

getting into the air and fighting Hitler. At my level of understanding of political matters the thought of war with Japan wasn't in the wind. In retrospect our attitude was remarkable. To put it mildly it was a hell of a shock on December 7 when we heard of Pearl Harbor. A few weeks later the Japanese hit Darwin and took Rabaul. Then we lost a division at Singapore. We had a war right on our doorstep.

Getting to the battle zone was possibly very dangerous. I have described the harrowing flights of multiengine craft across the Pacific. Naval aircraft usually joined their carriers in port. Army fighter pilots, or ground crews from any service, normally traveled in transports to the Pacific, often along with ground soldiers. No one who traveled in a transport enjoyed the voyage. It was hot, many men suffered from seasickness, and conditions were very cramped. In the pit of many stomachs, however, was the fear of submarines. American troopships, whether regular naval vessels, converted liners, or anything that could be pressed into service, rarely traveled in a convoy that was worthy of the name. Destroyers were desperately needed at the front, and lesser escorts were not available in large numbers. Frequently a small convoy would break up, with the ships depending on the massive size of the Pacific for protection. For the most part it worked. The Japanese submarines, though wreaking havoc on the U.S. Pacific Fleet in 1942, did not pose the feared menace to troop and supply ships. This, however, was not recognized at the time, and the men had to sweat it out. Any ship torpedoed in the far reaches of the Pacific had scant chance of any assistance. Marine ground crewman David Galvan had a very anxious moment while crossing the Pacific:

My squadron had been pretty well knocked out during Pearl Harbor. They scrounged together about 125 men and we were designated an "Expeditionary Force." We didn't know what that meant but did not like the sound of it. They put us on board a troopship with some other Marines that they had scrounged from Nicaragua or wherever they could find them for a Defense Group. After four days we lost our escort and were on our own with this troopship, maybe about 800 men and all by itself. One night we were all on deck it was so hot—near the equator—we're flying without lights but the moon was out and the guys were on deck singing "Don't Fence Me In" and that kind of thing. Then all the lights went on aboard ship. We were shocked into silence, we couldn't believe it. We all had our jackets on and headed for our stations but no signals were given for battle stations. After about fifteen minutes the lights went off. What happened was that there was a submarine out there tracking us. The captain made a decision: It was either Jap or American. If it was American he wanted it to know who we were. If it was Jap, he was going to get us anyway. We lucked out. This was about four or five days out of Efate. That's the scariest thing that happened to me aboard a troopship even though later I was under attack. That commander was smart. In March 1942 everybody was very trigger-happy. We were always testing our guns—whatever good that would do on a troopship.

World War II was a unique conflict in that the nations involved produced and consumed astounding quantities of weaponry that was technologically complex by the standards of any era. Even today only the most skilled mechanics can competently work on a huge World War II–era radial engine. Communications and radar systems, although analog, were complex, capable, and extensive. It is true that contemporary weapons are far more sophisticated, but because of their great expense and extreme complexity they are deployed in relatively small numbers. Conflicts prior to World War II, in contrast, relied on large numbers of relatively simple weaponry. World War II was thus a transition era between the age of rifles and the computerized battlefield. Naturally this kind of war required huge numbers of people with keen technical skills to build, maintain, and use the massed quantities of complicated weapon systems upon which modern armed forces depended. This was particularly true for the Western Allies. As the Russians, Japanese, and even Germans illustrated, it was possible to fight some of World War II with the weapons of earlier wars. However, in doing so those nations ran straight into the grim calculation that has shaped all modern wars: A government can choose to fight a war with money or blood. Painful casualties cannot be avoided when fighting a determined opponent. However, as Marshall Henri Pétain so correctly summarized twentieth-century war, "fire kills." If a country can afford the cost, it can greatly reduce the blood tax of war by employing firepower and advanced weaponry of all sorts. This was no mean factor in democracies desperate to avoid the carnage suffered during World War I. The United States and its democratic allies were rich countries for the era and chose to spend their treasures to equip their forces lavishly. It is no accident that Allied losses were far less than those suffered by the USSR and any of our major enemies.

Although it took time for mobilization to move into high gear, the Depression generation provided an almost perfect fit for the kind of war that the United States chose to fight. The trauma of Pearl Harbor immediately ended any political opposition to the conflict. (It did not end political disputes over the proper war strategy. Unfortunately for Japan many former isolationists and other Roosevelt opponents urged a stronger war effort in the Pacific. Naturally such sentiments were music to the ears of men such as Admiral King and General MacArthur. Whether such efforts helped prevent the Allies from finishing Germany in 1944 must always remain a subject for conjecture.) For the Allied air forces it was a priceless advantage that Western economies were firmly in the era of the internal-combustion engine. Furthermore, because times were hard, anyone with any technical aptitude maintained their own cars, trucks, and tractors to save money. And in a time before anyone had heard of a youth culture, young men were quite accustomed to physical labor. Barracks life was accepted if not loved. It is also safe to say that the hierarchy between generations was stronger fifty years ago than it is today, thus facilitating military discipline. It is also worth pointing out that for many young men the military world where decent food, adequate clothing, and some pocket cash were universal represented a step up the economic ladder. Much the same would have been true in Australia and New Zealand. Put simply, the Allied nations were relatively rich, almost completely literate, and brimming with healthy young people who knew how to use a monkey wrench. These conditions were perfect for fielding massive air forces.

Robert White, a ground crewman in New Guinea, had ample opportunity to observe ingenuity at work. In New Guinea, which was as far down the supply line as any theater of war, something that was not done on the spot would very likely not get done:

> Everybody did their part. You had the officers to blow the whistles—
> people like General Kenney, who was a good man. That shows
> MacArthur was smart because he listened to other people. For instance,
> he had a guy that figured out that you could cut a truck in half and
> stick it in a C-47, then weld it back together. There were so many
> people that knew machines. Farm boys knew trucks, tractors; they
> could fix anything. A lot of them were hunters, good shots. Some of
> them were clever at living off the land. I didn't realize how many skills
> our people had until I saw it in action. The common soldiers made
> things work, and given a chance they made things a lot more
> comfortable, which was important for morale. The war opened a lot of
> people's eyes.

Harold Maul, who ended his New Guinea tour in command of a
B-25 squadron, had nothing but praise for the ingenuity of men of
modest rank:

We got things done any way possible. We didn't ask permission to
create those strafers. We didn't ask permission to rewrite the book on
tactics. I couldn't have commanded the squadron without those ground
crew. They were tough, extremely smart, and worked like hell. Some of
the older guys who knew the ropes were also the greatest scroungers in
the world. I have no idea where they found what they found. In early
1943 an order from the adjutant general told us that we were supposed
to have separate rations for flight crew and ground crew. I said screw it.
We're all going to eat the same damn thing. The problem is that some
of it needed to be refrigerated. We didn't have any refrigeration and I
asked for a solution. The next thing I knew two of my sergeants came
up and said, "Major, if you can release a couple quarts of that medicine
you have under your bunk we can get a refrigerator." I had motor pool
give the gents a jeep on the spot. About two hours later they came back
towing a four wheel, walk-in, gasoline-generated refrigerator. We
camouflaged it to make sure the real owners didn't stumble on it. But
we had cold drinks, iced tea, all kinds of great things. Things like that
were important in New Guinea. Now only the old guys, the guys who
knew the ropes, could have done that. Screw the regulations.

The United States had another priceless asset for the air war: In stark
contrast to Japan, where aircraft companies suffered from a constant
shortage of skilled personnel, in America many women were well edu-
cated and found an invaluable niche in aircraft design. "Rosie the Riv-
eter" has won fame since the war, but her comrades at the drafting tables were helping to give the U.S. aviation industry unprecedented
flexibility. Norm Avery was a young engineer for North American and
recalled this contribution:

I wish I would have been older at the time so I could have better
understood the significance of all of the things that were taking place
around me. . . . So many of the pieces were right there at my fingertips
but I didn't see their significance. And now the exact way the pieces fit
together is lost to history.
    From its original plant of 1934 in Inglewood where I spent all of my
time, which wasn't very big, North American grew tremendously. The
employment grew with it. This was true with the entire arms industry,
and competition for skilled labor was fierce. You have to realize that

there were no computers in those days, and even the smallest alteration in an aircraft design required drafting new blueprints so people in the factory could make the changes. Changes big and small were taking place almost every week. This meant thousands and thousands of drawings. Originally the shortage of draftsmen was very serious. Soon we hired hundreds of young women. They were smart and meticulous, just about perfect for the job. Prior to the war there were very few women in the industry. By the end they were a very important part of the company. North American was not alone in that regard. They did important work and helped us tremendously.

In an odd way the poor economic circumstances of the late 1930s also aided the creation of the air arm. It was U.S. military policy to require two years of college for admission to flight training. Unlike in most countries American pilots and crucial flight crews were almost all officers. An experiment with noncommissioned (noncom) pilots was tried just before the war. The men proved fine, but the odd mix of rank ran against the grain of military discipline, even the looser variety that prevailed in the Air Corps. A pilot, for instance, might be a sergeant while a copilot was a second lieutenant. This situation did not sit well with the brass, so the sergeant-pilots were made first warrant officers and then given commissions. The USN and Marine Corps had a similar program, but the numbers of enlisted pilots never surpassed 15 percent of the U.S. air arm, an almost exact reversal of the Japanese ratio.

During the 1920s there had been a great increase in the number of state-supported universities. Tuition and board were very cheap in that era, and when the Depression came many young men and women either continued or began higher education simply because opportunities for young workers were so limited on the outside. Furthermore, good high schools were very good indeed. When the military began to accept exams for some of the time in college, tens of thousands of young men proved mentally up to the task. In the event, the United States alone trained 200,000 pilots and still more skilled crewmen such as bombardiers, navigators, and radiomen. It should also be noted that flight engineers had faced rigorous coursework, and gunners were expected to be able to fill in on more complex jobs if combat conditions required it. Considering the size of the air forces, the men destined for service in Australia and New Zealand matched American counterparts in aerial skills if not formal education. Altogether the Allies possessed splendid human resources to create a massive air arm and eventually made very good use of the opportunity.

The motivations of young Japanese men wishing to become aviators
were no doubt similar. Japanese pilots had performed well in the international races and feats of daring. The design of world-class civilian
aircraft was a great source of pride for the Japanese people, although
the specifications and even existence of military models were tightly-
kept secrets. Furthermore during the 1930s the Japanese air arm became a demanding and elite service. Although training would be brutally difficult, the life of any airman was far preferable to the bleak
future faced by infantry conscripts who learned to accept frequent
abuse from vindictive officers and noncoms. (Exceptions abounded in
this regard. Many Japanese officers, like good officers around the
world, took pride in caring for and earning the respect of their troops.
Nevertheless a Japanese enlisted man was at the bottom of the barrel,
the target of corporal punishment, and expected little better. As in so
many areas Japan had feet in two different centuries.) Regardless of
treatment, pay was poor and the work was hard in the infantry—good
reasons to avoid it. Prospects were little better for common sailors in
the rigid hierarchy of the imperial navy.

In one regard the situation in Japan was very different than in the
West. Although not fully mobilized for a world war, Japan was on a
war footing throughout the 1930s, particularly after war with China
began in 1937. The imperial fleet played an important strategic role in
the campaign, even though naval actions were minor. The frustrating
land war had little to recommend it for anyone who could possibly
avoid the infantry. (As events would prove, soldiers facing the Red
Army were sitting on top of a powder keg.) The air arm, however, was
deeply engaged in the conflict. Fighter pilots received adulation in the
press, and great hope was placed on the ability of bombers to force
Chinese leaders to see reason. Although I contend that the Japanese
drew the wrong tactical lessons from the war with China (see Chapter
6), there can be no doubt that the possibility of combat brings great
gravity to any decisions concerning military service. Japanese aircrews
were part of an elite service—and they took great pride in that. Surely
any of these young men who thought about the future would also have
known that the empire's military aircraft would be at the point of the
spear if larger hostilities came to pass.

It must be noted that Japan during the 1930s was not the Japan we
know today. In great contrast to the United States and the other Allies,
much of Japan's economy remained in an agrarian age. The young
men who could fix an ill-behaved Model T or tractor were few in comparison. As to high school and higher education, at least as America
knew them, they were much more developed in the United States than

in Japan. It was a bad omen when on March 23, 1939, the original Zero prototype was disassembled, loaded into oxcarts, and moved over poor roads to the large naval air base at Kagamigahara prior to its initial flight. There was nothing in Japan to rival a great base like Wright-Patterson. As one might imagine this was not an ideal society for supplying the thousands of skilled men required to support a large air force. Young Japanese of the era were tough, tenacious, and all too used to discipline. They were not, however, handy with the all-important monkey wrench. Many ground crews, having little familiarity with complex machinery, simply copied what they were trained to do and probably never grew to truly understand the advanced subsystems of a fighting aircraft. No wonder that Japanese officers after the war bitterly complained about Tokyo's inability to support aircraft in the field.

Furthermore it is safe to say that command rigidity inside the imperial armed forces was a serious problem. Whether or not it was theoretically possible to replace the Zero, Oscar, and Betty as the heart of the imperial air arm, Japan failed badly in its efforts. Allied tactical formations, originally proven deadly by the Luftwaffe, were not adopted by Japan until 1944. Japan's requirement for a large increase in training facilities was recognized early in the war, yet precious months passed before results began to appear. Although fighting a war with little margin for error, Japanese commanders again and again moved slowly, cautiously, and with little foresight. On the front lines soldiers and airmen proved capable of great initiative once freed from the heavy hands of headquarters. Rabaul was cut off in early 1944 but not captured by the Australians until after Japan's surrender. The Australians were startled to find how well organized the base remained and how healthy the garrison seemed. Mechanics at Rabaul were even capable of resurrecting a few aircraft from the scrap heap and wage a small guerrilla air war against advanced Allied bases.

Yet isolated Rabaul was the exception to the rule. It is difficult to imagine a Japanese air force having the skills and organizational flexibility to make major alterations on key combat aircraft at the front. And the tactical give-and-take that so marked Allied assessments of combat results was not sufficiently present in the Japanese forces. Tactics and doctrine were developed by men at the top, and those below were expected to put them into action. If something proved "broke" in the U.S. air forces the men on the spot would do what they could to fix it and inform higher command echelons after the fact. In retrospect it is striking how quickly Japan lost its qualitative edge over Allied forces. Although flying inadequate numbers of less than ideal aircraft,

American pilots of all services were more than holding their own before the end of the Guadalcanal and Buna campaigns in January 1943. The Allies kept refining their fighting techniques and gained as much as possible from weapons of limited abilities. The Japanese would stay with the status quo until it was proven hopelessly inadequate. Naturally when the Allies received superior weapons the roof fell in on the Japanese air effort.

Much has been written about the superb level of training found in the JNAF at the time of Pearl Harbor. A close look at the situation, however, shows a more complex picture. There is no question that before 1941 the Japanese air arm could be extremely selective in choosing men. (This was likewise true for American pilots before the emergency of 1940. These men did not undergo the draconian and perhaps pointless training regimen found in Japan, but they were an elite force and accumulated flying hours in droves. There were, however, very few of them.) Until war with the United States loomed after 1939, the Japanese army and navy fielded air forces of medium size. Still, the number of young men in Japan was large. Tokyo decided to pick the best men possible and, as aircraft would remain in short supply, saw no reason not to.

However, Japan was an authoritarian regime with a rigid social hierarchy. In fairness to Tokyo, the pool of well-educated and extremely healthy young men was far smaller than that in the West. Yet the methods employed to surmount this problem were by no means the best available. The IJN chose pilots from three pools. First were ensigns from the Naval Academy at Eta Jima. Indeed primary flight training and the study of aviation was a part of the general curriculum as early as 1920. Nevertheless, unlike the far-sighted admirals in the USN, IJN leaders made a serious mistake when integrating aviators into the naval forces. In Japan the cult of the big gun remained dominant until Pearl Harbor. Furthermore naval officers were expected to be seamen above all; carrier and air group commanders were not expected to be flying officers. Put simply a young academy graduate would undergo rigorous aviation training in addition to strenuous naval instruction and a full tour at sea. If he stayed in aviation his chance of later naval command was not promising. Instead of integrating naval aviators, as the USN had done, the Japanese segregated them. As one might expect this did nothing to encourage Eta Jima graduates to enter aviation. By Pearl Harbor officers and academy graduates represented only 10 percent of all JNAF pilots.

In 1928 Eta Jima graduates were joined in aviation by the Pilot Trainee Program, which enabled noncommissioned officers already in the fleet to apply for flight training. This helped but clearly would not provide the numbers envisioned for future expansion. A year later Tokyo instituted the Flight Reserve Enlisted Training Program, which directly recruited physically and academically gifted teenagers for ultimate service in the JNAF. These young men were fifteen to seventeen years old and initially were required to be primary school graduates; in 1937 the standard was raised to middle school. These young men were given a one- to three-year stint at sea and then sent to aviation training. All had to pass rigorous physical examinations and evidence excellent academic abilities. Like the men recruited from the fleet, the reserve youths were enlisted men. This meant that 90 percent of Japan's pilots were either enlisted men or noncoms.

In and of itself there was no reason why one had to be an officer in order to be a good pilot. Only the Americans routinely commissioned pilots. Yet one wonders if the Japanese cared about initiative and adaptability—traits that proved invaluable during war—and whether they would have recruited and indoctrinated young men who should have been in civilian school adapting to a less structured life. American pilots, too, were extremely young; most Japanese pilots were younger yet. American pilots who confronted Japanese land-based units after the shock had worn off from the blitz in Southeast Asia often commented about the radically different levels of skill and tactical judgment among Japanese pilots. Many others believed that if a Japanese unit lost its flight leader, its effectiveness plummeted. It is likely that both observations contained some truth. And the yawning divide separating officers from enlisted men did not help morale in the field. (It was very rare for a Japanese pilot to receive a field commission early in the war.) One must also wonder whether sea training, which lasted a year at least, was of much value to future aircrews. All U.S. air forces showed a pressing interest in getting men through training and into the air; the finer points of military etiquette could await another day. (I should point out that most aviators who gained naval command in the United States were Annapolis graduates and well trained in the basics of naval operations; one did not go directly from flight deck to command. A similar situation existed with young men from West Point. The issue, however, was that regular officers flying for any U.S. armed service could look forward to potentially rich military careers.)

In 1941 Tokyo began a major expansion of the reserve pilot program, but results did not appear at the front until 1943. Consequently the JNAF went to war with a well-trained core of fighter pilots and tactical aircrews but without a replacement apparatus that would accommodate a major expansion of the air arm. There is no question that many of these pilots ranked among the world's best. In some years before 1941 the JNAF graduated the absurdly low figure of 100 new pilots. In 1937 ace Saburo Sakai recalled that seventy-five men in his class were accepted out of a pool of 1,500. The initial aim of the harsh training regimen was to create the warrior mentality. According to Sakai, his first physical training instructor told the young men that "a fighter pilot must be tenacious and aggressive. Always." In addition to rigorous flight and ground instruction, cadets were put through a grueling physical program that included hanging from an iron pole with one hand, swimming, holding one's breath, walking on hands, standing on heads, diving off a platform onto the ground, and wrestling. Poor performance in this program could result in the shame of expulsion. (U.S. flight training later in the war including "preflight," which also included a heavy emphasis on sports and physical fitness. This was not a phase—once severe physical examinations were passed—that would often result in a "washout." Indeed many pilots before 1943 never went through it.) Sakai believed that such training developed an "amazing sense of balance and muscular coordination" that paid handsome dividends in combat. Americans likewise emphasized overall physical fitness but found that an artificial ordeal did not help make good pilots. The IJN must have agreed with the Americans, because as war progressed and the Americans increased physical instruction (one is tempted to think that the great lengthening of training in the United States reflected the fact that there was no obvious place for many of the late war pilots) the Japanese were dispensing with it. When push came to shove it was important to teach men to fly, which above all meant hours in the air training.

It is not possible to create an exact profile of the amount of training possessed by Japanese and American pilots at any given period during the war. Evidence exists, but the numbers are not consistent. Basic trends are clear enough. At the time of Pearl Harbor the IJN had a very well trained force with a core of superbly prepared carrier pilots. Captain Takeshi Mieno, director of training in 1945 for Navy Headquarters, told American interrogators after the war:

The flying experience of the JNAF pilots at Pearl Harbor averaged about 800 hours with a minimum of 300 and a maximum of 2,500. That level was maintained by the first line JNAF pilots until the Battle of Midway; the level fell off only gradually through 1942, but declined considerably in 1943 as field training was curtailed. In the Okinawa campaign, the average flying experience of pilots was between 200 and 300 hours, but that had been under instructors of less ability than earlier. Physical standards of flying candidates were lowered slightly during the war, and the washout rate in flying schools was reduced from nearly 40 percent to 5 percent.

Captain Minoru Genda, operational mastermind of the Pearl Harbor attack, presented a similar picture: "The strength of JNAF at the beginning of the war was 3–4,000 pilots. About 1,500 were trained for carriers. The average experience of the pilots varied between 800–1,000 hours. The minimum was 200–300. The Eleventh Air fleet that attacked Pearl Harbor had 600 pilots with average experience of over 600 hours. A squadron leader averaged about 2,000 hours. In 1945 the average was down to 400 hours with a minimum of 150."

Training within the army, unburdened with carrier operations, was less rigorous. Colonel Junji Hyashi, chief of staff of the army's 51st Training Division, told Allied officers:

JAAF had approximately 2,000 pilots with 300 hours training in '41. Shortage of training personnel kept a buildup down until 1943. By end of '43 we had 5,000 pilots. However, the quality of the pilots steadily decreased as the war progressed. Originally students had 100 hours of primary training but that was shortened to 30. Sometimes the total came to 100—same as primary originally. We needed pilots in a hurry. Also fuel shortages began. We assigned more and more cadets to become instructors and thus instructors were not as good. We tried to find men who were wounded and could not fly combat for that role. We also used school graduates not up to rigors of combat for instruction. There was no fixed rotation policy for pilots. Training divisions had about 750 planes and each graduated 300 pilots every 3 months. Cadets had lower physical standards as war progressed, but mental skills remained the same and there was no cause for degradation in that regard.

Figures compiled by the U.S. Fifth Air Force after the war show that Japanese pilots possessed adequate experience well into the war and indicate that the fall in performance came somewhat later (as compared to Japanese sources). At the beginning of the war, according to 5th USAAF intelligence, the average Japanese naval pilot had 600-plus hours of flying experience, which included training as well as experience picked up during operations; this was a formidable total by the standards of the time. By August 1942 the figure had dropped to 500 hours; by July 1943 to 400; by the beginning of 1944 to 300. Closer examination of the data paints a grimmer picture. According to U.S.

figures the IJN started the war with approximately 1,000 pilots who had more than 600 hours' flight time. This number held until August 1942 (the invasion of Guadalcanal), then began a steady decline until the category ceased to exist in July 1944. Pilots with more than 600 hours probably would have included many squadron and group leaders. Within U.S. forces, prewar elites, after the initial battles, were promoted, made leaders of the training program, and otherwise put to work improving the overall quality of the air forces. The Japanese, with their haphazard rotation policy, allowed such men to die out. Japanese pilots with 300–600 hours in the air at the start of the war numbered about 1,400 and increased to 1,800 in April 1943, dropping back to about 1,000 in early 1944. This category briefly rebounded and then began a steep decline in mid-1944 (the time of Japan's catastrophic defeat during U.S. operations against the Marianas) until it disappeared in February 1945. In May 1943 U.S. records noted a large influx of pilots possessing 200–300 hours of total flying time. As noted by Captain Takeshi above, this group certainly resulted from the large buildup of the reserve training program early in the war. Immediately this category became the largest in the JNAF as the more experienced men declined greatly in numbers. By mid-1944 some 3,500 pilots in this category were flying for the JNAF. Put simply Japanese pilots flying in mid-1944 possessed 50 percent of the average flying time of pilots flying in January 1942. After mid-1944 the JNAF almost ceased to exist as a skilled force.

Fifth Air Force conducted a similar study of Japan's army pilots. Across the board army pilots had less time in the air, although the JAAF must be considered a well-trained force until 1943. Some 650 pilots at the time of Pearl Harbor had 500–600 hours. (U.S. records did not include a category for men with more than 600 hours' flying time for the JAAF, although several individuals existed with well over that total.) The category wavered for the first year of the war, began a steady decline in early 1943, and ended in November 1943 when Wewak was demolished for the first time. Some 1,200 men had adequate totals of 300–500 hours. The curve followed the aforementioned category almost exactly, ceasing in March 1944. Until November 1943 the largest group comprised pilots with 200–300 hours of flying time. In November a new group appeared with less than 200 hours and immediately became the largest classification. This group peaked in July 1944 with some 2,500 men. By that time the categories representing pilots with more than 300 hours had disappeared.

The anecdotal accounts from Japanese officers and the U.S.-compiled figures were quite in order. (The U.S. study relied upon postwar Japanese sources, so there is no surprise there.) A few important points stand out. Japan did indeed have a strong cadre of elite pilots at the beginning of the war. However, early engagements, including those between carriers, prevented that number from growing as one would have expected. As clear from the Japanese accounts, the expansion program was begun too late and imperial top guns were being lost as fast as they were being replaced. When Guadalcanal and New Guinea heated up, the numbers of top pilots began a slow slide, which became a precipitous descent in mid-1943 for both Japanese air services. Still, when Japanese reinforcements arrived in large numbers they met Allied pilots who were on the opposite curve (i.e., increasing flight experience). And Allied pilots were not flown into the ground, as many Japanese were.

I must emphasize that the studies quoted are not precise and do not break out the different kinds of flying. Put simply an hour in a fighter was far more important than an hour in a primary trainer. However, as we shall see presently, American pilots in late 1941 and early 1942 received training that was no more intensive (in terms of time) until mid-1943. I would conclude that the reason for the turning tide in the Pacific air war lay less with a decline in Japanese pilot training than with superior Allied tactics, aircraft better suited to a war of attrition, superior antiaircraft, and much better communications. As a related point, I think it likely that the early Japanese air victories were less a product of aerial wizardry than a reflection of superior numbers, shock, and better fighters. As those advantages dissipated Allied airmen were able to stun their opponents in the period August 1942–July 1943. As soon as new Allied planes, better maintenance crews, and more squadrons entered the theater, the stunned opponent was being set up for the knockout, which came with considerable speed.

Elite Japanese pilots were assigned to carrier operations. No doubt their feats did much to build the fearsome reputation that the Zero developed in 1942. Also important, the prewar IJN rotated squadrons so that as many men as possible could experience combat flying in China. China may have been a tactical wasteland, but there is no question that combat experience of any kind, particularly if successful, builds confidence and, far better than training, identifies the pilots who will excel at war. (All air forces have stories of great aces that were poor student pilots. Manfred von Richthofen was one of the first. In the event, brains, nerve, and marksmanship proved far more valuable than acrobatic skills in combat.) In addition, the combat demands were not severe, thus enabling Japanese squadrons to ease new pilots into operations as they received further training. Giving the job of acclimating new pilots to the squadrons—although also employed, by necessity, by the United States early in the war—was a dangerous precedent. When put to heavy combat, squadrons lost the ability to maintain a plane as well as the pilot surplus. All too often, then, experienced pilots flew the available aircraft while the rookies were shoved into action when a veteran became a casualty or grew ill. Far better was an in-theater training system, soon developed by the USAAF, or regular squadron rotation supported by reserve units, as developed by the U.S. Navy and Marine Corps.

Very interesting testimony concerning the situation at Rabaul came from the postwar interrogation of Southwest Fleet staff officer Captain Toshikazu Ohmae, who served at the island bastion between June 1942 and December 1943. After that period Ohmae was transferred to the Central Pacific, where he watched U.S. forces crush Japanese defenders, already crippled, in the South Pacific. Ohmae commented on the brittle nature of Japan's reserve system when war came: "The Army had reserves in China, Manchuria and home defense. In Japan the Navy had training only. We were fully committed from beginning. At start of war, had 40 percent plane reserve in front area. We believed this was the best way to win as quickly as possible."

Japanese combat aircraft in 1942 wore out or were destroyed faster than they could be replaced. This melancholy math eliminated the JNAF reserve in short order. Ohmae pointed to the serious impact that losses of all kinds had on Japanese strength at Rabaul: "When we began in August of 1942 most of our pilots were very well trained with more than 500 hours flying time. But by 1 January 1943, only about 15 percent were left and we were receiving pilots fresh from school. They had only about 100 flying hours in combat planes: maybe 200 overall." According to Ohmae, the command at Rabaul undertook desperate measures to maintain strength. New pilots who arrived were not adequately trained, although those who lived no doubt added flight hours very quickly because of the distances involved in the Solomons campaign. Experienced naval pilots from other areas in Southeast Asia were exchanged for Rabaul veterans weakened by malaria and stress. In 1943 the army agreed to send major reinforcements, but this expediency proved a failure, according to Ohmae: "The Army had just come into Rabaul, but it was no help. Japanese Army units had no training in navigation and in any event these planes had too short a range."

Ohmae and other officers on the spot pled for the deployment of the JNAF's sole remaining source of good combat aircraft: the Imperial Japanese Navy's carrier air groups. Originally Tokyo refused the request, believing that it was essential to rebuild the air groups for a decisive battle in the Central Pacific, probably in early 1944. (The IJN got its wish: The Battle of the Philippine Sea in June 1944 proved a crushing American victory, almost demolishing the imperial navy as an effective force.) In March 1943 the situation at Rabaul deteriorated further when Fifth Air Force destroyed some forty Zeros that were attempting to provide cover for the troop convoy during the Battle of the Bismarck Sea. Believing that then-current trends would have catastrophic consequences, Yamamoto himself, in one of his last actions, ordered the deployment of Carrier Divisions (CARDIVs) 1 and 2 to Rabaul. In April the Japanese launched massed air strikes at Guadalcanal and targets in New Guinea. Huge reinforcements brought overall Japanese strength in the Rabaul area to nearly 700 aircraft, much the highest number of the war. It was sad commentary on the poor operational maintenance that the Japanese raids in April could employ less than half that total. Japanese losses proved heavy, and Yamamoto ordered the carrier divisions back to Truk.

The beginning of the end of Japan's aerial war effort took place when Rabaul's forces desperately attempted to stop the U.S. landings at New Georgia in July 1943. Ohmae stressed the decline in Japanese training. It should be pointed out, however, that the New Georgia campaign was the debut of several Corsair and P-38 squadrons in the Solomons, which was bad indeed for Japan. (Some of these units gained great fame. The Marine "Black Sheep" squadron and the navy's "Jolly Rogers" were the two most notable, but they were not alone.) Regardless of the exact equation, Ohmae described a catastrophe that once again led to the sapping of imperial carrier reserves:

In July, after the U.S. landings at Rendova, we attacked as best we could. Because of the very low level of the training of our land-based pilots, we lost three quarters of our strength and had only 40 or 50 planes left. We made an urgent call for reinforcements, and the CARDIV 2 air group was sent in about 25 July. It never went back to its carriers and was merged then and there with the 26th Air Flotilla. Thereafter a new CARDIV 2 air group was formed, but it was a completely new group. Originally the pilots of CARDIV 2 were very good with much experience. It had about 175 planes. At first it was based forward, but after your landings at New Georgia this became untenable and it retired to Buka, and finally, at the end of August to

Rabaul. At that time total Navy aircraft strength at Rabaul amounted to 100 fighters, 30 single engine bombers and 30–40 Bettys. We were receiving replacement Zero Type 52 fighters, which were very good, but the replacement pilots were very poor. In November 1943 the new CARDIV 2 was also land-based, coincidentally with your landing at Bougainville. It stayed in Rabaul for about two weeks, suffered 30 percent losses and then withdrew. Thereafter, it was reorganized and went to Singapore to train. It had only a few really experienced pilots.

Although it is impossible to precisely weight the relative importance of declining training standards along with growing technological and numerical inferiority, the Japanese war effort clearly began to crack in mid-1943. Critical to understand, however, is that when the Allies stabilized the situation and slowly turned back the Japanese thrust, they, too, were suffering from training deficiencies of all kinds and every imaginable shortage of combat equipment.

On the surface there appear to be some similarities between recruitment methods used by the United States and Japan. In practice the differences were great. Like the Japanese the USAAF, USN, and Marines relied on a combination of academy graduates, in-service transfers to aviation, a huge reserve element, and, for a while, a few noncommissioned pilots. Army officers who completed flight training obtained a temporary rank in the regular army that was good for the duration. However, the numbers of U.S. academy officers were higher than in the Japanese service, no doubt because many saw aviation as the wave of the future and an excellent road to promotion.

The USAAF and USN handled recruitment and training differently. In general, the USN was a much more developed service during the interwar period than was the army. As late as 1938 the army was numerically second-rate, eclipsed in size by a number of smaller powers. The USN, however, possessed a great fleet and much stronger backing from Congress. In 1935 Congress passed the Aviation Cadet Act, which authorized the USN to recruit flight officers (later ensigns) from U.S. colleges. If these men made it through training they did a three-year stint with the fleet. By Pearl Harbor the Navy Reserve provided half the aircrews in the USN. (As the navy also administered the Marine Corps, much was the same there.) As war progressed that percentage grew, for most aviators considered themselves combatants only for the duration and had no interest in making a career out of the service. As it worked out many changed their minds. Unlike Japanese counterparts, the Americans came out of colleges, not middle schools.

Although higher commands normally went to academy men, in general the distinctions at the crucial squadron level between regulars and reservists was far less dependent on service background than one's ability to fly. Prior to 1941 that strongly favored the academy graduates and other regulars. Many pilots who got their wings after 1939 had more than 1,000 hours of flight time (some much more). When Roosevelt called up the reserves and the huge training expansion began, the balance began to shift. Veteran pilots fought the first carrier battles and later did much to help fledglings. But as events developed the war was fought overwhelmingly by younger men who joined the armed forces in 1941 and later.

The USN, starting from a stronger position and envisioning a much smaller expansion compared to the USAAF (though large when compared to the Japanese), suffered less of the near chaos that so marked the army's breakneck enlargement. Faced with the crisis in Europe, Congress was quick to order a substantial increase in naval aviation. The senior service wisely allocated resources to the creation of training facilities, an intelligent decision that reflected necessity. In one respect the navy and army faced a similar problem: a severe shortage of modern fighting aircraft. Instead of rushing to build badly equipped squadrons, the USN allocated resources to training while awaiting the arrival of modern aircraft. As it was the task was prodigious. After the fall of France, Congress authorized an increase in the USN training program to 4,500 per year in 1941, 6,000 in 1942, and 15,000 in 1943. The original naval program reduced the training time from one year to seven months without—or so it was argued—sacrificing any quality. (Later the term was again lengthened.) Service training called for 300 hours of training, including eighty-eight hours of specialized training in modern types. After completion, those men who stayed in the USN were, in theory, to progress to the Advanced Carrier Training Group (ACTG), where they would receive the training necessary for effective carrier combat. Marine Corps pilots were not necessarily expected to follow the same regimen. In the event, many early-war navy pilots received advanced training ashore using obsolescent aircraft. Ultimately the great naval task forces that went to sea in late 1943 and crushed the Japanese in 1944 had a substantial active reserve of both pilots and aircraft. The new men fighting earlier, particularly those in the Marines, made do with far less.

From the outset the USN and Marines attempted to keep squadrons together. For carrier service, air groups (fighter, torpedo-bomber, and dive-bomber squadrons) were likewise considered an organizational whole. Originally those units included all ground crews, but the test of war soon proved that to be unfeasible. USN and Marine squadrons soon included only key support personnel, delegating the bulk of the ground crews to ship's company on carrier or to the air base on land. Yet in theory pilots and planes went into battle together and were rotated out together. (In practice Marine units received periodic replacements, and Marine unit rotation was a ragged affair.) There was much to favor this plan of action. It was, however, best suited for carrier engagements where the number of battles was relatively few and the "air bases" could return to base, where new air groups were getting final training.

The pace of USAAF expansion was far faster and started from a weaker base. In addition, much to the chagrin of USAAF leaders, thousands of modern aircraft ended up in the Lend-Lease pipeline. (Generals feared that shipments to Britain and then the USSR would not only hinder the army's growth but also be wasted if the Germans prevailed over either country.) The pace of expansion was truly prodigious: In 1926 the Air Service counted 900 officers and 9,000 enlisted men flying 1,000 aircraft, most of which were noncombat. When the Depression hit, the Air Service was commissioning 150 men per year as pilots. Wisely the army expended its resources, building sophisticated facilities like Randolph Field and Wright Field. (The Air Service had to look outside the ranks to construct such famous places. A 1926 law limited nonflying officers in the Air Service to 10 percent of the total force, severely limiting the pool of engineers and technical personnel.) During and after the 1940 emergency pilot training, the figures skyrocketed. In 1939 1,200 new pilots were authorized. In 1940 the number went quickly to 7,000, then to 12,000. Soon afterward the goal of 50,000 pilots per year by mid-1942 was proclaimed. (The army failed to produce such numbers but came surprisingly close: In 1943 the numbers did explode to 83,000 pilots and 240,000 ground crewmen. Soon it became obvious that the USAAF manpower expansion had exceeded what was reasonably necessary; recruitment became more selective and the numbers of recruits fell.)

The army did not attempt to rotate squadrons in the manner of the navy and the Marines. Distances were long to base and army planes were all land-based. Instead units were based in a given area and kept there; pilots were not. Although early in the war the USAAF undoubtedly pushed its small force too hard, a replacement pipeline appeared early. Crews saw more than their share of action but would rotate out before heading for psychological oblivion. In addition, all American pilots received a leave policy that few Japanese counterparts could have imagined. Men who rotated back added knowledge to the growing pool of combat savvy, in turn passed along to green aircrews. A surprising number of pilots volunteered for another tour after a good rest.

Even worse than in the USN, army training was hamstrung by a lack of modern aircraft. (The balance of forces in the South Pacific is examined in greater detail in Chapter 6.) At present it is enough to note that U.S. superiority in aircraft and crews at the time of Pearl Harbor was an illusion. Many accounts of the period do a poor job of distinguishing aircraft in the pipeline and those integrated into fighting squadrons. If one looks only at paper strength the United States outdistanced Japan in numbers of aircraft; in practice the opposite was the case. The defense of the Western Hemisphere, plans for operations in Europe, and squadrons allocated to the string of islands protecting the route to Australia lessened effective strength; moreover the army and navy were just beginning to receive the first-generation fighters in numbers. Thus at the time of Pearl Harbor the USAAF had a paper strength of sixty-seven combat groups (40–70 aircraft depending on type) with a manpower pool of 9,000 pilots and 60,000 ground crewmen. In practice, however, the army estimated that it had 2,800 firstline aircraft, of which only 1,150 were either in or ready for squadron deployment. This was not much for a nation facing a two-front war. USN pilots did not see substantial numbers of the grossly inferior Brewster Buffalo fighters until the summer of 1941. By Pearl Harbor the USN carriers were just receiving early-model Wildcats, and it was not until Midway that the F4F-4 Wildcat, the preferred carrier model, was standard.

All this had serious repercussions for training. USN pilots received some 300 hours of training prior to ACTG or advanced training with their squadrons. Army and Marine pilots were rarely as fortunate. Yet there is training, and then there is training. In 1939 the United States copied several other nations and created the Civilian Pilot Training Program, subsidized by the government and operated by private contractors. The idea was to provide elementary flight training for many men (and a small number of women) so they could serve as a kind of last line of defense. In practice many wartime pilots received their first instruction through this program, and found it to be most worthwhile.

Before looking more deeply at U.S. training it is valuable to consider the basic progression. Cadets began in elementary biplanes like the famous Stearman. Military pilots are very poor judges of training aircraft, because after piloting powerful and complex frontline machines the earlier models appear simple and easy to fly. In a sense they were. Although a biplane like the Stearman or a more complex monoplane like the AT-6 Texan was an easier aircraft to handle than a beast like a P-40 or Corsair, things looked very different to cadets. To a new pilot each step up the rung posed challenges. The military did wash out many cadets very early in training (often before they touched an aircraft), but the only way to tell a real pilot was to let him fly, an extremely dangerous process. As a pilot moved from primary to basic training he encountered aircraft that were more powerful and more complex. In the best of circumstances the training system was a type of mass production. The human material was good, but the type of slow and easy dual-control training that a civilian recreational pilot would receive today was neither feasible nor desired.

In the harsh world of military training, a washout was a psychological blow. However, the rigors of training were expected to prove the complex and subjective judgments of individuals by performance. This meant that many cadets were killed in training. Some were simply in over their heads; others showed the poor judgment of a rookie. With each step up the training ladder, their new mounts were faster, had higher wing loading, and higher stall speeds. A World War II fighter pilot would consider an AT-6 Texan a simple and forgiving aircraft. Someone confronting it for the first time faced a powerful, low-wing monoplane with a variable-pitch prop. When the time came to face single-seat combat models, dual-control training became impossible. Thus training was very much a matter of "sink or swim." Thousands sank and never resurfaced.

This raises a larger question: Were American pilots well trained for the war they faced in 1942–1943? The answer is complex. Men faced greatly different experiences during training. Some learned from splendid instructors, whereas others did not. Some were under intense pressure to get into the air; others had more flexibility. Furthermore wartime pilots tended to look at training with differing perspectives. In general I would argue that pilots believed they were not well prepared for the job they faced. Yet many understood the great pressure for combat pilots and believed that the military did a respectable job under bad conditions.

The more advanced training became, the more important it was for the men sent into combat. The leap between an obsolete warplane and a frontline model was usually considerable. No matter how many hours a pilot had tallied in trainers and obsolete fighting machines, the most important factor in combat was whether he knew the capabilities of the plane he was flying. It was exactly at this point that many early-war American pilots were weak. Marine fighter pilot Joe Foss was older and much more experienced than the average Marine pilot at the time of the Guadalcanal campaign. Foss was not pleased with the level of training given to the men who flew with him in the harsh days of late 1942:

Teamwork was learned on the job at Guadalcanal. When we arrived the average time that those guys had was about 200 total hours in the air. That was the average for the whole squadron, so some people had less: That includes basic training—everything. The actual time in the F4F that we were flying was very short before we went into combat. There was practice there, which was good. But in advanced training at Camp Carney we didn't have the proper planes to fly. We had some Brewster Buffalos and two or three Wildcats and a Texan. That was the total fleet and not much for forty pilots. I had more time in a Wildcat than anybody because I had gone through ACTG and I had 136 hours in a little over thirty days. I was king of the heap when it came to experience. I was the only Marine in ACTG and I had talked my way in. We went out and strafed, dive-bombed, did mock dogfights and carrier landings. We flew morning day and night—that's the way to learn about it. So I had a head start on all of the pilots in my squadron, including the commanding officer. He had a total of 1,800 hours in the air, I had 1,100 but the bulk of my time had been in the F4B4, F2F, F3F [predecessors to the standard Wildcat—EB] and through training. And that was zilch compared to what you really needed at Guadalcanal. Total time when you went through flight school was a little over 200 hours in those days. That's just enough time to get you in trouble. My younger partners out there didn't know much, and there were many ways to get killed. You could come up and have this mass of planes come after you—it wasn't on even terms, nothing "fair" about it. Those people sacrificed their lives keeping the enemy off the backs of our people whether they were trained to do it or not. They were dark days.

Although all airmen were taught the basic theory of flight, U.S. training was strongly oriented toward the job at hand. Some men were always aircraft junkies and immersed themselves in technical and theoretical matters. Combat aircrews were obviously interested in the flight characteristics of their weapons; such knowledge kept them alive. Technical specifications and matters of theory were often ignored in favor of lessons from the "University of Mars." Young pilot Robert DeHaven of Fifth Air Force, like many of his comrades in the illustrious 7th Squadron, learned to fly the difficult P-40 with considerable skill. That did not, as he recalled, mean he was prepared to design one:

I graduated from flying school on 4 January '43. I transitioned to a P-40 and had fourteen hours in one when on 20 February I received my overseas shipment orders and reported to the POE [port of embarkation] in San Francisco on 27 February. I boarded a ship going to Hawaii and was assigned to a Reserve Training Unit [RTU] where I was supposed to get more time in the fighter aircraft. After approximately a month I was sent to Charters Towers, Australia, where there was another RTU. The next step was up to New Guinea and combat in early May. In the two periods in Hawaii and Australia I accumulated just over forty hours of P-40 time. Which was the time I had when I first flew in combat. That wasn't very much.

We new pilots were very interested in anything that would help us achieve our missions and return in one piece. In that era of aviation, flight experience, good leadership, teamwork, and a certain "feel" were what helped you. I do not think many of us could have given lectures about the physics of flight. Fortunately most of us were too stupid to remember or even know about the laws of physics, so we went ahead and violated them anyway. We were like the bumblebee—it's got the wrong shaped wings, wrong shaped fuselage, and by all laws of aerodynamics it cannot fly. But of course it's a dumb insect and it doesn't know that so it goes ahead and flies anyway. We didn't know what the hell was going on, so we just went ahead and flew and did the job.

Navy pilots received, in general, better training than did men bound for other services. The unique demands of constant carrier operations and the long tradition of good training meant most carrier pilots received something more than the rudiments. (Early squadrons, however, did not receive the long preparation given to the new units formed for the new carriers that arrived in late 1943.) Even though carrier battles were rare, aircraft were in the air, weather permitting, any time the ship was at sea, patrolling for any possible danger. Every flight, of course, entailed a takeoff and landing, both delicate operations. However, as Tom Powell, an Avenger gunner on the *Enterprise*, pointed out after the war, the navy, too, had its problems due to a lack of aircraft:

When I got back to San Diego we originally didn't have any aircraft. So I was teaching the boots that were coming over how to make tie-down lines, signal flags, and things like that—I'd been in the navy for about a year. That was not the kind of preparation necessary to win the war. After we got our planes I originally served as ground crew. The aircrew and ground crew we were getting at first were totally lacking in any kind of advanced training. They were right from boot camp. When the *Lex* [USS *Lexington*—EB] got sunk we got a bunch of the survivors that came into the air group. They split them among the squadrons to sharpen up the new guys. We had guys off of the *Yorktown* [sunk at Midway—EB] that transferred in. Any ship that was sunk was picked over for veterans. At first we had the old Helldivers off the *Sara* to train with. Eventually we received our new Avengers. We were the first squadron that got TBFs and trained with them from the beginning. They trained some as bombardiers, gunners, ground crew, as well as pilots. We were the first complete squadron of Avenger aircraft.

According to Fred Cassidy, a crewman on one of the RAAF's feared Beaufighters, initial training in Australia was no better than in the United States, despite the knowledge picked up in Europe:

When Pearl came the RAAF knew they'd have to send some of us to the north against Japan. They had the Beaufighter already on the way out here. Britain had promised to send us some and they did, but they had no crews. So they kept some of us specialists at home to crew them. I was a specialist: a navigator, radio operator, and gunner. I had done all of those courses. They trained us in everything but flying. It was a two-seat plane, and apart from flying you did most everything else. When March came along the planes came and we were dispatched north. There was no real operational training. We were sent straight to Moresby. It was quite a shock when we went up there.

As the months progressed after the attack on Pearl Harbor, the U.S. training structure began to mature. Every possible theater had an insatiable appetite for aircraft. The result was a kind of mass production of aircrews and ground crews. For the most part the men involved possessed the abilities required. However, despite a certain belief in one's own immortality, the services realized that producing huge numbers of planes supported by huge numbers of men made "safety," at least in the modern sense, impossible. Aviation in the prewar era was far more dangerous than it is today; wartime requirements only amplified the hazards. The Allied air forces did not squander lives without thought, yet the needs of war necessitated an approach to men and machines that would be unthinkable today. Put simply life was cheap during World War II, a sad fact evidenced continually in the training regimens of all the combatant nations. The military realized that aggressiveness was essential on the battlefield and kept a loose rein on training. The sheer size of the enterprise added to the grim equation. And early ground crews, upon whom so much depended, were no better trained than men in the air. Training was hazardous for ground crews. There was always the danger of injury when dealing with heavy and complex objects. And whenever an aircraft crashed it likely happened at an airfield. A plane out of control was not easy to spot, and often the ground crews were sent running for cover in a split second. The result was a grim but necessary process: "survival of the fittest," which was in no command directive but implicit in mass warfare. If anything, bomber crewmen believed, in retrospect, that their training had not been ideal. Bombers were inherently complex, and it was necessary to forge some kind of team. The cry for bombers on the part of commanders at the front was deafening, and in training a crew the instructors usually had no idea where the men would be flying or what conditions to prepare for.

John Gallagher of the famous 5th USAAF 345th Bomb Group was training at a time when the call for B-25s and their crews was clamorous from commanders in the Mediterranean and Pacific. The result was tough going: "In training we piled up our plane, but luckily nobody was hurt. They had us back in the air the next day; they didn't want anyone to think this over. That happened all the time. There were more planes lost in training than in combat. Not people, but planes. We cracked them up all the time. It was mass production. It was unbelievable how many planes they made and how many crews they trained."

Charles Kittell also flew a B-25 for Thirteenth Air Force operating in the Solomons. His reflections on training show a keen appreciation for the unique nature of the war and inherent difficulty in the task:

We were well trained in terms of flying considering the situation. It was very important to get a large number of people out there. Each theater had its own unique demands. Strafing in the Pacific meant flying low. You have trees, buildings, hell, big boulders that were obstacles. If you graze something like that with one wing you are a dead duck. Plus they were shooting at you all the way up and down. But you learned all that when you got there. You learned how to stay alive. But every theater had its own discrete problems, so the trainers couldn't prepare you for every eventuality. Plus, we were learning all the time. What was considered a good tactical technique in training might well be superseded by something else when you got to the front. The cadets that I taught in early '45 missed combat because the war ended before deployment. However, had they gone to war, they would have been much better trained than we were. They were getting all of the knowledge that we had accumulated in Europe and the Pacific. Obviously this was knowledge we didn't have when we trained in late 1942. As far as flying you did as well as you could with the number of hours you had. Then you had to learn by doing.

In Chapter 6 I illustrate the impact that training had on combat operations. Indeed the development in the field of a simple but sound tactical doctrine well suited to imperfectly trained pilots was one reason that Allied forces were able to slow and stop the Japanese juggernaut before the Allies gained the upper hand in numbers and pilot quality. Here it is worth emphasizing that Allied training did not surpass Japanese training in length and quality until at least early 1943, and the American training machine did not operate at peak efficiency early in the war. Interesting testimony on this subject comes from the Military Analysis Division, found in the Strategic Bombing Survey (Pacific). Among the dozens of studies made for the SBS, one of the most general, but also most interesting, was *The Air Campaigns of the Pacific War*. This report represents more than history. Bright young officers attempted to analyze the war looking for lessons that might help guide the development of air doctrine for the new U.S. Air Force and the USN in the uncharted, and potentially radioactive, waters of the Cold War era. The authors were quick to credit strong performances but were critical of errors they identified on the part of Americans and Japanese. Although expressing general approval of U.S. training and finding it far superior to Japanese training, the authors of *Air Campaigns* also found significant areas to fault:

> However laboring under great pressure and in the fog of war, our military establishment did make some serious errors in its training programs. It must be borne in mind that the training problem was gigantic. The Air Force was expanding one hundred fold and the ground and naval forces were also expanding greatly. Even though a tremendous task was accomplished in the training program, for the sake of future national security those mistakes which were made should not be overlooked. The two most serious errors are discussed below.
>
> *The Numbers Racket.* In general, the emphasis of our training program was on quantity rather than on quality. In meeting deployment schedules and in prematurely committing forces to combat theaters, we became obsessed with the numbers of people and units produced rather than with the state of their training. Particularly during the first 2 years

of the war, air crews, specialists and units that would have achieved a
barely operable proficiency level when they were committed to active
theaters. This was false economy. It actually delayed rather than
accelerated the effective impact of our Air Forces on the enemy. Only a
moderate increase in the training given air crews and technicians would
have produced a much higher combat capability and thereby would
have reduced the logistic requirements and the over-all structure
required. We had not fully comprehended that a war of technology
depends more on the efficiency and the skill of a relatively small
number of people employing powerful weapons than on the sheer
weight of numbers of armed masses.

Utilization of Civilian Skills.   The second greatest weakness in our
training program was a failure, in many instances, to utilize properly
and build from civilian skills. This was not, however, exclusively a
training problem or failure. Many factors, including our draft laws,
worked to transplant highly qualified individuals from one line of
productive war endeavor to other fields in which their specialties were
not employed.

I quote this analysis at length because it contains much truth. The
authors were, however, looking for lessons useful in the future and left
some important historical factors by the wayside. As pointed out in
Part I of this book, it was vital to create an air presence in an area even
if it was not very effective because it would slow enemy action and
force the enemy to concentrate forces. And in the brutal math of attrition losses hurt the Japanese Empire more so than the Allies. Furthermore the Allied air arm did create training way stations close to the
front to help prepare men for the final plunge into combat. Nevertheless, as the SBS and much other evidence demonstrate, Allied air forces
were hardly working at peak efficiency during the first eighteen
months of war.

The SBS extract is striking because both sections emphasized the
failure to better train and organize specialists. The authors, in this regard, were not discussing pilots. (The desirability of better-trained aircrews was self-evident.) Instead one must infer that they were writing
about inadequate training of bombardiers and ground crews. After the
war the USAAF was most self-critical concerning its preparation of
bombardiers early on, particularly in the European theater. As we shall
see later precision skills were far less important in the Pacific, but no
doubt many bombing missions went for naught because of poor execution. More importantly World War II aircraft were challenging to

fly, but they were also challenging to maintain. Unlike an automobile the planes required constant inspection. If the crews didn't mind their p's and q's then the plane would either not fly or simply crash. During an era of shortage, a plane on the ground was a plane wasted. It might as well have been shot down, and planes counted more than pilots early in the war. In this regard I think that the SBS analysts are indeed correct: Too much complex technical training was given to young ground crewmen—regardless of their potential—in too short a period. And I do not doubt that a better "fit" could have been made between mechanically skilled men and maintenance positions. The military was notorious for putting a good shot behind a typewriter while putting the best typist in a rifle squad.

The Japanese suffered exactly the same problems—except worse. Whereas the Allies grew more competent at the skills necessary to "keep 'em flying," the Japanese grew less so (though neither was prepared for the war of attrition that developed in the South Pacific). The Japanese possessed a cadre of splendid pilots, but as they were lost (for whatever reason) it became clear that the new levies from home were decently but imperfectly trained. This process started shortly after Pearl Harbor and was well under way by Guadalcanal. At the same time the Allied units, cut to ribbons in the first few weeks of wartime, were catching their collective breath. The result was that by Guadalcanal two flawed air forces squared off in the South Pacific. Perhaps the Japanese held the qualitative edge in manpower initially, but Japanese aircraft were much more likely to kill their own pilots. The Allies responded somewhat clumsily at first but with increasing competence. As a result between May 1942 and May 1943 the opponents were close to equal in quality and quantity. Both badly needed on-the-job training. Neither had ideal aircraft. Neither had ideal maintenance. It was a campaign where the one-eyed did combat with the one-eyed. In retrospect we can see that it would be only a matter of time before the Allies would open their other eye, and the outcome would be sealed. The only question was how fast the Japanese air arm would collapse. In the event, a hard-fought battle turned into a complete rout, as Japanese air units throughout the Pacific were crushed with astounding speed. Had the war ended when Japan's air arm lost its effectiveness, Tokyo would have made peace in July 1944.

Morale

There are few subjects in military affairs more important or complex than morale. As every decent officer knows, the spirit to fight and endure hardship is essential to victory. Officers also know that morale has many facets. Men who believe—perhaps rightly—that the enemy has gained the upper hand fight at a serious disadvantage, for they now face not only their fear of death but also a belief that any sacrifice will be in vain. When a unit is on a roll, exactly the opposite effect takes hold: They become aggressive and normally more effective. Within the larger universe exists personal chemistry within units. No matter how confident they were, stress and the gnawing realization that their number might be up wore down even the most intrepid of fighting men. And men fought in groups. Fighter pilots, though alone in their planes, stressed solidarity and teamwork within the group. Attack aircraft had crews—men who had to work together effectively whether or not they liked one another. All men spent most time on the ground. Thus a unique form of discipline, influenced by the youth of many air leaders, developed inside the air arm (at least on the Allied side) that altered relations between officers and enlisted men (which is not to say that the divide was not ever-present). And then there were the living conditions. Beyond malaria and jungle rot, living conditions in-theater were crude, diversions few, women nonexistent, and creature comforts rudimentary. Everyone faced a miserable climate and boredom. None of these matters were mundane. Bad food might be less important than fear of death, but staring at dehydrated eggs for a year did nothing to lift spirits. All factors contributed, to some degree, to overall morale. Striking is how both sides adapted to dangerous and harsh conditions and tended to their missions for months and years on end.

One vital point should be made at the outset: In the first two years of war general political morale on both sides was excellent. Antiwar sentiments among segments of the population have been a fixture of American history—except for World War II. It is safe to assume that only a handful of men in the Pacific, no matter how badly they wished to get home, questioned the need and justice of the American cause. Admiral Yamamoto's carriers on December 7, 1941, did more for Washington's propaganda battle than anything the U.S. government could have done. Hitler's outrages merely added buckets of fuel to the fire lit at Pearl Harbor. Australians and New Zealanders faced the chilling possibility that Japan might attack or blockade their homelands. Fighting on one's doorstep is a quick way to make or break morale. Fortunately for the United States the other Allies in the Pacific responded with a determined, effective defense. On the Japanese side, the youngsters in the air arm viewed themselves proudly as elites of the Empire of the Rising Sun—the new samurai. Raised in an authoritarian and hierarchical society and indoctrinated in devotion to emperor and nation, the men of the Japanese armed forces threw themselves into the Pacific war with startling, almost frightening ferocity and tenacity. The pressures of war in the long run could and did wear down most men. Yet even if spirit waned in an individual heart, there is not a shred of evidence that men on either side lost the conviction they were fighting a just and necessary war. The difference, of course, is that the Allied servicemen were fighting the good war and that the Japanese—despite undoubted bravery—were living and fighting under a cruel, wicked delusion created by a criminal government.

Yet believing in the abstract that one is fighting the good war is only part of the equation: Patriotism and the belief that defeat was unbearable had much to do with motivating men to join the services and journey to distant, sinister places. Once in a combat zone, a variety of factors worked to raise and lower morale. In considering this question, I think it important to assume that almost every man had a limited reservoir of internal strength drained by fear, stress, fatigue, and environment. The important thing for leaders was to try to structure operations and provide the physical objects required to sustain spirit for as long as possible. In any event war is not the natural state among most men; the perseverance necessary to fulfill one's mission was finite.

Although distinctions are not always easy to discern, I think that the single most important component of combat morale was the fighting man's perception of his chances for survival. Much more than a simple fear of death, this melancholy factor reared its head in many places. There was also a sense of immense frustration brought on by the belief that sacrifice was not commensurate with the gains made. Most typically this condition characterized air units that were suffering sustained tactical defeats and serious casualties while rarely tasting clear victory. The reaction was to become tentative in operations, sometimes the worst possible response. This component of morale had a chronological symmetry. Early in the war Japanese air units, flush from victory after victory in the opening weeks of hostilities, believed themselves invincible. Some Allied opponents during those black months of early 1942 grew to agree. What was required—and achieved—by the Allies was the infusion of enough forces to stabilize the situation and turn a rout into a contest. For several months the enemies engaged one another with growing ferocity. Although the physical point of defeat for Japan was in the upper Solomons and New Guinea in 1943, the psychological dagger of the air war was at Guadalcanal. Sometime in early or mid-1943, depending on the local situation, Japanese morale began to waver and Allied spirits rose. This phase corresponded with the beginning of the Allied advance throughout the theater. The situation was, therefore, a psychological state that influenced behavior yet one based soundly on military reality. With the exception of some units that simply had terrible luck, most units slid downward because of forces that no one in the local area could control. In other words a unit could fly well and be led well and still come out on the short end in most engagements. This fact made the sting of defeat even worse, because it was compounded by the feeling of futility. Obviously such feelings were self-reinforcing.

This is one reason that the Allied policy of rotating aircrews out of combat areas was so important. Oft-defeated units were replaced by men who knew things were bad but were convinced they could do better. The men in defeated U.S. units had little chance to share their gloom with replacements; under any circumstances rotation was universal among combat crews (although conditions varied). Commanders relieved a small number of units completely; officers rotated other men who showed fatigue; veterans, even in successful units, served the informal role of instructor before rotation, but they, too, were gone soon enough. What happened was an unusual transfer of knowledge.

In contrast the Japanese allowed "invincible" veteran pilots to continue at the front until death or some unlikely transfer. Aviation author Henry Sakaida has written two interesting books containing brief biographies of Japanese army and navy aces during World War II. It is startling to discover how many served in the South Pacific and how many—especially IJN pilots—died there. (This situation stood in stark contrast to Allied and German experiences. Although several prominent aces like Richard Bong and Gerry Johnson died in accidents at war's end, most American aces survived the war. So, too, did many of Germany's top pilots. Overall Luftwaffe losses were appalling. However, those who learned the ropes were usually able to stay alive. It helped tremendously that the Germans usually fought over friendly lines. It also helped that German aircraft, although not as sturdy as U.S. planes, were not flying firebombs.) Japanese replacements, well enough trained and strongly encouraged, learned from veterans the true situation. Such matters cannot be quantified, but it must have been unsettling to new aircrews. In consequence the Japanese might have been struck by a wicked convergence: As Japan's air arm weakened, replacement pilots—with far less training—became more common. Combat officers in China prior to Pearl Harbor passed along to the youngsters in their command the idea that Japanese airpower was superior. This belief, well founded in local fact, increased morale and added to aggressiveness and morale early in the Pacific war. After

Guadalcanal and the devastation of air bases in New Guinea, veteran Japanese pilots played exactly the opposite role: The young men coming into the theater were not lied to—that was impossible—but they quickly learned that their chances of survival were very poor and began flying on that assumption. It can be little surprise that Japanese pilots began to fly conservatively, especially as they suffered stinging losses in every large engagement. In the meantime the veterans died, confirming the siren song.

Jim Morehead flew P-40s during the confused and hopeless defense of Java against strong Japanese forces early in 1942. From the time of arrival the unit was forced to fly poorly coordinated missions against superior forces in superior planes. In February 1942, after a series of blows inflicted by Japanese aircraft, Morehead's squadron commander was killed. As recorded in his memoirs, the event accelerated a near collapse of morale:

> Nothing worse can happen to a unit than to have it lose its commander, especially if he is well qualified, skillful and well respected. Whereas youth is normally optimistic about fate, forever feeling that if bad things happen, they will never happen to me, now there was a reversal. Unlike any combat circumstance I was ever exposed to, it switched. The attitude changed to: "I am a goner, the next one lost will be me, I know it will be me." How many times I heard "We're just flying tow targets. We are all on suicide missions!" Such conclusions were only logical. Anyone's arithmetic can figure out how many missions you are likely to last if ten go out and only five come back. When an alert stack is normally boisterous with laughter and wisecracks, silent anxiety was the mood in those days.

During an interview, Morehead made a very interesting point. During the downslide every mission takes a psychological toll whether or not the enemy is actually engaged. Pilots begin to attribute to their opponents great abilities, perhaps greater than they actually had. Morehead's men, for example, had heard—correctly—that some Japanese pilots would take a position just below an Allied aircraft's tail, where it was difficult to see. The pursuit might last miles, but whereas the Japanese pilot was flying at near-full throttle, the isolated Allied aircraft was probably at cruising speed. When close enough, the Zero would employ its excellent short-term climb rate and deliver a fatal strike at close range. Other fears were of more common tactics, such as enemy fighters attacking from the sun. If one believes one is losing, such threats take on a frightening reality, whether encountered or not. The result is psychological fatigue on the part of the defending pilot every mission out, as Morehead explained:

> Radar at Java was nearly nonfunctional, we often depended more upon native drums. Radar was also flawed when we moved to Darwin. We had so many false alarms it was hard to be effective. You wasted you time and psychological stress on missions that you didn't encounter the enemy. That helped wear us down. The stress is almost as great as an actual encounter. You're both expectant and afraid—it really raises the blood pressure thinking combat is near. When it doesn't take place, men are confused when the situation is uncertain. So we were wearing down our units even when we weren't fighting. Later I was a squadron commander in the Mediterranean. We had some bad times but normally we were confident because we were winning. Even when on the bad end of an engagement, the morale in our units was never remotely as bad as it was early in the Pacific war.

American commanders understand Morehead's ideas. In November 1942 5th USAAF commander General George Kenney relieved the 19th Bomb Group, sent them home, and dispersed the unit. In army practice such a move was difficult to contemplate, as a weakened unit would expect to await new planes and pilots. Yet Kenney believed that the 19th, which had been pounded in the Philippines, the Indies, and New Guinea, was completely exhausted. The few serviceable aircraft and newer crews received reassignment to other units; the veterans were allowed to go home.

It appears that exactly the same process took place inside the Japanese air arm. Although heavily indoctrinated, frontline warriors are the last to be deceived because the reality of the course of battle was dramatically in front of them to examine. The course described by Morehead was described more mildly by Minoru Genda, a top operational brain of the JNAF: "I think that as long as we were winning everything was fine and our morale was high, but that as soon as we became aware we could lose our morale would drop and we would lose our feeling of invincibility." More dramatic commentary came from the diary kept by Tetsuzo Iwamoto, perhaps Japan's highest-scoring ace of the war. Like the more famous Saburo Sakai, Iwamoto was also a petty officer who joined the naval air arm well before the war. During the conflict with China he was credited with fourteen victories, highest among the service. In mid-1943 Iwamoto was transferred to Rabaul. Always outspoken, the ace found the situation at

Rabaul serious and recorded his thoughts in his diary. In the first entry Iwamoto described an early mission during which his unit's old-model Zero had to escort a vain Japanese attack on the U.S. landings at Bougainville in late 1943: "With this antiquated plane we were expected to fight against the enemy's latest models that vastly outnumbered us. It was like being ordered to die. We had no choice but to obey orders and do our best." Shortly later Iwamoto expressed his general disgust: "Prior to the beginning of 1943, we still had hope and fought fiercely. But now, we fought to uphold our honor. We didn't want to become cowards. . . . We believed we were expendable, that we were all going to die. There was no hope of survival—no one cared anymore." Further comment on this subject comes from the interrogation of Commander Ryosuke Nomura, an experienced fighter pilot and staff operations officer at Rabaul between November 1942 and July 1943. For reasons that are unclear, Nomura's testimony was given in summary form rather than the normal transcription. Nevertheless the points made were very clear: "The Naval land-based losses in the Rabaul-Solomons-New Guinea areas were extremely high and finally resulted in the destruction of the cream of the Naval Air Forces. The high losses were attributed in the order named to: 1) Superiority of American fighter aircraft; 2) Breakdown of Japanese aircraft supply system; 3) Inability of the Japanese to replace experienced pilots and maintenance personnel."

As a result of the high losses, the absence of a pilot rotation system, and the withdrawal from Guadalcanal, Japanese pilot morale rapidly declined after February 1943. On several occasions the pilots were guilty of gross exaggeration of damage inflicted, and finally it was necessary to station watches at several points in order to verify pilot reports. Although the exaggerated reports were not used as a basis for planning, they were given to the press, which was encouraged by the commander of Eleventh Air Fleet to widely publicize them. The pilots continually discussed the relative merits of the Japanese and U.S. aircraft and were convinced in their own minds that they were flying greatly inferior machines. In the words of Commander Nomura, the Japanese pilots "had a horror of American fighters." It was generally considered that the Zero was about equal to the P-40 and F4F but no match for the F4U and F6F, which Japanese pilots particularly disliked.

Closely related to the perception of victory and survival were the almost indistinguishable problems of stress and fatigue. Fatigue, in the military medical definition of the term during World War II, was considered a psychological condition often caused or made worse by physical exhaustion. As was the case with morale, stress and fatigue varied among individuals. It is safe to say that ground crews, although often the victims of bombing attacks, were vulnerable to a different type of stress and fatigue than were combat aircrewmen. The situation also varied depending upon the type of aircraft flown. Leadership—good and bad—was a part of the equation. Despite wide differences in degree, stress and fatigue were a problem throughout the South Pacific. Depending on the experience, stress and fatigue could leave an individual in need of a little extra shuteye and good grub, or it could cripple the effectiveness of entire squadrons.

All Allied air arms were concerned about the issue, and it became the subject of a blizzard of reports. The best compendium of information on this subject comes from an official history published after the war by the Office of the Air Force Surgeon General, *Medical Support of the Army Air Forces in World War II*. Although an excellent work in general, a few of the findings are not confirmed by my research. The work presents a grim picture of the damage done by stress and fatigue to the USAAF in the Pacific. Much of the evidence was taken from the reports of several dozen psychiatrists and psychologists working for the USAAF surgeon general during the war. Psychiatry and psychology had great prestige during the 1940s in the United States. Possibly some of the gloomy depiction was colored by a seek-and-ye-shall-find mentality familiar to anyone in academia.

The most distressing information confronts conditions that existed late in the war. By 1945 far too many men had been pushed too hard in the Pacific. Just as importantly the United States, like every nation in the world, was growing war-weary as the conflict entered its last act. The surgeon general's study suggests that in the early months of war men were disheartened and confused because they did not understand why they were so quickly thrust from the comforts of home into world war. My findings are quite the opposite: Most men certainly did not like being sent to war, but in 1942 the basic necessity and justice of the conflict does not appear to me to have been widely questioned. (I have no idea how psychologists could have done meaningful studies in 1942 when the USAAF was undergoing a chaotic deployment and lacked an orderly medical apparatus.) Such caveats aside, the essential findings produced by the official history are fully supported by the veterans who participated in interviews for in this book. The South Pacific was without doubt a particularly grueling place to fight a war.

The evidence illustrating this problem is substantial. Throughout the war in Fifth and Thirteenth Air Forces some 20–30 percent of nonbattle casualties resulted from fatigue, stress, and other psychiatric problems. In times of sustained activity before major infusions of replacements the situation was even worse. In May 1943 the surgeon of the 5th USAAF 3d Bomb Group presented a dire picture:

> Combat crews show signs of operational fatigue and definite deleterious changes in mental attitude after six to eight months of combat. Combat crews with over ten months of combat develop severe operational fatigue and undergo changes in attitude toward flying to such an extent that the probability of ever restoring them completely is questionable. The future efficiency, health, and general standards of the AAF will be endangered by pushing these men too far.

If medical analysis was correct, the problem continued when men returned to the United States. Both Fifth and Thirteenth Air Force usually categorized returning aircrews as suffering from "combat fatigue" (whether or not they actually did) and grounded them for a period. Midwar the Office of Air Surgeon General in the United States found that 30 percent of returnees from the South Pacific suffered from chronic fatigue and most of the others were "badly played out even if they are not demonstrating actual symptoms." Commanders in the United States also concluded that the percentage of USAAF personnel rotating out from New Guinea who could return to full combat status for another tour was the lowest of any theater by a great margin.

Many pressures worked to wear down morale. (Obviously all assaults on morale were made much worse by the terrible medical situation.) Several studies confirmed that stress and fatigue were actually worse among ground crews than aircrews, particularly if they were stationed in rear bases. The danger in this case was the enemy of every army—boredom. Lee Tipton spent more than two years as an officer with 13th USAAF Service Command and saw plenty of low spirits:

> Recreation in a meaningful sense didn't exist. There was always a seashore nearby, but that's short-lived and didn't appeal to everyone. There was a lot of depression. It didn't become serious to the point that people had to be evacuated, but a lot of men were down, gloomy. Maybe I was lucky that we were so short-handed. In the twenty-six months I was over, except for a brief leave, I had three days off duty. So I was very busy and I think that was good for me. For a while I was in Brisbane for three weeks of chemical war school and saw how nice the lives the people were living. Some of us were jealous of that; jealous of the home front in a way. There were people that would do anything to get to the rear. We had a couple of doctors that were continually

putting each other on sick calls. I was given to the inspectors general
for a week to participate in the investigation. It was so obvious. Kind of
pitiful behavior for doctors.

The boredom got so many people down because they were stuck so
far from home. There was just no relief and it was hurtful to morale
and caused some first-class problems. Never saw much of either USO
[United Service Organizations] or Red Cross. Later on a few
Hollywood types came out, maybe three or four. There wasn't much of
a way to put on a show with all that rain. So morale was not very
good. It was the right of every GI to complain. But the feeling was that
the emphasis was being put on Europe to start with. But it was worse.
We felt that within the Pacific we were second cousin to Fifth Air Force.
Boredom could become a kind of desperation. You must remember we
didn't know how long this stuff was going to go on, when the war
would end. I was only in the [South Pacific] for twenty-six months but
they sure seemed long ones. . . . We didn't really know who was going
to win. Japan was a long way away.

Fred Hitchcock was a ground crewman for Fifth Air Force. Although personally well suited for inactivity, he recalled some of the
psychological pressures that made life difficult for many:

Boredom was not my personal enemy. I have lots of interests and
always have. However, some people that were shy, or introverted and
not very active mentally, could just get ground down by the routine, the
bad weather, and the bad food. Some people just couldn't get along
with others. We had a few diversions. . . . I think the people that
cracked were people that carried some troubles with them to New
Guinea. Most of us got through okay. . . . The war seemed endless.
There were slogans like "Join Mac and you don't come back" or
"Golden Gate in '48."

Several medical reports coming from the South Pacific contrasted
with the superior morale found in Marine and USN air units because
of their policy of regular rotation for both aircrews and ground crews.
However, Marine Tony Betchik, a Wildcat crew chief on Cactus during the worst of the Guadalcanal campaign, recalled that stress was a
problem as well for Marine ground crews. Note that Betchik mentions
a problem that afflicted all U.S. forces early in the war: When mobilization began and the armed forces exploded in size, the military did
not do an adequate job screening recruits for serious psychological illness. The numbers involved were a small percentage of men mobilized,

but they could be serious trouble at the front and cause the medical personnel difficulty:

> Surprisingly in our unit morale held up well. It's amazing what you can do when young. You don't think anything can happen to you. But it was rough. Because of the miserable climate, the Japanese raids, and the sheer work we didn't sleep much for weeks. And the diet was very poor. When I arrived I had thirty-two perfect teeth: On Efate I needed major fillings in seven. I attribute that to a bad diet. But fatigue made everything worse. You could tell stress was building in some of the men. People would withdraw, grow morose, pull into themselves. We also had some people who went "Asiatic" from the stress. Some had pretty serious breakdowns. There were a considerable number of them and they caused real trouble when they tried to evacuate them.
>
> . . . Toward the end of the year we could begin to evacuate those worn down by illness. Many of those men should have gone out earlier. At the end of the year if someone didn't report for duty after three days they pulled him out. They knew they'd pushed too hard.

Some ground crews were much more involved in coherent military operations and thus suffered much less from fatigue and boredom. Certainly one of the most important variables was whether the duty performed had a genuine, immediate purpose. By 1943 all combat units had a control center that constantly monitored the position of friendly aircraft in a given sector. Their information was passed on to all units in their group or, if the situation required it, to higher headquarters. Connected to both signal communications and radar, friendly units when flying required constant attention. Allied aircraft, after all, must know the location of other friendly units and be alert for an enemy attack. Howard Redmond was part of 49th Fighter Group Control Squadron and recalled that the war was exciting work:

> Morale in our unit was terrific. One of the guys I served with lives nearby and we often talk over this period. The thing that was so great about fighter control was that we knew what was going on. Most men didn't have a clue, they were told so little. Boredom was never a problem. Every day had new operations, new challenges, and we'd be tracking things hour by hour. We saw all the in-flight reports, so we knew a lot about bigger events in the theater. Pilots and higher officers frequently gave us a call. We participated and observed a great military campaign. I don't regret a minute.

Redmond's point about being "in the know" was no small matter. Particularly early in the war, many men had very little idea what was going on in the South Pacific. Partially this reflected the general disorganization of the time. Military intelligence also believed, with some reason, that a captured aircrewman would be less vulnerable to interrogation if he did not know very much. Many units produced mimeographed one-page "newspapers" that contained major headlines and innocuous news of the local area. As time went on this situation loosened up. Some men received a newsmagazine from the United States, or their families sent them hometown newspapers. Radiomen could sometimes pick up information from Australia or the Japanese. A South Pacific edition of *Stars and Stripes* eventually got going. By 1944 many Americans in New Guinea were avid readers of a small Australian military newspaper, *Guinea Gold*. But many men fought the dreary war in the South Pacific with very little knowledge of what was taking place outside their immediate worlds.

Fatigue and stress afflicted aircrews also, although the form it took was often different. One point that the medical history made was the serious erosion of morale due to the lack of a definite rotation system in the USAAF. Better prepared, the Marine and USN units employed regular unit rotation from the beginning of the war, although men on Guadalcanal and those flying from carrier decks could hardly wait for a specific date. The combat situation often determined their timing of rotation. Yet it is true that the USAAF's policy was vague indeed. A genuine rotation schedule was not implemented until late 1944, and even then it was not ironclad. Part of the army's procedure was no doubt influenced by geography. The Fifth Air Force in New Guinea (and the units flying in China) were at the end of a very long supply chain. The Marine Corps, in contrast, was closer to major bases in the New Hebrides and employed far fewer units than did the army. The carriers required periodic stops at Pearl Harbor for refitting, and this proved a perfect time for rotating air groups. Perhaps army leaders simply made a mistake. General MacArthur was famous for telling his men they were there for the duration, and a tour in the Pacific for a ground soldier could seem interminable. (It is perhaps significant that Thirteenth Air Force in the Solomons did more to see that pilots had leave together, and eventually it established a center on Guadalcanal where personnel could be checked for stress prior to leave.) Army combat units in Europe after D-Day also relied on the pipeline and have received criticism for the policy ever since. Yet USAAF leaders were no fools. Although tours were long and no definite end usually in sight, army crews were rotated (after long tours) when replacement pilots became available.

Rich Walker was with the 13th Bomb Squadron of Fifth Air Force. A squadron commander who flew B-25 strafers and A-20 attack planes, Walker and fellow bomber crewmen faced the highest degree of battle danger among USAAF personnel. (Some of the Marine fighter squadrons at Cactus and their USAAF counterparts fighting in New Guinea before mid-1943 suffered similar losses.) Walker's perspective concerning stress is also of interest because of his later service in the U.S. Air Force. As Walker remarks, most men faced danger tenaciously, but some went over the line, sometimes with tragic results:

> We had a rotation policy of a kind. Fifty missions generally sent you home. It just depended on how badly they needed pilots. If they had a surplus it was less, if they had a shortage they raised it. I could have gone home but I was squadron commander and decided to stay around. Looking back I think I simply wasn't very smart. I should note that I had heard about places like Tahiti before the war and I was thrilled to be sent to the Pacific—that proves I wasn't very bright. Yet to the extent that you can enjoy a thing like that I did. I can't really tell you why I stayed.
>
> There were many occasions when I saw crewmen or pilots starting to go over the line. One kid came to us as a copilot early on. We transitioned to A-20s and checked the pilots out as A-20 pilots. But we couldn't check him because he just lacked any confidence in himself to fly it. So we transferred him to another B-25 outfit. He'd come back almost every day to see his friends and I knew he wanted to return. So finally he came and said, "I can check out in that A-20" and be transferred back to our squadron. He did check out and I transferred him back in. His brother was a Red Cross worker in our area. In this kid's first A-20 mission he came off the target and just kept flying straight. He never turned toward home but just disappeared over the horizon. None of us had any idea of what happened to him. When we came back and landed his brother was waiting to congratulate him on his first mission. It was heart-wrenching to look at that guy's face and tell him that his brother didn't make it.
>
> I can think of another guy. I was air coordinator on some of the amphibious landings. I was the guy who controlled the attacking aircraft supporting the landing. We were landing on an island called Numphoor. The Japanese were firing out of emplaced guns in cliffs. The navy called naval artillery in. I brought my squadron in. I was supposed

to go in first and drop a bomb to mark the target and the rest of the guys would attack it. I got a radio message from the fleet telling me, "Get that guy to quit firing; he's plastering our own ships." He started firing way out, way before the beach and kept right on firing and flew straight into the cliff. He never deviated left or right or pulled up. Whatever went on in his mind is just beyond imagination. But this kid was a real sincere, religious kid. Maybe the terror got to him, but it looked to me like he just deliberately flew into the cliff. Maybe it dawned on him he'd fired on our ships. Maybe he froze. The problem was that you never got to talk to someone who cracked like that, so motivation remains a mystery. . . .

We've learned a lot since then. Later in my career I flew for SAC [Strategic Air Command]. It was like night and day. The group at SAC was extremely technically informed and very intelligent. Very different than the regular guys we fought the war with. After flying with SAC I would look back and wonder how any of us survived the war. At SAC we were tested by the shrinks and we also knew much more about flying. We did things like aero refueling and intercontinental flights— stuff you couldn't imagine in 1943. A long mission on a B-25 would be about five hours max. We'd go thirteen routinely on a B-52. That wasn't much more than ten years after the war, but it was a different world.

B-24 flight engineer and gunner Carl Camp ended his tour in mid-1944, a period when Fifth Air Force badly needed replacements. As Camp recalled, combat efficiency suffered:

Nobody had much respect for Dugout Doug [a derogatory nickname for General MacArthur—EB]. He was a ground general trying to run an air force. We went by hours, not missions. They had raised the number just a week before we got there. Later they raised it twice more. It was just like the book *Catch-22*. So MacArthur more or less abolished the rotation, or at least it seemed like it. It was true [that] replacement crews were hard to come by. So you're going to fly forever until you get killed, seriously wounded, or go crazy. There was a pseudomutiny. People didn't refuse to fly but they'd abort at the drop of a hat. If anything went wrong with a plane, we'd abort. The flight surgeons knew what was going on and they let people sit out sick. The crews were burned out, it was that simple.

The official medical history notes that problems of fatigue and stress were less common among fighter pilots than among bomber crews.

Officials attributed this fact to lower casualty rates (which was usually but not always true), as well as to the ability of the fighter pilot to better control his own fate. A bomber—if it carried out its mission—flew a specific course and stayed on the bomb run until clear. Fighters could engage or not with greater freedom and in all cases had more ability to make evasive maneuvers. Furthermore a fighter pilot was ultimately responsible for his own aircraft and his own life. A B-24 pilot, for instance, had ten or eleven men with him. No doubt the distinction was real. However, fighters flew more missions than bombers, and their pilots were not immune to the factors that ground down their comrades in bomber units.

Ralph Easterling served a long and distinguished tour with 5th USAAF 49th Fighter Group. When it was time to finish Easterling recognized that fact:

There are some people that really enjoy combat. Modern-time gladiators in a sense. Most people know that war was maybe necessary but that it isn't natural, that there is a better life in peacetime. You'd go over eager to do your job. As time went on you'd encounter close calls. Friends would get killed. You expected this; it wasn't a surprise. But you began to mature. You'll do your duty, but you feel that if there are others to take my place and I have done my tour that it's time to join the normal world. War is exciting and touches anyone that goes through it. But peacetime life, work, and family is more natural. Common sense starts winning out over aggressiveness and feelings of invincibility. Some showed shell shock or fear, but I think far more men showed more common sense. . . .

Stress can come from many sources: Just as much from things on your mind as the enemy out there. If someone did collapse the flight surgeon would handle it. After all the squadron didn't want someone in the air who didn't want to fly. But everybody had a different limit. I know I looked forward to rotation. It was 100 missions; I put in 120. At the end of my tour we had an air raid. We were all in our little shelters and the bombs were coming down and I said to myself, "What the heck am I doing over here? What's this all about?" A couple of months later our squadron commander said, "I can cut your orders to go home or promote you to captain: What do you want?" I said, "Give me home." It wasn't fear, but it was just time to get out. I still enjoyed the flying; to be honest I enjoyed combat. But I was getting to be more of a realist. I was thinking more, maybe subconsciously, of what could happen. I got home and met my brother, who had been a navigator in Eighth Air Force. He had almost

the same type of experience. He was asked the same question by
General [Ira] Eaker himself and he had turned down promotion and
accepted the rotation home.

Robert Croft was one of Easterling's squadronmates in the Seventh
and offers similar reflections:

Most of us were confident and continued to do our duty. But stress was
there. We had one guy that just could not stand it. He lasted about
three months. He had come over with us, but just went off his rocker
and they put him in a hospital in Australia. We never heard anything
more from him. We had others that would get rattled. Some rest or a
leave would normally help those guys. It could get to you especially if
one of your good buddies had just been shot down in front of you or
that kind of thing. There were 14 of us that landed over there and only
6 came back. That's not something you can shut out of your mind
completely, even when you're young and invincible.

   Over the long haul things start to go on mentally. To be a good
fighter pilot you have to think that you're the best there is. Period.
"Nobody can fly as well as me." As time went on and you got closer to
when you knew you were going home you began to *hope* you were the
best pilot. First you knew it, but later you hoped it. Sometimes you'd be
a little afraid of a mission: You'd think I've only got another four or
five weeks left, I hope I don't get shot down now. That went through
your mind. Most of the time that kind of thing was on the ground.
When you were up in your plane it was business. . . .

   When I left my feeling was of great relief. You were glad to get out of
it but you hated to leave the guys that you were with. Fortunately four
of us came back together. We had gone over together. It was supposed
to be five, but one was shot down the day before he was supposed to
come home. Thankfully he was rescued and came back about two
weeks later. It was mostly just a tremendous feeling of relief to be away
from being shot at. Naturally there was also the excitement of getting
home to your loved ones.

As Don Gordon testifies, stress was also a problem with some carrier
pilots. Although early-war training left something to be desired, carrier
units were the best-trained and most-often rotated units in the U.S. air
arm. Gordon flew from *Enterprise*, arguably the most illustrious warship in naval history. No units, regardless of pedigree, were immune
from the pressures of war:

We had a couple of pilots that you could tell were being pushed a little too far. One told the skipper that he felt like pushing the nose over and diving into the ocean. They sent him back. And then we had people who were just plain stupid. They didn't have the capability. You might talk to them and think they were the greatest pilot in the world. They had no fear but no ability. They didn't know how to take care of themselves. They would do things like taking seven or eight passes at the carrier and finally taking wires when they made the cut. The problem was that you never knew who was good in a wartime situation and who was not until the actual experience took place. Look at Joe Foss. We were told that Foss was not the greatest pilot in the history of peacetime aviation. Then he was sent to the fighter squadron at Guadalcanal. That his was his forté, the place for him to be. Maybe he didn't set records in training, but he certainly proved he could fly in combat—they didn't come any better. But you never knew with a new pilot until the pressure was on.

Every airman in the Pacific had to confront fear of death and the deaths of comrades. Considering the terrible physical conditions of the theater and the risks involved, it is no surprise in the least that stress and fatigue plagued all of the combatants in the South Pacific. What I find surprising is that so many men continued on despite the horrible environment. It is safe to say that every unit in the theater, even the most illustrious and experienced, had its bad days. It is likely that most individuals had bad days. Nevertheless most Allied and Japanese air-crews did not shirk and continued to slug away at each other with no letup for two years.

It is never simple to generalize on matters concerning fighting spirit. Nevertheless several general factors were at work to keep many men out of harm's way for very long periods. One factor was the sheer resilience of youth. Another was widespread fatalism. In many cases there was a strong desire to prove oneself a worthy member of the squadron and a feeling of responsibility to one's comrades. Simultaneously, however, the conscious awareness of the inevitability of casualties also caused most men to keep a unique emotional distance between themselves and com-rades. Last, many men learned to compartmentalize stress and fear, thereby enabling them to avoid debilitating terror. It was also a great ad-vantage if the unit was well led and possessed a good flight surgeon.

Almost every combat veteran I contacted for this project mentioned the importance of youth for survival in an intensely hostile world. Don Gordon of *Enterprise* puts the point very well:

War was fought by young people. It was absolutely central to it. The war started with pilots of maybe age thirty-five or older running the situation. We thought our skipper Flatley was quite old at thirty-two. [James Flatley was a famous leader and tactician on the early-war *Enterprise*.—EB] I was twenty-one. When I was thirty-four I had a squadron of my own. These kids come back and they're ready for their next flight, three or four a day. This goes back to my point about thinking too much. Younger men thought less—that was good. Young people just have no doubts, no reflections. They don't think, they do it. You can't dwell on things. If someone was lost, he was lost. You didn't talk it over. You just get up and take off again.

John Gallagher, who manned a turret of one of the 345th Bomb Group's B-25 strafers in New Guinea, puts things simply: "We were too young to be scared." Gallagher also explored another issue often brought up by veterans. Young crewmen accepted death but convinced themselves that the victim would be someone else:

At the beginning when you're young you think going to war is a big deal, you don't understand the real consequences. You're going to get killed maybe, but most kids don't really believe it. There was a huge difference between men that were nineteen and twenty-five. Kids thought, "Nothing's going to happen to me, it'll be the other guy." The older men were more realistic. In my case it was true—it always was the other guy. The thing that really sticks in my mind about the war is the fact that I was so very lucky to get back. There were so many places where things could have gone the other way. I think a lot of veterans feel this way.

Phil Caputo, another 5th USAAF B-25 crewman, expands on Gallagher's thoughts:

It is so hard to explain war because it has its own rules, it's not like peace. There is no peacetime similarity to the type of feelings you confront in war. You're young. You were frightened—very frightened— but very excited at the same time. You were well trained but everything is happening fast. There was an exhilaration to things that are sweeping by you. But you have to stay levelheaded. And you kept your sense of humor. I look back on things like that and wonder how I did it. Young people are so blind. I guess that's why they wanted eighteen-, nineteen- year-olds: all healthy and none of them thought they'd ever die. You knew somebody was going to die. You *knew* it every time you went out. But you never believed it would be you. And everyone else thought the same thing. I'll tell you something that may sound strange, whenever you heard of a guy going down, or saw it, for a moment you were joyful that it wasn't you. It was like a quota, or lottery. It wasn't you. That feeling didn't stay long but everyone had that reaction.

As Caputo further explains, one way of avoiding thoughts of death was not to talk about it:

I saw a guy almost get punched or worse. This crew were going out on a mission and one guy says, "Hey, wouldn't be funny if we all hung our jocks today?" Another guy almost went berserk and wanted to kill him. So did most of us. It was like a jinx: You never talked like that. But after a while it gets to you. You want to see your name on the board to go on a mission, but there's a little fear there when you do. But you know you got to finish so many missions so you want to get it over with and go home. But you get that little chill: Is tomorrow my time? Is it going to be me tomorrow? But you always felt it was going to be the next guy and everyone thought it. One time a plane was downed, and luckily several crewmen were picked out of the water. But the others in the squadron thought we had gone down. By the time I got back the guys had already cleaned out my locker. When a guy goes down they don't take his personal things that go home, but anything that you can use. His flight jacket, photos, gadgets, who knows. So I had to get it all back again. "Sorry guys, I'm not dead." That night I walked by this guy who was reading with a flashlight. He hadn't heard about the mistake and he almost passed out: He really thought I was a ghost. He almost passed out. I am not kidding.

So nobody liked to hear talk about dying: It was bad luck. I knew a guy who came over with me. At first he had more missions than I did, but flight engineers were in real demand so I began to fly a lot more. I ran into him a little later. He had only sixteen missions. He'd just received news that his wife had given birth to a son. He said he didn't think he'd ever see the child. I told him sure he would, no trouble. You never talked long about that. Well, he never saw his son. He was dead in a few weeks.

As 5th USAAF B-25 crewmen J. W. Kennedy recalled, youth was a powerful anecdote for war, but nothing could banish fear:

Each man had his own ideas. Each man was convinced, he thought, that it was going to be the other fellow that would get hit and he was

going to make it. You didn't think about yourself getting hit or you
tried not to. A lot of guys had nightmares. I sure did. I used to have
nightmares about going down burning. I never wanted to burn to
death. They'd wake me up. But you went back to sleep. . . . So there's a
great deal of meditation. I don't know anybody who wasn't scared. At
least I didn't meet anyone that wasn't scared. I was scared to death so
many times but you just couldn't admit you were afraid.

Fred Miller, also a 5th USAAF B-25 crewmen, concluded that what
the civilian world considered maturity could in fact be a danger in
combat:

I found that a lot of the married men didn't come back. They were a
little older or had more responsibility. There might have been a little
hesitation. It wasn't good to think if you were a pilot. There were a lot
of young war widows. That was my observation. Being cautious wasn't
always safe. Their mind was at home with their wife or baby and not
where they were. They'd get to daydream, and one split second and
you're gone. Trouble comes fast because you're moving so fast.

The struggle against fear—inherent in any war—was conducted in
many ways depending upon the individual. I think that it is safe to
conclude that most combat personnel relied on several levels of defense. One of the most common was a simple fatalism that is familiar
to any student of war. Although it is impossible to prove, my small
sampling of men facing death indicates that older aircrews, perhaps
wiser than their younger comrades concerning casualty rates, relied
more on a passive acceptance of fate than a feeling of youthful invincibility. No doubt many younger men combined youthful optimism
with an identical sentiment. The idea that a man in combat was always
vulnerable to random chance was very rational. Contemplation of this
melancholy thought is as old as military history. In modern warfare
the opinion has more validity than ever. Although World War II airmen were among the last warriors to frequently see their opponents in
combat, the skies during a melee were impossible to monitor fully.
Enemy antiaircraft might miss time after time but get lucky enough
once to destroy an attacking aircraft. Add to the equation the possibility that one's airplane might suffer a mechanical failure or become a
victim of unpredictable weather (not to mention simple crew error),
and there was good reason to look at any wartime mission as a throw
of the dice. Logically once a man accepted his position in the air war
it was natural to accept the reality that it was impossible to control the

variables that might lead to death. The result was to attempt to banish such thoughts from the mind as long and as totally as possible.

Marine fighter pilot Joe Foss, who was older than most of his squadronmates, was a confirmed fatalist: "I was scared every mission. Anyone who says he wasn't was either lying or a fool. However, combat was a bad place for a worrier. If you started counting the odds of your chances of survival and acting according to the odds you wouldn't have gotten out of a covered hole in the ground. There was no really good place to be around there. So you got into your airplane and attacked the enemy. There really wasn't any other way." Ian Page was one of the first New Zealand pilots on Guadalcanal. He flew his Hudson patrol bomber in the thick of the engagement. Like Foss—who was on the Canal at the same time—Page was an older pilot and found the acceptance of the fate of battle as the best psychological defense mechanism:

> I'm a fatalist now. If something is going to happen, that's that. It was
> no different on Guadalcanal. There were people being killed around
> you all the time. Our crew lived with itself and was very close. My crew
> never showed any symptoms of stress that I could detect. You have to
> be a fatalist to exist in active service. . . . On a conscious level everyone
> knew the dangers. If you dwelled on them, made them vivid in your
> mind, you couldn't carry on, do your duty. If you worried about dying,
> that might cause you to die. It was much better to keep going with as
> much skill and care as possible.

Fear within the individual heart is at the center of combat. One of the most elusive questions is how warriors are able to confront and even use fear while avoiding the throttlehold of terror. Unfortunately I think it very likely that those struck by terror during battle are not often with us to share their experiences. (Artillery bombardment, as described earlier, is a very conspicuous exception. The men on Guadalcanal who endured the bombardment in October 1942 often describe a passive, awful terror. Guadalcanal was, in every respect, an exceptional battlefield, even by the standards of the South Pacific.) In air warfare terror in the heart of a pilot, or if it passed through to the entire crew, might well lead to destruction. The trick was to compartmentalize fear—which was universal—from terror. The psychology involved is impossible for a civilian or a historian to fully understand. Yet a grim logic appears: When struck by fear the "adrenaline rush" (as I have heard described by veterans of three wars) temporarily amplifies the fighting spirit regardless of the consequences to fighting effi-

ciency. Terror very likely leads to paralysis and doom. R. W. Kennedy,
a B-25 crewman who arrived early in the war and saw some very bad
moments, commented on this situation:

> We were too young to be scared. I've done a lot of self-analysis after
> the war to discover where my marbles went. I've decided that when you
> get into a real rough spot, terror hits. If you survive the instant of terror
> it's pure luck. But then the terror subsides and fear takes over. Then you
> can think in fear: follow a logical course. Look at your options and
> decide the odds are still with you. So you found you could function
> with constant fear. And nothing much happened except that it affected
> your digestive tract. But every once in a while the terror tries to rise up
> and destroy you. It doesn't do that so much in the air. It more likely
> hits before your next day's flight. Because you *know* you're going to get
> it on the next run, but you keep going. That's the way it goes.

Marine Cactus fighter pilot Jacob Stub recalled a similar reaction:
"Before a flight you could get pretty tight. After landing you'd look
back and feel relief and tension. However, when in the air you're so
busy that you don't have much opportunity to get scared."

A major defense against fear was the refusal to dwell on the deaths
of comrades, and I think that in a long war such behavior has proven
extremely common. Three conditions made this reaction even more
common among combat airmen in World War II than it was for men
serving in other combat arms. First, training was extremely dangerous. Combat training of any type was hazardous, but none remotely
approached the dreadful peril faced by airmen prior to entering combat. The overwhelming majority of men to come into a combat zone
for the first time had already known several men killed or badly injured while preparing for war. No new combat airman—no matter
how youthful—could fail to know that he was in a dangerous game
and that many men were going to die. Men died in large numbers
without combat; battle, it must have been plain to see, was only going
to make things worse. Second, men by and large did not witness their
comrades' fates. It was surprisingly rare for one pilot to see another
from his squadron go down; he was more likely to hear the grim news
upon landing. Some bomber crewmen saw friends die from fighter
and flak damage, but they were much in the minority. Related to this
point is the third observation: The most common place to find close
friendships was inside a bomber crew. As it was military policy to
keep all or parts of the crew together whenever possible, close friends,
simply put, shared the same fate. Most of the bomber crews came

back, friends intact. About a third did not, and many friends perished together.

It was quite rational, therefore, to keep a certain emotional distance from squadronmates. The fighting men, I think, by and large liked each other because they had so much in common. Yet all of them— even the most inexperienced—knew that empty seats in the mess tent would appear with regularity. It was essential for the fighting integrity of the unit—and thus the individual safety of each airman—not to allow grief to paralyze one psychologically. Fighter pilot Joel Paris reflects on this melancholy fact:

> Dreadful things happened all the time. I've seen movies where someone is killed and everybody in the squadron gets all bent out of shape and upset because Joe gets killed. Well, it wasn't that way at all. You do feel bad about someone getting killed, whether they died in combat or due to some mistake they made themselves. But you didn't form such close friendships. It was protective, I think, to keep you from being devastated. You really didn't get that close. You never knew when the guy was going to be around anymore. In a year's time you had so many killed or badly injured, maybe twelve or fifteen. Count in serious illness and half a squadron's gone every few months. So you couldn't afford to get too upset when somebody buys the farm. You'd have a toast at the officers' club and split up the belongings. That was it and you went on with your business. It happened to me. I got hung up on the way back from leave and word got out that I had gone down. More than one man died on the New Guinea–Australia ferry run. I got back about a week later; it took me days to find all my stuff.

Robert DeHaven's reflections were similar:

> It was not possible to survive in a combat environment if a man allowed himself to be shattered by the death of another. It was simply too common. When a man in your unit died there was always a postmortem. If something had gone wrong in combat we wanted to know what it was. That was an important part of improving the skill of the squadron. If a pilot's own error was at fault it was good to be reminded of behavior to avoid, to always stay alert. Unfortunately, it was common that no one knew with any precision what had taken place. Yet there was nothing morbid when a comrade perished. We made a salute in his honor at the bar in the officers' club. Then there was a race to see if their Aussie flying boots or other valuables were left behind. What there was was divided up.

I should note that the division of property that almost always followed the death of an airman was not a crass act. Belongings that had
personal meaning were returned to the family. Often his friends would
examine letters and trinkets to make sure nothing (such as a letter to a
married pilot from a mistress) would cause needless pain at home. The
remaining items were Spartan—flying boots would be major treasure—and best used by the men there.

For some men the difficulty of facing death was made worse by discussing it. Most men considered it bad form or bad luck to talk about
death. (No doubt there were many exceptions.) Yet sharing thoughts
was difficult with those around you. It was even more difficult to share
them with those back home. J. W. Kennedy's units, like others at the
time, suffered serious casualties relative to strength. This meant death
to you and those close to you. Kennedy found it painful that it was impossible to share such thoughts:

> So you carry on, come back, and meet your friends. Your friends know
> the situation as well as you do, and nobody is interested in discussing
> tomorrow's casualties. So you write a letter home. You can't say where
> you are or what you do. You can't tell them what you have done. Mail
> was censored, but much of the censorship was personal, not military. So
> you write letters about watching the ants. That convinces your parents,
> or in some cases wives, that you're still alive and that it's not all that
> bad. And you remember that one of your jobs is to keep the morale up
> at home. So what's the point of scaring your loved ones half to death?
> They can't help if things go wrong. So you keep your fears to yourself.
> And we're too big and too brave to talk about it to other men. So you
> live in your own private little hell.

Some found solace in religion, attending church services regularly or
on special occasions, but it does not appear that overt religious faith
was the norm. However, the cliche that there are no atheists in foxholes contains much truth. As several veterans noted, although men
did not often discuss spiritual matters—not an unusual trait for people
so young—many "internal dialogues" concerning divinity took place.
Kennedy has an interesting observation on this subject: "There were
church services, but it was not a religious army. A minority went to
services regularly and more on holy days. But I don't think chaplains
were overworked. However, there was a lot of informal praying done,
usually around a tough target."

Men could fortify themselves with small bits of superstition. Good-
luck charms of all kinds are as old as war and were ever-present in the

South Pacific. They might be photos of loved ones, religious symbols, or even a rabbit's foot. As Robert DeHaven observes, the most interesting type of charm was the nose art found on almost all USAAF planes. (Navy and Marine regulations discouraged or forbade the practice.) And although squadron crests and nicknames often projected some image of military menace (like the famed "Jolly Rogers"), such was rarely true with nose art. As DeHaven explains, there was good reason for this difference:

> There were superstitions of all types. Personalizing the aircraft I believe was one of them. The subjects chosen were almost always things that the pilot found life-affirming. Wives, girlfriends, or women in general were very popular. Perhaps there was some reference to someone's hometown or something humorous. Some men chose something that was private. It was a form of talisman. No one could wish harm to the subject, so no harm would come to the airplane. I should add that the crew chief often had some kind of symbol of his own on the right side of the plane. . . . If there was a good artist around, the nose art could get quite elaborate. It was also common for men to refer to their airplane with a feminine pronoun, just like a boat.

The flight surgeon played an important role in the physical and emotional well-being of every combat squadron. During early years of flight it became obvious that men flying above low altitudes are subject to unusual physical stresses. Consequently during the interwar period much research was conducted in the new field of aviation medicine, most of it physiological in nature. However, it was soon obvious that any air arm was wise to monitor closely the psychological state of anyone entrusted with a dangerous and expensive military aircraft. The specialists in the field were few in number, but most military services developed courses tailored for standard physicians, which allowed many to be assigned to dispense the special care required of aviators as well as tending to standard disabilities. Allied forces deployed flight surgeons on the squadron level.

Flight surgeons were trained to be watchful for men who were being pushed close to their limits. On-the-job training was no doubt more helpful than stateside course work, because stress and fatigue proved so ubiquitous in combat theaters. Flight surgeons in the South Pacific, who of course confronted the medical calamities that accompanied service there, needed no studies from psychologists to tell them that a combination of physical battering and stress was a dangerous brew. It was a difficult position. On one hand commanders of high rank in-

formed the medical brass of the serious personnel shortage that afflicted the theater, particularly in the first year and a half of war. On
the other, flight surgeons—like all doctors—had a responsibility for the
well-being of the men in their charge.

Sometimes the job of the surgeon was simple enough. If a patient
suffered from debilitating disease or serious injury he was simply removed from the theater. If an aircrewman, particularly a pilot, demanded to be grounded there was very little to do other than to
ground him. (It was army policy to reassign such men to ground duty.
This system was highly criticized by psychologists who worried that
other men would feel they were carrying an unjust load, thus lowering
the morale of those still flying. Stress, many experts argued, was con-
tagious.) Sometimes battle casualties demanded rapid action on the
part of the flight surgeon. Exactly this circumstance triggered a dramatic action by Dr. Victor Falk, the flight surgeon of a U.S. Marine
Dauntless squadron sent to Guadalcanal during the October crisis. Because the situation was desperate the squadron was dispatched before
completing training, and they suffered serious losses with little to show
for it. Dr. Falk assessed a psychological and operational downward
spiral and simply grounded the whole squadron—undoubtedly a wise
move. Dr. Falk later described the situation:

> Lack of training was key to our troubles. When we left the states some
> of those fellows had half a dozen or ten hours in dive-bombers. The
> story was that we would go to New Caledonia and have additional
> training before combat. We were in Nouméa for forty-eight hours, and
> some of our men were on their way to Guadalcanal. Some of our men
> were able to accomplish their mission despite their poor preparation. It
> was in their character; they had the natural skills. They were eager.
> Almost everyone made a real effort to do their job. But most were not
> ready. We had at least two planes simply fly off into the clouds and
> never return. . . .
>   We had the worst casualty rates of any of the squadrons. I had about
> eight commanding officers in the eight weeks we were on Guadalcanal.
> We picked a very bad day to arrive—it was that night when the
> Japanese bombardment took place. As losses mounted there is no
> question it was also preventing the men from improving their skills.
> They were looking for fighters and concerned about antiaircraft and not
> concentrating on the target. So we were losing men badly and not
> accomplishing what we set out to do. The morale was very bad. I
> finally grounded all of the survivors. That was literally unheard-of at

that time for a medical officer who had nothing to do with command. I
talked with our colonel and he said he couldn't do it but that I could if
I thought it was a necessity. I did, so I grounded them that minute. I got
them out of there one or two per day along with the casualties. This
was mid-November and another squadron came up in relief. We would
have been up for relief under any circumstances in the near future, but I
saw no reason to risk men that clearly had been battered. I stuck
around for an extra couple of weeks and one day got on a plane and
left. It was all quite informal. I have some very grateful friends among
the survivors.

Normally, however, the flight surgeon had to deal with situations
that were much more ambiguous. It was not common for a man to
simply ask for relief. The surgeon had to be aware of signs of fatigue.
Surgeons had the right to authorize early leave or extend a leave and
often exercised that right. Surgeons also had to deal with men who
complained of medical maladies that might be real, might have been
compounded by stress, or, more rarely, might have been bogus. Perhaps the most difficult job was to help keep the squadron on an even
keel psychologically. Ultimately a flight surgeon was often the man responsible for rotating an individual, whether or not the order had arrived. Although no easily obtainable records of such actions are available, from anecdotal evidence it is clear that action by the flight
surgeon was a major part of pilot rotation in the South Pacific, particularly in the USAAF.

Lloyd Boren arrived in November 1942 in Australia to man one of
the tired B-17s still available to Fifth Air Force. At this early period in
New Guinea rotation was almost arbitrary. The flight surgeon served
as a substitute for policy: "There was no established policy of rotation
when I was there. The flight surgeon had the ability to pull people out
of combat. He was the person who pulled me out when I got back
from hospital. We loved our Doc. If he thought someone had too
much he'd pull them off. He didn't want someone that had been seriously wounded to go back to combat. Not every flight surgeon would
do that, but Doc was smart. We needed him then."

There comes a time in the service of many fighting men when an unusual psychological process sets in. On one hand, because the man had
seen much combat, the technical skills are actually at a very high level.
On the other the man is being sent to the well too often. The reaction
is not to flee but to become both careless and aggressive. (One combat
soldier who served a long tour in Vietnam called this reaction "fight-

ing mean.") The man might be in danger of simple breakdown. More likely he is in danger of being killed. A wise flight surgeon saw this develop and moved to prevent possible tragedy.

The 41st Fighter Squadron that Edwards Park flew with in New Guinea arrived early and remained in the fight until the end. Park was an early arrival and flew more than his share of missions. Park described the work of a good flight surgeon:

> We lived on surging adrenaline. I used to ask the doctor, "What's the adrenaline doing to me, Doc?" He was a funny man, sardonic from Texas. He'd say, "I don't know, Ed, but we're going to find out aren't we?" We'd ask him about atabrine and sterility, and he'd say, "I don't know, let me know when you find out." We generally begged him to find us bonkers enough to send us home. He just laughed. He'd say, "If you think you're crazy, then you're not. I'm watching you, you're still the cream of America's youth, you're still good. You can go out there and die for your country."
>
> The flight surgeon decided that many people had too much. He got me home finally. I had gotten ragged as hell and very weary. I was operations officer by then and senior flight commander, even acting CO [commanding officer] for a while. He finally got me out. I trembled, that's really what it amounted to. My hands shook, my knees shook. When I saw the enemy I felt better. The anticipation I hated, but meeting the actual fact made me feel good, made me feel easy, knowing what to do with the circumstance at hand. There were times when I'd go out of my way to pick a fight. I was actually more aggressive than previously. But some of the new pilots must have been worried about following someone who was jittering around as much as I did. I am almost certain that I would have been killed had the doc not sent me home. It was a very common pattern, I think.

For more than a century commentators on combat have stressed the importance of group expectations to individual behavior in battle. I would not challenge this assessment in any way. It is important, however, to distinguish between respect and affection. In general it was important for aircrews to gain and maintain the respect of comrades on the aircraft and within the squadron. (Obviously in the case of fighter pilots it would be the latter.) Yet the individual relationships that formed varied greatly in depth. Most individuals made close friends, who may or may not have been part of their own crew. Some crews developed an unusual chemistry and formed deep bonds. Some—probably most—had a more businesslike relationship. As we shall examine further shortly, the issues of rank and discipline weighed heavily in such matters. Regardless of the nature of the relationship the fear of letting down comrades helped to overcome the fear of physical danger.

Veteran B-25 pilot Harold Maul expresses the importance of fulfilling the responsibility to his crew and squadron:

> I was scared to death every goddamn mission I flew. Anyone who said they weren't is a liar. The thing that keeps you going is how you look to your friends. That's really important when you're young. You want their respect in the worst way. Your stomach may churn and your asshole might be tight but you pushed through it. I flew over fifty missions. More than was required, but as squadron CO it wasn't possible for me to crap out and refuse to fly. . . .
>
> I wasn't commanding it at the beginning, I was still a second lieutenant. But I had my crew; I couldn't leave them. Your crew was part of you. Officers and enlisted men shared the same hazards and had to depend on each other, so we had to get along. You made sure everyone to the extent it was possible knew how to do necessary jobs— how to lower landing gear, things like that. It was a different atmosphere than in a fighter unit.

Beyond the importance of proving one's worth in the eyes of comrades there was also a sense of teamwork that developed within units. The type of aircraft flown affected such group solidarity, but it existed in all units that were in fighting trim. It is important to note that many men trained together prior to deployment to the battlefield. When forming new squadrons and groups, all the U.S. air arms formed fresh units together in the States. Not only did pilots learn to fly with each other; a bomber crew ideally stayed together throughout the tour. The same was true for USN and Marine units. Over time this sense of unity dissipated. As noted, the U.S. Army did not rotate units but relied on the replacement pipeline to fill depleted units. Under good circumstances a bomber crew would be replaced by a new crew that trained together. (It was very possible that an experienced pilot might break in the new crew until a new replacement pilot came in or the copilot was given the bird.) In the press of operations, however, many men were thrown into an unfamiliar world more or less alone. Also skilled personnel like bombardiers and navigators might be in short supply. If such was the case, the skilled ones would move to the plane that needed them most. (As we shall see, flights of bombers often navigated and dropped bombs on instructions from the flight leader, so not every plane required a full crew; every flight officer was

expected to be competent in basic navigation.) All air services hoped
to have a reserve available to compensate as soon as possible for
losses and illnesses.

Edward Brisck was a 13th USAAF B-25 pilot in 1943 and stressed
the importance of crew and squadron solidarity:

> There was a personality difference between fighter and bomber crews.
> You were a team and got close in that way, almost a professional sense.
> I can't remember anyone who didn't meet our expectations. You never
> had recriminations about someone not doing their job. We gave a
> briefing before a flight and the crew did it. You were responsible for
> your crew: That made a major difference.
>
> We were well led. We never had any problem I was aware of with
> breakdowns of crew. . . . All [the commanders] were really nice and
> very competent people, great leaders . . . [and our squadron
> commander] was always in the forefront of everything that happened.
> The crews got along well: Personal animosities were not in the open
> that I could see. It's not like we were a bunch of happy kids: Far from it
> considering the job we were doing. But everyone seemed to get along.
> The theater was part of it too, no doubt. I might have gone insane in
> England when they were having those terrible losses. In our squadron
> there was real camaraderie and our losses were not terrible. Things
> worked well all around.

Single-engine tactical bombers like the Avenger and Dauntless created a minigeography that affected the men who flew in them. As we
shall see later, bombers were segmented by noise and flying position,
whereas fighters accommodated only the one pilot. Tactical bombers
had a unique internal design that almost certainly affected the relationship between pilot and crew. In both the TBF and SBD the pilot
sat up front inside an isolated compartment, his crewmen behind a
bulkhead. In addition, unlike U.S. Army bombers, where several officers were aboard, in a tactical bomber only the pilot was commissioned. This meant that their pilots and crews might have a professional yet distant relationship. In a war where rank meant
surprisingly little among aircrews, the hierarchy remained inside Marine and USN tactical bombers. By no means do I imply that the services suffered because of this; there were hundreds of aircraft, and
exceptions abounded. Nevertheless the distance between ranks was
probably greater in a tactical bomber than anywhere else in the U.S.
air arm (though the huge influx of reserve pilots surely tempered the

situation). Tom Powell, an Avenger gunner flying from *Enterprise*, recalled the distinction:

> Rank was important in the navy when I joined before the war. There was a real divide between officers and enlisted and very little fraternization. This broke down during the war inside the squadrons somewhat. The crewmen and the pilot were together quite a lot—it wasn't like an officer of a whole division on a large ship. I think the people preferred having a regular officer as opposed to some of the ninety-day wonders we got that didn't know what was happening. However, we rarely saw our pilot except when it was time to fly. The radioman and I were enlisted. We lived in different camps on shore. The radioman and I had nothing to do with the pilot, really, unless we were flying.

Robert Wyllie was an Avenger pilot on *Enterprise* during the same time Powell served. His recollection is similar:

> We talked with the crew via the intercom. We couldn't see each other during flight. You didn't talk much; very seldom, really. There was good reason for that: Everyone had their eyes open and needless chatter served no purpose. Our relationship was professional, nothing social, really. We had very little to do with the ship's officers. Our friends were fellow aviators. You'd be friends with the fighter or dive-bomber pilots but not the ship's company. The enlisted men had their own circle. This was true on ship and on places like Espíritu. However, in the air you depended upon each other and all of us knew it. A mistake could cost us all dearly.

Fighter units developed a different chemistry. Although alone in the plane, tactical teamwork was an essential component of Allied fighter combat. Also, fighter pilots naturally spent most of their time on the ground. They lived with squadronmates and depended upon each other in battle. It is true that the USN and Marines did a better job of squadron rotation, but by the end of the tour there were many new faces under the best of circumstances. The USAAF relied on the pipeline. Replacement pilots usually came up from theater training centers in small groups. They may or may not have known each other. As with bomber units, early-war fighter units formed and trained together in the United States. Yet fighters flew many missions, and squadrons often went up together. In many instances a close camaraderie developed. Edwards Park flew a long tour with the 41st Fighter Squadron on New Guinea and reflected on this matter:

All of us shared the foul conditions of New Guinea. We were all young. There was a lot of black humor. We scoffed at a lot of things—the war, the brass, the military, general strangeness of our life. There were a lot of inside jokes—things that a single word could trigger people to break up with laughter. Sometimes someone would make a remark over the radio and start the whole squadron laughing in the air. Planes would straggle all over because the pilots were cackling. It was a band of brothers.

Australian and New Zealand units undoubtedly had a somewhat different atmosphere. Both countries possessed a strong streak of perceived social equality, and pretense was not appreciated. British officers, accustomed to a more orderly universe, learned that different rules applied when dealing with Commonwealth cousins. Discipline required for war was recognized and followed; had it been otherwise Anzac forces of all types would not have gained their excellent reputation. Yet no one would mistake New Zealand and Australia for old Prussia, and a type of informality was the rule. As Beaufighter crewman Fred Cassidy recalled, the major distinction in RAAF units was not between rank but between air and ground. Anzac pilots were not necessarily officers. Cassidy points out that flying in the rear seat of a Beaufighter required the skills that normally brought a commission in U.S. service:

> Officers and enlisted men were quite separate on ground staff musterings—staff, motor pool, typists, and so forth. This was not true with the aircrew. We had an aircrew mess. Fliers were not automatically commissioned in the RAAF. Many were sergeants. It wasn't until you put in many missions or did something special that you received a commission. Out of a thirty-man course of pilots you might get four commissioned and twenty-six made sergeant. Later on more would gravitate toward commissions but many never got them.
>
> In our squadron we had an aircrew mess: Everyone shared it regardless of rank if you flew. You had the same privileges around the place except you didn't get saluted. The ground staff musterings had a sergeants' mess and an officers' mess. The ground staff didn't eat with us. So among aircrew there was a low level of rank-consciousness. Half the time we didn't wear rank. I got commissioned in 1943. But you didn't take much notice of it in the RAAF. It wasn't the be-all and end-all like it was in the RAF. Some of my friends who went to England were very critical of the way things ran in the RAF. You might even have a two-man crew like a Beaufighter. If one was commissioned and

one wasn't they didn't mess together or even see each other. There was no real rapport like we had. In a combat theater I think it is a very silly way of doing things. The education of pilots and navigators were usually better than, say, a simple gunner. You had a lot more responsibility flying rear-seat in a Beaufighter than you might in a Dauntless. After a period probably 60 percent of pilots and navigators were commissioned, but a simple gunner was almost never in that category. These days of course all aircrew are officers.

One special relationship existed in all air arms that merits notice. Unless facing some kind of temporary personnel problem, every combat aircraft had its own crew chief, a skilled ground crewman who serviced one specific plane. This system was employed to ensure that each aircraft received the constant routine maintenance required. It also reflected the fact that each aircraft had a personality of its own. As 5th USAAF fighter pilot Perry Dahl recalled, the chief was a man of importance:

> You had your own airplane and your own crew chief and assistant crew chief. The relationship was pretty close; the officer-airman relationship was always very evident. Of course officers were in a certain area, so we didn't fraternize at all with the enlisted personnel. He was more like a mother, and he was normally older. I was nineteen years old, for example, and my chief was maybe twenty-nine or thirty, or thirty-five or fifty. Because you know in those days we were fighting for our life, and everybody wanted to get into the war. So these guys were kind of mothers. When we came back from a strike all these crew chiefs were out in the line watching when our formation came in. . . . So as the airplanes would pitch those crew chiefs would be there counting because they knew what flight you were in. . . . And whenever there was a hole in one of those flights, when only three guys would pitch out of a flight, they would all sweat out their airplane. Because they had an association a little bit with the pilot, but more than that I think they had pride in their equipment. They'd think maybe that they did something wrong.

Unquestionably Allied maintenance standards increased following a ragged period early in hostilities. (At worst Allied maintenance was superior to that received by the Japanese.) Nevertheless a wise pilot took interest in his own plane. As David Vaughter of the 6th Trooper Carrier Squadron notes, "You had to be careful because after a while you get the feeling that somebody up there is watching out for me. I worried about that when I worked for Eastern Airlines, too. There are a lot of dead pilots who thought that. You can never let your guard down or trust your luck. I always gave my plane a good look." Vaughter squadronmate Ernie Ford held the same view: "The saying went, 'There are bold pilots and old, but no old bold pilots.' I always did my own preflight whether the flight engineer did it or not. I did that right up to the time I retired from the Air Force. It is amazing how many things a good flight engineer can miss."

The relationships that existed between individuals in the Allied air arms was very closely related to rank and discipline. This subject is always interesting, because no large institution in the modern world relies more on hierarchy than does the military. In theory—and often in practice—the military exercises extraordinary control over the men in service. In the Allied air arm (I believe that much of the following was also true for the Japanese) rank and discipline took on a different form than was found in most other branches of the services. Two closely related reasons accounted for this. First, because the prewar air forces were so small until well into the 1930s, the men who led air units into battle were young, as there simply were not enough veterans to go around; flying personnel were startlingly young. (In this regard the infantry was not much different. The grizzled noncoms featured in film did not often stand up to the frightening physical assault waged on ground forces by the jungle. The army, however, was designed to be officer-heavy to manage a greatly enlarged land army, so field-grade officers were men of greater age than were found in aviation.) This factor deprived air officers of additional benefit they might have received from being older than the men they commanded. A twenty-three-year-old captain, common enough in the air services, might speak with less authority to a twenty-two-year-old subordinate than would an older officer. In addition, many men in the air arms held technically skilled positions. As is true in all technical specialties, officers outside the guild, so to speak, are far less likely to challenge a man on a subject that a superior officer might know nothing about. More important among aircrews, especially pilots, was the creation of a kind of parallel rank system. To pilots skill in the cockpit tended to count more than the insignia on the shoulder. Furthermore the environment made spit-and-polish a near impossibility, so even a strict or mean-spirited individual had a tougher time inflicting the hated Mickey Mouse routines on the men. It is safe to say that most pilots saw that it was in their interest to be on good terms with ground crews, and few appeared to concern themselves with needless displays of authority. A pilot with a good reputation quickly gained respect among fellow pilots as well as ground crews. Respect, for most fliers, was more important than outward manifestation of rank.

Ground crewman Robert White has some interesting observations concerning rank in the USAAF:

The Fifth Air Force was very young. We had a case of an officer who got off a plane, he was about twenty-eight and a general. They had a different kind of rank than "stars and bars"—the most important thing was to fly and know about airplanes. Most pilots I met had no desire to tell other people what to do. They were fliers. You respected their rank but they weren't standard officers that liked discipline and authority. The pilot was interested in working on his plane. He'd invite his mechanics for a little test-ride. Usually the mechanics liked the pilots. But we didn't have much work, really. I had general duty: Any work somebody needed to be done. We went out to the jungle and cut down trees. Once we built one of New Guinea's famous outdoor cinemas where men sat in the rain and watched old films. We put up a sign that said, "No Colonels will be admitted to the movies without their parents." A lot of pilots, especially fighter pilots, were in their early twenties. We saw all the other big brass over time—MacArthur, Kenney, and Eichelberger. Doolittle visited once and Stillwell later in the war. I thought Stillwell was a GI cause he wore a fatigue hat. General Arnold showed up once. The biggest kick was seeing Lindbergh when he made his tour of the South Pacific. But the brass weren't really part of our life. It was a bunch of kids running a war.

Howard Redmond served in the 49th Fighter Group Control Squadron and was in frequent contact with group officers and fighter pilots checking the situation. Redmond's world was one that probably existed only in the air arm:

There was total informality. Nobody pulled rank. Hell, nobody wore rank. We knew who they were, but you never saw a proper uniform. The controllers were officers and pilots. At first controllers were all pilots. One of them was reputed to have slept through the Wheeler Field raid, and I believe it. He'd sack in on the cot until someone called him with something important. Everyone wore shorts and moccasins. All of the controllers were captains and we all knew each other. All the sergeants called each other by their nickname. We were told that another unit was told not to fraternize because we were bad for discipline. That wasn't our way. Our master sergeant went by the roster for work details—he'd start at the top of the roster, not by rank. They'd all come over together. The same was true on the line. Richard Bong used to come in sometimes to watch things. He didn't know us by name but was very informal, a very nice guy. He knew the controllers by name and would bullshit with them. He was a quiet farm kid from Wisconsin. I also remember seeing Gerry Johnson and many of the other aces. None of them acted like royalty.

Robert DeHaven gives a fighter pilot's view on the issue raised by Redmond:

I think that it was natural and necessary to wish for the respect of fellow pilots. Ultimately the only way to gain this respect was by performance in action. No one approached their mission in the same way. There was certainly an element of fortune involved. I knew fine pilots who never received credit for a large number of kills. However, it did not take long before everyone in the squadron knew who was doing the job and who, for whatever reason, was holding back. It was tremendously rewarding to do the job correctly and know that men close to you realized your contribution.

Discipline was likewise different in the air arm compared to the other services. Although mistakes were made, air units did receive some of the best men their countries could ship out. There were fewer men of the lowest ranks, as there was less use for them, and few men who wished otherwise were forced into combat. Many saw combat come to them (yet the Japanese were never able to bring the necessary force to shatter morale among Allied ground crews). In addition, in the strange world of the South Pacific the familiar military discipline often proved pointless. The theater was too ragged for formal inspection. Moreover many officers who might have been prepared to lead an infantry company were completely in the dark when confronted with the strange world of radar, fighter control, airstrips, hordes of incomprehensible aircraft, and thirty-year-old generals.

Fred Hitchcock, among his other duties on the ground, manned the control tower of the base at Gusap and places forward. The U.S. Army, at least according to Hitchcock, had a difficult time finding the right man to lead their unit. In theory they were in the rear but in practice often saw the enemy at close range:

My outfit was the best and worst in some ways. We weren't a combat outfit like the Marines but by the time we'd finished the war we'd seen more air raids than almost any combat troops because when the Japs bombed us, they bombed the airstrips and we were at the airstrips. You have to remember the scale involved. If you think about bombing Boston it would be quite an area. If someone bombed Gusap they didn't send that many planes over but the target would be the control tower, the strip, the planes around the strip, and some tents: That was it. Every air raid was not miles away but right where we lived.

Any good officer will say that discipline and leadership are two sides of the same coin, and probably on this issue military history can lead to distortion. With the exception of a handful of very charismatic generals in the twentieth century—Rommel, Patton, Montgomery—very few servicemen had deep feelings toward the brass. In the South Pacific only two top commanders gained serious attention from their fighting men: Admiral William Halsey and, more prominently, General Douglas MacArthur. A closer look at these legendary figures sheds light on the leadership issue we're discussing. As we will see, leadership—good and bad—is not always what it appears.

Although Halsey was not directly an air commander he was intimately involved with the struggle at Guadalcanal, not the largest air campaign in the South Pacific but unique nonetheless. Fought when Japan was still in many ways ascendant, the U.S. expedition could have concluded as a debacle. U.S. and Australian air units defending Port Moresby in early 1942 were likewise under the gun, but defeat there would have meant a strategic rather than material blow, as Allied ground forces there were so small. The ante was raised in turn by Japan and then Australia in the summer of 1942, but by autumn any possibility of Japanese victory in New Guinea depended upon a crushing imperial victory at Guadalcanal. No wonder Tokyo looked at its setback in the Solomons with such horror—it also meant delaying indefinitely another great push toward Port Moresby. And as Tokyo well knew, an Australian-U.S. advance up the New Guinea coast ultimately posed a mortal threat to the defensive perimeter protecting the resource-rich East Indies.

Regardless of the epic battle along the Kokoda Trail the U.S. command was fixated by the agonizing risk taken on Guadalcanal, which was apparent to every person on the island. Cactus crew chief Tony Betchik merely echoed the worst fears of 12,000 men in October 1942 when he admitted that "we all feared defeat and capture, I think. We were afraid they were going to leave us there. We believed that Halsey and Roosevelt saved us. For a while we were almost cut off." The leadership of Halsey and others gave the Americans on Guadalcanal an unusually savage determination to succeed. The flag was at stake—

and so was the existence of the men involved. Fighter pilot Roger Haberman described a desperate time that was unique in the American experience in the South Pacific:

> The men at Cactus were absolutely dedicated to what they were doing. There wasn't a single slacker, not one. There were a couple of guys that broke down because they couldn't handle it—that was something else. There was a rotation policy, but it was not set in stone. We went up and flew until relieved. I was there from October 9 to November 11 when I got shot in the leg and evacuated. The outfit that I was with was moved out less than a week later. Out of the forty pilots we had fourteen killed and four wounded, two broke down, and the rest had malaria. So we were ravaged when we left. We were no longer effective. But we had held on.

Douglas MacArthur has generated more historians' ink than any U.S. leader of the Pacific war. The defeat of MacArthur's forces in the Philippines in 1942 and his role in altering U.S. defense planning in 1941 have received mounds of criticism, greatly amplified by his subsequent showdown with Truman in Korea. It is difficult to argue that MacArthur's men showed great affection toward him during the Pacific war. He lacked the common touch that turned some soldiers—say, those under Montgomery or Rommel—into fanatical supporters. In addition, MacArthur was a fierce opponent of many military leaders in Washington and often unforgiving toward direct subordinates. Neither quality helps win the approval of historians.

As is often observed, in many ways MacArthur was an individual from a different era of history. (Which is not to say that MacArthur lacked charm. He did not lead from the front day by day, but he was very close during important events. He spent more time with common soldiers and seamen than did any Allied theater commander, and those who received the personal "MacArthur treatment" were often awed.) Yet respect for MacArthur's leadership among those under him in the Pacific war grew tremendously with time. Many of the veterans who participated in this project mocked MacArthur's vanity. However, when compared to the USN's bloody slugging match in the Central Pacific, Mac's men came off lightly and inflicted tremendous blows to Japan. MacArthur, in the view of Southwest Pacific veterans, did not waste men—and he won. In my opinion, MacArthur's conduct of operations between mid-1942 through VJ-Day showed uncanny skill and timing. In addition, probably more than any other leader of similar rank, MacArthur ran his campaigns around airpower. No doubt this reflected the disaster suffered by his air units in the Philippines combined with an all-too-clear understanding of what enemy air superiority could do to a defending force. Fifth Air Force in particular became identified with MacArthur. Fifth veterans—like many of those who served in his ground units (whom I interviewed for an earlier work)—are strongly in MacArthur's corner today. Fighter pilot Joel Paris speaks for many:

> The war in the Pacific really was secondary. We were kind of marking time until the big war was won, then we'd go over and clean things up in the Pacific. Fortunately MacArthur, being the egotist he was, hurried things along considerably. Instead of holding he marched the war back to the Philippines. Throughout he showed remarkable economy of force. I didn't like him as an individual, but he was one hell of a general. I saw MacArthur half a dozen times during the war and at no time was he showing any particular concern for his own well-being. Compared to most men of his rank MacArthur spent a lot of time near the front. He certainly wasn't living in luxury or opulence when I saw him and his staff. MacArthur watched a parachute-drop in the Markham Valley in a B-17; I don't think Eisenhower did anything like that.

Jack Williamson was a junior member of MacArthur's HQ staff who helped organize the air movement of the commander and various VIPs throughout the Pacific. Although he rarely dealt with MacArthur, Williamson's comments demonstrate the broad approval among lower officers near the general's orbit:

> We thought Mac was the best. He was aloof and didn't have much to do with the command back in Washington. But where the battle was he was there. A lot of people don't understand this, but MacArthur put himself at risk many times. Four-star generals don't do that often. He'd stay up late at night studying maps, and because he grew up there he knew Asia. He knew how to fight the Japs. He let the jungle kill them so we didn't have to. He didn't get into many bad battles, certainly not compared with other theaters. He saved a lot of our lives. And that was part of his style of command, not an accident. Nobody even knew how many Japs we bypassed. We also bypassed a lot of planes.

During the war some of MacArthur's fiercest critics were in Australia. MacArthur was commander of Australian forces, although he was very careful to allow local command to remain firmly in Aus-

tralian hands. Under the command structure of Southwest Pacific
Command, Australian General Sir Thomas Blamey was commander of
Allied ground forces, a fact that represented Australia's dominance in
the land campaign for New Guinea. Yet MacArthur never ceased to in-
furiate the Australian public and much of its military. It is true that in
official communiqués an Australian victory was referred to as a "victory by Allied forces." It is also true that MacArthur made impolitic
references to Australian fighting skills during the Kokoda campaign.
(Australian commanders were likewise concerned at that stage, but the
sting was much worse coming from a foreigner who had just abandoned an army in the Philippines. One could argue that MacArthur,
because he had lost an army in the Philippines, understood Japanese
fighting techniques better than Australian commanders back from the
Mideast, but that point is rarely made in Australian circles.) Despite
the bitterness that continues among Australian historians and veterans, it is difficult to pinpoint strategic movements of consequence
where Australian and American views differed during the New Guinea
campaign. Indeed many of Australia's greatest victories came under
MacArthur's leadership during 1943.

Still, MacArthur did not like interference from anyone, and his ties
within the Australian government were a strain. When given adequate
forces MacArthur was quick to exclude Australian participation in the
Philippines campaign. Instead he directed a large Australian army to
mop up in New Guinea and the Bismarcks. He did ask Australian
forces to spearhead the last major Allied amphibious landing of the Pacific war when they attacked the Balikpapan oil fields in Borneo. Why
Australian leaders wished to shed blood over the Philippines is an issue
I do not understand. Many of the areas left to mop up were under
Australian prewar control. (New Zealand units participated in this
campaign also.) One wonders how many Australian soldiers were
eager to engage in a major campaign in the Philippines, where their nation had no interests, for the sake of national pride. Instead
MacArthur directed them to Borneo, one of the most strategically important positions in Asia. As it was, MacArthur was counting on Australian assistance if an invasion of Honshu was required.

MacArthur, I believe, realized that Australia and New Zealand were
growing weary in 1944. Their homelands were safe, European commitments continued to chew up Anzac manpower at alarming rates,
and both countries had been in the conflict since 1939. Fresh U.S. units
were coming into the theater, such that supplies rather than manpower
limited operations. The decision was whether to employ experienced
Australian units who had seen more than their share of fighting,

poorly experienced Australian divisions, or poorly experienced U.S. divisions. Logistically—as to both strategy and politics—the Philippine decision was a simple one.

In the air war MacArthur's relations with the Australians followed a similar route. One of General Kenney's first decisions—strongly supported by MacArthur—was to squelch a poorly conceived plan to integrate Australian and U.S. aircrews. The bulk of the RAAF was engaged in defending Australia, and when the time came Fifth Air Force gave valuable assistance to the Australian effort to demolish and isolate Japanese forces on Timor. Australian units under Kenney's overall command were always under at least two layers of Australian officers. As we shall see, when push came to shove in 1943 the RAAF, like the Australian Army, played a crucial role in demolishing the Japanese position in the South Pacific. Following Japan's retreat from Rabaul in early 1944 the RAAF lost its relative importance, as its aircrews were now understandably expected to support Australian efforts in the mop-up. The timing was unfortunate in this respect. Due to a short supply of second-generation U.S. fighters, New Zealand did not receive Corsairs until 1944. Australian fighter units soldiered on with their P-40s and Spitfires until Australian industry began producing the great P-51 late in the war. By the time Anzac air units had first-line aircraft the air war had passed them by. Although the Corsair was a magnificent fighter-bomber, it required enemy opposition to create aces.

Ground-pounders, in my experience, were quite willing to allow another unit to capture a city and win glory—if it lessened the blood spilled in their own unit. New air units were more aggressive. Yet between March 1944 (the final destruction of Wewak) and VJ-Day the fighters of Far Eastern Air Force (which resulted from the June 1944 combination of 5th USAAF and 13th USAAF) were almost all engaged in ground attack. Anzac units missed a brief and fierce fight when the JAAF committed everything in the battle over Luzon. During those few weeks the fighter pilots of FEAF had several harsh fights, and the B-25 strafers again proved their worth. Yet the battle was short, and American fighters returned to attacking ground targets and small ships. Even the fearsome U.S. carrier task forces—roaming with impunity and insolence throughout the Japanese Empire—often found few opponents. The kamikaze campaign was a tragic, brutal, and vain response to a hopeless military situation. However, it highlighted the complete bankruptcy of the imperial air arm in late 1944. Anzac infantry missed nothing in the Philippines, and Anzac air units missed little also. For Australia and New Zealand to have participated in the

major air battles after the victories at Rabaul and Wewak and before
the Philippines would have required Anzac aircraft carriers and the
massive supply trains that enabled them to work. For that they needed
British assistance, as U.S. carriers were choked with men and aircraft.

There was, in other words, a certain symmetry between the Anzac
contribution in the South Pacific air war. For a year and a half the war
of attrition between the Allies and Japan was between ground-based
aircraft. After that time—except for the interlude in the Philippines—
the war revolved around the great carrier task forces. Yet when the
new carriers arrived in late 1943 and throughout 1944 the war was all
but won—only the timing was in doubt. When the RAAF and RNZAF
did their most valuable work in 1943 they were an integral part of a
fiercely contested air war near their doorstep. During that critical period the coalition among the Allies demonstrated great effectiveness.

MacArthur had a role in forming the joint war effort, particularly
between the United States and Australia. Group Commodore William
Garing, who led Australian forces at the crucial Battle of Milne Bay in
September 1942, was a strong supporter of MacArthur:

> I liked MacArthur. I had to deal with him and there's no doubt that he
> was the only man that could handle the Australian government. Our
> General Blamey couldn't because he was too close to the scene, too
> involved in the internal politics. The great thing that MacArthur did
> was to push the Australian government and get the war effort going.
> He was controversial when he came because he had left an army at
> Bataan. However, there is no doubt that he shifted the emphasis of the
> air and land effort away from Sydney and toward the north. I saw the
> confusion at Milne Bay and believe that without MacArthur's
> leadership, we would have been possibly vulnerable in the north. At the
> least, the war would have lasted longer. Heavens, he had confidence.
> When he arrived in Australia the Pacific was a shambles. Within weeks
> he was making preparations for an offensive that eventually led to
> Luzon. MacArthur was not a fine diplomat but had great strategic
> vision.

Halsey and MacArthur possessed a common trait: Although both
greatly appreciated the need for airpower of all kinds, neither one was
an airman. In Chapter 6 we will examine the order of battle, but for
the moment we can note that a significant psychological and sometimes physical distance existed between most men in the air service and
their top commanders. Certainly the best known and most liked was
the ever-busy and ebullient General George Kenney, 5th USAAF com-

mander. His forward commander, the flinty but skilled General Enis Whitehead ("Enis the Menace" to many), was more respected than loved. I think much the same could be said about the fine Marine commander at Cactus, Ray Geiger. USAAF commanders in the Solomons such as Nathan Twining and Millard Harmon served with great distinction, but it is unlikely that their pilots spent very much time debating their relative merits. The Australian command structure was often marred by controversy, but there is no reason to think that the arguments affected day-to-day operations.

I believe two reasons exist for this lack of identification between the men and the brass in the air services. First, air force commanders were no different than any other officers of high rank. They were few in number, and those under their command were many. Kenney made it a point after moving his headquarters to New Guinea in 1943 to tour as many units as possible. Still, it was a rare day to see a top officer. The situation was no different in ground armies. I have talked to veteran soldiers of three different wars who did not remember the name of their divisional commander. Some sailors on large ships could go weeks without seeing the captain. (Successful admirals like Aaron "Tip" Merrill and Arleigh Burke did gather a special loyalty from their men; they were, literally, in the same boat during battle.) Just as important, I think, was the pace of the air war. Ground campaigns, even if protracted, ultimately had clear winners and losers. Naval battles likewise were either won, lost, or drawn in short order. The air campaign, however, was never easy to measure. To be sure, as one side or the other was ascendant its air superiority allowed the seizure of forward bases. Yet the air fighting itself was largely a pounding war of attrition. The major Japanese base during 1942–1944, after all, remained Rabaul. After slugging it out for two years it must have been obvious to Allied fliers that they were slowly gaining ascendancy. It would not have been clear that the Japanese were cleverly being stretched, weakened in subtle ways, and made vulnerable to rapid collapse. For most of the campaign, therefore, measuring success and failure would have been a subjective process for airmen and ground crews. Most would have been concerned with the world inhabited by their own squadron and group. Indeed it was at this level that leadership most keenly showed itself in the South Pacific air war.

There were dozens of officers throughout the theater on both sides who provided inspirational leadership based on accomplishment in battle, good judgment, and an ability to demonstrate skill to and concern for men under their command. It would be impossible to do them all justice. Yet in the U.S. air arm I think the most respected and skilled leader was Colonel Harold "Joe" Bauer. An experienced flier before the war, Bauer was given command of the Marine fighter squadron VMF-212. In that role he prepared some of the greenest pilots flying out of the miserable base of Efate for much more serious duty. During a short stay at Cactus in early October Bauer scored several victories. When his squadron was transferred to Cactus in the worst days of the battle in mid-October, Bauer brought in his squadron to relieve exhausted units. On its approach Henderson VMF-212 ran straight into an attack by nine Japanese Vals directed against *MacFarland*, a converted destroyer that was bringing in fuel and ammunition to replenish the serious losses caused by the Japanese battleship bombardment two days earlier. Although *MacFarland* was hit with serious loss of life, Bauer shot down four of the Vals, a feat for which he was awarded the Congressional Medal of Honor.

Soon after that General Geiger appointed Bauer head of fighter operations at Cactus. In theory this meant that Bauer was not expected to fly. Although thus grounded, Bauer urged his fighters to engage the dreaded Zeros directly and, in general, brought a breath of fresh air. The admiration that Bauer gained was dramatic and almost universal. Significantly Bauer was a great favorite with the ground crews, not a normal state of affairs considering the great difference in rank. Tony Betchik had no love for officers but made an exception for Bauer:

> The officers had their world and we had ours. We had very little rapport with them. Rank has its privilege and it's always been so. It's necessary to a degree because you need a boss in war. . . . There were a few exceptions. I had the highest regard for Colonel Joe "Butch" Bauer. I heard later that somebody called him "Injun' Joe." I never heard the nickname on the Canal: We called him Butch. He flew my planes and was the only one who would take time to talk to the ground crew. He was the best Marine officer I served under. Many on the Canal thought he was the best pilot there.

More importantly Bauer galvanized his hard-pressed fighter units. It is probably no accident that after Bauer gave his instructions to "engage Zeros," the kill ratio over Guadalcanal shifted in favor of Marine and USN pilots. Fighter pilot Roger Haberman offers a typical assessment of Bauer's leadership:

> Morale was vital in October because that was the crisis point for Guadalcanal. The soldiers could see many of the fights, and watching

them fend off the Japs was a big boost to them and to us. Bauer was an absolute rock. He was responsible for the mental attitude of the fighter pilots, and fortunately he was a very strong individual. He was so goddamn strong that I would have done *anything* he recommended. I don't care what it was—if he said fly down the smokestack of a battleship, I would have done it. He was a real motivator.

I didn't know him or anyone outside our unit prior to arrival. But he made an impression fast. Everything was verbal. We didn't have any chalkboards. We all spoke the same language. He'd say, "Get 'em: Do this, do that." We'd talk about tactics and so forth. For example, we're sitting at ten o'clock in the morning waiting for them to come in. We know they're coming and we know our radar would pick them up. Bauer would be sitting there playing cards, smoking a cigarette, loafing, waiting for the phone call. Maybe reading some beat-up books that sat around. The field telephone was hanging on the tent pole. It rang and Bauer would pick it up, and we'd hear him say "Sure, okay, all right." After he hung up, he'd turn and say very quietly, "Okay fellows, let's go: Let's get them." Everybody is so tense. Some bit their fingernails. I didn't. I figured if death comes it comes, screw it, and you didn't want to waste energy tightening up your nerves. But this was a classic example how he'd handle his people. If you've got forty pilots, forty students, forty workmen, forty anybody, you don't talk to everybody the same way. You change the way you work as you learn your individuals. But he worked this way. He didn't rile anyone; everyone had confidence in him. He just communicated confidence and command. That's amazing, particularly in a life-or-death circumstance. He learned who the people were under him. In a circumstance like that you know you have their *maximum* attention; it doesn't take long to figure out who's who. That's when you work as a group. The forty pilots were divided up into flights. You get to know the people as you fly with them, as you talk with them. You get to know how they're going to react, and how you're going to react. That's called developing a team. And Bauer did that—he developed a team. The squadrons would do anything he said. He was so smooth, so intelligent. He was in charge of operations. He didn't have to fly.

On November 14, 1942, imperial forces suffered a disaster at Guadalcanal. Urged by Tokyo, Combined Fleet, despite serious misgivings, made one last stab at victory. The Marines and soldiers had decisively defeated major Japanese land assaults in mid-October. Therefore Yamamoto dispatched a large surface force, containing two battleships and several smaller warships, to cover the arrival of a convoy carrying the initial wave of a fresh division to renew the offensive. On the night of November 13 a U.S. cruiser task force, despite terrible losses, sunk one of the Japanese battleships and threw the operation into confusion. Not expecting defeat, the Japanese troop convoy approached Guadalcanal and came under withering air attack from the Marines at Cactus and pilots from *Enterprise* who had been shuttled in for temporary duty in the crisis. As the Marine and USN pilots (aided by army P-39s and B-17s) began to devastate the convoy, Bauer could not contain the urge to join the battle. Ironically he met his old friend from the *Enterprise*, James Flatley, before taking off. Teaming up with Thomas Furlow and Joe Foss, Bauer's group headed for the transports. When near the ships Bauer was jumped by a Zero, which he promptly destroyed with a head-on shot. Foss believed that the debris from this victory damaged Bauer's Wildcat. (That was a genuine possibility; as Japanese fighters often flamed, a close engagement frequently meant passing through wreckage.) Perhaps Japanese antiaircraft struck home. In any event Bauer bailed from the plane. With night falling, Foss and Furlow returned to Cactus. A later search turned up nothing, and Bauer was gone.

The following night the United States Navy effectively finished the campaign in another violent night battle. Despite losing several precious destroyers, USS *Washington* demolished the second Japanese battlewagon. What remained of the Japanese convoy was crushed the following day. For those close to Bauer, his loss gave a bitter taste to one of the great victories of the Pacific war. Haberman reflects: "Bauer was an operations officer and didn't belong out there. It was tragic, damn it, and no one liked it a bit. But that was the kind of guy he was: He had to go out and see what was going on so he could plan his strategy and check conditions."

Bauer's deeds were unusual and probably could have only taken place in the extraordinarily intense conditions that existed during the crisis at Guadalcanal. Yet Bauer was not the only veteran, serving in theory in operations, who lent a well-appreciated hand to the men under his command. In Fifth Air Force the first commander of the famous 49th Fighter Group was Paul Wurtsmith. Kenney soon appointed Wurtsmith to head 5th USAAF Fighter Command. By the end of the war Wurtsmith was a major general. (Wurtsmith was another in a long line of USAAF notables who perished in an air accident soon after the war was over.) One of his successors as 49th Group leader was the much younger Robert Morrissey. As 7th Squadron pilot Robert DeHaven recalled, all these men helped build the morale of the group:

The theater in New Guinea was much smaller than in Europe. There were advantages in this regard. Pilots had a personal contact with their leaders that I don't believe happened in the larger theaters. I met Kenney many times. You could talk to Kenney, push for changes, and he'd listen. There was active participation of key senior players. Both Wurtsmith, who was a brigadier at the time, and Morrissey would put their symbols of rank on the desk, put on lieutenant bars, and fly missions. Gestures like that gave a great boost to morale.

Group Commodore William Garing did much the same thing during the bitter battle for Milne Bay in September 1942, which ultimately resulted in Japan's first major land defeat of the Pacific war. Garing was thirty-five years old when given command of Australian fighters at Milne and was not expected to fly. Indeed his pre-Pacific specialty was operating flying boats. Regardless, Garing flew, as he explains: "It was often done for group commanders to fly in combat, even though that was not their real responsibility. I flew fighters at Milne Bay on occasion. I certainly wasn't the best fighter pilot in the RAAF, but I believed it would help morale at a time of great confusion. If the commander flies, even a few times, the others say, 'If he's flying that's okay with me.'"

Ultimately the most important leaders were the squadron and flight leaders inside the units. Some of these men—Bauer, Thomas Maguire, Pappy Boyington, Tom Blackburn, Robert Westbrook—were notable aces. (Many aces and many good pilots did not wish command.) Most were not. Seniority, judgment, a certain aptitude for paperwork, the ability to cooperate with others, and connections with superiors were among the various qualities looked for in a squadron commander, not a simple tabulation of victories confirmed. Obviously somewhat different criteria were employed for choosing leaders of bomber units, but I think in all combat units judgment and maturity (even at age twenty-three) were more important than aerobatic skills when finding leaders. It is safe to say, however, that most of these men were exceptional pilots.

Leaders were important in combat as well as on the ground. James Edmundson began his long and successful Air Force career as a squadron commander for 431st Bomb Group of Thirteenth Air Force. He expressed a simple but effective philosophy followed by the best combat leaders:

All of the standard things are important for leadership in the air. You try to listen to your men. You share much of their life. You make their lives as pleasant as possible. More important you must convince them that you are competent; that you know what you're doing. Therefore, as a squadron and later as a group leader, I thought it was vital to lead from the front. We were all in the same boat—I wasn't in the rear. There was no rear. As group leader I didn't have to go on a mission, but I was there on the tough ones and I think good group leaders shared my feeling. It's also important to realize that we were young for men of our rank. The promotions, especially early in the war, came with tremendous speed as the USAAF expanded and casualties took their toll. You have to be air leaders, and you have to be out in front. You can't run a flying outfit from the ground.

At a certain level leadership had no connection to rank at all. To maintain good morale squadrons required many cocky young men with a to-hell-with-it attitude buoyed by a good sense of humor. Dozens of the veterans who helped me in this work mentioned a good sense of humor as one of the most valuable attributes for maintaining spirit under grim circumstances.

Not only did the terrain and climate guarantee a rough tour; so did the fact that the theater was distant from base and near the bottom of the supply priority list for every possible commodity. Fortunately the young men proved remarkably resilient despite being faced with a foul environment. Naturally the situation was at its worst early in the campaign. Bombardier Lloyd Boren found New Guinea most distasteful when he arrived in late 1942:

I was over there for fifteen months and that was just as long as I wanted to be. The weather and living conditions were extremely bad. I was watching the movie *Memphis Belle* not long ago, and the crew is living in England in Quonset huts with wooden floors wearing dress uniforms at a dance. Now I fully respect the great dangers faced by the men in Europe. But God, when I think how we lived, it was pitiful. We lived in tents with dirt floors. There wasn't enough lumber to go around. We had one long mess-hall tent where officers and men ate. At that time there was little division between officers and enlisted. You were too close; it just didn't make any sense. Most of us wore a pair of shorts and boots and that was it for your uniform. Not a parade ground, no insignia. I was black all over from the sun.

Living in the Solomons early in the war was no better than camping out in New Guinea. Men who served in the upper Solomons like New Georgia and Bougainville cursed the beastly climate, where one Marine said, "It was always raining either up or down." Dauntless pilot LeRoy Smith came to Guadalcanal just after the Japanese were expelled. Smith was a Marine and, like most in his service, had little love for the navy. However, as Smith and later thousands of servicemen discovered, the navy became the carrier of treasure when the supply pipeline allowed. As Smith recalled:

> Things changed after I arrived. When I got there we were in the standard four-man tent with mud floors. Food was wretched. The first week I was with them when we lined up to eat you got to choose between one utensil. You could choose a spoon or a fork because there weren't enough to go around. Sometime after the Japanese were cleared out of the Canal the navy loaded up a transport on the East Coast with umpteen F4Us, SBDs, and P-40s and got it to the Pacific. After that arrived the holes were plugged. When I got there they were still fueling out of fifty-gallon drums. Parts were cannibalized from wrecked planes or worn-out aircraft. This supply ship arrived around the same time that the new carrier *Essex* did in late 1943. When the *Essex* arrived it was Christmas for people on Guadalcanal. Those ships can carry a year's supply of everything—from oranges to turkeys. It was like some saint had come to Guadalcanal. Things that people would have sold anything for were there in large quantities. Things like Coke and canned fruit. Right before I arrived, some recreational supplies were arriving—things like volleyballs, baseball gloves, basketballs. You get the picture.

Most men in the South Pacific lived in tents. The beastly hot, humid nights of the area made these less than ideal. The hordes of mosquitoes and other insects made things worse. From the beginning servicemen tried to raise their standard of living. As was typical of combat soldiers throughout history, the men in the South Pacific confronted circumstances that civilians would have found hideous. Slowly they constructed a world replete with luxuries, if one can use that term. The most important, outside of decent food, was a floor. In the South Pacific if one lived in a tent without a floor it meant that one often lived with mud underfoot. This was uncomfortable and extremely unhealthy. The problem was that lumber was extremely hard to obtain because cut logs were designated for rear bases and, in theory, for buildings of high medical value like latrines. In practice stolen lumber was near the top of what developed into a long list of valuable items available on the South Pacific black market. Those men lucky to have connections elevated the floor of their tents and affixed wood. As the months passed and a base was not provided an electrical generator, they became prime items for barter. In practice this meant that a tent-dweller might have a single sixty-watt bulb for four men. Large saws capable of providing a supply of lumber were sent to the theater. This was an obvious response, as one thing that the South Pacific had in abundance was lumber. Yet the results of the output were odd. Many of the trees near bases were large, and those nearby probably contained shrapnel from enemy bombing raids or the remains of friendly antiaircraft fire. That led to broken saw blades and injured men as metal struck metal. Still—and this is the odd part—men with access to local lumber used some of the most beautiful and valuable woods in the world to build floors and latrines.

Food was another standard by which men in World War II judged their life, and on that count the situation was awful. Allied forces on Guadalcanal faced serious food shortages only for a brief period. In September the Marines sustained themselves largely on captured Japanese food. In Malaya the Japanese called captured British food "Churchill supplies." On Guadalcanal the large food cache intended for the Japanese pioneer battalion fell into Marine hands. The poetic justice is obvious, yet it was not until November 1942 that food shortages ceased to become a difficulty. With that exception, Allied units never faced hunger as an enemy. (Japanese units could not say the same on several battlefields.)

However, a monotonous and bad diet over many months proved a major problem for Allied morale. In our era, for the first time in history, many people in the industrial world suffer health problems due to the overabundance of inexpensive foodstuffs. The diet endured for months on end by a serviceman in the South Pacific would be almost unimaginable to a modern civilian. Nothing was fresh. Breakfast might be prepacked pancakes with sugar-syrup or despised Australian marmalade. Remaining meals took advantage of whatever was available from the companies—operating in the golden era of canned food. Some goodies were controversial. I have talked with many men who today both like and despise Spam, one of the most universally served foodstuffs. Vienna sausages, another common delight, were likewise received with divided opinion. If there was anyone who developed a taste for dehydrated vegetables, he has not contacted me. Much of the food came from Australia and New Zealand. Naval personnel, normally accustomed to the best food in the armed forces, faced New Zealand mutton, a task few relished. When not supping on Spam, U.S. units might receive Australian Bully Beef, a greasy canned meat despised by nearly all who confronted it.

To make matters worse, poor food in very poor conditions was an invitation to food poisoning. The "GI drizzle" was a common enough fact of life and made existence only that much harder. (If combined with dysentery, any food poisoning became immediately serious.)

Sad but true, average serviceman faced the worst imaginable health hazards while receiving the worst food supplied by Allied governments. Theft and temporary flight were merely partial solutions. David Galvan, before moving on to Guadalcanal to help service the planes at Cactus, served a brief time at Efate, one of the worst locales. Although not a cook, he was temporarily drafted into the service because all three squadron cooks came down with malaria. Galvan described the scene:

> So I became an enlisted man's cook. When one [cook] recovered I became the officer's cook. That lasted a couple of weeks. I didn't want to be a darn cook. It was hot to work over a stove. They had a big tent and all the flaps were up and there was a wood floor. It was nothing to find rats in the big sacks of coffee. One guy that made it dipped this big bucket into the bag and dumped it into a big cauldron of boiling water, larger than five gallons. He poured it in, and by god there was a rat swimming. He picked it out with a dipper and kept making the coffee. The food was dried eggs, dried milk, and canned food, and it was bad. That wasn't my fault.

Perhaps it was coincidence, but Galvan, after the crisis passed, was relieved from service on Guadalcanal with severe cases of malaria and dysentery.

Avenger tail-gunner Jess Scott was in the theater several months later than Galvan and learned quickly that the way to good food was to become friends with someone in navy supply. Best of all was to become useful to someone in the Seabees, famous across the Pacific for fine engineering and an uncanny knack for free enterprise. Scott recalled:

> Now in the New Hebrides where we'd go periodically for refits, training, etcetera, there were some Seabee units that had access to the frozen foods coming into the theater. I made connections with all the cooks and bakers, guys who wanted rides in the planes, then I took our crews over to see the Seabees and we had terrific food: fresh rolls, pies, ice cream, everything. But nothing lasts forever. One time we were down there and they'd opened a new field in the bush on New Caledonia. It must have been fifty miles from Nouméa. All we had to eat there for two weeks was

Spam and dehydrated potatoes and orange marmalade—period. We
didn't have any bread to put the marmalade on. What a wretched place.

Because basic supplies were rare and many men were desperate to
improve their often squalid existence, theft of supplies was common
throughout the theater. Bases posted guards, and not to thwart Japanese infiltration. (Although that was a problem at some bases in New
Guinea; usually infiltrators tried to steal food, however, not inflict
damage.) Instead they were trying to protect supply dumps from U.S.
servicemen.

The massive "diversion" of supplies began in the earliest stage of the
war. The desperate need for almost anything provided the motive for
seizing supplies, and the chaos made the job easy for those with some
nerve. Chuck Novak, a crew chief with 68th Squadron, arrived early
in the war in Australia. A few months later his unit was moved to
Guadalcanal. As Novak recalled:

We didn't steal anything; we borrowed it. I am not sure how anything
got to its destination. When ships came in with supplies we tried to
look and see who was going to pick them up. So we'd go over and
paint our truck the same color as theirs and pretend to be them. We'd
load the truck up and drive off. Half the time we didn't know what we
were getting. Once we ended up with a supply of left shoes—don't ask
me how that happened. We got a lot of Spam. It was American
ingenuity. We were independent and we could think; it's something to
be proud of.

After mid-1943 the Allied supply situation quickly improved, and by
1944 even the South Pacific was receiving unusual bounties.

When the war entered 1944 surprising changes took place in parts
of the South Pacific. At major bases mosquito control made the areas
much safer, and the Seabees and Corps of Engineers made them much
more comfortable. The Americans employed thousands of natives to
grow fresh fruits and vegetables. By the end of the war Espíritu, even
Guadalcanal, would have been hot and muggy but tolerable. Yet this
simply signified that the South Pacific was becoming a rear area. Even
as such improvements were taking place the air units were moving ever
farther up the coast of New Guinea, into the Admiralties, and began
operating against the Indies and Philippines. The USN's new carriers
began their rampage against targets throughout the Pacific. What that
meant to the men involved in the air war was that living conditions improved only by a matter of degree. By the time conditions in the rear

had greatly improved, combat units had moved forward again, probably several times. By any reasonable definition, Allied servicemen fighting the air war faced harsh conditions from beginning to end.

Because the men in aviation knew the hard edge of the environment,
there was widespread respect and sympathy for soldiers fighting the
ground war. Many of the veterans who contributed to this work remarked, often with amazement, on how horrid was the world inhabited by infantry in the tropics. Airmen knew that regardless of relative
risks their life on the ground was far less punishing than that faced by
someone carrying a rifle during one of the brutal jungle battles.

B-24 navigator John Mullady's comment is typical:

It was a miserable place to live with the heat and disease. Insects, oh
God, they were all over the place. We all pitied the ground-pounders.
Later we went up to Palau, which the army was taking. Those soldiers
looked utterly miserable. They had spent thirty days on the line. They
were filthy and many had that 1,000-yard stare. It was a terrible scene,
one of the worst that I saw. What a horrible place for a ground war.
You were never dry. You'd sweat while it rained.

C-47 crewman Edward Brown served a year after Mullady but
shared the same feelings:

You had to feel for those poor guys on the ground. I pulled a whole lot
of those infantrymen out of the front line back to the hospitals in the
rear. They had one hell of a time. The mud, the rain, the disease, and a
war on top of it, it was just amazing. I don't know how they did it. We
all respected them for it. If we could get home if nothing else we could
sleep on the planes. We had it a lot better than the infantry did and we
all knew it. I never heard a one of those wounded bitch. They took it
like men. I was proud to serve with them.

•   •   •

Unfortunately there is not a great deal of information concerning
morale and living conditions confronted by the Japanese contesting the
skies over the South Pacific. Rabaul was an extremely well developed
base by Japanese standards; outlying fields and the Wewak complex
were much more crude. Of one thing there is no doubt: As the war entered 1943 Allied air attacks and U.S. submarines began taking a toll
on Japanese supply vessels. The living conditions facing Japanese airmen, never better than those of their Allied opponents, could only

have grown more grim. After being leapfrogged many Japanese air and ground units became paramilitary farms with little or no military utility. Units in unlucky places faced starvation and conflicts with indigenous populations. The growing calamity in the South Pacific was summed up by the widespread comment in the JAAF that "nobody returns alive from New Guinea." They might have added that few were to return from Rabaul before war's end.

Chapter 6 illuminates why the air war in the Pacific became such a vicious affair. Suffice it to say there was little love lost between Japanese and Allied airmen, although grudging respect for the enemy was widespread. Occasionally men found out they had some things in common. Fighter pilot Edwards Park described such an event:

> The Japanese were warriors and had been at it a long time. They considered it that way, that war was for warriors. It was hardship all around. Many Japanese kept diaries and we had many translated if they fell into our hands. We read them with great interest. I remember one guy had been ferrying a Tony down from Formosa into Wewak and on his first day he got into a skirmish with a big flight of American planes coming over. He got tangled with some yellow-nosed P-47s and tried to drop his wing tank and one hung up. He said he got out as soon as possible. One of our guys said, "I was the guy he was after. I remember a wing tank hanging and a Tony doing a fast split-S out." It was a very funny feeling. We all kind of wondered what happened to him. I think most of us hoped he lived. He was one of us in a way. He said it was horrible at Wewak, the food was lousy, that he couldn't stand it and wished he was out of there. We always talked about bad food, no women, the same things. It was good for us, made us human beings for a little while.

Day-to-day defenses against the triple assault of climate, boredom, and stress were not easily attainable for men in the theater. Simply put men found what meager diversions were available: They drank a lot, looked forward to leave, and hoped for rotation. Off-duty diversion was an important part of ground life depending upon one's position. Chief engineers, crew chiefs, and some pilots spent time with their aircraft between missions. When the unit was active, which was often the case, tending to aircraft consumed great amounts of time. Yet even for those in responsible positions the weather and course of battle imposed extended lulls in action. For many aircrews and ground crews the world was painfully slow, even if operations were regular. Almost everyone spent much time on housecleaning and other domestic tasks. There was no regular laundry service (though some units made arrangements with natives), and care for the tent was left to the men. Projects to improve quality of life occupied many hours; because of the heat none were done quickly.

From Pearl Harbor to VJ-Day various board games and card games were popular. Some units may have preferred one game to another, probably reflecting a shared enthusiasm on the part of a couple of men who eventually interested others. Bridge was popular in some units, not in others; chess and checkers had fans everywhere. All units had hard-core readers, and thousands of books made the trip to the South Seas. Other men found diversion in a small flood of old magazines.

If I were to create an image that best represents the misery, futility, and black humor of the South Pacific it would have to be a night at the movies in the South Seas. Every unit had a projector and, because movies were circulated by airplane, there was a good supply. However, what men learned to accept as a theater almost defies the modern imagination, accustomed to late-twentieth-century multiplexes. Lee Tipton of Thirteenth Air Force described a scene that dozens of other veterans also mentioned. What is startling is how normal Tipton and others make it sound:

> We had movies at night. A movie theater consisted of a dozen coconut logs and a cover about the size of an umbrella that covered a movie projector. And then a screen about the size you'd find in someone's home for a slide projector. That was our entertainment. We'd sit there in the rain. You'd get used to that. Some wore ponchos, but they were so darn hot that many guys just sat there in what passed for a uniform. The rain was a little cooling. Of course there was the mud all around. The darkness around the screen was total, and sometimes it was difficult to hear what was being said when the rain picked up. But men just sat there on those logs and became immersed in the film while getting soaked to the bone. When vehicles became more numerous, it was very common for men from other units to come up and see the film if it was better than the one showing at their theater. There was no popcorn and no ushers.

Soon after Pearl Harbor Hollywood began to churn out war movies, and many made the journey to the South Pacific. As USN ground crewman Dan Harper recalled, wars on the screen did not generate the same reaction as the real thing:

I can't recall any propaganda movies per se, but the Hollywood
productions had a lot of political content. John Wayne running around
shooting Japanese and this kind of stuff. We'd laugh at the technical
ridiculousness of these movies. I remember one where John Garfield
played a pilot who was shot down over the jungle. He picked up this
.50-caliber machine gun and was running around the jungle shooting
this .50-cal from the hip. That was very difficult to do unless you're
nine feet tall. We giggled and laughed at it. But it was something to do.

Depending upon the unit and time of year, gambling was popular. It
should be remembered that money, at least in the civilian sense of the
word, had far less meaning in the South Pacific than it did in the any
other theater of war. Except for a package of cookies there was almost
nothing to buy. There were no women, so courting and prostitution
were impossible. Perhaps recognizing these circumstances, military
paymasters in the South Pacific were often late, although I have heard
of no one who believed they did not receive what was due them eventually. Obviously this situation encouraged those men who enjoyed a
game of chance. J. W. Kennedy of Fifth Air Force was one of them. As
he described it, "Money was of no value so they didn't bother to pay
you. You got paid every three or four months and that was the signal
for the start of the all-night card games and crap games and they continued until 10 percent of the squad had 90 percent of the money."

Kennedy also pointed out that many units had mascots. As with nose
art, the army was more tolerant of personal quirks than were the USN
and Marines. (On paper there was good reason to do so: Airmen were
told when they made the jump up the coastline that they could not bring
pets with them because of fear of disease; this was one of the most
widely disobeyed orders in a disorderly theater.) In any case many units
and even many plane crews adopted pets, usually dogs but including a
collection of God's smaller creatures. Like pets in a college fraternity
house—where most pilots and crewmen should have been—odd stories
abound. I hope they are true. J. W. Kennedy provides a fine story:

We had little ceremonies. Somebody had three bulldogs that someone
else had picked up in Australia. They were named Rabaul, Gasmata,
and Soupta [names of Japanese air bases—EB]. The dogs would fly and
the crew chief would put the dog's name on the manifest when we
boarded the airplane. Soupta's plane went down. When they got this
manifest they saw "General Soupta" and all hell broke lose. It didn't
sound American so they got it into their heads he was a Dutch liaison
officer and they were searching everywhere in New Guinea and northern

Australia to find out who this general was. When they found out it was a dog letters came down about not listing animals on the manifest. Ours was a young pup named Rabaul. We were called up, lined up in class-A uniform, or whatever we could get that looked like a class-A uniform. When the dog lifted his leg to urinate, the adjutant issued the orders, the dog was brought forward, and the tinsmiths had made a Maltese cross with a piece of ribbon. That cross was hung around the dog's neck and he was awarded the DSC: Distinguished Squirting Cross. Those were the crazy things we did to keep up our spirits.

Naturally the men liked music. Early record albums were popular items, often played on manual phonographs. Airmen had access to radios, setting them apart from most servicemen in the Pacific. Receiving any program required a good radio, as there were no DJs in Dobodura. Airmen had radios in their aircraft and advanced communications nets at the base. There was military intent to this technology, but it also offered the opportunity to listen to tunes, whether on the ground or in flight. Fred Hitchcock, who had extensive experience with radio communications, was a connoisseur of what was available in the South Pacific. Few mastered the art as well as Hitchcock, but a little news and music was greatly appreciated by many:

I had a second radio set at Moresby and later at Gusap going all the time to listen to programs. I'd keep it low if we were taking messages. There was a show from Australia by a guy named Mike Collins who had a program of news and music and I listened to it religiously. Great show, and for some reason nobody I've talked to can remember it. There was Armed Forces Radio, of course. Sometimes they'd take a ballgame and eliminate all of the delay between pitches, so you could broadcast the whole thing in about twenty minutes. If someone came in from communication who knew the score, we tell him to shush.

I would listen to the various foreign broadcasts given by the enemy on short-wave. You could often get these very clearly. We called it Zero Hour, what was later called Tokyo Rose. They'd start up with a recording of Arthur Fiedler's rendition of "Strike Up the Band." They'd have little comments; she was called Anne on the program and would talk about our girlfriends and other men seducing them. I listened to Rose for several years, and stories about her predicting military actions are rubbish in my experience. When everyone in the Japanese military knew an American unit was in the area she might say something, but stories about Rose having supernatural powers and strategic insight are just not true. But the music was good.

The other programs were interesting. My favorite was "Reggie Hollingsworth and the News." Reggie was an Australian traitor and he would come on sounding like Churchill broadcasting from Tokyo. There was another program that was dedicated to war analysis. They were very clever. One was dedicated to "Japanese bases behind American lines: Springboard for new offensives." The idea was that if any of these places we bypassed got supplied they'd be roaring forward again. Then there was a show they called "The Postman" that short-wave sets in the U.S. picked up. He'd start out playing the piano, some sad tune, and send messages from POWs. As we moved up from Australia we got new programs. One of my favorites was "Radio Saigon: The Voice of France in the Far East." This French lady would come on and talk about French literature and music and such things. It was her opportunity to break into show biz, I guess: There was no propaganda. Once in a while we'd get Radio Shanghai, but that was tough to get. Radio Manila I didn't learn to get until late in the war. There was no printed guide to these frequencies so you had to fiddle around until you found something. Later I could get loud and clear Radio Jakarta, Batavia.

In the prewar military, athletics was a major part of unit life. Tournaments in football, baseball, and boxing were common. The Army-Navy football game was viewed as something like a small-scale war—except that the outcome was more important. After Pearl Harbor these amusements almost disappeared. The chill of a real war going badly did seem to dampen enthusiasm for team sports. (Professional baseball was temporarily transformed by enlistments and the draft.) Yet when the Allies stabilized the front and began to gain ascendancy some of the old habits returned, but without the prewar intensity.

Howard Redmond recalled that in late 1943 there was an intersquad baseball tournament pitting the enlisted men and officers of each squad against each other and an additional team from headquarters. According to Redmond, although the enlisted and HQ personnel were playing against men who had some of the best hand-to-eye coordination on earth, the victor was often uncertain.

Vices—though it's a stretch to define them all as such—were commonplace in the South Pacific. Although an unlikely notion today given the sinister reputation of the tobacco industry, cigarette smoking was common in World War II. (No doubt the health dangers were not well appreciated at the time, but I have seen cigarettes referred to as "coffin nails" in war letters.) Cigarettes often came with rations and were available at low prices, usually about fifty cents per ten-pack carton. In fact cigarettes were so common that they had little barter value in U.S. units.

As one might expect, many men picked up the habit during the war. Servicemen from World War II, Korea, and Vietnam (still a smoker's war, despite the Surgeon General's report) have told me that cigarettes served as good antidotes to boredom and stress. Men commonly smoked while in the air unless near something flammable. A great deal of flying in the South Pacific was done at reasonably low altitudes, which made the vice easy to indulge. But even while flying at higher elevations tobacco fans often indulged, even though that meant negotiating with the oxygen apparatus, which was essential above about 13,000 feet. Fighter pilot Joel Paris had some trouble because of this:

> Many men smoked in fighters all the time. I was an avid smoker. They put us on 18,000 CAP. [Combat Air Patrol—routine defensive patrols of base areas that rarely led to contact with the enemy after 1943 because Japanese attacks were infrequent. When Japan was on the ascendant or a carrier engagement was imminent, CAP was often tense work.—EB] Why that altitude, I do not know. We'd go up there for three hours or so. At 18,000 you have to wear an oxygen mask; you can't go too long without it. But you can't light a match. It will light, but it won't flame. I couldn't stand it without a cigarette for the whole flight. So I'd take off the mask, reach down, and turn the little knob on the mask to 100-percent oxygen, open my lighter in front of this mask, light the lighter and my cigarette. If you're not careful the mask catches on fire. That happened to me. There I was trying to beat the thing out on my knee. Suddenly I realize, "Jesus Christ, burning rubber is hot." I put out the flame but the mask was all filled with soggy melted rubber. You do the best you can. I disconnected the mask, put the hose in my mouth, and for the rest of the mission sucked on this hose because I'd burned up the mask. That's what I'd go through to smoke a cigarette. Believe me, I wasn't alone. That was from sheer boredom, not excitement.

Almost every army in history has relied on some substance that alters the perception of reality, typically alcohol. Many in the South Pacific were friends of the bottle. (Few men had heard of marijuana during that period; perhaps that was for the best, as weed would have grown at prodigious rates in that climate.) Although no solid data is available concerning the Japanese servicemen and the bottle, Americans frequently captured sake and very good beer from overrun Japanese depots. In one form or another booze was therefore commonplace in all Allied air units. (The USN at sea was dry, but much time was spent in port; smuggled liquor, often by officers, and pure medicinal alcohol were difficult to control.) But we should keep this subject in perspective: I am not suggesting that the air war was fought by drunks. Supplies were surprisingly abundant but never limitless. More importantly a clear head in combat had obvious value. Serious alcoholics were few and were treated as medical problems. (Many addicts concocted a variety of methanol-based brews that often caused serious medical problems.) Instead I think that the airmen probably drank as much as other young men, whether of that era or today. Youth can sustain such self-abuse, and most outgrew the desire to party after returning to peacetime, work, and families.

Choice in beverage was undoubtedly linked to service and rank. Those serving on the ground, particularly enlisted men, were on the short end. Although the sheer quantity of beer and hard liquor that passed through an air base put ground crews in a better position than someone in the regular army and Marine Corps, beer and commercially produced liquor were in short supply. Consequently those serving on the ground relied on ingenuity and self-sufficiency. Those who were skilled—often from the hill country of the U.S. South—put up stills. Less potent but easier to produce was a variety of jungle juice, usually based on fermented raisins; coconuts could also be used. Sometimes the techniques were combined. Medical alcohol was desirable if the proper barter could be found. Although a crewman on a B-25 on New Guinea, James Buchanan shared a taste for the South Seas "vin ordinaire" that graced the table of many enlisted men:

If we had raisins we'd make our raisin jack [one of the most common homemade brews in the tropics—EB] with coconuts. You'd drill a little hole, put in some raisins, seal 'em up, and wait about ten days and drink it. You'd open the coconut and light a match and if you got a blue flame you knew it was ready and that it was good alcohol, not wood. We also drank a lot of hospital alcohol. That stuff was 190-proof. We'd go down to the hospital and buy some from the medics or trade something. War souvenirs were good barter. If a medic had access to larger hospitals he knew that nurses liked silk and we had used parachutes. So everybody had it now and then. We'd melt Charms candy and mix it together with some water. Grapefruit juice was better but you could use almost anything to mix it with. I drank a lot of it, that's probably why I have a bad stomach. Sometimes if you got going we'd take some hits of the stuff straight—it would make you blind for a while. It was something else. Something else.

The one person who did not need medical alcohol was the flight surgeon. Bourbon was considered a medicine, and men were given two ounces upon returning from a mission to calm their nerves. (Some enterprising men tried to sneak their ration into a canteen and horde it for a proper drunk, but that was not encouraged.) On occasion a flight surgeon might give an extra ration to someone who appeared particularly edgy. "Medical" alcohol also frequently appeared upon pilots' birthdays or other holidays. No wonder the flight surgeon was normally highly thought of.

For those who were in the right place, which included many pilots and aircrews, the preferred drink was commercially made beer and hard liquor. If more humble beverages were available, like Australian wines and liquors, they would do. As LeRoy Smith remarks, "We drank anything we could get our hands on." The real stuff (as opposed to homemade brews) was extremely valuable in the South Pacific. Air units, however, were in a unique position—they had airplanes. Despite the deadly serious mission, it was a rare unit that could not spare a plane. Fighter units might "adopt" an overage tactical bomber or transport for "utility use." Access to a multiengine aircraft meant access to Australia, if one served in New Guinea, or New Zealand if in the Solomons. Both destinations promised booze and beer and were places where money had some meaning. (There was also a lively barter for American cigarettes or other goods.) Flights between Allied nations and the front were commonplace. Men going on leave went to one or the other. Ill individuals were often evacuated for better care in large hospitals. Critical spare parts had to be kept in stock. And as Robert DeHaven remarks, "It was poor economy of effort to have aircraft arrive in our theater empty." In other words many flights between the rear and the front carried beer and liquor in quantities varying from a few bottles to a planeload. Even men who did not drink got into the act. Pilot Charles Kittell of Thirteenth Air Force reflected that "I never had a taste for beer or liquor. But other men did. I would get my share and trade it for a case of Pepsi, which was a real luxury out there." Booze, in other words, was a kind of legal tender.

Aircraft had other advantages for those who liked a drink. Ice machines are reasonably simple contraptions and appeared in the theater after 1944 in numbers (as did ice-cream makers). Yet the young man's drink is beer, and prior to seeing ice, which some units never did, the men had to choose between drinking it warm—hot is probably a better term in the tropics—or using ingenuity.

Joel Paris and many others discovered the value of their high school science lessons. Compressed gas could be used as a coolant, and the air cools the higher the altitude. These were useful lessons in a fighter squadron:

> When we had the '38s we had a 300-gallon external fuel and baggage tank, and they'd open up the door on that thing and fill it with beer. We'd take it up to 40,000 feet and fly around for fifteen or twenty minutes or so and get it freezing cold and haul ass back to the field. Everybody had a cold one. We also used to use CO_2 cartridges for the same thing, but they raised hell 'cause we used them all up. The cartridges were intended to be used for putting out fires, and we were cooling beer with it. The P-38 solved that problem because we could get it high enough and fast enough.

So young aviators drank a lot in the South Pacific—no surprise there. All squadrons were given periodic stand-downs, when they knew they were not going up for at least a day. This often precipitated a serious party. It is impossible to guess how often the gentlemanly drink at the officers' club was later supplemented by a hit on the flask, nor can one guess how many tent-dwellers shared a bottle. In one regard, however, military aviators had an advantage over other young drinkers recognized by almost no one. (Young workers in hospitals are an exception.) A good antidote for a hangover is oxygen, and oxygen is something that was available in all combat aircraft. Many men admitted that sucking on the oxygen system on the ground helped clear their heads. LeRoy Smith described the dark shadow that must have intruded upon many wartime parties in a combat zone:

> Marines never drank. It was forced upon them. People like Pappy Boyington I think could fly better drunk than sober. My squadron was next to his, and I saw him in the bar often. Rest of the men were like other fighter pilots, but Pappy was really a hell-raiser. On the night before a mission or at early dawn a lot of men would go out and sit in their cockpit sucking on that oxygen. It was amazing how well that cleared up the head. Psychologically if you were going into Kavieng [the feared Japanese base—EB], and a week before you'd gone there and lost five of sixteen planes, the diversion of sucking on a little oxygen was great.

Men also enjoyed receiving and sending mail. Receiving mail, once the military situation was stabilized, was well done by all of the services unless a unit was transferred to another base. For most men, such as Carl Camp, mail was a great lift:

Mail came in nearly every day. It was a bit irregular. Sometimes it wouldn't come in for several days and then a whole load would show up. But I'd say somebody got mail almost every day. Mail was very important. Everything you've ever read about mail or seen in the movies is absolutely true. It was crucial for good morale. It was terrible on the guys that didn't get letters very often. A letter could make your day. It didn't have to be much of one: Maybe just some chit-chat from someone you loved or a friend from home. It would lift your spirits.

General MacArthur, probably realizing how much intelligence his headquarters had gathered from captured Japanese orders and diaries, was unusually stringent on what could be sent out. Censorship from the front, as things usually went, was arbitrary. Edward Brown, who helped crew a C-47 in New Guinea, commented, "I'd send letters home and try to avoid anything sensitive and have them arrive cut to shreds. The only thing left was a salutation." MacArthur's apparatus was not extremely efficient. As Fred Hitchcock relates, mail to the states was cleverly done and not always carefully watched: "Most of the letters home were V-mail. It was clever. They were written on a piece of paper with an APO (Moresby was 929, Gusap 713) number. We couldn't use any location names. Then they'd photograph them. They could get dozens on a piece of film. They'd fly them to the states, develop the film, and send it from there. One of our fellows wrote home: 'Censorship prevents me from telling you how bad things are.'" Robert DeHaven likewise suffered little from the scissors wielded by headquarters clerks:

Diaries were discouraged for infantry because of intelligence concerns. We had no such restrictions in our squadron. Censorship was not obtrusive. It wouldn't have taken much intelligence to put the information I wrote home about together with the information my family was getting from the newspaper to know to be able to tell virtually within spitting distance where we were stationed. Even if it was combat. "Somewhere in New Guinea" became a oxymoron. If you were in New Guinea you were "nowhere" by definition.

Normally a great boon, mail in some circumstances could injure a serviceman as badly as a wound. Men in the South Pacific had a fragile emotional life almost by definition. All saw their share of death and misery firsthand. I think this fact made them, like other combat soldiers in other wars, unusually vulnerable to bad news from home, associated by most with stability and affection. The most common bad news—beyond perhaps the death of a parent—was the Dear John letter. Many were of little consequence, as many servicemen had mere "understandings" between themselves and their stateside girlfriends who perhaps someday they would wed. As time passed affection waned, and a broken relationship might be a good excuse for a bad mood or downing a bottle. However, if a man at the front placed great importance in the relationship, particularly if the couple was engaged or married, a Dear John letter could wreak emotional havoc. Lee Tipton in 13th USAAF Service Command had to deal with censorship and did not like it: "One of the disgusting, demeaning, and saddest things I had to do was to censor mail. I hated it. I worked around people and then had to read their mail. I felt rotten. The Dear John letters were rough. It was all a one-way street. Our men weren't saints but they had no opportunities to stray because there were no women. Sometimes the bad news was not unexpected. In some cases it came out of nowhere. As I saw more than once, it could be devastating."

Fred Hitchcock saw the same emotional calamity as witnessed by Tipton. In addition, Hitchcock recalled that World War II was also a family war:

One of our men's brothers was a pilot in New Guinea and they wrote each other frequently. Then his brother was killed. The guy sat in his tent crushed. We lost a lot of men during the war, but the sense of loss was completely different. None of us knew what to do. There wasn't anything to do. I thought that guy should have been sent home right then—one casualty in one family was plenty. Another fellow got a Dear John letter. He was crushed so badly that he couldn't handle it. The flight surgeon tried his best but eventually the man was sent home on medical disability.

In a land offering up a powerful enemy as well as wicked forces of nature, the best possible remedy for a blow to the emotional armor was relief. Rotation was slow enough under the best of circumstances; the next-best solution was leave. Leave usually went from the Solomons to New Zealand and from New Guinea to Australia. As war progressed Sydney became a port in the storm for Americans serving in the upper Solomons.

Still, there was a dramatic divide, in terms of leave policy, between the ranks and services. The USN and, to a lesser degree, the Marines were not liberal in granting leave but treated ground and air crews almost the same when it came to rotation. This offset the need for regular leave. That being said, general ground crews, or men not associated directly with a squadron, in the navy and Marines were rotated far less often and did not receive leave as often.

This division was harsher in the USAAF. Regular, predictable rotation was never USAAF policy for any personnel. Rotation was informal, usually after a certain number of missions or hours in the air, accounting also for factors like combat damage and distinction in missions. Leave was thus used as a replacement for regular rotation. Ground crews received leave, though often less frequently than airmen. It depended upon whether one was directly attached to a combat unit or was assigned to a rear service unit established at the various bases. Someone connected with a combat unit was treated well when it came to leave. Someone in the rear might be in for a long stay. I would guess that there were thousands of ground crews in the USAAF who spent more than two years in the theater and received less than one month's leave.

Army aircrews had a much better situation. Although combat situations dictated events, it was common for aircrewmen, especially pilots, to receive a leave every three or four months. USAAF psychologists studied the issue early and recommended nine days as ideal. If leave was too short, the individual was likely to spend much of it getting to and from his destination. If leave was longer, he was less likely to want to come back. Psychologists even recommended that squadrons give returning crewmen two or three days off after leave because the army expected and wanted men to play hard during their breaks from combat. This recommendation was probably a good one, as anyone returning from leave was physically tired from traveling in 1940s-era planes and trains.

Likely by war's end the U.S. armed forces had worn out their welcome in New Zealand and Australia. The ratio of foreign troops to native population made for a bad mix, and of course there were many instances of individual transgressions, which merely amplified animosity held by New Zealanders and Aussies toward Americans. It is certainly true that Anzac servicemen, whose leave policy was, ironically, less liberal, held an understandable grudge against the horde of American servicemen who inhabited their home nations throughout the war.

Nevertheless it is rare to hear bad remarks from American veterans aimed at their allies in Australia and New Zealand. Combat personnel had the deepest respect for the skills and sacrifices of Anzac personnel. More to the point, most Americans felt a strong cultural affinity with the two nations. New Zealand was smaller and more rural, but those very qualities delighted American servicemen hailing from farms and small towns (as well as those from urban areas, as city boys liked New Zealand because it was different). The reverence expressed for New Zealand in retrospect is startling. Australia was almost universally loved unless one was stuck in one of the northern Australian air bases. (One soldier described the area near Townsville as a combination of Libya and New Guinea; today it is one of the most popular tourist destinations in Australia.) Americans were not known for such reverence, and if anything Australians were even less inhibited by display and class position. Whatever the problems that existed between MacArthur and Canberra, the American-Australian alliance, on a basic level, must be considered one of the most successful in world history. Thousands of war brides from New Zealand and Australia testify to that fact. So does the pattern of return pilgrimages. American servicemen have revisited European battlefields in droves, and regular tours return veterans to Vietnam. Likewise thousands have returned to New Zealand and Australia. But it is the rare American who wishes to revisit the Solomons and New Guinea. It tells much about this theater of war that veterans choose to revisit the sites of their (often short) leaves rather than the locales in which they toiled for flag and country. In their own way they revisit not battlefields but places that were, for a short time, a link to their civilization—a link to home.

Yet despite the heat, despite the mud, despite the disease, boredom, and stress of his existence, every fighting man in the South Pacific air war was defined by the great battle swirling around him. That is, after all, why so many youngsters were shipped overseas. It was to fight this battle, and thousands were yanked from their homes and plunked down in one of the most miserable places imaginable. The success and failure of that battle—as almost everyone knew—would have undeniable influence on America's place in history. To exist in that environment required ruggedness, tenacity, and ingenuity. Similar talents were needed in the air. But they had to be complemented by tactical judgment, skill in the bloody craft of combat, and a fierce desire to destroy the enemy. And so it is to the world of air combat that we now turn.

PART THREE

FIRE IN THE SKY:
AIR BATTLE IN THE SOUTH PACIFIC

Worried War II was a massive enterprise that required the mobilization of nations, constant technical innovation, a complex intelligence apparatus, and the strategic allocation of huge forces. Recognizing the life-and-death stakes of the conflict, combatant powers employed, to the extent that it was politically possible, their finest industrialists, economic planners, political leaders, and military commanders to achieve victory. The gathering and allocation of manpower and industrial might was not only a rational process; by necessity it had to show the talents of nations' elites. It was not a place for fools and dreamers, although they existed. Instead the war, once executed, rewarded competent planning, solid political leadership, massive industrial mobilization, and the will to win. All of these qualities rewarded intelligent innovation and political-military foresight. And the qualities gathering at the top to fight war with maximum efficiency required a rational framework within which intelligent people could act.

The central paradox of war is that political, economic, and military mobilization—all rational and presumably intelligent decisions—will stand and fall upon battle. Battle throughout the centuries—and World War II is an excellent example—has followed a simple dynamic: Combatants allocate resources for a strategic purpose; they organize forces in a strict hierarchy; military units have a chain of command reaching down to the lowest level, simply because in battle men are asked to undertake exceptional actions. It is a rare human who wishes to kill someone he has never met. It is even more rare for someone to wish to die, especially if the cause is political, not personal. As shown by World War II the result was an intense, combustible mixture of planning and chaos. During the war the real importance of good organization and proper deployment was that the better-prepared side would survive the slide into chaos that characterizes all serious battle. Unless force levels are greatly out of proportion—a situation that rarely existed in the South Pacific—strategy and tactics existed to give one side an initial edge that would hopefully carry through the engagement. The order and precision that military forces replicate in training, for good reason, will never stand up indefinitely to the helter-skelter of pitched combat.

Air warfare is extremely difficult to chart. The qualitative and numerical balance of forces is a critical part of any military equation. Yet that equation is especially difficult to solve in the context of air forces. In some ways air combat in World War II harkened back to the medieval era of armored knights: For every participant there were many squires who prepared him for battle. However, every plane inevitably wore out, requiring maintenance, which could ground it for days or weeks, or a full reconditioning, which meant it was sidelined indefinitely. Even aircraft in good condition required maintenance and periodic reservicing on the ground. If an aircraft was put into full-scale battle (as opposed to, say, patrol or reconnaissance), the chances of its needing repair were far higher, as systems had to be checked and common damage mended.

In practice—for those wishing to understand the history of the campaign—this means that numbers were and remain tricky at best. What military men call "paper strength" (the numbers of aircraft available in theory) rarely matched the numbers that could be put in the air. If battle was sustained this was even more true. Therefore a unit with a paper strength of twenty-four fighters rarely fought with that many; if engaged for several days running, the unit might put eight in the air. This does not mean that the pilots were killed, just that they could not fly until their aircraft was made airworthy. Slightly damaged aircraft were quickly restored to working condition by men who grew increasingly skilled at fixing sophisticated machines. However, a missing spare part meant an aircraft could be down indefinitely. Unit records that are available do not always record the precise number of aircraft that were airworthy and the extent of damage to those on the sidelines. In addition, when a mission began, units often suffered an "abort"—the premature termination of a flight or mission for whatever mechanical reason—which made continuation either dangerous or suicidal.

Likewise it is difficult to track paper strengths. Units and pilots entered and exited the theater constantly. If, for instance, a U.S. Marine fighter squadron was deployed to New Georgia in 1943, it is valuable to know when the unit arrived and when it was ready to fight. It is also valuable to know if it replaced another unit when it came forward. Analyzing Japanese strength is even more difficult, as Japan redesignated the numbers of its combat groups and brought in carrier-based units.

Another factor complicating the analysis is that World War II air warfare rarely had a geographic or numeric point of reference by which to judge victory and defeat. In the South Pacific many land campaigns were long, yet the march to victory could be charted by an army's moves (successful or unsuccessful) toward a strategic objective. Progress, or lack thereof, could be monitored simply by looking at a map or reading the battle reports. Likewise naval engagements usually had "winners," or at least strategic winners, because one could compare the result of battle against opposing sides' objectives going in. Savo and Tassafaronga were clear Japanese victories because their forces decimated the USN. The mid-November battles off Guadalcanal were brutal Japanese defeats because the imperial objective—bringing in troops to renew the island battle—was crushed. And whereas the great land campaigns in the South Pacific lasted months, the great naval battles lasted a few hours. Still, in both instances it was possible to discern winners and losers. Carrier battles were perhaps the most dramatic of all. They lasted two days at most, and a draw or victory was apparent simply by counting carriers sunk and damaged and planes shot down.

None of this was true in the South Pacific air war. Had one side prevailed decisively with its carriers, the two-year land-based struggle between Japan and the Allies would not have taken place. Yet because the carriers were best able to destroy or disable each other, huge air forces gathered in the Solomons and New Guinea. Although days passed between engagements, the air war was one of attrition. Strategically the connection was more easy to discern. Without air superiority of some sort the Allies would not attack an objective. Every step up the Solomons, every move up New Guinea indicated that the Allies were gaining the upper hand over their Japanese counterparts. Some air battles in the area were large by any standard. Most were medium-size engagements. Regardless there was no single day that turned the tide. Instead it was a process of relentless pounding, where both air and ground factors interacted to allow the Allies to achieve the decisive edge, which they employed with devastating effect in late 1943.

Air battle itself is the most difficult form of combat to describe. The units almost never knew exactly where they were fighting, although that would not have mattered anyway. Combat in the South Pacific took place over the jungle or ocean, neither being a good place to lose. The aircraft moved at speeds that had no precedent in war until that time. Low-level bombers might well exceed 200 miles per hour, and fighters often engaged at more than 300 miles per hour. At such speeds it was easy enough for an aircraft, or a pair, to lose physical sight of a battle that lasted for only a few minutes. It is essential to realize that almost none of these warplanes carried radar, and if a pilot lost sight of his unit he tried to navigate to a rendezvous point or simply headed for home—easier said than done.

The events during those few minutes were perhaps painfully obvious, shattering even. Fighters were flying through the exploding debris of their victims, shots being fired, hitting home—or perhaps hits were suffered. If the battle was serious both sides had to worry about being jumped. So even as pilots recorded individual victories (some verified by gun-camera films), it was all but impossible to crush a major enemy unit in the air. One side might win a tactical victory one day, only to give it back the next. Even the men involved cannot give a precise accounting of the battles, and the records were not always models of accuracy. Consequently it is impossible to re-create an exact chronicle of the air battles in South Pacific, even if one believes the records (which I do not in every case). What is possible, I hope, is to identify the patterns of war in light of the innumerable battles that took place during two years. Yet describing air combat is like holding mercury, the events fluctuate so. If successful, we shall stare a unique, vital form of war square in the face.

One must appreciate the chaos that reigned, to varying degrees, over basic air-combat doctrine at the time of Pearl Harbor. This is important, because a general tactical doctrine is crucial for allocating forces, training crews, and planning combat operations. Under the best of circumstances doctrine will change to reflect changes in technology and national interests. However, because technology was advancing so quickly in the five years prior to war, combat air doctrine was a moving target, so to speak. When the air forces in the South Pacific went from theory to deadly combat, there was precious little to guide the men whose lives were on the line. To a startling degree the craft of air war, particularly for ground-based units, was a matter of on-the-job training.

The United States Navy had approached airpower more intelligently and diligently than had the Army Air Corps during the interwar period, but until Admiral Yamamoto's carrier strike force ended the argument at Pearl Harbor the relative importance of the aircraft carrier was a matter of spirited contention. Even among air-minded admirals the technical revolutions taking place in radar and communications led to great uncertainty concerning the best way to run a carrier battle. (In fact there was no real consensus until 1944.) The Japanese, despite their spectacular tactical success at Pearl Harbor, had never engaged enemy carriers. When the Battle of the Coral Sea took place in May 1942, the Americans and the Japanese were leaping into the dark.

Land-based units on both sides had less guidance. It must have been a sobering thought to postwar airmen, but the tactical doctrine projected for every type of combat aircraft in 1939 was proved seriously flawed or complete nonsense by 1943. As late as 1935 some air forces questioned the utility of fighters altogether, based on their maxim—"the bomber will always get through." As noted earlier the dreadful threat posed by bombers did lead to a spectacular renaissance in fighter design. Still, most air forces thought of fighters basically as bomber interceptors that would defend specific points of great importance. Many prewar airmen, because of the great increase in fighter speed, doubted that fighter-on-fighter combat would prove feasible. Tactical doctrine, as I shall examine further, so concentrated on interception initially that fighter combat was thus crippled. Moreover, no one thought of fighters as being powerful ground-support weapons. Confident that speed and altitude would protect its bombers, no air force saw the crucial importance of fighter escort. (The Luftwaffe was closest to realizing this but tried to solve the problem in the wrong way, developing a multiengine heavy fighter to accompany long-range bomber raids; in battle the Me110 proved easy meat for Allied pilots. The Bf109, a fine fighter, was a poor escort because of its short range.) Attack aviation, demanded by ground generals, was very poorly thought out by airmen. As a result ground support had to be "learned by doing" at the cost of hundreds of infantrymen lost to friendly fire and bungled support missions. Although it is amazing in retrospect, many air leaders believed that heavy and medium bombers flying at high to medium altitudes would prove deadly to moving ships. In the event, even slow-moving merchantmen proved difficult targets, and warships were almost invulnerable to attack from above 6,000 feet. To compound the problem no air force genuinely appreciated the extraordinary versatility and utility of combat transport aircraft.

Through no fault of their own, airmen could never truly realize the importance that radar and radio communications would play. The technology was new, unreliable, and in some cases highly secret. Techniques that became central to Allied and German combat practice such as vectoring (guiding fighter units to an intercept point) were in their infancy when war broke out. The surprisingly elaborate communications networks that appeared on the Allied side—even in a "minor" theater like the South Pacific—and did so much to amplify the combat power of all types of aircraft existed only in embryonic form. (The Pearl Harbor surprise, at a tactical level, would have been unlikely had the best available radar-communications network been in place.)

Every air force gave lip service to gaining air superiority as the first goal of any air campaign. No one could argue with the general concept. However, as early operations proved, no one had a decent road map for gaining superiority in the air. (The Germans had good fortune early in hostilities when opponents left aircraft close to the front—a reflection of their limited range—thereby allowing the Luftwaffe to destroy them on the ground. Soon Germany's enemies became far less obliging.) In the event, it proved difficult to force battle against an enemy force if bad odds dictated that the defenders run to fight another day. It also proved difficult to knock out runways for more than a few hours or a day by simply dropping bombs. If notified that an attack was imminent, enemy tactical bombers would simply take off and fly away, leaving bombers with little to strike other than easily repaired dirt and steel matting that covered the fields. Nighttime bombing attacks, never employed in large numbers in the South Pacific, could rarely achieve the accuracy required to do harm. In the end and after much trial and error, the Allies found that the only way to gain air superiority—and it was never total—was to launch blistering assaults from every weapon at their disposal over an extended period. New weapons, inspired by Allied engineers in the field, were developed to destroy the merchant shipping serving Japanese bases and to devastate unwary airfields. These Allied bombers were accompanied increasingly by fighter escorts, thus forcing Japanese aircraft to either rise to the fight or allow the bombers through to do their worst. Furthermore the air and land campaigns became completely intermingled. A leap forward in the Solomons or up the coast of New Guinea forced Japanese aircraft to operate from a shrinking number of bases, where they became even more vulnerable. In the end this sustained, costly, multifaceted offensive was successful, but only after two years of the kind of fierce combat that encourages the development of sophisticated warmaking.

A word on Japan: Imperial forces had been at war in China for the four years prior to Pearl Harbor. They used the opportunity to gain combat experience and hone a group of skilled small-unit tacticians. In a larger sense, however, Japanese airmen learned and adopted a series of incorrect lessons from the Chinese conflict. The Germans were wise

enough to use Spain as a laboratory in which to develop effective tactical formations, which gave them an early edge in air combat during
the later war. Although the Japanese developed techniques that were
perhaps suitable to China, where their air arm (despite some bad moments) was never seriously challenged, these failed miserably against a
more-powerful enemy. (Significant is that Japanese carrier tactics, un-
influenced by China, were excellent in many ways.) Poor Japanese
fighter tactics succeeded in China and during the weeks after Pearl
Harbor because of good pilots and nimble warplanes in numbers, not
intelligent battle technique. Unlike many air forces around the world
the Japanese recognized, thanks to some hard days over China, the importance of bomber escort. Yet because Chinese bombers rarely posed
a serious threat Japan created fighters that were inferior as interceptors. Japanese bombing tactics proved grossly inadequate when the
crunch came at Guadalcanal. Japanese tactical bombers, effective during the early carrier battles, proved ineffective deathtraps when operating from land. Worse still, the general success of Japanese airmen in
China did nothing to prod them toward improving their communications apparatus. When fighting after Midway shifted from a Japanese
blitzkrieg to a harsh contest, the Japanese showed a marked reluctance
(or inability) to reexamine their battle tactics and so paid a heavy
price. By the end of 1943 the plain predictability of Japanese actions
gave a major advantage to Allied forces. Therefore—despite four years
of battle experience in China—overall Japanese air-combat doctrine
proved even more inadequate than the Allies' doctrine at the outset of
the Pacific war. Unlike the Allies, however, the Japanese showed little
flexibility when things went bad and, undoubtedly, received less than
was possible from available forces.

Analyzing battles is complex due to innumerable variables. One of
the most important of these is the numerical balance of forces. It is not
possible in this work, which covers two years of fighting, to precisely
depict the relative numerical strengths. And although the difficulties
are many, the most obvious is that the balance of forces changed as
war progressed. Early in the war, when force levels were relatively low,
the Japanese possessed a healthy advantage of usable aircraft in the
theater. By the end of 1942 a numerical equality was reached, with the
Allies slowly gaining an advantage thereafter. In mid-1943 the Allies
received major reinforcements and gained a substantial numerical advantage in both the Solomons and New Guinea. Another problem is
actual strength versus paper strength. This disparity arose from two
problems. The first was simply an inadequate supply of aircraft at the
moment. The second was serviceability, or the percentage of assigned

aircraft that can fly during a given day or week. Sometimes a serviceability deficit was an inevitable but temporary function of flight. Aircraft needed periodic maintenance, after which the airplane was back
on the flight line. In some cases shortages of spare parts as well as poor
repair facilities might render a plane useless for an extended period,
meaning it was as good as destroyed. It did not matter much *why* an
aircraft was not in the air, a lesson the Japanese learned more brutally
than did the Allies. In any event it is safe to say that it was a rare air
commander who did not want more planes, more parts, and more
good ground crews. Despite such problems it is important to reconstruct an approximate numerical balance at various points in the campaign, because it had an immense influence on the outcome and duration of the South Pacific air war.

It will be helpful to offer the lexicon defining the complex air forces
in the South Pacific. In the U.S. air arm the building block of fighter
units was a two-plane tactical unit, known as the *section* or *element*.
The section had a leader and a wingman. (The two-plane element was
a fixture in fighter units; the other categories were also generally used
in bomber units.) Two sections composed a four-plane unit known as
a *flight* or *division*. The next unit up the pecking order—the
squadron—is the hardest to define. Depending upon the type of aircraft, squadron strengths varied greatly. A PBY squadron often had
eight planes; heavy and medium bomber squadrons usually possessed
ten to twelve; Marine and U.S. Army fighter squadrons mounted between twenty and twenty-four machines. The largest squadrons were
USN carrier fighter squadrons, which comprised thirty-six to thirty-
eight planes. A large carrier carried two eighteen-plane SBD
squadrons (one was designated as a *scout-bomber squadron*, but the
planes and roles were interchangeable), as well as a twelve-plane TBF
squadron. Navy and Marine land-based tactical bomber squadrons
were roughly the same. Ideally a squadron had *reserve planes* and *reserve pilots*. For much of the campaign in the South Pacific,
squadrons were understrength or at least had no reserves. Although
good pilots were always at a premium, a squadron normally had
more pilots than planes.

Above the squadron was the *group*. Army and Marine land-based
groups possessed the same type of aircraft. A USAAF bomb group, for
instance, would have four squadrons of bombers, usually of the same
type. A USAAF fighter group had three squadrons, but as noted they
were larger than bomber squadrons. (Army *transport squadrons* were,
by their nature, extremely flexible because they might be operating in
large numbers or, more likely, singly as the task demanded.) Navy

groups had squadrons of differing types of aircraft. For instance, Naval Air Group 10, aboard USS *Enterprise* in the fall of 1942, had fighter, dive-bomber, and torpedo-bomber squadrons within its complement. In the USAAF the echelon above the group was the *air force*, of which two—Fifth and Thirteenth—served in the South Pacific. (In June 1944 the two combined to become Far Eastern Air Force.) Navy *air groups*, being wedded to their carriers, served under various task force commanders at sea or higher administrative units in the rear. The rough equivalent of a USAAF air force in the Marine Corps was the Marine *air wing* (MAW), of which two served in the South Pacific—First and Second.

Japanese organization was somewhat different, although there were similarities, which makes our task somewhat easier. The terminology was complex, and the same unit had different operational and administrative titles. Those interested in pinning down the terminology should refer to some excellent specialized works (see, e.g., Francillon; Hata and Izawa, in the Bibliography). I confine the discussion to Japanese terms of the most basic units, because they often appear in secondary accounts. For the most part I have tried to use the closest Allied term for an equivalent unit.

The major difference between Japanese and Allied organization is that imperial air units were based on multiples of three, whereas most Allied units were based on multiples of four. The smallest component in Japanese army and navy units was the three-plane *shotai*, the equivalent of the Allied section. Above this basic level paths diverged. In the Imperial Japanese Navy, three *shotai* made up a nine-plane *chutai*, or division. Two or three *chutai* created a *daitai*, or squadron, of eighteen to twenty-seven planes. A number of squadrons, usually three, made up a *kokutai*, or air group. (A group usually included different types of aircraft, very much like a U.S. carrier air group. But, perhaps to confuse future readers and historians, a Japanese carrier division was designed for two ships, reflecting the Japanese practice of employing fleet carriers in pairs or groups of pairs.) As in the Allied forces the group was probably the most important operational unit, with the squadron a close second. Japanese Army organization followed a different progression, the *chutai* (division) being left out. This meant an IJA squadron had nine to twelve planes. The IJA air group was called a *sentai* and usually had three squadrons. (In other words, this made an IJA air group one-third the size of its IJN counterpart.) Four groups made up an *air brigade*, or *wing*, which was a mixture of bombers, fighters, and reconnaissance planes. Two or three wings created an *air division*. Two or three divisions formed an *air army*.

In analyzing the numerical balance of forces it is best to divide the two-year period of study into segments that coincide with major changes in force allocation that in turn coincide with larger military events. Absolute precision is unattainable, but it is possible to see an overall escalation of force on both sides. This was typical of force levels in World War II. Even the countries mobilized for war before hostilities, principally Japan, Germany, and the Soviet Union, found their military economy unprepared for the magnitude of the struggle. This problem was much worse for democratic nations like Britain and the United States, which had been sleepwalking for at least a year before 1939. The size of forces among all combatants continued to rise until 1944, when Germany and Japan began to waver. The question, therefore, was not one of increasing force levels but rather which side would increase force levels fastest. That being said, it is important to realize that if relative force levels and strategic objectives were in synch a great deal could be done with forces that, by late-war standards, appear small.

In the time frame between Pearl Harbor and the Allied offensives against Guadalcanal and Buna-Gona (December 1941–August 1942) the Japanese possessed an advantage in air forces that, fortunately for the Allies, was never coordinated with strategic objectives. It is certainly true that Japanese air units, especially those belonging to the IJN, sliced through most of the opposition during the first three months of war. Japan's commanders were, in retrospect, harmed by a surplus of riches (see Chapter 1). With the carriers raiding Darwin, then Ceylon, the land-based units had a large area to occupy and several possible routes of advance. In addition, during this period the Zero fighter and Betty bomber were beginning to increase in production, allowing units equipped with older aircraft to refit with newer models.

The air war in the South Pacific began when the Japanese based at Rabaul (seized in January 1942) began raiding Port Moresby, New Guinea. Japanese aircraft based on Timor raided Darwin. In early February the Japanese began building forces at Rabaul and New Guinea. At Rabaul the chief force was the 4th Air Group with twenty-seven new Betty bombers and a like number of new Zeros. In early April units of the famous Tainan Air Group appeared at Lae in New Guinea and Rabaul to support bomber attacks on Moresby. A second front based on the 3d Air Group in the East Indies opened a sustained air offensive against Darwin. Altogether these forces represented some 100 aircraft. It was 4th Air Group that suffered the stinging February defeat when fifteen Bettys went down in an attack against a U.S. carrier raid. However, it was soon replaced and reinforced. In April 1942 the Japanese made the major commitment of placing the headquarters of Eleventh Air Fleet at Rabaul, implicitly making Rabaul the center of Japan's land-based air units for an extended period. More aircraft continued to arrive throughout the summer until Rabaul had two major air flotillas (25th and 26th) along with numerous seaplanes and reconnaissance aircraft. Counting the aircraft in the Indies (not under command of 11th Air Fleet) the Japanese possessed more than 200 aircraft on paper for operations against New Guinea and northern Australia. Some of the units in the area, such as 3d Air Group and the Tainan Air Group, possessed some of the world's best pilots. Never was the qualitative difference between imperial forces and the Allies so great. In addition, the Japanese had the geographic advantage of interior lines. It was a relatively simple matter to redeploy formations from Southeast Asia, China, and Japan to Rabaul. In addition, carrier strike groups potentially stood behind the land-based units like predators looking for unwary prey.

Against this force the Allies began hostilities with a handful of miserable and ill-suited aircraft. Fortunately Roosevelt made the bold decision to strip U.S. units forming in the United States and send precious fighter planes and units intended for the Philippines to Australia and islands between. (In retrospect this left Hawaii very poorly defended, but Washington thought it worth the risk to send major forces to an uncertain fate in Australia. General Marshall and others dedicated to Europe First thought the allocation was excessive. MacArthur, naturally, thought it far too little and far too late.) Yet even with the lightning speed that the United States decided to allocate major forces to Australia, it took several months to set up shop.

When the Japanese turned their eyes toward Port Moresby, which could have been so easily seized in February 1942, they originally saw nothing. The situation changed quickly. Canberra, even before MacArthur arrived, saw that the need for fighters was pressing and obvious. In February a transport arrived carrying seventy-five P-40s. Australians, like the British, did not like to designate airplanes by numbers, so they put them into commission as three squadrons of Kittyhawks. Despite American fears that Canberra had given up on northern Australia, the RAAF wanted one squadron to go to Sydney, one to Townsville, and one to Moresby. The squadron sent to Moresby in early March—the first serious Allied unit to engage the Japanese after the crushing defeats of earlier weeks—had a veteran leader, but the pilots were green. Nevertheless the new No. 75 Squadron engaged the Japanese in several sharp engagements with never more than twenty-four aircraft, often far less. Inflicting some damage on crack Japanese air units, the small collection of Australian pilots created an air presence that the Japanese could not ignore. Japan's chance to walk into Moresby was gone. U.S. heavy bomber units gathering at Townsville began raids at about the same time but with limited impact. Yet here again Japanese fighters were deflected, and the eventually huge collection of antiaircraft guns began to assemble at Rabaul and other major bases. In the same month 8th Squadron of the U.S. 3d Bomb Group joined No. 76 Squadron. The American debut in the South Pacific was made by men flying the A-24, an army version of the SBD. The Dauntless was a splendid plane in carrier battles but—like its Japanese counterpart, the Val—a flawed weapon against ground targets for reasons I examine later. Soon RAAF No. 75 Squadron left Moresby. However, it joined another new Kittyhawk squadron, the RAAF No. 76, and together played an instrumental role in drubbing a Japanese attempt to take Milne Bay in late August 1942, handing imperial forces their first land defeat of the war.

In early April two squadrons flying P-39s for the U.S. 8th Fighter Group arrived in Moresby. The U.S. 49th Fighter Group deployed to defend Darwin. None of these aircraft were supplied with sufficient spare parts, and despite orders from General Arnold himself damaged aircraft soon became the main source for spares. Bombers proceeded to Townsville, where they began dangerous and largely ineffective raids against Rabaul, Kavieng, and other Japanese bases at night. Fearful of Japanese attack, heavy bombers used Moresby as a point to refuel, not as a base for operations.

Recognizing correctly that Allied air efforts in northern Australia and Moresby were not being used well, MacArthur appointed Major General George Kenney to command the newly formed Fifth Air Force in early August 1942. Though a very shrewd commander with an excellent grasp of technical issues, Kenney did not know the actual state of his forces. Although the creation of Fifth Air Force was implicitly done to aid MacArthur's drive into New Guinea and free U.S. operations from Australian support, Kenney found out quickly that the substantial forces sent to Australia in early 1942 were worn out, battle casualties, or mechanical cripples. In August Kenney demanded an accounting of his aircraft. The answer was depressing: According to records 481 aircraft were present in Australia; only 141 were judged combat-ready. (This did not include a loss from April to July 1942 of 171 aircraft. Of this total, enemy action downed 61 fighters and 22 bombers in combat as well as 10 planes hit on the ground; 73 aircraft were lost due to accidents.) Of these aircraft Kenney found he had 75 fighters, many of an inferior type (P-39), 43 heavy bombers that did not have a good base or a well-defined role, and 33 medium bombers that were not yet the deadly machines they would become in a few months. The RAAF had an additional 60 fighters on hand and some good planes, such as the Beaufighter, expected to arrive in September. However, most would be used to defend Australia and not move north in the near future. By August 7, 1942, when the Marines and United States Navy struck Guadalcanal, the Japanese had a numerical and qualitative edge over U.S. forces in the New Guinea theater. Their edge did not last long.

When U.S. forces invaded Guadalcanal the military equation in the South Pacific changed overnight. The initial landings were covered by 238 aircraft flying from the decks of three U.S. aircraft carriers. After some very sharp fighting against Japanese planes thrown into the fray from Rabaul in the first two days of the invasion, the carriers left. (Heavy bombers from Espíritu also attacked Japanese positions on Guadalcanal. On the eve of the invasion Fifth Air Force sent its battered 19th Bomb Group on a night raid against Rabaul; despite claims of serious damage done, Rabaul's air units were untouched.) It was clear from the outset that the Americans had to create a powerful land base on the island or it would be impossible to cover supply convoys bringing reinforcements and supplies to the Marine invaders. The need for air cover was made even more emphatic when a Japanese cruiser task force made a daring sortie from Rabaul and inflicted a shocking defeat near Savo Island, sinking four Allied cruisers in the first of the violent night battles off the coast of Guadalcanal. (Almost unscathed in the battle, the Japanese force lost one cruiser, sunk by a U.S. submarine on the return voyage.) It was also soon obvious that the Japanese were not going to give up Guadalcanal. Instead they sent in vessels laden with troops to disembark only a dozen miles west of the Marine perimeter. Consequently the Americans needed planes on the spot not only to protect their own supply convoys but also to hinder Japanese reinforcements.

As in New Guinea initial force levels were grossly out of balance with those available for the front. In theory there were several hundred planes, counting USN carrier aircraft, in the South Pacific, Hawaii, and the West Coast. In actuality commanders had to work overtime trying to decide where they could find even a minimal force for Guadalcanal. The U.S. Navy—probably wisely—refused to strip a carrier of its air group for land use. There were a limited number of Wildcats, SBDs, and U.S. Army fighters on the various South Pacific islands seized several months earlier. However, the supply line to Australia and Nouméa had to be defended, and Wildcat fighters, without drop tanks, could not fly directly to Guadalcanal. Wildcats and SBDs were in short supply, and the Marines—also wisely—did not want to strip planes from squadrons being formed on the West Coast of the United States. The only possible savior was Admiral Nimitz, who had Marine Air Group No. 23 at Pearl Harbor. Just recently refitted with precious Wildcats and new SBD-3s, MAG 23 was put aboard the small escort carrier *Long Island* and sent to the South Pacific. Most pilots were rookies but some men had flown Marine fighters in defense of Midway Island in June. On August 20, with Henderson Field finally complete, MAG 23 flew in with one fighter squadron of nineteen planes and one squadron of twelve SBDs. Such was the beginning of the air war in the Solomons.

The command arrangement in the Solomons was complicated, as all of the American services were involved, soon aided by New Zealanders. The overall area commander was Admiral Thomas Ghormley, who was replaced in October by the more dynamic Admiral William Halsey. All air units came under the control of Commander, Aircraft, South Pacific Force (ComAirSopac). The first man to hold this position was Rear Admiral John McCain. Although his stay was short, McCain was a tireless advocate for building up Guadalcanal's air strength to turn it into a sinkhole of attrition for Japan's air arm at Rabaul. In September McCain was promoted and moved to King's staff and replaced by Rear Admiral Aubrey Fitch, who served ably through the remainder of the campaign. The air units on Guadalcanal (soon dubbed the "Cactus Air Force," as "Cactus" was the code name for Guadalcanal) were put in the able hands of Brigadier General Roy Geiger, commander of 1st MAW. Worn down by the brutal environment of Guadalcanal, Geiger was relieved by his former chief of staff, Brigadier General Louis Woods, who led Cactus until victory in February. (Geiger's career was far from finished: On Okinawa he became commander of U.S. Army and Marine ground forces after the original commander, Simon Buckner, was killed in action.) Having an organizational chart that was probably unique in World War II, the Cactus Air Force, although dominated by Marines, also included fliers from the navy, the USAAF, and the RNZAF. (Some American servicemen were better at war than ethnography. Several veterans have expressed appreciation for the excellent performance given by Australians at Cactus. All of the "Australians" on Guadalcanal hailed from New Zealand. The Aussies had a full plate defending their shores and fighting in New Guinea at this period.)

Between August 20, 1942, and February 9, 1943, when the Japanese completed the evacuation of what was left of their battered and starving army from Guadalcanal, the Allies and Japanese heavily reinforced their air arms in the Solomons. Both sides had to replace a steady stream of combat casualties, aircraft damaged by accidents, planes that took off and disappeared, and dozens of men and planes that simply wore out. Indeed their operational strengths varied wildly depending upon the pace of combat and the stock in the replacement pipeline. Taking advantage of interior lines the Japanese initially built up air strength faster than Cactus could. On August 7 Eleventh Air Fleet at Rabaul, with some units stationed in New Guinea and momentarily out of the equation, had an operational strike force of 24 Zeros, 32 Bettys, and nine Vals to throw at the U.S. landing. In two days of attacks the Japanese not only proved their edge in fighter combat but also that their bombers were sitting ducks for fighter attack and antiaircraft. With the Betty force crippled and more fighters needed, Rabaul began gathering forces. By mid-September Rabaul's forces had inched up slightly. In October major reinforcements arrived, and the Japanese could strike with 48 long-range Zeros and 62 Bettys. Another 29 short-range Zeros were available for convoy escort, patrols, or use over New Guinea. Cactus had likewise grown, but not as quickly. In late September Geiger commanded 36 Wildcats, 25 SBDs, seven Avengers, and three P-39s. B-17s and USN PBYs from Espíritu flew reconnaissance.

In October, finally alert to the dreadful danger posed by Guadalcanal and Cactus Air Force to Rabaul and, indeed, their entire defensive perimeter, the Japanese made an all-out attempt to crush Cactus and then destroy the Marine perimeter. After an intense series of air battles IJN Combined Fleet deployed two battleships and several smaller warships to systematically bombard Henderson Field. In the aftermath Cactus Air Force had shrunk to nine Wildcats, eleven SBDs, and nine P-39s. When the situation was most bleak, the remaining aircraft, aided by B-17s, inflicted heavy damage to a major Japanese troop convoy. A gasoline barge came into the Canal, relieving a worry nearly as great as losing all of the airplanes. In addition, a new U.S. fighter squadron landed. The great Japanese ground offensive had failed miserably, leaving the Marines and arriving U.S. Army troops stronger than ever. From this point it was downhill for Cactus.

Combined Fleet, in retrospect, committed one of the great blunders of World War II at Guadalcanal. Yamamoto and his superiors in Tokyo wanted to rebuild forces for a decisive battle expected in late 1943 or early 1944. Consequently, with the possible exception of the carrier battle at Santa Cruz in October, Combined Fleet never committed the heart of its surface fleet to the Battle of Guadalcanal and was very wary in its use of carriers. But there was a window of tactical opportunity that Yamamoto and the others refused to open: Japanese submarines, often maligned in postwar literature, during September and October largely reversed the miracle of Midway. Imperial subs sunk *Wasp* and damaged *Saratoga* and the fast battleship *North Carolina*. (It is possible that *Yorktown*, at Midway, might have been saved had not an I-boat slipped it a fatal fish.) The carrier balance that had shifted in America's favor after Midway was nearly equal, and Combined Fleet had greatly superior surface forces. Had Combined Fleet been willing to risk an all-out commitment to Guadalcanal it may well have been able to shell Henderson Field into oblivion, allow Japanese transports to proceed to Guadalcanal, and put the Marines under siege. In my opinion had Japan defeated the United States at Guadalcanal General Marshall and his supporters, after seeing that Australia and New Zealand had adequate defensive forces, would have shut down the South and Southwest Theaters completely. Japan then could have waited, gathering all of its strength in the Central Pacific until U.S. shipyards readied a new fleet for a drive that everyone expected. As it was, the two-pronged Allied attack past Rabaul and into Southeast Asia made a coherent defense of the Central Pacific impossible. It is likely that the Pacific war, though having the same outcome, might have lasted many months longer, with enormous repercussions for the postwar world. Such a strategy would have been risky for Japan. Considering that Guadalcanal was fought just as Germany was defeated at Stalingrad, however, the cautious strategy Japan followed might well have been the worst possible mistake.

Yamamoto could also have urged withdrawal from Guadalcanal and fought a Fabian battle in the Middle Solomons, where all of Rabaul's aircraft could have been employed. Instead Combined Fleet fell between two stools, expending many aircraft and losing a painful number of warships. No matter how many air and sea battles were tactical victories for Japan, as long as Cactus survived and Japan bled it was only a matter of time before the gathering logistic momentum, already flowing to the South Pacific, would give the Allies a decisive advantage. The Japanese did not intend to squander some of their finest resources on Guadalcanal, yet they did so. Reluctant to risk all at Guadalcanal, they took a series of half-measures that never could complete the job. Put simply, with Japan so battered the Allied advances up the Solomons and New Guinea were far easier.

While these dramatic battles were taking place a more subtle process was at work. U.S. transports and escort carriers were bringing a sizeable air force to New Caledonia and the New Hebrides Islands. Increasingly it was possible to move combat units into Cactus. Marine and USAAF units were growing not only in strength but also in sophistication with a much larger supply of fuel and parts on hand. On November 12 the first eight USAAF P-38s moved to Guadalcanal. Already the growing complex of fields was home to USAAF B-26 and B-17 bombers, at least for shuttle missions. Marine pilots were anxiously awaiting the arrival of the Corsair. In the short run, temporarily reinforced by planes from *Enterprise*, Cactus reached a peak of combat power on November 12: forty-seven fighters, twenty-three tactical bombers, and ten medium bombers.

In November the Japanese Eleventh Air Fleet attempted to aid Combined Fleet in one last, badly supported bid to take Guadalcanal. Several new units had come in, but some veteran units had been forced out of battle. The famous Tainan Air Group, the unit that boasted several legendary Japanese aces and earned the respect of all opponents, was sent back to Japan, where it was reorganized around ten surviving combat-ready pilots. When it returned in the spring of 1943—renamed No. 251 Group—it was a new and lesser unit. Before the last Japanese offensive Rabaul hosted 105 Zeros, thirty-seven Vals, and thirty-six Bettys. Rabaul's air force was to help protect the last large Japanese troop convoy destined for Guadalcanal. During November 13–15 elements of Combined Fleet and the USN engaged in a series of nighttime surface battles matched in our century only by Jutland for their ferocity. Rabaul's contribution was shattered early when the Bettys and Vals were battered by fighters and antiaircraft. After the mid-November battles Combined Fleet convinced Tokyo that Guadalcanal must be abandoned. The shattered Japanese air units at Rabaul, except for those needed to help hard-pressed Japanese land units in New Guinea, stayed home for six weeks. Both sides attempted to build up.

At this point I would like to highlight three related topics that mark the campaign in the South Pacific until Japan was driven from the field. The first is the use of carriers. The entire campaign in the South Pacific was possible only because neither side was able to gain a decisive advantage in carrier strength. Had Japan, after Midway, had some bad breaks and suffered another serious defeat at either the Battle of the Eastern Solomons in September 1942 or the more bloody Battle of Santa Cruz in October 1942, there is little doubt that Combined Fleet would have had to abandon Rabaul. Had imperial carriers and submarines fully reversed the verdict of Midway, Guadalcanal would have become a catastrophic defeat for the United States. In the event, neither happened. After Santa Cruz both carrier forces were so badly battered that neither wished to risk another engagement. This was a vital consideration in 1942, as a carrier task force carried many more aircraft than did any land base.

As it was, both sides held their breath when carriers engaged and counted up victory points after battle. (In my opinion the Americans won all the carrier battles of World War II. Every carrier battle was precipitated because one side was supporting an invasion or supply convoy and the other side tried to stop it. Because the U.S.-protected convoys achieved their objectives—and thus the Japanese failed in theirs—strategically the USN came out on top. Guadalcanal was worth far more than the fate of any single warship, particularly with new vessels nearing completion in U.S. shipyards and air groups training in vast numbers.) Yet the concern here is how the two fleets employed their carriers in the battle for Guadalcanal and, later, the battle for the Solomons. The United States Navy, even when things looked bleak, refused to permanently base any USN aircraft on Guadalcanal. The merits of this decision could be argued either way in retrospect. However, events forced a compromise. In September the *Saratoga* was torpedoed but survived. Almost its entire air group was moved to Guadalcanal, where it remained for a critical month during September and October. Later, when *Wasp* and *Hornet* were sunk and *Enterprise* was disabled, smaller numbers of USN planes found themselves working out of Cactus. Most of the pilots and aircrews were evacuated by air and sea transport after a short tour, but Geiger never allowed a combat plane to leave the Canal if he could avoid it. During the November battles the great carrier *Enterprise* had one of its finest moments. Although the huge carrier was partially disabled at Santa Cruz and the USN did not wish a fleet engagement, the bulk of the flight group was shuttled to Guadalcanal, where it inflicted heavy damage on the last Japanese naval offensive with little loss. When the battle was over *Enterprise* retired, in this instance bringing most of the aircraft along.

The Japanese were likewise reluctant to employ carrier planes from land bases. Combined Fleet knew all too well that its damaged carrier air groups, particularly after serious losses at Santa Cruz, needed retraining and refitting if they were to engage the Americans again in a general naval battle. However, the November defeats—their significance already clear to Combined Fleet—had jolted Tokyo. (Japanese military headquarters in Tokyo were often weeks behind frontline units in accurately appreciating strategic reality. Bad news moved especially slowly—news of the catastrophe at Midway was not shared fully with IJA leaders until weeks had passed. Soon thereafter the army hid the looming disaster at Buna from the navy. This was not a healthy situation and contrasts markedly with the close and steady gaze given to events in the Pacific by Admiral King and his staff at the Pentagon. Roosevelt himself was very well informed concerning news from the front.) Imperial forces, both army and navy, received orders to do everything possible to defeat or delay the Allied drive up the Solomons and through New Guinea. The few thousand extra Japanese infantrymen who could have stopped the New Guinea and Solomons campaigns before they began in the first weeks of 1942—but who the army claimed were impossible to deploy—were suddenly made available on a scale that dwarfed Admiral Inoue's requests for extra troops immediately after Pearl Harbor: Rabaul and New Ireland became fortresses; Bougainville was given a large garrison and islands in the Middle Solomons were heavily reinforced; a major Japanese army was deployed in New Guinea to face the Australians and Americans after their bloody but stunning victory at Buna; fearing the Allies might use Darwin as an offensive base, the Japanese army put a sizeable garrison on Timor. In this environment it was difficult for the IJN to hold back precious reserves.

Although there were dissenters at every step, the Japanese began land-basing carrier groups at Rabaul in late 1942. Combined Fleet was preparing for one of the most brilliant naval operations of the Pacific war: the evacuation of the remaining land forces at Guadalcanal under the nose of a sizeable U.S. air and naval force. Yamamoto threw two small carriers and a number of surface vessels into the mission. More significantly, 100 Japanese army aircraft made a short debut in South Pacific combat, and sixty-four planes from *Zuikaku's* air group, still recovering from serious losses at Santa Cruz, were land-based at Rabaul for a brief period. Because of the audacity of the Japanese move and U.S. bungling, Japanese forces pulled off the coup with few losses (although the Bettys suffered as usual) while sinking a U.S. cruiser in the bargain. Counting the carrier machines, the Japanese employed nearly 400 aircraft during the week-long engagement.

Buoyed by unexpected success (if an evacuation of an important point can be considered such) Yamamoto decided to base almost all of Combined Fleet's active carrier resources in the Rabaul area in early April to launch a massive attack on Guadalcanal and New Guinea. As Combined Fleet was painfully aware, both MacArthur and Halsey were gathering ships, men, and aircraft to push farther the Allied offensives in New Guinea and the Solomons. With luck, Yamamoto believed, a lightning air offensive of great size might catch the Allies napping and create a mini–Pearl Harbor and delay plans for a further advance. Not counting float and reconnaissance planes, the Japanese deployed 96 Zeros and 65 Vals from their carrier groups in addition to the 86 Zeros, 27 Vals, and 72 Bettys of Eleventh Air Fleet at Rabaul—a total of 346 combat aircraft.

The results of the operation (usually referred to as I-GO) could hardly have justified the disruption to carrier-group reorganization and training. On the alert, a major U.S. cruiser task force at Guadalcanal was just able to get out of range when the first blow fell on April 7, when 157 Zeros escorted 67 bombers of various types against ships near Guadalcanal. Three days later 71 fighters and 21 bombers attacked Allied shipping at Oro Bay southeast of Buna. On April 12, 131 Zeros escorted 43 Bettys on a raid against Port Moresby. The air assault ended on April 14, when 127 Zeros and 23 tactical bombers struck Allied shipping at Milne Bay. Japanese pilots claimed many ships sunk and dozens of enemy aircraft downed. The reality was quite different. Intercepted on each raid by Allied fighters, confronted by advanced antiaircraft, and lacking the skills of the early war, imperial forces came away with a very small bag. The Allies lost a U.S. destroyer, a New Zealand corvette, and three merchantmen sunk (none carrying troops or essential cargo). Allied fighter losses were less than twenty. Depending upon which figures one wishes to use, the Japanese lost between 40 and 61 aircraft. Despite the euphoria among pilots and some of his staff, Yamamoto was not impressed with the operation and ordered the carrier aircraft back to Truk on April 17.

The fact that so little was accomplished with so many aircraft against so many targets was a vivid illustration that a new stage of the war was beginning. Japan's April air offensive was its last meaningful offensive in the Pacific war, and it had come up nearly empty. In addition, the IJN had to accept another bitter blow from their failed attacks. Yamamoto had moved up to Rabaul to direct operations personally—his first trip to the combat zone. While there he decided to inspect the forward bases on Bougainville. With U.S. code-breakers having deciphered some of the Japanese code yet again, U.S. P-38s of the 339th Squadron based on Guadalcanal launched an astounding long-range raid that succeeded in jumping and downing the two Bettys carrying Yamamoto and his staff. The legendary admiral and many top officers died in the Bougainville jungle.

The necessity of gutting carrier formations did not end with Yamamoto's death. In July, when U.S. pressure on the central Solomons was eating up Rabaul's available aircraft, officers of Eleventh Air Fleet were able to persuade Combined Fleet to commit all of CARDIV 2 (aircraft from the carriers *Junyo*, *Hiyo*, and *Ruyho*) to forward bases on Bougainville. This was at least 92 warplanes, although it seems that some additional aircraft also went to Kavieng. Immediately ensnared in intense combat, none of these aircraft returned to Japan. In the meantime a new CARDIV 2 was organized in the rear. In January 1944 it, too, was dispatched to Rabaul and was destroyed in two weeks. Also present for the battles near Bougainville in November 1943 were the 150 aircraft of CARDIV 1 (*Shokaku, Zuikaku,* and *Zuiho*). After losing half of its aircraft, CARDIV 1 retreated after two weeks. However bad things looked at Rabaul, the timing could hardly have been worse. Just as the U.S. Navy was bringing its new, extremely powerful carriers into service, almost every carrier group in the IJN was squandering men and machines in an obviously lost cause.

The behavior of Admiral Halsey was quite different. As his land forces built up, Halsey felt confident enough to actually weaken his carrier force and did not consider inserting carrier air groups onto U.S. land bases in the Solomons. Because *Enterprise* was wounded and tired, the Americans sent the great ship to the United States in February 1943 for a complete refit. By this time the unlucky *Saratoga* had a splendidly trained air group. The Royal Navy agreed to aid the *Sara* in 1943 by dispatching HMS *Victorious* to the South Pacific for the summer of 1943. Halsey correctly believed that the Japanese did not wish a fleet engagement in the Solomons but could hardly rule out the possibility. Instead he employed his two carriers—which would cooperate with increasingly powerful Allied land bases—near the periphery of action. Although there were some alarms, a battle never took place. That fact, however, translated into a victory for Halsey, as he was now advancing toward Rabaul while his comrades in Pearl Harbor were assembling the new fleet (much of which Halsey later commanded) that would crush Japanese air and naval forces during 1944–1945.

Second, the Guadalcanal campaign also illustrates the cruel and unavoidable dynamic of attrition in air war that characterized all theaters. Aircraft were not unique in this regard. Ground units consumed men at a wicked pace during combat, and naval shipyards had to work full-bore to produce new bottoms to replace those that had been sunk. The appetite for men and machines during World War II was so intense that it can distort our view of the conflict in retrospect. When a contemporary student of Guadalcanal examines a photo of a single Wildcat serving at Cactus, he or she is looking at an object that existed at a moment in time. If thinking about the six-month campaign on the Canal, however, it would be much better to view the photo as representing a plane that was sent to replace one mechanically identical that flew from the same place but had been destroyed in combat, ditched because of lack of fuel, crashed due to pilot error or an unseen hole in the runway, or had simply worn out. Moreover unless that photo depicts a moment late in the campaign, the observer is likely viewing a machine that would eventually suffer one of those fates. That, in a nutshell, captures the dynamic of attrition.

Although military numbers are rarely precise, we have unusually good ones to illustrate the grim flow of events at Guadalcanal. Authors John Lundstrom and Richard Frank have conducted careful studies of both U.S. and Japanese losses during the Guadalcanal campaign. Let us recall that it was a very rare day when Cactus Air Force could get more than sixty aircraft into operation. Until the temporary reinforcements during the February 1943 evacuation of Japanese forces, Eleventh Air Fleet at Rabaul was doing well to count 120 aircraft more or less airworthy. Attacks on Guadalcanal rarely exceeded sixty planes. Frank, who employs much of Lundstrom's research, concluded that the Allies lost 615 aircraft during the entire campaign, including the carrier battles, and that the Japanese lost 682. Because the Allies were flying closer to base and could ditch more easily, and because they flew fewer major attacks in multiengine bombers, which had large crews, Frank estimates that the Allies lost 420 men killed; in comparison the Japanese lost two to four times as many.

It is reasonable to ask why such a huge disparity existed between present-for-duty strength at a given moment and overall campaign losses. In the first place, as examined earlier, both sides brought in new units. The Marines and USN were careful to rotate squadrons for leave and rebuilding (with the Marines dispatching replacement pilots). USAAF units on Guadalcanal, like their counterparts in Fifth Air Force, relied upon new units and replacements. The Japanese also dispatched some tired units home or to less active theaters. (Interestingly Captain H. Komoto, a staff officer of 23d Air Flotilla covering Timor, noted that in October 1943 his best pilots were sent to the Solomons and replaced by battle-fatigued pilots from Rabaul. Yet the Japanese had no regular system of rotation and relied upon the deployment of new units. According to Vice Admiral Jinichi Kusaka, commander of Eleventh Air Fleet throughout most of the Pacific war, Tokyo supplied Rabaul with an average of fifty replacement aircraft per month, 80 percent of them fighters, from spring 1942 until early 1944. It is also important to note that both sides had more pilots than aircraft. Thus if planes were available and properly serviced they were soon in action and vulnerable to loss. The requirement for both sides was to bring the number of aircraft and number of pilots into an effective relationship. Ideally a squadron should have an operational strength but include a reserve of both pilots and aircraft in good condition. By the end of the Guadalcanal campaign neither side had achieved such a balance. Japanese units in particular were usually far below allocated aircraft strength. The answer was the production of both planes and pilots. As events in the South Pacific soon showed, the Allies were able to achieve that balance while the Japanese were left increasingly behind.

Third, the Guadalcanal campaign illustrates how a high percentage of aircraft were lost to noncombat mishaps (usually called "operational losses") as opposed to being downed in battle. The primary dangers were bad weather and poor fields, yet other mishaps could cause an operational loss. A minor pilot error or mechanical failure during takeoff or landing could easily damage or destroy an aircraft. (During takeoff, when the engine strains toward maximum power, is when a mechanical problem becomes most likely. Landing any World War II plane under the best of circumstances was a bad moment to let the mind wander. Naturally many pilots when coming home were exhausted—a bad combination.) Maintenance men also made mistakes that could show up during a flight. Navigation errors were always possible. There was even the possibility—not great but present—of colliding with a squadronmate. There was always the problem of young pilots hotdogging it—trying to impress or amuse friends—and crashing fighters at tree-top level, which meant instant death. Many men died that way. It is probably also true that more men survived an operational failure than a calamity in combat. Still, the operational bottleneck for both sides was battleworthy aircraft, not men to fly them. So to a commander a loss was a loss, regardless of what caused it.

Figures abound from the Allied side illustrating the dreadful toll of operational losses. According to the figures compiled by Richard Frank, the Americans during the Guadalcanal campaign, including all services and including the carrier battles, lost 264 aircraft in combat and 451 to operational losses. In the classic *History of Marine Corps Aviation in World War II*, author Robert Sherrod tabulated the individual casualties suffered by Marine Corps aviators during the entire war. The largest single category of men killed was 815 who perished in training or squadron formation in the United States. Those killed in action totaled 794. (Another 1,136 wounded in action amplifies the combat nature of overall casualties.) Men killed in operational losses overseas numbered 560. Another 319 airmen were missing in action (MIA, a subject I will revisit); twenty-five went missing while flying outside combat zones. Author Thomas Miller, working with sometimes incomplete squadron diaries, attempted to tabulate the fate of

the men who fought on Cactus. (These numbers exclude carrier engagements and the ugly losses suffered by USAAF long-range bombers
throughout the campaign.) According to Miller Cactus lost forty-six
men shot down, the vast majority being killed as a result. Another
thirty men were lost due to operational accidents—usually crashing or
ditching; two planes were lost to friendly fire from U.S. destroyers.
Several of these men survived, but their planes did not. Another sixteen airmen were missing in action. (I do not include here the several
men killed or wounded during bombardment on the ground.)

The problem of operational losses obviously afflicted Thirteenth Air
Force as well. In a contemporary report prepared in mid-October
1943 by Thirteenth Air Force Fighter Command for the period June 1,
1943–October 1, 1943, intelligence recorded thirty-two fighters lost in
combat and fifty-seven lost due to operational reasons. (Interestingly
the P-38s suffered only three combat losses and fifteen operational
losses, whereas fifteen P-40s were lost to enemy fire and thirteen to accidents. What this says about the two fighters is difficult to assess. The
Lightning was undoubtedly the superior fighter, but it also may have
been going through teething troubles made worse by the difficulty in
maintaining the big ship.) Another set of figures tabulating pilot deaths
for the same period showed that twenty-six died in combat, eleven to
operational failures. This shows that by 1943 a decent percentage of
American pilots downed were recovered alive and also illustrates that
an operational loss was less likely to be fatal.

As for U.S. forces the danger of accident was higher in New Guinea
than in the Solomons. According the official history of Australian air
operations, Fifth Air Force by April 1943 had, on paper, received
2,284 aircraft, of which 772 were ready for action. (Presumably this
included planes receiving normal service. No American figures from
this period give Fifth Air Force an operational strength anywhere near
as high.) Losses in this period, according to Australian figures, were
538 to accidents, 385 to enemy fire.

U.S. figures amplify this picture. At the end of the war Fifth Air
Force was preparing a report for its operations throughout hostilities.
(These loss figures, which I found at Maxwell, are not the same as
those reproduced in the Fifth Air Force study included in the Strategic
Bombing Survey. It seems that the SBS decided to handle operational
losses differently. The figures I found at Maxwell include losses that
were perhaps aircraft repaired or retired due to wear.) According to
Fifth Air Force intelligence it lost 2,928 aircraft in the Pacific war: 803
to enemy action and 2,125 to operational failures. The tables are broken down by month/year and type of aircraft. Some interesting figures

surface: Between September 1942 and January 1, 1944, combat losses for bombers totaled 164; operational casualties were 122. Combat fighter losses were recorded as 111 in the same period, and operational casualties were 291. (Transport losses were consistently weighted toward operational casualties.)

Beginning in January 1944 this trend changed. From January 1, 1944, to war's end Fifth Air Force intelligence (by this time Far Eastern Air Force) claimed 266 bombers lost to enemy action but 579 lost to accident. Fighter losses remained heavily in the operational category. After January 1944 until VJ-Day Fifth Air Force Fighter Command lost 248 ships in combat, whereas 579 went down due to accident. It should be noted that an MIA category was not included in these figures; it is likely they were added to the operational losses. I do not believe that these figures, derived from squadron reports soon after the war, are precise. The total picture, however, is quite clear: The big increase in accidental losses after 1944 is perfectly consistent with the flow of battle. After early 1944 FEAF increased greatly in size while Japanese forces declined. Kenney, however, always pushed his units hard, and the chances for mishaps grew as the theater expanded.

A smaller sample fills out the picture. Recently veterans of USAAF 49th Fighter Group compiled a comprehensive chronology of their unit's service in the Pacific war. Although not fully complete, the book contains a good breakdown of losses by type. In the period April 1942–June 1944 the group historians tabulated the deaths of ninety-six men. (Obviously this does not include pilots who lost or damaged aircraft but survived—probably the majority in most units.) The historians record thirty-two men killed in action, eighteen missing in action, and forty-six killed in operational accidents. Interestingly, thirty-nine of the operational deaths occurred early in the war in Australia and included eighteen men lost in two ferry accidents in transports. Seven of those killed in action perished when the Japanese destroyed a PBY serving similar duties. Once in New Guinea the totals of killed and missing were virtually identical.

The figures available indicate that Japanese forces suffered considerably fewer operational losses than did U.S. forces. Richard Frank has argued that Japanese operational losses during the Guadalcanal campaign were half those suffered by the Americans. The postwar interviews conducted by the Allies for the SBS include many anecdotes of high operational losses for imperial aircraft flying from the crude satellite fields near Rabaul and especially by the IJA aircraft operating out of Wewak. Losses of replacement aircraft due to ferry losses appeared high. Yet the figures for the Japanese air arm are not as convincing.

Frank also contends that the Japanese suffered fewer operational losses because their pilots were more experienced throughout most of the Guadalcanal campaign; I doubt that, even for this early engagement. Japanese pilot quality was dropping from the beginning of the struggle for Guadalcanal and continued thereafter. Japanese replacement pilots in late 1942 were as well trained as the Allied rookies, but neither group was ready for what awaited. In addition, Japanese aircraft, because they were on the offensive, had no navigational aids and possessed very poor communications among aircraft under even the best circumstances. We must remember that imperial aircraft were flying more than 500 miles to strike Guadalcanal, and mistakes in navigation or an encounter with bad weather would have presented dangers much more serious than those faced by Allied planes flying near their bases.

Still, it is possible that Japanese military aircraft carried a hidden strength: Because they were so light, imperial fighters as well as bombers had low wing-loading and low stall speeds; in practice this meant they were easier to take off and land. In late 1944 a large body of American and British test pilots, combat pilots, and engineers tested a variety of Allied fighters and included a mint-condition late-model Zero for comparison. Many of the Americans who flew the Zero were impressed by its smooth handling characteristics and ease of landing. One test pilot even suggested that Japan create a civilian small-plane industry after the war. And because Japanese aircraft had excellent range a lost Japanese pilot—unless he was stretching range on, say, a raid against Guadalcanal—consequently had more time to locate familiar ground.

Although these technical factors explain some of the disparity between Japanese and Allied operational losses, others may have been at work. In the mid-1970s professors Ikuhiko Hata and Yashuho Izawa wrote a detailed account of Japanese naval fighter units and several biographies of aces. Although marred by some of the same absurd victory claims that even Japanese officers were wary of accepting during the war, the work has much valuable information. In particular Hata and Izawa attempt to list the individual fate of every JNAF fighter pilot by training class. Each pilot was listed as killed in action, killed by accident, or survived. Because of incomplete records they were able to account for officer pilots only up until the June 1944–July 1944 class. They were able to track enlisted seamen-pilots, a much larger group, until the June 1942 class. The youthful enlisted trainee groups were followed until the class graduating in November 1942. The fates of these men were grim indeed. Altogether the authors cataloged 1,035 killed in action, 138 killed in accidents, and 245 survivors. It is important to emphasize that this group includes perhaps only a quarter of the men trained by Japan to fly against the Allies and is limited to IJN fighter pilots. (Bomber crews that were decimated are not included, nor are the men who flew for the IJA. I should also note that I did not add the many killed who graduated in classes before 1936, on the assumption that many met their fates prior to Pearl Harbor.)

Anyone who has studied military casualties should be staggered by such tremendous casualties among this group. A kill rate of 83 percent—among any group—is extraordinary. Considering the time frame there is no question that so many perished in the South Pacific simply because it was by far the largest combat theater of the Pacific war until 1944. Numbers such as these—and they appear to be accurate—suggest a near suicidal urge to accomplish a mission regardless of the realities of the moment. Japan did not have an air-sea rescue system worthy of the name. As in other Japanese services, surrender was not acceptable for most pilots. It is very telling, I think, that I have never encountered an MIA category in any Japanese source. It is possible that many Japanese fighters who did not return, regardless of reason, were listed as killed in action. It is also possible that many young Japanese pilots—if low on fuel, damaged, or lost—might have sought any possible enemy target to attack regardless of their chances for finding one. If a Japanese plane did not return from a mission there was no chance the pilot could put it on the ground a few miles from base and survive—a classic operational loss by American standards.

I think it is also important to consider the consistent complaints from Japanese air officers regarding ground maintenance and spare-parts supplies. Japanese combat records are, apparently, detailed. However, it is still unclear whether a full roster of serviceable and non-serviceable aircraft appeared in most cases (as was the case in many Allied situation reports) along with average rates of operational aircraft. When the Allies began offensive operations in early 1943 an aircraft that was nonoperational for any reason (often minor) was an obvious target for ground attack. Japanese ground losses after 1943 often exceeded 20 percent (and sometimes pushed 50 percent) after a major Allied attack. Aircraft that suffered even slight difficulties were good candidates for bigger problems during flight. An American ground crew might well get a tired or damaged plane off the ground and have the pilot regret it after something failed. Many Japanese aircraft in this category may well have stayed on the ground where, unless repaired soon, they were destroyed by Allied bombers.

In retrospect the trend is clear: The air war in the South Pacific was becoming an attritional slugfest. At the time, however, commanders had to pursue a war that was moving far faster than anyone had anticipated. For the moment in the Solomons the pace of battle slowed while the Japanese prepared to defend positions on New Georgia and nearby islands and Halsey planned his attacks on them. Air battle did not cease. However, before and after the futile Operation I-GO, the attacks began to go the other way. Guadalcanal was harassed, but Allied units began steady attacks against Japanese positions in the central Solomons. While they did so American strength blossomed.

Gaining such strength, the Americans reorganized their air effort during the waning days of the fighting on Guadalcanal. On January 13, 1943, the Pentagon authorized the formation of the USAAF Thirteenth Air Force under Major General Nathan Twining. Because the Solomons were targeted for a major offensive, the Pentagon also directed that a subcommand be established under Fitch's ComAirSopac. The new echelon, with typical military elegance, was named Commander, Aircraft, Solomons (ComAirSol). ComAirSol was one of the most integrated command structures of the Pacific war, including officers from all U.S. services and New Zealand. Originally it was commanded by Rear Admiral Charles Mason. Illustrating the multiservice nature of the Solomons campaign, Mason was succeeded by Rear Admiral Marc Mitscher in April; Nathan Twining was promoted from Thirteenth Air Force in July and turned over the position in November to U.S. Marine Major General Ralph J. Mitchell. In 1944 command alternated between Marine and U.S. Army generals. In March 1944 Mitchell relieved Fitch as ComAirSopac. Rear Admiral Mason's command was responsible for the direction of all the land-based aircraft (with the exception of reconnaissance) for all services in the Solomons. Fitch was left the daunting task of supervising the growing flow of men and supplies into the theater. Carriers at sea were always commanded by Admiral Halsey and his task force leaders.

With this reorganization came a major increase in force levels during the first quarter of 1943, and an important actor became the newly formed USAAF Thirteenth Air Force. During the battle for Guadalcanal the few USAAF P-39s present rarely engaged Japanese aircraft, although they served stoutly in a ground-support role. By April 1, 1943, however, the USAAF was building a powerful and balanced force. Deployed by that date were two heavy bomber groups, a medium bomber group, and two fighter groups. With Guadalcanal in U.S. hands, USAAF bombers increasingly began to stage out of the major base complex being constructed on the Canal. One fighter squadron, the 339th, was the first fully operational P-38 unit in the Pacific and became one of the most successful squadrons in the theater. Other fighter units lived with P-39s and P-40s for another year, but now that U.S. bombers were on the attack they could fly low cover for bombers with Corsairs and Lightnings above them, putting them very much into the grim game. The Thirteenth also gained its first squadron of what would become a group of invaluable and sought-after C-47s. Add into the mix a patrol squadron, and Admiral Halsey had a nice addition to his strengthening air arm.

In the three months after evicting the Japanese from Guadalcanal, Marine squadrons were rotated; many veteran units were redeployed or given extended rest. In their place Halsey brought in four new Marine fighter squadrons, two Avenger squadrons, and two dive-bomber units. Two Marine transport units added valuable flexibility. Based on Guadalcanal or the nearby Russell Islands (seized in February), those units did not suffer the incessant attacks suffered at Cactus. Instead they trained, patrolled, and launched regular attacks on targets in or near New Georgia, the next obvious target for Halsey's force. A decent supply of spare parts and greatly improved facilities increased the effectiveness of the Marine force. So did new aircraft. Although the Wildcat had a few more months to fly in the South Pacific, in early 1943 the new Corsairs began to appear in Marine fighter squadrons, with many more on the way to Espíritu.

In late April 1943 Admiral Halsey received more good news. RNZAF No. 1 Fighter Squadron arrived at Guadalcanal to join the Hudson reconnaissance unit already there. Like the navy and Marines the RNZAF believed in rotating fighter squadrons regularly (though reconnaissance units stayed much longer and employed replacements). Therefore RNZAF fighter strength in the Solomons was never great at any given moment, yet it was continuous, and RNZAF Kittyhawks earned great respect from the U.S. tactical bombing units that enjoyed the comfort of their escorts. Upon the final offensive at Rabaul the RNZAF had the equivalent of a composite air group based on New Georgia, which included two fighter and one reconnaissance bomber squadron—a sizeable contribution from a country deeply engaged in Europe and not as large as many U.S. cities. RNZAF antisubmarine patrols continued over a wide area of the South Pacific. In late 1943 a squadron of PBY reconnaissance and air-sea rescue aircraft deployed near Guadalcanal.

The Guadalcanal campaign took much of the heat off of Allied forces in New Guinea and Darwin. Still hampered by a serious shortage of aircraft and support groups, neither Fifth Air Force nor the

RAAF increased numerical strength between summer 1942 and spring 1943. Dramatic changes in deployment, however, did take place. Many squadrons of Fifth Air Force, as well as RAAF No. 9 Group under Kenney's direct command, moved out of defensive positions at Darwin and near Townsville to Port Moresby. Those units did their best to aid the Australian army's dramatic counteroffensive over the Kokoda Trail and soon gave everyday support to the horrid siege of Buna-Gona. By December some bomber units staged directly out of Port Moresby, and fighter units used Dobodura near Buna. Attacks on the Japanese bases at Lae and Salamaua became routine. During this period attacks by Bettys nearly ceased because of the horrible losses taken at Guadalcanal. When the JNAF intervened at Buna, which it often did during November and December, it had to fight Allied aircraft operating at low altitudes. Allied P-39s and P-40s, so often crippled earlier because of poor performance above 18,000 feet, became deadly enemies below 10,000 feet.

Worse yet—from the Japanese point of view—General Arnold had relented from his earlier refusal to allocate modern fighters to the theater. In late summer the first shipment of modern P-38 Lightnings began arriving in Australia. Because the aircraft was so unusual ground crews faced a major turnabout from the more familiar P-40s and P-39s. One pilot trained in P-38s was shocked to find that ground personnel had put the ailerons on the wrong wings. By January two squadrons had converted to P-38s, and a third joined in May. As in the Solomons, as these second-generation fighters grew proficient at high-altitude combat the effectiveness of the older planes at lower elevations increased.

Fifth Air Force and the RAAF, however, began to scream for reinforcements. The view of the Pentagon was that too many aircraft had been sent to Australia in 1942 as it was. Although two transport groups arrived in theater, no new units made their way to northern Australia and New Guinea. One of the earliest arrivals, 19th Bomb Group, had been so badly battered in the Philippines, East Indies, and Australia that Kenney took the unprecedented step of sending the unit home to be disbanded. The wear and tear on Fifth Air Force was tremendous. Its yeoman P-40E models were wearing out quickly. The 90th (heavy) Bomb Group, which had a full strength of sixty planes, was down to fifteen by January 1943. A study done on Fifth Air Force immediately after the war indicates that in every category, except for transports, its effective strength fell between June 1942 and April 1943. Fighter strength in January 1943, for instance, was about 150 operational aircraft, mostly P-39s and P-40s. The percentage of nonoperational aircraft rose alarmingly during this period, often more than 50 percent of the total force. Fifth Air Force, in other words, was winning the battle for New Guinea, but it was doing so because the enemy was occupied elsewhere. Still its units were falling apart; something had to change.

At this time the RAAF was at the center of a confused but important debate over Australia's effort in World War II. In late 1942 Australia possessed thirty-one squadrons of all types of military aircraft. Canberra, with Prime Minister Curtin very much involved, demanded enough aircraft from the United States and Great Britain to equip forty-five squadrons in 1943 and seventy-two by 1944. In theory MacArthur supported that goal. In practice Kenney, who was also desperate for aircraft, told Washington that Australia lacked the manpower to support more than forty-five squadrons. Despite promises from Washington Australia gained a mere sixty Kittyhawks throughout 1943 in addition to twelve PBYs. And Kenney proved correct about Australian manpower: In March 1943 RAAF No. 9 Operational Group, flying in New Guinea, was already short 1,000 men; similar shortages were seen across the board in the Australian military. Facing up to such limited resources, Curtin made it clear to Churchill and Roosevelt that Australia's war effort would be directed toward the Southwest Pacific, the area from which Australia proper was being threatened. This was, of course, very good for MacArthur: Australian ground forces were the backbone of the withering assault launched on the Japanese in New Guinea during 1943 and early 1944. Canberra's decision, understandable given the circumstances, also led to a great what-if of World War II. After the successful operation against Lae and Salamaua in September 1943, Australia was no longer under any direct threat, and militia units were being prepared for modern war. Had the three elite Australian divisions (7th, 6th, and 9th) been deployed to Europe for D-Day, Montgomery would have possessed an additional corps of superb infantry with which to bludgeon German forces. The fact such a move was not seriously considered illustrated the sobering impact of the Japanese offensive and Australia's changing role in the world. For the moment, however, the RAAF was there to support its Pacific drive and cost the Japanese dearly.

During the first four months after defeat at Guadalcanal Japanese forces at Rabaul increased in size. In the Rabaul vicinity the IJN's land-based air units maintained a paper strength, mostly fighters, of some 150–200 planes throughout most of 1943. Between January and July 1943 they were joined by 75–100 aircraft from the Japanese Army Air Force. In addition, the IJN kept 50–100 planes at the bases at Lae and

Gasmata, intended for operations against Fifth Air Force. Despite considerable reinforcements from aircraft dispatched by Combined Fleet's carrier units, in April 1943 Japan had lost its numerical edge, although not by a large margin. On the other side of the coin the Japanese (at least until the air attacks from Fifth Air Force and Halsey's force could coordinate on Rabaul) maintained their advantage of interior lines and could move forces, in theory, from one front to the other. During this time the kill ratio increasingly tipped in favor of the Allies, though Japanese forces could still make Allied attacks costly and dangerous. It was Japan's potential strength—greatly reinforced by recent memories of Japanese victories—that made both MacArthur and Halsey very cautious before moving forward again. Not only did both commanders want more men, ships, and supplies; they also demanded more aircraft.

By early November 1943 another significant rise in force levels took place on both sides. During this period, however, U.S. industrial might was beginning to show its power, giving the Allies the advantage in both quality and quantity. The numerical buildup also corresponded with major changes in a strategic situation that left the Japanese—although this was not clear in Tokyo—flirting with military catastrophe.

The principal beneficiary of the ceaseless escalation of combat force levels during fall 1943 was Fifth Air Force. After pleading and pestering from Kenney, MacArthur, and the Australian government, the USAAF sent significant reinforcements to New Guinea. Two new fighter groups were added to the order of battle. (One, 475th Fighter Group, was the first all-P-38 group to arrive in the Pacific Theater; boasting some of Fifth Air Force's best pilots, it soon began compiling its impressive record.) A few other squadrons abandoned their worn-out Airacobras and P-40s and received a steady stream of P-47s and P-38s. The best of the P-40 models, the N, replaced some of the older versions. Nevertheless, although paper strength of 5th USAAF Fighter Command crossed the 600-plane mark in August 1943 for the first time, there were 200 old fighters still on the roster. Many probably did not belong there. According to Fifth Air Force figures published immediately after the war, operational strength never crossed 375 in 1943 and was usually less, even during the buildup. Yet the gain was great. Operational strength had been stuck at about 175 between August 1942 and June 1943. Kenney also received a new medium-bomber group, the 345th, which operated many of the low-level strafers that were proving so effective. Other bomber units received some new machines to replace old ones; heavy-bomber groups were receiving B-24s to relieve badly worn B-17s. A new B-24 bomber group also arrived in Australia but was put under RAAF operational command near Darwin when it was decided that strategic bombardment in that theater should be a two-way street. (In fact it became a one-way street: Japanese attacks on Darwin ceased and Allied forces began to assault targets in the Indies, eventually doing substantial damage.) Some A-20 tactical bombers began arriving, with more promised. Fifth Air Force also received two new groups of C-47s, which were becoming essential to the Australian land campaign in New Guinea.

Kenney naturally wanted more of everything. He was particularly adamant that he receive more reserve crews (ideally two crews per plane). Washington promised more but claimed that fewer reserve crews were necessary for the growing transport force. Kenney acidly pointed out that the transport casualty rate was as high as a fighter unit (they saw less of the enemy but were in the air so often they saw more weather). The Pentagon compromised and agreed to send additional reserve crews to the theater. It would have been better to have more reserve crews and reserve aircraft, but Fifth Air Force would have to wait for spring 1944 before Arnold loosened the USAAF purse strings again and substantially reinforced Fifth Air Force.

Kenney's airmen soon had excellent places from which operate. Engineers discovered a splendid location in the Markham Valley called Tsili Tsili, putting even short-range fighters within range of Lae and bigger craft within range of Wewak. In June U.S. troops seized two islands, Woodlark and Kiriwana, between Buna and New Britain. With almost no casualties Fifth Air Force had ideal locations to build fighter bases to protect daylight bombing raids against Gasmata and Rabaul. Another hammer blow fell on New Guinea that summer. Quickly driving the JNAF from its old haunts at Lae and Salamaua, and pounding the new Japanese Army Air Force at Wewak in August, MacArthur dispatched General Thomas Blamey and his Australian veterans on a brilliant amphibious campaign against Lae itself during September 1943. At the same time unopposed paratroopers seized Nadzab, another ideal site for an airstrip. Within weeks Nadzab had become another Dobodura (which itself was receiving continual expansion, for it would serve as the main base for attacks against Rabaul).

The Allied air offensive against Rabaul had to await the arrival of Admiral Halsey's powerful air armada. It was the policy of both MacArthur and Halsey to avoid unescorted daylight bombing attacks (a lesson not yet learned by U.S. bombers in Europe), and so Halsey's fighters and tactical bombers had to get bases closer to their ultimate target. In July and August, as part of a naval-ground campaign that ranged from bungling to brilliant, Halsey's forces seized New Georgia and Vella Lavella in the Central Solomons. Japanese aircraft contested the New Georgia operation in force, received a bloody nose, and achieved little. Supported by fighters from his new bases, Halsey moved against Bougainville in November. Seizing a good perimeter in an unoccupied part of the island far from major Japanese garrisons, USN Seabees and the Army Corps of Engineers soon turned the area at Torokina into a major air base that army divisions surrounded with powerful defensive positions. Finally both MacArthur and Halsey had positioned their air forces within striking range of Rabaul. Utter calamity for Japan ensued in short order.

Like Fifth Air Force, ComAirSol received substantial reinforcements throughout the summer in preparation for the great strike against Rabaul. Because both Marine and USN squadrons received systematic rotation, some of the units that entered the theater replaced others that left. However, many squadrons given leave in the summer and fall were back at work in November. Marine squadrons that arrived in the theater after April and before January 1944 included twelve fighter squadrons, three TBF squadrons, and six SBD units. Thirteenth Air Force received no more new groups; however, it did receive new squadrons to fill up understrength groups. Included were two heavy-bomber squadrons and two transport groups. As in Fifth Air Force, the Thirteenth did receive many replacement aircraft. One heavy-bomber group discarded old B-17s in favor of new B-24s, and one squadron traded Airacobras for P-38s. Inspired by the success of the low-level B-25 strafers, many of Thirteenth's Mitchells received a similar field modification.

In the fall of 1943 the USN entered the struggle for the South Pacific in force. During early 1943 the new U.S. heavy and light carriers were organizing for combat some months down the road. But the USN had produced more squadrons than its major carriers could use, which made surplus aircraft and pilots available. Admiral King was not concerned about European commitments, so the extra units appeared on the bases that had been seized by Admiral Halsey during the summer. The squadrons were usually independently deployed, a fact that made almost no difference in the diverse command structure found under Halsey's forces. The most famous squadron was VF-17, the "Jolly Rogers," which employed the navy's first Corsairs on land bases because the aircraft had not been deemed carrier-ready. Although VF-17 has received much attention since the war, it was joined by two SBD squadrons and two fighter squadrons employing the new F6F Hellcat. A huge force was approaching the Japanese fortress from the east. After the war U.S. records claimed that of the 740 aircraft potentially available for operations against Rabaul, at least 480 were ready on any given date.

By late summer 1943 it was obvious at Rabaul and Tokyo that Japan's position in the South Pacific was hanging by a thread. In hindsight the Japanese should have seen all too clearly that their delaying campaign in the Solomons and New Guinea was turning into a trap for land garrisons and a place where it would lose priceless aircraft and irreplaceable warships. To slow down MacArthur's drive toward the Philippines or Indies (the Japanese assumed the former) imperial forces were crippling their own ability to confront the new U.S. naval menace, a threat supported by a large and well-trained amphibious landing force growing daily at Pearl Harbor. Once Lae and New Georgia were lost the Japanese should have done everything possible to withdraw forces from the South Pacific and move them into the Central Pacific and Indies. In light of losses inflicted by U.S. submarines and Allied aircraft, surely that would have been no easy matter. Yet supply ships continued to enter Rabaul in large numbers until October 1943, and a few sailed in until February 1944; merchant ships arrived in the Wewak area until March. In addition, there was a huge number of small ships and barges that had been used to deploy the great Japanese garrisons in the first place. What the Japanese needed was a redeployment and a period of calm to prepare for the inevitable hurricane brewing in both the Central Pacific and South Pacific. A strategic withdrawal, even if incomplete, would have provided that. It was folly to dispatch more planes and warships to Rabaul and eastern New Guinea, but that is exactly what Tokyo decided to do in late summer 1943. MacArthur and King, whether they knew it or not, were paralyzing Japan's ability to build up defenses in more critical areas. Although the ultimate battles in the Central Pacific were violent affairs, they were all won, and—even if victory was inevitable—casualties could have been worse than they were. It is worth pointing out that Japan had as many men defending Rabaul and Kavieng as they later did on Okinawa. The 250,000 troops in or on their way to New Guinea (not to mention the 100,000 men garrisoning Rabaul, New Ireland, and Bougainville) could have been used to bring major reinforcements to spots like Saipan, Guam, Iwo Jima, Borneo, and Okinawa. At the same time, Japan's deadly destroyer and cruiser force was wasting away in the face of Allied air and naval actions, just as they were needed to hunt submarines and support fleet operations. The Japanese were turning a strategic error into a strategic disaster.

Yet the JNAF had been ordered to delay the Allied drive up the Solomons and do what it could to hinder Fifth Air Force in New Guinea. Thanks to replacement aircraft, the transfer of pilots from the

Indies, and the remains of the CARDIV 2, which had been transferred to Eleventh Air Fleet, Rabaul had a strength of roughly 240 aircraft in October 1943. Most were Zeros, although many tactical bombers and reconnaissance aircraft were included. At the same time, the Japanese had reinforced fields at Buka, Kara, Kahili, and Ballale on or near Bougainville. A Japanese staff officer to Admiral Kusaka, commander of air units at Rabaul, estimated deployments to these bases during 1943 at 230 fighters, seventy-five tactical bombers, and thirty-two Bettys. Many of these planes were lost prior to October, so it is not possible to estimate their strength in the fall of 1943. All bases, however, were operating and fighting until driven back to Rabaul during or just before the Bougainville invasion. By August there were no more naval aircraft based on New Guinea due to the destruction of the Japanese position at Lae. However, the southwestern New Britain base at Gasmata remained responsible for countering Fifth Air Force. Although reduced to a minor facility, Gasmata received major reinforcements during December to counter Halsey's attack on Cape Gloucester, raising the force to approximately 100 aircraft. As already noted, substantial numbers of aircraft reinforced Rabaul and environs from Combined Fleet's carrier divisions. CARDIV 2 intervened in the Bougainville campaign and lost half its 150 aircraft. Altogether the Japanese had 500 aircraft in the Rabaul area by early November and would receive more. However, they were fighting Fifth Air Force as well as Halsey's airmen in the Solomons, and Japanese aircraft did not fly at full strength any more than did the Allies. In terms of operational military aircraft, especially fighters, it is likely that Rabaul's defenders were outnumbered by at least two-to-one and usually more. Those were poor odds for the Japanese. Unlike imperial aircraft at Guadalcanal, Allied planes were within easy striking range of Bougainville and then Rabaul. Allied planes were more numerous, technically superior, and flown by pilots who were increasingly gaining a qualitative edge. If one combines the quantitative two-to-one edge with the qualitative edge in both aircraft and pilots, the balance of forces had reached a point where massacre was inevitable.

The doomed Japanese airmen at Rabaul had received—in theory, at least—extensive help in the summer of 1943 from the Japanese Army Air Force. The JAAF had begun deploying aircraft to Rabaul in late 1942 and had participated in several battles. When the army began moving large numbers of troops to New Guinea, it was natural for Tokyo to move army aircraft to support them. In the spring of 1943 Japanese troops occupied areas near Wewak on the New Guinea coast and commenced building airfields. Unlike services under Halsey's command, Japanese army and navy air units never cooperated well. A division of labor began in 1943 that left the defense of New Guinea to the Japanese army air arm and the Solomons to the Japanese navy. As huge army garrisons existed near Rabaul, such a division made no operational sense whatsoever. Nevertheless the old Pearl Harbor attitude that the IJN was responsible for the South Seas continued long after any strategic rationale for such had passed.

Therefore the Japanese 4th Air Army began a redeployment from Rabaul to the newly constructed complex of bases near Wewak in June 1944. By August the move was complete. On paper 4th Air Army had two air divisions, the Sixth and Seventh, to defend New Guinea. On paper 6th Division had 180 fighters, thirty-six reconnaissance aircraft, and 108 bombers, or a total of 324. Seventh Division had eighty-four. In addition, army units in the theater received roughly sixty aircraft each month as replacements. That was paper strength. In practice the Wewak complex hosted maybe 250 aircraft of all types. No doubt the 4th Air Army's order of battle on paper comforted officers in Tokyo and the hard-pressed generals fighting Australians in New Guinea. However, operating from crude fields with poor aircraft, 4th Air Army was vulnerable to devastating attack. With Japanese leaders having no conception of how quickly the Australian army and Fifth Air Force could move up the Markham Valley, this collection of warplanes would provide Fifth Air Force one of its most spectacular victories and provide Allied air forces a host of useful lessons to employ against Japanese bases throughout the remainder of the Pacific war.

However costly it was in terms of aircraft and men, by October 1943 the Allies had gained the equivalent of a checkmate in three moves against the opposing Japanese forces. Still, the balance of forces we outline above reflected many factors. Undoubtedly the production of aircraft and the training of men were important. Yet every war has a rhythm all its own. The technical differences between the opposing aircraft, especially fighters, were never decisive in and of themselves, and neither was the numerical balance. The Americans had survived at Guadalcanal despite bad odds. The Japanese fought strongly for a year until their forces collapsed in a matter of weeks. The air campaign in the South Pacific was thus like any other military campaign: It comprised a multitude of battles that formed and were shaped by patterns of aerial combat. The air war required victories by every type of air unit, yet nothing could be done until fighters—so often maligned before the war—made sectors of the skies death zones for Japanese aircraft. Once this was accomplished, strikes by bombers and fighter-bombers against the imperial defenses became devastating.

6

Deadly Geometry:
Fighter Warfare in
the South Pacific

A World War II fighter pilot lived at the nexus of his personal skills, the capabilities of his aircraft, and the laws of physics. In practice these factors were deeply intertwined. Thus it is somewhat artificial to isolate the various factors of aerial warfare. Still, it is wise to try. If we can obtain a general appreciation for the dynamics that shaped fighter operations, then we can better understand why the war in the South Pacific was fought in the way it was. We can also appreciate some of the subtle but profoundly important components of the air war that allowed one of the antagonists—the United States—despite some technical disadvantages and initial numerical parity, to maul Japanese airpower within a year of invading Guadalcanal.

Like all great battlefields the killing zones over the South Pacific had distinct physical characteristics that influenced combat. The passage of time and the changing nature of aviation have dulled our ability to appreciate the extraordinary sensations experienced by any airman of World War II. This situation reflects daily life today. Anyone who has ascended a hill or driven through a mountain range can visualize, for instance, the importance of high ground to land battles. All of us are familiar enough with the elements to grasp the importance of severe cold, deep mud, or desert sun. Preserved battlefields in the United States and Europe draw millions of visitors and are dramatic because they illustrate across time what the fight looked like and how it developed. However, except for the sailor and seaman, few people understand the enormous variations of wind and sea and supplies that confronted participants during World War II naval battles.

In a similar vein almost everyone flies this day and age. Yet commercial aviation has gone to lengths to isolate passengers from the sensations of flight. Airline management knows very well that people get uneasy if buffeted about the cabin. That is one reason the use of jet aircraft caused a huge increase in the number of people willing to fly: In the thin air found at very high altitudes, where jets fly, the ride is far smoother. And except for takeoffs and landings sounds are not conspicuous. Many other people fly in the relatively safe environment of civilian aviation, supported by a huge network of radio and navigation aids, in private and corporate planes designed to be reliable above all. And although no sensible person would argue that these advances are not helpful to civilization, such creature comforts obscure the stark differences between modern air travel and World War II air combat.

Combat in a World War II military aircraft was intensely visceral. There was constant noise and odors. Fighters, even bombers, performed maneuvers that glued airmen to their seats and would terrify any civilian today. Aircraft were vulnerable to mechanical failure that could instantly kill the men aboard. Pilots often flew powerful aircraft well beyond their capabilities and suffered oblivion. At some point many engaged enemy aircraft at close range in deadly battle. The realm of the World War II fighter pilot can only be appreciated by those who fought the war, the few military pilots of the postwar era who encountered close air-to-air combat, and, to a lesser extent, the small number of dedicated enthusiasts who keep World War II aircraft flying today at great expense. And yet these men and their dangerous machines played a central role in the greatest military conflict in history. That role was more important in the South Pacific than in any other theater. Regardless of geography, climate, disease, and morale the crunch in World War II came during combat.

Fighter Formations and Missions

During World War II the primary mission of fighters was to either kill or protect bombers. The fact that fighters also proved in certain circumstances to be excellent ground-attack planes was an unexpected but welcome bonus. Regardless of whether the pilot's immediate job was to protect or destroy bombers, enemy fighters usually constituted his greatest obstacle to success and the greatest threat to his personal survival. Consequently, in practice, fighter pilots had to face the hazardous and complex job of destroying other fighters.

Battle tactics and weaponry are always related. However, the fighters of 1942 and the support technologies had evolved so quickly that pilots had little precedent to guide the development of a coherent set of battle tactics. On one level ample experience existed: During World War I pilots on the Western Front fought a massive war that included fighter melees that in 1918 matched in size large engagements that took place during World War II. Yet in some respects the important lessons of World War I were forgotten, not analyzed, and consequently not refined. For instance in World War I there was no effective communication between aircraft other than hand signals and aircraft gyrations. Yet flight leaders realized it was vital to approach the enemy from an advantageous position. Indeed squadron commanders in 1918 looked for the same edges as a later generation would: altitude, surprise, and concentration of force. Consequently all of the air forces developed increasingly sophisticated flight formations. Once the point of contact was reached, however, it was every man for himself. When the dogfight started, a cool head, marksmanship, and flying ability counted for everything.

During the interwar period air forces continued to emphasize taut, sophisticated formation flying for groups and aerobatic maneuvers for individual pilots. There were good reasons to train pilots in intricate formations. Groups are difficult to assemble in the air, and if they are to rendezvous with another unit elsewhere they must congregate accurately and quickly. Furthermore political and military leaders around the world were deeply worried about mass bombing attacks on cities. Fighters during the interwar years were called "pursuit" planes. As the name implies, air forces continued to develop the type almost exclusively as an antibomber weapon. Bomber enthusiasts and many skeptical politicians, knowing that fighters had not performed well against heavy bombers flying at night during World War I, openly questioned the need for the type. The secret development of radar and the design of very fast fighters in the late 1930s ended any doubt concerning the fighter's future. It reinforced, however, the emphasis on rigid formation flying. All of the world's air forces used, for their basic tactical unit, the three-plane section flying in vee-formation (sometimes called the "Vic"). The flight leader flew slightly in front of the wingmen positioned to his rear-right and rear-left. The three planes flew close, almost wing tip to wing tip. Airmen believed the vee-formation allowed a well-coordinated, massed attack on bombers. Large formations were constituted many ways, but the most popular was a vee of vees.

The fixation on bombers crippled the development of sophisticated antifighter tactical formations. Although everyone recognized that the great increase of speed and loss of maneuverability resulting from the abandonment of the biplane made massive 1918-style fighter shootouts impossible, airmen continued to assume that a fighter engagement would develop into a series of one-on-one combats if they engaged at all. What was considered inevitable, however, were units of enemy pursuit aircraft engaging during patrol missions over the front lines. Pilots in the small, elite, very well trained fighter forces of the 1930s practiced complex aerobatic maneuvers and intricate angles of attack. Whether this was ever good policy is open to question. It was very bad policy for a large force composed of imperfectly trained pilots. Ironically during World War II in the Southwest Pacific the fighter pilots of Japan and the United States traded places relative to their national character. Japanese pilots, growing up during a time when a militaristic regime pounded a group ethic into the national consciousness, developed tactics that emphasized the individual in air combat. Their American opponents, coming from a land that prided itself on respect for individualism, made a military art form out of deadly but well organized and disciplined small-group tactics.

Much of this development was due to historic circumstance. Japanese pilots amassed much experience during hostilities with China and short engagements with the Red Air Force. The Chinese air effort was a feeble affair and, if anything, encouraged Japan's great emphasis on individual dogfighting skills. The introduction of the Zero, one of the great dogfighting planes in history, only encouraged trends that led to calamity.

The Japanese, however, did develop a significant refinement to the standard vee-formation. The Japanese three-plane section, the *shotai*, was much more flexible than other varieties of the Vic. Instead of flying in rigid position, the two wingmen flew much farther back from the leader. While the flight leader held a steady course, looking for the right place to engage, the wingmen weaved right and left and up and down behind him. This gave the formation much better defense from surprise attack because the weaving fighters were able to check blind spots. The tactic was enhanced by the bubble cockpit mounted on both the Zero and Oscar, allowing excellent pilot visibility. When the flight leader engaged, instead of going in simultaneously and firing as one aircraft, the wingmen trailed the leader, each attacking in succession. When several *shotai* participated in the same attack against an unwary target the impact was devastating. Yet once engaged or, worse yet, if the *shotai* was the victim of attack, then Japanese pilots fought individually. The system worked well for several years. Consequently its flaws were hard to see. Japanese fighters, above all, failed to develop disciplined techniques for deployment at the squadron and group levels. If put on the defensive the Japanese proved to be at a serious disadvantage. In 1944, three years after other air forces had done so, the Japanese converted to the four-plane formation. However, by then the number of good flight leaders was so small, and U.S. machines so superior, that changing tactics did little good.

In the late 1930s U.S. tactical doctrine was very much in line with the defective policies followed in most air forces. Yet American observers—including General Kenney, who was in Europe during 1940—of the debacle in France and the Battle of Britain saw plainly that the U.S. air arm needed rehabilitation quickly. In the months before Pearl Harbor U.S. designers greatly improved the oxygen system for the aircrews and hurriedly worked on self-sealing fuel tanks and improved armor for fighters. They also improved the design of the .50-caliber machine gun, raising its rate of fire. Fortunately for the United States these designers were learning valuable lessons just as they were developing the new aircraft that ultimately won the air war in World War II.

American airmen privy to information from the Battle of Britain were also quick to note that the vee-formation proved a failure early in World War II. It was far too rigid and largely wasted the assets of the wingmen. If the flight leader was forced to make a tight maneuver, the formation unraveled. Collision between wingmen was a perpetual danger. Wise minds in the Luftwaffe, assessing their experience in the Spanish Civil War, had foreseen all of these problems. Before 1939 German fighters abandoned the vee-formation. In its place they adopted the famous four-plane *schwarm*. In a *schwarm* planes were separated by 600–1,000 feet, roughly equal to turning radius. It was made up of a flight leader and his wingman accompanied by a section leader and his wing. They were positioned almost exactly as four fingertips outstretched. Because of this, the Americans called the formation the "finger-four." During an engagement, the *schwarm* usually broke up into two sections. Indeed it was the two-plane element that made the *schwarm* so successful. The section leader flew the fighting plane; the wingman's primary job was to guard the leader's tail. This was an ideal setup for initiating inexperienced pilots. Their job, though still very hazardous, was kept much simpler. As the wingman developed his skills the pair could use a myriad of tactics—offensive and defensive—depending upon the situation. Until the British began using similar tactics after the Battle of Britain, the Germans profited handsomely from these superior techniques.

American pilots had additional incentive to rethink their fighting
techniques for the coming war. In the spring of 1941 the eccentric but
brilliant General Claire Chennault, who had been in China since 1937
and knew the Japanese well, began warning his superiors in Washington about the new superfighter just introduced by Japan. Some officers
dismissed Chennault's claims, believing them exaggerated, which they
were to a certain degree. Others, fortunately, took the warnings to
heart. But Chennault was a tactical genius, and when the American
Volunteer Group—the legendary Flying Tigers—began flying in
earnest immediately after Pearl Harbor they were far better prepared
than any other U.S. unit to fight the fearsome Zero. The Flying Tigers,
admittedly an elite unit, compiled a respectable record against Japanese aircraft of all types, including the Zero and Oscar. The difficulty
of Chennault's achievement was illustrated during the first weeks of
war when Zeros pounded U.S. and Allied squadrons in the Philippines,
Malaya, and the East Indies. Some of these squadrons were equipped
with obsolescent aircraft. Others were simply not prepared and attempted to face the Zero with defective tactics. In any case the Japanese cut them to ribbons.

After these debacles U.S. officers were more ready to listen to Chennault. Commanders quickly circulated a document prepared by Chennault's intelligence personnel outlining the lessons learned by the Flying Tigers, which flew the early-model P-40B, the least capable of the
P-40s, while fighting Japanese fighters:

Concerning the P-40 and Zero the Universal rules are: 1. Take
advantage of the sun and clouds whenever possible. *Keep Looking
Around*. Never remain intent on a target, a flight of the enemy, or even
one part of the sky for very long. Danger might be coming from any
direction. Take one last look before making an attack, and take another
good look as you break away. If possible, also take a good look around
just before you come within firing range of your target. Basic tactics
adopted with P-40s against Japanese fighters of superior
maneuverability: 1.) *Never Use Climbing Maneuvers* unless you have
excess speed from a dive because the Jap plane can outclimb you. 2.)
Use the P-40's best characteristics; namely—speed, diving and fire
power (head-on runs). Never use maneuverability. Avoid aerobatics
because the Jap planes can do them faster and in much less space.
Never Dogfight Them. 3.) Altitude is good life insurance. If the enemy
has two or three thousand feet altitude advantage on you, turn at right
angles to his course, or even directly away from him and avoid him
until you have enough distance to climb safely at least to his altitude.

Climbing straight up into an enemy formation at 150 MPH is almost a sure way to lose pilots and equipment. 4.) If you have to bail out while the enemy is in the vicinity, wait as long as possible before opening your chute, because if a Jap sees you, he will machine-gun you. 5.) Be patient; use the clouds and sun, and wait until you have an altitude advantage before attacking. If you have to dive away from the attack, it will take you twenty minutes to get back into it again. If you have an initial altitude advantage, you can dive, fire and climb again and repeat at very close intervals, thus doing more damage.

In a nutshell Chennault's officers described the techniques used to destroy Japan's fighter forces in the Pacific. (The Flying Tigers were also early converts to the two-plane unit.)

By the start of the war the two-plane element and finger-four were already used in many U.S. fighter units. The British were having second thoughts about the Vic, passing along information to the Americans. Brilliant fighter tactician John Thach of the *Enterprise* fighter group was one of America's native-born fliers to work out an alternative to late 1930s formations that were proving inadequate to war in the 1940s. After the war Thach gave credit to Chennault's warning for prodding him and his comrades to come up with superior formations to even the playing field against the formidable Zero:

It was in the spring of 1941 that we received an intelligence report of great significance. The report described a new Japanese aircraft, a fighter, that performed far better than anything we had. Some of our pilots just didn't believe it and said, "This can't be. It is a gross exaggeration." . . . I felt we should give it some credence because it sounded like a fighter pilot who knew what he was talking about. As it turned out, this Japanese plane did have a climb of about three thousand feet per minute. It could turn inside of anything and it did have a lot more speed than we did, even carrying more gasoline. This was the Zero. I decided we had better do something about this airplane. . . . But without that intelligence report that was said to have come out of China, I think we would have gone right along fat, dumb, and happy, and eventually run into the Zero and not had nearly the success we did have. We would have been far worse off. In fact, we would have been in far worse shape in the early battles of the war.

Once American units converted to the two-plane element and the finger four they became the most dedicated adherents of structured formations in preparation for combat and continually stressed the importance of fighting in a unit. The unit varied in size depending upon the type of mission and whether it was preparing for a fight or going to the attack, but at minimum the doctrine of the two-plane element became something like a mantra, passed on throughout every unit in every service in the U.S. air arm in all theaters.

There was no single type of fighter formation followed by every squadron in every service, although the pair was the basic component in all of them. Beyond that there were many variations. Some squadrons later in the war replaced the finger-four with a diamond-like formation. Some squadrons, especially if numbers were short, flew in formations that were not models of geometric precision. Unless a long way from the enemy, formations were not always static. No formation wanted to be jumped by attackers, and so scanning the sky was everyone's duty. Particularly when clouds or the position of the sun became factors, it was possible, although not likely, for a large enemy group to get quite close prior to being spotted. Therefore if a squadron had up four flights together, the last might periodically weave across the sky as a rear guard for ambush. (If the rear flight was jumped it would dive toward the front of the formation while the lead flight turned to support, putting the attackers in a tricky situation.) Some flights delegated this duty to the two rear aircraft, as recalled by Robert Croft: "In the flight of four your third and fourth men would weave back and forth behind the first two. The pilot in the third slot was always your second senior pilot, the first was senior. You scissored back and forth all the time. The elements were not always in alignment: sometimes slightly below, sometimes above, sometimes off to the side." Yet despite the variations a U.S. squadron formation might well have looked like that described during the war by Elliot Summer of the famous 5th USAAF 475th Fighter Group. Summer joined that unit in fall 1943 and described a mature and battle-tested sixteen-plane formation that would have closely resembled many Allied units across the South Pacific:

> The squadron consists of four flights, Red, White, Blue, and Green, flying in a diamond formation. White flight flies on the right flank slightly below and behind Red flight. Blue flies left flank above Red and behind White. Green flight flies the lid directly behind Red. The altitude difference between the low flight and top flight is not over 1,500 feet. The space between flanks is about three-quarters of a mile. This provides for maximum visibility and protection. When attacked, Red and White provide mutual protection, as do Blue and Green.

Especially interesting testimony concerning American formation flying and combat tactics came from Fifth Air Force. In early 1944 with many new pilots coming off the assembly line Fifth Fighter Command decided that it would be a good aid for advanced combat training to gather reports concerning successful tactics or possibly fatal mistakes from the men they considered best informed. The Americans writing these reports were all extremely competent tacticians and included some of the most successful fighter pilots in the Pacific theater. Contributions came from top aces and masters of their craft such as Richard Bong, Gerald Johnson, Thomas McGuire, Robert DeHaven, Cyril Homer and Charles MacDonald. Other pilots with lesser "scores" but with a reputation for good sense and leadership were also included. Published during the 1970s as a paperback book, the document, in my estimation, is one of the best looks under the skin of air combat produced during World War II.

In the 5th USAAF collection, I do not think a single contributor failed to stress the importance of keeping an appropriate formation depending upon mission and the imperative of keeping the two-plane element together as long as possible during combat. For instance, Captain Allen Hill of 8th Fighter Group wrote, "A two ship element is five times as powerful as two single airplanes flying alone, and ten times safer." Gerald Johnson of 49th Fighter Group in his long and interesting report made a list of "musts" for both offensive and defensive action: On both lists were the recommendation of "Maintain elements at all costs." Colonel Charles MacDonald, the brilliant if eccentric leader of the 475th Fighter Group, made the point using, I am sure, an element of hyperbole, "The main reason we beat the [enemy] is because we work as a team, using the good qualities of our planes and keeping him from using the good qualities of his own. I think if the Nip had P-38s and we had Zeros, we could still beat him because the average American pilot is a good team worker and is always aggressive."

Ralph Easterling, also of Fifth Air Force, reflected on these matters many years after the war and emphasized the importance of tight organization. As he noted, it was necessary not only to attack the foe but also to keep one's own units from creating self-inflicted chaos:

You must realize that each encounter in air-to-air combat was different. Most of your missions did not include combat with enemy aircraft. When it did happen it was fast and never duplicated itself. That's why we stayed with our basic formations because they were sound and versatile: stay with your flight if possible and your two-plane element if

at all possible. You did do some maneuvering but you usually kept your
cockpit level and speed up. That was one good way to avoid getting hit
by fire from one of your own planes too or hitting one of your own.
Friendly fire is part of war—that's why recognition was so vital. We
were trained to recognize within one-thirty-second of a second. People
don't believe it but it was true. You had to move fast in that
environment and you sure didn't want to fire at your own aircraft.

The stress put on organized formation and a handy wingman was
hardly a 5th USAAF exclusive. As noted, it was USN doctrine before
hostilities and appeared at Guadalcanal. Joe Foss claimed that wingmen saved his life twice. One was the sort of freak accident that
claimed more lives than we shall ever know:

You bet it was important to keep wingmen together. I was fortunate in
having a wingman that stayed by me. And others would hang in with
you, too. If you lost your wing in a dogfight you hooked up with
someone: you didn't ever head off alone. Boot [Thomas Furlow, cited
several times—EB] started off with me. If he got separated someone else
would be with me in a flash if they saw just one plane. I'd do the same
thing myself. One time my oxygen mask came unhooked and I passed
out in the dang plane. I remember it like yesterday. I was sitting in a big
chair totally relaxed and listening to the radio, and then I started
waking up because somebody was yelling "Pull out! Pull out!": that
was Gregg Loesch. He followed me right down, he was flying wing
with me as I'm headed down after I'd let go of the controls and he
could see what was wrong. I was laying back or hunched over. When I
realized what was happening I pulled out right on the side of the hill
there on Guadalcanal, right on the side of the mountain, and he pulled
up right with me. We went right into the clouds and as I was rolling my
eyes around trying to focus on the instruments we pop out again and
both of us were close and here's a Zero in front of us. I was a little
closer and got him: and Gregg said, "After all that work you get the
Zero, I don't get a shot." That was one of the easiest ones I got: The
guy just floated by, he didn't know we were there, and didn't have any
idea we were down there. That was an episode where without my wing-
right there I would have been splattered all over Guadalcanal.

In another instance, Foss, flying over Guadalcanal, received some
crucial information from the ground, which, with the help of
squadronmates, saved the day:

Radio communication were vital to our tactics. When I was shot up Joe Renner was on the ground. He said, "There's a plane up there that's smoking, on fire." Of course everybody that was within radio range kicked their plane around and looked for fire. No one called me to tell me that I was smoking. I look back and found out it was me. On the ground the guy is yelling for me to bail out. I was thinking maybe I should. So I pull up and get the canopy open getting ready to bail. Then I look up and see these two Zeros, one of them just heading for me. I dropped right back into the cockpit and hooked up again, and yelled, "Greg, Ruddy," and the two Zeros made a run on me and they really powdered me good. I was going away from them and losing altitude. Then the two Zeros pulled up right in front of Greg Loesch and Rudy Ruddell and they just picked them off—poing, poing. I just went peacefully down and made a dead-stick landing.

From the American point of view it was fortunate that tactical changes enhanced the few advantages possessed by the first-generation U.S. fighters such as the P-40 and Wildcat. Better armed and more rugged than the Zero, both aircraft, particularly the P-40, had a good rate of roll. They could, in other words, change direction quickly, particularly at high speeds. This allowed a variety of two- and four-plane maneuvers intended to lead a Japanese fighter attacking one plane of the element into the guns of his wingman. The variations on the theme were endless, but the most famous was first developed by famous USN pilots and tacticians John Thach, Butch O'Hare, and James Flatley in the summer of 1941 in response to the ominous warnings coming from Chennault. Thach and comrades demonstrated the new tactic with deadly effect during the Battle of Midway, after which its fame spread instantly. The Thach weave is still part of the fighter pilot's playbook and can be seen as representative of the type of defensive tactic used by American pilots desperate to compensate for the Zero's superiority in maneuver.

In a classic Thach weave a two-plane section separated slightly wider than the full turning radius of the plane (in the case of Thach's Wildcat, about 1,000 feet). The two wingmen watched each other's tail. If an attacker was seen the spotting wingman turned sharply toward his partner. Understanding the meaning of the move, the wingman under attack likewise turned sharply toward his comrade. The abrupt turn made an accurate shot by the Zero almost impossible. If the attacker followed the fleeing Wildcat, hoping to turn inside his quarry and regain a good shooting position, he ran directly into a frontal attack by the second Wildcat. Note that an aggressive American pilot welcomed a frontal, or head-on, attack against a Zero. Although the Zero's twin cannons were dangerous, the Japanese aircraft was too fragile to stand up to six .50-caliber machine guns firing at point-blank range. If both planes hit their quarry, the engine would be the likely target, not the cockpit. Because Zeros burned easily, it was a bad position for a Japanese pilot. If the Wildcat missed the attacking plane, both American planes would roll again soon after they passed each other, setting up an identical maneuver in the opposite direction. Often the victim of the engagement would be a another Zero that began following the second Wildcat. Even if no Japanese aircraft were harmed, the Wildcats stood an excellent chance of weaving through a hazardous position and, when the time was right, disengaging. At that point they had the option of going home or seeking another fight under better circumstances. The same technique could be used with a four-plane flight, with the individual two-plane elements weaving in tandem, doubling the chance of a Japanese attacker being struck.

Frequently in war one factor interacts with another and multiplies the favorable or harmful nature of the initial factor. As we have just seen, tactical innovation amplified the few but important areas of technical superiority possessed early in the war by U.S. fighters over the Zero. Second-generation U.S. fighters had different qualities—excellent speed and good high-altitude performance perfectly suited to the formation tactics devised by American pilots in 1942. In addition, all could outturn and outroll a Zero and Oscar at high speeds. (The Corsair had an especially good roll rate for such a fast aircraft.)

The areas of U.S. technical superiority in individual fighters were amplified by U.S. superiority in two vital support technologies: onboard radios and ground-based radar. The radios carried by World War II fighters were heavy and vulnerable to damage or breakdown. Nevertheless they were nearly indispensable for battle maneuver based on the two-plane element. Pilots were all trained to use visual cues and flew close enough to see them. Because of breakdown, every experienced pilot flew several missions without a radio. Yet the whole point of the new tactical formations was to allow coordinated maneuver not only prior to engagement but also during battle itself. Pilots flying in a standard finger-four formation were scanning every possible angle of the sky over and over. Regularly looking for a visual cue from the flight leader was wasteful. More importantly it was essential that everyone be able to hear simultaneously the call of "bogeys at nine o'clock high." (Some radio terminology would be helpful. Pilots developed a remarkably effective shorthand to describe the location of an object sighted in their three-dimensional realm. When flying in formation they used the clock as the horizontal reference. For instance a target at three o'clock was directly to the right. The terms "low" and "high" meant simply that the object was above or below the flight. Thus the message "bandits at twelve o'clock low" meant that enemy aircraft were directly ahead and below the flight. The friendly flight, therefore, is in ideal attack position. Conversely the message "bogeys, six o'clock high" meant that enemy fighters are above the flight and to its rear. The flight is in serious danger and, if properly led, would react instantly. Because surviving was far more important than killing to sane pilots, the term "six" became an all-purpose description for the zone behind an aircraft. (In theory an important difference existed between the terms "bogie" and "bandit." The latter was an identified enemy aircraft while the former was an aircraft of unknown origin. In practice in the South Pacific the terms became intermingled.)

As well illustrated by the examples above, during melees pilots routinely used their radios for defense and attack. A Thach weave or other defensive maneuver was best initiated by a radio command. If a pilot received a message from his wingman to "break right" he would put his fighter into a violent, abrupt defensive turn to the right whether he saw an attacker or not. If a pilot detected an attacker moving toward him from the rear, he told his wingman to "clear my six." If his wingman responded immediately and a bit of time remained, the pair might proceed to set a trap for the attacker by crossing each other's path in a "scissors." A second cousin to the Thatch weave (and because simpler, probably more widely used), a scissors (which had dozens of variations) went into operation when a defender made a quick change in direction toward his wingman, which would hopefully throw off the enemy's aim. Unlike a weave, in the scissors the defender banked in the direction of his wingman but at a much lower angle, trying to keep up speed. If the wingman was close enough he would be turning toward the attacker and try to close upon the attacker's rear quarter. The attacker had to break off or risk imminent attack himself. It was not uncommon for others to get involved in the scissors. At some point one side would try to break off. In addition, as I shall examine, any formation could easily fall apart during battle. As no one liked to fly alone in World War II skies (the era of the World War I lone wolf was long gone), pilots would use their radio to try to find comrades in such situations. With luck the unit or flight might re-form. For all of these reasons and more, radios were a tremendous help before, during, and after battle.

Radios of all types were a new technology and vulnerable to damage from the terrible climate in the theater. Furthermore they were vulnerable to pilot error, as were so many other factors. Robert DeHaven recalled some of the difficulties of air-to-air communications over New Guinea skies:

Communications were very important but they had to be used wisely and that was not always the case. When you tried to gain an element of surprise you maintained a strict radio silence. If, on the other hand, you were on the deck and running for home, balls to the wall on power, and feeling every second things were getting rougher, then the conversation got very pointed and very pleading: "Where are you guys? They're blasting my ass. Are there enough enemy for all of us?" There were some great comments depending on the situation. However, communications were so vital there was a dedicated comm link so everyone had their chance to talk if necessary. But it was vital to use good radio discipline and present a message clearly. There was nothing more disconcerting when flying a Thach weave than to hear someone over the radio yell "Zeros" without telling you where they were. You and rest of the flight start looking around all over. Such mistakes did not aid a unit in combat.

There were technical problems also. Probably the most aggravating and most debilitating condition that could take place was a stuck microphone button somewhere in the flight. That created an open circuit that only one man can use, but he didn't know anything was wrong. Nobody else can get into the flight circuit. So you think you're still in communication but you're not. You've simply got an open frequency that is spoiling everyone else's ability to talk or to talk to each other. In other words one pilot has inadvertently screwed the whole communication net of the whole flight. And that happened. So we had good reason to learn all of the standard hand signals and messages sent by waggling wings and so forth. And the radio mikes were uncomfortable. We got these little round blisters, about three-quarters of an inch in diameter on our neck on one side of your larynx. When you built up enough moisture and salinity you'd get a burn where they were located on either side of your throat. It looked like Dracula had been with us. Eventually this was replaced by the much more comfortable facemask, which enabled you to get ambient air, which was fairly cool at most altitudes. We stopped using throat mikes in late '43. The people in ETO [European Theater of Operations] never used them as far as I know: they had VHF and mask combination. Their gear was significantly better than ours. The Pacific was at the bottom of the list except when it came to Bully Beef. We got top billing for that.

Japanese technicians skilled at repairing radio sets were in short supply. It is common to see photos of Zeros flying from Rabaul without a radio mast at all. Frequently the *shotai* leader would have a radio for communications with base. Plane-to-plane, however, the pilots relied on traditional visual cues. It would have been a rare *shotai* that would have had three working radios. U.S. after-action reports, even those written early in the war, often noted very poor teamwork on the part of Japanese fighters. These reports were unquestionably accurate and often reflected the fact that many Japanese pilots were using World War I communications in 1942 and 1943. Poor plane-to-plane communications undoubtedly hurt imperial forces badly in the long run. It might also help explain the unusual Japanese approach toward fighting formations.

Japanese formations above the level of the *shotai* mystified American pilots during the war and remain difficult to explain. If there was any structured formation designed for aircraft to support one another, American pilots could not recognize it. In after-action reports from all parts of the South Pacific throughout the study period Allied pilots described Japanese units as "gaggles" of birds or "swarms of bees." Regularly American pilots would see Japanese aircraft doing various aerobatic maneuvers or engaging in mock combat. A typical description was written during the war by William Gardner, an ace with the 5th USAAF 8th Fighter Group, "My first contacts with the enemy were in the latter part of 1943. The Jap fighter formations were loose and could be recognized in the distance as a swarm of flies. Many of the planes would flip momentarily on their backs for a good look underneath, and others would be rolling."

If the situation was right such lack of order proved no obvious handicap. Elite Japanese pilots were known for becoming so closely attuned to the behavior of their experienced wingmen that they instinctively acted in concert. Such a situation would require tremendous training and proved impossible to sustain as attrition took its toll. Yet early in the war the Japanese "flying circus" tactics, as Robert DeHaven called them, made for some very tense moments. Roger Haberman reflected on the opponents he met at Cactus:

The Japanese pilots were good. When we went out for a fight, what I called a "go-around," we could tell immediately if there were army or navy pilots. You could tell immediately if they were navy because they'd press more, more persistent. I couldn't describe a tactic they used. They came at you like a swarm. They were all over you, absolutely all over. I never could discern a pattern in their attacks. That was a big difference. We'd stay together if possible. If there was a single enemy, even if you had the drop on him, you didn't go after him because you'd get creamed by someone else.

Robert DeHaven also had respect for enemy formations regardless of the seeming chaos:

It was true they flew in gaggles. I don't think that it was necessarily because of poor pilots, although some were obviously not well trained. In 1943 we had some men who could have used more training also. I think they were trying to take advantage of known capability of their aircraft. Japanese planes were uniformly more maneuverable than ours. So they would try to goad us, try to break up our formations so they could attack bombers if we were on escort, the most likely mission to cause a major engagement. They would dart in and dart out. They would use random maneuvers. Any American who tried to follow could be in immediate trouble. . . . And the enemy's good men could fly. The fighters at Lae had lost many of their top people when I arrived, but they were still capable of doing a dance of death against anyone not watchful. The P-39s were at a terrible disadvantage. That was shameful, no real contest.

No doubt American opinion of Japanese units reflected a degree of fortune. A newly arrived and rebuilt unit at Rabaul might well contain some excellent pilots. It would also be possible for an American unit to encounter Japanese replacements that were not ready for the daunting task at hand. Many contemporary reports expressed something close to contempt when describing the foe. In early August two flights of 13th USAAF P-40s and a pair of Marine Corsairs tangled with a larger force of Zeros toward the hard-fought campaign for Munda Point. One of the army pilots, Lieutenant Lucien Shuler, claimed multiple victories in a confused melee. According to the after-action report, "Lt. Shuler stated that the quality of the Jap pilots was the poorest of any he had ever encountered. In many instances they took no evasive action when under fire, and flew as though completely bewildered. All their passes were made singly, with no semblance of any formation. Their groups scattered in all directions when the P-40s attacked." 5th USAAF P-38 pilot Perry Dahl also had a very low opinion of Japanese tactics:

In my judgment the Japanese lost the air battle from a purely strategic view because they employed poor tactics. I think they had good pilots, I think they had good equipment, but their tactics were deplorable.
You'd be flying and you'd see something in the distance. I couldn't tell whether it was a flight of Zeroes or a flock of buzzards. And you would go in there, dive through their formation and you'd scatter them to the winds. We never broke down to less than an element and of course we criss-crossed each other's tails. But you could fly through a hundred of those dang guys and keep each other clear and come through unscathed. You could cut one out of the herd sometimes. But the Zeros didn't have anything like that. They didn't seem to keep their wingmen. They felt that the name of the game was to get into a one-on-one dogfight, and we didn't play their game. We maintained our two aircraft element integrity.

Ralph Easterling believed their methods of combat sometimes reflected factors not directly related to battle:

Radios could be invaluable. On the P-40 we had a radio behind the pilot [and] some armor plating. Under the pilot was armor and there was a little half-inch sheetmetal coming up the side. The Japanese radio equipment to the best we could tell was much lighter and not protected, and their pilots had no protection to gain a weight advantage. They played to their strength, which was nimbleness. Many Japanese pilots didn't wear parachutes. That was not an option in American service—you wore them, period. Being without a parachute would be like flying barefooted.
    We were more businesslike. It wasn't glory, it was a job. I guess we were more interested in killing rather than dying. Their intent in going into battle was quite different than ours. They would do things that struck us as nuts. And, of course, their aircraft ended up doing mass suicide attacks. Many people now can't really understand that or grasp it. I can't say that many of us did at the time either.

Whatever reason the Japanese had for organizing their units into incoherent flocks, it led nowhere. It seems likely that one reason was that their air-to-air communications capability was so poor. The one advantage in flying in units that appeared chaotic is that it allowed Japanese units to observe the entire sky. As I examine just below, it was always bad to be caught in an unfavorable tactical situation, but it was infinitely worse if the enemy was very close when first sighted. By rolling and gyrating, Japanese fighter units probably sighted large

Allied units (large meaning squadron-size and larger) in most cases. Once sighted the Japanese fighters, using conventional hand and wing signals, could ready for the defense or prepare for an attack. Yet the Japanese were often one step behind the game. In many instances relatively small Allied units could scatter a larger Japanese assembly. Likewise numerical and tactical advantage rarely yielded great results for the Japanese. C. L. Jones, who met the Japanese in 1942 over Moresby when imperial forces were ascendant, later had occasion to reflect on this situation:

> I met the great Japanese ace Saburo Sakai a few years back in Fredericksburg, Texas. He was a wonderful, nice guy. He said when they were attacking us out of Lae they took the radios out of the Zeros to keep them light. They took everything out. Can you imagine that? As a fighter pilot I can assure you that is stupid. Now we always were concerned about weight. But giving up radios? Sometimes ours didn't work, either, but it was worth the bother. An unreliable radio was much better than no radio. Those guys were awfully good, but I can see why they didn't last long in combat.

Whatever the reason for creating the "gaggle," many Japanese units attempted to shift to the U.S. system of formation-flying in 1944. This was particularly apparent over the Philippines. However, the move was far too late. A Japanese formation would hold for a moment and fall apart as soon as battle commenced. In this period of the war Japanese pilot quality had declined dramatically, and a tactic that perhaps should have been implemented in 1942 was ineffective. Interesting testimony on this matter comes from Lieutenant Kunio Iwashita, who was interrogated immediately after the war. Involved in much late-war fighting, he ended the war as a test pilot. According to Kunio, many in the imperial forces realized the superiority of the Allied system but did not have the human resources to counter it: "We needed a long range high altitude fighter very much. I think that the P-38 was very good as it shot down Japanese fighters very easily. We admired the American fighter flying formations. We used bicycles for ground training in some cases as this helped in the development of formation flying. But our young pilots could not fly these formations. How to train these pilots for this type of flying is an important question."

I should point out that at the time Iwashita was fighting Americans over the Philippines the Japanese pilot-training program was a shambles. Earlier in the war, when U.S. forces were receiving green replacements, the finger-four and stress on the two-plane element was a boon.

Whenever possible a rookie flew wing with a veteran. Often this arrangement went to living quarters. A four-man tent might have three replacements and one veteran. The experienced man was expected to pass on the details that could make the difference between success and calamity. Under most circumstances the veterans were glad to comply. Not only were they helping America to prevail in battle; replacements usually meant that some of the veterans would be rotated home.

The Japanese problem went deeper even than poor formations. In addition to short-range radio communications, Allied fighters carried long-range sets that put them in touch with ground controllers back at base. In practice this added the benefits of radar, which was not carried by World War II fighters, to the flight. As illustrated dramatically during the Battle of Britain, radar rendered extraordinary advantages to defenders. Radar installations available in the Southwest Pacific were not as powerful as the large, permanent stations used by the British in 1940. Yet thanks to massive research and development in Britain and the United States, radar evolved at breakneck speed during World War II. By Pearl Harbor major U.S. warships, particularly carriers, were fitted with air-search radar. In the summer of 1942 Americans constructed an eighty-ton radar installation in northern Australia. As time passed the Americans built large radar bases throughout the Pacific, capable of handling extended operations, navigation, ferry flights, and training. At the time of the crisis in New Guinea and Guadalcanal, however, Allied units had to do with small Australian radar sets and the first portable U.S. models. Small radar sets were delicate and required skilled operators. Weighing about 3,000 pounds, they and their operators fit into air transports. Much larger sets were installed in both theaters very early in the campaign. Radar was operating at Henderson before U.S. aircraft were there. The range of these small sets was about 150 miles. By themselves the radar stations would have been much less valuable than they proved. They were supported, however, by the famous Australian Coast Watchers, who manned 140 outposts by midwar.

Radar was always important to U.S. fighter operations, but it was most useful when the Allies were on the defensive. Its greatest advantage was that it allowed ground controllers to vector fighter groups toward targets. In practice, fighter units, particularly at Cactus, were often first alerted by signals from the Coast Watchers. This enabled squadrons to prepare for battle. The radar available was crude by later standards, yet it gave defenders the range and bearing of attackers and, by gauging how soon the contacts appeared on the sets, a rough idea of altitude. Fighter squadrons could then scramble and be guided to the target by ground controllers. (I do not wish here to evaluate grand tactics of the carrier engagement, but vectoring fighters during a naval engagement was a difficult task simply because the carriers—which fighters defended—were on the move, making coordination a challenge. Much work was involved to refine the technique at sea.) This advantage was crucial at Guadalcanal because it allowed the slow-climbing Wildcats to reach attack position in time to intercept. As it was, because Bettys were very fast at high altitude, the Allies had little room for error. Regardless of the problems with the technology, the U.S. defense of Guadalcanal would have been impossible without radar. The only alternative would have been to fly a standing patrol in a likely place at a likely time. If not judged correctly, such an intercept would fail. Worse yet many aircraft would have been caught on the ground or jumped by Zeros on the way up or on the way down to refuel.

Initially the intelligence network was of less value at Moresby, as the Owen Stanley Mountains blocked long-range acquisition. Australian P-40s required good fortune to reach equal altitude before engaging the enemy. American P-39s, with a terrible rate of climb, simply could not reach attack altitude. Much to the frustration of the pilots, for several weeks it was standard practice for P-39s to take off and flee seaward, earning them an uncomplimentary title—the "fishing fleet." When they had crawled to adequate altitude they would turn back, usually to find the skies empty of Japanese raiders. Sometimes, however, they met high-flying Zeros, with potentially terrible results. However, once the Australians pushed the Japanese over the Owen Stanleys and the Allies set up at Dobodura, the situation changed. Radar sets at Dobodura could cover approaches to Moresby as well as Japanese attacks on Allied forces besieging Buna. Later, in the Solomons, radar stations set up immediately upon landing proved invaluable in thwarting Japanese air attacks against landings at New Georgia and Bougainville.

It would be simplistic to assume that a few dozen radar sets held the fort for the Allies; instead they created a surprisingly elaborate air communications network that kept track of all friendly flights in a wide area. A hostile unit, naturally, was immediately vulnerable to interception. Howard Redmond was part of the 49th Fighter Control Center and recalled the importance and complexity of the operation:

The controller was an officer who would vector fighters to a target. I was a noncom and my job was to keep track of the friendly planes coming in and out of the area. So when a target appeared on the plotting board, which came in from the Signal Corps radar that worked with us, then the controllers would ask those of us tracking friendly movement if we had anything coming in. If we did, fine, if we didn't it might be enemy. We'd get constant reports of flights and destinations. A C-47 was taking off at Nadzab and going to Dobodura. If we couldn't identify it and the pilot didn't have his IFF on [Identification Friend or Foe, a simple electronic beacon aboard an aircraft that indicated whether another aircraft was friendly; it was an imperfect technology at the time but is now an essential part of air operations.—EB], they'd send up a flight of fighters real fast to investigate. The controller's job was to scramble fighters, vector them, or handle anyone that needed help. The controller in theory also controlled the flak [antiaircraft—EB]. If it was definitely enemy he'd instruct the flak to fire at will. I kept track of our planes to help the controller identify something in the sector.

The Japanese communications network was crude in comparison, although it often worked adequately. The Japanese did not need Coast Watchers. There were dozens of islands in the Solomons and countless places along the coasts of New Guinea and the Bismarcks to place observation posts. Japanese land radios were excellent, so a manual sighting could be relayed quickly to a base likely under attack. Because of the relative paucity of targets in the South Pacific, it did not take much guesswork to determine which base or facility was going to receive a visit from Allied aircraft. In addition, the larger bases had radar, though not very reliable and in short supply. It had a range of about 150 kilometers, shorter than the Allied technology. So a large raid, particularly if it included heavy bombers flying at medium altitudes, would not come as a surprise. The big problem with the Japanese system was the lack of a control apparatus. Because airborne radios were so poor, vectoring was difficult, to say the least. Instead the Japanese had to rely on standing defensive patrols that, if fortunate, were in the right place. Zeros and Oscars could stay in the air a long time, but the crude warning system broke down, and it was possible that patrolling fighters would be caught on the ground or at low elevation when forced to refuel. Against low-level attacks the Japanese, as we shall see, often found themselves in the direst straits.

Maneuver and Melee

Explaining the nature of World War II air combat is complex and carries a touch of irony, as the numbers were puny in light of the staggering scope of World War II. In the South Pacific it was a rare day if 100 aircraft were involved in an engagement. Usually it was half that number or less. Furthermore the combatants could usually spot one another at some point during the encounter. Because of the weaponry involved combat took place at close range, usually inside 300 yards. Yet the physical record of the course of an air battle does not exist outside a sketchy outline on a printed page, usually prepared by an intelligence officer well after battle. Because of the great speeds involved, an air battle—almost always brief—usually spread out over a large area. Anyone who has examined the complicated charts of a naval battle, which took place at a snail's pace compared to an air showdown, and only on two dimensions, can imagine the impossibility of graphically representing a running battle after the fact based on combat reports. More so than any form of combat, battle in the air defied the ability of the camera to capture it. We have thousands of gun-camera shots depicting the moment of death for a fighter or a fleeting portion of an enemy's pass. We also have thousands of photos taken by bombers showing the destruction wrought. Yet we have no film that depicts an aerial action in anything like its entirety. This is no surprise, as existing technology would not allow it. Even so, eyewitnesses to a major engagement never saw more than a fleeting fragment of events around them, even if action was a stone's throw away. Consequently we must rely on contemporary and retrospective accounts of pilots to paint a coherent picture of World War II fighter combat. Reproducing the action in its frightening, deep texture is impossible, yet it is possible to identify factors that shaped battle and essential trends found in a majority of engagements.

Before analyzing battle, I think it is worthwhile to describe the pace of fighter combat in the South Pacific. As just mentioned it was not common for more than fifty planes to do battle in the theater. Although the battles might not have reached the scale sometimes found in Europe (a fifty-plane tangle between fighters would have been a major battle for Europe as well) the pace of combat grew for more than two years, and there were very few lulls in the action. Air warfare, like other forms of battle in World War II, was above all a struggle of attrition. For most of the time between spring 1942 and winter 1943–1944 neither side was completely dominant (until the final weeks), which in itself amplified the element of attrition.

Using figures collected by the army and respected researcher Frank Olynyk, I compiled a list of all of the victory claims made by U.S. fighter pilots flying for Fifth Air Force, Thirteenth Air Force, and the Marine Corps. (Navy figures for the carrier battles have been done by John Lundstrom and, by definition, are dramatic but episodic. The absolute numbers of planes lost in the carrier battles were tiny compared to the land-based struggle. I have squadron totals for the few USN land-based squadrons, but not a breakdown of dates of kill claims, the real information sought. Here again the numbers would not have been large because, with the exception of VF-17's 154 claims, other land-based USN squadrons played a short and secondary role in the South Pacific. I also included army victory claims made by squadrons that joined Thirteenth Air Force prior to its formation in January 1943.) Not wishing to include an examination of events in the Philippines or East Indies in this work, I began the total with March 1, 1942 (the deployment of 5th USAAF squadrons to Darwin), then continued the tabulation through May 1, 1944, when the fallout from the Rabaul battles was complete and the Marine Corps and Thirteenth Air Force ended their part of the air battle. (Fifth Air Force, joined by the Thirteenth, continued active throughout 1944.) I broke down the two years into two-week segments.

The totals I arrived at (leaving a small margin for error) were 1,437 victory claims by pilots of Fifth Air Force, 428 claims from Thirteenth Air Force, and 1,504 from the Marine Corps. I wish to evaluate the overall losses and their causes later, but for the moment keep in mind that firm victory totals for air-to-air combat will never be known for any theater in World War II. Consequently I do not intend to guarantee the numbers of the claims themselves, yet they serve as an excellent indicator of violence. A two-week period in which 200 Japanese kills were claimed was most probably more violent than one in which thirty kills were claimed. As one would expect, the most violent periods almost always coincided with major military moves. Guadalcanal was a fierce fight. So was each Allied move up the Solomons. Every MacArthur-ordered advance by Australian and U.S. troops up the New Guinea coast was preceded by a major air offensive from Fifth Air Force. And in considering the ferocity of fighting over Guadalcanal, New Georgia, Bougainville, and Rabaul it makes sense that more fighting took place in the Solomons than over New Guinea. (Personally I was surprised the numbers were so close.) These figures are for fighter victory claims only and do not include aircraft damaged, "probable" kills, and planes downed by bomber gunners, antiaircraft, and noncombat factors. Many of the Japanese aircraft claimed by American pilots were bombers and reconnaissance aircraft, but probably three-quarters were fighters.

Two points stand out vividly from the figures tabulated. First is the overall escalation of air combat in the South Pacific. In the first two-week period (beginning March 1, 1942) Fifth Air Force claimed five victories (the other two forces were not in action at all). The highest two-week total between March and August 1942 was twenty-four, and normally the number was closer to ten. When the Guadalcanal campaign began the numbers soared. Marine figures were often over sixty and hit 112 in the last two weeks of October 1942. From the Allied side there were frequent lulls in the action. For instance until the Japanese temporarily ceased attacks on Guadalcanal in mid-November 1942, Fifth Air Force recorded only four claims in two and a half months. Conversely during the Buna campaign and for February-March 1943 Fifth Air Force was very busy, whereas the Solomons were quiet. Second, during two years of combat a general lull throughout the theater was rare. If the Solomons were not hot then New Guinea was, and vice versa. In June, with the Japanese under pressure to prepare for the New Georgia operation (some of their last major air offensives of the war took place during this period) Fifth Air Force received its last time-out. After mid-1943 both theaters were usually intensely contested. To illustrate the relative increase of combat: The highest victory total claimed by American pilots during the Guadalcanal campaign (112) was during the second half of October 1942. No other two-week period during Guadalcanal surpassed 112, and most were far less. A year later figures soared. The most violent two-week period (263 claimed victories) was December 1–15, 1943, with Fifth Air Force busy in the Cape Gloucester area and Wewak and forces in the Solomons attacking Rabaul.

Thus the longer the war went on, the greater the number and size of battles. No matter what the actual victory figures were, this was ominous for imperial air forces because they were less able to replace pilots and, more importantly, planes unless they stripped other Pacific areas of strength (which they did). The Japanese also received little rest after Guadalcanal. There were two-week periods between February 1943 and May 1943 when Allied kill claims were puny (for February 15–March 1, 1943, American pilots claimed one victory), yet from the invasion of Guadalcanal until the abandonment of Rabaul and nearby bases the Japanese had to wage a fierce two-front war. And toward the end of 1943 Japanese enemies often attacked the same targets—usually Rabaul—thus eliminating the advantage of interior lines. Prior to this period the JNAF often had to move air units from one threatened sector to another. Japanese army units ultimately faced Fifth Air Force with little support and so suffered immensely.

Another interesting point can be gleaned from the figures. Between April 1, 1942, and January 1, 1943, the three U.S. forces claimed 682 victories. This does not include the 133 Japanese aircraft John Lundstrom claimed fell to USN fighters in the carriers battles of 1942 (including Midway). Thus, even allowing for significant overclaims, the figures suggest that the Japanese suffered serious losses against even first-generation U.S. fighters such as the Wildcat and P-40. Indeed by the time the more powerful and superior second generation began to arrive in force in early 1943 Japan was already on the defensive. However inferior early U.S. aircraft appeared on paper, it was they who blunted the Japanese advance and were beginning to turn the tide prior to the arrival of much better models.

On either side units were in the air often. Sometimes weather kept aircraft grounded, no doubt to the great relief of pilots. On other days small engagements took place in which each side took few or no losses. Yet over the long haul combat between fighters was unavoidable. And in those engagements, although the exact figures will never be clear, hundreds of fighter aircraft on both sides went down due to a number of causes.

The type of mission flown by a fighter unit influenced the odds that it would encounter enemy aircraft. In general fighters flew five types of missions. The most common was the routine patrol (at least in number of missions, if not planes involved). Patrols were routinely small and tried to prevent harassing attacks on air bases and detect enemy reconnaissance. Aircraft on patrol were also on the lookout for enemy naval action. Carriers (Allied and imperial) flew a standing patrol at all times when at sea, searching for submarines and the odd enemy snooper. Occasionally a patrol would intercept an attack. More likely it would stumble upon enemy reconnaissance or harass an enemy submarine. The fighter patrol system was usually kept close to base, as other long-range aircraft were better suited for reconnaissance. The air patrol was thus the equivalent of a standard patrol in land combat. Rarely anything was encountered but patrols were essential nevertheless, as the enemy would be tempted to take advantage of any blindness. Yet much had changed since World War I: Enemy bases in the South Pacific were at least 200 miles apart, and a local patrol was unlikely to encounter the enemy patrol, a staple of combat in the Great War. Most patrols were risky mostly because they produced fatigue and boredom, always dangerous for a fighter pilot.

Occasionally a patrol would run into a fighter sweep, the second type of mission. Typically a quick fight ensued. In the fighter sweep, units would pass over likely targets looking for a fight or, better yet, unwary victims. The Japanese used sweeps at Guadalcanal on occasion to fool U.S. units. Radar could tell that aircraft were on the way but was not good in identifying types at long range. As Japanese bombers began to take unacceptable losses, the JNAF would launch an attack and, well before reaching target, send home the bombers, hoping for a shootout with Cactus Wildcats, which they were confident of winning. This tactic worked on occasion but also led to some stinging defeats. Later Allied units would send fighter units over enemy bases, usually to coordinate at some phase of a bomber attack, hoping to intercept Japanese fighters on the way up or down. Sometimes it worked, but usually it did not. The fighter sweep in Europe was a controversial tactic early in the war but gained favor when it became possible for fighters to jump German interceptors. It became a more effective tactic when fighters developed into devastating bombers in their own right. Often in Europe fighters would cover fighter-bombers and make Luftwaffe air bases into deathtraps. On occasion the Allies did the same in the Pacific.

There was an asymmetry of combat odds that made sweeps rarely effective in the Pacific. Early in the war Allied units rarely went out of their way to tangle with Zeros; their interest was in attacking bombers. Fighters, after all, by themselves could not threaten Moresby and Cactus. Later that all changed. If sixteen Corsairs swept a Japanese base there was little incentive for imperial aircraft to attack them knowing that the kill ratio was not likely to favor the defense and, if it did, the overall combat punch of the enemy would be reduced little. Yet a combat sweep picked up by enemy observation posts or radar might lead an aggressive commander to take off and attempt an ambush. There were no safe missions in World War II.

The third mission (rare but likely to lead to engagement) was troopship defense or attack. During every amphibious landing made after February 1942 in the South Pacific, enemy aircraft attempted to attack shipping. Merchant and troop ships were the best targets, but warships presented a great lure for any bomber formation. Fighters could not accomplish this mission alone, but as shown by the February 1942 catastrophe that befell Japanese Bettys, tactical and strategic bombers needed fighter protection. The Allies attacked Japanese invasion convoys aimed at New Guinea in early 1942 with indifferent success. They also hit the convoy attacking Milne Bay. Convoy attack became a Japanese specialty because of the general course of operations. Japanese bombers attacked American shipping and troops at Guadalcanal, New Georgia, Bougainville, and every step up the New Guinea ladder. All the bombers had fighter escorts, and some attacks caused the largest air battles in the South Pacific. It is testimony to the arrogance (or desperation) of Japanese planners early in the war that convoys sometimes had very poor fighter protection. At Milne Bay in September 1942 RAAF P-40s smashed Japanese ground forces and never saw a Zero or Betty intended to attack their base of operation, even though it was desperately close to Japanese ground forces. Six months later Fifth Air Force crushed a Japanese troop convoy in the Bismarck Sea, in effect isolating Lae. In that case, however, Zeros were present in large numbers, and a great fighter battle ensued. When U.S. invasion convoys attacked targets in the Solomons and New Guinea, air commanders knew that fighters would be with tactical bombers seeking to bomb shipping.

The fourth type of combat mission was bomber escort, which was likely to bring about fighter engagements. It proved possible—and wise—for early Allied units to avoid contact over Moresby. (The RAAF was less likely to do this, because its fighters climbed faster and its squadrons were led by experienced airmen. Retreat does not come easily to Australian forces of any kind, although had the RAAF pilots been flying P-39s the situation might have been very different.) However, during the Guadalcanal campaign Cactus had two simple jobs: to make things hot for Japanese surface ships bringing men and supplies to the island; and to shoot down Japanese bombers. If the bombers were shot down or, more likely, prevented from delivering their bomb load, Cactus would survive. If Cactus survived, the Japanese troopships were not safe near Guadalcanal and the Japanese army had to rely on pitiful replacements and supplies delivered on inferior vessels like converted destroyers, barges, and small luggers. Everyone within a thousand miles of Guadalcanal understood the equation, and such knowledge explained the fierce fight for the field. The air and naval battles peaked near Guadalcanal in October and November when the Japanese attempted to reinforce their garrison with proper troopship convoys. Substantial imperial fighter cover was employed for both attempts. Once vanquished on Guadalcanal, the Japanese had to face the same equation on battlefields closer to home: Air superiority over Guadalcanal meant American victory there. U.S. bases on Guadalcanal and the nearby Russell Islands doomed New Georgia. With New Georgia in hand, Bougainville was helpless. Once U.S. fighters set up on Torokina, then Rabaul and Kavieng were dead. Simultaneously Fifth Air Force had begun systematically devastating Japanese land bases at Buna, Lae, and Salamaua. The fierce attacks by their bombers, a small number of A-20 attack planes, and later the famous "strafers" began to demolish the Japanese air network in New Guinea and separate it from western bases in New Britain. Knowing that unopposed bomber attack meant the death of every Japanese air base in New Guinea the Japanese attempted to intercept the bombers. It was the obvious necessity to defend one's air base or watch it die that caused most fighter engagements in the South Pacific, and if one wishes to determine the reason for a given fighter clash a bomber was probably involved somewhere.

The fifth mission was direct support of ground troops and ground attack. I will examine this topic in Chapter 7. For the moment it is sufficient to point out that this risky task became more important and extremely common as the war progressed. Because Allied fighters were so much tougher and could carry a greater load, ground-support sorties were far more frequent among Allied fighters than Japanese.

Although no two air battles were the same in the South Pacific I believe they can be broken down into three major components: observation, unit maneuver prior to combat, and melee. Observation was influenced by mission type, pilot skill, and formation. Assuming the typical prebattle observation took place, formation maneuver was largely a matter of coordinating units to prepare for attack or defense. Both of these phases were greatly influenced by the type of mission that both sides were flying. When melee began, two factors immediately came into play. One was the tendency for an air engagement to go from high altitude to low. The other was for chaos to overwhelm order. A well-executed battle that began with trim formations in good battle position at altitudes above 20,000 feet often ended, even if things went well, with aircraft scattered across the sky at low levels and often alone.

It was vital to see the enemy as soon as possible. One disadvantage of long missions and sustained combat was that pilots simply got tired and it was more difficult to stay alert. Yet men on both sides were trained to scan the skies at all times in search of the opposition. Rubbernecking, or simply sweeping your head in constant motion, was an occupational necessity. As I mentioned earlier, the sky in the South Pacific, although almost always dotted with clouds, was unusually clear, allowing visual contact at great distance. Although everyone was expected to keep their eyes open, some pilots had exceptional eyesight or an innate ability to distinguish movement at great distance. Such men were an invaluable asset. Robert DeHaven described initial contact:

> You could see the enemy at quite a distance. You'd first see very tiny dots or spots. Some people were able to see those tiny dots much more quickly and more precisely than most pilots. There were several men in my memory that, before I'd even scanned the sky, could see the contact and identify the type of aircraft. Over the radio you'd hear something like "six bogeys at ten o'clock high." If they were in formation that

meant bombers. If not in formation, which was the unique Japanese way of doing things, it was a gaggle of fighters. A visual contact had a real impact on the squadron. Some wit of the past said "nothing focuses the attention like knowing one is about to be hanged." Seeing the enemy certainly focused the attention. Everyone knew that a fight was near.

C. L. Jones agreed on the importance of seeing the enemy as soon as possible: "The secret of seeing an aircraft was more than eagle eyes, and I thank the lord for a pretty good pair. But you had to know what you were looking for. Frequently it was a tiny glint coming from the sun off the canopy. You can't really see the planes, you see this glint. That takes some experience to pick up. Rookie pilots are looking for planes—experienced ones look for specks of light or tiny flecks against the clouds. That can save your life."

Once visual contact was achieved a fight was not inevitable. If the distance was great enough it was usually possible for one side or the other to flee if the position was bad or there was a great disparity in numbers. In an escort mission, however, it would be difficult for the es-corting side to avoid melee regardless of conditions, because the very reason for being there was to engage fighters going after the bombers. An escort flight did not necessarily have to be within sight of bombers. (Bombers and fighters often took off separately and then ren-dezvoused.) If the flight sighted was on an interception mission de-fenders might feel forced to engage enemy fighters before they found the bombers. If bombers were in view, it was obviously important to strike interceptors prior to their attack. And if one side had a distinct advantage in position and was sighted at relatively close range, it might have been possible to force an engagement. Second-generation U.S. fighters had the edge with superior speed and high-altitude per-formance. Many fights ensued, no doubt, simply because the Allies and Japan were at war and fighters were made to attack the enemy. The challenge was made and accepted.

In any event what normally ensued after contact was an aerial chess match that did much to decide the outcome of the battle. Timidity was not a trait often found among World War II squadron and flight com-manders; intelligence and prudence were prized in leaders. However important aggressiveness was, if it lapsed into rashness men could eas-ily die. Indeed if contact was made and the relative position of one's group poor, the first thing to do was to gain altitude. Robert Rowland, commander of 5th USAAF's 348th Fighter Group, which flew P-47s, emphasized the importance of patience: "Never try to assume the offensive while below and under enemy fighters. Gain an equal or greater altitude by climbing out to one side and then come back into them." Robert DeHaven echoed Rowland: "If your situation looked unfavorable it would have been standard procedure to either change the tactical situation to your favor, or if that was not possible, to disengage and fight another day. Quite commonly the decision not to engage was not criticized in any way. It was simple—in a bad situation the strategy was to survive, and if you were in a bad situation the tactic was don't mix it up." As recalled by C. L. Jones, serious consequences could befall a pilot who makes an overaggressive decision to fight:

All good fighter pilots were aggressive. Some were exceptionally so. My dear friend Bob Faurot was like that. He was one of our really fearless leaders until he was lost. He came three or four months ahead of us. When I came back from combat they assigned me to a fighter replacement unit. I would have to give talks to the new pilots and fly with them. I used to cite my four flight leaders when I first went to the 39th Squadron as examples. Tommy Lynch was our leading ace. He was cold-blooded. I think he was the best fighter pilot in the Pacific. In combat he was calculating. Bob Faurot was a great leader, too. He was a good pilot, the guys really liked him, and he was fearless. But I preferred flying Tommy's wing compared to Bob's because when Faurot saw the enemy he'd say "Tally Ho! There they are, let's get 'em." He'd climb up straight underneath them and try to attack. Now that's risky against a Zero. You want to maneuver and find a good position to begin your attack before closing. You can't just go charging forward. Skill and cunning had to be combined with aggressiveness. A leader should never forget he's responsible for three guys along with himself. You must put the four of you into position to start work. Lynch would do that.

Bob was shot down in the second day of the Battle of the Bismarck Sea. On the second day we lost three P-38s, which was almost unheard of. We lost Bob Faurot, a fine pilot named Hoyt Eason, and another man—all in Bob's flight. I remember that day vividly. We made two sorties, one in the morning and one in the afternoon. It was a bright day, a lot of aircraft fighting and ships below. I'm convinced old Bob just got carried away and took his flight right into the middle of the fight and kept them there in that pack of hounds. He shouldn't have done that—he was much too low and the enemy present in large numbers. Three of them were shot down in no time at all.

I got caught, too. I looked up and saw some P-38s circling high above, and I'm down there in the middle having fired almost all my ammunition and having a fine day of it. I haven't a clue where my wingmen are because this was a huge melee in Pacific standards. I look behind me on the right and left and see three Zeros ready to knock me out of the sky. I remember what I said over the radio because I didn't often use bad language. I looked up and said, "Hey, you goddamn P-38s, come down and help me." Charlie King, the flight leader above, comes on and says, "Jonesie: You didn't say goddamn?" He's laughing and I'm scared to death. Both Charlie and I were Catholics. We didn't use the Lord's name in vain but that day I was in bad shape. I saved myself. I rolled the '38 on its back and went down in a spiral with engines going full throttle. We were about 12,000. I pulled out right above the water and headed for home. I was out of ammo and heading home down on the deck with nobody behind me. And suddenly I see a '38 going in my general direction with one engine smoking. Before I could get to him he splashed into the water, skips once, and boom. I thunder across the water and his tail was sticking up and I saw his number and thought I saw a yellow life vest. I made a 180 turn and fly over the wreckage and call for a PBY rescue. That was Hoyt, one of the three shot down, and a fine fighter pilot. I got off the call, but we never saw him again. That happened often. We were really sad about losing all three of them.

Obviously what constituted a good tactical position prior to battle depended greatly upon mission and type of aircraft. In general, however, both sides sought the advantage in altitude and relative position. (Seizing a position in the sun was always desirable, because the glare could almost blind a pilot being attacked. But because the sun's position rarely corresponded with the mission of the interceptors and fighters and because such formations were large, sun position was a luxury that could not be counted on.) The reason that altitude was of such great importance is worth a brief examination. A staggering array of maneuvers was available to the pilot of a World War II fighter. Each was capable of doing things that would snap the airframe of a civilian aircraft like a matchstick. The problem, from the American point of view, was that Japanese fighters could perform their maneuvers quicker and at a slower speed. This latter attribute was important. A cursory look at aeronautics explains: Viewed from the side, the wings of an airplane, like those of a bird, are curved and tapered on the top, flat underneath. The thrust generated by the propeller creates an apparent wind that strikes the wing. Due to the curvature in the wing, air moving over the top of the wing flows more quickly than that passing underneath. Because of the Bernoulli effect (a concept of fluid dynamics), the faster-moving air on the top creates less pressure than does slower-moving air along the bottom. The disparity in pressure creates lift, which is the counterpart of gravity. When the plane moves through the air it creates friction, or drag. Thrust and drag are also natural counterparts. When flying at a steady speed in perfectly level flight the twin counterforces that govern performance—lift-gravity and thrust-drag—are in equilibrium.

Any maneuver, regardless of how slight, that alters this equilibrium will cost the aircraft either speed or altitude. A plane can exchange altitude for speed by diving; when a plane climbs the opposite takes place. In this case the elevators on the tail move upward, causing the nose to rise. When the angle of the wing relative to its flight path changes (the angle of attack in aviation parlance) the Bernoulli effect is amplified, causing more lift. Drag, however, is also increased, slowing the aircraft down. In a climb, therefore, due to the result of the twin forces of drag and lift, the aircraft rises due to lift but also slows due to drag. Something similar takes place during a turn. When an airplane turns, or banks, the lift generated by the wings is no longer parallel to the ground. The force of gravity, however, still is. Airmen distinguish between actual weight of an aircraft when flying level and "apparent" weight of an aircraft when banking. The tighter the bank, the more the wing drops and the higher the apparent weight. More lift, therefore, is required. The pilot accomplishes this by raising the aircraft's nose, thereby increasing the angle of attack and, hence, lift. The result, however, is that the airplane slows down. In a hard defensive turn, or break, the pilot rolls the wings until they are perpendicular to the ground and pulls back hard on the stick. The result is an abrupt high-speed turn that has saved many pilots' lives. It also bleeds off speed at a tremendous rate. To one degree or another, speed and altitude are the trade-offs during maneuvers.

This had tremendous implications for combat in the Pacific. If a U.S. aircraft, even second-generation models like the P-38 and Corsair, made an attack run on a Japanese fighter and the latter went into an evasive maneuver (e.g., before the attacker achieved firing range or after he missed the initial shot), many American pilots could not resist the temptation to follow. Some squadron leaders admonished fellow pilots never to follow a Japanese fighter unless the attacker could maintain a lead, or the ability to aim in front of the Japanese plane. The problem is that the Japanese pilot might be good, and so another break could take place or the attacker could miss the shot. In either case the American fighter was slowing as a result of maneuvering.

Some squadron leaders thus instructed men never to follow a Japanese aircraft past a certain point on the compass, perhaps 90 degrees, regardless of lead. At the point of fire, however, such a decision was ultimately up to the pilot. If the speed dropped too far, an American pilot was in trouble, as his advantages (e.g., in level speed, climb rate, and dive rate) required some time to gain inertia. The slower the plane was flying, the more time it took. Even a very fast diver like the P-47, if it had bled too much speed, would thus be extremely vulnerable to attack from above. And an Oscar with a good head of steam could outdive a Thunderbolt if the latter began the dive at slow speed. In short the Japanese wanted to slow the pace of battle, whereas the Americans wanted to step up the pace.

When an engagement was imminent two things usually took place. First, aircraft would increase speed. Fighter planes cruised well below top speed (so-called military power). Although aircraft lack transmissions, like automobiles there is a speed at which the engine operates at maximum fuel and flight efficiency. When flying at full tilt fuel consumption doubles and great strain is put on the engine (something like going over the redline in a sports car). By mid-1943 most fighters had a throttle setting called "emergency power" or some such, usually based upon some kind of water or alcohol injection into the cylinders, which cooled them enough to allow the engine to operate far above specifications for a very short time. This ability was almost never used by wise pilots for offensive reasons, as it overstressed the engine. (An engine overhaul was usually standard after emergency power was employed; a pilot was required to report its use to the ground crew.) As Robert DeHaven explained emergency power, "It was a short-term remedy for a serious situation. This was not a normal combat tool, but a defensive one. The manifold pressure went up very high. It gave you a burst of speed which could save a pilot. But it did not last long. You could expect something to blow up in a few minutes. As you can imagine, use of this measure unless necessary was seriously discouraged." Yet fighters sought to keep speed up, which was central to U.S. tactics and important to the Japanese as well. Even though the maneuverability of Zeros and Oscars suffered at high speeds, it was in their interest to keep up speed at the start of engagement. It allowed a formation to add some precious extra altitude before shooting began. Speed allowed Japanese pilots to complete complex and lethal vertical maneuvers. It also allowed them to attack the unwary American who had begun to fly too slow. And Japanese pilots knew it was far easier to slow a plane down than to speed it up.

Second, a change in formation occurred, at least on the part of the Allies. Again, there was no set of procedures that covered every aerial battle. What took place over Guadalcanal did not necessarily replicate itself over Wewak. Yet the American version of the finger-four was not an attack formation, and neither was it ideal for defense (although it could function in either mode). It was an excellent formation from which to shift quickly to the situation at hand. Because speed increased, the distance between aircraft also increased. A flight might increase its width and attack line abreast, or with all aircraft flying parallel. Or the basic formation might simply be spread out. Planes would start to roll and scissor, as pilots became wary of the unseen enemy. Thus given an advantage or equality in altitude some expert Allied pilots favored changing from the finger-four to a string, wherein the four-plane flight leader would line his aircraft behind, all maneuvering to gain an opportunity to attack a target initially with little banking. This transformation would take place in all flights. Thomas McGuire, commander of the powerful 431st fighter squadron of Fifth Air Force, advocated the approach: "I like the squadron to drop from escort formation to string formation as soon as the enemy is sighted. We use a string of flights made of four ship components. Each man should be back six to ten lengths with an interval about double that between flights." Charles MacDonald, who commanded McGuire's 475th Group, concurred: "When we get over target the flights fall into the fighting formation. That is, each flight forms itself into a loose string. These strings are mutually supporting, and when they are weaving and criss-crossing present an extremely hard nut to crack."

By definition one side or another had altitude advantage, however slight, at the beginning of an air battle. It was at the point of fire that the technical deficiencies of Japanese fighters began to do terrible harm to the imperial cause. The unique situation at Guadalcanal hid some of these difficulties. Marine fighters naturally wanted to down the bombers (as was true with all interceptors throughout the war). The Japanese, for reasons I examine later, attacked at altitudes that were much too high for effective attack but made interception hard. Like later U.S. escorts, Japanese fighters flew at several echelons above, equal, and below the bombers they were protecting. Because Wildcats were not well suited to high-altitude attack many were trapped into the mistakes outlined above that caused loss in speed and vulnerability to the gaggle. However, even at that stage, Wildcats—and all first-generation U.S. fighters—could, if they saw the danger in time, go into a high-speed, curving dive that no Zero could possibly match. Granted, a U.S. fighter that dove out had a difficult time regaining an attack position, but it could fight the next day; Japanese aircraft caught in the first pass might well suffer catastrophic damage. Unless a cloud was handy, diving out was a treacherous maneuver for an imperial fighter. (This was not always the case, however: As the campaign wore on U.S. fighters of all sorts became wary of attacking a lone Japanese fighter. It was not unknown for a single plane to serve as bait, luring U.S. fighters low and thereby making them vulnerable to attack from above.)

If U.S. second-generation fighters enjoyed the altitude advantage the Japanese were indeed in trouble. In fact with a head of steam they could make a pass through a Japanese formation, go into a shallow high-speed climb, and repeat the process two or three times. The object was to knock down some enemy if possible and to bust apart the Japanese formation (which was almost always successful). Then American squadrons would spread out into flights and into elements. Perry Dahl described the way things went between P-38s and Zeros if events followed the script. His description could well have been used to illustrate an engagement between Corsairs and Zeros as well:

> The Japanese did a lot of acrobatic stuff like loops and cloverleaves to get away from you and very fancy maneuvers as opposed to just kicking the rudder and diving. . . .
>
> In my judgment in combat if you can make that thing fly sideways and inside-ways and inside-out and backwards you are in good shape. Plus, they had the seat pointed wrong on the fighter. You should be looking back all the time. Because that's where they are going to get you—the six o'clock. All of my airplanes except one or two I got from their six o'clock position. I think I would have got six or seven more if I'd learned that sooner. I was trying to do the stuff they taught you in flying school, you know. You compute the speed of the target, and you compute the range, and you are leading with so many radii, the 100-millimeter gun sight, and all this kind of stuff. I'd line that all up, but by the time I fired my guns wouldn't work. Or by the time you clear all that out you look and there the guy is diving at you from a six o'clock, so you have to break off. But I learned. When a guy came by me and offered a 90-degree deflection shot, I didn't shoot at him. For one thing he might not see me, and the odds of hitting him were pretty slim. But I'd go after him and I'd close within 300 yards astern, and I never fired until he filled up the whole radii of the 100-mil sight, which means I was well within 300 feet. That close—300 feet—you fire at him and blow him out of the sky. That really was effective. Head-on was good, too. I'd take a head-on with them anytime. That 20 Mike Mike [20 mm

cannon—EB] was quite a weapon. You know the P-38 had all forward
firing .50s, and the cannon, all right in the nose. At 300 yards their
bullets met in a six-inch circle. And that's a lot of firepower at 900
rounds a minute. I'll take anybody on with that firepower, including a
tank. Nose to nose! Ha! But like I say, it took me a long time to learn.

But the P-38 couldn't turn. So what we did was keep our speed up. We
always tried to get an altitude advantage, but if not, even then we'd dive
and we'd keep up a lot of air speed, never let the air speed get below 350
mph, never, ever below that. Because if you did and a Zero closed in on
you he'd have you before you could accelerate and get away from him.
. . . I always swore, and still think it's true, that if a Zero pilot ever saw
you, you'd never shoot him down. What we'd do is sandwich him: He'd
be turning away from one guy and the other guy would nail him. You
know, shooting down an airplane is a spectacular occurrence.

C. L. Jones went from an early P-39 to a P-38 and much preferred
the second aircraft. He described the basic tactics employed at the beginning of a melee:

I'd let the Zero do all the little maneuvers in the world, but if you had a
'38 and saw him and came down on him with good altitude advantage
you'd take your shot and if his little tricks worked you'd sail right on
by, climb, and try again. You'd keep it up until you or your wingman
hit him. You knew he couldn't match your dives or climbs.
Maneuverability and combat characteristics had to suit the
environment. A lot of things fit the circumstances that wouldn't fit
others. We had speed, climb, and much better high-altitude
performance. We could go anywhere we wanted. It was important to
avoid fighting on their terms: a low-altitude melee.

Melee and dogfights were brief, usually less than five minutes. Many
pilots on both sides went through hours of combat and actually spent
only a few minutes within shooting range of an enemy aircraft. Analyzing this period is something of a contradiction in terms, because it
was the pinnacle of chaos in air warfare. However, it was during melee
that most combat losses between fighters took place, so it is essential to
try to create some kind of structure that explains the fate of so many
aircraft while respecting the fact that no two combats were the same.

Once aircraft came into shooting range two things happened almost
invariably. First, the larger formations fell apart. Second, the fight either ended quickly or continued at a progressively lower altitude. The
disintegration of formations was taken for granted by both sides. The

ideal result of the first or second pass by fast U.S. fighters was to break up the Japanese formation, making individuals and pairs vulnerable to attack by the Americans' two-plane element. It was a Faustian bargain, because a good Japanese *shotai*, if the Americans were not cautious and fortunate, often benefited from the same outcome.

To understand this dynamic it is important to look at the question of gunnery and surprise. Perry Dahl's description that victory during fighter combat was a "spectacular occurrence" was no overstatement. The visual images held by veterans of air combat must defy expression in words, and it was extremely difficult. By World War II standards Dahl, with nine victories, was a great ace. However, he flew 900 hours in combat to get his kills. Richard Bong, who flew with Dahl on rare occasions and was America's greatest ace in any war, flew more than 300 missions to record his forty victories.

World War II fighters were gun platforms. Whether they carried machine guns or cannons, their striking range was limited to a maximum of 1,000 yards. In practice, however, the killing zone was much smaller. Anyone who has done target shooting knows it takes practice to reliably hit a target at a fraction of the theoretical range of the gun; it is more far difficult yet to hit a moving target. In aerial combat both gun and target are moving very fast. World War II fighters had electric gunsights that could compensate for the position of the pilot's head in the cockpit (a World War I pilot using an old cross-and-bead sight had to peer from directly behind the sight to avoid visual distortion), but they did not have an automatic "pipper," or visual cue, that showed the pilot where to aim based upon the movement of both aircraft. (One was developed late in the war and gained detractors and supporters; gun turrets had an automatic sighting system, discussed in the next section.) The sight would inform the pilot where the bullets were going to go if the aircraft was on a true course, as well as the rough range of the enemy.

The difficulties inherent in gunnery were technical, a reflection of the imperfect training given World War II pilots, especially during the first two and a half years of war. First of all in most fighters the main armament was mounted on the wings (.50-caliber machine guns for the Americans, 20mm cannons for the Zero). Separated by several feet if the guns simply fired straight, the bullet streams would be wide but lacked punch. So guns were adjusted so that bullets would strike a convergence point in the distance (typically 1,000 feet, though exact range varied upon pilot preference). Up to that point the bullet stream would converge inward; once past the bullets would scissor outward. Because a P-38 had its armament in the nose, convergence was not an issue. In other words, except for the Lightning, fighters were emitting cones of fire, not a single stream of bullets. Robert DeHaven explained the situation:

> It is very hard to hit another aircraft in flight, particularly when you're using converging gunfire. By definition it gives you one point of maximum impact at a particular boresight range, normally about 250 yards for the .50-caliber. Inside that boresight point and outside, you were hitting with misses. Whereas in a P-38 you had parallel fire with the four .50s and the 20mm going straight out in front of you. You didn't have worry about a boresight point, you always had maximum fire in the normal stream. A good shot could strike a target at a somewhat greater range in a P-38 than any other fighter for this reason.

Pilots often disagreed on this issue. A narrow cone of fire was extremely effective—if it struck home. A broader cone of fire raised the poor marksman's chances of hitting a target. In practice a high percentage of kills took place inside the convergence point. Naturally at extremely close range the problem of convergence didn't come into play as much.

The closer the range the greater the kinetic energy from a round of ammunition. A single .50-caliber bullet hitting home from fifty yards did far greater damage than a lucky hit from 500 yards. (A cannon, with its explosive shell, was less influenced by range.) Thus even if the convergence point was set at 300 yards an enemy aircraft inside the zone was actually in great danger because more air contained bullets; it did not take many rounds to do serious or fatal damage to a Japanese plane. Some Marine units in 1943 ceased using armor-piercing rounds simply because they believed that standard lead shot (abandoned by many squadrons, especially in Europe), which had a tendency to splatter when it struck, was more likely to strike a structural failure point or fuel tank than an armor piercing round (which might make a clean hole through the enemy's fuselage). Incendiary rounds were always a part of the mixture on both sides because of the catastrophic effect of fire on a plane. From the Allied point of view, then, there was much to be said for throwing a lot of lead into the air and hoping that some would find home. The expert marksman, in contrast, knew that a short burst near the convergence point might yield devastating results.

Fighters fired at one another under one of three general conditions. The best circumstances (for the attacker, that is) was if the strike aircraft was flying at a steady course at a target that was also flying at a steady course. When that situation took place the major variables of hitting the target, always conditioned upon pilot skill, were the actual course of the attacker and the degree of deflection as it approached target. World War II fighters were overpowered, and almost all suffered to one degree or another from the force of torque caused by the propeller. When altering speed or altitude, even by small degrees, the aircraft became unstable. All fighters had trim tabs that could be adjusted to refine flight characteristics, yet the state of trim was upset easily. One result was a slight skid, even during a mild maneuver. One of the simplest instruments on every instrument panel, the needle and ball informed the pilot whether the aircraft was flying straight and true. Great pilots manipulated trim tabs during combat and kept their aircraft stable during combat; many others relied on feel and close range. Yet the issue was vital. It might appear to a pilot that he had a perfect bead on a target. Yet if his plane suffered even a small degree of yaw (sideways movement), which was difficult to detect, the attacker might think he was firing straight while in truth he was firing slightly to one side. It is no wonder that instructors trained pupils to fly smoothly and avoid abrupt maneuver when making an attack run.

If the aircraft was stable and flying true, the pilot still had to account for deflection, or the angle of the attacking plane in relation to the target. Deflection angles are often discussed in books about air combat, although they simplify the reality. A full-deflection shot was 90 degrees, or perpendicular to target. Due to the speeds involved an attacker shooting at high deflection had to dramatically lead his target so that bullet and victim arrive at the same spot at the same time (as a hunter leads his quarry, aiming just in front). Under any circumstances this was a difficult shot to make. To complicate matters, in order to properly lead a victim one had to move the nose of the aircraft prior to firing, which raised the possibility of creating yaw. Add to this the facts that the attacker was closing rapidly and had little time to aim, and it becomes easy to see why pilots found it more effective to fire at lower deflection angles. The ultimate shot, which was very rare, was a zero-deflection shot from the enemy's six, in which the attacker was directly behind the enemy and flying at exactly the same angle. Deflection was not an issue, and if the attacker was stable and at close range the chances for a hit were excellent. The other zero-deflection shot was a head-on attack. In this case both attacker and defender were approaching at a horizontal angle relative to the earth but at very high speeds. Obviously with each aircraft closing at more than 250 miles per hour, there was little time to make the shot and little chance of striking with surprise. Yet the head-on pass was used frequently by

American pilots with devastating effect. In practice, however, a zero-deflection shot was extremely rare.

A 20-degree shot was considered a good bet from front (eleven to one o'clock) and rear (seven to five o'clock). But things were more complicated than that, as it was extremely rare for a plane to attack another flying at exactly the same angle to the earth. The attacker was either below the target or above it. Sometimes the angle difference was slight, other times severe. This made a tough job tougher, for deflection then became a three-dimensional problem. If an attacking fighter flying perfectly straight had a theoretically perfect dead-six attack angle, he could miss only to the left or right. When attacking from above or below the attacker could miss left, right, up, and down. No wonder that the great Fifth Air Force ace Thomas McGuire cautioned new pilots, "On deflection shots, pull your sight through the [Japanese plane]. Most shots in deflection are missed by being over or under rather than by incorrect lead." Thus hitting an aircraft even under the best circumstances was a daunting challenge.

That challenge was complicated further in two difficult but common situations. In the second scenario, a stable attacking plane faced an enemy that was in maneuver. Assuming that stable flight was achieved before shooting, the difficulty in striking home was magnified by the slightest change in direction. If the target began to bank, then the attacker would have to adjust for a shot that included both vertical and horizontal deflection, which could throw the aircraft slightly out of stable condition and create yaw. It would be like shooting skeet from the bed of a moving pickup. The bullet stream would have to bracket a large area and would inevitably curve, decreasing the chance for a hit.

Worse yet was attacking a plane that was in full evasive maneuver. In that circumstance the firing aircraft would have to maneuver with the target. If both planes were in a radical set of maneuvers the attacker, if the defender moved toward him, might be allowed a snapshot, or a split-second burst fired at close range. If the snapshot hit home, the defender was probably a goner; more likely it would miss, as two aircraft engaging in radical maneuvers were not likely to hit one another without a blunder or dumb luck. Bullets, simply put, flew all over the sky in greatly expanding arcs, unlikely to strike anything. For the alert attacker it then became crunch time. An American could avoid further maneuver—fearing loss of speed—gain altitude and try again. Perhaps, however, the attacker had made a mistake in judgment and had no option but to dive. If the attackers were Japanese, a bungled assault would alert the radio-carrying Americans, allowing them to break off, gather speed, and return for another blistering assault. In any case it was not in the American pilot's interest to continue a dogfight. This factor made the Pacific Theater a different game than Europe, where the aircraft were much more similar and a U.S. fighter might well accept the challenge to maneuver. Robert DeHaven discussed this point:

> There were two distinct theaters of air war: one was Europe, the other the South Pacific. They were vastly different. A standard tactic, for instance, in Europe, was a defensive Lufberry circle. That was used very effectively up through the Mustang period even though the Mustang was much more maneuverable than the Bf109 and Fw190. They did more traditional dogfighting, air-to-air combat. If you tried to do that in a P-38 in the Pacific, even when we got maneuver brakes and hydraulic ailerons, you still couldn't get into circle combat and expect to survive. You just didn't do that.

Simply put, it was very difficult for one fighter to hit another in combat, something that could be overcome with excellent marksmanship. Superb marksmen were rare, and some pilots claimed hunting during their youth had proven helpful. Joe Foss believed much of his success over Guadalcanal was due to his days hunting in South Dakota.

No doubt Foss had a point. Skeet was a popular pastime among fighter pilots if conditions allowed. Yet as Foss himself pointed out, even though he was a very veteran pilot for the period, he was not properly trained in the craft of aerial marksmanship:

> If I was as smart when I started as when I ended I would have had double the kills. The biggest mistake I made at first was shooting out of range. The enemy looked closer to me than they were. If you shot at a Zero out of range and he saw you shooting, he just left the area. He just left you sucking smoke. He'd be flying straight up and you weren't going to be following that baby. He was out of there. So I learned you better get them when they were close.

Bill Harris, one of the top aces of Thirteenth Air Force, spent a brief stateside tour in early 1944 with other army pilots working on a postdoctorate of sorts. One of his classmates was Richard Bong, who Harris described as the "best shot I've ever seen." When both returned to combat they added to their scores. Yet great aces like Harris and Bong were not the only ones benefiting from a greater emphasis on gunnery training.

USN pilots during the interwar period prided themselves on advanced attack techniques and training on high-deflection shooting. No doubt such preparation helped the great tacticians like Thach, O'Hare, and Flatley. As a Marine Foss also received USN training in prewar days. Yet the average naval aviator who saw action in the South Pacific was far from a dead-eye marksman. Maneuvers like the effective but delicate overhead attack on bombers were quite beyond most pilots' skills, and the technique was rarely used when war went into the mass-production stage. Navy fighter pilot Don Gordon did two tours on the *Enterprise*, fighting both at Santa Cruz and the Philippine Sea (June 1944). When rotated back to the States Gordon became an advanced instructor for hordes of well-prepared youngsters waiting to join the navy's great task forces. Gordon was a hunter but found that training was more important:

> Shooting was hard. Many pilots would completely miss towed target sleeves. And it had to be towed at a realistic speed or it would come apart. You couldn't tow a sleeve much over 150 mph, much slower than actual combat, so it's a poor exercise. It does acquaint the pilot with the guns and how fast they fire. I did a lot of hunting as a kid and still skeet-shoot. I think that was very good training.
>
> I had a cruise in F4Fs and had some kills there, then a tour in F6Fs and had some more. I then went back to the States to serve as an advanced instructor. My first groups of students went up to battle the target sleeve. I shot 8–10 percent. My students shot 4–6 percent. The next flight I was 15–16 percent and my students 6–8 percent. The next flight I was up to 25 percent and my students at 12 percent. I was learning that I had been trained wrong at first, but we were getting better. It's all range definition. You have to be close. In combat the target looks awful big but he's still way too far away. But I improved. When the students were finished they were better trained than my group had been in 1942.

Note how both Foss and Gordon emphasized the most common gunnery mistake made by fighter pilots was not poor deflection shooting but firing too soon. Many pilots, including the 5th USAAF aces, cautioned about wasting long-range shots at high deflection because that would only alert the enemy that he was a target. Thomas McGuire's maxim was to "go in close, then when you think you are too close, go on in closer."

Regardless of the difficulties of getting in close—not to mention how one might define "close" in the first place—jamming guns were a problem, especially early in the war as ground crews played catch-up. As Thomas Furlow recalled, a jam was not unusual over Cactus: "Often at least one of your machine guns failed. It was a rare day when all six functioned without flaw. There were a lot of jams. Sometimes you'd have three guns on one wing, none on the other, or two on one and one on the other. You never knew for sure. That was a good reason to fire in short bursts. And you tried to get very close. I'd imagine about 200 feet—it was never the same. You had to be fairly close or you simply couldn't hit them." Robert DeHaven, who also encountered his share of jammed guns early in the conflict, found longer ranges preferable, especially when flying the P-38: "There was an old cliché about the fighter pilot being interviewed and being asked how close he got to his prey before he pulled the trigger and he answers, 'Close enough to hit him over the head with my oxygen mask. And then you hose them down.' Sometimes it was exactly like that. I saw many planes downed at point-blank range. I flew through the debris of one kill I made and damaged my own aircraft. Ideally, however, I would say between 200 and 250 yards was a good range if the attack position was good." However, whether the attack distance was 100 feet or 250 yards, this was very close combat. The key to shooting down a fighter, it would seem, was to get close and obtain a good firing position. How would a pilot do this?

Surprise, for one thing. Some aviation authors have argued that a high percentage of aircraft were killed by surprise attack. I would agree, but only if the term "surprise" is properly defined. Most every pilot would emphasize that the skies were no place for the lone hunter. Most formations, even in the South Pacific, were not small. Unless on routine patrol or ground support in an area where air dominance was present, a fighter mission would usually include a whole squadron. If a major raid was in the works, the entire group might fly. Every pilot was expected to keep his eyes peeled for enemy aircraft. If on the defensive, what he could not see the early-warning systems (the "eyes" of radar) would, with varying degrees of effectiveness. The result was that in the South Pacific it was unusual for a major unit to be caught flat-footed. Still, many enemy formations were not spotted soon enough to prevent them from striking with an altitude advantage. If a unit was escorting bombers, particularly if on close support, there was little alternative than to accept the challenge.

And then hell broke lose. Because there were so many targets, if an enemy unit scattered, the attacking flights would separate and pursue victims. Soon the flights broke apart. (Breaking down also prevented congestion and lessened the possibility of friendly collision. In a high-speed chase, too many aircraft could easily get in one another's way. For this reason, if an American unit had the advantage in numbers and altitude, it was standard to attack with one or two flights and keep the remainder in reserve as high cover.) Every aircraft had blind spots. Even within a flight or two-wing element it was impossible to keep track of everything taking place. Indeed the reason that Americans so emphasized the importance of the two-plane element was to compensate for that fact. Therefore, even though most everyone knew that a fight was under way, there were opportunities for a keen or lucky pilot to land a blow on a pilot occupied by the limited area he could see and evaluate. Roger Haberman reflected on this aspect of air combat:

> During combat you often don't see what happens in front of you. You get so interested in what's taking place off to one angle that something appears and it's gone before you can react. You never get the whole picture because there are too many people involved. You only see a small part. In January on my second visit to Guadalcanal we went up to Munda. We put on a "go-around" with Japanese fighters. Marion Tate was in Foss's old front four and a double ace and didn't come back and nobody saw what happened to him. Nobody saw him in trouble, being chased, nothing. He was in the group and just disappeared. Nobody saw him hit the deck, smoke, nothing. You're so goddamn intent on what's going to happen to you and what you can shoot down that you don't notice what happens to the other guy. We were right there in the air with them.

Robert DeHaven expressed similar thoughts based on his experiences in New Guinea: "You didn't get jumped by large numbers of aircraft in the Pacific one way or the other. However, we shot down planes by hitting them where they couldn't see us or before they could react. I personally think that for the most part that they did not know until they were hit or about to be hit because the combat was so close in. It was simply a matter of getting the advantage of speed and altitude and then hit and run." Ralph Easterling, also of Fifth Air Force, echoed DeHaven: "You usually saw each other from some distance and then closed. But it was never possible to keep track of everything. So being aware of a specific aircraft, particularly if it was shooting at you, might come only at an instant before. Sometimes you didn't have much warning at all. The enemy could jump you or they get jumped and have only a fraction of time to respond." Thomas McGuire put it simply, "It is always the one you don't see that gets you."

Because of the possibility of getting jumped, American pilots were eager to maintain both speed and altitude. Speed management was important, of course. If coming from above, a fast plane like a Corsair could easily overrun an enemy if it approached too quickly and especially if it attacked in a high-speed dive. And at full speed even the easiest maneuver was a challenge. Yet it was the rare pilot who got fancy. There are accounts of desperate American pilots who cut the throttle, hoping that the Japanese attacker would fly past. Sometimes P-38 pilots cut the throttle on one engine to create an unexpected and dangerous defensive maneuver. Some pilots at low speed attempted to use their dive flaps or even landing flaps to execute a very tight turn. Such moves were not encouraged and were usually employed by rookies or masters, and then only rarely. For the most part, then, the array of maneuvers employed by American pilots was relatively small.

Pilots on both sides used the basics, of course. The chandelle was a slow, climbing turn that led to a fighter changing direction, gaining altitude, and losing speed. There was also the Immelmann, which was a climbing half-loop that left the aircraft at a higher altitude and flying at a different direction. A defensive staple of both sides was the split-S, a kind of Immelmann in reverse. When conducting the split-S the pilot rolled the fighter on its back and pulled back on the stick. While heading down the pilot might do a half-roll to change direction. Regardless the result would leave the fighter moving in a different direction, at a lower altitude, and at higher speed. (The split-S was a typical trade of altitude for speed, combined with a directional change. Although the split-S was used by everyone, the P-38 required much more altitude than did the P-40 and Corsair, much less the Zero.) All these maneuvers could be made more quickly in a Zero and in less space. If a U.S. plane went into a split-S or any type of dive, it was usually for defensive reasons. Thus the staples of U.S. tactics were the shallow dive and shallow climb with as few major maneuvers as possible, all to keep up speed. It is a cliché among fighter pilots that "speed is life," but it was true when fighting aircraft as nimble as Zeros. For most good American pilots there was virtue in simplicity. As Joel Paris put it, "Air combat in the Pacific consisted of a relatively small number of relatively simple maneuvers executed at exactly the right time."

Sometimes one side or another, usually a U.S. Corsair or Lightning squadron, could pull off the textbook attack, keeping the altitude and speed advantage at all times, score several victories, and break off after a day well done. Rarely was a melee so simple. The greatest of pilots had a second sense concerning the relative location of enemy and friend, but they were rare. Even when considering the absolute masters of fighter combat, I doubt if any did not flirt with destruction from enemy fighters. The Japanese had maneuvers and tricks of their own. A good *shotai* might attempt a move the Americans called the "Prince of Wales." During this three-plane maneuver the *shotai* leader would wait until the attacker was almost in range and then pull into a loop while his two wingmen turned abruptly toward the attacker. If the American did not resist temptation and continue forward at very high speed, one of the three Japanese fighters would get a good shot. More likely there was a nearby Zero that the American simply did not see while pursuing a target. There was no certainty that his wingman would see it, either. Therefore, there was a basic decision that had to be made by most pilots in a major fight. Because it was vital to get close to an enemy to destroy him, and because it was preferable to attack an enemy that did not see you, this almost always required some kind of maneuver. Because maneuver required a loss of speed or altitude and, when attacking, tended to concentrate the pilot on the target, the risk was always there of an unseen enemy inflicting a blow. For the average pilot there were no safe kills.

When attacking an enemy formation there was no formula one could rely upon to find an unwary victim. One technique recommended by John Loisel of the 475th Fighter Group was to avoid stragglers and attack the thickest part of the enemy formation: "Head for the main body of the enemy if you are leading a flight or a squadron. Disregard the stragglers. In my experience at hitting enemy formations, a few wingmen have seen me coming and taken evasive action, but where the enemy was concentrated there were several who obviously didn't know of our presence. Plow into the largest bunch you see. After such an attack the enemy will be forced to break up." Cyril Homer, another 5th USAAF ace, concurred and advocated a deadly tactic called the "zoom-climb": "Make sure that if you do attack that you are not being followed. No matter how well you look around you, you will not see all the planes in the area. You sometimes feel as if they come out of nowhere. In the case of the enemy being below, judge his speed before coming down on them. As you come down roll around, clearing yourself. Do not try to dive *on* him—instead, dive under and up from the rear, for this is his blind spot."

Good shots and aggressive American pilots from the beginning of the war looked for the opportunity to make a head-on attack. Often this was the concluding part of a defensive move. If a Japanese aircraft gained the six position but was not in range to fire, the U.S. aircraft would use superior speed to gain distance and then simply turn around and head straight for the adversary. The shot had to be made in less than two seconds. In many circumstances the Japanese plane would break away and the U.S. fighter sail past. Sometimes the Japanese fighter would either accept the one-sided duel or simply do the wrong thing. The result would be one of the most dramatic encounters in fighter combat.

The head-on attack was part of the American repertoire of basic combat techniques since being recommended by Chennault. No doubt hundreds of fragile Japanese aircraft perished under the punishing fire of American guns. Richard Bong was noted for favoring the technique. Yet the best description of a head-on attack was given by Charles Lindbergh. In mid-1944 Lindbergh spent several months in the South Pacific helping pilots and technicians of both the army and Marine Corps get more range out of their aircraft, a mission he accomplished with great success. With no publicity at the time, Lindbergh flew several combat missions with the Marines and USAAF. While visiting Fifth Air Force he found himself near Biak, the scene of serious airfighting. Lindbergh was in a two-flight formation. As might be imagined considering his fame, Fifth Air Force provided him some good company. In this case one of the flights was led by Charles MacDonald, one of America's finest pilots. Lindbergh had an extraordinary mastery of words and described the brief and deadly encounter vividly:

I tripped my gun switch, brightened the ring sight, nosed down to follow in attack. To my left a Japanese plane disappeared in haze and cloud. A second was banking sharply toward the airstrip under the protection of the ground guns. We dove toward the strip, unmindful of puffs of smoke and invisible steel fragments that were zipping around us.

Tracers spurted from MacDonald's fighter, a beam of death that forced the Japanese pilot to reverse his bank. A thin trail of smoke informed us that one of the bullets hit, but the enemy showed no loss of maneuverability or power. Miller, Blue 2, fired a short deflection burst against wings that were almost vertical in the air. My Lightning was next in line. I watched the red balls of the rising sun on the enemy plane grow larger, shrink from round to oval, then disappear as the wings cut toward me, knife-edged against the background of gray haze. It was to be a head-on pass. I centered the plane in my ring sight and squeezed finger against trigger. Streaks of fire leapt from my fighter's nose out of four machine guns and one cannon. Raise the tracers— creep them leftward—flashes on the target as my bullets hit—but the wingspan widened in my ring sight. The enemy's guns were firing, too. I held the trigger down, head on with no deflection. There was a rattle of machine guns and streams of tracers. Slightly climbing, slightly diving at five hundred miles an hour we approached, hurtling into an eternity of time and space. The cowling in my sight expanded. Enemy cylinders grew fins. I hauled back on my stick as I sensed our closeness. The Japanese plane jerked upward too! Was the pilot trying to collide? I yanked back with all my strength, braced for the crash. There was a bump but it was only air.

By how much did we miss? Ten feet? Five? I was zooming steeply. I banked left and saw ack-ack bursts ahead, reversed the bank and swept my eyes over sky and earth looking for aircraft. I saw only friendly Lightnings. No one but my wingman was on my tail. I saw the plane I had just shot down. My enemy was in a wing-over, out of control. I watched his nose drop. His plane twisted as it gained speed. The rising suns diminished in sized. Down. Down. Down. The sea had not seemed so far beneath us. Down. A fountain of spray, white foam on water, ripples circled outward, merged with waves. The foam subsided. No mark remained.

Life had balanced on a razor edge during that encounter. If I had been ten feet behind, my enemy would have rammed me. At the speed I was flying, ten feet was less than a tenth of a second. Bullets were ripping back and forth at the rate of thousands per minute. It took only one to kill. The slightest difference in our rates of fire might have reversed the outcome of the combat—had my controls been a mite less sensitive, my guns a shade less accurate, my bullets of slightly smaller caliber. . . . I had the advantage that the most modern weapons give. My enemy did not.

Because maneuver of some sort was required to get close enough to the enemy for a good shot, a countermove from the other side was common, particularly if an American aircraft had, in the desire to destroy the enemy, allowed speed to slip. The response when attacked by the enemy was to regain speed, and that meant getting rid of altitude. Japanese aircraft often maneuvered downward to escape attack. Even if an American attack began with a classic series of passes followed by a slow climb and a return pass, physics does not allow a perpetual-motion machine. Either the time required to gain altitude after repeated passes would ultimately cause the opposing sides to lose contact (it was obvious for the Japanese to head down in such situations), or the Americans would have to close and mix it up if the fight was to continue. So just as surely as squadrons broke down into flights and flights broke down into elements in a melee, so did the altitude of the fight usually decrease in short order unless one side decided to call it quits. As Robert DeHaven noted, "Fights that started at 20,000 feet did not stay there long. The only really effective defensive maneuver the P-40 had was the dive out. You simply went straight down. Nothing the Japanese flew could stay with it except the Tony, and you could get away from that. So the altitude advantage disappeared quickly enough." Joel Paris added that at the end of the process, if one did not break for safety, a fight became extremely hazardous: "Any time you initiated a fight at altitude, it was no time before you were heading toward the deck. That was just natural."

On the deck one badly wanted a good wingman or some friendly aircraft with more altitude to help out if things turned ugly. It was a dangerous place to be. Many pilots, some of them excellent, brushed a wing to the ground or water on the deck, usually with fatal results. Don Gordon had an encounter on the deck during the Battle of Santa Cruz and witnessed the impact of a slight error:

> I was out there with another one of our guys lined up with me, and as we were orbiting the ship I saw this Kate torpedo-bomber coming. He was down on the water. I was out of ammo. The guy with me gave me a thumbs-down, meaning he was out—he didn't have a radio due to damage. So the easiest way to get away from this guy was to meet him head-on. I got right down a few feet off the water. I wasn't going to hit him or anything. He must have looked up and saw me and turned left. He cut his wing in the water and that was it. The ship saw him go in so I got credit for the victory. That was a bad place to make a mistake.

The deck was also a bad place to lose speed against a nimble enemy. Obviously such situations were tailor-made for the Zero and Oscar. Yet even a Japanese plane would flounder if it had lost too much momentum and was close to stall speed. If the enemy had more speed available, he could gain position. If this happened and no one was there to give aid, the defender was in desperate trouble. As Robert Morehead described it, someone on the deck at low speed was "out of speed, out of altitude, out of ideas, and out of time." When writing during the war, Robert DeHaven suggested trying a violent skid and noted that "a prayer comes in handy, too."

The chaos inherent in a melee was probably best illustrated by the commonly experienced empty sky. Although pilots on both sides were cautioned never to fly alone, the breakdown of order was so extreme and so rapid that most every veteran fighter pilot in the South Pacific

experienced it (no doubt made more common by the usual cloud formations even on clear days). Regardless of the course of events, the result was the same: An engagement would begin with many aircraft in
full view and a few minutes later a pilot is flying utterly alone with not
a friend or enemy in sight.

Joel Paris reflected on this eerie occurrence:

When firing began combat was at very close quarters. Very close.
Definitely. And it could happen real quick. You'd be in the middle of a
fight, and they're fighting all around you and suddenly you look around
and you're the only sonofabitch left. Everybody's gone, disappeared.
Nobody's left around but me. It's kind of funny, really. You're so intent
about what you're doing and suddenly you look around and you're
alone or almost—maybe you've got a wingman if you're lucky. We did
teach that real religiously that you wanted to fight in pairs at least.
They were pretty good about that. That was one of our disciplinary
emphases: stay together, stay together, stay in pairs. But you separated
anyway. I was often by myself after a fight. The sky is big and things
happened so fast.

Robert Croft agreed: "When you get into a melee you lose cohesive-
ness. That's inevitable and we even planned for some of that to happen. It's amazing how crowded the sky can be and an *instant* later it's
empty, absolutely empty. There are clouds, the sun and everything
moves so fast. And suddenly you're the only guy there. You search all
around and no one—you're alone."

As should be evident, a fighter melee in the South Pacific had a blow-
counterblow dynamic that was unmistakable. If one wished to engage,
the risk was there of getting hit. Nothing could alter that simple fact.
Edwards Park had an interesting observation concerning this flow:

There was a blow-counterblow tempo to a dogfight, what we called a
"soiree." One plane would hit a target and an enemy wing would hit
him. This required what modern pilots call "situational awareness,"
knowing where the other enemy are. You're concentrating on one thing,
pursuing a target, and the enemy could be close by, perhaps done a
wingover, or in a cloud, or maybe right next to you, but you don't
notice him, maybe you see just a blur in your peripheral vision. And all
of a sudden you're taking shells. It was very confusing and bewildering.
And the better you were the better you understood where you were and
who was around you. The first combat I was in we were attacking a
bomber. I totally lost my element leader on the second pass. The first

pass I was right with him. The second pass I was being a good clean-cut American boy ready to die for his country and I went in a little farther than the leader did on this pass. He peeled off and I hung for a second and a half longer shooting. And then I peeled off and looked for my leader. I did a nice flying-school chandelle, which was absolutely the wrong thing to do, and picked up 144 bullet holes. So that was the wrong thing, exactly what a new pilot does. I should have stayed with him and let him show me how close to get. We got the bomber anyway, although I didn't know until later.

The air war over the Pacific was well documented on a certain level. After every mission the squadron intelligence personnel debriefed the pilots. Paperwork, like everything else in the South Pacific, was handled haphazardly, and a standard debriefing was an informal affair. Nevertheless a major air action was rare enough, and squadron officers did their best to interview all participants and piece together a narrative of events. (The procedures involved to claim and verify a kill were done separately.) Squadrons sent their reports up the chain of command. Most after-action reports that did survive were accumulated at a higher headquarters for analysis and distribution to other squadrons. The accounts rendered were honest and largely accurate. Keep in mind, however, that the personnel were describing events that moved very quickly; much was missed. Furthermore people see what they want to see. If a pilot fired at an aircraft and hit it, it was easy enough to see it fall smoking to earth. However, what looked like smoke could have been exhaust, and the aircraft, seemingly careening toward oblivion, could have been in a spin or power-dive. Moreover a successful mission made the squadron and pilots look good to officers up the chain of command. But the fact remained that the job of intelligence officers was a serious matter. They took testimony from as many participants as possible. Braggarts are not appreciated by squadronmates, and most men did their best to report the truth as they saw it. Consequently the first-person accounts of fighting are not perfect renditions of past events. Yet looking closely we are drawn much closer into the extraordinary world of World War II fighter combat.

Two dramatic descriptions of that violence came from the Solomons. Like Fifth Air Force, Halsey's air command was collecting reports of particularly instructive engagements to use for training purposes. Flying in a multiservice command, they made liberal use of Marine, USN, and USAAF reports. A long but interesting report described a major engagement during the Munda campaign in mid-1943 in the

Solomons. American pilots were better trained than a year before, and many squadrons were equipped with Lightnings and Corsairs, both better than the Zero. All U.S. units at this stage of the war were well versed in four-plane formation tactics. Nevertheless Japanese fighters included some of their last elite squadrons, and Japan was still a most formidable opponent.

One furious engagement during summer 1943 was recorded by Major William Fraser, commander of the elite Marine Squadron VMF-112 based at Henderson. On June 7 the 112th was finishing its third tour on Guadalcanal. The Japanese picked that day to launch a large attack on Henderson, knowing that U.S. fighters based there were devastating Japanese forces farther up the Solomons as a prelude to the invasion of New Georgia. As Fraser had ended the day alive— but without his fighter—he recorded events as an instructional aid for his pilots or, as Fraser put it, "I'm writing this in the hope that others will avoid my errors and come out with a good score—and a whole skin." Although the Marines had been warned of the incoming attack, as Fraser relates the Japanese got the jump on them. Fortunately for the Marines, at high altitude the Corsair, not the Zero, had the edge in agility:

The Zeros came in to our right about 30,000 and were flying in three plane flights stepped back almost to a column. Above them were six more planes, slow rolling and looping—looking around, I guess. Someone yelled "they're behind us" so we executed a left turn. I saw six of them diving down to a level slightly below us and coming up in back of our last man. It's a good thing that we had our speed because the Zeros apparently underestimated it and leveled off. The first two were in column astern and I headed for them, as I made a left turn. I put on the master gun switch, added RPM, blower and throttle, and felt I was ready. My boy executed a gradual diving turn, then straightened out in a very steep dive. My old Corsair closed on him like the dickens, though. I gave him a burst from 500 yards, allowing a little for bullet drop, and saw the tracers hit the plane. [A smart pilot would never fire at another fighter from 500 yards: Fraser, however, because of greatly superior speed, was closing fast and drawing a bead. Note the Japanese aircraft was using the American-style dive, no doubt to bring the fight to an altitude where the Zero was more at home.—EB] A couple of little black puffs of smoke came from his wing roots but he didn't burn as I expected. He rolled slowly to the left and I rolled with him, shooting as I went. I was overrunning him, though, and very uncomfortable on my back, so I rolled out of it, turned and tried to find him again, but, "no go." Stan Synar, my wing man, saw him spin in— so I guess I killed the pilot. After turning I saw another Zero go by ahead of me and I was about to take off after him when Synar went screaming by me, closed very fast, and blew him up in flames. Synar and I were at 8,000 feet then, and we joined up and headed back up.

The Japanese high-altitude attack had failed. The return engagement for the Marines, however, was not so successful.

We were at 18,500 and looked for the rendezvous. How wrong we were! They had 25,000 feet. Synar was flying nice formation on my wing, when suddenly he dove under me because he had a Zero on his tail. At the time, I thought that he had seen the enemy BELOW, so I cocked up on my left side to see where he was going so I could follow him. I heard one shooting behind me. There were a bunch of Zeros in the sun. So I quickly kicked the bottom rudder, rolled, and figured that I had lost him. I hadn't though; he followed me for quite some time as you'll soon see. But anyway, as I was doing this nosedown roll, another Zero went under my nose, and 2,000 feet below, headed in another direction. I straightened out and got on his tail but he was out of range. He pulled up in a gradual STRAIGHT climb, about 1,000 feet per minute—probably to set me up in a good position for his buddies. *Beware of Zeros flying straight.* The first one went straight, I followed, and it turned out there was another on my tail. That time, though, Synar had shot him off. This time there was another on my tail. I chased the straight-flying Zero, "poured the coal" to the Corsair, and we simply walked up on him like nothing at all. He saw me overtaking him and pulled up into a loop. I followed, gave him a few bursts, but they didn't have fatal effect—just smoke puffs again. We just have been indicating 170 knots when he pulled into that loop. Try it sometime in a Corsair and see where you end up—yes, that's just where *I* was, fresh out of air speed and on my back. I had given him a burst halfway up, though, and he flamed on top. Then, I cut the gun and pulled back on the stick—she almost spun, because I could feel the stall at the tips, but she finally fell off on a wing.

Fraser pulled off an extraordinarily risky maneuver: He stayed through a loop, stalling at the top, and hit his enemy. He came close to a spin, which in a Corsair was something to avoid. However, stalling in combat is always dangerous, as Fraser found out:

I was trying to get myself oriented to get back in the ball game when, suddenly, there was a bang in the accessory section and tracers were flying by. Immediately, I rolled right and dove. The oil pressure went to 40 lbs. Remember that guy following me? Well after being hit, I headed down from 18,000 feet when the same Zero got on my tail again and started shooting. I rolled right, nose down, and dove for a layer of clouds at 8,000 feet, wondering when the motor was going to jump its mounts. After going through the cloud I again headed west, throttling back and lowering my RPM; the oil pressure read 0. No sooner than I had done this than that 20mm started bouncing off the armor plate; he was STILL there. I rolled right again and dove from about 7,000 feet to about 300 feet and got squared off to land. The motor was vibrating badly, backfiring, and finally the prop froze still. I landed in deep water 100 yards off shore. It was a neat landing. Everything was just dandy EXCEPT I was in terror of being strafed. The Zero—still chasing—closed on me and bounced a few more off the armor, and then swished back and forth looking me over. I thought he was waiting to strafe me in the water, but I guess he was out of ammunition.

As the point of the report was educational, Fraser tried to summarize his mistakes:

Let's look at my mistakes. Remember when the Zeroes first attacked us from 30,000 feet? Well, I should have been able to see them, but I didn't. That part of it has been corrected. Now that Synar is LEADING my division and I am on his wing. Synar is a First Lieutenant and I'm a Major, but I would much prefer to be an ex-division leader than an ex-Major. I secretly suspect that Synar has radar antennae in his ears and a scope for eyes, because he picks up planes long before I can. When I asked him about this trait, he says he looks into an area, looks for any movement, and then shifts his gaze to another area; he doesn't try to sweep the whole sky at once. Next on my list; maybe I should have cut my throttle when I was overrunning the first Zero, but I'm a great advocate of having high speed. Let me suggest that if you feel uncomfortable for any reason, just dive out and look over the situation. If everything is ok come back in again. You have plenty of speed and you have enough gas to enable you to take your time. These Corsairs can run away from any Zero built.

When I was first attacked in the second engagement, I should not have straightened out on the tail of the Zero below me; either I should have looked for Synar while I was diving, and joined up with him, or, not finding him, I should have gotten out altogether to see what was going on. Instead I tailed in behind the bait and played sucker.

Although you've heard this before, I'll repeat it. STAY TOGETHER. If you are following one of your buddies and an easy shot goes by, ignore the bait and follow the other Corsair. . . . As Colonel Bauer used to say, "They're still making Zeros in Tokyo, so there will be plenty to go around."

Fraser and his wingman took great liberties in the battle just described. This was possible because they were flying Corsairs and not Wildcats. Both the advantages and limits of the new U.S. aircraft were vividly shown in a rash attack made on a Japanese bomber formation by Captain James Swett and his wingman, Lieutenant Harold Seal of VMF-221 on July 11, 1943, near Munda. Swett's two-plane element was the last uncommitted unit in an eight-plane attack by Marine Corsairs. Although Swett and Seal's adventure was short, it was just one portion of a running battle involving several formations that lasted more than an hour. Observe that Swett and Seal's attack was a quick pass made with very fast aircraft. Under such circumstances two aircraft could, and frequently did, cause serious harm to a much larger force. And yet as Swett and Seal found out, battle always has risk. Lieutenant Seal was an experienced pilot and Swett an ace. Captain Swett began the account:

At 1700 [hours] we received a radar contact of a large formation. Nearly an hour later we sighted the bogey heading toward Munda. . . . I estimate that there were from twelve to fifteen bombers in a "Vee of Vees" with about ten or twelve Zeros above and behind them. The bombers were at about 20,000 feet and the Zeros at about 2,000 feet above and spread all over the sky, not in any definite formation at all. I picked the last Betty in the starboard echelon, firing for his engines. I could see I was getting hits, but the bomber did not burn. I had to split S to roll out and avoid collision. I rolled over again about five or six thousand feet below and went into a cloud. [Note that Swett started his pass at 25,000 feet and ended just above sea level.—EB.] When I came out of the cloud I saw a Corsair which was smoking badly. I was two or three miles astern of his beam. There were three Zeros about a mile behind him in a spread-out A-B-C formation. I caught up to the last Zero and put a six or seven second burst into him. He began to pull up and lost his starboard wing about halfway out from the wing root and fluttered into the water. The other two peeled off and went back. The

Corsair ducked into the clouds and I lost him. During the chase I called to him: "smoking Corsair, get out of that thing." After the other two Zeros left I tried to find him but was unsuccessful.

Then I spotted a Betty low on the water and heading about 130 degrees. I thought he had only one Zero for cover. . . . When the Zero got out of position I went for the Betty, firing for the motors. I was about fifty yards behind the Betty when I hit him. He nosed over and hit the water. I pulled up over the splash, made a turn and headed for the clouds to get out of the way of the Zero, but found another making a pass at me. He made a high side run on me when I was at about 1,000 feet. He got my motor right away—I could see the holes appearing in the cowling. I got into a cloud and in the middle of it the engine began sputtering and I found I had neither oil nor fuel pressure. Then it quit. I got squared away and headed in the general direction of home, making a water landing about five miles off shore. The ship made a good landing. The hatch stayed open and the plane skipped along nicely. It gave me plenty of time to get out. But there were two Zeros firing bullets into the water all around me so I dove right overboard. I didn't even inflate my Mae West [the inflatable life jacket worn by fliers—EB] and left my chute in the plane, getting into the water as fast as I possibly could. The tail of the plane stuck out of the water for about ten minutes and I spent my time ducking around behind it every time the Zeros came by. They were coming in on opposite courses and I was quite active for a while. After about five minutes they left and I was able to inflate my life jacket.

The Zeros that struck Captain Swett had either followed him down or had been flying high cover for the Betty on the deck. In either case, although they were very close, Swett did not see them. The smoking Corsair heading off into the clouds, of course, was Swett's wingman, Lieutenant Seal. Like his flight leader, Seal had an interesting afternoon:

We sighted the bogies at nine o'clock at about 25,000 feet and about five to seven miles away. Bombers were in front with low and high Zero cover, the latter about 2,000 feet above the bombers. Jim headed right for the formation in about a 20–30 degree dive. I followed. I saw the Zero formation break up and the bombers turn northwest. Swett was headed directly for the bombers and when he got about 1,000 yards from them, Zeros started to get on his tail. I was about 1,000 yards from him and thus able to attack a Zero behind him. As soon as he got within range I turned and shot him. The Zero burst into flames. Then I

A famous RAAF Wirraway supports Australian troops in the Buna area. A converted trainer, the Wirraway proved very effective when flying low and slow and could help spot and attack Japanese infantry positions in dense terrain. The RAAF developed sophisticated air-to-ground support techniques sooner than did their American allies. (Australian War Memorial)

A shattered Zero captured at the small Japanese airstrip at Buna in late 1942. The Buna strip, a tiny affair, was the first Japanese base to go under in the South Pacific. (U.S. Air Force)

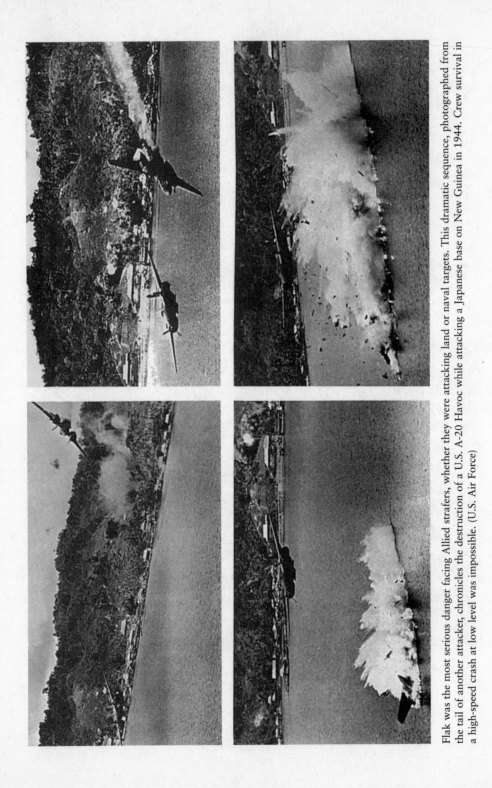

Flak was the most serious danger facing Allied strafers, whether they were attacking land or naval targets. This dramatic sequence, photographed from the tail of another attacker, chronicles the destruction of a U.S. A-20 Havoc while attacking a Japanese base on New Guinea in 1944. Crew survival in a high-speed crash at low level was impossible. (U.S. Air Force)

This spectacular sequence records a devastating skip-bombing attack made on a Japanese frigate. The attack was made in 1945, but many similar attacks were made throughout the South Pacific in 1943 and 1944. (U.S. Air Force)

13th USAAF B-25 bombers have just launched a medium-altitude strike against Japanese positions on Bougainville. Low-level bombing tactics were famous in the theater, but medium-altitude attacks were effective against facilities and runways. (U.S. Air Force)

A U.S. Army 40mm Bofors medium antiaircraft gun guards Wau. Radar-controlled aboard ships, the Bofors on land was often aimed manually. Possessing a huge punch, excellent range, and rapid fire, it was one of the most widely used weapons of the war, employed in some version by every combatant. (U.S. Army)

Because they posed such a serious threat to aircraft, antiaircraft positions became prime targets for air attack. This Marine 90mm position on Bougainville was hit by a Japanese raid in November 1943, with several men killed. Judging from the wreckage in the area, this raid was far more successful than most made by Japanese forces on U.S. beachheads. (U.S. Army)

Skip-bombing B-25s have destroyed a Japanese freighter (background) in early 1944 off the New Guinea coast. A Japanese frigate is straddled and about to sink. The bomb visible at the bottom was dropped by the same aircraft that took the photo. (National Archives)

(Above left) Tetsuzo Iwamoto. Japan's highest-scoring ace fought from China until war's end and lived to tell the tale. His tour included a stay at Rabaul. Japanese victory claims were less formal and rigorous than those accepted by the Allies, but postwar sources credited Iwamoto with some eighty kills during the war. (H. Sakaida)

(Above right) Junichi Sasai. A rare officer-pilot in the JNAF, Sasai was highly respected within the elite Tainan Air Group. Credited with twenty-one kills, Sasai died over Guadalcanal. (H. Sakaida)

(Above) Robert DeHaven of the 49th Fighter Group stands in front of his P-40. DeHaven was credited with fourteen kills, ten in a P-40, an extremely high figure for a first-generation fighter. His other victories were scored while flying a P-38 Lightning. (R. DeHaven)

(Left) Gerald Johnson of the 49th Fighter Group, credited with twenty-two kills. Johnson served a brief stint in Alaska, where this photo was taken. (Barbara Curtis via John Stanaway)

(Left) Joe Foss, with his trademark beard, relaxes at Nouméa in December 1942 before his second tour at Guadalcanal. Foss was credited with twenty-six kills, all at Guadalcanal, an extraordinary total in less than three months of flying. (U.S. Marine Corps)

(Right) The famous Marine squadron VMF-121 of Guadalcanal takes a short rest at Nouméa. Contributors to this project include Thomas Furlow (rear, second from left), Joe Foss (with beard), and Roger Haberman (smoking pipe). (U.S. Marine Corps)

(Above) Pilots of the elite Tainan Air Group at Lae during happy times. Before the invasion of Guadalcanal, when this photo was taken, Japanese pilots had an edge wherever they flew. (U.S. Marine Corps)

(Right) Charles MacDonald. A brilliant leader and tactician, MacDonald was credited with twenty-seven kills while flying for the famous 475th Fighter Group of Fifth Air Force. (G. R. Roberts via John Stanaway)

On August 8, 1942, one day after the U.S. Marine landing on Guadalcanal, Rabaul sent a large force of torpedo-carrying Betty bombers against the invasion fleet. The Bettys caused minor damage but suffered terrible losses from U.S. antiaircraft. Note how low a torpedo attack was made. (National Archives)

A U.S. carrier raid on Rabaul, November 11, 1943. In this, one of a series of raids, the USN planes crippled so many Japanese warships that Rabaul ceased to exist as an imperial naval base. Large Japanese aerial counterattacks from Rabaul gained nothing. The return of the U.S. carriers, after a year-long hiatus, was a disaster for the Japanese Empire. (U.S. Navy)

turned to look for Swett again, thinking he was headed for the
bombers, but I couldn't see him. I continued after the bombers,
thinking I might be able to see him after I had taken a shot at a bomber
and gotten closer. I never did see him again. I headed for the last
bomber in the entire formation. I was coming up astern of the bombers
and only one or two hundred feet above them and when I got about
400 yards behind him I started firing. I shot about 100 rounds from all
guns, seeing the bullets going into the fuselage, wings and motors but
nothing happened. All of the bombers were shooting at me but none of
them hit me. Then I felt bullets going through the front of my plane
and out of the corner of my eye I saw two Zeros attacking from above
and left. I split S out and dove straight down. I dove all the way down
from 25,000' and began to pull out at about 6,000.

I started to climb again and saw no planes at all. When I got my
altitude back the bombers were a good distance from me and I knew I
couldn't catch them. But there were about ten Zeros below and about
three miles from me. I saw no friendly planes. While climbing I called
Swett but heard nothing. Two of the ten Zeros were off to one side and
more or less by themselves. They were about 4,000 feet below me and
separated by about 2,000 feet in altitude. I dove down and got the top
Zero. It blew up. I continued in the same run, still firing, gave my plane
a little left rudder and got the second as well. He began smoking, then
flamed and went down. Then I again felt bullets going into the front of
my aircraft. One came into the cockpit and went through my radio. I
could see three Zeros coming from my right, one of which had me
perfectly bore-sighted [firing at point-blank range—EB] and was
shooting the hell out of me. I did a "split S" and dove down and while
diving Zeros were making runs on me from all sides. I almost rammed
one. I kept right on going and then saw a cloud for which I headed. As
I was diving I saw oil going over the top of my hood. The gauge read
40 lbs. I looked in the mirror for pursuit but saw no one. I went right
through the cloud, being afraid to wait in there with my low oil
pressure. When I came out I continued my dive right down to the
water. When I leveled off I was making about 360 knots. I looked back
again and this time saw four Zeros about two miles behind me. They
were in line astern. [One following the other, as described by Swett
above. It was at this point that Swett was closing from the rear and
attacked one of the pursuing Zeros. As often happened, Seal did not
realize it.—EB] I held 360 knots for about two minutes and then my
speed dropped to 250. This I was able to hold for about 10 minutes.
The oil pressure stayed at 40 pounds all this time. I wanted to throttle
back and change to lower RPM but was afraid to do so and left it at

2,000 with full gun. When I checked on my Zeroes I found I was now about four miles ahead of them and pulling away gradually. Two then turned back but the other two kept after me. I was going to try to make home, thinking the other two Zeros would give up after a while. I was then about 25 feet off the water. About three minutes later, with oil all over the front of the plane, the air speed began dropping off. It fell to about 140 knots and the oil pressure to 0. The cylinder head temperature was sky-high. I couldn't see the Zeros but I could feel them closing in behind me and then I saw bullets hitting the water in front of me. Bullets also went into my wings, but my tanks did not blow up. I knew I was going to have to make a water landing so I locked my shoulder straps, making sure that they were fast by sitting back and pushing forward again. Then I felt bullets hitting my armor plating. They must have hit the plating with two or three hundred rounds. Then I found there was no pressure on the controls when I pulled back on the stick so I immediately put down 50 degrees of flaps and kicked hard right rudder. I hit the water at about 90 knots and the whole dash board came up and hit me in the face. I wasn't knocked out and immediately looked down to unfasten my safety belt, but found it was already undone. Blood was running down my nose and water was up around my waist when I started to climb out of the plane. I got out all right and blew up my life jacket. At the same time I saw the two Zeros go over my head and turn back. They did not strafe me.

The landings at Guadalcanal initiated a furious response from Japanese aircraft based at Rabaul and Bougainville, as well as a series of carrier engagements. In these early, crucial battles the Marine and USAAF airmen at Henderson fought for their lives. On successive days Japanese forces launched large attacks on Henderson Field. The two engagements illustrate vividly the tremendous importance of possessing an altitude advantage at the outset of an air battle. Once possessing the initiative, skilled pilots do not give it up quickly. And on Guadalcanal, with large numbers of combatants flying toward a single obvious target, the engagements showed vividly the blow-counterblow nature of combat.

On October 2, 1942, radar reported a large raid headed toward Henderson. Every available Marine Wildcat scrambled, thirty-six in all, and headed skyward to gain attack position. While they were on the way up radar reported that the targets were approaching too quickly to be bombers. Zeros were coming, hoping to draw Wildcats into battle:

Major J. L. Smith [a famous Marine ace—EB] led the first division through a layer of clouds, topped at 23,000 feet, and then a second smaller "pancake" cloud with a top at 25,000 feet. The Wildcats were leaving vapor trails and were silhouetted against the cloud layers. When Smith emerged from the smaller cloud, about eighteen Zeros with a 2,000 foot altitude advantage dove on Smith's division and on through the pancake cloud, hitting the other divisions emerging from the first cloud layer. Enemy planes were very systematic, and attacked every plane in the division almost at the same time. . . . Smith crash-landed behind Marine lines and walked to base. . . .

Major Dobbins, in command of the second four-plane section, broke through the cloud bank at 23,000 feet and was met by four Wildcats diving fast. Dobbins believed that the Wildcats had located Bettys and were attacking, and nosed over to follow them. Then the Marines saw a wrecked Grumman falling with the formation and tracers passing their cockpits. Dobbins went into a vertical dive and escaped. His wingman also dove, saw tracers and watched his cockpit fill with oil and smoke. He crash landed with his engine destroyed. Another pilot in the division was spotted on the ascent, but not seen again. He was killed, and his plane found demolished in a large crater near Marine lines, but his body could not be removed. Another Marine section spotted six Zeros near Tulagi. The Zeros saw them approach and reversed direction. The section leader pursued, hoping to catch them at the end of their maneuver. However, he failed to gain position and headed into a cloud. His wingman did not follow. The next day Marines found the Wildcat. The pilot had a broken neck and was dead.

Major Robert E. Galer led the third division behind Smith. When they emerged from the clouds at 23,000 feet they were immediately attacked by seven to ten Zeros coming down in an overhead attack. Two or three Zeros came down high from the right. Galer and his wingman were in a dogfight with several Zeros and no way out. The two made runs on Zeros on each other's tail trying to upset the Zeros' attacks. Galer's wingman disappeared. His plane hit and smoking, Galer's wingman had bailed out but made field safely. Another Grumman passed through and smoked a Zero that was attacking Galer. Galer blew up a diving Zero. However, after Galer destroyed the Zero, another got on his tail, got him bore-sighted and shot Galer's plane from wing tip to wing tip, through the cockpit and through the engine. The engine quit immediately. Galer made a forced landing at sea. Armor no doubt saved his life.

The Marines lost six aircraft and four pilots killed in a few minutes, a terrible loss for the small force at Henderson. Note that the Japanese attack from above broke up one U.S. flight after another, throwing all of them into disarray. Note also that the Zeros caught the Wildcats while they were ascending. This compounded the situation because an aircraft in a steep climb is vulnerable, almost incapable of instant maneuver. The real culprit, however, was the radar system. The Wildcats were climbing after bombers. When it became obvious that the enemy formation consisted of fighters, it should also have been obvious that the Wildcats were not going to reach superior altitude in time.

The next day a smaller flight led by Captain Marion Carl, who soon became one of the Marine Corps's most famous pilots, turned the tables:

Radar contacted enemy flight 145 miles out at 12,000'. The Wildcats reached 34,000 before the raid arrived in the vicinity of Henderson Field. The enemy flight split about 100 miles out and what was probably a flight of 10 or more bombers turned back and went out of the screen going N.W. At least eleven Zeros approached Henderson at 10,000'. Captain Carl saw the Zeros below him when he was at about 30,000 and led the squadron down in a loose spiral, keeping between the Zeros and the sun. When he was about 1,000 feet above them they turned northwest towards their base. They apparently saw the Wildcats at that time, but the Grummans were in position for attack and Captain Carl hit the first Japanese division of five Zeros.

Carl went down at high speed from about 30 degrees behind. He attacked the right rear Zero, fired a short burst at about 100 yards and the Zero exploded. The Zeros began maneuvering violently. Carl pulled out of a steep dive with all guns jammed and had no further contact. Lt. Winter dove behind Carl, and had to pull up to avoid striking the plane shot down by Carl. As the Zeros began to scatter, one pulled up right in front of Winter and almost stalled. Winter flattened out on the Zero's tail and fired at about 100 yards but missed. The Zero did a wing-over and Winter blew him up at about 25 yards. [A wingover is an abrupt half-loop done to change direction and gain altitude. Because the plane pulls up it is a terrible move to make with an enemy on the six. Zero pilots often did wingovers to gain tactical advantage. The opposite of the wingover is the split-S. Either the Zero pilot did not see Fraser or was acting on reflex and was literally killed by task overload.—EB]

Lt. Fraser, flying wing on Carl, dove down in a slow spiral. He had never seen Zeros in such good formation before. Fraser took the plane to Carl's left. The Zero pulled up in front of Fraser who opened up at not over fifty yards. The Zero blew up, one wing came off. Fraser tried avoiding the wing but a small piece hit the windshield and cracked up. Fraser still had good speed, and saw a Zero trying to get on another Wildcat's tail. The Zero saw Fraser coming and pulled up in a loop: Fraser looped right behind him shooting on the way over. Because of his speed he could stay with the Zero. He came out of his loop close to and on the Zero's tail and blew him up. Fraser headed for some clouds, searching for Zeros. Although he saw none, several 20mm bullets struck the bottom of his cockpit. He got into the clouds and was not hit again, but the Jap must have hit his gas line and his engine began burning. . . . Fraser was picked up by a destroyer and dropped on the beach soon later.

As one can see, if one side seized the initiative in an air encounter it could hold on to it for a brief but crucial period. Neither of the engagements described above lasted more than a few minutes. Both were characterized by good pilots getting the jump on other good pilots. Confusion resulted on the side attacked, and that confusion cost aircraft. However, it is also important to see that in both cases the attacking forces, even though possessing great advantages, suffered losses. In a World War II fighter battle, pilots had to close to kill, and when they closed they risked counterblow. The bloody attrition that was the hallmark of both world wars was very much in evidence daily in the skies over the South Pacific.

Another factor was sometimes at work during combat. Here the problem was not fatigue but the result of the inevitable adrenaline rush. Military psychologists have long noted a condition called task overload. Overload results from the simple fact that people are not capable of performing several tasks at once with equal efficiency. Robert L. Shaw, our finest contemporary analyst of air combat, has described the condition brilliantly:

First the operator devotes less attention to each task in an attempt to complete them all. At some point, however, this process leads to neglect of one task which renders the operator ineffective in that area. Depending on the perceived relative importance of each task, the operator then must either concentrate on the completion of one task to the detriment or exclusion of the others, or drop it altogether in favor of a more critical task. The longer this overload condition exists the more tasks are discarded to allow the operator to concentrate on the perceived most critical element, eventually resulting in what might be

called "task fixation." . . . Add to this situation the stress of air combat,
and the predictable result might be described in layman's terms as
"Going to hell in a hand basket."

The implications of overload were immense. During an aerial melee
the pilot was bombarded with stimuli. He had to monitor his own aircraft (fighters are particularly prone to problems when flying at top
speed), watch his wingman, and keep alert for dangers around him. If
confusion and fear overwhelmed the pilot, the paralysis could set in.
Undoubtedly many "unseen" enemy aircraft that destroyed a victim
were in plain view. One conclusion is obvious enough: Decent training
was essential for a fighter pilot. An inexperienced pilot had much to do
just keeping his powerful aircraft in flight. It was a tremendous disadvantage in combat if the pilot had to think about the enemy and also
how to keep his own plane in the air. Conversely a pilot who had
logged enough hours to fly his fighter by instinct was far better
equipped to react to the lethal and rapidly evolving environment of air
combat. Some men were simply naturally good pilots. Many officers—
American and Japanese—have pointed to the great decrease in pilot
training that took place in Japanese forces after 1943 and used that decrease as an explanation for much of the growing calamity facing
Japan in the air. Overload explains one reason lack of training could
be so harmful. (It was also another advantage of the highly structured
U.S. approach toward combat flying.) Frequently American pilots observed an almost suicidal lack of action on the part of Japanese fighter
pilots. Some of these men, unquestionably, as Shaw would put it, were
"going to hell in a hand basket."
    Robert DeHaven witnessed at very close quarters the results of an
enemy pilot freezing in the middle of battle. He described events that
took place in late 1944. There can be no doubt that other victims, both
Japanese and American, suffered a similar fate:

If one does not have mastery of the aircraft, very bad things could
happen. Obviously much depends upon overall circumstances of
combat. For instance in the Philippines we were encountering
consistently very poorly trained pilots or men with limited experience.
However, they had the newest issue of Japanese technology: the George,
Frank, and Jack. These were fine aircraft on paper, but the pilots didn't
really know how to use them. [I should add that any of these second-
generation Japanese aircraft would have been harder to fly than a
Zero—not good for a rookie pilot.—EB] As a result there were at least

two occasions in my own experience where it looked like the enemy simply gave up. On one occasion I attacked a Jack. He was diving straight away from me instead of trying any evasive maneuver at all. I closed, fired, and he simply blew up. I flew through the debris and some of it became enmeshed in my airscoops. But he never made a gesture to disengage. He obviously knew I was there or he wouldn't have dove out. He suffered from panic, or perhaps resignation. Perhaps some young man simply threw his hands over his eyes or was trying to crawl out. But he did nothing meaningful to try to save his life.

During the war Gerald Johnson, who ultimately commanded the 49th Fighter Group, wrote about the declining quality of Japanese pilots and witnessed similar incidents:

The Jap fighter planes have all been very maneuverable and when flown by an experienced pilot become a most difficult target to destroy. Fortunately, however, the majority of Japanese pilots encountered are not of this caliber. They are excellent stick and rudder men, but their weakness is that all their maneuvers are evenly coordinated. They make use of sharp turns and aerobatic maneuvers, seldom using skids, slips, or violent uncoordinated maneuvers in their evasive tactics. Another characteristic of the younger pilots is their definite lack of alertness. In many recent instances we have engaged enemy fighters and they have made no effort to evade our initial attack, evidently because they didn't see us.

Pilots have reported that in addition to being "surprised," many of the Jap pilots are either frightened or bewildered once their formation has been split up, and they make little or no effort to evade attack. I have destroyed several fighters recently when they have tried to dive away or make shallow climbing turns. Any of these . . . could have taken a shot at me if he had utilized his superior maneuverability and climb.

Since the war there have been many books published on World War II aces and their aircraft. This is understandable, as aces have fascinated military aviation enthusiasts since the time of Immelmann and von Richthofen. I think that this surplus of works has obscured the role of the vast majority of pilots who did not reach ace status and has led to an overemphasis on the role of fighters. Yet a look at some numbers, I think, is revealing. Just after the war, famous military journalist S.L.A. Marshall published his book *Men Under Fire*, in which he contended that very few infantrymen did most of the fighting. The debate over whether Marshall was correct and, if so, why continues today. The air war seems to offer testimony on the controversy.

I have tabulated the confirmed victory claims of several Marine and Army squadrons active in the Solomons and over New Guinea. I counted only victories confirmed through the spring of 1944, a period corresponding with this study. Again, it is not my intention to substantiate any victory figures. Most studies from all theaters of World War II indicate that enemy losses were not as high as those claimed. Nevertheless the Japanese air arm was punished brutally in the South Pacific, and there can be no doubt that hundreds were shot down in fighter combat. What interests me is the approximate breakdown of kills within squadrons to ascertain the importance of both aces and pilots who made multiple kills. Unfortunately I do not have any numbers on pilots who had no kills whatsoever, although they no doubt represent a large number. (As we shall see, many had no kills for reasons beyond their control.)

One obvious point highlighted by the numbers is that the type of aircraft flown was an important part of the success of a squadron. The 67th, which was stuck with the export version of the P-39 during the Guadalcanal campaign, was effectively excluded from the great air battles. They had fifteen victories claimed from the start of the war until June 5, 1944, on which day four of their overall total were claimed. The 41st of Fifth Air Force had better P-39s, but the plane was the least able of U.S. fighters, and its poor range hampered it even further. Until March 1943, when it transitioned to P-47s, the 41st had claimed sixty-three victories. The P-40 units of Fifth Air Force did considerably better. Until June 1944 7th Squadron had 108 confirmed kills and 8th Squadron 147. (Both units claimed several more kills when given P-38s at about this time of the war.) As one might expect, pilots flying the second-generation fighters, particularly the Corsair and Lightning, were at a distinct advantage. The 9th Squadron, stablemate of the 7th and 8th in the 49th Fighter Group, had been given P-38s in late 1942 and by June 1944 claimed 198 enemy downed. The 339th squadron of Thirteenth Air Force, despite a nearly six-month hiatus in mid-1943 while it refitted and redeployed, claimed 134 victories. The 13th USAAF's 44th Squadron had 125 kills despite being pulled from action for six months at the end of 1943. The 431st Squadron of Fifth Air Force's illustrious 475th Fighter Group, although entering battle in the summer of 1943, was given credit for 116 destroyed enemy aircraft by March 1944.

The Marine Corps squadrons were in a somewhat different situation. The early-war squadrons, which flew Wildcats, engaged in the extremely intense Guadalcanal campaign. No USAAF P-40 or P-39 squadron saw anything like that sort of concentrated combat. VMF-121 was the highest-scoring squadron of the Guadalcanal campaign. Except for some short leaves, the unit was at Guadalcanal from October 1942 to January 1943. When one considers that the Japanese usually had the numerical advantage during that period, the pilots of VMF-121 flew in what modern pilots would call a "target-rich environment." Equipped with Corsairs, the squadron also had a short tour in June 1943. Overall the unit was given credit for 201 kills, mostly over Guadalcanal. Because of their efficient rotation system, few later Marine squadrons saw the sustained combat faced by the early units at Cactus. They also had more competition from a growing number of Marine Corsair units and the efficient P-38 squadrons of Thirteenth Air Force. However, the Corsair units established formidable records. VMF-214, the famous "Black Sheep," downed 127 Japanese aircraft over the Solomons. Despite a late arrival in the theater VMF-112 claimed eighty-six victims in a few weeks of combat. VMF-215 had a somewhat longer stay (September 1943–February 1944) and claimed 139 victories.

If we dig a little deeper we discern some interesting patterns. The first is the great importance played by pilots with multiple kills. Forty-ninth Fighter Group as a whole from the war's start until June 1, 1944, recorded 463 victory claims on the part of 195 pilots. Out of this total there were twenty aces, who accounted for 160, or 35 percent, of total kills. Ninety-six men claimed one aircraft. The chances of a pilot with one kill claiming another were very good, but the higher up the victory ladder, the fewer the pilots. For instance, twenty-five pilots claimed three aircraft each for a total of seventy-five. As for the aces there was a very definite divide. Many of the men on this list added to their scores later in the war. Also several pilots flew P-40s during this period, whereas others flew P-38s. Yet there were only five double-aces (ten victories); one, Richard Bong, had twenty-one kills at that time.

In other words 367 of the group's 463 kills (79 percent) were accounted for by the 99 out of the 195 pilots who had more than one victory confirmed. Other army squadrons show a similar importance for aces and multiple kills. In the 41st 15 of the 41 pilots with confirmed victories possessed 59 percent of the squad's 63 victories. In Thirteenth Air Force's hot 339th Squadron 51 pilots recorded kills; seven were aces, accounting for 43 percent of the squadron's 134 victories. The 26 pilots, counting aces, with multiple kills accounted for 87 percent of the unit's score. The 342d squadron, a P-47 outfit flying for Fifth Air Force, claimed 70 enemies downed. Its three aces (out of 22 pilots with kills) claimed 20; 94 percent of overall claims came from the 18 pilots with multiple kills. Several other USAAF squadrons show a similar pattern. One might say that the pilot who destroyed the imperial air arm had three Japanese flags painted on the side of his fighter.

Two USAAF squadrons I investigated show a somewhat different profile; both were P-38 units from the outset. The 44th Squadron flying for Thirteenth Air Force had a confirmed score of 125 enemy destroyed, 65 of them claimed by aces. Pilots with multiple kills accounted for 81 percent of the unit's total. The 431st Squadron of Fifth Air Force, in the period of this study, compiled a score of 116 kills, 60 of which came from aces, 82 percent attributed to men with more than one victory. I do not think that these units deviated very much from the overall USAAF pattern as much as it may appear. The 431st had eight aces out of 39 pilots claiming victories; the 44th had nine aces out of 46. This was a higher percentage of aces than found in the other units and leads one to conclude simply that because these two units benefited from superior aircraft throughout, they simply shot down more planes and thus had more aces.

Marine figures tracked the army pattern. Hard-fighting VMF-121 had 201 victories, 105 claimed by aces. A very high percentage (92 percent) of the squadron's victories came from pilots claiming more than one kill. Perhaps reflecting the intense combat, 41 out of 57 pilots had credit for at least two planes destroyed, a very high percentage. Most kills were in Wildcats, but, as mentioned, the squadron was in the middle of combat more intense than found in most periods of the war. The Marine pilots flying Corsairs in the Solomons during 1943 were very likely engaged in some massive air battles and had superior aircraft. This led to a large number of victory claims relative to the number of planes operational and hence a large number of aces. VMF-112, which did several stints in the Solomons between November 1942 and August 1943 in Wildcats and Corsairs, had 86 victories, 44 attributed to aces. Seven of the squadron's 29 pilots credited with kills were aces. The same pattern shows up in VMF-214, the famous "Black Sheep." Of the 127 kills credited to the squadron, 71 fell to aces. There were nine aces out of the unit's 43 pilots with victory claims. Men with multiple kills accounted for 83 percent of the squad's score. An extreme example was VMF-215, which served in the Solomons throughout the final onslaught against Rabaul, a time of desperate fighting. In VMF-215 there were 10 aces among the 30 men who were credited with a kill. The aces accounted for 105 of the 139 kills credited to the squadron. This meant that 93 percent of the unit's victories came from those with multiple kills.

Ever since World War II the military has tried to identify the profile of a good fighter pilot. The superbly trained men flying modern jets, in my opinion, operate in such a different environment than the mass conflict of World War II that I have no intention of drawing generalizations across time. A few factors stand out, however. First, much of the damage inflicted in air-to-air combat was inflicted by a minority, which in the South Pacific, at least, does not appear to be as small as indicated in some aviation literature. (I should reiterate that military figures do not list those pilots who had no victories, surely a large number. So I search only to identify trends, not to provide a reliable statistical analysis.) Joel Paris reflected on this fact of life: "The real fighting was done by a small number of people. I guess the same thing happens in the infantry. There are a lot of people along with those fighting, but they're really kind of company. I've known fellows that flew dozens of missions and never blew the tapes off their guns." Probably the single most important quality held by a fighter pilot (assuming he was a competent pilot) was aggressiveness. As I have tried to illustrate in my analysis of aerial melees, getting close enough to shoot down an aircraft often left one vulnerable to counterblows. Pilots knew this, and those that accepted the dangerous reality had an advantage if well led and lucky. Those with a high degree of skill, good judgment, and an aggressive temperament were obvious candidates for making ace. But a decent pilot willing to mix it up was a dangerous opponent even if his technical skills were not exceptional. Conversely the chaotic nature of air battle usually left a way out. It would have been very easy for a U.S. wing to make an attack pass, keep the speed up, fire some bursts, and call it a day. Many American pilots who flew escort missions remarked on the reluctance of many Japanese units to close with the escorts and bombers. Instead they stayed on the periphery and tried to dart in but were very quick to retreat. Those willing to throw the dice were not only likely to make a kill but also, in an active theater, to make more than one. They may also have been more likely to die in combat. Robert DeHaven reflected on this matter:

Even today—the Israeli Air Force is a fine example—there is a premium on aggressiveness. This has always been true in fighter combat. It is an extremely important trait for a successful fighter pilot. I don't mean blind heroism, but rather taking advantage of a situation by virtue of aggressiveness, training, experience, and a desire to succeed. I've seen combat where a friendly plane is overtaking an enemy plane and would press only so far and then break off for no definable reason. On one occasion I asked the pilot why he broke away and he asked, "Did you see that Zero coming in from the starboard side?" I said no. Perhaps his actions were sound combat tactics—when under attack get out. In his case it meant breaking off from a successful attack because he was about to be attacked himself. And yet he might have hung on for another two or three seconds to make sure his assessment of the threat was accurate. Or he could have ignored it and pressed his attack. Things always moved very quickly. What you see in your peripheral vision might be a Zero, it might be a friend, it might be nothing at all.

Some pilots probably did not belong in the theater at all. Don Gordon met some aboard the *Enterprise*, in the main an excellent group of fighting men:

Some guys would panic. They shouldn't have been in fighters. You could tell who they were. You could tell who wasn't going to survive. They filled a seat. It's sad, but they filled a seat. When I had squadrons I told some pilots, and this is God's truth, that you're filling a seat but you're not capable here and you better watch your ass. One guy made admiral: I told him to get out because he would not live, and he did. This was after the war. He was a splendid officer, made admiral and I didn't. But he was not a fighter pilot. A symptom would be trying to be too smart. They think, but they don't develop habits of flying intuitively. If you are flying from a carrier you can't think. You have to prethink. It all has to be preplanned. If you're "too smart" you think about the situation as it happens. That's too late. I had good friends lost in combat because they were trying to think how to fight a Zero. You don't think, you do it.

There were other important reasons for not compiling a record of kills. Some men were unlucky enough (or perhaps lucky, depending on one's perspective) to be posted in an area where there was little combat. After Rabaul fell there were many Marine and USAAF squadrons that had little or no contact with the Japanese until the Philippine campaign began in late 1944. Considering the fact that his tour was only three months long and that he flew a Wildcat, Joe Foss's record of twenty-six kills was remarkable even for Cactus, which produced many aces. Yet in the spring of 1944 he did a second tour and, like most of the men in his new squadron (VMF-115), did not engage an enemy. There was also the possibility that a decent young pilot might get stuck with a poor element leader. Some pilots believed that the role of the wingman was to protect the leader; the leader would do the killing while the wing kept the element safe. This may have been good tactics, but it did not make for high scores until a pilot gained enough experience to lead his own element.

Concerning aces, most were probably fine pilots with a healthy dose of aggressiveness. Yet the difference between five kills and three might kills may well have been luck. Sometimes when an enemy plane went down and two pilots claimed the kill, they would flip a coin or cut cards. Or one man might run into a particularly inexperienced Japanese unit and knock down someone who did not manage to wiggle the aircraft's rudder due to panic. In a similar vein someone on patrol might jump a Japanese floatplane doing reconnaissance. It is true that the number of aces was not high. But it is also true that a very high percentage of those who made ace scored between five and seven kills. These men were intrepid pilots and invaluable to the war effort, no doubt; they were not necessarily more greatly skilled than someone with three or four flags painted on the fuselage.

The great aces, I think, were in a very different category altogether. If an American pilot in a first-generation fighter scored ten or more victories, then by my definition he was a great ace. For those flying second-generation fighters, a more realistic total might be fifteen, perhaps twenty. These men represent a handful out of hundreds of pilots who flew in the South Pacific, yet they fly at a different level than their contemporaries. All were technically fine pilots; all were good shots; all knew how to balance risk against the possibility of victory. Although by definition the great aces saw much combat, it was rare for one to perish in a dogfight. In the melee they were masters of the situation. Yet perhaps because of their aggressiveness several died in accidents or because of ground fire. Richard Bong and Gerald Johnson perished in accidents shortly after the war; Thomas Lynch and Paul Westbrook died attacking Japanese warships. As shown above, the percentage of Japanese fighter pilots killed was astounding. Yet even after doing battle in flying tinderboxes for years on end, some of the best made it home. Tetsuzo Iwamoto, perhaps Japan's highest-scoring ace, fought throughout the war and survived. Hiroyoshi Nishizawa, another pilot claiming the title of top Japanese ace, was killed in a transport that was shot down by Americans.

It is difficult to ascertain the degree to which making ace motivated combat pilots. Some pilots were probably put on a fast track by their commanders to gain publicity for their units and to encourage Washington to allocate more resources to the theater. In total several thousand fighter pilots fought on both sides during the South Pacific campaign. Any form of competition between the pilots for glory and publicity would, I think, be rare. Because of the massive scope of World War II and a changing attitude toward warfare, individual heroes played a much smaller role than was the case during World War I. It is likely that Manfred von Richthofen was the most famous individual combatant of the Great War. Eddie Rickenbacker was one of the most famous men in the United States during and after World War I. Yet the great aces of World War II—Bong, Hartmann, Johnson, Purdy—are known only to aviation enthusiasts. World War II was dominated by generals like Patton, Montgomery, MacArthur, and Rommel, not by men of lesser ranks. Furthermore the simple ferocity of World War II encouraged, at least in Allied countries, a grim and businesslike approach to war. Accomplishing one's mission and thus killing the enemy were a part of the equation, but achieving anything beyond local-hero status was out of the ordinary. Roger Haberman had interesting comments on this point:

The number of kills was very secondary—you wanted to stay alive. This was true with Foss and everyone else. I led Foss's second section. He led eight and I led the back four. There wasn't any talk at all about whether he got twenty-two or nineteen or three. He comes down and talks to the intelligence people and they tally the score. But we were interested in none of that. You wanted to keep you and your buddies alive. I never heard a word about a Congressional Medal of Honor or any of that type of bullshit. You're just interested in doing a journeyman job and staying in one piece. Any fighter pilot that was indulging in competition for numbers or having his flights set up to pad his kills was full of it. He had the wrong attitude. That's not the way to win a war. Your job is to get the job done and not count the damn chips. I am adamant on that. You were not there to get numbers, you are there to achieve your mission. I never heard Foss even mention it. Not once. He'd brief intelligence and that was that. We were there to do the job and stay alive. That included fighting the Japanese. But the mission was first, and you couldn't do your mission if you were dead.

Yet the fraternity of fighter pilots was relatively small. Even in the South Pacific (a small theater for the war) several million men in all services participated. The number flying aircraft of all types, much less fighters, was in the low thousands. And at the levels where such things counted most—squadron, fighter group, even air force—only a few hundred men flew at any given time. The respect of one's peers was vital in all services. Fighter pilots were one of the few groups that could quantify to some degree their success. In addition, the fact that they fought alone at the point of fire gave their war an individual nature unique in World War II. Therefore I think it safe to say that doing well—physically demonstrating by becoming an ace—was important to many men. It was not, as Robert DeHaven explained, simply a matter of competition but an expression of survival and the satisfaction of victory:

> I think most of the young men involved would have said it really wasn't such a big deal, to get five kills and become an ace, but it really was. Aces didn't come that quickly or easily. Certainly by a wide margin the number of people that flew and engaged in aerial combat who did not become aces outnumbered those who did by a large factor.
>
> But you must understand that it was not a scoring contest. It was the satisfaction in achieving victory and surviving. Combat was exciting beyond description. The smell of cordite that would seep into the cockpit of any fighter was almost like an aphrodisiac—it was "*eu du combat.*" When you engaged the enemy, and had made a kill, sometimes landing with bullets in your plane, you were filled with a euphoric high that was not explicable. There was the satisfaction of victory and also the deep fulfillment that you had survived. When you landed, especially if your wingman was home with you, there was a feeling of the deepest satisfaction.

Pilots who were reported as missing in action represent a huge category of losses in fighter combat and can never be properly accounted for. Because they exist in such large numbers, I must examine the MIA issue.

As noted, intelligence did not always make the distinction between MIA and operational loss. As also noted, according to figures available on U.S. operations the number of missing was very high. The Japanese, perhaps sensibly, did not have a category for MIAs, concluding that if a plane did not return its pilot and crew were killed in action. Yet I think investigating the issue brings to light the grim and random tempo of combat operations in the South Pacific. By definition I cannot identify the fate of those who were classified, usually forever, as MIA. Yet aided by the data available and some common sense, I think it possible to reconstruct the fates of many who never returned. Considering this cumulative tragedy, I want to exclude the obvious categories that I have already examined: accidents on takeoff and landing; bad weather; and navigational error (getting lost).

The most obvious fate of an aircraft gone MIA was likely that it fell
to enemy fire without a friendly pilot witnessing the event. Every pilot
knew that it was dangerous to fly alone, yet at the conclusion of most
engagements there were aircraft flying solo. It is likely that some of
them never made it home. While flying off *Enterprise* during the Battle of the Philippine Sea during June 1944, Don Gordon scored the
sort of kill that in U.S. records would have been listed as MIA: "At the
Philippine Sea I saw a lone Zero about 500 feet over my head. I went
into a loop, fired at the top, and shot down the Zero. He never knew
I was there. Then I came home. So I was never really in a dogfight during my service."

One can only imagine how often such a fate befell a lone fighter during a long campaign. However, there must have been other causes. Because fighter aircraft were so powerful they were inherently dangerous
to fly. An inexperienced pilot, confused during combat, was in danger
of putting his fighter into a dangerous situation. Stalls are common in
flight and easily handled (although never recommended in combat). A
spin is a different matter in a fighter, particularly an inverted spin. Two
particularly dangerous situations were created when a pilot experienced a snap roll or an accelerated stall. A snap roll might start when
one tried to hold a tight turn with too much elevator, bringing the aircraft into a stall. One wing will stall before the other and the plane
rolls violently in the direction of the stalled wing. Unlike a normal
stall, this would take place at high speed and throw the aircraft into a
wicked spin. The spin may be "inverted" (the aircraft is upside down
or flat) and extremely difficult to recover from without a cool head
and some altitude. Young RNZAF pilot Bryan Cox, who during training was just beginning his career in the P-40, went into a mild snap roll
and very nearly died:

On reaching about three thousand feet and approaching Palmerston
North I decided to make a right-hand climbing turn and
overexuberantly moved the stick over to the right and slightly back.
The unforgiving P-40 objected; without the slightest warning it rapidly
cartwheeled to the right. From my many experiences of flick-rolling
Harvards [the U.S. T-36 standard trainer for Allied forces—EB] I
instinctively checked forward on the stick and applied left rudder—
which stopped the rotation after only 90 degrees of roll—and found
myself inverted with the easily recognizable white profile of the T & G
Insurance Building framed in the windscreen! Instantly assuming that
the flick had occurred from a combination of too low an airspeed, and

too much back pressure on the stick along with high wing-loading, I held the aircraft inverted but allowed the nose to drop to gain a safe airspeed before attempting to roll the right way up again. On rolling level at about 1,000 feet right over Palmerston North I climbed away, carefully checking the airspeed and handling more gingerly!

Luckily for Cox the snap roll had not taken place at high speed and he had done what was called for. One mistake in this situation and Cox would have died. A relative of the snap roll was the accelerated, or high-speed, stall. A high-speed stall can be induced in a number of ways but requires either a steep bank up or down, which increases the apparent weight of the aircraft, combined with any weight instability of the aircraft or overly abrupt move of the stick. An overaggressive recovery from a power dive could cause an accelerated stall. The result can be a spin, which in a World War II fighter could take 10,000 feet to recover from assuming the pilot kept his head. USAAF flight manuals recommended bailing from any aircraft in a spin at less than 5,000 feet. If the spin was flat or inverted the situation was worse, as the pilot had to essentially reverse the standard spin recovery procedure or add additional measures such as cutting the throttle. A standard stall in combat, usually caused by trying to climb too quickly with too little power, was a bad situation by itself. A spin in a heavily loaded fighter, often with very badly distributed weight, was a dreadful danger. If a pilot was in combat and suffered a spin, particularly at altitudes lower than 8,000 feet, he could flutter to oblivion in seconds and no one would see him die. (The precise details are murky, but the great ace Thomas McGuire died in a high-speed stall at low altitude when his flight was jumped by a single Oscar. McGuire was not in immediate danger but tried to bring his heavily laden P-38 into attack position to save a wingman. Pushing the controls too hard, the wing dipped and McGuire crashed.)

There was also the danger of running out of fuel, which no doubt led to MIAs. Japanese Zeros escorting bombers to Guadalcanal had already learned the importance of fuel conservation. As the Americans went over to the offensive, they had to hone the art also. In the 5th USAAF study, many unit leaders stressed the importance of stretching the legs of a fighter's range through careful flying. (Lindbergh was in the area to assist.) But any long mission left pilots with a tiny margin for error. Just as many Japanese aircraft ran out of fuel attacking Guadalcanal, U.S. aircraft found the shoe on the other foot as they moved forward. Americans never operated as far from base as did the

Japanese attacking Guadalcanal from Rabaul, yet no American fighter had the exceptional range of the Zero.

In July 1943, Lieutenant George Henry Smith's flight of Navy Wildcats was operating out of Guadalcanal supporting the U.S. drive up the Solomons. (Smith's unit, VF-21, came off an escort carrier and did two short stints while land-based on Guadalcanal and compiled a fine record during the fighting over New Georgia.) Rendova, part of the New Georgia island group, was a relatively distant objective for a Wildcat patrol. Smith quickly faced a calamity that was repeated hundreds of times, often with a fatal outcome, in Pacific skies. Note that Lieutenant Smith, due to bad weather, was very low on fuel before getting lost. Note also that confusion set in, making a dangerous situation worse:

On July 14th at 1330 our eight Wildcats took off from Guadalcanal on a routine combat patrol over Rendova. There was a heavy weather front on our flight path so we turned south to get around it. Our Wildcats came onto station at 1545 by approaching Rendova from Simbo Island. When we arrived there, flying at about 200 feet, both my wing tanks were dry and I figured that if we had to go south of the storm again I wouldn't have gas to get back. The section leader agreed we couldn't stay around much longer, and turned the lead over to me. We went down the coast of New Georgia. The leader of the other flight wanted to cross New Georgia to the North and our flight leader took over again. I had tried to go over the clouds but at 20,000 feet there was no top so I came down again. It looked awfully bad up north to me and I was pretty sure I didn't have enough gas to go up there so I asked permission to return to base alone. They gave me the lead instead, so we continued on down the New Georgia coast. We couldn't find a landmark, so I took a heading of 150 degrees. . . . Then the whole formation just broke up. . . . It was about 1900, and I knew I would have to come down so I just gave them the dope and hoped they would get it. I tied my emergency kit and canteen to my chute straps, snapped my shoulder straps, opened the cockpit cover, turned on my landing lights and made a power landing with full flaps and wheels up. The tail hit, then the nose hit a swell and the ship nosed over. I released my safety belt and just sort of dropped out into the water. The plane sank in about 10 seconds.

Wildcats, like several other USN aircraft, had a large raft embedded in the fuselage but on impact they often did not come loose, particularly if the plane sank quickly. Smith's larger rubber boat failed to come to the surface, and he was forced to make due with the small raft that was part of the parachute apparatus. Currents and winds controlled the tiny vessels. Unlike some pilots, Smith was not fortunate enough to meet the friendly inhabitants of the Solomons. His companion was the South Pacific:

In my jungle backpack I had three cans of pemmican, two chocolate bars, a canteen of water and some vitamins. In addition, I had the regular plane emergency kit of a canteen, three cans of pemmican, one chocolate bar and malted milk tablets. I had my own canteen, a .45 pistol, knife and my rubber raft. I saved half my parachute for a blanket. I got pretty cold sitting in the water. I decided to ration what stores I had with me. I allowed myself four mouthfuls of water, one can of pemmican, two malted milk tablets and two vitamin tablets a day. I stuck to this as long as my rations held out.

The next morning an American reconnaissance plane passed overhead but didn't see me. Later two more flew close with no response. In the early afternoon of the second day, with the sea completely calm I heard a noise like breakers and suddenly saw whales spouting. One came up and nudged the boat with his nose and slid underneath it. He was the first of several over the next days. I tried to spear fish with my knife, but since there weren't any prongs, they wouldn't stay on. I did get one by scooping him into the boat as I slashed him. It was tough, dry and hard to swallow. Fish wouldn't take a hook either. I tried to shoot them, but that was impossible. I made a sieve out of my mosquito net and caught some of the minnows that were always swimming underneath the boat. I ate them alive like one of those college boys you hear about and they weren't too bad. Soon my water supply was nearly gone. All afternoon and night of the 18th there were rain squalls so I was able to collect drinking water. The sea was terribly rough, however, and I was pretty badly bounced around. The waves break over the bow and keep slapping you around—it's torture. I got a lot of salt water sores. There is only one position you can take on a boat like that. All you can do is slouch in that position or sit straight up.

On the 20th, soon after a Japanese plane passed by, an albatross came and sat on the edge of the boat. I shot it with my .45 and skinned it the way you would a rabbit. I cut its throat and squeezed the blood into my canteen cup with a little water to keep it from coagulating. It was pretty good. I ate the liver of the bird, but the heart and meat were tough and stringy. The lungs have some moisture in them which helps to quench your thirst and below the intestines there is a pouch of fat

which is good to eat and which I used for oiling my gun. It was cold
and rough that day and there were fifteen foot waves. A sea gull came
and sat on my hand. The next day more gulls came and sat on my head
and toes. Another American patrol plane passed overhead.

On the 24th I saw my first shark. It rubbed the bottom of the boat
and I shot at it but to no avail. I shot two more birds, and learned that
the meat was better if you let it sit for a while. My water was running
low, but luckily it rained in the morning. Another shark passed by. So
did a Japanese plane. Another albatross came and sat on the edge of the
boat for about four hours. I stroked his neck and talked to him and he
pecked at my hand. He was Oscar, my friend. It rained all night and I
filled my canteens. But I dropped my canteen cup into the ocean.
Luckily I found a coconut, cut it in half and used it for bailing and
storing bird meat. The 28th was a bad time as several large sharks
followed the boat the entire day. Another was there the next day.
Fortunately he left because my raft capsized later. Everything was tied
down, so I lost nothing.

Although not clear from his austere account, Lieutenant Smith undoubtedly knew he was facing doom. He was growing weaker, out of
sight of land, and running out of supplies; the elements were gaining
the upper hand. As described below, Smith found salvation. Dozens of
allied amphibious aircraft were dedicated to pilot rescue and were frequently supported by U.S. submarines. If possible warships searched
for a downed flier if a Mayday was heard close by. Note that the size
of the ocean and the relentless power of the waves made saving a comrade a hazardous and potentially deadly business:

On August 1st at 0900 a New Zealand patrol plane flew past at 800
feet, turned, and circled. They dropped a New Zealand life jacket about
30 feet away. It contained a flashlight, emergency rations, twenty
rounds of ammunition, a stainless steel mirror (my metal one had been
worthless for a long time due to corrosion), cigarettes, a flare pistol and
a note saying "Good luck, will send Dumbo soon." ["Dumbo" was the
name for the PBY Catalina, America's outstanding long-range
amphibious reconnaissance aircraft.—EB) On the next day the weather
was so bad, I expected no rescue. It was terribly cold and the boat
capsized again.

By August 3rd I had begun to lose hope, thinking I must have drifted
out of the position reported by the New Zealander. At noon, however, I
saw three PBYs approach. Two passed by. I shot my flare pistol and the

third saw me. All three circled for about an hour and a half, dropping float lights. The waves were well over 10 feet, and I doubted they could land. Finally one landed some way off. I couldn't see the plane because of the swells, and he couldn't see me. The other two planes circled over me, and the third taxied in my direction. As soon as I saw him, I paddled like hell and they took me aboard. The crew was seasick, but the pilot, Lieutenant Hamblin, decided it was too rough to take off. They gave me grapefruit juice and fried two steaks for me with peas and coffee. I hugged the PBY crew. I knew I was safe. Even if the PBY broke up, they had those big ten-man life rafts with equipment and supplies. Those rafts even carried a little still for making drinking water. We could have been pretty comfortable. They put me in a bunk and wrapped me in blankets until I was warm. We rode out the night and it got rougher. It seemed very bad the next morning but Hamblin took off. We arrived at base about ten o'clock. Sometimes they pass out medals for bravery and skill. Those fellows on that PBY had both.

Smith was in the water for three weeks. The tropical climate, so often a malignant foe to all combatants in the South Pacific, saved him. In a colder area he would have died of exposure. In a drier area he would have died of thirst. And yet the warmth that saved Smith, sadly, must have prolonged the agony for many forlorn pilots who were never spotted and simply floated away into oblivion.

I must make another important but sad point concerning fighter combat in the South Pacific. The Pacific war from start to finish was one of the most vicious conflicts in our century. The land war, in great contrast to other theaters of World War II, descended into something like a war of annihilation with Japanese soldiers refusing to surrender and, in response, American troops refusing to take prisoners. Although air combat lacked the violent immediacy of ground-fighting, fighter pilots on both sides for the most part fought with tremendous brutality. On an abstract level, I think, men on both sides grew to respect the enemy's combat prowess. The arrogance that marked Allied assumptions prior to Pearl Harbor evaporated during the Japanese blitz of the first months of the war. Allied fighter pilots were all too aware that their opponents had good aircraft and excellent skills.

This matter leads to the larger issue of feelings held toward the Japanese on the part of American airmen. This is a complex matter and generalizations are precarious, to say the least. On one hand there was genuine respect for the obvious bravery of the Japanese. This view was

expressed after the war by Major General Richard Carmichael, who
during the conflict served as commander of General Kenney's 19th
Bomb Group and spent a year in a Japanese POW camp:

> We always respected the Japanese. I never looked down on them. They
> were formidable. We had a lot of respect for their pilots. The best
> Japanese pilots were the Navy pilots in the beginning. We were against
> Navy pilots every time we ran up to Rabaul. In the first part of the war,
> those were real fine pilots. They wasted away their really trained pilots,
> I guess, within the first year or so. . . . I don't think anybody had any
> doubt in their minds that they were up against a real smart, aggressive
> enemy.

On the other hand racial hatreds and the legacy of Pearl Harbor had
an undeniable impact. LeRoy Smith reflected on this years after the
war but also made the simple yet easily forgotten observation that
Americans and Japanese lived on the other side of what was, in cultural terms, a much larger world than today's:

> We didn't have much good to say about the Japanese. Everybody knew
> they were brave or crazy. Some of the guys just hated them. When we
> first took Guadalcanal, we captured a bunch of construction workers
> who were building what we called Henderson Field. I heard stories that
> guys would go up on a little hill with their rifles and take pot shots at
> the prisoners in the pen down below. I never saw it, and maybe it didn't
> even happen, but it gives you an idea of how some guys thought. Hell,
> a friend of mine a little while ago ribbed me for driving my old
> Japanese pickup. But you should remember we were really distant from
> the Japanese. Most Americans didn't know a damn thing about them or
> their country. It wasn't like the French and Germans, or Russians and
> Poles who were neighbors and always fighting wars. I don't think I had
> ever seen a Japanese before I entered the navy before the war. America
> was a big island then. There was a lot we didn't know.

Much the same, no doubt, could have been said about the Japanese.
Regardless of feelings of cultural antipathy, nations do not normally
go to war to faraway countries because they do not like the people involved. The fighting personnel of both nations were stationed at the
end of the earth, from their point of view, struggling over land that
none of them had ever heard of for causes that were most abstract.

In addition, the military regime governing Japan showed a remarkable callousness toward the lives of fighting men. Assuming that every-

one would do their duty, and that their men considered death in war an honor, the Imperial High Command did much to waste some of their most precious human assets. There was no policy of rotation for units and individual pilots. Units were reassigned, and if one was demolished its remnants might be sent to Japan for rebuilding. No doubt wise commanders found excuses to reassign pilots when their performance began to deteriorate, as happens in almost every case at some point. Normally, however, Japanese pilots served until they were killed, wounded, or evacuated because of disease. In addition, there was no formal policy of air-sea rescue for downed pilots. Commander M. Okumiya was a squadron leader on Rabaul with 2,200 hours of flying experience. Wounded, he was promoted and reassigned to staff duty in Tokyo. Immediately after the war, Okumiya told American officers: "Pilots generally had parachutes, life preservers and rafts. Seaplanes, subs and destroyers were sometimes used to search for downed fliers. But this depended entirely on the will of the division commander. There was no organized system at all. This was one of the big differences in your approach and ours. Your whole philosophy was different. Approximately 20,000 naval pilots were trained during war, and approximately 9,500 of them were killed."

The Japanese indifference toward their own men quickly was manifested in their treatment of the enemy. One of the intellectual errors concerning the Pacific war, at least in its early stages, was that racial hatred was central to the mutual butchery that ensued. This, in my opinion, was a minor factor. Far more important was the impression passed on from man to man on the front that the Japanese asked no quarter and gave none. The closer Allied pilots were to combat, I think, the worse was their opinion of the Japanese as humans.

Like all American servicemen fighter pilots were infuriated by Pearl Harbor. The Allied defeats that followed were viewed as a kind of mugging. Even worse, I think, all of the Allied pilots had heard horror stories—many true—of brutal mistreatment and executions of prisoners of war. Wake and Bataan, which show the Japanese in a miserable light in retrospect, were exaggerated by the eternal military grapevine. Although the details are not exact, apparently the Japanese executed some thirty American fliers captured over Rabaul. It was common practice for American fliers above the rank of lieutenant not to wear insignias into combat, because they feared that if downed and captured they would be tortured by the Japanese military police to learn military intelligence.

From the point of view of a fighter pilot, however, the treatment afforded a pilot who bailed from a stricken aircraft was of utmost im-

portance. Warfare is an ethical swamp, and this issue is a perfect example of the deadly ambiguity facing men in the field. In retrospect it
is obvious that aircraft and not pilots were the limiting factor in operations in the South Pacific. This was probably true in other theaters as
well. At the time, however, this would not have been at all clear.
Fighter pilots would have known better than anyone that a skilled opponent was a military asset well worth denying the enemy. If one side
was attacking the other, seeing a plane go down and the pilot in a
parachute meant that the pilot might well be in battle again quickly. A
violent logic would argue that killing the pilot along with the aircraft
was a justifiable military act. Unlike prisoners taken in a ground fight,
if a pilot parachuted over his own lines he was likely to be back in action. A certain logic would argue that killing the pilot was as important as killing the aircraft.

A comparison between the Pacific and European Theaters in this regard sheds light. In practice, although few European Theater pilots
like to discuss it, many men were shot in their parachutes. An overly
excited or fatigued pilot, especially one who had lost a wingman, was
an obvious candidate to smoke an enemy before he reached safety. Yet
on the Western Front men in 'chutes were relatively safe. German pilots over Britain in 1940 usually allowed RAF pilots to bail safely, perhaps because the war between the two nations had yet to reach the violent crescendo that later developed. When the Allies went on the
offensive in Europe there was an obvious deal between the opposing
sides. Luftwaffe pilots and German troops on the ground usually imprisoned the huge numbers of Allied airmen who parachuted out of
stricken bombers. In return Allied fighters allowed German fighter pilots to float to the ground even though they knew many would be up
in the air again within days. Most of the great German aces in the
West were shot down several times. Killing those men on the way
down would have saved many Allied planes, but the Luftwaffe would
have taken its revenge in spades. Consequently the two sides concluded that they had a vested interest in conducting a harsh air war
with some trappings of ancient chivalry.

This bond born of violent necessity was never made in the Pacific
war. The Japanese made it a practice to shoot Allied pilots in their
'chutes from the start of the war and never ceased the practice. It is impossible to say to what degree this policy reflected circumstance or military ethos. Although it is difficult to ascertain the extent to which
Japanese military ideology penetrated the intelligent men flying fighters, there can be little doubt that they shared in the cult of death that
permeated the Japanese military. To give or show mercy in traditional

bushido was a complex subject. When the warrior code was mass-produced for the nation after the Meijii Restoration the idea of surrender was considered something close to treason or, worse yet, of cowardice. From this logic terrible things flowed. Suicide in the early stage of the war was not the norm for Japanese pilots. Most pilots carried parachutes knowing that they could land in friendly hands. (Even over Guadalcanal there was a Japanese zone of control until imperial forces were expelled in February 1943.) But not even that expedient was required. Simple pilot armor was available early in the war, yet few men took advantage of it. If an honorable and sacred death was preferable to captivity, then it followed that destroying enemy aircraft and crew was likewise acceptable because the victims had sacrificed honor. We will never know how the Pacific air war would have developed had the Japanese followed the Luftwaffe practice of allowing downed pilots to live. However, in practice the imperial forces began a vicious correlation of killing that did not end until VJ-Day.

Whatever the motivation, it was a common for Japanese pilots to shoot helpless victims. During the large air battle of June 7, 1943, some of which is related above, Corsair pilot Lieutenant Samuel Logan experienced the practice but lived to describe it:

I saw two Zeros chasing a New Zealand P-40. I followed them down trying to close in on the tail of the Zero. When I was about 500 yards away, my plane sudden began to vibrate and shake. I pulled up the nose but it continued to stall and shake worse than ever. I hadn't seen any tracers but I turned and saw that my rudder was mostly shot away and that I had very little elevator control. The nose kept dropping. Suddenly I saw a Zero go past me from behind. I hadn't known one was there. My plane was getting out of control so I opened the greenhouse, got out, and crawled back along the fuselage, clear to the tail. I didn't have a chin strap on my helmet, so it blew off with my goggles, and for a while I couldn't see a thing. I jumped but made the mistake of pulling my rip cord too soon. It worked OK and I was at about 20,000 feet. I was trying to pull up into the seat of the chute when I heard kind of a "put-put" behind me, the noise of a machine gun fire. I swung around in my chute and saw a Zero making a run on me from behind firing with two machine guns. He missed but went so close under me that I had to jerk up my feet to avoid being hit by the prop. When he passed by, he did a wing-over and made a second run on me. I was trying to collapse the chute to speed up my descent, but couldn't do it. I was pretty high and weak from lack of oxygen. He missed again and then wheeled around and came back for a third run with both guns firing. I

was busy trying to spill the air out of the chute, and I now had it
partially collapsed. This time though, I didn't think to pull up my feet.
The prop hit me. I thought at first my feet were gone, but then saw that
only the heel had been taken off my left foot. He made another run
before the New Zealand P-40 I saw before came along and chased him
off. It seemed to take ages to hit the water, and I had to fight to keep
from passing out. Several Corsairs and P-40s were around so I figured
I'd get picked up soon. I put a tourniquet on my right leg. The big toe
and the one next to it were on, but all the outside and rest were cut off
just above the ankle—kind of a sideways cut. My left heel was cut too.
I gave myself two morphine surettes and I took four sulfa tablets. The
morphine started to do its work, things began to go dim, and I lay back
and relaxed.

Lieutenant Logan was quickly picked up. His foot was later ampu-
tated. However, as we can see from another account, this practice was
not a Japanese specialty. In August 1943, during one of the big air
battles of the Munda-Bougainville campaign, a large group of inexperienced Zero pilots tangled with veteran American Corsair and P-40
pilots who went on a rampage. U.S. Army Lieutenant Lucien Shuler,
a P-40 pilot, was in the fight. Already an ace, Shuler added to his
score:

Lt. Shuler made a pass on another Zero, from the left-rear quarter, he
fired and the Zero rocked its wings and fell off in a roll to the right. Lt.
Shuler followed in the roll, firing as he went. The Zero pulled out into a
shallow dive, Lt. Shuler fired from behind and the Zero started burning.
The canopy came off, and the pilot stood up in the cockpit. The
parachute opened, pulling the pilot out of the plane and into the cone
of fire from Lt. Shuler's guns. When last seen the parachute was
blazing.

Robert DeHaven put well the thoughts of many veterans of the air
war in the South Pacific:

In my memory there was nothing racial to explain the intensity of the
hatred of the Pacific war. It never came up. This is hard to explain now,
but absolutely true. We considered them a despicable people but it
wasn't the same thing as racism. We learned from the performance of
the enemy. There were no prisoners. They didn't believe in it. I saw the
strafing of an American pilot in a parachute. We retaliated and the
result was a mind-numbing involvement in the Pacific that I don't think

existed in Europe. The war was very personal, not machine versus machine. Sometimes you could see the enemy in their cockpits. It was fleeting, but I looked two of them in the face. The days of chivalry were certainly over in the Pacific. Everything was amplified. There was Pearl Harbor and the other savage events of the war. But it involved us, too. When we returned from a mission we faced dust, mud, heat, insects, and all of the things that made New Guinea a miserable place. Any man had times when he very much would have preferred to have been somewhere else. But the Japanese had started the war so our danger and physical suffering were because of them. We were in New Guinea, the end of the world, because of the Japanese. We held that against them. There was no remorse when an enemy pilot died.

Joel Paris shared DeHaven's thoughts but with even more feeling:

The war was nasty in the Pacific. We never let anybody reach the ground alive unless they were coming down over our own territory where they'd get captured. If we could help it they were going to die. It would be stupid—we were there trying to kill them. If they got on the ground, they were going to be up tomorrow. Ours was a war of annihilation. In Europe it was a little more restrained in the air. We were intent on killing them and they were intent on killing us. None of our pilots reached the ground alive if the Japs could kill 'em. We didn't give any quarter and they didn't either. We had six or eight pilots shot down over Japanese lines and captured. Not one survived the war. I don't have much grief for the Japanese. I was working on killing them until the war ended. I've never forgiven them for Bataan and the POW camps. No apologies. They were so cruel. Even before the war some people talked about how civilized the Japanese were. How could they do what they did? They showed cruelty to everybody, not just to us.

The world of fighter combat in the South Pacific, like much of war, defied concrete description. The varieties of men and motives were as broad as the theater was large. Edwards Park, in his splendid autobiographical account of the war in the theater, not only described the types of men involved but also touched on an affection held by many toward the machines that they flew into combat:

There were many pilots I knew who honestly loved what they were doing, who could not rest easy until they felt they had flailed the skies and loosed a hail of bullets at every enemy plane that ever flew. They would complain when they had a day off; they would moan when their

mission did not invite combat. I knew these young men and some of
them I quite liked. But I never understood them.

There were others who were devoted to the whole exercise of flight
to the exclusion of everything else. They tended to abhor combat
because it might be injurious to their planes, but they would accept it as
a technological plateau that their machines were built to achieve. They
could talk about nothing but aviation; they were doing what they loved
and knew best though admittedly not the way they'd like to do it.

Most of the men I knew were civilian groundlings at heart who
joined up quite simply to fight for their country, whatever that meant,
and went bouncing through this strange and savage environment with
varying degrees of tolerance and endurance. Some found themselves
flying fast little aircraft and firing guns. Some were sent home for
psychiatric treatment. Some were naturally good at it, but hated it;
some were naturally poor at it, but loved it.

Steve [a squadronmate—EB] was quite good at the job because he
worked at it. He also had a dimension of responsibility that fitted him
for command. Guppy [another squadronmate—EB] was very good at
the job (he became an ace) despite the fact that he despised every
minute of it and plotted incessantly to find a way safely out. I was quite
poor at it most of the time and more or less resigned to being marked
for destruction. But I was saved by a breathtakingly lovely brown-grey-
green Airacobra with a delicious smell all her own who accepted me
with resignation and then incredibly, with a stirring of her pure metallic
soul that can only be called a kind of love. She saved me again and
again, and she nurtured me and equipped me, at least for survival. Yes.
Nanette. I still remember you, Nanette.

Despite a long and brutal campaign, marked on both sides by a multitude of tactical successes and failures, one inexorable trend became
clear in 1943: Japan was going to lose the contest between fighters in
the South Pacific. What had started as a Japanese victory slowly turned
into a catastrophe for Tokyo. As usual, Robert DeHaven put the situation well and succinctly: "Starting in 1943 the P-38 and our other
modern fighters posed tactical problems for the Japanese that they had
no answer for. Compound that with the growing inexperience and aircrew degradation suffered by Japan, their situation was absolutely
hopeless."

But worse was to come for Tokyo. With their fighters stalemated or
defeated they could not prevent the Allies from making the full use of
their airpower. Air transport kept alive a major Australian land campaign in New Guinea and proved invaluable elsewhere. Allied photo

and reconnaissance units watched every move made by Japanese naval units. Worst of all, by checking the power of imperial fighters, Allied fighters made the skies safe for Allied bombers. The fighters may have opened the door to the Japanese Empire, but the bombers kicked it in.

7

Making History:
Bombers in the South Pacific

One 8th USAAF veteran of the violent strategic bombing campaign against Germany told me that "fighters make headlines but bombers make history." Although the scale of war was much smaller in the South Pacific than in Europe, this statement was quite accurate. Unless acting as bombers themselves, the clouds of fighters on both sides ultimately served to protect or stop a bombing campaign. From the humble Australian Wirraway to the heavy B-24 Liberator, bombers had the potential to project power. Command of the sky in and of itself was of little value. What made control of airspace valuable was what advantage the combatant could derive from it. In the South Pacific almost all advantages were gained from bombers of all types. Small in number but huge in importance, long-range bombers were the best reconnaissance aircraft. In a theater where the terrain made the use of massed artillery extremely difficult, bombers of all types served as a vital adjunct to land campaigns. Unless prevented by fighters or antiaircraft, tactical bombers were a mortal threat to warships needed to secure sea-lanes. Any military aircraft could threaten the merchant shipping required to launch amphibious landings or supply garrisons—a tremendous power in an environment where no military unit could survive for long if isolated. Last, if the numbers of aircraft and the geography allowed it, bombers could cripple enemy air bases. The direct assault on enemy air bases, a task far more difficult than anyone had foreseen, was central to eventual Allied victory in the theater. Imperial forces saw the flow of events and did their best to stop it with increasingly inferior means. The Japanese air arm was not so much shot out of the sky as it was dismantled piece by piece.

Although both sides hated each other and conducted the air war in the South Pacific without thought of mercy, there was an unusual, almost abstract quality to the course of operations. If war in our era has ever resembled a chess match, it was in the South Pacific. Except for some of the Australian-led attacks into the East Indies, no air missions were "strategic" in the broadest sense of the term. Neither side could strike at sources of vital natural resources, much less the direct means of production. No cities beckoned to tempt either side to break the other's will by assaulting civilian populations. Carl Camp, a gunner on a 5th USAAF B-24, knew this as well as MacArthur when he observed, "I flew in a heavy bomber, but strictly speaking we were not involved in strategic bombardment. There weren't any strategic targets like you found in Europe or in the Pacific later. Big or small, all of the attack planes played a tactical role. We just varied in technique." The strategic framework existed; it was, however, one step removed from the front.

What was at stake, once it was clear that Japan would not be able to attack or isolate Australia, was whether Japan could hold its defensive perimeter and force the expected major Allied offensive into a single and predictable course in the Central Pacific allowing for the almost mystical "decisive battle" to be fought under circumstances most advantageous to the Japanese Empire. From the Allied point of view, smashing the Japanese positions in the South Pacific would open a yawning breach in the imperial defensive line. This breach would multiply greatly the strategic quandary facing Tokyo. Facing an eventual American drive into the Central Pacific was menace enough. Having to simultaneously prepare a defense against an Allied move into Southeast Asia was a strategic nightmare. (There was also the possibility of Britain and China reopening fronts in Burma and the Chinese mainland.) An Allied move into Southeast Asia would deprive Japan of the resources required to operate an industrial war economy. An American thrust into the center posed a direct threat to the home islands. Frederick the Great once commented that "to attempt to defend everything is to defend nothing." Any Japanese leader would have understood the Prussian king's dictum. If the Allies could not be contained in the Solomons and New Guinea, a long distance from points of inherent value, the empire's defense became a problem with no possible solution. No wonder throughout 1943 and early 1944 Tokyo poured several hundred thousand troops, dozens of precious warships, and more than a thousand aircraft into the theater to stop or delay Allied momentum.

A quick look at the map in the Pentagon, however, showed a mirror image. Although not planned originally, a large force was gathering in the South Pacific. The United States Navy's drive into the Central Pacific would be constrained by the absence of specialized landing vessels, not a lack of troops. Indeed the Japanese troops being rushed into New Guinea and Rabaul could just as well be directed toward the Marianas or other island chains. Admiral King, who loathed MacArthur, might think of bypassing the Philippines, but many other officers in all services saw the obvious benefit of seizing at least portions of the great island chain. The man who knew this best was Douglas MacArthur. Admiral Halsey participated with skill and vigor against the Japanese in the Solomons. Once in place, it would be very difficult to either move or leave idle the force growing in this most unexpected of theaters. Therefore the bombers in the South Pacific, although all directed at narrow military targets rather than grand strategic objectives, were very important pieces in a very important chess match.

Bombers were one of the prime manifestations of a rich man's war. All were extremely specialized and required top-notch crewmen to gain full advantage of the respective aircrafts' power. Multiengine bombers proved a burden in every way. They were complex to design, very expensive to build, and a maintenance nightmare. A heavy bomber had four engines, a crew of ten or eleven, and complicated subsystems. One can imagine the numbers of men on the ground required to keep these huge (for their time) aircraft flying. The margin of error for ground crews was thin indeed. There was more to go wrong on a bomber, and with so many men aboard the results of error became more tragic. Good maintenance personnel were always at a premium, and bombers received the lion's share. Also bombers gobbled supplies of all kinds. Naturally they needed far more spare parts than did fighters. They also required immense quantities of fuel and hundreds of tons of bombs. Sadly bomber losses were heavy—it was certainly the most dangerous task routinely given an airman. To make matters worse, operating complicated and very heavy airplanes over long distances and at low altitudes made bombers vulnerable to accidents of all kinds. However, despite the huge investment in men and treasure they could fly and see far. More importantly they could project power and were thus at the heart of the air war.

Ironically nations that built large numbers of bombers did so fully realizing that most of the bombs dropped would miss their target. Under the best of circumstances it was difficult to hit a target with a bomb or a torpedo. In the South Pacific the conditions were rarely ideal. Tactical and medium bombers attacking ships and airstrips often had to contend with fierce antiaircraft fire. Allied pilots attacked Japanese warships with great caution. Japanese pilots, if they did not attack with similar caution, accepted brutal losses from antiaircraft alone. Airmen attacking enemy bases found that their targets were hard to put out of action and necessitated multiple strikes, often extending over many months. Bombers of all sorts supported ground campaigns in one way or another, and in the dense terrain common in the South Pacific targets and damage wrought were difficult to identify and assess. And during operations bombers were unfortunately capable of inflicting damage to friendly forces. They were also frequent recipients of friendly fire from their own antiaircraft, even fighters.

The great advantage of bombers was their reach and, put simply, their ability to drop bombs. Since World War II there have been hundreds of books published about aircraft and air campaigns, but few pay the slightest attention to bombs. I can understand why this is so. The subject can be technical, dealing with ballistics and explosive effect. In addition, a huge variety of bombs were produced during the war. Nevertheless a brief examination of the subject quickly illustrates why air forces on both sides spilled so much blood and treasure attempting to bring bombs to the target. They were, in every way, an extremely powerful weapon.

I will confine my description to bombs carried by Allied aircraft, although with slight variations the points are valid for the Japanese air forces. With one notable exception, two points stand out about all of the bombs used. First, they were large weapons. In determining size, the only useful comparison is artillery shells. A round fired by the ubiquitous 105mm howitzer, the standard U.S. field piece in the Pacific, weighed thirty-three pounds. The 155mm howitzer, found in much smaller numbers, fired a projectile of ninety-five pounds—the weight of a small bomb. Only large naval artillery fired rounds that were as heavy as commonly used bombs. An eight-inch naval gun armor-piercing round weighed 335 pounds. A sixteen-inch gun of the type found on a battleship could fire a projectile weighing just over 2,000 pounds. Yet it was rarely possible to use naval guns to their full effect in the South Pacific (much less in Europe), and bombs had advantages even when both could be employed.

Bombs, in contrast, weather permitting, could be dropped over a huge area and packed a powerful punch. Barring the famous twenty-three-pound fragmentation bomb (the parafrag, which we shall examine later), bombs were an order of magnitude larger than artillery shells. The smallest bomb widely used weighed 100 pounds. A multiengine bomber would drop at least ten such small devices. A bomb of this size was most commonly used in large quantities against areas where enemy troops were operating but could not be specifically identified. Ground targets were nearly impossible to locate, but none could withstand a direct hit from the smallest bomb, and neither could nearby light infantry positions. The idea, therefore, was to drop as many as possible and hope that some hit home. Very few did, but the grim math of war assured that some would strike a random target. More common were 250-pound bombs used by bombers of all types against a range of targets; it was commonly mounted on fighters. Probably the most common bomb was the 500-pound general-purpose (GP) bomb that was dropped by second-generation fighters and all bombers. Officers liked the 500-pound weapon because it could leave a deep crater on a runway and wreak terrible damage to anything other than a warship larger than a destroyer. For normal use the 1,000-pound bomb was the heaviest employed in the South Pacific. There were no massive concrete targets that required something heavier, and tactical bombers could carry one over a limited range, multi-engine bombers two or maybe more. Some 2,000-pound bombs found their way into the theater, but the trade-off between the number of bombs that could be carried, and consequently the percentage of likely hits, was not considered good.

There were exceptions. Some bombs were field-altered to ensure that detonation would occur just above ground level, and some very large bombs were given time-delay fuses intended to prevent Japanese ground crews from filling a crater on an airfield. The most important deviation from the norm concerned armor-piercing bombs, carried by any aircraft attempting to attack a heavy warship. An armor-piercing bomb, usually 1,000 pounds, was a slightly altered naval artillery shell. (Indeed, the navy supplied armor-piercing bombs to the army, whereas GP and other types were given to the navy by the army.) These were an SBD specialty, and a handful of dive-bombers with 1,000-pound armor-piercing bombs did terrible damage to the warships of Combined Fleet during 1942.

Bombs had another important advantage over artillery. A shell fired through an artillery barrel is subjected to tremendous heat and stress. And an artillery piece must be able to fire thousands of rounds without mishap. Consequently an artillery round requires a heavy casing, which lowers the amount of weight of the shell given to explosive power. This is not a problem if one wishes to pepper an area with shell fragments. However, the greater the amount of explosive, the greater the amount of shock created by the explosion. A bomb designer worked within different limits. A bomb left the aircraft with very little stress or friction. Consequently if the designer wished, it was possible to devise bombs that carried very little casing and a large amount of explosive. The result was a shock wave that often created its own fragmentation by destroying buildings, trees, and anything else in its path. The standard 500-pound GP bomb carried about half its weight in pure TNT. Some bombs had lighter casings and a higher percentage of explosive to maximize blast. Fragmentation bombs had heavier casings that were designed to break apart. Later bombs used more complex explosives like amatol, which increased blast by 25 percent. Crews in the South Pacific took whatever they could get.

Because bombs were dropped from a passive position, they could be designed to kill men and damage targets in three ways. One was shock. Because the amount and type of destruction varied, choosing the right weapon for the mission was difficult. However, shock effect, for our purposes, is probably best measured by the ability of the bomb to cause damage at a certain distance. The damage itself was done by a tissue of air propelled by the explosion; it had tremendous pressure initially but dissipated rapidly. According to U.S. Army figures, an enemy in the open would suffer a ruptured eardrum from a 100-pound bomb dropping within a radius of thirty feet. If a 500-pound bomb was dropped the radius increased to forty to fifty-five feet. A 1,000-pound bomb would rupture an eardrum within an eighty- to ninety-foot radius. Killing was a different matter. A 100-pound bomb would kill 50 percent of men in the open at a radius of ten feet. A 500-pound projectile had the same effect at fifteen to eighteen feet. A 1,000-pound bomb would kill half the enemy within a radius of thirty feet. (Please note that these figures are based on radius, not diameter.) Obviously there was a law of diminishing returns here, familiar to any study of mortality and weaponry. Yet the exchange was all too clear. There were many solo bomber missions in the South Pacific, but for the most part the bombers came in units. All of these figures given for shock—and let us remember that a man with a broken eardrum was probably out of the campaign—were multiplied many times by the fact that so many bombs were dropped.

Secondly, bombs killed with fragmentation. Fragments came from two different sources. One was from the casing of the bomb itself, usually a soft metal. The other was the debris blown into the air by the shock wave. Fragmentation bombs heavier than 100 pounds were almost always aimed at enemy infantry (whether attackers could see the enemy or not), aircraft on the ground, and antiaircraft installations. Officers knew that most of the men would be prepared for air attack at air bases and important places in an infantry position. Therefore bombs were set to explode above the ground. The results were wicked and explain better than any anecdote why smart soldiers dug deep. If a 500-pound bomb exploded twenty or thirty feet above a small area, the chances for injuring a soldier who was in the open or a shallow foxhole (what the military called a 10-degree fortification) were 100 percent. A deep trench, particularly if made with angles, reduced the chances of casualties to less than 30 percent. No field fortification could prevent complete catastrophe if there was a direct hit, but digging a trench as deep as a man is tall made the victim far less vulnerable to air attack. Yet with enough bombs falling some men on the ground would die or suffer wounds—whether physical or psychological—regardless of precautions. If a bomb struck an enemy advancing to the attack above ground, the results could be catastrophic.

In practice many men on the ground, because they were exhausted or foolish, did not take advantage of well-dug trenches when faced with frequent small nighttime raids. (The famous "Washing Machine Charlie" was responsible for these hated visits all over the Pacific; no doubt the Japanese had their own name for our solo raiders.) This explains the great popularity of the field-modified daisy-cutters, which were designed to detonate inches above the surface. Usually used at night when single and small raids took place, daisy-cutters were deadly for many a man who decided to ride it out in his tent. The effectiveness of this simple tactic soon taught most men to head for protection during a minor night raid, greatly increasing fatigue. A daisy-cutter, if the fuse mechanism functioned correctly, was also effective against unprotected aircraft, vehicles, and other equipment above ground.

Last, bombs were used to destroy buildings and create craters. Like artillery shells, bombs had simple but effective fuses that allowed the crews to set the weapon to explode above, on contact with, or below the earth. The technology was not perfect, and many bombs dropped proved duds. The fusing mechanism in a World War II bomb was simple but designed for safety. Huge numbers of bombs were stored together, and one errant explosion could put a group out of action for weeks. An errant fuse on a flight was fearsome to the crew. It was better for everyone that a bomb could be armed only on board the aircraft and near the target. Duds were far preferable to unstable weapons that could destroy a bomber or worse. Nevertheless the fuse mechanism usually worked and gave officers the option of controlling the altitude at which the explosion took place.

Buildings in the South Pacific were of extremely light construction, so the major consideration was in trying to erode runways and associated targets. Communications and maintenance facilities proved to be some of the most valuable targets for eroding an airstrip, and they were easy enough to destroy if they could be identified. Geology intruded to a degree. Hard, dry sand was almost like concrete and difficult to crater. Mud, like water, carried shock waves very nicely. I think it is safe to say that most airfields in the South Pacific fell into the medium to soft soil category for making craters. Hitting an actual runway was a job for larger bombs if at all possible. If a bomber or fighter dropped a 250-pound bomb on a Japanese runway with a fuse setting of .025 second, the bomb would penetrate nine feet below the surface and upon detonation create a crater twenty-six feet in diameter and thirteen feet deep. The defenders would need to fill this hole with seventy cubic feet of soil to repair it. (Any bomb damage could create soft spots on a dirt field, making it dangerous to taxi.) A 500-pound bomb with the same fuse settings would create a crater thirty-three feet wide and sixteen feet deep, requiring 150 cubic feet of soil to fill it. A 1,000-pound bomb created a crater forty feet by eighteen feet, needing 290 cubic feet of soil to repair. Knocking out a field took tremendous effort. Ground crews would find the means to fill enough holes to get aircraft off the ground. Yet in the long run sustained bombardment destroyed the integrity of the strip and made it difficult to use safely.

To deliver bombs it was necessary to have bomber pilots. I have been unable to discover whether the services attempted to fit the right breed of cadet to the role of bomber crewman (as opposed to fighter service) during World War II. During the prewar era bomber pilots were something of an elite in most air forces. In the Japanese service tactical bomber pilots included some of the best men available; Nell and Betty pilots were also held to very high expectations. Much the same could be said about the American service. With the huge expansion that took place in all air forces during 1939–1941, this situation may have changed. When the air forces were relatively small during the late 1930s, pilots received rigorous training and flew many hours. Once expansion began, the training system was flooded in all countries. Many of the "old codgers," as Joe Foss described prewar veterans, received promotions and were soon flying a desk where they were able to institutionalize their finely developed skills. And despite prewar doctrine, the importance of fighter pilots was made evident during the Battle of France; the Battle of Britain made them godlike.

Consequently when huge numbers of junior birdmen began to appear there was a heavy preference for fighter service. In American service all cadets received psychological as well as physical screening. Other nations lacked the confidence in the social sciences, but there must have been some kind of subjective character evaluation done somewhere along the way. Allied services normally asked cadets what type of service they would prefer. Yet because aircraft and pilot expansion was straining the respective resources of all nations, it was likely that many men were assigned to single-engine or multiengine advanced training on the basis of immediate need. So I have not been able to ascertain whether it was chance or design that put a man at the yoke of a bomber or behind the stick of a fighter. Depending on the time or place, perhaps both were the case. The men who went through the process could provide no answer, but in speaking to veterans some felt deliberate selection was at least part of the process, whereas others felt that the pipeline had a momentum all its own.

If postwar aviation literature is any indication, fighters have indeed received more than their share of the headlines. Yet it would be a mistake to believe that the first team went on to become fighter pilots, whereas bombers received the leftovers. New Zealand bomber pilot Ian Page mentioned that good judgment was certainly required on the part of a man responsible for a crew, and the crewmen were hardly passive passengers. Because they so often flew long distances, good navigators were important. A top-notch bombardier was considered pure gold by those in the business. A good gunner could save an aircraft in battle. There was also a great premium put on superior flying skills. Flying a bomber did not usually include maneuver the way a fighter pilot understood the meaning. And there was no premium placed on dogfighting ability. Yet bombers were heavy and vulnerable to every danger posed by the laws the physics. Bombers often suffered engine failure, making them tricky to fly, to put it mildly. They were big targets and therefore attracted more than their share of battle damage. Pilot skill varied greatly in all of the services. Yet a good bomber pilot was a good pilot indeed. I once attended a symposium on the strategic bombing campaign against Germany. Someone asked a Mustang ace what he thought was the most difficult task that could face a pilot in his theater. The former fighter pilot answered in an instant: "Landing a crippled B-17."

Bombers on both sides represented a gamble in combat. Like most weapon systems they usually missed their targets entirely. Many missions achieved partial success. However, even more so than fighter missions a bomber attack had to be figured as a major investment by either combatant. Yet despite hundreds of failed or marginally effective flights, when bombers were in synch with the mission, crew skill, and geography, they could crush enemy forces in strikingly short order. A well-placed bomb could obliterate an enemy infantry position in an instant. If the target was a warship, victory might take a few hours. If the target was a major land base, a well-honed bomber offensive proved capable of changing a campaign of attrition into a month-long period of annihilation. When military men spoke of airpower in the Pacific, they referred to the power of bombardment.

A Confused Start

The rain of bombs that was to eventually fall throughout the South Pacific started on a very humble scale and could not be considered a great success on either side. In March 1942 the still small Japanese land-based force bombed both Darwin and Port Moresby. From a technical point of view those operations were conducted with skill. The few RAAF and U.S. fighters available to defend the targets were roughly handled by Japanese escorts, and Japanese bomber losses were low. Allied reinforcements moving quickly into the area learned to fear the sound of the air-raid siren and were quick to head for the comfort of a deep slit trench. Yet during this period both Moresby and Darwin improved their facilities, however slowly, and received reinforcements. Of the two targets Moresby was by far the more vulnerable. In a sense it was protected by its own crude facilities. Although later turned into an effective port, Moresby was initially a pier and two airstrips. Offloading of ships had to be done offshore via smaller vessels. There was, in short, a lack of obvious targets. Had the Japanese bombing force at Rabaul been large enough, it perhaps could have flattened the pier and town and slowed the improvements of the airstrips. As it was, medium bombers at Rabaul rarely numbered more than two dozen during the early months of war, and the imperial carriers were busy elsewhere. To make matters worse, Rabaul's bombers, in addition to periodic losses due to raids on Moresby, suffered serious losses when they made the aggressive but futile raids against a U.S. carrier raid during February. Nell bombers based at Rabaul repeated the disaster on a lesser scale during the Battle of the Coral Sea. Attacking an Allied task force of cruisers and destroyers on May 7, 1942, with both torpedoes and high-level bombing, Japanese airmen reported a great victory, sinking several warships. In fact they had not landed a single hit and suffered four bombers shot down, one ruined, and another four damaged. Weakened, they continued their attacks against targets in New Guinea. With more new bombers coming off the assembly lines and now becoming somewhat concerned about the growing Allied strength in Australia, Tokyo slowly built up Rabaul's strength during the spring and summer. As events would prove, they were going to need it.

The strategic setback suffered by Japan in the Coral Sea is much more clear in retrospect than it was at the time. The land-based attacks yielded a steady if modest number of Allied fighters shot down. Bombers could claim damage on targets, even if it proved minor. Japan's real failure was to recognize Allied weakness in the theater and jump on it immediately. Until Midway there was no reason for concern in Japan's eyes. The South Pacific could wait. Yet Allied servicemen in New Guinea at the time looked at the situation differently. Rumors of Japanese invasion were constant, and many men were ready to go bush. In Australia the possibility of a Japanese landing, especially in the north, seemed very real.

It was during these bleak days that the USAAF began bombing Japanese targets in the South Pacific. Most of the early efforts were made by B-17 bombers that had originally been sent to Australia to reinforce the 19th Bomb Group that Washington had so hoped would either deter or delay an invasion of the Philippines. Lloyd Boren was a bombardier for a B-17 that flew for 19th Bomb Group during the short time it served in Australia. He recollected the type of mission flown that at the time would have been considered a success:

Our main target in those early days was shipping in Rabaul Harbor and those three airstrips there. We'd go in individually. We only flew in formation twice, and that was with the 19th. The rest of it was individual plane raids. Rabaul was always hit at night. We flew up from Australia to fuel at Port Moresby. It wasn't safe to leave a plane there for long, so we had to time it well. We would take off at intervals of five or six minutes and attack individually. You'd never see another plane. We'd go through the low point of the pass through the Owen Stanleys, near Lae. We'd circle the target to get our bearings and go in at different altitudes, usually pretty low. Nine times out of ten there was enough moonlight so you could see the ground and shoreline pretty well; we weren't that high. Sometimes one of us would get caught in a spotlight and look like a giant ice-cream cone in the night.

One time we went over to bomb one of the strips at Rabaul. We ran into a terrific storm and flew right through the middle of it all the way to Rabaul. As it turned out we were the only ones to get through; the others turned back. To show how good the navigator was, we broke out at about 500 feet. I thought we were about at 1,000. We had 500-pound bombs. When we broke out of the clouds we were going right straight down the runway. Our lights were on full and lighting up the airstrip. So we opened fire with our machine guns and I dropped one bomb after another, and they hit bing-bing-bing right down the line and we kept on going. They didn't expect us that night, especially so low. That was awfully low to drop bombs; the plane would pop up every time one went off. We sprung the bay doors and they wouldn't close. We were lucky to get out of that one alive. But it sure was a neat job of navigation.

As Boren recalled, if a night mission was conducted properly, a B-17 had an excellent chance to come home:

Japanese flak at that time was terrible. They couldn't hit the side of a barn, especially their ships. We'd go over Simpson Harbor at Rabaul at 5,000 feet, which isn't too high. But the bursts almost always went off below us. We were seldom hit by a ship. At the Rabaul fields they weren't much better. When they'd get someone in a searchlight they'd get him in a ring of searchlights. We'd watch the plane trapped and you could see all the bursts around it because the Japs were firing everything they had at it. The tracers would look like it was coming straight at you. But we had a saying that if you could see the tracer it wouldn't hit you. That wasn't too comforting. We were hit several times; sometimes we never heard it. There was so much going on inside the plane, so you didn't really notice things being so busy. When we were inside those lights the pilot was blinded, so I had a much better view right out the nose. I'd tell him to dive to the right or to the left, go up, go down. I'd use the bombsight on shipping until I figured that they would turn as soon as they saw the bombs anyway. So we survived, but usually so did they.

Hard-pressed, 19th Bomb Group returned to Australia in the summer of 1942 and was given some daylight missions against Japanese positions. The most prominent was launched on August 7, 1942, when what remained of the group, sixteen planes, attacked Rabaul in support of the Guadalcanal invasion. Despite General Kenney's later claims, there is no reason to think that the attack accomplished anything, if, for no other reason, Rabaul's strike force was on the way to Guadalcanal. During this period U.S. bombers suffered heavy losses, many to accident because their aircraft and pilots were weary. The 19th began to disintegrate, and its replacement, the 43d, was not yet in place. It was a low point for Allied fortunes in New Guinea. Lloyd Boren, who was a bombardier on a B-17 for the 19th in Australia, saw the situation at its nadir:

One of my last flights was in a '17 called the "Old Man" with a picture of Uncle Sam on his nose. We had been hit about two weeks before by flak over Rabaul. Two of us got purple hearts out of that one—mine was minor. They sent us down to Sydney. The unwritten law in the squadron was to send anyone just back from Sydney on a twelve-hour recon mission to sober you up. So they put us in the Old Man, put in an extra bomb-bay tank of gas and four or five hundred-pound bombs on the other side and said take off. We were supposed to scout around. Our first target was Gasmata. Funny-looking strip. We were told that Gasmata had been bombed out. We were flying about 2,000 feet and had a photographer with us. You could look down and see the bomb craters on the runway. I was the only one who could see down at that moment and I could see too clearly several fighters taking off right over those craters. We got hopped by about nine of them. I immediately salvoed everything including the bomb-bay tank and all our bombs. We got into one hellacious fight. We would have never gotten out of there except for the clouds. We got into the clouds twice and broke out. The second time we broke out a fighter was right on us and wounded all four officers—myself, the navigator, copilot, and pilot. I got one bullet through the shoulder and cannon fragments all over me. The pilot got a cannon shell right through his left leg and portions of his back were covered with shrapnel. The copilot had one piece of shrapnel just miss his jugular vein, but he could still manage okay. He got us into the clouds and we stayed there until we knew they were gone. We got back to base as soon as possible. We couldn't make Moresby so we stopped at Buna at Dobodura. The engineer and copilot landed the plane. The navigator was cut up, but he managed to get us back. The doctors operated on us by flashlight that night near Buna.

The next morning they sent a C-47 over to pick us up. They brought us back to Moresby. The pilot and I were put on a hospital ship and taken to Sydney. At the time I was wounded I didn't feel anything. It happened so fast that it felt like someone was pushing me against the wall. It just shoves you, but no pain. I looked down at my flight jacket and saw the blood pouring out of the sleeve. It flew all over the navigator, and then it started to hurt some. They shot me up with morphine and as soon as possible they cut the blood flow off with a scarf and let it loose every once in a while until they got me wrapped up. But we got back.

Tactically Allied attacks did little to damage enemy capabilities. Some ships were damaged, and some fighters went down when attacking U.S. bombers. Men on the ground had to fill in craters on

runways. Yet raids did not hamper Japanese operations in any substantial way. If anything the attacks against Rabaul and Lae had done
nothing other than increase the desire on the part of Tokyo to finish
Allied resistance in New Guinea. However, the few B-17s were beginning at an early date to be the eyes of the Allied effort. This is not the
place to analyze the complex Allied intelligence apparatus, which included code-breaking, signal intelligence, Coast Watchers, and conventional analysis of interrogations and artifacts. Often, in the South
Pacific, none of these sources provided information. Even when they
did it was necessary to make a physical sighting of the target for military operations to commence. B-17s and later B-24s served this task
splendidly on many occasions. So did the famous PBY reconnaissance
plane flown by navy and Marine pilots and eventually used by Australians and New Zealanders; even the army flew some. Yet in all theaters, especially New Guinea, steady long-range patrols by heavy
bombers discovered many enemy movements. It was a B-17 that first
spotted the Japanese construction of an air base on Guadalcanal. A
similar plane first spotted the Japanese convoy heading for catastrophe in the Bismarck Sea.

However, reconnaissance aircraft had several jobs. One was simply
to keep track of the enemy, a vital operation during naval and air campaigns. Indeed many military analysts have argued that reconnaissance, ever since a French pilot in 1914 provided information essential
for the monumental victory on the Marne, is the single most important
role played by airpower. Another was to map a battlefield for ground
troops, through standard cartography and photomapping. Photomapping, common but inferior, meant that a plane simply photographed a
potential battlefield. These photos were the norm early in the war and
were employed throughout the conflict. Photos were always valuable
for identifying enemy strong points and provided basic geographic information. However, land commanders far preferred accurate maps,
yet they operated in a theater that had yet to be mapped well. If complex photos taken with special cameras were given to cartographers
they could be turned into maps, and true cartography with current
photos of enemy positions was the best combination. Therefore many
early Allied forays into Japanese territory were not designed to attack
but to identify the lay of the land for ground commanders.

Early in the war on New Guinea, Fifth Air Force established the 8th
Photo Squadron, which included a small number of B-17s and the first
P-38 fighters to arrive in the theater. Kirkwood Adams was a gunner
for a B-17 in the 8th Photo and learned that it was a dangerous occupation:

We were sent most often to Rabaul. We also flew over the Admiralties: We were the first plane in there. We didn't map New Guinea itself but flew over areas like Finschhafen. We'd go before a raid and after a raid to try and get results. We'd also map areas prior to infantry attack. We'd come in low on those missions to get a good look at gun emplacements, etcetera. A guy would take a great big camera and aim it out the side window. We'd go over Rabaul high: count the ships in one day and come back the next and keep tabs on shipping that way. We flew at 30,000 feet, but the fighters could reach us if they had time. We went over a couple of airstrips on Bougainville, from high they went by as you blinked your eye. Anyway there was a big puff right above us. Just one big puff. It was a fighter I'm sure. The Japs must have figured out what we had in mind because the plane that came in the next day was met right off the coast by a flight of Zeros. I almost cry when I think about it. They got back but out of the ten crew three were dead. The fighters came in from the front and killed the pilot. The copilot and engineer steered it. Then the navigator got killed. The radio operator had to navigate. When they got back to Moresby the plane didn't have any hydraulics and 130-some cannon and machine gun holes in that thing and it still made it. We had P-38s that took off and just never came back, but that was the worst day for our B-17s.

5th USAAF officers did not like seeing their bombers used as dedicated reconnaissance aircraft. They did, however, use single bombers for attack-reconnaissance throughout the war. Sometimes—but rarely—one of these planes attacked a target successfully. More importantly they brought back invaluable intelligence throughout the conflict. Yet in order to free bombers for other duties Fifth Air Force employed its handful of early P-38s for photomapping and reconnaissance. These were early models of the breed that had unreliable turbochargers and were not considered adequate for combat operations. Some had been rejected by the RAF from European service for a number of maladies. Yet if they operated properly they could fly very high and very fast, something no Japanese fighter could do. Originally stripped of armament the early P-38s were well suited to the task. In addition to offering superior cruising speed and altitude, the big Lightnings were able to carry complex photographic gear.

Fred Hargesheimer was one of the first pilots to fly the new but dangerous Lightnings. He described their arrangement: "We had trimetrogon horizon-to-horizon cameras for mapping. Three cameras: one vertical and two oblique. We could map a strip maybe forty to sixty miles wide from about 10,000 feet. That was the primary mission at first because the maps were so miserable. They had us working hard over the Owen Stanleys and down to Buna. At 30,000 feet you could see an awfully long way in the South Pacific." As Hargesheimer related it, during clear weather there were few secrets held by the Japanese in the Rabaul area: "We did some target assessment over Rabaul but more often we were taking pictures for a target compilation group that chose the targets for the bombers. A lot of bombers carried their own bombers for damage assessment. We'd often see new groups of ships that had come in. Often you'd watch aircraft taking off from the strips. By that time we'd have our pictures and be on the way home." (An interesting footnote: Hargesheimer was eventually shot down, was rescued by native peoples, and spent much of the postwar era on New Britain establishing and running a school for the children of the people who had saved him.)

Soon, good horizon-to-horizon photos were turned into maps by cryptographic engineers in Melbourne. These products, so badly missing in the terrible battles of Buna and Guadalcanal, were invaluable. A photo was indistinct at best, whereas an accurate map was a ground officer's bible. To get maps and photoreconnaissance required skill, luck, and courage. Vince Murphy of the 8th Photo recalled the unusual challenge (because of immature aircraft) and pain suffered by pilots in his business:

Up at 30,000 feet we flew very nearly between compressibility and stall. [This was a poor characteristic of first-model P-38s and was solved for combat versions.—EB] Then again, nobody else was up there with you. The trick was to keep looking around and if you saw anyone else to get the hell out of there. Morale was difficult with everyone on his own. Because of individual missions, when you had a casualty someone just didn't come back. You never really knew what happened. Sometimes people showed up days later, but usually nothing. So you had to go on and try to figure out what went wrong the best way you could. But it was important work. We carried complicated trimetrogon cameras. The photos were developed and turned into maps by the cartographic engineers in Melbourne.

Later in the war Fifth Air Force began protecting its reconnaissance aircraft with escorts. Murphy is not sure it was wise:

We lost quite a few pilots when we were flying individually. We rarely knew what happened to them. Kenney said he didn't want to lose any more of us because we were too valuable and specialized. So they gave us escort. Now, our fighters didn't go out alone. They went in flights of four, so we had five planes instead of one. Now every time we went up all hell would break loose because the Japs would see five planes. They'd say, "Hey, there's a flight up there, let's go up and mix it up a little." So we got a lot more interceptions and a lot more confusion in the missions. . . . Our original plan of flying fast and high, taking photos, and getting out was a good one.

Gunner Jim Eaton served first with the 19th Bomb Group and then was transferred to the 43d Bomb Group given the newly formed Fifth Air Force. Eaton had pulled strings in Nouméa to make sure he was not "left on the beach" and secured assignment to Australia. As Eaton reflected, June 1942 did not prove a happy time Down Under:

It was a nightmare for everybody in this period. First, you had no idea what the Japanese were going to try next. They had all the decisions to make and the muscle to back it up. We didn't know anything and had nothing to do anything with. When we got there, as it was explained to me at the time, we were prepared to abandon most of Australia and retreat to a circle around Canberra and Melbourne and the Japs would take over the rest of it. That was a drastic picture but we believed it at the time. At the Coral Sea we stopped them but didn't beat them. There was something near panic when the Japanese marched on Moresby. Finally the Aussies stopped them and shoved them back. It was a tense time.

To get to Australia Eaton had volunteered to serve in the ball turret, sometimes called a "ventral turret." The ball was mounted on the bottom of the aircraft and was considered difficult to operate. Although not aware of the fact at the time, Eaton and others like him slowly made a point that had very serious consequences for Japanese fighter pilots: The Zero was too fragile and poorly armed to be a good interceptor. Eaton's B-17E, a new model in the summer of 1942, had one of the new automatic gunsights that amplified the power of turrets in U.S. bombers. Eaton's ball turret was a retrofit, and some B-17Es carried manual sights. As Eaton often flew single-plane high-level daylight reconnaissance missions, he had good reason to use the awkward-handling firepower:

Sperry built our turrets. They did early autopilots and developed a hydroelectric turret system. They used direct control from handles or yokes, if you will. If you wanted azimuth elevation you moved in a certain direction and you got azimuth, if you moved in the other direction you got elevation. So they went up or down or around and around depending on how you pushed the levers. The Sperry people added a computing sight. When tracking the target the computer would measure the angular velocity. You'd aim the turret until you'd see the target in the radicle of the sight. By framing it and knowing its wingspan you automatically told the computer the information it needed to figure range. It interacted with lead angle and drop of projectile over the distance fired and so on. So by tracking the target you're aiming the sight and also positioning the guns so when you fire hopefully the bullets will reach the particular point the same time the target does. It was really an analog computer. This was a predigital era.

Like many combat pilots, Eaton discovered that hitting a target was difficult at best:

No matter what sight you were using, hitting something required a lot of luck. After the war I remained in the aerospace field and years later I was part of the development of much more sophisticated devices. But I suppose that the WWII devices were a lot better than having a bunch of totally green guys shooting at ducks. How many do you have to shoot at before you learn lead? Move that situation into a 30,000-foot altitude and 500-mph closing speed and things happen in two or three seconds. You don't have time to sit there and compute anything in your head. So the sight gave the gunner some chance of doing his job. But really if he hit anything it was pure luck. We finally threw out all of the prewar theory of aerial gunnery—fire short bursts, only when you had time to compute the lead, etcetera, etcetera. My God, if you do that the guy is on the other side of you turning back before you've fired a shot. The ball gunner fired twin .50s. The name of the game was to try to find some way for the enemy to fly through your garbage. You learned to anticipate his moves. For instance, you'd see a burst of smoke come out of the exhaust stack—okay, he's just increased throttle and getting ready to close. A Zero could turn left but couldn't turn right well because of engine torque. So if you had one on your left wing he'd do a 270-degree turn to come at you. A guy on your right wing did a very fast 90-degree turn. At three o'clock or nine o'clock. We learned years later they had to fly a pursuit curve—they had to anticipate where you're going to be also. It was not as simple as it looked. Otherwise we'd all be dead.

The Japanese approach would start at about 2,000 yards or under. Our range was about 1,000 yards so they'd stay out of range until closure point was reached. Then they'd come into, hell, maybe 100 feet of you. Depending on how effective you were of giving them a little caution—telling them, "A little more of this and you're going down in flames." So the idea was to get a lot of lead out there and hope to get the enemy pilot's mind off of what he was trying to do—destroy the bomber. Every fifth round was a tracer. The tracer was there to remind the enemy that he was in danger the closer he got. After a while I learned my job was not to shoot down enemy aircraft. My job was to keep them from shooting us down. Just keep them from closing, from getting close enough to hit. Every new gunner that came along I preached: "Jack, your job is to keep them *away* from us. We want to be the guys to come home. It isn't to see how many of them we can shoot down. We're here to defend the aircraft and that's it."

Single recon planes were target practice both for Japanese antiaircraft crews and fighters. So frequently we were flying with seven or eight fighters chewing us up for thirty or forty minutes at a time. If it was easy for them to hit you, there would have been no single recon flights because they would have shot us all down. But it wasn't easy. We didn't appreciate that at the time, because we didn't understand a proper pursuit curve. But you'd still get some "gravel on the barrel" when the bullets went through the airplane. It sounded like gravel hitting the side of a barn. But that would be maybe one round out of 100 being fired at you. Planes did go down, but the B-17 was a tough aircraft and we had a good chance if everyone did their job.

Flying at very high altitude alone, Eaton pointed out, required attention to detail for the safety of the crew:

The guy in the ball turret was by himself. He knew best what was going on underneath the plane but didn't know a thing about what was going on above, in front, or anywhere else. It was loud inside a bomber so you communicated with the intercom. After you'd flown together for a while you knew when to say something and when to keep your peace. Flying at altitude we learned to check every crew position. The pilot would come on and say, "Hey, waist gunner: What's going on?" That started everyone talking. You'd listen to the guy that was half-silly because of oxygen deprivation. You could tell it just by listening. If he didn't talk, you got to him in a hurry—oxygen deprivation at 30,000 feet could kill someone. These little behavior characteristics that were not widely known to outsiders but served veteran crews well. The main problem was knowing when not to talk. When you were on a bombing run, under attack, or something serious, you didn't talk unless there was something new you could tell us. Like "there's twelve more fighters coming" or whatever else you could spot while looking around and enjoying the scenery.

Eaton on one occasion went on a flight that broke all of the rules being learned by B-17 crewmen who would give them a good chance to return in one piece:

The guy who was the pilot that particular mission violated all of the orders being given prior to the takeoff. We were ordered to check the number of ships at Simpson Harbor. This was 20 November 1942. Something big was going on down the Solomons. We had orders to stay at altitude—don't come down no matter what. Don't stir the pot. We start taxiing out on the runway and the aircraft gets bogged down on the mud. Took an hour for a track to get over there and pull us out. The pilot and copilot changed positions. The copilot had replaced our regular copilot who was sick. So the new guy, who we didn't know, was first pilot. . . . At this stage of the war this wasn't unusual. Patchwork crews were very common. Later men would train together and develop more cohesion. We were replacement parts at that time. But everything was a mess and we were used to it. We started down the runway, everything fine. We got off the ground, up over the Owen Stanleys, approached Rabaul from the east going west so we'd be on our way home when we passed over. The next spot we were supposed to check was Gasmata. Before we reached Rabaul the weather socked us in very quickly. We're at 32,000 feet and we can't see a thing. The pilot flies up toward Kavieng negotiating with the navigator for a course and rate of loss of altitude that would take us over Simpson and break out over the overcast at exactly the right time. This is the pilot's version of events. We didn't know where the damned overcast would stop. The pilot wasn't supposed to be going low and we don't know this guy. We get through this exercise, break out of the overcast, we look around, and, my God, we're flying formation with twenty Zeros. They're as surprised as we are. We're right over Simpson. There are two big aerodromes and the place is full of warships. [In November 1942 there would have been many warships indeed at Rabaul because of the great surface battles of the month.—EB] Instead of going back up into the overcast and getting the hell out of there the pilot takes a power dive toward a little cloud over the middle of Simpson Harbor. I'm in the ball turret. This was about noon. We're in this little cloud and [the pilot] tells the navigator to give him a heading that will get us out of the harbor. The navigator, an experienced guy, says don't turn now: Go straight. We broke out of the cloud. Now I had lost the door to my turret in the power dive. We peeled the damn paint off the wings in the power dive. We certainly didn't take any pictures because nobody was nuts enough to be hanging out the window with the plane hurtling downward. We didn't learn a thing about the fleet that day. So we got out of the cloud and the Japs had evidently given up on us.

Now during the day's briefing we'd been told that our troops had captured the strip at Buna. So our new pilot decides to pay our respects to the guys at Buna. Off we go. I won't get into my turret because it didn't have a door on it and I couldn't keep my headphones on. As we approached the runway at Buna I see nine Zeros flying right on the deck. I don't know what they were doing, strafing or what. I get back into my turret and we start maneuvering through the valleys and low over the jungle trying to clear out. The Zeros were with us all the way. We got credit for shooting down three of them. We weren't supposed to be there at all. We get home with the right wheel . . . shot out. I got out, went up to the pilot, asked his name, and told him I wasn't ever going to fly with him again. So everything goes wrong and I end up with a Silver Star.

As the war continued the job of Japanese interceptors grew harder. Some skilled and intrepid Zero pilots learned the exacting technique of the head-on pass and continued to devastate American heavies. However, U.S. fighter escorts became more and more common. The B-24 Liberator, which became the most often used heavy bomber after 1943, lacked some of the B-17's structural strength, but it carried more modern armament and flew in larger formations. As Liberator gunner Carl Camp recalled, Japanese fighters never found the answer posed by American heavy bombers:

The Japs weren't that brave, at least the army pilots. A lot of times the fighters would just veer off. The navy boys were pretty good. But none of them were team players. They were all prima donnas. They'd all make their own runs. A lot of times that's what led to their doom. They had a little trick I saw several times. The fighter would go into a snap roll down through our formation firing at the same time. All those bullets are flying out there like as though you took a water hose, grabbed it four feet behind the nozzle, and just swung it around—it throws the water everywhere. The Japs would be throwing ammunition everywhere. But I never heard of anyone being hit while they did that. They did that first. Then they'd climb up to one side of you. Then one at a time, like kids jumping off a rope swing, they'd come down through the formation. That meant the gunners could concentrate on one at a time. It was stupid, really. It made our job a lot easier. As long as they wanted to do that it was fine with us.

We'd call them all Zekes. In truth there were Zekes, Tonys, and Oscars. From a distance they all kind of looked alike, especially when they're going through you with a combined speed of several hundred miles an hour. You see the meatballs [the painted rising suns—EB] and you can see them firing—that's a pretty good hint. . . . Sometimes we saw a welcome variation. The Jap fighter would come flying through our formation with a couple of P-38s on their tail. That was a fine sight and made for a good day.

In the war of attrition the Japanese won a small victory in 1942. In the fall of 1942 it was becoming obvious to General Kenney that the 19th Bomb Group was getting tired. This was a sensitive issue at the time, because Kenney himself had only received his position in July due to MacArthur's displeasure with the U.S. air effort in New Guinea. The 19th had been pounded since the beginning of the war. Seeing little done of consequence and tasting numerous defeats, the aircrews of the group that had started the war were losing heart. Furthermore their aircraft, which included some of the most vulnerable models of early B-17s, were growing overtired. In November Kenney made the unprecedented decision to send the entire group back to the United States. Crewmen like Jim Eaton and Lloyd Boren, who had arrived after the early calamities, received assignments to new squadrons. The last commander of the 19th, Richard Carmichael, in a postwar interview put the situation simply: "The 19th was a problem for General Kenney—old crews wanting to go home and a new commander, General Kenney, wanting to fight. They had done their part. So they finally sent us home in November and December 1942."

Perhaps Carmichael, Kenney, and all of the frustrated B-17 pilots of 1942 would have felt better had they known the problems they were causing for the Japanese. Interesting testimony on the vexation caused by American heavy bombers even early in the war comes from Masatake Okumiya, who during the war was a staff officer of CARDIV 2 and consequently served in several carrier battles and on land in the Solomons during the brunt of the Allied assault against Rabaul. After the war Okumiya became an officer in the Japanese Self-Defense Force and spent several years studying the calamity suffered by Japanese airpower in the Pacific war. According to his postwar account, Okumiya believed that American heavy bombers posed a problem that threatened Japanese operations and that they had no good answer:

Sun, the great Chinese strategist [Sun-tzu, reputed author of the fourth-century B.C. classic *The Art of War*—EB], once said: "Those who know the enemy as well as they know themselves never suffer defeat." This historical statement was never proved truer than by the probing missions of the B-17 and B-24 bombers which endowed the Americans with a tremendous advantage in the far-flung Pacific war. For years the Japanese Navy had followed a strategic concept laid down by tradition: that a small Japanese force could achieve victory over superior enemy strength only so long as we were informed of the enemy's strength and movement, while ours remained hidden. With the B-17s and B-24s thundering constantly over our ships, airfields, and staging areas, the situation was reversed. We were in the position of the traditional enemy and handicapped by the same limitations we had always regarded as the opponent's weakness.

By September of 1942 the reconnaissance-mission flying B-17s and B-24s had become a grave problem, and the Japanese Navy tried every possible means of destroying the troublesome raiders. With the Guadalcanal campaign in full swing, our fighter pilots became desperate, but failed to achieve any notable advance in increasing the number of destroyed American bombers. . . . On numerous occasions the Boeings flew undaunted on their bombing and reconnaissance missions despite the attacks of Zero fighters which swarmed about them and which the enemy's heavy machine guns too often destroyed.

Okumiya also quoted the account of Lieutenant Commander Mitsugu Kofukuda, commander of the IJN 6th Air Group based at Buin during the Solomons campaign concerning the B-17:

The four-engine B-17 and B-24 bombers were, generally speaking, the most difficult enemy aircraft for the Zeros to shoot down. Because of their excellent self-sealing fuel tanks, they were extremely difficult to set afire with the Zero's 20mm. cannon shells. Our fighter pilots soon learned that the B-17s and B-24s could rarely be destroyed unless the pilots or vital parts of the aircraft were hit and rendered useless. The fierce resistance with which the heavy American bombers opposed our fighters, unlike that of our own land based medium attack bombers which too often fell easy prey to enemy fighters, was a most serious problem. In my opinion, which is shared by many Japanese combat officers, the ability of the B-17 and B-24 to defend themselves and carry out their intended missions despite enemy fighter opposition was a deciding factor in the final outcome of the war.

Considering the unfavorable balance of forces existing in New Guinea, Allied bombers had done a creditable job of exerting pressure. Late in the year, as we shall see, they did much more damage.

Yet during the fall of 1942 the first great challenge, outside of the two carrier battles of Coral Sea and Midway, for either side to employ airpower as a decisive offensive tool was given the JNAF when the Americans attacked Guadalcanal. There are four missions bombers could accomplish in the South Pacific: reconnaissance, supporting ground troops, sinking ships, and destroying enemy air bases. When Guadalcanal became the center of the storm in the Pacific war, the imperial air arm failed totally in each of those tasks. By doing so JNAF leaders, despite extraordinary tenacity and courage on the part of airmen, shared fully with Yamamoto and others in Combined Fleet in the catastrophe at Guadalcanal.

In retrospect I think that the Japanese paid a serious price for their deep integration of land-based airpower and fleet movements. From its inception the JNAF was conceived as an adjunct to Combined Fleet. Ideally this was an excellent organizational arrangement for a conflict where naval, ground, and air operations would be so closely intermingled. Yet when the crunch came at Guadalcanal the major decisions were made by naval officers. There was no Japanese equivalent of Kenney or Geiger. The principle of attack overwhelmed the basic questions of how best to accomplish the tactical objectives. Given enough time to plan, the Japanese practice of leaving tactical decisions to relatively low-ranking operational wizards like Genda worked well. When it was necessary to move quickly for high stakes the decisions were made by officers whose experience and sentiment were still wedded to the big gun. This does not mean that the Japanese underestimated the importance of airpower. They had pioneered the offensive use of naval aviation (see Pearl Harbor). Yet when faced with a situation that did not fit the script the IJN proved incapable of altering operational procedures to meet the circumstances. Frequently it showed poor attention to operational detail that high-ranking airmen would have seen at once. They were far too slow to ask what was wrong and too quick to respond by simply increasing the size of their forces and attempting failed methods again on a larger scale.

The matter of reconnaissance was a vivid case in point. After Midway the Japanese should have anticipated a major American move somewhere in the Pacific. Yet the pioneer units at Guadalcanal continued construction of their air base at the typical languid Japanese pace. Amazingly the officers of Combined Fleet and at Rabaul were absorbed by the IJA's offensive over the Owen Stanley Mountains directed at Port Moresby. Valuable air resources were at Lae, and a small airstrip for temporary use was in operation at Buna, the ultimate source of Japanese supplies for the venture. At Tulagi the JNAF had several Zero floatplanes, and there were other seaplane tenders scattered throughout the Solomons. Regardless no systematic reconnaissance was undertaken despite the fact that Midway had given the Americans a temporary advantage in carrier strength. It may well be that the magnitude of the defeat at Midway was not well appreciated throughout the Japanese military, as bad news traveled most slowly in Tokyo. The situation is particularly remarkable when it is considered that U.S. B-17s, fearing that the Japanese were about to finish their base at Guadalcanal, were already launching raids on what would soon become Henderson Field.

The result was that Vice Admiral Kelly Turner's invasion fleet, supported by the largest Allied task force yet assembled, including three aircraft carriers, arrived off Guadalcanal and Tulagi and achieved complete surprise. It is impossible to say what Combined Fleet would have done had it realized the peril even twenty-four hours in advance. Certainly there would have been a major search for the U.S. carriers. More importantly, however, because they were as surprised at Guadalcanal as the Americans had been at Pearl Harbor, Yamamoto and his staff had no opportunity to ponder the single most important question posed by the Allied attack: Should Japan defend Guadalcanal? Rough-and-tumble airmen like Kenney and Geiger might well have pointed out the terrible strategic problems that would be faced by any sustained attack coming from distant Rabaul. They certainly would have been screaming for advanced bases on and near Bougainville "sooner than absolutely possible." In the event, like good warriors, the Japanese launched an immediate air assault that failed miserably and followed up with an air campaign that displayed an array of tactical errors and did more damage to Japan's land-based air arm at Rabaul than it did to Cactus.

Guadalcanal, more than any major military campaign of the Pacific war, illustrates the old military dictum that victory goes to the side that makes the fewest mistakes. At sea the Allies did much to squander their immediate advantage, whereas Mars smiled on Combined Fleet for months. An audacious move by the intrepid Admiral Mikawa led to the humiliating Allied defeat at Savo Island. A confused carrier battle in the eastern Solomons could well have ended a major Allied victory but finished a slight tactical win for the USN. Japanese submarines then began their extraordinary run of success in Torpedo Alley, sinking one carrier, damaging another, and sending a new fast battleship and heavy cruiser back to Pearl Harbor. In October the carriers faced off for the last time, and *Hornet* went down to a brave and sustained attack by Japanese aircraft. In the meantime surface ships of the two navies were engaging in their long-anticipated battle. Despite prewar plans, however, the engagements were at night, sporadic, and incredibly violent. On many occasions the Japanese gave the USN a lesson on surface night-fighting, but the big showdown came in November; the IJN was left licking its wounds.

Yet the fighting skills and good fortune given to Combined Fleet at Guadalcanal could not compensate for the thrashing delivered to the JNAF by Allied aircraft based at Cactus, protected and ably supported by the aircraft carriers of the United States Navy.

When Rabaul received radio messages from stunned garrisons on Tulagi and Guadalcanal at dawn on August 7, 1942, there were seventy-two combat aircraft on the field. Planning for a raid on Milne Bay, twenty-seven Bettys were already loaded with bombs. The loaded aircraft, along with eighteen escorts from the elite Tainan Air Group, were immediately ordered to strike. Before a bullet was fired the Japanese had made their first mistake. It was a 565-mile flight to Guadalcanal but the weather was good, yet there was no possibility of launching two attacks on a single day. The waters around the island were swarming with warships and transports. If there was ever a time for a well-considered air strike this was it. With warships present and U.S. carriers definitely present, an hour of thought might have been wise. Perhaps more could be learned from the garrison concerning ship dispositions. Even though it would have meant a substantial delay, the Japanese made a terrible error in not replacing bombs with torpedoes. Instead one of the most important air strikes of the Pacific war was ordered immediately aloft. They were spotted at once by an Australian Coast Watcher, and the Allies were warned. U.S. naval radar soon picked up the raid. Fortunately for the Japanese their American opponents were new at the game, too, and most of the Wildcats available were kept above the carriers. Those made available to protect the transports and surface ships off Guadalcanal were not well positioned. Consequently the Japanese escorts did very well against the outnumbered U.S. fighters. However, the point of the raid was the destruction of U.S. ships: If the carriers could not be attacked, then the transports must be struck. The Bettys approached their target at 12,000 feet, dropped their bombs, and proved what B-17 pilots could have told them—you must be very lucky to hit a ship with a bomber flying above 6,000 feet. All the bombs missed. Although the Americans lost ten Wildcats, they destroyed all sixteen seaplanes at Tulagi, shot down four Bettys, caused two to crash-land, and damaged several others. To add insult to injury two Tainan pilots perished, and Saburo Sakai, their leading ace at the time, was wounded so badly that he was out of combat for more than two years. The mission was an abject failure, the first of many humiliating defeats when Japanese bombers attempted to interfere with Allied landings in the Pacific.

On the same day, Japanese officers ordered the kind of pointless gesture that helped the Allied cause immensely throughout the war. At Rabaul there were sixteen Val dive-bombers. Nine were ready and loaded with twin 60kg bombs designed for attacking ground targets. The Val could not reach Guadalcanal and return from Rabaul. So instead of preserving precious combat aircraft and experienced crews, Japanese officers ordered the nine to attack. The pilots were told to try to return to the undeveloped field at Buka on Bougainville. Rabaul also dispatched a destroyer south of Bougainville in case some of the Vals or damaged aircraft needed to ditch. The Vals pressed their attack and managed to hit a U.S. destroyer, the only damage done to Allied ships that day. Six were shot down and three ditched. Only three crewmen survived. It was the kind of gesture that some Japanese officers relished. It was also an absurd waste and an insult to every airman in the IJN. (On more than one occasion U.S. aircraft pushed their attack beyond operating range and suffered losses because of it. However, when they did so, they were pursuing carriers that had been identified and the planes were properly armed to do them harm. The Vals at Rabaul had no such vital target and were not well enough armed to sink or even seriously damage a large ship.)

Although not sure of American intentions, Japanese officers from Yamamoto on down knew that they would rarely see a target as large as the fleet off Guadalcanal. Reinforcements came into Rabaul on August 7, and another attack was readied for August 8. This time the Bettys carried torpedoes. They also eluded most of the U.S. fighters. However, the Coast Watchers had seen this attack also, and when the Japanese raid arrived the U.S. transports were under way and surrounded by a powerful escort of cruisers and destroyers. When faced with a barrage of antiaircraft of a magnitude they had never encountered, the Betty formations fell apart. One U.S. destroyer took a torpedo but survived. (The destroyer *Jarvis* was apparently hit again the next day while withdrawing, with the loss of all hands.) The major success of the day took place when a Betty crashed into the transport *Elliott*, which was beached and later sank with moderate loss of life. Two hours later shocked Japanese officers watched a handful of Bettys return. During the ten-minute engagement at Guadalcanal the Japanese bomber force was shattered. Twenty-three planes reached the target. American gunners and a handful of fighters destroyed seventeen Bettys, caused one to crash-land, and took down another Zero. The five surviving planes were all badly damaged. A total of 125 bomber crewmen died on the mission. In two days Rabaul's heavy strike force was in ruins.

All too slowly the serious nature of the Guadalcanal operation dawned on Tokyo. Some officers argued that it was a "reconnaissance in force" and nothing to worry about. The annihilation of an elite IJA attack force of 900 men on August 21 ended that dream. On the same day, the Marines began landing fighters and dive-bombers on Henderson Field; within weeks Fighter One was also in operation. A Japanese attempt to bring in a troop convoy was foiled days later during the Battle of the Eastern Solomons. Although it was a USN victory, the Marines proved they could sink ships while the Japanese proved they could not. Even as the entire Guadalcanal operation hung on a thread for two months, the outline for U.S. victory was already clear. With Japanese carrier groups mauled by their engagements with U.S. carriers, Japanese land-based planes had to prevent the Americans from establishing a kill zone against the Japanese transports carrying reinforcements required to destroy the Marines. In that task the JNAF failed completely.

Because of the great range involved, the Japanese had to depend on Bettys to neutralize Henderson. Although Tokyo sent substantial reinforcements to Rabaul, including their best bomber units, the numbers involved in a given raid almost never surpassed twenty-four bombers. Viewing the Japanese offensive with the perspective of what was required by far more powerful Allied forces to destroy an airbase, imperial efforts bordered on pathetic. A Betty flying from Rabaul would usually carry one 250kg GP bomb (the fuse settings are not clear) along with two 60kg daisy-cutters. Later Allied aircraft attacking air bases would have carried a single 500-pound bomb along with two 100-pound fragmentation bombs, considered to be a reasonable armament for an SBD; a twin-engine bomber or TBF would carry much more power. Under the best of circumstances, then, the Bettys flying from Rabaul were carrying an armament suited for a P-38 on a ground-support mission. Allied officers of a B-24 squadron would have laughed at the bomb load carried by a Betty.

The Bettys were trying to destroy the runway with the large bomb and destroy aircraft on the ground with the daisy-cutters. Given the extreme difficulties of long-range attacks, the Japanese method had a certain logic. However, Betty attacks throughout the Guadalcanal campaign were fatally crippled by the inability of Japan's officers and airmen to devise an appropriate means to deliver ordnance on target. Instead the JNAF employed the worst possible tactics in light of this crucial mission. Bettys (if records are correct; some U.S. fighter pilots challenge them) attacked at altitudes of well above 20,000 feet. Often records claim that they dropped at 24,000–27,000 feet. Perhaps such tactics worked against poorly defended Chinese cities, but they were absurd against a prepared air base.

To provide some perspective: U.S. daylight bombers over Germany usually dropped bombs at 18,000–24,000 feet. Americans were attacking factory complexes far larger than an airfield and dropping loads dwarfing those carried by the Bettys. The Japanese tactic had two results. First, when fortunate enough to make a hit, Bettys rarely did serious damage. Because there were dozens of such raids between August and November, on occasion the bombers would get lucky and detonate a fuel dump or destroy some aircraft on the ground. (Ground victims were almost always damaged or destroyed aircraft in the bone-yard near Fighter One—planes able to fly left the ground when a raid was detected.) More likely, however, they missed the target completely or inflicted damage that was easily repaired by the ever-present Seabees. Marine fighter pilot J.A.O. Stub was at Guadalcanal at the height of the battle and recalled, "There were many air raids. Occasionally some damage was done, but I cannot recall that our operations were seriously harmed by any of them."

It is difficult to explain why the JNAF adopted tactics that almost ensured the major objective would fail. Along with great range the Betty's advantage was excellent speed. At high altitude a Wildcat could catch a Betty only with difficulty. Yet because of the Coast Watchers and radar, Marine and U.S. Navy fighters exacted a deadly toll. John Lundstrom, who uses figures conservatively, estimated that USN and Marine fighters alone destroyed sixty Bettys over Guadalcanal between August 7 and November 15. Richard Frank, who studied the campaign to its end, argued that the Marines and USN fighters downed 125 Bettys. This would not include aircraft lost to antiaircraft fire and accidents. The equation becomes more complex when the Betty and Zero are examined in tandem. Zero escorts were able to fly above Betty formations and took a toll on defenders when they enjoyed the altitude advantage. Yet neither the Zero nor the

Wildcat were good high-altitude fighters. At any altitude above 20,000 feet the Zero lost much of its advantage in maneuverability. Obviously higher-altitude operations gave Wildcats an even better opportunity to use their superior dive speed if in trouble. If Bettys flew so high to avoid interception, they were, at the same time, crippling their Zero escorts.

It is also possible that the Japanese were stung by the spectacular success of U.S. antiaircraft on August 8. U.S. shipping left Guadalcanal two days later (hastened by the Japanese victory at Savo Island). However, they brought in powerful antiaircraft defenses for Henderson. The U.S. Marine Third Defense Battalion, which was deployed near the airfields, had radar-controlled 90mm antiaircraft guns along with a number of 40mm Bofors automatic cannons and 20mm Oerlikon cannons—essentially a land-based destroyer. In early November they were joined by the Ninth Defense Battalion, which took up positions near the new bomber field at Koli Point. Army units brought in similar weapons. The 40mm and 20mm weapons had done most of the damage on August 8. Their effective range was roughly 6,000 feet. The 90mm, however, theoretically could hit a target at 30,000 feet. (The American 90mm was similar to the famous German 88mm gun that caused so much damage to Allied bombers in Europe.) Radar control was an undeveloped technology at the time for land-based weapons but, like the tracers from Jim Eaton's ball turret, puffs of lethal flak debris were good reason to stay away from the target. U.S. antiaircraft on Guadalcanal did not down very many bombers and damaged several, but if it helped keep the attackers too high every round was worth it. Jim Norris was a ground crewman for the army's 76th Squadron on Guadalcanal. Like all men on the line he was theoretically at ground zero for Japanese bomber attacks. He recalled the futility of most Betty raids:

I don't think any of us really knew why the enemy bombed from such a high altitude. Maybe they were afraid of our fighters or trying to stay away from flak. But keeping the Japanese at a higher level was a tremendous advantage. The Japanese accuracy at 20,000 feet was very poor. Very often they'd miss everything and the bombs would drop out in the jungle. Sometimes they missed by a couple of miles and their bombs were probably closer to their own lines than ours. There were some times when we were almost out of business but those were due to mechanical failures, lack of parts, accidents, or planes downed in combat. The only time we were really shaken was by the battleships in October, and even then we got things going.

Obviously Allied fighters did not face great tactical problems when attacking Japanese bombers of any type. The Betty had a 20mm cannon mounted in the tail, so cautious fighter pilots attempted to attack it outside the 30-degree arc covered by the cannon from the rear. Beyond that almost anything would work. Good shots liked a pass from the front quarter. Veterans might launch a tricky overhead pass. Yet the .30-caliber machines guns carried as the main defensive armament were not feared by Allied fighters, and they would attack from any angle if the opportunity arose. Many Allied pilots found the slow rate of fire of the 20mm did not protect the bomber from a fast run in from the six aimed at the Betty's wing root. Poorly armored and a flamer, the Betty had to rely on its good speed for protection—and that was not enough. Other bombers were easier targets than the Betty. Losses for imperial bomber crews were serious throughout the war.

It is sad commentary on the performance of Japanese bombers during Guadalcanal that the worst moment for Cactus was caused by a naval bombardment. The Americans survived that trauma and maintained their killing zone near Guadalcanal even during the darkest hours. During the Japanese land attacks days later there were no Japanese aircraft to support imperial troops. Beyond some strafing of U.S. hill positions, Japanese aircraft played no role in the merciless ground-fighting. Japanese troops fought without air support. More importantly they fought without the supplies that the IJN should have provided them because Allied airpower at Cactus prevented shipping from landing its cargo. To make matters worse, if a transport could get close to Guadalcanal there was a desperate shortage of landing craft, which made unloading a much longer process. The Americans, too, used smaller vessels at first as a temporary expedient. During the day, however, U.S. transports, covered by Cactus fighters, slowly began to trickle in to Lunga Point. Unlike the modified destroyers and barges routinely used by the Japanese, the Americans brought in genuine transports. The Japanese were reasonably successful in landing men, but the Americans were landing firepower. Considering the fact that the Japanese had to attack with men against fire, the debacle suffered by imperial troops in October was inevitable.

The growing futility of Japan's effort was illustrated in the air by actions directed toward Henderson in late October 1942. For weeks the IJA had concentrated a large force around the Marine perimeter and planned a decisive assault for October 25. Although the Japanese had managed to land a large force with destroyers and barges at night, at great cost to a handful of transports, they were poorly supplied in all categories and woefully deficient in artillery. Combined Fleet planned a major sortie to support the offensive with a massed attack on Cactus that would include attacks from land-based and carrier-based aircraft. Furious air battles began several days prior to the finale over Henderson, during which U.S. fighters, despite insufficient numbers, did very well. On October 25 the Japanese sent eighty-two aircraft of all types in six waves against Cactus. Despite being outnumbered, the Americans inflicted serious losses on the attackers and lost only two fighters. The fields were almost untouched, although some Japanese Vals bombed the boneyard where wrecked U.S. aircraft were stored near Fighter One. It was all for nothing. Unharried by Japanese aircraft, the Marines had smashed the Japanese ground attack the night before.

In those violent weeks in October over Guadalcanal and nearby seas, two trends came into sharp relief. First, the American airmen showed an ability to sink ships, whereas the Japanese did not. The second point relates to the first: Even before superior Allied aircraft entered the theater, Allied naval and land units had greatly improved the power of antiaircraft armament. The tactical alignment, from Japan's point of view, proved as bad as could be imagined. Tokyo's nimble but light aircraft were soon to be challenged by big, rugged, and superior Allied bombers and fighters. Simultaneously the Japanese would lose the ability to challenge Allied forces on the deck because of withering flak that posed mortal danger to fragile Japanese aircraft. As fortune would have it, these technical trends coincided with the Allied discovery that one of the best ways to sink ships and destroy ground targets was to strike just above the treetops. On October 25 Yamamoto expected to hear the message that Japanese troops had captured Henderson. The message never arrived. However, starting at this time in both the Solomons and New Guinea, Allied bombers began to do what the Japanese bombers proved they could not. Soon enough a hail of bombs helped to throw Japan completely on the defensive.

Allied Bombers Take Control

The superior ability of the Allies to project airpower by late 1942 had a twin defensive-offensive component. Despite hundreds of volumes dealing with aircraft and pilots, very little attention—except on the part of some naval historians—is paid to the subject of antiaircraft. This is unfortunate because antiaircraft, called "flak," was almost certainly the greatest killer of bombers on both sides of the Pacific war and a tremendous danger to fighters. As I examine below, Japanese gunners did slow but steady and painful damage to Allied aircraft. Yet there is no doubt that in this field the Allies had a great advantage at sea and over land bases. I should also add that all dedicated antiaircraft guns in use by either side were powerful weapons. Any aircraft struck by fragments or a smaller cannon shell was in danger. Obviously the fragility of Japanese aircraft played to Allied strength in this area, whereas many an Allied airman made it home in their tough planes despite taking a wicked hit from Japanese flak.

Antiaircraft came in three varieties: heavy, medium, and light. At the time of Pearl Harbor the two sides were quite evenly matched concerning both naval and land-based antiaircraft. This is another way of saying that both sides were woefully deficient in a vital weapon system. On December 7, 1941, the primary USN naval antiaircraft weapon was the extremely unreliable and despised 1.1-inch cannon and the .50-caliber machine gun. Some of the most modern vessels had the new heavy five-inch guns in sophisticated mounts. However, most five-inch guns were in open, single mounts with no complex fire-control system and not able to traverse or elevate well enough to be decent antiaircraft weapons. They were considered defense against destroyers and torpedo boats, not aircraft. Pearl Harbor and the Coral Sea, to put it mildly, quickly changed opinions throughout the American services.

The United States Navy made mistakes prior to Pearl Harbor and made more thereafter. Yet if USN leaders identified a problem they could move with great speed and ingenuity to solve it. Admirals saw immediately that naval antiaircraft was inadequate. The 1.1-inch gun did not work, and the .50-caliber machine gun was, as one sailor told me, a "revenge weapon"; if it did shoot down an attacking airplane, it did so at such close range that the attacker had already dropped his bomb or torpedo. As a result orders went out to retrofit every possible warship and combat transport with as much antiaircraft as possible.

The heavy naval antiaircraft gun was the famous .38-caliber five-inch gun. The 5–38 could fire a seventy-pound high explosive projectile up to a range of 18,000 yards. It was rated at fifteen rounds per minute, but a good crew could fire twenty. Beginning in mid-1942 the 5–38 was given a radar fire control, which would not only direct the shell but also set the fuse on the round. Like all heavy flak, a shell fired from a 5–38 was intended to explode and hurl fragments over an area of several hundred feet, not to strike the aircraft like a single bullet. (Any aircraft struck directly by a five-inch gun faced immediate destruction.) These guns became ubiquitous in the USN. A *Fletcher*-class destroyer carried five guns in single mounts; a cruiser mounted eight. A new fast battleship like the *South Dakota* carried ten twin mounts for a whopping total of twenty. Carriers were given special attention: *Enterprise* carried eight, and the *Essex*-class had twelve. (Later in the war the five-inch projectiles carried the proximity fuse, which exploded when it sensed a metallic object within a certain range. It was a deadly device but not widely distributed until late 1943. The first Japanese plane downed with the device was fired upon by the great cruiser *Helena* in January 1943.)

It is important to realize that warships rarely traveled alone, and an aircraft carrier always had several escorts. Given the great range of the 5–38 any attackers would be under fire from several ships. Although such numbers are illusive, it seems that the early-war 5–38 was less effective than those equipped with better radar later in the war. Regardless any pilot coming under heavy antiaircraft fire a few minutes before attack is going to be uneasy. Undoubtedly many attackers received damage; some were destroyed outright. Yet there was a substantial bonus. Air attacks were very brief, violent, and chaotic affairs. It was vital to see the attacker as soon as possible. Many gunners manning the light antiaircraft that had no fire control used the puffs of smoke caused by the 5–38s as a way to first spot Japanese raiders that would appear as tiny specks but grow larger with great speed. The heavy flak gave a sure sign of direction and altitude of a raid. (It also threw up a blizzard of explosions and caused a deafening sequence of cracks as the terribly loud five-inch guns fired dozens of rounds aboard ships, adding to the confusion of the moment. Many American gunners in exposed mounts were punch-drunk from the noise made by the 5–38s after an attack.)

An attacker that made it past the heavy guns would have to face deadly medium antiaircraft—the versatile 40mm Bofors cannon. A Swedish design the United States had licensed before the war, the Bofors was produced by the thousands. It was one of the most successful weapons of the century, and variations serve throughout the world today. The 40mm fired a two-pound projectile up to a range of three miles. By late 1942 the Bofors was also radar-controlled. Feeding a clip containing eight rounds, a good crew could get off more than 100 rounds per minute. Starting the war with none, *Enterprise* finished the war with forty Bofors; *North Carolina* entered Tokyo Bay in 1945 carrying ninety-six; a humble destroyer in midwar carried three twin mounts. The Bofors shell carried a contact fuse, which meant that it exploded only if it hit the target. If it did, however, destruction of the victim was almost certain either immediately or within a very short time. Only the stoutest bomber, of which Japan had none, stood a good chance of surviving a hit from a Bofors.

The last line of defense in a late-1942 fleet unit was the 20mm Oerlikon cannon. A Swiss design adopted by Britain before the war, the

Oerlikon was first built by the United States in mid-1941. By late 1942 the 20mm had replaced the .50-caliber machine guns on all frontline vessels, and for good reason. Loaded with a drum magazine holding at least sixty rounds, the 20mm could in theory fire 600 rounds per minute. With a crew of three, one man loading the magazine as it quickly emptied, the 20mm threw out a large number of shells. Very much like their 20mm counterparts on the Zero and P-38, a 20mm round would cause serious damage if it struck home. The 20mm guns were manually controlled by their crew and fired over a simple sight. The great advantage of the weapon was its small size and light weight—less than 100 pounds. Consequently it was possible to put 20mm guns in almost any unoccupied position on a vessel without fear of upsetting its stability. For that reason it is difficult to tell how many 20mms were on any warship at a given moment. They were a standard retrofit whenever a ship came into port, the basic doctrine being the more the better. A sailor on the cruiser *Boise*, which was damaged at the Battle of Cape Esperance in October 1942, assured me that when the ship was returned to the United States for repairs, Admiral King himself came aboard, found every place on the deck where poker games took place, and put in a 20mm. A midwar destroyer would carry ten Oerlikons, larger vessels far more. The USN authorized the fitting of thirty-one Oerlikons on its prewar cruisers by May 1943, but the actual number varied by ship. When the Bettys from Rabaul attacked Turner's transports on August 8, 1942, several transports were fitted with a dozen Oerlikons, more than carried by either the *Repulse* or *Prince of Wales* when they were sunk by Japanese Nells and Bettys in December 1941. Simply put U.S. vessels were becoming naval fortresses. Bombs and torpedoes could still sink and damage them, but as the weeks passed during the Pacific war it became more difficult for Japanese aircraft to get close enough to attack them.

The improvements in U.S. naval antiaircraft were shown by the three carrier battles. At the Coral Sea the Japanese lost some thirty aircraft and several more damaged. Japanese losses at the Battle of the Eastern Solomons in August 1942 were similar, although they sunk no U.S. carriers. In October during the Battle of Santa Cruz, when more U.S. ships were carrying enhanced antiaircraft weapons, Japanese losses soared to 100, including well more than half of both torpedo- and dive-bombers. Japanese airmen did sink the *Hornet* but at the loss of the planes shot down and damaged that approached an entire IJN air group. At the time Combined Fleet believed it had won a victory. What it could not know was that from that point forward Japanese aircraft would prove of little value against major U.S. warships until the desperate kamikaze campaign began in late 1944. And because U.S. warships escorted transports, Japanese air strikes—as predictable as the dawn—failed miserably to hinder any landing in the Solomons and New Guinea.

The Japanese also increased antiaircraft on their vessels, which made them dangerous to attack. But their weapons were often less powerful and usually less numerous. No Japanese warship carried radar-assisted antiaircraft weapons, so the advantages in quality and quantity were solidly in favor of the USN. This was also true for land bases. Some Japanese gunners proved the primary enemy of Allied bombers, but they were in the minority when considering the number of antiaircraft weapons given to Japanese bases.

U.S. land units also increased antiaircraft strength. When the U.S. Marine Ninth Defense Battalion landed on Rendova during the New Georgia campaign it had three batteries of four radar-controlled 90mms. Supporting the heavy armament were Bofors, 20mm cannons, and .50-caliber machine guns. All major Allied air bases also received powerful antiaircraft defenses. Often batteries never hit a plane, but it was a rare day when Japanese bombing attacks did serious damage. Any attack that was hurried or confused was compromised.

The Japanese did not often attack U.S. antiaircraft positions on Guadalcanal because of their understandable fixation on the airfields and aircraft. Furthermore if Bettys could not reliably hit an airfield, they were going to have less success at high altitude against smaller positions. When the Allies attacked New Georgia, however, the Japanese launched one of their largest air offensives of the entire South Pacific campaign. With the Bougainville bases operational and flying much closer to their bases, the JNAF could use Vals and Kates against U.S. positions. Zeros were available for the risky job of strafing. The Ninth Defense Battalion's antiaircraft and artillery positions were a prime target when the Japanese aircraft struck. While furious fighter battles took place overhead, Japanese aircraft attacked the Rendova beachhead on July 2 and July 4. As Frank Chadwick, a flak gunner with the Ninth, recalled, the war between aircraft and antiaircraft positions was at close range and violent:

On July 2 the Japs launched a big air raid on Rendova. They knocked out two of our 155mm guns. One of our men was in a foxhole that took a direct hit. There was nothing left of him at all. We all knew what had happened to him, but he was listed as MIA until after the war. There were dive-bombers, Bettys, and Zeros. The bombers came over first and hit the gun position. The dive-bombers attacked the beach positions. When the bombers cleared out the Zeros came in and strafed us. The planes were about fifty feet off the ground. Their canopies were back, their goggles were up, and some had white scarves on—you could practically reach out and shake their hands. The Japs did have spirit. I was on the 40mm and was almost killed, which scared the hell out of me. I had big holes from shrapnel through my dungarees; the holes were charred from the hot shrapnel going through. We lost the electrical generator for the controls of one of the guns, and a sergeant who tried to fix it was electrocuted.

On that first afternoon we had a 20mm gun set up when that first wave came through. The Japs hit the gun and killed all four of the crew. Four more guys came in, moved the bodies out, and were firing when the second wave came through. It took nerve to take out four of your buddies' bodies to face a second wave of planes. I think we were all crazy at the time. Strafing and things like that happen so fast that it doesn't bother you until it's over. Most planes come in at treetop level. You see the firing of the guns on the wings, you see the bombs drop from the plane. You see the pilot's face. You are talking fifty, sixty, ninety feet away. It happens in a blink of an eye. And a few minutes later you start shaking and look for your cigarettes. You're pretty well trained, too. You do what you're supposed to do. Later it sinks in.

On July 4 the biggest raid took place. I don't know if they were after our position or the tanks behind us about 300 feet back in a coconut grove. They dropped two strings of bombs in front of us and two behind. Nobody got hit, although there was shrapnel flying all over. There were fuel and ammunition dumps burning and some of the 20mms and 40mms on the beach were knocked off. We were in our foxholes watching those fifty-five-gallon drums of aviation fuel fly through the air and explode. The raid probably lasted half an hour but seemed like forever. All agreed it was the most impressive July Fourth yet. But during a low-level air attack the crews stayed at their guns, nobody headed for their holes. On that day a group of eighteen Bettys got beat up and we think the 90mms took most of them out. Rest of the planes came across the beach. You stand your ground and just keep putting up the lead and try to bring them down. We shot down many aircraft on Rendova that day and in the days following. There was a big mountain on Rendova, always covered by clouds. Between eleven and one o'clock you could rest assured they were coming down onto the beach positions through the clouds. On clear days they came in from the northwest, right across the beach, sweep across the channel, and head for home. A supply logjam developed on the New Georgia beachhead, and it was a prime target. The Japs hit those concentrations

of supplies near the treeline every day. That's why they targeted our
90mms so often because we were firing at them. Of course, they weren't
fond of our artillery hitting Munda, either.

For the Allies the New Georgia campaign was a painful enterprise
that cost them dearly before the airfield at Munda was taken and the
rest of the island secured. Yet the Allies set a pattern there that was repeated many times over. A powerful fleet, covered by large numbers of
fighters and a cloud of bombers, struck the beachhead. The Japanese
would attack, take serious losses, and most Allied naval units would
retreat from immediate danger, only to reappear in support of supply
transports. In the meantime commanders immediately installed land-
based antiaircraft units. When Japanese aircraft appeared, which they
always did, they had to battle the fighters, attempt unsuccessfully to
attack the ships, and then be faced with the choice of either breaking
off the attack or continuing to do battle against fighters and land-
based antiaircraft. The equation was a bad one for Japanese forces,
and they lost the air battles over every beachhead, allowing Allied
bombers in their turn to continue a relentless attack against imperial
ground forces.

We can get an idea of the power of U.S. antiaircraft from the postwar interrogation of Captain Takashi Miyazaki, a group commander
and then senior staff officer at Rabaul for almost the entire campaign.
When asked what threats were most severe to Japanese aircraft flying
from Rabaul, he answered that Allied fighters posed the greatest danger to Japanese fighters. That observation makes sense considering
that Zeros confined ground attacks to the occasional strafing run and
rarely got within range of warships. As for bombers he estimated that
the worst danger came from naval antiaircraft, the second worst from
land-based antiaircraft, the third from fighters, fourth from ground attack by Allied bombers, and fifth from bad weather.

While the Japanese were losing the ability to harm Allied warships,
the Americans and Anzac units were honing their ability to sink ships
and support ground offensives. Throughout the South Pacific the single most important key to Allied victory was to prevent the offensive
as well as supply missions on the part of Japanese ships. In practice it
was not possible to stop movements by the very fast Japanese cruisers
and destroyers entirely, although Allied planes could make some parts
of the theater very dangerous to move through.

Because of the many accounts of the Battle of Midway and battles in
1944, it would be easy to underestimate the difficulty of sinking ships

with bombers. Like all bombing missions most attacks came up empty. However, when struck with a bomb or torpedo any ship was in mortal peril. Obviously there were variables involved—the strength of the ship, whether the ship was under way and could maneuver or was at anchor, the amount of flak, and the availability of fighter cover. Nevertheless any ship under way proved a challenging target, and on-the-job training was required before aircraft could exert fully their inherent advantages.

Prior to the end of the Guadalcanal campaign a curious division of labor existed between American and Japanese forces on the vital techniques required to sink ships. Obviously the Japanese had proven effective at hitting battleships at anchor at Pearl Harbor. And thereafter their splendidly trained early-war carrier groups proved able to launch skillful and courageous attacks, best represented by their sinking the carriers *Lexington*, *Yorktown*, and *Hornet* during the great battles of 1942. Attacking major warships was the task JNAF pilots had been trained to do before the war. Although heavily defended, carriers were large targets, vulnerable because they carried huge amounts of aviation gasoline, and not able to maneuver like a nimble destroyer. Although not as well trained—or so many authors have told us—the Americans during the same period sunk four heavy and two light Japanese carriers and a heavy cruiser to boot. No doubt Allied intelligence had much to do with success, yet so did the skills of American carrier pilots.

What interests me is the relative lack of Japanese success in attacking Allied small warships and transports from the air. Certainly the technology and technical skills were available in the early weeks of the war, when Japanese aircraft of all types dealt heavy blows to American, Dutch, Australian, and British shipping. However, from the beginning of the war, whether it was because of doctrinal emphasis on attack, poor antiaircraft, or defective intelligence and air-to-ground coordination, the Japanese did a poor job of guarding their own transports and an even poorer job of sinking Allied counterparts.

At the risk of suggesting a pattern where one may not exist, I find it interesting that in January 1942, when Japanese forces were completely dominant, they allowed a small contingent of ancient U.S. destroyers to launch a nighttime torpedo attack against anchored imperial transports, sinking four and damaging three. It is true that Japanese forces were expanding at a tremendous rate, yet it is also true that the only time Japanese surface ships got near Allied transports was during Savo Island, where they successfully fought their way through a heavy cruiser screen, and Leyte Gulf, where Halsey made a rare slip. The dreaded Japanese surface-launched long-lance torpedo filled the waters off Guadalcanal and other points in the Solomons with destroyed U.S. warships, but none found their way home to an Allied transport.

After Balikpapan in 1942 the Allies continued to contest landings and attack transports. When the Japanese landed at Lae and Salamaua in March 1942 their invasion fleet was attacked by two U.S. carriers. Although unprotected by Japanese aircraft, three transports went down under ultraheavy attack. Perhaps greater damage should have been done, but the American aviators did a better job at Lae than did Japanese aircraft against Allied transports during the entire Pacific war. In May another raid sunk a Japanese destroyer and transport off Tulagi. In August 1942 U.S. B-17s badly damaged one transport unloading at Japan's bungled attempt to take Milne Bay.

In contrast Japanese airpower did almost nothing to prevent the buildup of Allied forces in New Guinea during the early months of war despite the pitiful forces MacArthur and Canberra could mount. In the event, Japan did not plan to invade Darwin, and the Allies did not plan to launch a drive from the area. Slowly small ships, often only a few tons in displacement, unloaded Allied garrisons at Moresby and Milne Bay. The Allies were using the small-vessel strategy not completely unlike that employed by Japan at Guadalcanal. However, there was no Japanese equivalent of Cactus to stop them, and they made a pitiful tropical dump into a dangerous military base.

Guadalcanal amplified the trend. As already examined Allied forces suffered little from Japanese attacks on the landings despite the fact that they received little direct fighter cover from the three U.S. carriers present. Regardless of many tragic mistakes, the Allies saved their transports at Savo and even decided to continue to unload for a few more precious hours. Initially the Americans, like the Japanese, relied on very small vessels for supplies. However, within a few weeks transports came in covered by aircraft from Cactus and warships. At Guadalcanal geography aided the Allies. Waters between Espíritu and Nouméa were far from Rabaul. Japanese ships coming from Rabaul approached American bases. Yet the Americans were soon able to bring in supplies and in October brought in an entire infantry regiment, complete with artillery, via transport. The Japanese also wished to reinforce Guadalcanal with transports, which could carry far more men and equipment than could destroyers and barges. Yet from a very early period both transports and escorts proved vulnerable to the aircraft at Cactus. When U.S. carrier aircraft flew in support, the situation became even more dire for Japan.

At Guadalcanal the American weapon of choice for sinking Japanese ships was the Dauntless dive-bomber. The SBD had already proved its worth most dramatically at the Coral Sea and Midway. The small, rugged aircraft was easy to produce and appeared in enough numbers to allow Cactus to maintain at least a minimal supply. USN carriers all had large flights of SBDs and usually carried reserves. It did not carry the bomb load of the German Stuka that caused Allied ships such grief in the Mediterranean, but it was much more maneuverable and could carry a 1,000-pound armor-piercing bomb, large enough to penetrate any Japanese ship of the time. More often the SBD carried a 500-pound bomb and perhaps a pair of 100-pound bombs on its wing. A nimble aircraft, it had twin .50-caliber machine guns firing forward and a twin .30-caliber mount in the rear. A few Japanese fighters and several reconnaissance planes fell to the SBD in air-to-air combat.

Yet it was in the bombardment role that the SBD justly won its fame. The USN had been interested in dive-bombing for years prior to the war and trained some splendid pilots who specialized in the craft. Some of these men helped win the Battle of Midway. Although Marine and USN pilots received the same combat training, it is safe to say that USN pilots developed an edge. On a carrier, combat was sporadic, which left time for training and patrol work. Many of the Marine units thrown into Cactus were green as grass. Early in the campaign Marine SBDs were not greatly successful when they had the opportunity to attack nimble Japanese destroyers moving up the Slot in the few hours of daylight available. Yet many proved quick learners, and on several occasions during the Guadalcanal campaign Cactus received assistance from SBDs dispatched from several carriers.

As might be imagined, dive-bomber work was difficult and dangerous. Marine SBD pilot LeRoy Smith flew in the Solomons during 1943 against Japanese land bases. He arrived just after Guadalcanal was seized, but the basics of dive-bomber technique remained the same throughout the war. Although no two attacks were identical and procedures from unit to unit were somewhat different, Smith described how a World War II pilot made a bomb run in a Dauntless:

> The SBD had a perforated dive flap. When you prepared to dive, it's your instinct in a dive-bomber to push the stick forward and keep pushing it and get yourself going down. However, we were taught a better way by a fine commander named Calhoun. He got us to peel off

and roll on our back, which is a little abnormal because flying inverted
feels strange. However, it lets you get on your target much easier. It also
misled the gunfire from the ground because as you passed over the
target they were firing in front of us. They often got one of us that way,
but unbeknownst to them we were preparing to reverse and got a good
dive on them. When you roll and pull through you pop those dive flaps.
You can move your stick around a little because it restricts the speed.
On TV it all looks pretty easy, but when you're up there it's as knit as a
button hole and the flak's going off around you. When you push over
to find that spot on the ground you need all the time you can get.

At the start of the dive you wanted the maximum altitude possible so
you could reach dive speed of 350 MPH and still have a little time to
adjust the plane on the way down, maybe an extra second or two. But
that was also influenced by what you were carrying. If you had a
1,000-pound bomb, you were near stall speed at 16,500 feet or so. You
didn't want to be there because you'd be flying so slow and make a
good target. So you'd start a little lower. The faster you're going the
tougher it is for the gunner. When you're up at about 360 MPH it was
time to hit the dive brakes. We had a sight—something like a big
hunter's rifle. We did a lot of skeet shooting to learn to put your guns
or bombs ahead of where you were aiming. When you roll over and
pull through you're trying to bring that sight to bear on the target.
When a bomb is hung under a plane carrying too much right rudder the
bomber skids and the bomb goes the other way, so you can throw the
bomb and never hit the target. By getting on that scope you could see
that the plane was stabilizing and the bomb would drop straight.

How high did you drop? Whatever was appropriate. A lot of guys
didn't come back because they tried to lay it right in there. Most of our
training was for a drop at 1,500–2,000 feet but in practice a lot
depended on the amount of antiaircraft. Flak made some guys think too
much so it was smart to give a little margin of error. Remember, you're
heading for the ground at high speed. When you are coming down you
get to the point where you think you've got everything lined up with
the tube and drop. But the plane "mushes" and will go down another
500 feet or so. That's why a lot of people never made it back. Because
of the speed and weight of the aircraft they just didn't pull up in time.
So I'd say you usually got rid of your bomb at 2,500 or a little lower—
somewhere in there. Conditions varied. A lot of our men hit the target
okay—they went right into the ground with their bombs. You're just
hanging, pulling as hard as you can on your stick and you've pushed
the throttle to the firewall to get the hell out. It didn't take a lot of
pressure if you did things right. The mechanical advantage was such

that you could pull out with a couple of fingers. Now a spin could take both hands because when you're in a spin—you never wanted that. The earlier dive-bombers took more stick pressure. I flew all of the Dauntless models. Each was a little easier to fly.

There was another sensation, a thrill involved. When you dumped your bomb and committed yourself to pulling out you closed the dive flaps—this is all almost one motion. When you close those flaps the plane becomes quite streamlined, so it's a little like a slingshot, giving you an extra pull to get out of there. That was one of the great advantages of those perforated flaps.

Cactus and USN pilots soon created the transport kill zone that crippled the IJA's attempt to break the Marine perimeter. Japanese attempts to get transport convoys through to Guadalcanal often triggered major naval engagements. The Combined Fleet sortie that led to the Battle of the Eastern Solomons in August was triggered by a Japanese attempt to support a convoy through to the Japanese ground force beginning to assemble between Cape Esperance and Tassafaronga Point, only about a dozen miles from the Marine positions guarding Henderson at Lunga Point. The Japanese carriers were beaten off, and eight SBDs from Cactus found the Japanese convoy led by the brilliant and tenacious Rear Admiral Raizo Tanaka on August 25, 1942. One Dauntless seriously damaged Tanaka's flagship, the cruiser *Jintsu*, putting it out of the war for months. Another SBD dealt a lethal bomb to a Japanese transport and a third seriously damaged yet another. A destroyer stood by to take on survivors. Although Japanese commanders often showed a crass insensitivity toward the fate of their own men, Japanese destroyer captains time and again went to great risks to pick their comrades out of the water. On this occasion disaster struck from an unlikely source: a flight of B-17s passing overhead. Knowing that the B-17s had a poor record for accuracy, the Japanese destroyer continued to collect survivors. On this day the luck was with the American heavies, and a flurry of bombs sent the imperial destroyer to the bottom quickly. The convoy shattered with more danger awaiting if it continued, Tanaka ordered it back to Rabaul. The Japanese troops would have to sneak in by barge or destroyer. (As luck would have it, the next day a flight of Bettys sunk a converted U.S. destroyer-transport; everything happened during Guadalcanal at some time or another.)

In October the SBDs continued to show their worth. On October 12, 1942, the morning after a U.S. tactical victory during the nighttime Battle of Cape Esperance, a multiwave attack from Cactus found a contingent of Japanese destroyers again attempting to aid a stricken Japanese warship. Two destroyers went down, one with heavy loss of life.

Worse was to come for Japan. At perhaps the single most dangerous hour for Cactus, American airmen, ground crews, and Seabees showed astounding grit and ability to improvise. Planning a large land attack against the Marine perimeter in late October, the Japanese planned to bring in a convoy of six fast transports. They were heavily escorted by warships. Worse for the Americans, a major Japanese task force based around two battleships headed for Guadalcanal, intending to bombard the forces at Cactus. The next day Cactus would receive heavy air attack and the convoy would unload. The plan almost worked. The battleship bombardment of October 13 devastated the aircraft and fuel supplies at Cactus. The following night imperial cruisers attacked again with less effectiveness. For two days steady Japanese air attacks appeared over Guadalcanal. During one, much of what remained of the Cactus fighters was on the ground, yet American antiaircraft made things very hot for the raiders, and their bombs drifted into the jungle. The next raid was met by the Wildcats missed by the first, and more Bettys died.

Furiously Seabees repaired the fields, fuel was flown in by transport from Espíritu, a forgotten cache of gasoline was found buried, and every possible plane was readied for attack. In a combined attack that included every imaginable U.S. aircraft, three of the six Japanese transports were sunk and the other three were forced to withdraw before fully unloaded. All of the infantry landed, but some 50–30 percent of supplies, depending on the category, never got ashore. (It was during this action that Jack Cram launched his torpedo attack with a PBY. At least one and perhaps two of the transports were sunk by B-17s. An exact accounting is not possible because so many different types of U.S. planes took part.) In the following days Japanese destroyers rushed to build up IJA strength for the big push. All made their runs, although six were damaged, some by strikes from the *Hornet*. On October 25 Yamamoto sent in more warships to support the final push by ground forces that were already defeated. Marine gunners from the shore damaged a Japanese destroyer who was no doubt expecting to see Japanese troops at Lunga Point. At about the same time Cactus fliers crippled a Japanese cruiser, which was finished off by a B-17 or a P-39 while burning and dead in the water, and severely damaged another destroyer.

Strategically the Guadalcanal campaign was lost in late October, although Combined Fleet gained some solace at sinking *Hornet* during the Battle of Santa Cruz, which was a dramatic footnote to the defeat of the IJA's offensive against the U.S. perimeter. The Japanese had hurled the IJA, Combined Fleet, and a horde of aircraft only to come up short. Had imperial forces possessed an extra regiment and some decent firepower and had the Japanese been able to prevent reinforcement of the American garrison, the battle might well have ended the other way—with devastating political consequences in Washington.

By October Tokyo had begun to panic. The Australians had driven back the Japanese expedition to Moresby, and an attack on Buna was imminent. The danger of debacle at Guadalcanal was clear, and no top leaders—Yamamoto included—would face defeat after so much Japanese sacrifice. (Some of the lower-ranking officers near the front had already become pessimistic, but voicing doubts within the Japanese military was a difficult proposition.) Thus Tokyo sent out orders to send major reinforcements to Guadalcanal to defeat the Americans. The most violent chapter of the campaign for the U.S. Navy was near. So was proof positive that the kill zone around Cactus was stronger than ever.

Yamamoto's plan was to use a powerful surface fleet, using what was left of his carriers on the periphery, to suppress Cactus. Once Cactus was down, then Japanese surface bombardment and air attack would keep it down, thereby keeping open a corridor for the several convoys of merchant ships that would be required to rebuild a new Japanese army on Guadalcanal with enough heavy equipment to destroy the perimeter. This dream died quickly when USN warships, ably assisted Cactus airmen, prevailed in a three-day naval bloodbath (November 12–15, 1942) off the coast of Guadalcanal. Japan's defeat at that last great engagement at Guadalcanal was primarily due to the efforts of the seamen aboard the warships that engaged formidable imperial forces in two merciless nighttime surface engagements. It was the job of Cactus to illustrate once again what would happen to Japanese ships found in the daylight within range of bombers, especially SBDs.

Cactus received an important reinforcement for the last major act of the campaign. Throughout the campaign aircraft from various U.S. carriers either made strikes in nearby waters or stationed and operated scattered groups temporarily from Cactus. (As noted, *Saratoga*'s flight group served nearly a month after the ship was damaged.) The November battles were heavily influenced by the presence of the strike aircraft from the *Enterprise*. Although it was damaged at Santa Cruz and was the only heavy U.S. carrier in the theater, Rear Admiral Thomas Kinkaid and Halsey coolly decided to commit most of the carrier's strength. Understandably reluctant to risk his ship in a classic strike, Kinkaid stood off from the immediate zone, launched a series of strikes, and ordered his tactical bombers and some of their escorts to land at Guadalcanal and become a powerful, albeit temporary, adjunct to Cactus. It was a splendid exercise in the use of airpower, and results matched any reasonable expectation.

The first victim was the Japanese battleship *Hiei*, which had been badly damaged during the night battle of November 12–13. Without steering it steamed a slow circle near Savo Island. Soon it was the target of attacks from B-17s, SBDs, and Avengers from Cactus. The airmen at Cactus soon learned a hard lesson. Battleships proved reasonably easy to disable but could be extremely hard to sink. As the day wore on *Hiei*'s crew, despite being hit by bombs from a B-17 and several SBDs, appeared to be winning the effort to regain control of the ship's steering and perhaps allow it to slip away at dusk. A healthy rain squall, which ruined accurate dive-bombing, added greatly to the Japanese battleship's chances for survival. Ultimately, however, a flight of Avengers from the *Enterprise* attacked at about 3:00 P.M. Several torpedoes had been launched earlier and hits recorded, but Japanese records indicate that none detonated. This time, however, imperial fortunes declined and two exploded, one causing fatal injury to the vulnerable rear of the ship, crippling its steering and beginning another major onrush of water. After dark, with destroyers taking survivors, *Hiei* was scuttled, inflicting a serious psychological blow to Combined Fleet. In addition, half of the battleship bombardment planned for Henderson was now gone.

Although the Dauntless proved a ruthless foe to Japanese shipping, the Avenger also played a role. During the later stages of the Solomons campaign it was most often used as a tactical bomber. Yet on occasion it could revert to its original purpose. As with all bombers, the biggest problem facing Avenger pilots was to hit the target. A torpedo run would seem to be an easier proposition than was a dive-bomber attack, because the pilot is wrestling with only two dimensions rather than three. In truth it was an extremely difficult maneuver that required nerve, good technology, and luck.

Robert Wyllie flew an Avenger off the *Enterprise* during the Battle of Santa Cruz and described an early-war torpedo run:

> At Santa Cruz four of us attacked a cruiser but we missed him. In the open sea, unless you surround the son of a gun, you probably can't hit a warship. He can turn faster than you can get around him. We had a little sight that looked like a tin can, but I don't know if anyone used it.

You'd line up two crosshairs and give it the enemy's speed and your speed and try to get to about 1,000 yards. Before Pearl Harbor nobody thought there would be a war so weapons were badly tested. I don't think our training was ideal, either. But those lousy torpedoes were completely inferior. We'll never know how many hits were made that simply did not go off.

Tom Powell was a TBF gunner flying off the *Enterprise*. His aircraft made a run on the *Hiei*:

We were under 200 feet or so when we launched our torpedo—very low. . . . They taught the pilot . . . to go in and come in from high altitude, weaving around, going up and down, and when they got within range and then you go down, level, get your speed down to where you can pickle it, you pickle it. The pilot told me that when they went out, instead of banking they'd do skid turns on purpose: the plane was pointing in one direction but it was actually going sideways through the air, you might say, to confuse their gunners. They called it "jinxing," skidding around. You'd change your attitude in relation to the ship. When all was done you'd be running parallel on the way out—you didn't want to go over them. Some did, it depended upon how the ship was maneuvering. If the gunner got close enough he'd fire at the ship, too. But in most cases you're out of effective range. Now we did strafe the transports later on at Guadalcanal. We could see them being struck by our incendiary bullets, starting little fires.

Hiei was going very slowly in circles—its rudder had been damaged the night before. The trouble was that all our fish were set shallow for carriers so when launching them in against a battleship it just hit their armor blisters, not the most effective way of doing things. After we pounded on it, they ran another strike from the island after we landed there. They credited George Wells with hitting *Hiei* in the stern and that really put them in a mess—knocked out a pump station. They scuttled it that night.

I believe we hit the *Hiei*. Whether or not it exploded I can't tell you. There were all kinds of troubles with the torpedoes. They'd hit but didn't go off, a defective weapon. I think that's why we started doing more bomb work than torpedo work—the problems with them broaching. At least we couldn't sink ourselves with our own torpedo the way the submarine *Tang* did.

Wyllie and Powell were correct: The prewar torpedo debacle, which crippled a major weapon system carried by submarines, destroyers, and aircraft, was arguably the worst moment in the history of U.S. military technology. The comparison of U.S. models to their Japanese counterparts during this time of the war was humiliating. But even though the weapon was defective, it was not inert, and a few Japanese ships fell victim to U.S. torpedoes. When repaired and improved in 1944 they proved a fearsome weapon when teamed with the rugged Avenger.

After finishing off *Hiei* the men from Cactus and the *Enterprise* were given an opportunity to hand Combined Fleet another stinging defeat. On the night of November 13–14 six Japanese cruisers closed on Henderson, and three conducted an intense bombardment. In stark contrast to the October attack, Japanese gunners destroyed only two planes and did minor damage, again pounding the boneyard. The Japanese, although they did not realize it, were in a terrible situation. Their "victims" at Cactus were very much alive. Worse yet there were SBDs from the *Enterprise* awaiting launch.

Six SBDs from Cactus caught the Japanese warships in the morning, one inflicting serious damage to the heavy cruiser *Kinugasa*. A short while later a two-plane scouting expedition picked up the Japanese formation and radioed its position to the *Enterprise*, which forwarded the information to a flight already inbound. Shadowing the fleet for an hour, the two scout SBDs decided to attack. Pilot Robert D. Gibson chose the *Kinugasa* for his run:

> Making a good attack was not easy. The practice bombs we used in
> training did not act the same as real ones. It was extremely important
> to start the attack anticipating where the target was going to be,
> because they were taking evasive maneuvers. You have very little
> leeway on the pitch of a bomb. When you got close, at 270 knots with
> your dive brakes open, you only had a few seconds and not much
> chance to maneuver on the target. So you had to be well set before you
> went in. On the way down you're under antiaircraft fire. People would
> get excited—you'd fire your .50s at the target and watch the tracers
> through the bombsight. On the pullout the rear gunner would try to
> shoot things up with his .30s, anything to keep the enemy diverted.
> Things worked right against *Kinugasa*. I stayed with it lengthwise,
> made my drop, and put one down the stack.

Dead in the water, *Kinugasa* went down soon after Gibson's strike. Soon the remainder of the *Enterprise* strike arrived and damaged two heavy and one light Japanese cruisers. Admiral Mikawa's once powerful cruiser flotilla was effectively out of action.

Marine and USN tactical bombers achieved a tremendous but predictable victory near Guadalcanal hours after Gibson and comrades had mauled Mikawa. The entire object of Combined Fleet's large surface sortie was to create a secure lane for transports, which would bring a new division and tons of supplies to the battered Japanese army on Guadalcanal. Destroyer wizard Raizo Tanaka commanded eleven destroyers that escorted eleven large transports. By Japanese standards the transports were large vessels, some 5,000–10,000 tons. Like Turner's transports they all had considerable antiaircraft. Unlike U.S. transports, however, when battle erupted the antiaircraft failed badly. Accurately identified by an Australian Hudson as a troop convoy rather than warships, Tanaka's convoy suffered a worse fate than Mikawa's cruisers and for the same reason. Counting on the destruction of Cactus and being provided false intelligence that great damage had been done, Tanaka tried to shepherd his convoy of 8,000 troops and supplies toward Tassafaronga. Once it was obvious that the Americans faced transports and not Combined Fleet, Cactus and USN dive-bombers attacked with ferocity in the early afternoon. Although the actual tally is somewhat murky, two transports took TBF-launched torpedoes during the attack, and another four went down to Dauntless bombs. A badly damaged transport disengaged but later sank. Tanaka's destroyers rescued several thousand men and took them back to Bougainville. Yet despite his better judgment Tanaka was ordered to land his remaining four transports at Tassafaronga whatever the cost.

On the night of November 14–15 Combined Fleet threw its last reserves into the area. Although the Japanese showed again their skill at night actions, another Japanese battleship was sunk, and Cactus, filled with reinforcements from *Enterprise*, was ready for a strike. They did not have to go far. Tanaka had wisely beached his remaining four transports during the early morning, knowing that none were going to survive. The four hapless troop transports suffered an attack that lacked precedent during the Pacific war. Stationary targets at Tassafaronga Point, just miles from Henderson, the beached ships were attacked by Marine artillery, every aircraft in the Allied arsenal, and a U.S. destroyer at point-blank range for more than an hour. Seeing the ships were quickly sunk, U.S. aircraft shifted to the supply dumps that had been off-loaded that night. Because Tanaka's destroyers had been quick to rescue survivors, fewer than 1,000 Japanese troops died during the journey. Yet the 2,000 men who were landed, because they brought so few supplies, actually made things worse for the Japanese army, which suffered from lack of food and ammunition more than men. Soon the newly landed troops served bravely as rear-guard troops as Tanaka returned again—this time to evacuate the defeated Japanese army.

The Guadalcanal campaign ended with the destruction of Tanaka's convoy. Many officers had long harbored doubts about Japan's prospects at Guadalcanal. After the November defeats Combined Fleet looked for a way out. It did not help that during December several other Japanese warships attempting to supply Guadalcanal were sunk or damaged. In the end Japanese submarines were pressed into supply duties; one was sunk in such shallow waters that American divers recovered valuable intelligence from its ghastly innards.

Ironically the IJN feared the army would accuse it of letting down on its side of the war effort. Indeed a Japanese army attack in September 1942 had probably come closer to winning the Guadalcanal campaign for Japan than had all of the movements made by Combined Fleet. Yet the army had also to look at "its" theater: New Guinea, which was also under terrible pressure. By year's end the decision was made to leave Guadalcanal and attempt to defend Buna. Once Tokyo accepted defeat at Guadalcanal the imperial government made the decision to send a flood of troops to New Guinea and the Solomons to give Combined Fleet time to prepare for another decisive battle against the Americans.

The Marine and USN tactical bombers played a great role in the Guadalcanal victory. They showed their strength by being relatively numerous because they were small, fairly nimble, accurate when attacking a discrete target like a ship, and able to operate from almost any airfield. Both the Dauntless and Avenger continued to play an important role in the Solomons campaign until the destruction of Rabaul. Indeed during 1943 U.S. aircraft destroyed more Japanese destroyers than they had during 1942. Both aircraft were very useful against land targets, although losses were high.

In contrast tactical bombers in the South Pacific, when the engagement became a battle between land bases, showed a serious defect. Japanese Kates and Vals proved vulnerable to U.S. fighters and antiaircraft. Both of these warplanes, so valuable early in the war, became nearly worthless deathtraps for Japanese pilots after Guadalcanal. American SBDs and TBFs were much more rugged, yet they suffered from some of the same grim math that laid low Japanese tactical bombers in the South Pacific. American pilots had great respect for the Avenger and Dauntless, and many came home in badly damaged aircraft. Yet nothing could change some basic physics: Tactical bombers were much closer in size and structural integrity to fighters than they were to bombers. This was especially true for the Dauntless. Although each had a rear gunner, defensive armament was poor compared to that of a true bomber. Speed and performance was actually less than that of a late-model B-25, except for maneuverability. In short SBDs and TBFs were dangerous aircraft to fly and remained so throughout the campaign.

As mentioned earlier, it is wise to judge a weapon system both defensively and offensively. Considering the physical makeup of the aircraft it was natural that both Dauntlesses and Avengers were vulnerable to Japanese fighters. The extreme ruggedness that made a B-17 difficult to shoot down (but often ineffective) did not exist with smaller aircraft. They lacked defensive armament, and the guns available to a Dauntless were a pair of .30-caliber machine guns on a mount (the pilot fired two .50-caliber machine guns in the wing). Veteran pilot Harold Buell believed this arrangement provided excellent defense if the SBDs could maintain formation:

Our gunners were very effective if you flew the proper formation. The rear gunner's value was in formation. The way most of my friends were killed in combat was in one of two ways—they either got caught by themselves or with one wingman and were shot down by Zeros or they were downed by flak. I found very quickly that once you got anywhere between three to six planes together in good formation and wouldn't break your formation, fly tight, turning into the fighter runs, the combined fire of those twin mounted machine guns was a lot of lead going out there. If they came in front, we each had two .50s firing forward through the prop. So if you flew tight, and I mean tight formation, six planes moving as one; then your formation becomes one great big flying fortress. We were especially tough if we stayed low and close—then they couldn't come in under us. So they'd have to dive down toward us. It got so the Jap pilots would look for loners. They'd shoot someone down before they re-formed in the formation. And there were always your characters who went to strafe on their own after the operation. None of my people did it: I wouldn't allow it. Those were the ones who got it.

Yet the SBD was vulnerable. Soon after sinking a Japanese cruiser, pilot Robert Gibson had refueled at Guadalcanal and was in pursuit of Tanaka's convoy along with six other SBDs. They were jumped by a flight of Zeros sent to defend the transports. Three SBDs went down and two were badly damaged. Gibson described events:

We went back to Henderson, refueled, and got another bomb. We went
back with *Enterprise* group. Near the target we were shot up by Zeros
from a carrier. They came in overhead and hit five of seven planes. I got
back with seventy holes. Our rear guns frequently jammed and when
they did we were defenseless. The secret is to come in at high speed,
drop, and split. At that moment we were sitting there and the CO was
reluctant to push over. He was just waiting at ninety-five knots and
Zeros chewed us up.

Attacking with a dive-bomber was very dangerous and not everyone
could do it. You could see guys start to crack: They'd show it. You
knew they'd get killed. They'd freeze when they got tight and that was
the end of it. I was there for fourteen months, flew 900 hours, and went
down twice. The danger doesn't strike home unless you're in a tight
spot and you think you're dead. Then you start worrying in a serious
way. I was seventh senior pilot in the squad before Guadalcanal and
second after it. I had to appoint people to flights. Rather than making it
even-steven I'd fly the guys I could trust. If I figured they were afraid, I
didn't put them into flights. I figured they'd get killed. You had to keep
your head and never become careless. I wanted to see pilots totally
married to weapon systems. Then it becomes totally instinctive and you
have survivors. The careless did not stick around.

Tom Powell manned the .50-caliber turret carried by an Avenger.
The turret, compared to the twin-.30 mount carried by the SBD, fired
far fewer rounds, and had a smaller magazine. However, it was a more
elaborate mount, and the .50-caliber round was far more powerful
than the .30. Powell described how the TBF gunnery system worked:

The Avenger was a good plane. I was gunner in a single .50-caliber
General Electric turret. In front of you was something that looked like a
.38 pistol. To move your turret you moved that pistol grip anywhere
you wanted. It wasn't a very fast turret because it was electric. Some of
the army bombers had hydraulic devices and moved rapidly, but ours
moved more slowly. It had a reflector sight. It was two rings with a
pipper in the middle that lit up. They ran us through regular gunnery
school at first. They gave us 300 rounds of shotgun ammo and then
they had about a week of recognition. When we got on ship they told
us to forget everything we'd learned and go into what they called
"apparent speed sighting." You'd take your pipper and put it on the
plane that was coming in on you and at maximum range. It would take
him about three seconds to cover the distance you and your .50-caliber
shell would go. So you'd put the pipper on him and say a word like

"Japanese" and see which way he moved from that dot. He might be pointed in one direction but you led him according to relative movement. That was very effective. Two red rings with a red dot in the middle. Say this plane is making a run on you from above-right at a slight angle. His nose might be pointed toward you as he fires, but he's flattened out more and as he goes through that dot he looks like he's going sinking, flat. So you go down below him, not where you think his nose has pointed. Apparent direction or apparent speed setting. We started firing this way in Hawaii before we went aboard ship. I think the training was good. Our group was good.

Powell's VB-10 group was indeed good. However, everyone had a bad day sometime at war, and VB-10 was jumped by Zeros during the Battle of Santa Cruz. Powell described the attack and defense on a bad day for U.S. aircraft:

Santa Cruz was an odd deal. The fighters that jumped us in the TBFs were supposed to be guarding their own dive-bombers. But they couldn't stand to see us go by underneath them without jumping on us. We were flying right wing on the skipper when he got shot down. We had two shot down on the first pass and two others were damaged so badly they had to return to the ship and ditch. So we lost four out of eight right there. There were about nine Zeros.

The Zeros came in from above. According to later books I read they had seen the *Hornet*'s group go by but had stayed with their planes. They saw our smaller formation but couldn't resist the temptation and shot us up. I understand that some of their dive-bombers didn't make it through to the *Enterprise* because their fighters were gone. There was no protection for a dive-bomber. When they jumped us the fighters dropped their belly tanks and some lost fuel pressure and altitude. They were below us by the time we got cut up pretty bad. So we were ineffective at first.

The Zeros came in real close. One was making a pass at a nearby plane and he flew right underneath me and I could see the pilot clearly. My shipmate was pouring some .30-cal into him. When I was debriefed they asked how many Zeros were there—I said three. They said there were more than that. I said, well, I saw three all the time. We used cone fire. Everybody on one side would take anything coming from one side and so forth. Everybody was putting tracers into a wing root on one and he burned. Some guy would claim the plane. I said you can have him if you want but I don't know how you can claim him when you got four lines of tracers going into a plane. Who shot him down? It

didn't make any difference. At the time the most important thing was
he was wasn't shooting at us anymore.

Vulnerable to both fighters and antiaircraft, as well as the usual operational dangers, airmen of both sides who manned single-engine tactical bombers had one of the most dangerous jobs in the Pacific air
war. Powell's VT-10 would have normally flown twelve planes, with
three men aboard each. Under most circumstances they had reserves,
and individuals were rotated in and out for a variety of reasons. VT-10
did three tours, two on *Enterprise* and one on *Intrepid*. Throughout
the war VT-10 lost twenty-five men killed and two taken prisoner. In
addition, throughout the war twenty-nine TBFs of VT-10 were forced
to ditch. Considering the size of the squadron, this is a very high total.

Only good flying and a well-staged attack could lessen the odds of
falling victim to antiaircraft fire (discussion below). It was almost essential, however, for tactical bombers to fly with fighter escorts.
Medium and heavy bombers received escorts when possible but would
fly alone if necessary, something rarely done intentionally with tactical
bombers. It was well worth the effort, for during scattered engagements throughout the drive up the Solomons during 1943 Marine SBD
units sunk another ten Japanese destroyers, destroyed many small supply vessels, and, along with TBFs, became an integral part of the continual assault on Japanese air bases and support of Allied ground
troops.

Allied fighter pilots throughout the war argued about the best way
to escort bombers. If flying advanced fighters, many pilots argued in
favor of distant escort, whereby much of the escort flew well in front
of the formation, seeking out enemy interceptors to bounce or at least
disrupt their attack. Every bomber crewman who has ever spoken with
me favored close escort, whereby the fighters stayed in immediate sight
of the aircraft they escorted. As the war went on the Allies accumulated enough fighters to do both. If a raid was large enough there
would be escorts flying well above the formation, another layer at perhaps 18,000 feet. In one of the few bones of contention between services, sometimes Marine commanders put P-38s at 18,000 feet and
Corsairs above them. This angered USAAF pilots believing they would
be less likely to get kills. More importantly 18,000 feet was a bad altitude for a P-38 to begin an engagement. With their turbosupercharged
engines the Lightning, like the P-47, was designed for high cover. After
bitter words with pilots from Thirteenth Air Force, USAAF P-38s received their share of high-cover missions. Ideally there would also be
low cover, or aircraft flying very close to the bombers. This was an ex-

cellent place for the old soldiers of the theater like the P-40 and P-39. LeRoy Smith liked his escorts low and close:

> Our flight was attacked by Zeros several times, but my plane was lucky. We had New Zealand P-40s cover us when we flew out of Munda and the Canal. They were fabulous people and top pilots. They also wore these fleece-lined flying boots that every American aviator craved. I got several pairs for my squad by trading liquor for them and it made me popular for a few days. We had a lot of American pilots there, too, but they'd be off chasing the Zeros in their Corsairs and P-38s. But the New Zealand pilots would stay right with us. We'd fly in vee-formations and the P-40s would just scissors right between us, stay in nice and close.
>
> The Japs would make a quick run and real fast our P-40s were on them. If things lasted more than a minute our high cover, if it was there, was also down on the Japs. The Zeros started higher, but someone would get them if they attacked us. The Japanese would stick maybe half a dozen planes high and off to the side of a formation and try to sneak in, but it was tough for them. The escorts did not follow us through our attacks—that would have been an undue risk. So we were most vulnerable when we were pulling out of our dive. You're a sitting duck. The plane was so methodically slow that the Jap fighters flew right by their targets half the time. Our only advantage was that after we had dropped we were right on the deck. This made it impossible for the Japs to attack from below, which they liked to do if they could. So if the rear gunner settled down and the escorts picked you up again quick, the enemy didn't have a lot of time to make their run. But that was tense and had you looking around. However, when we returned to base, the New Zealanders would sometimes put on a show for everybody. It was great to see—when those P-40s would return from taking care of us and they'd come over as a squadron. They were always much lower than any other fighters. And a guy would do a giant loop and land right out of the loop. And they'd all peel off that way. They had more guts than good sense. Zoom, zoom, zoom. It was incredible to watch. They came back with banana leaves in the windscoops all the time because they'd just scoot the ground and the treetops. Crazy, but those were fine pilots.

In the long run sinking ships was every bit as important in New Guinea as it was in the Solomons. It is true that there were no major naval engagements in the confined and dangerous waters between New Britain and New Guinea. Indeed until the area was properly charted in 1943 the U.S. Navy was most careful when entering it and would not risk transports in the reef-infested waters off places such as Buna. (The arrival of shallow-draft landing craft like LSTs and LSIs in 1943 was a tremendous addition to MacArthur's forces.) Yet when land-fighting started both armies were completely dependent upon sea transport, and not just for conventional military supplies but for the essentials required to keep an army alive. If isolated from supply, an army in New Guinea would have to retreat rapidly, disperse, or simply disintegrate. As Admiral Inoue had feared in 1942, Australia was an obvious base for an attack on Japan's maritime perimeter.

When the Australians stopped the Japanese overland drive for Moresby, any chance to close down the Southwest Pacific Theater disappeared. Realizing the danger in late 1942 the Japanese army made the decision to begin a major reinforcement of troops to the Bismarcks, Bougainville, and above all New Guinea. The garrison at Buna was expected to extract a painful cost from the Allies and provide time for the Imperial Japanese Army to reinforce New Guinea proper. Initially they were ordered to hold the area of Huon Gulf and Vitiaz Strait (Lae and Salamaua) because this was the area closest to New Britain and Rabaul. However, the abilities of the Japanese army to fight and Japanese aircraft to fly from New Guinea bases were completely dependent on the ability to supply the men. If Fifth Air Force and the RAAF could learn to sink ships as well as the navy and Marines were doing, then they could cripple the Japanese defensive. Because land communications were so bad everywhere in New Guinea, it would take weeks or months to bring supplies forward if they had to be landed outside air range. Conversely if the Japanese could make the waters off New Guinea treacherous for Allied shipping, then they could slow the Australian land advance to a crawl. The Japanese called Guadalcanal "Starvation Island." Ultimately New Guinea would far better deserve that name—and for a far larger number of Japanese servicemen. There would be no Admiral Tanaka to rescue survivors.

Neither Fifth Air Force nor the RAAF was well situated in mid-1942 to sink ships. Fighters were still by and large interceptors, not the fearsome fighter-bombers they became in late 1943. Bombers were just arriving in theater in substantial numbers. The Bristol Beaufighter, which proved a ruthless weapon against small shipping, had not yet arrived in force. The Hudson was a reconnaissance plane first, a bomber second. The very promising A-20 was arriving, but only in tiny numbers. Furthermore during the interwar period neither the British, who influenced the Australians, nor the USAAF developed a cult of the dive-bomber. Fifth Air Force had a squadron of A-24s, which was the army designation of the Dauntless. However, they were thought of as ground-support weapons, not antishipping aircraft, and the crews never received the rigorous training those in the navy enjoyed. The Fleet Air Arm, after reclaiming the Royal Navy's flight decks in the late 1930s, did show a serious interest in torpedo attacks. (Ironically during the RAAF years, naval aircraft had been so badly neglected that the obsolescent Swordfish flew throughout the war. No wonder Fleet Air Arm was delighted to get Corsairs, Wildcats, and Avengers via Lend-Lease. Nevertheless British torpedoes worked, and Swordfish were responsible for the propaganda coup of the sinking the *Bismarck* and inflicted the humiliating strike on the Italian fleet at Taranto, something that did not go unnoticed in Japan.) Yet only the Beaufort could carry a torpedo, and supplies of both were short and techniques most uncertain. The USAAF did experiment with torpedoes slung under B-25s and PBYs but was not satisfied with the results. Not realizing they were receiving a miserable weapon, the Australians accepted a stock of U.S. aerial torpedoes.

Worst of all, by fall 1942 it was clear that standard B-25s, B-17s, and B-24s were not very good at sinking ships. Despite a tactical doctrine that went back to the days of Billy Mitchell, the idea that the multiengine bomber attacking from high to medium level with the sophisticated Norden or Sperry bombsights could hit a moving ship proved gravely flawed. Had the prewar Army Air Corps had the money to conduct thorough exercises, perhaps that terrible error would have been made clear, perhaps not. Whether feasible or not, coastal defense was a mission that the prewar Congress would fund. In such situations a cash-starved military service will usually find a way to please those who hold the purse strings.

Heavy and medium bombers were inherently poor at sinking ships for two reasons. First, especially when flying at the theoretically correct altitude of 18,000 feet or higher, the lag between drop and impact was long enough for even a merchant ship, much less a nimble warship, to take evasive action. When Jim Eaton served with the 19th Bomb Group early in the war he learned more than he wanted about Billy Mitchell's foolish doctrine when put into practice by B-17s:

There was a basic fallacy of high-level bombers attacking surface vessels. We had been trained and trained to bomb from 30,000 feet or even higher in B-17s. That was high but okay for a stationary target, but against a moving target like a ship it was a flop. Dropping from high altitude gave the ship an opportunity to wait till you dropped, watch the trajectory of the bombs, and evade: a hard right, a hard left, or all stop. All the captain had to do was just change his direction and avoid the point of contact. It took us much too long to figure that out.

Harold Carmichael was closer to the situation than Eaton and discussed the failure some years after the war with great candor:

Hell yes there were exaggerated claims for B-17 attacks early in the war. We couldn't hit the side of a barn. As a matter of fact, the only reason I wasn't court-martialed is because of our inaccuracy in bombing. In the Battle of the Coral Sea, I had a responsibility for that 435th Squadron at Townsville. Some of my airplanes were trying to support the navy at the Battle of the Coral Sea. One of them tried bombing a ship. Of course, the pilot thought it was Japanese, but it was a U.S. cruiser. But, as I said, we couldn't hit the side of the barn so fortunately we missed it. We missed all those ships in the harbor at Rabaul and those claims of Collin Kelly sinking a battleship were a bunch of exaggerations.

The second reason heavy and medium bombers were ineffective against ships was training and experience. Army doctrine allowed for difficulties in hitting a moving ship. The answer, they thought, was a close formation dropping bombs in unison under direction of a masterful bombardier. That way the spread of the bombs would be so great that a hit would be likely. In fact as the war went on, heavy bombers did make more hits against ships, particularly when they lowered their altitude considerably. They were never ideal weapons, but they were dangerous if managed by skilled individuals. Such men were hard to find in Allied air forces early in World War II. (The mystique of the bombardier developed during hard experience over European skies. Just as some men could hit fighters and others could not, some bombardiers had the touch. A few no doubt made it to the Pacific and inflicted considerable damage to Japanese shipping.)

Something else was clearly needed for Fifth Air Force. Just as necessity is the mother of invention, Kenney and some key subordinates did not exactly throw away the book on bombardment, but they certainly wrote a couple of new chapters. The most important was to refine new ways to sink ships with the aircraft at hand. Kenney had spent some of his prewar career in attack aviation, where extremely low-level attack was the norm. Pushing the edge low in army attack became the equivalent of cutting a dive-bomb attack to the lowest possible margin. A keen student of the air war in Europe, Kenney was interested in British experiments using low-level attacks against shipping with heavy bombers. An aide, William G. Benn, shared Kenney's enthusiasm (and perhaps started it). In any case Benn was given command of the 63d Squadron of the new 43d Bomb Group and ordered to develop night-time low-level attacks for use by B-17s against shipping. The techniques varied somewhat. One called for a simple drop of less than 2,000 feet that was expected to hit the target. The other called for dropping lower and allowing the bomb to strike the water before it turned vertical, to skip like a stone into the ship's hull. With a slight delay in the fuse the bomb would drop slowly and blow out the side of the ship. In November a B-17, despite suffering serious damage itself, sunk a Japanese destroyer near Buna during a nighttime skip-bombing attack. By itself the victory was small, yet it encouraged skip-bombing advocates and thus proved a bad day for Japanese fortunes.

It was during this period that 5th USAAF engineers began to modify their A-20 attack planes and a squadron of B-25s to the famous low-level strafer configuration. In the B-25 the bombardier was removed and replaced by eight forward-firing machine guns. The responsibility for bomb release was given to the pilot or, sometimes, the copilot. Kenney called these new aircraft his "commerce destroyers," realizing the great importance of creating his own kill zone for Japanese ships. It is not clear to what extent the experimental skip-bombing techniques for B-17s were directly related to the development of the strafers, but the connection seems obvious enough. It is possible that Kenney, Benn, Pappy Gunn, and others were working on a parallel course already suggested by British practice. In the event, it did not matter. Kenney embraced both the strafer and skip-bombing and made them tools not only to attack ships but also to demolish Japanese air bases.

When the Australians and Americans began their attack on the Buna beachhead in November they approached a tactical nightmare. Japanese engineers had constructed an ingenious network of field fortifications that were barely visible to ground troops, much less to airmen. The single most important task for the air forces was to keep the Buna position unsupplied, a difficult proposition. The distance between New Britain and Buna was far shorter than the Japanese run up the Slot to Guadalcanal. And the Japanese garrison at Buna was there only to hold on, hopefully, until victory had been achieved in the Solomons; the need for supplies was not great. To make matters worse, the Allies were still not good at sinking ships off the coast of New Guinea. In November some small convoys of transports and barges made it to Buna. More ships arrived at Lae. Damage inflicted by the Allies was originally small, but as November wore on the tide turned. Australian Beaufighters proved deadly opposition to any Japanese supply barge found. U.S. and Australian bombers began to pick off small transports one by one. As we shall see, the small Japanese airstrip at Buna was one of the first to suffer the lethal 5th USAAF treatment. By December the Japanese Buna garrison was effectively isolated. This process accelerated in November when the Allies got their major base at Dobodura, very close to Buna, in operation. Eventually the Japanese garrison at Buna-Sanananda, despite desperate and horrible fighting, collapsed as much from starvation as from combat.

The New Guinea air war and much of the campaign turned on a pin in March 1943. As part of the campaign to reinforce its position in New Guinea, the Japanese army authorized a convoy of eight transports, escorted by eight destroyers and a large fighter escort, to proceed from Rabaul to Lae. Employing clever signal intelligence and reconnaissance, Fifth Air Force was waiting. Accounts of the famous Battle of the Bismarck Sea vary greatly, but it appears that air strength on either side was limited. As the Japanese hoped, bad weather periodically blanketed the area. At most the Japanese fielded eighty escorts. In turn Fifth Air Force had some 150 aircraft to make the attack. (Some accounts incorrectly give Fifth Air Force a much larger force; either side's fighter escort would not have exceeded twenty at any given moment.) Half of the Allied force was P-38 escorts. Yet even without a dive-bomber and a successful torpedo launch Fifth Air Force delivered a stunning defeat to the Japanese.

The destruction of the convoy began on March 2, 1943, when the 43d Bomb Group sent out all its B-17s in three waves, sinking at least two and maybe three transports. Notably the Fortresses dropped at 8,000–6,000 feet. Two Japanese destroyers picked up some 800 survivors and ran them quickly to Lae. They proved to be some of the few survivors from 7,000 troops carried in the convoy. It is possible that some of the destroyers were damaged, as their antiaircraft fire next day was less than expected. On that next day the massacre began. In waves, and sometimes simultaneously, B-17s, A-20s, Beaufighters, and B-25s struck the Japanese convoy, attacking from medium altitude and skip-bombing. In a fine example of the Japanese repeating a defective tactic, many of the fighters went after the B-17s (this had happened in the Solomons more than once) while more dangerous opponents operated unmolested at lower altitudes. In short the transport convoy was annihilated and four destroyers sunk. Unlike the Guadalcanal debacles, Japanese destroyers were unable to act effectively to rescue men. With four sunk outright, the others were damaged and under intense attack and had to run for their lives. They rescued perhaps 2,000 men, some no doubt fellow destroyer crewmen. After the ships went down Allied aircraft strafed lifeboats and men in the water for the rest of March 3, finishing the job the next day. A few Japanese sailors and soldiers were rescued by destroyers and submarines, but the rest were killed or drowned. The exact figures will never be known, but the number of Japanese troops and sailors killed at the Bismarck Sea was roughly 5,000 more men than were lost (by either side) in any one of the great naval engagements off Guadalcanal.

The Bismarck Sea was the debut of the B-25 strafer and Bristol Beaufighter. Both had been in action previously, but never with such effect. Fred Cassidy was aboard a Beaufighter at the Bismarck Sea:

When attacking ships we liked to come in from the front. It was our goal to put the bridge out of order. You would begin the approach sideways, maybe three-quarter speed, perhaps 220 knots, and about four miles off. Then we'd run parallel. We'd make a big wide turn, get into line astern, usually a flight of maybe three. We'd start at the back of the ship and make a big sweeping turn and come in from the front and begin the dive from about 500 feet. The ship would be about 600 yards in front. You'd let go with your cannon at maybe 100 yards from the ship, aim straight at the bridge, and turn straight off. You'd pull up over the mast. You'd watch the ship kind of disintegrate. In the Bismarck Sea battle we strafed from the front. The ships were careening in all directions. I saw a 500-pound bomb level with our starboard wing going at the same altitude and same speed that we were that a Mitchell had just dropped, maybe twenty feet off the water. You also had to dodge bomb-splashes at the Bismarck Sea because the Liberators and '17s were dropping from 6,000–10,000 feet and they'd make huge splashes when we were about twenty feet off the sea. These splashes were thirty to fifty feet across and followed by a tremendous spout of water. We had to fly through those. The damage done to the Japanese was devastating.

Veteran B-25 pilot Garrett Middlebrook had an unusually close ringside seat to the Bismarck Sea debacle:

After the Bismarck Sea we converted to eight .50-calibers in the nose, which were awesome, absolutely awesome. It was absolutely unreal what they could do. I saw it often, first at the Bismarck Sea. This was a very interesting mission for me—it was the only one I flew as a copilot of the sixty-five I flew during the war. Midway through the mission I thought I was fortunate. The pilot was doing all the work and I was a witness to history being made—we knew this was a big show that would live in the history books for 100 years. During the battle we circled out there waiting our turn to go in, a good mile away. The A-20s went in first, and then the strafers of 30th Bomb Group arrived. They went in and hit this troop ship. What I saw looked like little sticks, maybe a foot long or something like that, or splinters flying up off the deck of the ship; they'd fly all around . . . and twist crazily in the air and fall out in the water. I thought, "What could that be? They must have some peculiar cargo on that vessel." Then I realized what I was watching were human beings. It was a troopship just loaded. When the third group hit them two of the ships went in and unloaded with those sixteen machine guns and most likely the turret gunner upstairs was having a little fun, too. I was watching hundreds of those Japanese just blown off the deck by those machine guns. They just splintered around the air like sticks in a whirlwind and they'd fall in the water. Soon afterwards we attacked a destroyer that was fleeing. We didn't have the nose guns but hit him square with two bombs at mast level.

After the war former Rabaul staff officer Masatake Okumiya described the anguish caused by the Bismarck Sea among Japanese leaders:

The effectiveness of enemy air strength was brought to [Admiral Yamamoto] with the news of a crushing defeat which, if similar events were permitted to occur in the future, promised terrifying disasters for Japan. . . . Our losses for this single battle [Bismarck Sea—EB] were fantastic. Not during the entire savage fighting at Guadalcanal did we suffer a single comparable blow. It became imperative that we block the continued enemy air activities before these attacks became commonplace. We knew we could no longer run cargo ships or even fast destroyer transports to any front on the north coast of New Guinea, east of Wewak. Our supply operation to northeastern New Guinea became a scrabbler's run of barges, small craft and submarines.

After the Bismarck Sea the Japanese had to send convoys much farther up the coast out of air attack range, for the moment causing immense difficulties in getting them to the front. Yet troops sent forth were hardly safe. After the war Japanese officers at Rabaul estimated that 20,000 troops were lost during sea transit in the Rabaul–New Guinea area. As the months went on U.S. submarines operating in Southeast Asian waters and off Truk began to take their grim toll in addition to ships and barges destroyed by aircraft.

After the Bismarck Sea the skip-bombing, or "masthead," attack techniques continued to make USAAF and RAAF bombers dangerous to Japanese warships. Marine TBFs and 13th USAAF B-25s teamed up to sink two imperial destroyers near Vella Lavella in August 1943. A few weeks later a pair of Japanese destroyers had the misfortune of running aground near Cape Gloucester; before help could arrive a flight of Kenney's skip-bombing Mitchells sunk them both. Perhaps the most satisfying work was done by some B-17s of the 43d Bomb Group. On the night of April 3, 1943, they launched a skip-bombing attack against Japanese warships at Kavieng, damaging one destroyer and almost sinking the heavy cruiser *Aoba*. The latter vessel, much needed by the Japanese, was out of combat for months.

A significant part of the bombing campaign against shipping was waged against small coastal vessels and barges. The Japanese had made wide use of barges running out of New Georgia at night to help supply units at Guadalcanal. As the waters throughout the South Pacific became more dangerous for transports, the importance of smaller vessels grew apace. The Japanese were able to send transports into Kavieng and Rabaul from Truk and Southeast Asian bases without great risk of air attack. (As just noted, U.S. submarines were, increasingly, another matter.) Indeed Simpson Harbor had large numbers of merchant ships until Marine and USN tactical bombers, operating from Bougainville, got close enough in late 1943 to make things dangerous for any Japanese ship. Until that time transports would off-load at Rabaul or Kavieng and supplies for garrisons in the Solomons and New Guinea would be put on barges, what the Japanese called *daihatsus*. These small vessels would try to run along the shoreline of islands where they were hard to see and sailed at night when possible. Yet an attempt to assure absolute safety would have crippled the effort, so the small craft might well be sighted at dawn, dusk, or even during daylight. In addition, they would put in along coastlines during the day but could not count on camouflage to hide them perfectly from prowling Allied aircraft. At night, to add a considerable degree of tension and violence to the enterprise, Japanese barges and coastal transports had to face attack from radar-equipped U.S. PT boats that prowled likely waters in a deadly game of cat-and-mouse. (It was not always easy to tell the cat.) Some of the barges had makeshift armor and antiaircraft cannons. Some had the support of small, wooden Japanese warships that were larger than PT boats but smaller than an Allied destroyer escort. In addition, some could proceed at a brisk pace, considerably faster than most transports. Yet all were small, made of wood, and unarmed or poorly armed; even the most formidable were vulnerable to air attack. To make matters worse, attack at the mast-head was the best way to go barge-busting.

Only in the Pacific war could such vessels have taken on such importance. The Japanese army was made up of mostly leg infantry. Imperial forces believed that night attack and superior spirit could compensate for lack of mechanization and medium artillery. This was making virtue of necessity. If possible the Japanese would have been delighted to have more heavy weaponry. However, without the ready availability of large transports, a light infantry war was forced upon the IJA. This hurt it often in battle but greatly simplified matters of supply. What the Japanese troops needed was food, basic ammunition, medicine, and a handful of amenities to help morale. Barges and similar vessels could provide such supplies even if the amounts were inadequate. If cut off from their *daihatsus* a Japanese force was in mortal peril. Because of the compelling interest in this form of transport, most barges were manned and controlled by the Japanese army. (This was also true with many U.S. transports; the difference in size, of course, was extraordinary.)

Barge-hunts became one of the most common missions for Allied aircraft of all types in the Solomons and along the New Guinea coast, especially fighters. No air force prior to World War II considered using the pursuit plane as a bombing platform, which explains one of the major reasons that light bombers like the A-20 and dive-bombers were developed. In the Battle of Britain some elite Me110 twin-engine "fighter" units were given the mission of low-level attack of sensitive targets—one of the few roles played reasonably well by this seriously flawed design. Soon Luftwaffe leaders added some Bf109 units, despite a very small bomb capacity, to the effort, and they proved a serious problem to the RAF. (The Germans called these units *Jagdbomber*, or *Jabo*, best translated as "fighter-bombers.")

In this issue as in so many others the USAAF had been retrograde, originally not calling for bomb racks on fighter designs to prevent the development of drop tanks. Private contractors and lower-ranking officers realized this was an error, and the proper fittings were installed, thus making it possible for an early-war U.S. fighter to carry a bomb and, ultimately, a drop tank. The major problem for early-war fighters was lack of horsepower. Marine Wildcats rarely bombed but could carry a 250-pounder; P-40s eventually could squeeze on two 250-pounders but usually carried only one; a P-39 wheezed under the weight of a single 250-pounder. Yet each warplane had tremendous firepower in their machine guns, enough to sink a small barge or shred a larger one. As we shall see, strafing was also commonly used for ground support, a category in which the Japanese were left behind yet again. Some attempts were made to fit Zeros with bombs, but the extra weight so degraded its performance, and the plane was so fragile, that the Japanese left the bombing to the bombers. Zeros often strafed, but Allied antiaircraft made it less and less productive. Much later in the war Japanese engineers did fit a 500-pound bomb to Zeros for kamikaze attacks (easily done, as there was no need to top off the fuel tanks or load a full complement of ammunition).

When the second-generation Allied fighters appeared they could carry prodigious ordnance, particularly if range could be sacrificed. It was not uncommon for the late-model P-38 and Corsair to carry 2,000 pounds of bombs (depending on the type). The USAAF experimented with fitting two torpedoes under a Lightning, a project no doubt best left for dead. In early 1944 Allied planes began receiving powerful five-inch rockets, giving a fighter the theoretical power of a destroyer's broadside. Strafing shipping was the riskiest mission a fighter pilot faced, but as the Japanese fighter arm slowly eroded, enough quarry for Allied fighters became hard to find. Fighter pilots thus found themselves more and more often on the deck.

By 1943 a fighter sweep often included keeping a sharp eye for barges and small transports. Robert DeHaven described sinking one:

We had missions where we were instructed to search for "targets of opportunity." That included the coastal shipping the Japanese were using to supply troops in New Guinea. There was nothing complex involved in the technology. To aid our attacks, there were dive-bomb indicators, painted white stripes emanating roughly on the position on the fuselage or on the wing root so the pilot could see from a normal sitting position. Those three angle indicators were 20, 40, and 60 degrees angle of dive. The steepest eventually went into a split-S when you pulled through. The dispersal was the least on the steepest dive.

I sank a little coastal tanker. There were two flights of P-40s with 250-pound bombs strapped on the center shackle and we saw this little tanker unloading something—lord knows what. It was partially camouflaged with local flora and we set up a dive-bombing run. I was leading the second flight of eight aircraft each. I made my split-S over the target and made my approach and threw off the bomb when I thought it prudent—they were shooting at us—which made me uncomfortable. I didn't know anything until I'd pulled out when my number-four man yelled "You got him!" When I rolled back and cocked the airplane to take a look I could see the smoke billowing up from the forward hold. He sank right there. As far as I know he's still

there. I want to emphasize that the hit was absolute, pure, and
unadulterated luck. The other men knew that, so I was no hero. This
was definitely not the Battle of Midway. It was perfectly possible that
the vessel was grounded. It may have been sunk by someone else, but I
did have a witness. But we didn't count those sorts of things at that
period. Late in the war some pilots stenciled trains to their planes when
we were flying out of Okinawa. By that time, it was rare to see a
fighter.

Because of their large numbers fighters were a serious danger to
barge traffic. But even tough U.S. fighters lacked the structural
strength of a medium bomber and were more vulnerable to antiaircraft. Two of the most prominent American P-38 aces, Robert Westbrook of Thirteenth Air Force and Thomas Lynch of Fifth Air Force,
both died due to antiaircraft fire while attacking small vessels. Consequently the best weapon for barge-hunting was a strafer or a Beaufighter.

Charles Kittell of Thirteenth Air Force often flew a strafer over the
Solomons, where barges were very common. As he recalled, there were
risks involved:

We attacked barges and small ships. The Japanese would set up little
traps. They'd park a barge and set up flak on like approach runs and
try to nail you. So you kept your eyes open. [C.L. Jones believes that
Thomas Lynch fell to such a trap.—EB] But we did a lot of barge-
hunting. After a while they were down to nothing but barges. We'd find
them scurrying between the islands. They'd hug the coast and that was
protection because the trees grew right into the water. The barges rarely
shot back and if you caught them, it was trouble for the barge. . . . We
had eight or sometimes twelve forward-firing .50s, each one pushing
out 750 rounds a minute, and that .50-caliber was a mean shell. That
was a lot of destruction coming at you. When you fired them all at once
the plane would shake. The barges were wood and not very strong.
We'd just blow them to pieces.

Fred Cassidy flew a feared RAAF Beaufighter. With its multiple cannons it was probably the last aircraft on earth that any Japanese soldier or sailor on a barge would want to see moving into an attack run:

One of our major jobs was to patrol the coast early in the morning or
dusk and shoot up these barge supply lines. They'd move early in the
morning or at night. They'd hull up in the day. They'd find these little

inlets along the coast to hide. You had to try to spot them—after a while we'd get pretty good at it. The barges were maybe twenty to thirty-five feet long and supplied the Japanese army all up and down the coast of New Guinea and New Britain. The danger was they'd put these things into little alcoves along the shore with overhanging trees. So they were very hard to strafe. You'd come in steep, get at them, and get out fast. We lost several aircraft trying to strafe these damn things and just crashing because their positions were so awkward. If you found them over the water then it was good—any barge was finished. You'd come in side-on and as you strafed the Japs would jump over the other side as we shredded their barge. Later we put a little scattergun on the rear of the plane, a .303 at the back and you'd spray them. I don't think you did any damage but you'd give them a fright. We attacked destroyers twice. That wasn't a good idea. You didn't want to trade fire with a genuine warship unless it was necessary.

Japanese losses of small ships were extremely heavy, although the numbers will never be known, simply because it is unlikely that anyone ever knew exactly how many of them were in operation. Often of local construction, as many as 6,000 were built. In May 1943 Japanese figures conceded the loss of 600 barges. Large numbers of new crew and maintenance personnel throughout 1943–1944 indicate a very high level of attrition. After the war Fifth Air Force claimed nearly 600 barges and small vessels sunk in Rabaul waters alone.

The barge war illustrated the bravery and ingenuity of the Japanese war effort along with its futility. Whatever success the Solomons campaign achieved as a delaying action would have been impossible without the *daihatsu*. The same boats kept large units in New Guinea alive in 1943. Yet wooden boats against Beaufighters, B-25 strafers, Corsairs, and the entire array of Allied aircraft represented an unequal struggle if attackers could cover points of departure, points of landing, and areas between. When barges' lines of communication were cut or frequently interrupted, the Japanese had to retreat, as they did from the middle Solomons. If orderly retreat was impossible as it was, then only headlong flight or disintegration was possible in the jungle. The imperial troops fighting to defend Salamaua and Lae were wasting assets, being set up for the kill by MacArthur and the Australians.

At worst the loss of a functioning supply line meant oblivion. The Japanese garrison at Buna-Sanananda was pounded by Allied air and ground forces but finally died of starvation. However, Buna was not the only garrison that collapsed due to strangulation—Guadalcanal was Starvation Island. Imperial pilots echoed soldiers when they said,

"No one returns from New Guinea alive." Japanese soldiers often kept diaries. The Australian official history of air operations during the Buna campaign quotes a succinct note that illustrated the impact of the Allied campaign against Japanese shipping: "With the dawn the enemy starts shooting all over. All I can do is shed tears of resentment. Now we are waiting only for death. The news that reinforcement had come turned out to be a rumor. All day we stay in the bunkers. We are filled with vexation. Comrades, are you going to stand by and watch us die? Even the invincible Imperial Army is at a loss."

The Imperial Japanese Army was indeed at a loss. In an island war like the South Pacific losing control of the sea-lanes was a death sentence. With the Imperial Japanese Navy in retreat, the campaign was decided; as yet undetermined was its length and cost. That would largely depend on how successful Allied aircraft were in aiding ground units and how well they could destroy or neutralize Japanese air bases.

Helping the Ground-Pounders

Battle histories are never the same as campaign histories. In most accounts of the air war in the South Pacific the high points in combat violence—Guadalcanal, the Bismarck Sea, the final assault on Rabaul—receive most of the attention. Yet an overview of combat missions from official histories emphasizes how much of the bombing campaign in the South Pacific was devoted to supporting land operations. The aces got the headlines, dive-bombers sunk warships, and the strafers were the darlings of the medium-bomber force. However, day in and day out Allied aircraft spent much of their effort to help ground troops prevail against a tenacious foe in a bizarre and malignant terrain.

Air and ground commanders in the South Pacific had to face an unpleasant paradox concerning ground support. On one hand there were few theaters in the entire war where accurate ground support was more valuable than in the South Pacific. The reason was simple enough: Because the terrain was so difficult and supplies often short, ground units in the theater could not count on the degree of sustained artillery support that would have aided operations in other arenas of combat. The amount of artillery available in the South Pacific varied from place to place. Where fighting was confined to a small area, as it was on Guadalcanal, the Americans were able to assemble a respectable number of 105mm and 155mm howitzers, which proved invaluable throughout the campaign. The Japanese were not as fortunate. The ability of Cactus to hinder Japanese supplies caused imperial troops to fight without true artillery support. Their field artillery (i.e.,

Pistol Pete) was used as a tool of harassment and fired only a few hundred rounds. Japanese field units had to rely on pack howitzers and mortars, which were useful weapons but lacked the invaluable punch of massed field artillery. The Japanese hoped night attack would negate U.S. artillery, but because the Marines and soldiers were on the defensive the likely areas of attack were registered long before battle. During their attacks Japanese infantry faced a wall of fire that repulsed every assault. The same grim equation made Japanese infantry thrusts almost suicidal for the remainder of the Pacific war.

However, in European terms the numbers of artillery pieces and their size were small. The U.S. 155mm howitzer was a heavy weapon in the Pacific but would have been considered medium artillery in Europe. The widely employed 105mm howitzer and its Australian equivalent, the famous 25-pounder, were light artillery but carried most of the load in the Pacific. On occasion naval artillery was available, but for the most part ground forces in the Pacific relied on light batteries, adequate for the task if available in large numbers. However, if there was fighting inland, then artillery was extremely difficult to obtain because ground communications were so bad. U.S. and Australian infantry fought the horrible battle at Buna-Sanananda with only a handful of artillery pieces. Later fighting on the Huon Peninsula and in the Markham Valley—mostly by Australian troops—was likewise undertaken with insufficient artillery. The Australians proved extremely clever at getting their 25-pounders to the front, but never in the numbers they would have liked. To make matters worse, the South Pacific was poor tank country. In fact many U.S. officers believed before Guadalcanal that armor would have no role in the Pacific; they were proved very wrong very quickly. The Japanese army was weak in anti-tank weaponry, to say the least, and if a tank could operate in the jungle it became lethal. Yet there were too many places where armor simply could not operate.

The terrain that prevented the employment of massed firepower in turn gave defenders a tremendous advantage. Because communications were so poor and the jungle so dense, much fighting took place along the few trails that existed, thus channeling an infantry attack and helping defenders deploy at likely spots. Hacking through dense jungle made cohesive advance and attack nearly impossible. (This factor, along with stout American defense, led to the Japanese army's defeat on Guadalcanal during its great ground assault in October.) There was no genuinely open ground in the South Pacific. There were ridgelines with little cover at the top over which soldiers could gaze a considerable distance, unless it was pouring rain. However, down the ridge a few hundred yards, perhaps even a few hundred feet, was impenetrable jungle.

The beastly terrain provided positions where field fortifications could make the determined defender almost invisible. Japanese construction engineers were seriously inferior to their Allied counterparts, but Japanese combat engineers were extremely clever and excellent fighting troops to boot. They were expert at constructing deadly machine gun positions out of tough jungle wood; their favorite was the fibrous coconut log. Allied attackers frequently found such positions at a range of some fifty feet—after being fired upon. Even at point-blank range, however, it was not always possible to locate the defensive emplacement. Mortars and pack howitzers, behind the front lines, were almost impossible to locate. What resulted was some of the most intense and ruthless close-range infantry combat of World War II. The only thing that prevented certain calamity to attacking infantry was the fact that the defenders likewise had difficulty in spotting targets. An entire infantry company could literally disappear in tall kunai grass or foliage if it hit the dirt under fire.

It follows logically that the same terrain factors often thwarted the use of airpower in support of ground troops. When airmen talk about air support for ground operations they speak in terms of "interdiction," or isolating the battlefield. As we have just seen, sinking Japanese ships and barges served such a role in the South Pacific. Airmen also embraced attack missions aimed at likely targets a few miles or more behind the lines, such as artillery positions and visible field fortifications. In the prewar period officers assumed they would have maps and accurate reconnaissance to help them identify such targets. Still, the mission that no one was genuinely prepared for prior to hostilities was close support, that is, hitting targets very close to one's own lines, perhaps 1,000 yards. The jungle made all such missions a challenge and dangerous for both airmen and friendly infantry alike.

Before the war Allied air forces lacked a well-thought-out system of air-ground communications. Lightweight field radios on the ground and reliable radios on aircraft were just coming into widespread use prior to the war. It is hard to fault the prewar officers, as the coordination of artillery and forward observers had not yet moved into the radio age. Indeed prewar artillerymen did not like to employ any barrage that was within 1,000 yards of their own men. By the end of the war, however, gunners were employing techniques that their 1930s counterparts would never have considered. Even the Luftwaffe, which did more than any other air force to coordinate ground and air attacks, preferred to attack prechosen targets that were several thousand yards or many miles behind the lines. (French artillerymen learned that lesson the hard way during the Sedan calamity of May 1940.) Inexpensive, common-sense measures, such as the use of small aircraft like the L-4 (the famed Piper Cub or, more generically, the Grasshopper) for artillery spotting, came about through field experimentation and was not part of prewar doctrine. Harold Maul was flying bombers in New Guinea early in hostilities and reflected on the overall confusion:

> I flew a couple of close-support missions in an A-20 and it was a mess.
> We didn't have the techniques then. We tried to base our runs on
> ground flares. Hell, they'd fire them and then the Japanese would fire
> the same color. We didn't have any communication with ground troops,
> no forward observers. This was early 1943, let alone '42. They'd never
> worked this type of operation before, neither the army or navy, they'd
> never done it. All the services before the war were strapped for money.
> At the Louisiana maneuvers I saw wooden machine guns and phony
> tanks. We dropped flour sacks out of B-25s and this was just before the
> beginning of a world war. Good God, it was really pitiful.

Although the Japanese did not drop sacks of flour on their troops in 1941, they also did not closely integrate ground and air operations. During Tokyo's blitzkrieg after Pearl Harbor Japanese bombers struck targets of value, such as airstrips, with great effect. It was during this period that the strafing Zero became a justly feared weapon in an environment with poor antiaircraft. Yet in these early campaigns it was the shock effect of Japanese bombers, rather than the actual damage done, that helped propel Allied forces into total retreat. Rather like the early inability of Allied infantry in Europe to combat tanks, the mere presence of Japanese aircraft weakened resolve. Japan's extraordinary victory in Malaya would have been impossible without the Japanese air arm.

The great victories of early 1942 were never replicated by Japanese bombers and fighters. During the Guadalcanal campaign the imperial air arm was expected to neutralize Cactus, which it could not do, but rendered no direct assistance to the Japanese army's attacks on the Marine perimeter. Put simply, throughout the Pacific war there was no Japanese close support. Japanese aircraft attacked ships, airfields, and landing craft but never in conjunction with a ground attack. Perhaps in some circumstances this reflected poor judgment; more likely it was an obvious reflection on battlefield realities. Because the Japanese army lacked firepower it had to attack at night. Japanese aircraft could not attack at night. Therefore their efforts were confined to attempting to destroy ships and aircraft. Yet Australian officers that defended Milne Bay and the Kokoda battles were pleasantly surprised to see the Japanese not contribute even a handful of combat aircraft to support imperial assault forces.

It is more difficult to assess early Allied ground-support missions. Guadalcanal was geographically one of the most unusual battles in history, with both armies having supply points within sight of each other. Obviously this meant that as long as Cactus was operating, U.S. forces held a tremendous advantage in attacking the foe and defending the perimeter. However, as in so many jungle battlefields, the terrain shielded the targets. The Americans employed a very simple approach, reflecting the fact that they had few ideas as to the exact locations of Japanese ground forces. If American intelligence knew that Japanese destroyers or barges had landed at Cape Esperance or Tassafaronga, Marine SBDs and TBFs would bomb the beach areas the next day, hoping to destroy supplies and kill Japanese. In addition, the 67th Fighter Squadron, which flew the P-400, an inferior breed of the P-39, dedicated itself to ground attack. It was a rare day when more than five aircraft of the 67th were in the air, but their field was within a few miles of their target. The P-400 was a poor fighter above 10,000 feet but had considerable firepower. They were like harpies on the backs of Japanese ground forces. Flying sortie after sortie, dropping small bombs, and expending as much ammunition as was available, they killed and wounded large numbers of Japanese troops. In mid-September, during the Battle of Bloody Ridge, three of the 67th's fighters caught retreating Japanese in the open at dawn and smashed the unit. As the campaign progressed, aircraft of all types attacked the Japanese bridgeheads. When the United States Army finally attacked out of the perimeter in December, SBDs, P-39s, and TBFs helped attack isolated positions in the hills discovered by advancing infantry. SBD crews found that depth charges worked well on exposed positions.

Guadalcanal was not a victory for tactical airpower, but it did not have to be once Cactus and the U.S. Navy had achieved superiority. The first real test for aircraft in a ground campaign came during the nightmare of Buna. In November 1942 Australian and U.S. forces had penned up some 8,000 Japanese infantry and engineers inside a several-square-mile triangle based at Buna, the small village where the Japanese force had originally landed. The Buna battlefield terrain was malarial mangrove swamp and proved one of the most miserable places of all to fight. Japanese engineers, left behind during the army's advance, had weeks to develop fortifications. There was also a small advance airstrip that could handle Japanese fighters (it was never intended to be an advance base). The U.S. 32d Division advanced up the New Guinea coast while the Australians pursued what was left of South Seas Detachment that had attacked Moresby.

The Americans soon discovered—much to the shock of some naive officers—that Buna was a tactical nightmare because crack Japanese combat engineers manned difficult positions. The survivors fleeing from the Australians, and a few hundred reinforcements, made the area between Gona and Buna even stronger. Although Allied troops were greatly superior in numbers, they had entered a disease zone that had few parallels on earth. Worse, they were attacking a fanatical and well-entrenched enemy without appropriate weaponry. The U.S. Navy believed that the waters near Buna, which were indeed badly charted, made the passage of warships impossible. The Japanese had made the voyage, but Allied ships refused. The result was that troops were shipped up the shoreline in a rag-tag group of vessels, less sophisticated than most Japanese barges, and not followed by ships that could have provided artillery. The 32d Division, alone among large American units during World War II, had to fight a major battle without field artillery. To make matters even worse one of the first convoys of crude vessels was attacked by U.S. bombers, killing some key officers. The Australians were not much better off. Some clever Aussie engineers figured out how to dismantle a handful of 25-pounders and send them by air transport to Buna. (The Australians also solved the problem of sending up light tanks via barge, something beyond the skill of the Army Corps of Engineer; those tanks were crucial in the final assault.) At the beginning of December, as the disaster began to loom in Allied headquarters, the issue was whether Buna would have to be taken in a World War I–type bloodbath or whether Allied airpower could break Japan's back.

It is difficult to precisely identify the mind-sets of the Australian and U.S. commanders as their troops approached the entrenched enemy without land and naval artillery. In MacArthur's headquarters pessimism was not encouraged, because MacArthur did not allow it. Whether that reflected MacArthur's personality or his fanatical desire to draw more resources to the Pacific matters little. Kenney was a splendid leader overall, but he was also MacArthur's man. In October Kenney wrote a letter to his superior, General Hap Arnold, expressing his views of the bare bones of the Pacific war:

Tanks and heavy artillery can be reserved for the battlefields of Europe and Africa. They have no place in jungle warfare. Artillery in this theater flies. . . . In the Pacific we have a number of islands garrisoned by small forces. These islands are nothing more or less than aerodromes or aerodrome areas from which modern fire-power is launched. Sometimes they are true islands like Wake or Midway, sometimes they are localities on large land masses. Port Moresby, Lae and Buna are all on the island of New Guinea, but the only practical way to get from one to the other is by air or by water: they are all islands as far as warfare is concerned. Each is garrisoned by a small force and each can be taken by a small force once local air control is secured. Every time one of these islands is taken, the rear is better secured and the emplacements for the flying artillery are advanced closer and closer to Japan itself.

As a strategic sketch of the war in the Pacific, Kenney's letter, which anticipated MacArthur's later operations, proved a brilliant outline to victory in the South Pacific. If understood as a tactical guideline for the battle facing Kenney and MacArthur at Buna, it anticipated the quintessential Pyrrhic victory of the Pacific war. In short airpower was unable to deliver anything like what Kenney and other Allied officers had hoped at Buna.

The obvious tactic was to simply attack every possible square inch of the Buna triangle. When Dobodura began operating in early December, it was a short flight to Buna. One quick casualty was the light airstrip built by the Japanese. With the Owen Stanleys acting as a guard for Allied aircraft flying toward Buna rather than shielding Japanese attacks on Moresby, Japanese naval aircraft that dared used Buna soon regretted it. Even P-39s at low altitude could deal heavy blows to Zeros trying to defend imperial forces at Buna. After the airstrip was blown to bits Allied aircraft of all types dropped bombs and strafed every corner of the Buna battlefield. Kirkwood Adams, a gunner on a B-17 employed by 8th Photo Squadron (one of the most important air units at Buna because of the lack of maps and photos of Japanese positions), recalled the result:

We used to go up to Buna every day. That was a real mess. But they needed maps of the area; nobody knew what was there. We went in low. It was terrible—you could tell that from the air. I'm glad I wasn't in it. It looked like the surface of the moon. Bomb craters all over—just stumps of trees left. There was total devastation. Things were so uncoordinated then. I think we bombed our own troops as often as we bombed the Japs. You couldn't see any kind of terrain lines. They were fighting so close.

Willis Connor was a radio operator for the U.S. 32d Division and expressed the fears that American troops felt toward Allied air strikes:

> They had no maps. Pilots couldn't see the second river on their photos because of jungle. We'd call in coordinates based on the assumption that they could. So we suffered a lot of friendly-fire casualties and would watch our planes dropping supplies to the Japs. They had no idea how to use close air support. One day we asked for support at eight o'clock. The planes didn't come so we delayed until noon. Still no planes. We jumped off and went into enemy-held territory. Then the planes arrived late and began attacking our own guys who had advanced. We were scared as hell when we heard an A-20—you could hear them a mile away they were so loud. When the plane opened up the recoil slowed it down, then would speed up again when it didn't fire, then slow down again. I'd hear those bullets go "bump-bump" against the tree. I made myself very thin.

The Australians had the best air-ground communications network in the South Pacific during this period of the war. Nevertheless, as Beaufighter crewman Fred Cassidy recalled, failure or success was largely a matter of chance:

> We did a lot of close air support but it was "by guess and by God." The jungle from the air all looks the same broadly speaking. We would be given a description by the army liaison officer. He'd say something like, "I want you to strafe on this coordinate and you can recognize it because there's a really tall tree and a little hut and a rock and two rocks and another hut and a big banana tree. If you strafe 500 yards to the southwest of that point you're right on target." When you got up there, there were fourteen places that all looked like the target from the air, and that was the problem we had—how to identify where we were. So they started using mortars with smoke instead of looking for vegetable patches next to the hut. They'd toss those mortars in the air when they heard us coming. We did a lot of that, especially near Buna-Gona.

Perhaps the most notable participants in the Buna air offensive were the Australian Wirraways of the RAAF No. 4 Squadron. Only in the twisted battlefield at Buna could Wirraways have succeeded. The aircraft was an Australian version of the extremely common AT-6 Texan trainer. When the Allies established an airfield at Dobodura, near

Buna, and fighter cover was made available, the skilled Australian pilots made surprisingly good use of the plane.

The Wirraway could carry only a 250-pound bomb. It was, however—as befits a trainer—very gentle to handle at low speed and low altitude. According to the Australian official history, the real values of the Wirraway were in supply and as a target drone. The Wirraway could be fitted with a supply canister, which it would drop to Australian troops who could use anything they could get. By flying low with an observer in the second seat found in all Texans, a Wirraway crew could identify antiaircraft positions when they were fired upon—a bit like playing aerial matador. (This was not unique as the war grew more intense.) Wirraways did drop bombs and destroy targets, but of more value they were in real-time communication with the tiny battery of Allied artillery at Buna. Firing in the dark those weapons were useless, but if given some coordinates by a Wirraway they could possibly drop a shell on an enemy emplacement.

In truth the Wirraway was a dead end, and the RAAF knew it. At Buna its greatest contribution was likely psychological rather than material. Air Commodore Garing, who commanded all Australian aircraft in the theater, reflected on air support:

No. 4 Squadron was quite effective. It was a dedicated army support squadron. It got a heck of a lot of praise. They made it their job to know where the army was and find out how they operated. They were using Wirraways. They were under my control overall, but operationally their activities were left up to the army and the squadron commander. Because of the ALOs [air liaison officers—EB] they were almost under army command. But the situation was so effective that only someone who was very stupid would have attempted to alter it. You must have some very close support aircraft for the army. The troops generally think that unless you're flying over the top of them you're losing the war. Of course that's not the case, it's the opposite. The Air Force should spend the bulk of its effort isolating the battlefield, cutting off the enemy's supplies, hitting his bases, bombing installations, keeping the enemy troops from being able to fight you. Shooting down enemy aircraft is good, too. But flying close simply to show force is not a good use of airpower. You have to be in after the enemy, and those targets might be hundreds of miles ahead of the army.

It is difficult to say whether Garing was correct. In the narrow sense Kenney certainly was not. Aircraft, despite Kenney's implied claim, could not effectively strike a specific target in a jungle battlefield at the end of 1942. Kenney was right, however, in that isolation of the battlefield in the South Pacific led to victory. Yet ultimately many of the men flying the first squadrons for Fifth Air Force dropped bombs on the Buna-Sanananda battlefield. Australian aircraft were prominent in the attacks. And as anyone who has viewed photos of the battlefield can testify, the bombing did turn the landscape into the surface of the moon.

There was a problem with judging the effectiveness of an air campaign against ground troops. Unlike air-to-air combat there is no obvious indicator of success. Moreover a World War II air offensive alone could not break entrenched ground positions. Yet if the ground was hammered and hammered—as it was at Buna and many other South Pacific battlefields—simple odds would suggest that some enemy positions were struck. If faced with malnutrition and disease the enemy garrison had to face surrender or death. Because surrender was impossible for Japanese forces at this stage of the war, one can imagine the kind of impact the steady pounding had on morale, even sanity. It is impossible to gauge how much longer the Japanese would have resisted had they not been bombed. It was surely an inefficient way to do the job, but the only alternative was to allocate the entire task to the infantry supported by its pitiful battery of guns. When the Sanananda garrison finally collapsed it did so in less than a day, and hundreds of starving Japanese soldiers walked about in a daze. Many committed suicide; others were shot; a handful became prisoners. Such was war in the South Pacific.

The Buna example of blind and semiblind area bombardment was repeated during several ground campaigns, although each campaign evidenced an improvement in techniques and weaponry. The assault on New Georgia in July 1943 had an uncanny resemblance to Buna. The 8,000 defenders knew that the Allied objective would be the airfield at Munda Point and so created a fortified zone around it. The terrain was not the grotesque malarial swamp of Buna, but it included some of the densest malarial jungle in the South Pacific. On paper the Allies were better prepared. They had conducted decent reconnaissance of the shoreline and had photomaps of the objectives. Admiral Halsey provided adequate supplies to the Marine battalions, and the 43d Division was given the objectives on New Georgia. The 43d, the main attack force, was landed some seven miles from Munda. It did not lack for artillery: Along with the full complement of organic batteries, the Marine Ninth Defense Battalion, with its lethal 155mm Long Tom guns, landed on the island of Rendova within easy range of Munda. Yet the power of the jungle to slow and blind attackers, com-

bined with a particularly well conducted defense, made the campaign
a miserable affair. Ultimately a second U.S. Army division and a part
of a third had to be deployed to finish the job, very much contrary to
Halsey's original wishes. It was almost as violent for ground forces as
Guadalcanal; Halsey's commanders pleaded for air support and received it throughout the battle.

The original job for aircraft was to defend the invaders against intense air attack. Once that was accomplished, then bombardment
from Marine tactical units and bomb groups from Thirteenth Air
Force commenced in earnest. Although dedicated air-ground liaison
teams were already in use by the Australians, there were still none on
New Georgia, so eight were patched together with volunteers. As is
made clear by Robert Sherrod, the author of the most authoritative
history of Marine Corps aviation in the Pacific war, air support was
still very crude in the theater:

> Execution of air-support missions was primitive compared to the
> smooth operation which had been perfected by the time Marine planes
> undertook such work in the Philippines. Of 44 requests for such
> missions, 35 were made the day before the execution. Of 7 requests
> from the front lines 3 of these were not executed; 24 came from the top
> ground command at Rendova or well back of the front. . . . The ground
> troops were afraid of the bombers—the close-in jungle fighting meant
> that in many cases the enemy might not be more than a few yards
> away; therefore, the small number of requests.

The result was that U.S. and New Zealand aircraft attacked and
strafed Munda the way Fifth Air Force hit Buna. In the six-week campaign the Marines alone flew thirty-seven attack missions that included nearly 2,000 sorties, most by TBFs and SBDs and the remainder by 13th USAAF bombers. Harold Raney was a gunner in a TBF
and described the techniques involved:

> Several of our missions were to support the ground forces on New
> Georgia in July. We'd go in the morning and pattern-bomb an area in
> front of where the troops were. So we'd drop about 9:00 A.M. After we
> left the troops would attempt to move forward into Japanese territory
> toward Munda. The tactics were simple. Our plane would drop our
> bombs and the next plane would drop his bombs a little further ahead.
> After four planes dropped their bombs, the next wing would drop their
> bombs about fifty feet to the north of where we were. We hoped this
> would help the advance, rather like artillery shelling from the air. We

were pattern-bombing. There were no individual targets you could aim
at. If you dropped enough bombs, you'd hit something. The Munda
area was heavily cratered. And fighters would strafe, too. We also acted
as artillery spotters for army artillery. We'd help them register their
targets, then they would cease firing and open up at night. That whole
place was really shot up. But the Japanese never molested us. When we
were spotting, we were sitting ducks.

New Georgia was a U.S. defeat in all but name. Halsey quickly re-
deemed the situation by landing New Zealand and U.S. troops on the
nearly undefended island of Vella Lavella weeks later. This brilliant
move cut off the remaining Japanese garrisons in the middle Solomons
and forced another Guadalcanal-style evacuation. Once Vella Lavella
had solved the problem of the middle Solomons, Bougainville was obviously the next target.

The Marines and 13th USAAF bombers helped support the invasion
of Bougainville in November 1943. In March 1944, long after Rabaul
was abandoned, 12,000 men from the large Japanese garrison in southern Bougainville marched overland to the Torokina perimeter and
launched a massed assault. Torokina was defended by two dug-in U.S.
Army divisions supported with tanks. The Americans employed massive
firepower, including heavy air strikes and naval artillery, to crush the
pointless Japanese attack in one of the largest single land battles that
took place in the South Pacific. By this time the Allies were learning
more sophisticated techniques of ground support. LeRoy Smith yielded
the back seat of his SBD to an army artillery spotter who was helping
warships employ their fire to maximum effect against the Japanese side
of the lines. According to Smith it was a harrowing experience:

During the Japanese attack on Torokina I flew spotter missions. Here
comes an army joker with his maps, and he says, "Put me at 3,000 feet
parallel to the beach." He was spotting for our warships. I'm knitting
button holes, I'll tell you, because those damn shells from offshore were
coming over my head. I'm looking for them down below and there they
go about a few hundred feet over your head; it was quite a surprise.
You could see the trajectories, or you think you see it, anyway. It was
like a blur. Then you look over there and see this hunk of ground just
rise up. When shells from a warship hit the ground you just can't
imagine how much dirt it disturbs. When I landed I was scared shitless.
I kept thinking about that "to whom it may concern" telegram that
would be sent home about me because one of those shells went a little
low. But I made it and the army beat up the Japanese pretty bad.

Despite this series of events, the main theater for ground support
was in New Guinea. The smoke had barely cleared at Buna when
fighting flared up at the Allied air base at Wau southwest of Lae. This
battle ignited a nonstop ground campaign in New Guinea that remained bitter until the fall of 1944. An Australian force moved up the
Markham-Ramu Valley, which for New Guinea offered good room to
maneuver. Periodically the drive was held up along ridgelines. Simultaneously MacArthur, with his growing sea power directly under his
command, ordered a series of amphibious attacks behind Japanese
lines, always forcing a Japanese retreat. Ultimately, between the two
offensives, a very large Japanese garrison was trapped on New Guinea.
Mopping up isolated positions continued until war's end, although at
a languid pace.

A bomb run in New Guinea terrain was never a joy. U.S. heavy and
medium bombers when making conventional runs preferred attacking
at medium altitude—6,000 feet or lower against a ground unit. (They
would hit a more heavily defended air base somewhat higher, but
rarely above 12,000 feet.) As 5th USAAF B-25 crewman Fred Miller
found out, dropping high-explosive bombs posed a danger to the attacker as well as the target:

> We had one mission to attack the Roosevelt Ridge near Salamaua in
> mid-1943. It was scheduled to be a big attack of thirty-six planes. But
> only four were able to bomb because it was so misty and foggy that
> most planes couldn't find the target. Because visibility was so poor we
> dropped down to under 1,000 feet and dropped our 500-pound bombs.
> You're not supposed to drop that type of bomb below 1,500 feet unless
> it has some kind of delay. The concussions made the plane go up and
> down like a jumping jack as the bombs went off. That puts your heart
> in your mouth, believe me. We all got Air Medals for that. They told us
> that we did some serious damage. I sure hope so. That was a tough
> mission.

Carl Camp flying on one of the 90th Bomb Group's Liberators had
a very similar experience a few weeks later in an area just north of
Miller's mission:

> We flew at lower altitude than in Europe. Lowest I ever got was 3,000
> feet above terrain. We were dropping 2,000-pound bombs and we
> could feel the concussion, it was knocking our airplanes all over the
> sky—that's low. It was supposed to be 6,000 feet above terrain but we
> went in at 6,000 feet above sea level and the target was on a small

mountaintop at 3,000 feet above sea level in New Guinea. We were cutting it pretty thin. That shook us all up.

Because Australian troops did most of the campaigning, the RAAF in particular expended a great deal of its energy striking Japanese positions of all types. Attacks were pressed particularly hard when extended, and bitter battles festered along mountain ridges that offered some of the most treacherous terrain in the Pacific. American troops played an important role on some occasions and became prominent after mid-1944. For a year and a half, however, the ground war in New Guinea was fought primarily by the battle-wise Australian army. Fifth Air Force contributed thousands of sorties and tons of bombs to the Australian ground campaign. As Robert DeHaven recalled, the stout P-40s of 49th Fighter Group spent much time attacking the Japanese in the mountainous New Guinea jungle:

Air ground support was one of our primary missions and responsibilities. We considered it a necessity. I would guess a clear majority of missions would have been considered ground support. In many instances an air-to-air fight resulted when Japanese fighters would try to prevent us from attacking their ground forces. We bombed and strafed every type of target available in that terrain. Many of our missions were close support, in direct proximity of the front. These were difficult missions to execute, but the Australians had organized things pretty well. Most of the terrain became well known to the Australian troops, because fighting would stall on a given front for several weeks. There was an Australian liaison officer assigned to at least the group level throughout Fifth Air Force. We were given preliminary briefings on photomaps—the targets along those ridges were chosen by the Australians. When we arrived in the area, the identification of ground target was made with white phosphorous mortar rounds. Everything was done with physical cues because our air communication capabilities with the P-40 were quite limited and often nonexistent when the radios failed. We would attack with small bombs and strafe.

We all admired the Australians. Despite MacArthur's claims that everything was accomplished by him personally, the dirty work was done by that small but very tough Australian army. I had the honor to visit one of their forward positions at Shaggy Ridge in the summer of 1944. [Shaggy Ridge was part of one of the ridgeline stalemates that marked the Markham-Ramu Valley campaigns. It was located just north of the U.S. airstrip at Gusap and due west of the coastal village of

Saidor. Fighting was particularly prolonged and nasty in the Shaggy
Ridge area.—EB] The visit was arranged by the Australian liaison. It
was rugged terrain, almost difficult to describe. I have photos of that
time. The pilot that went with me, Lieutenant Green, went over this
rope bridge, and on the photo you can see the chasm the bridge
spanned. It was a sheer drop of what looked to be hundreds of feet. I
don't know the actual decent, but anyone falling to earth was dead. A
rope bridge is not what most Americans would consider a bridge. I
wouldn't cross it today. I admit that I was uneasy about that bridge
back then when I was fearless and immortal like all the young pilots.
The Australians prepared quarters for me, which consisted of a
hammock strung between two trees. We had Bully Beef for dinner. The
Aussies were delighted to see us and took us right up to the departure
point on the ridge. If you went a step farther, you carried a rifle. One of
the most welcome treats came from the Australian Salvation Army
representative who was right on the ridgeline dispensing hot tea and
hard biscuits. In the Markham Valley there was a truck run by the Red
Cross and they charged you for a cup of tea. I respected any man that
could endure ground combat in New Guinea. But the Australians were
something special. I was proud to assist them.

The attack on Japanese forces by air did not really end until VJ-Day.
As noted, Anzac squadrons assisted their troops' slow advance against
bypassed garrisons in the Bismarcks, at Bougainville, and on New
Guinea. U.S. forces brought into the area were sometimes given some
live ammunition target practice by attacking stranded Japanese installations prior to being deployed to more active theaters. (Except for a
few very intense weeks when Japanese fighters contested the skies in
late 1944 and during the kamikaze campaign at Okinawa, it is likely
that when units did advance they were employed in ground support intermingled with periodic barge-hunts.) Several crewmen doubted the
wisdom of this campaign. After Rabaul was isolated completely, in the
spring of 1944, no real damage was done to the Japanese war effort by
attacking bypassed positions. The isolated Japanese garrisons were, in
essence, prisoner-of-war camps. Furthermore no combat mission was
without risk. Accidents, foul weather, and Japanese antiaircraft continued to pose a threat long after imperial aircraft and ships had abandoned the fight. In spring 1944 J.A.O. Stub was sent on his second
tour to the island of Emirau, just north of Kavieng, to fly a Corsair
with VMF-115. There were no air or naval targets in the area, so the
squadron made ground attacks on a defeated foe. Stub, like others,
doubted the value of many missions:

Most of war is waste. Our missions out of Emirau, except for the normal patrols, were wasteful, almost silly. In the summer the Japanese at Rabaul patched together a couple of aircraft and attacked Manus in the Admiralties, which were nearby. Everyone got all excited. You'd of thought the whole Japanese fleet was out there, but it was simple harassment. There was no reason to launch any major attacks, but we did. We worked with PBJs, the Marine's name for the B-25. We would come in with bombs and strafe flak positions and the PBJs would follow and bomb. We hit Kavieng, which still had very strong flak. I think they were running a gunnery school down there, because some of those gunners were good. That's how it was in the war. Everybody wanted to get into the act. I think a lot of the pilots did, some out of pure boredom. The officers wanted to order sorties and drop bombs because it would show up on the score. Sometimes we escorted the PBJs on some long-range missions, which were very uncomfortable for a fighter pilot—that parachute you're sitting on feels like a brick after a couple of hours. I'd like to think that some of those raids did damage, had a purpose. The war as a whole was certainly a necessity and winning essential. But, from a military view, a lot of what we did was pointless, even ridiculous, at that time and place.

•   •   •

Most officers and servicemen would probably agree that the most wasteful and tragic occurrence in combat is friendly fire. It is a problem as old as war and has become more common as engagements have taken place at greater distances with automatic and indirect-fire weaponry. Modern technology, despite much funds and thought expended, has not ended the danger. During World War II ground officers expected friendly-fire casualties to be 8–10 percent of the total in a battle. In the air war, because those involved usually saw each other, the percentage was probably less. Yet the danger of friend killing friend always existed in many guises.

An obvious moment of peril was a close-support mission. Artillery short rounds were a common cause of friendly-fire casualties; the same problem troubled airmen attacking close to comrades on the ground. A small error on the part of the airman or the individual directing fire on the ground could easily lead to an attack striking the wrong target. The culprit could be an errant bomb or a strafing run slightly off-target. Robert Croft also flew many missions in support of Australian infantry and recalled one that turned out badly:

One ground attack sticks in my mind. We were working out of a place
called Gusap. The Australian infantry was pinned down in the
mountain area north of us. They called for ground support. We were to
be guided to our target by a set of colored panels. One of the
Australian units put their panels in backwards so we strafed them
instead of the Japanese. I remember that vividly. They had just put their
panels in backward—green, yellow, red. They were supposed to be red,
yellow, and green. You strafed toward the green, so on that day we hit
them. We didn't know it at the time because all you were going by was
the panels. We didn't have radio connection with a ground-support fire-
control in those days. That's why we used panels. An Australian officer
came down to our squadron and apologized to our squadron for doing
it wrong. It was a great thing for him to do. We had killed some of his
men, but he didn't want us to feel as though we were responsible. I've
met officers that would have tried to blame us. It was a terrible thing.
But even with today's technology it happens. There were friendly-fire
tragedies throughout the theater. American planes would make passes
on each other. The Tony and P-40 looked very much alike. A Betty and
a B-26 were almost identical from a distance.

The reason that the artillery short round was so dangerous was that
attackers were usually not as well dug in as defenders and were thus
more vulnerable to fire. The same unfortunate process was at work
during a close-support mission. As Fred Cassidy recalled, "Unfortunately we sometimes got our own blokes. That was not nice. Sometimes
people would bring back our empty shells back to our base to show
how close we'd come to them. That was most common early in the war
and you couldn't tell who was to blame. It was bad for morale, let me
assure you. It was also inevitable in that terrain. And no one in command ever requested that we cease our missions." Cassidy was echoed
by Robert DeHaven: "Friendly fire was greatly regretted but accepted
as an inevitable penalty for the type of war we were fighting."
As indicated by Robert Croft above, it was possible for friendly aircraft to fire on each other or be fired upon by ships even if in plain
view. Target identification was an art, and only a very few men were
really good at it. During the war the military circulated a magazine on
the subject that included many photos of new friendly and enemy
weapons of all kinds. Each magazine included quizzes that challenged
the reader to match a photo with a list of possible aircraft supplied at
the bottom of the page. I have been studying military history for
twenty-five years and have personally seen almost all of the major
fighting aircraft from both sides on several occasions. Taking these

tests is a genuine lesson in humility. The very few I have passed have taken long examination. During the war, when taught identification, men were trained to identify friend or foe in an instant. In truth, from a distance, it was rare when one had the opportunity to view a possible target from a clear angle. Joel Paris had more than his problems with friendly fire:

Friendly fire was a terrible problem. I've told people many times that I was shot up five times by our guys before I ever got a bullet hole in me fired by the enemy. Shot up by my own people at different times by different people for different reasons. Both ground and air. A B-24 shot me up good—that was the first time. Then a naval vessel got me, they were really bad. Anybody that got near a warship was in danger from them. The ground troops hit me two or three times. The worse thing was that if somebody fires then everybody fires. If they see an airplane it must be an enemy. They just shoot. I was dropping some recon photos to troops that were hitting the beach at Biak Island. I flew real slow with the flaps down to throw out this canister of pictures on the beach with a streamer on it. There was this LST, I waved at him and saw him swing this .50 around and aim it and start firing. I wasn't more than 300 or 400 feet from him. When he started firing everybody and his brother started shooting. I came back a few minutes later and was going about 400 MPH when I dropped the pictures. I don't know where they went and can't say that I care much.

There were natural enemies on the battlefield. Ships feared aircraft, and the motto was "better safe than sorry." Small procedural errors could lead to calamity. Jim Geyton of *Enterprise* recalled that before IFF became reliable and in general use a quadrant of the ship was considered a "safe" zone where flak gunners would await positive identification of a lone aircraft before opening up. The zone, perhaps the port quarter one day, the starboard bow the next, changed regularly. One day a B-25 crew mixed up the quadrants and fell to the ship's 5–38s. As Paris mentioned, wise pilots kept a safe distance from any ship. Fighters also looked at unidentified fighters as enemies. Several pilots mentioned that "everything looked like a P-40." The Australian Wirraway was in particular danger because the T-6 Texan, upon which it was based, was a dead ringer for a Zero and Oscar. The great ace Gerald Johnson mistook an RAAF Wirraway and shot it down. Fortunately the RAAF pilot escaped without injury. Johnson, in a display of GI black humor, painted an Australian flag on the side of his P-38 to join the growing rows of rising suns.

As Frank Chadwick recalled, danger arose when fighter and antiair-craft action became intermingled, which often happened at Guadal-canal and throughout the Solomons. Chadwick described an en-counter off Koli Point on Guadalcanal:

On Koli Point two planes approached down the beach, right off the deck. One of our guys on the 20mm opened up and got them both. The first one was a Zero and the second was a Wildcat in hot pursuit. We fished the Marine pilot out of the drink, and he was mad as hell. But you can't tell who's coming at you at that altitude and the Japs often snuck in and strafed the beach. When someone is shooting you don't really have much time to think—this all takes place in a couple of seconds. So Buck Jones, our gunner, put a Jap flag and an American flag on the 20mm. Our colonel was ticked at that and we had to remove the American flag. If we'd got an army plane they probably would have let us keep the flag.

Perhaps the most common cause for friendly-fire incidents between aircraft was simple panic from lack of training. Ground soldiers knew that a nervous sentry was as dangerous as the enemy on most occa-sions. Perhaps the man was inexperienced, perhaps fatigued, or per-haps he should not have been in combat. But many men died because of simple negligence or panic. Al Rothenberg flew a Navy PBY over the Solomons and almost perished due to an inexcusable error:

When flying patrol a B-17 overtook me. It wasn't more than 100 yards away. I waggled my wings. The waist gunner started shooting and put three holes in us before I guess the pilot told the idiot to stop, "No, no, you moron, wrong target. That's one of ours." This was in broad daylight. He probably thought we were a Kawanichi. On rare occasions patrol planes would run into one. But the Kawanichi was a four-engine plane. I didn't think anything else in the world looked like a PBY with our high wing. Heaven only knows. But I was infuriated.

Error played a major part in World War II; so did intelligence and adaptability. Of all of the aspects of ground support given in the South Pacific, without doubt the most important was yielded by Allied troop carrier squadrons, which employed principally the C-47. As was so often the case during World War II, the importance of air transport was not correctly anticipated prior to war. All air forces had transport craft, but they were considered utility planes that would be useful for moving officers and important supplies from point to point. The interest in paratroopers also increased the interest in transport aircraft. For the most part air forces employed military versions of civilian aircraft. Ruggedness and relative ease of maintenance—qualities demanded by early airlines—matched exactly the requirements for a good combat transport. The Germans found the venerable Junkers Ju52 a reliable transport and employed it throughout the war. Picking the DC-3 as the basis of a military transport was a simple decision for the Americans, and eventually British, Canadian, and Anzac forces clamored for C-47s.

The tremendous potential of transport aircraft was overlooked because no one realized how many airplanes were going to be built in the war. A C-47 could carry about twenty-five men (thirty in a pinch) or a few thousand pounds of supplies. Normally the loads were less than that. But armies and navies thought in terms of the load capacities of ships and trains, which were infinitely greater; even a large truck could carry nearly as much as a transport. Yet none of those transports could fly. Some 13,000 C-47s were built during the war (another 2,000 built under license in the USSR), and this reliable aircraft, capable of making dozens of flights between overhauls, increased the load-carrying capacity of airlift substantially.

This was a weapon that had to be deployed in huge numbers to achieve maximum effectiveness. And so it stands to reason that this situation put the Japanese at a serious disadvantage. Yet technology was not a factor, as Tokyo had licensed the DC-2 before the war and had some adequate transports of its own. But the Japanese aircraft industry failed to produce adequate numbers of twin-engine bombers, and in the attack-oriented imperial military, transport construction was thus a low priority. Ironically, considering the miserable performance of most army bombers and the poor overall track record of the Betty, the Japanese might well have had priorities reversed as Japanese shipping began to disappear. Whatever the case, the empire fielded several hundred transports spread throughout the Pacific. The Allies concentrated hundreds and finally thousands of troop transports in the theater.

And in no theater of war were transports more valuable than in the South Pacific. During the Guadalcanal campaign C-47s supplied gasoline (on desperate occasions) and supplies of all sorts. Just as importantly, on the return they carried the wounded and disease-stricken servicemen. The Solomons, once the IJN had been kept out of the American rear, did not depend on transports for basic supplies after Guadalcanal. Yet they always served as a good means for bringing in particularly valuable supplies and continued to provide invaluable service within the medical apparatus.

In New Guinea transports were so important that one could argue
that the role of the fighter was to make the air safe first for the transport and then the bomber. During the Australian counteroffensive
against the Japanese that led to the epic pursuit over the Kokoda Trail,
U.S. transports tried to drop supplies to Australian troops. When U.S.
and Australian forces began to isolate the Japanese stronghold at
Buna-Sanananda, supply-drops became central to the fighting. Because
roads always remained primitive at best, the supply-drop became a
staple of land warfare in New Guinea. It might take days or weeks for
supplies at a base to be brought to the front; only a drop would work.
Amazingly the U.S. Army Air Force had given no thought to dropping
supplies from the air. Specialized parachutes did not appear until
1943, so the pilots and ground crews had to develop suitable techniques on the spot. David Vaughter was a young C-47 pilot in New
Guinea and described the problems posed:

When we first went in to drop supplies we didn't have any training. I'd
never dropped anything in the States. We had dropped some
paratroopers but never supplies. Frankly, we didn't have a clue as to
what to do. There was no book on the subject, so we wrote our own.
At first, we and some of the other early-arrived squadrons went at it
wrong. Until Buna we dropped Australian supplies. The Aussies packed
it up and wrapped it in beautiful wool blankets covered with burlap.
We dropped everything from ammunition to canned fruit.

The first crews given this duty told us to go in as low as possible and
make sure we had enough speed to go over the trees: approximately
150 knots. This was for safety, because we might have to turn to do it
again. If you went too slow, you could stall the airplane, which is a bad
idea at low altitude. Well, we were actually in there skip-bombing
supplies at ten to twenty feet elevation at 130–150 miles an hour. We'd
kick the stuff out the door and it hit the ground like shrapnel, almost
blowing apart. Sometimes the supplies would ricochet off the ground
and fly down the hills. We often averaged only 20 percent recovery. If
everything was demolished, we'd have to do it again. Gradually we
learned that logic was leading us astray. It made sense to drop low.
However, we learned that the optimum altitude for supply drop was
around 300 feet. We flew higher, and also as slow as we could, maybe
eighty to ninety miles per hour. The supplies then had the opportunity
to lose forward momentum and fell almost straight down. This more
than compensated for greater height, and lost material dropped
considerably. When they requisitioned parachutes for this duty, there
were times when we had 100 percent recovery.

The Allied discovery (by engineers prior to the Japanese attack in the summer of 1942) and subsequent development of Dobodura as an airstrip was the turning point for operations in New Guinea. When the Australians had pushed the Japanese back into their perimeter at Buna, U.S. engineer units knew exactly where to build a good airstrip. After a small group of indigenous laborers and engineers cleared some kunai grass, C-47s began to arrive with heavier equipment such as large lawn mowers. The Australians discovered that it was possible to cut small bulldozers in two parts with welding torches, put them on C-47s, and repair them when landed. (They used the same technique on a few 25-pounders; later they lightened the piece so it could be deployed without surgery.) Dobodura immediately served as a base where Allied fighters could cover the battle at Buna. More importantly it served as an indispensable point of supply for Australian and U.S. infantry. Soon it became the entry terminal for thousands of Australian troops. The Kokoda Trail over the Owen Stanleys was the worst possible route of reinforcement, and the small port of Nassau Bay was far from the battlefield. Dobodura was the far better place from which to bring in troops. As on Guadalcanal, there was little point of bringing transports in full and leaving empty. Thousands of disease and battle casualties, who suffered under the most primitive medical conditions ever faced by Allied forces during World War II near the front, were saved by evacuation via Dobodura to the hospitals in Moresby and Australia. With the defeat of the Japanese at Buna and Guadalcanal the construction of Dobodura brought the war to the northeastern coast of New Guinea and set the stage for strategic advances that followed in 1943.

None of this happened, however, before a major scare at the obscure outpost of Wau. Between the jungle and mountains of the Owen Stanleys, the mangrove swamps near Buna, and more fierce mountains along the northern coast of New Guinea lay a valley along the Markham and Ramu Rivers. In this landscape the most spectacular example of the value of combat transport took place during the battle at Wau in late January 1943. Inland from the Japanese base at Salamaua, Wau was a gold-mining settlement, the only outpost of Western civilization existing in the New Guinea interior. Because the mines needed supplies, Wau possessed a serviceable airstrip. When war broke out Wau served as a base for Kanga Force, a small band of Australian irregulars. Kanga Force had made a series of raids, varying greatly in success, against Japanese positions at Salamaua and Lae. In January, with the Buna campaign developing into a major defeat, the Japanese attempted to salvage something by seizing Wau.

It was a shrewd move by the Japanese. If they could hold Wau, then they could forestall an Australian thrust up the river valleys leading into the Huon Peninsula. Wau also sat astride the series of tracks and trails that led to every point of significance in the area. One route led to Port Moresby. Although longer than the Kokoda Trail, it was easier to traverse. Because the import of defeat at Buna and Guadalcanal took several months to sink in for the command apparatus in Tokyo, the Japanese army still entertained hopes of starting another drive on Moresby. Even if an offensive proved impossible, a position at Wau would either delay further Allied moves in New Guinea or force the Australians to retake Wau. The latter prospect would have been extremely unappealing immediately after the savagery at Buna.

Guided by a German miner who had spent his life in the area, a Japanese force of 3,000 moved inland on January 14. Although Kanga Force had some sporadic contacts, the Japanese were six miles outside Wau before the Australians realized a major assault was under way. A race began immediately. The Japanese attempted to push through rugged terrain and take the Wau airfield. The Australians had only 500 defenders at the outset. For their part they had to hold the airfield and fly in reinforcements as fast as possible. Often the field was under fire.

Already one of the most difficult strips to land on under the best of circumstances, Wau was an uninviting prospect in the middle of battle. Ernie Ford recalled the situation:

At the end of January 1943 things got hot at Wau. The Japanese had infiltrated a large force and reached the edge of the airfield. Aussie defenders were desperate for reinforcement. I think almost every transport in New Guinea was involved. But we had to wait for the weather. Weather was always tough in the Owen Stanleys, and Wau was surrounded by hills and mountains. It was often fogged in. We had Aussie troops ready to go at Moresby, and they wanted to get in bad. Luckily the weather broke just as the Japanese were closing in on the field and off we went. Planes came in every few minutes. Sometimes we had to circle so the Aussies could clear Japanese troops from the edge of the runway. When we got down, the Aussie troops got out on the double. During the first days, they went right into battle. Of course, they didn't have far to go. There were mortar rounds and small arms fire coming in. I can tell you we got out as fast as we could. But as long as the weather held, there was another load waiting. After a week or so, the Aussies threw the Japs back.

At the height of the battle on January 31, forty transports made seventy-one flights into Wau. Within two weeks Australian troops outnumbered the Japanese and smashed the attack. Kokoda, Buna, and Wau, however, were just the beginning. During 1943 Australian troops fought a major offensive in the Ramu Valley while depending largely on air supply. It was one of the most successful employments of airpower in World War II. The drive also helped lead to the construction of air bases, which led to a death sentence for the JAAF in New Guinea. Simultaneously with the Australian drive Allied forces in the Solomons and Fifth Air Force began to pummel the Japanese air units in the Rabaul area. Although powerful in the Solomons and New Guinea in July 1943, the Japanese navy and army were on the edge of disaster. Within six months Rabaul was destroyed and the JAAF air units in New Guinea were reduced to cannon fodder.

The Destruction of Japanese Airpower

Although it took the better part of a year (to late 1942), the Allies collected an adequate number of aircraft and developed proper attack techniques; once that occurred they were able to disable and destroy Japanese airfields. Naturally such attacks on the fields forced Japanese aircraft—assuming they had warning to make a choice—to flee or rise in defense. Although on occasion Allied attacks were badly organized and vulnerable to a hostile reaction, Allied fighters—particularly Lightnings, Jugs, and Corsairs—were quite glad to mix it up. Consequently the destruction of Japanese airpower was accomplished in the air by fighters and on the ground by bombers.

There are some important points to consider when analyzing the brutally efficient destruction of imperial air bases in the South Pacific. First, unless a base's line of supply could be cut or greatly reduced, or the base itself seized by invasion, a well-constructed base was a tough target. Fields could be bombed and defenders shot from the sky. However, if they so chose the Japanese could send reinforcements of aircraft and ground personnel and get the field back in action. The sophistication of the field complex was another vital factor. No Japanese base, Rabaul included, was well constructed by U.S. standards, yet the Japanese proved excellent at making do. Thus some Japanese forward bases were much more complex than others. A good one possessed more than one strip, some kind of taxiway, and revetments under the jungle cover. Buin, Buka, and Kahili on Bougainville were good examples and proved challenging targets. Some fields, like Munda on New

Georgia and Buna in New Guinea, comprised little more than a strip and a few tents. Sometimes pressed into emergency service, such fields proved easy to blow to shreds. In general all of the New Guinea strips were considered inadequate by the Japanese, and Wewak, the largest of the bunch, proved extremely vulnerable when the time came for Fifth Air Force to strike.

It was also important for the Allies to get as close as possible to their intended victim. Confident that their radar, antiaircraft, and fighters could protect Allied bases, commanders wanted to breathe down the enemy's neck. If the attackers were close, then multiple attacks could be launched on the same day, thereby increasing chances for catching the enemy on the ground. Likewise damaged raiders had a better chance to limp back to base and secure rescue if they went down. A nearby base also made the important task of barge-busting more feasible. Last, we need to understand that attacking fields was probably the most dangerous mission of all in the South Pacific air war: The Japanese had time to prepare, and they knew that the Allies would come. Major fields had large quantities of antiaircraft guns, substandard though still deadly. Add Japanese fighters to the equation, and Allied bomber pilots targeting places like Kahili and Kavieng knew they were in for an uncertain ride.

I should also add that the Allied approach toward attacking Japanese airfields—like the overall Allied effort—was usually a fine combination of aggressiveness and prudence. They employed no set technique. If a major mission was planned and the required numbers of planes were available, then the Allies attempted to find the right mix to take advantage of each type's strengths. They also frequently attacked multiple targets, making concentrated fighter defense more difficult. If a smaller group of aircraft was available, commanders were likely to send it out unless the risks were prohibitive. Put simply, the Allies plastered every target in sight with everything in their arsenal and did not relent. Yet Kenney and the other commanders in the Solomons did not take foolish risks. There was never any illusion about the ability of bombers to operate successfully without fighter escort. On rare occasions later in the campaign Kenney or the Australians flying out of Darwin would send heavy bombers on long-distance raids deep into the East Indies or Dutch New Guinea. The raids were not sustained, however, and helped force the Japanese to keep some fighter defenses in areas where they were not normally needed. (Kenney wanted Arnold to station B-29 superheavy bombers at Darwin to attack the oil fields in the Indies, but Arnold turned him down; considering the unhappy fate of those given to Chennault, Kenney's idea might have had merit.) Allied forces also used B-24s for long-range armed reconnaissance missions, where they would stay high, and relatively safe, unless they spotted a ship to attack. Such missions aside, fighters always went along with the bombers. It is true the rendezvous between fighter and bomber formations did not always work as planned, and sometimes coordination was simply ill-timed. Yet Allied escorts greatly lessened the menace of Japanese fighters. This policy was well in place months before Allied bombers in Europe adopted it.

It was a sad coincidence for the Japanese that many of the techniques the Allies developed to destroy ships were ideal for assaulting airfields. Originally this meant dive-bombing, glide-bombing with TBFs, and fighter-bomber attack. Although the ferocious combined low-level/high-level attack proved invaluable against major imperial bases, smaller ones had been ravaged by Allied attackers even before the strafers entered the game.

What's more, by the time the Allies went over to the offensive against imperial forces they also possessed an excellent air-sea rescue system that only got better through 1943. PBYs, flown by all of the Allied air forces in the South Pacific, were central. PT boats and submarines also helped when possible, and destroyers plucked many a flier out of the ocean. Dozens of valuable pilots were saved as a result. (Throughout the war it is estimated that PBYs saved some 540 pilots—enough to equip several aircraft carriers.) The positive effect on morale can be imagined. On the Japanese side, in contrast, a surprising disregard was paid to this matter. Interrogated after the war, Commander Masatake Okumiya was an experienced combat pilot until seriously wounded. After recovery he was promoted to a top JNAF staff position at Rabaul. Immediately after the war Okumiya told American officers, "Pilots generally had parachutes, life preservers and rafts. Seaplanes, subs and destroyers were sometimes used to search for downed fliers. But this depended entirely on the will of the division commander. There was no organized system at all. This was one of the big differences in your approach and ours. Your whole philosophy was different." In his later memoirs Okumiya claimed that Japanese pilots had great respect for Allied PBY crews, as they often saw them rescue pilots within artillery range of Japanese bases or in positions where the vulnerable PBYs might come under fighter attack.

The first Japanese bases to become deathtraps were in New Guinea. When the Guadalcanal campaign removed so many JNAF fighters from New Guinea, Allied bombers pummeled the small base at Buna, which was quickly eliminated, as well as the fields at Lae and Salamaua. Both of those bases, on the Huon Gulf in New Guinea, were under constant pressure during the Buna campaign and thereafter. Both were under IJN command, and during this time it was concerned with the Solomons. Periodically the Japanese would attack an Allied base, but for the most part the attacks were a one-way street. Still, the Japanese were able to stage aircraft out of Lae for several months, and Salamaua became a good target for Allied aircraft. Salamaua, closer to Allied bases, caught the worst of it. As Robert DeHaven recalled, "I'd like to have an Australian dollar for every bullet I pumped into the airstrip at Salamaua coming out of Dobodura. We did a good job because when we finally captured the place we decided not to build a base there." DeHaven was quite correct: Allied engineers decided that the shredded position at Salamaua was not worth resurrecting for anything other than an emergency strip.

Lae was also becoming a dangerous place from which to operate Japanese aircraft. During the Buna offensive, the little Japanese air interference that existed came from Lae or, less likely, from Gasmata on New Britain. The Buna battlefield was a frustrating target for bombers to attack. But the Lae airbase, once home of the famous Tainan Air Group, was a different story altogether. Bombers of every sort paid their call. Particularly ruthless were RAAF Beaufighters. The Australian official history described the situation in late December 1942: "So heavy were the Allied air attacks on Lae that when six Beaufighters and five RAAF Bostons made low-level sweeps over the aerodrome on the 7th December, the crews found it difficult to distinguish undamaged enemy aircraft on the ground because of the amount of wreckage that littered the target area."

In late 1942 a damaged strip did not mean a dead strip in New Guinea. Zeros offered battle at Lae until its conquest in June 1943. Allied aircraft at Dobodura were also within range of Japanese planes from Gasmata and secondary airfields at the western tip of New Britain. Yet the Japanese were being pushed back, and those aircraft that dared operate risked destruction on the ground and in the air. When the Bismarck Sea battle ended in complete debacle for the Japanese, one of the smaller freighters was filled with replacement aircraft and replacement parts for aircraft at Lae. When the ship went down, so did the base at Lae. The Australians had little trouble with Japanese airpower when they seized Lae in September 1943 with assistance from the U.S. Navy.

An unusual symmetry developed between the campaigns in the Solomons and New Guinea. I already described Japan's vain attempt to open an air base at Munda that was quickly smashed by the combined effort of every Marine and USAAF bomber in the Solomons. Only a handful of Japanese aircraft ever operated from Munda, which had engaged the efforts of hundreds of Japanese pioneers. On the neighboring island of Kolombangara, where the Japanese deployed a sizeable land garrison with limited amphibious capabilities, only a small field was built. The Japanese positions on New Georgia and Kolombangara existed only to delay Allied operations toward Rabaul.

In any event, a few weeks after New Georgia fell the New Zealand–U.S. landing on Vella Lavella put the Allies between Japanese units in the middle Solomons and their base at Rabaul. The result was the headlong flight of Japanese ground units, which were evacuated by destroyers and barges.

In the summer of 1943 the air war throughout the South Pacific was about to escalate further. After the costly conquest of Munda, the Seabees made good use of an invaluable point on the map. As LeRoy Smith recalled: "When the Seabees got through with Munda they just flattened the mountain and you could have landed four B-24s side-by-side. It was huge: You could come back dragging your ass in the water all shot up and you had something to come back to. They ran right up to the water." Vella Lavella became a valuable air base, and the immediate target then became the complex of bases built by the Japanese on and near the island of Bougainville. They included Buin and Kahili on Bougainville proper, as well as Shortland Island to the south and Buka to the north. Within this complex rested much of Rabaul's air fleet, and these bases received much of the reinforcements that the IJN agreed to send Rabaul in late 1943.

At the same time—within days, even—Fifth Air Force and its RAAF component were preparing to do battle with a new enemy. A brand-new Japanese Army Air Force was ordered to assemble on four poor strips near the village of Wewak. Both the Japanese army and navy were reacting to what they well knew would be the order of the day: no retreat. In September 1943 the Imperial War Council endorsed a heavy reinforcement of the South Pacific theater. Large numbers of Japanese troops came from Manchuria to New Guinea. Aircraft from Malaya to Formosa were ordered forward, many directed to the "safe" fields at Hollandia.

During the summer of 1943 Japanese and Allied forces had traded blows during a number of air and sea battles. The Japanese had certainly begun to slip in the kill ratio as their aircraft became less capable and less numerous. Perhaps had the Japanese army and navy been better coordinated, the catastrophe threatening them both would have played out better in the end.

Still, I doubt there was anything that Japanese commanders could have done given the September 1943 Imperial Order requiring that the

Southeastern Area be held as long as possible so that Combined Fleet could prepare for a decisive battle in the Central Pacific. Ironically September was a time when the Japanese could have fled Rabaul and Wewak in good order and with purpose. In pursuing a lost cause in a sensitive place the Japanese merely ensured that they would not only lose the battle but also abandon any reasonable means for keeping the Allies away from the real gold of the theater for weeks and months. Instead the imperial air arms in the Solomons and New Guinea were like a rabbit caught in a snare: Movement was impossible, and there was little to do but await the executioner.

By August 1943, as Kenney prepared for the demolition of Wewak and Allied units in the Solomons readied groups for the destruction of the Bougainville fields, the Allies had assembled the necessary weapons and battle techniques to destroy airfields. In the coming engagement the B-25 strafers of Fifth and Thirteenth Air Forces proved more effective against airstrips than ships. They were made more deadly by the deployment of a simple weapon that General Kenney himself had helped develop before the war while working with attack aviation: the parafrag. It was a twenty-three-pound fragmentation bomb attached to a small parachute. To allow strafers and A-20s to launch large numbers of these small bombs quickly, special racks were devised by Pappy Gunn in Australia. Factory models improved on Gunn's work, and Washington forwarded tens of thousands of parafrags to the South Pacific, mostly to Fifth Air Force.

Rich Walker flew a B-25 strafer for the illustrious 5th USAAF 3d Bomb Group and attacked several Japanese fields in New Guinea. As he recalled the strafer was an effective weapon, but it did have its quirks. Walker also recalled an unexpected benefit of the parafrag:

We could fly on one engine. A B-25 was pretty iffy on one, particularly one of our homemade strafers. They destroyed the balance of the plane by putting all that weight up front and pulling the bottom turret out. That changed the center of gravity. They had a slide rule you were to use to figure your weight balance. We sat there one day working the slide rule, and hell the slide nearly fell out of the rule. So we threw it away. There was another problem with the strafers. You needed armorers to load those guns and replace those barrels. In theory if you fired in bursts the guns wouldn't overheat and the barrels would last for a long time. But our pilots would hold those firing buttons down and that would eat those barrels up. When you get excited closing on a hot target you're not going to let up. He's shooting at you, you're shooting at him; you are going to pour it on hard. I remember those tracers looked like they were going through a twenty-foot arc, flying all over the place. When we came home from a mission they sometimes had to replace all eight barrels. We had tracer, armor-piercing, and incendiary bullets.

Often we had antiaircraft guns as a target, to protect the B-24s who would fly high and try to hit big targets and installations. First, they'd send in recon so we had a pretty good idea where the flak was. Then it was up to us to find them, attack them, and suppress them. This set up a face-to-face duel. A lot of times it was a matter of whether you'd get them before they got you. The crews had guts and would stay with their guns in my experience. We'd use parafrags for this type of work along with strafing. We carried dozens. The bombs were small and were scored to break up into one-inch squares upon detonation. You could lay them down for half a mile. The parachute was about six feet across, just enough to slow the bomb down and prevent detonation under the plane because they'd follow along your flight path when you first dropped them. I've got pictures taken from the rear of the plane of those parachutes hanging over the positions and the Japanese gunners diving for cover. We found something out about parafrags. When you're in the jungle you have a lot of trees. These things would hang in the trees and they had a contact fuse. They wouldn't go off until they hit something. When the wind would blow the branches would sway. Sometimes those things would go off two or three days after they were dropped and then get dislodged and hit the ground. I'm sure that was demoralizing for the Japanese. It was a very effective weapon.

Perry Dahl escorted many strafer missions and saw their deadly effect on Japanese airfields:

Escorting B-25s was really great because they were very, very destructive. We loved to fly with the B-25s. They went in low and fast. You almost always got in a fight when you were with them. I might add that the parafrag and the planes that dropped them were instrumental in winning the air war over there. I escorted many B-25 missions to drop parafrags. The B-25s would kick parafrags out for what seemed like three days. Over the runway you'd see these things falling down, little bombs, about twenty-five pounds. But many of them. Everything that was on the runway had little bitty holes in it. Afterwards when we took the Japanese base and moved into it there'd be Zeros and other Japanese planes stashed all over in the woods, back in the jungle and everywhere they could hide, full of these little bitty holes, all from the parafrags. It was kind of hazardous because they'd go in very low and

[they] got smart. There would be flak towers alongside the runway so that normally the B-25s would go underneath the flak towers and the Japs would really lower the boom on you. But you almost always found that the destruction, the havoc really was tremendous with those parafrags. I mean they'd wipe out *anything* that was on the runway. And then we'd come in. We'd roll in, strafing with incendiaries. Man, those planes on the runway would really go up. I must have shot up twenty to thirty planes on the ground.

Yet many of the Japanese planes on the ground were inoperable before being destroyed by these raids, as the Japanese would place destroyed planes in revetments and near treelines. Still, because Japanese maintenance was poor, it did not take a serious blow to ground a Japanese plane. And once an airfield was under sustained assault it was not likely that a grounded plane would ever fly again. This was particularly important, as increasingly the airpower bottleneck for the imperial air arm was the number of aircraft, not a lack of crewmen. As Perry Dahl also pointed out, the lack of flexibility and depth in Japanese industry prevented them from replying in kind. Japanese bombers made frequent raids on Allied forward bases and sometimes slipped in with little warning. They, too, had a parafrag, but it was distinctly inferior:

I was on the runway just ready to take off when a Zero came over. I saw this guy and pulled the canopy down. I just sat down in the airplane because we had armor around the cockpit and I didn't have a chance to get out. He dropped some parafrags. The rack that they were hanging on hit the nose of my airplane, so all of the parafrags flew over me and landed on the runway and knocked out a few airplanes. But we got one of our guys in a half-track, we had one on the side of the runway to protect us, to just run down the middle of the runway. So he drove down the middle of the runway, blew up about four or five, and then I took off right behind him. When I came back I saw there were an awful lot them that didn't go off. They didn't look twenty-five pounds, they looked like maybe eight- or nine-pounders: little bitty things, and with little propellers on the front. And he dropped them either too low or something, because most of the propellers didn't have time to arm. It was kind of a Mickey Mouse thing. I think about eight of them went off, put a couple of holes in a few airplanes, but just skin damage. So they weren't too effective. Not nearly as effective as ours.

The offensive that destroyed Japanese airpower in the South Pacific began in August 1943. Initially the Allies possessed a numerical advantage, but not a great one—at least on paper. (The serviceability of Japanese aircraft steadily declined during this period, making it difficult to estimate actual strength.) Fifth Air Force had received some new units and many new aircraft during the summer, as had Marine and USAAF air commanders in the Solomons. Yet the Japanese army was gathering a large force in the Wewak area, doing much to even the odds.

Fifth Air Force had good reason to move against the four fields near Wewak. The scheduled September invasion of Lae would be within range of several Japanese bases, and a major new player was not welcome. Fortunately for the Allies some clever intelligence and rapid action helped their cause. The Japanese had assumed that Wewak was relatively safe outside Allied fighter range. Shipping came into the area, bringing the men and materiel required to finish the new strips. No one in the IJA had reason to fear that the Allies understood the extent to which they were reinforcing land and air strength at Wewak as well as Hollandia, a coastal village to the west. But Allied codebreakers and experts at signal intelligence had accurate information on the units being moved into the area, their potential strength, and dates of arrival. Thus armed with excellent intelligence, U.S. engineers and Australian light bush forces cooperated on some clever deceptions. A small expedition of engineers was sent to find a location for a fighter strip, and one was found at the village of Tsili Tsili a few miles west of the Markham River. With native assistance Australian forces quickly cleared a short strip for transports, which was operating within days; engineers began receiving light construction equipment. During this time Allied engineers were visibly active at another inland site, Bena Bena, to the northwest. This drew Japanese air attacks and a furtive land attack. With Japanese attention thus drawn to Bena Bena, the strip at Tsili Tsili accepted its first fighter unit and deployed a powerful defense force. Meanwhile Kenney's planners, now assured of fighter support and an emergency strip, planned for a heavy strike at Wewak, timed to hit just after the arrival of substantial JAAF units. The Japanese finally discovered Tsili Tsili in early August, but the ruse had been executed. Some air attacks were mounted, but they merely served to illustrate that Japanese bombers did badly against U.S. fighters; they did little damage.

Wewak, like many areas along the New Guinea coast, had been harassed before. However, it was seriously assaulted for the first time on August 17, 1943, with a force of nearly 200 aircraft, representing a good percentage of Fifth Air Force's overall long-range strength. The first wave—B-24s—attacked at night. Apparently they did enough damage to the runway to prevent aircraft from taking off, but on the first day it made little difference. There was no radar at Wewak in August, and Japanese observers who spotted incoming B-25s down the coast telephoned Wewak itself. In a bizarre twist of fate, the telephone lines between intelligence and operations at the base were inoperative. The intelligence officer on duty ran onto the field trying to sound an alarm just as the strafers hit and destroyed forty aircraft on the ground. That was merely the first raid on Wewak. In the following weeks Wewak and many other targets were struck hard. In the process Fifth Air Force refined a deadly system for attacking airstrips. It proved so successful that the Japanese army air arm bled badly in New Guinea while inflicting very minor losses on Allied ships and airstrips.

As usual it is difficult to generalize about tactics, because each target was different and mission size varied greatly. However, in outline the 5th USAAF system for a large assault revolved around combining an advance attack by heavy bombers, followed by a strafer attack, with both covered by powerful fighter escort. Ideally this process would be repeated several times in a short period. Heavy bombers over time did tremendous damage to the facilities required to keep airfields running. In the short run, as shown by the August raids over Wewak, they could drop heavy bombs on the runway. If warned, a light Japanese fighter could often maneuver around craters and take off, but craters could slow the movement of the fighter to the strip. More importantly craters could prevent bombers from getting into the air. Japanese pioneers and servicemen worked hard to fill craters, and a field incapacitated or crippled one day could be in operation the next. However, Japanese pilots despised crude New Guinea runways, dangerous under the best of circumstances. When pounded by several raids, particularly by heavy bombs, runways became perilous to operations. The immediate danger, however, was a coordinated low-level raid coming out of nowhere. In that case fighters that did get off the ground still had to face a strafer blitz and fend off the bristling Allied fighter escort. This was a terrible combination for Japanese fighter pilots and bomber crews alike, and it no doubt presented a terrible physical and psychological burden to those on the ground. Ultimately antiaircraft and ground fire proved the most effective airfield defense, but it was not enough.

During the first raids in August the strafers struck hard, destroying forty planes on the ground in two days. Fifth Air Force claimed 175 aircraft destroyed on the ground in August. Rich Larsen of the 345th Bomb Group flew a 5th USAAF strafer:

It was much better to come in low because we moved so fast. They didn't hear us until we were upon them. The treetop level, I felt as safe as you could be. And I think the others did, too. They don't hear you and they don't see you. They may hear a rumble, but by the time they realize what it is you're on top of them, unless they have a view of you getting ready for your attack. At 5,000 feet you're in their sights for a long time. They can pump a lot of lead at you. Of course if something happened low there was nothing to do. We lost aircraft from ground fire, but I preferred low-level. There were some who didn't share that opinion, I know, but they were in the minority. We were pretty secure from fighters, too. The Japanese technique was to come straight down at you and go right through the formation and go right back up. And then turn around and go right back up and go through you again. Hit you from top and bottom. With strafers they couldn't do that. They had to come in from the side or rear. If a fighter makes a slip at ten feet above the ground he's done for.

When you pressed that fire button and fired all those machine guns the plane vibrated like crazy—that's a lot of lead flying out there. We'd go across abreast—wing tip to wing tip with maybe a whole squadron. So we'd make only one pass over the target. We'd keep the element of surprise. We'd sweep over the target, with twelve planes strung out maybe half a mile. Everybody was firing their guns. All you could see was a glow of flame about five–ten feet in front of the airplane. A blaze of fire coming out. Later on I thought, if you were on the ground, or sitting in an airplane, or in a ship—we'd fly two or three planes abreast against them—that it would scare the living bejeezus to see that kind of firepower coming at them.

Fred Miller was a crewman on a 5th USAAF B-25 and was convinced that lower was better:

Air bases were the most dangerous target because of the flak and small arms. Like Wewak—there was this little rise and on top was an ack-ack gun. It went off right in front of me. There weren't any windows on the side, and I could feel the heat from the blast on my face. That's how close we were to that gun. I don't know how it missed us, maybe it couldn't depress far enough so it fired over us. We had a saying that if you didn't hit any trees on the way in we were too high, if you didn't come back with green on the wing tips you might get clobbered. So on this mission I looked and saw that the planes on both sides of us were fifty feet lower than we were and I thought, "Oh, lord." We had a substitute pilot that day. I think, "We're going to get it." All of a

sudden we dropped straight down: I thought we're hit. But I think that
flak position showed our pilot what we meant by flying low. He told
me later that if I hadn't told him about how low to go he wouldn't have
believed it. He said he thought he was low until he saw all that black
smoke in front of us.

Phil Caputo manned the top turret on a strafer and had the kind of
freakish and instantaneous experience that could come from mowing
the grass:

Antiaircraft wasn't that big of a threat because we came in so low.
Light ground fire was the real danger. They had these little pits with
machine guns and light antiaircraft guns in them. You'd see the
parafrags float into them. The gun crew would look up watching these
things float down and jump. You'd have to be lucky to make it out. But
once we had a guy killed with a single shot. It was from some kind of
small arm. A bullet went right through his neck. It could have been a
pistol for all I know.

We had a few wounded, but that was pretty rare. It was much more
likely to live or get killed. I had a real scare. We were flying low, very
low, and some of the planes ahead had already dropped their bombs. I
turned to look over my left shoulder and my turret was covered with
blood. We were going fast and it was fresh: The air had blown it over
my turret and then blew it off. The moment I saw that blood I started
looking down at my own body, checking for hits. I'd heard you could
be hit and not know it, so I was frantically looking for a wound. Then
it dawned on me there was no wind rushing into the turret so I must be
okay. This all happens in seconds. It was instinct. I thought it over and
decided that a bomb hit someone on the ground and threw him up into
our prop. An arm or leg hit the turret. I didn't see anything, just the
blood, and the pilot flying wing staring over at me. We were that low. It
was hard to explain that kind of thing, it was so strange.

With the successful invasion of Lae and the seizure of Finschhafen a
few weeks later, Fifth Air Force seized three new bases that sealed the
doom of Wewak and, later, Hollandia. Lae and Gusap proved useful
for fighters. The real find was Nadzab, which over time replaced Dobodura as the major forward base for Fifth Air Force in New Guinea.
The August raids did not finish off Wewak. However, Colonel Rinuka
Kaneko, a staff officer of 8th Area Army, which controlled the Japanese 4th Air Army at Wewak, claimed shortly after the war that the
number of aircraft operating from Wewak dropped from a peak of

250 to 160 in three weeks (not factoring for reinforcement aircraft lost during the period). According to Kaneko the force was rebuilt to 200 aircraft until Fifth Air Force renewed the attacks in November. A final blitz during January-February reduced the total to well below 100. By April, 4th Air Army abandoned Wewak and 6th Air Division, which made up its heart, was considered destroyed. When the Americans struck Hollandia in June, the JAAF suffered another terrible loss.

The extent of the JAAF defeat at the hands of Fifth Air Force can be better appreciated by the postwar testimony of Lieutenant General Torashiro Kawabe, a top member of the JAAF staff in Tokyo until promoted in March 1943 and made commander of the entire JAAF in Manchuria. According to Kawabe, when he arrived in Manchuria there were some 1,500 aircraft manned by well-trained pilots and ready for battle. They did not have top-line aircraft and were an obvious reserve for pilots and maintenance personnel. Because operations in New Guinea became such a sinkhole for JAAF forces, Tokyo felt compelled to strip an entire theater and redeploy its forces to the Philippines, where they could better be allocated to fill the gaping holes appearing in the JAAF order of battle in late 1943. Torashiro spoke of it:

In July or August of 1943 the bulk of the planes were moved out of Manchuria. The reason for that was that most of the planes that were sent out to other fronts [from Japan] had been lost, and it was as replenishments that the planes were moved. Before I assumed my post in Manchuria, in about February of 1943, that was the first time that the Manchurian Air Force was called upon for planes and they went straight to Rabaul. The first ones sent out after I assumed my post went from July to August 1943 and, as I recall their destination was the Philippines. I never was aware of their destination. They just called for the planes and I turned them over. . . . As you know, the Solomons and Guadalcanal were followed by a move farther north, and the air strength from Malaya and that area was called on for replenishment in the New Guinea Area. They put up a very bad showing there, one after another being wiped out and leaving the general Philippine Area empty of planes. That was why the General staff ordered that the Philippine Area be reinforced, and it could also be called a replenishment center. The airplane production in the homeland was satisfactory. It was on the up-grade at that time but the training of personnel was not adequate and that was the reason that they had to call on such forces as from Manchuria. . . . But of the planes produced in the home country, we couldn't have one hundred percent of them in action at the destination.

One of the reasons for that low percentage of planes reaching the destination which were operational was that, unlike the United States, the maintenance bases en route were very poor. Only a small percentage actually became operational at the destination. . . . For the last six months that I was there [Manchuria] the actual planes which could be considered operational were nil—practically none.

As Fifth Air Force began to dismantle the JAAF, Halsey's airmen began a withering assault on the Bougainville base complex that guarded Rabaul. In many ways the reduction of Rabaul was Halsey's finest hour. By late 1943 the planning and logistic momentum was shifting toward Pearl Harbor and a proposed drive up the Central Pacific. Even at this late date it seemed to many that only one avenue of approach for the Americans was possible against the empire. Yet the geographic and military momentum was leading the Allies, whether some in the Pentagon wanted it or not, to the best possible solution: a twin advance against a weakened enemy.

The geographic momentum was simple enough. As MacArthur was quick to point out, Australia had provided an invaluable base. Australian troops and land-based airpower existed to take the Allies into the Philippines and Southeast Asia. (MacArthur's desire to leave Australia out of the Philippine operation was just becoming clear.) Once Fifth Air Force was in Luzon, all of Japan's island empire would be worth nothing. Furthermore MacArthur was learning how easy it would be to take large areas of territory by using a combination of powerful land-based airpower and fleet units. MacArthur's small Seventh Fleet did an extraordinary job considering its size. In addition, if Washington allowed MacArthur's forces to wither on the vine, they would not only condemn Anzac divisions to relative inactivity but also neutralize an American multidivision land force, increasing in quality with every month, a viciously effective air force, and an Allied navy that was proving good at making landings at important places. Those were excellent strategic assets to throw into the military dustbin.

From MacArthur's point of view King had made an agreement with MacArthur to attack or neutralize Rabaul, and he meant to hold King to it. By August the Pentagon had concluded that a direct attack on Rabaul was no longer necessary. Commanders of Seventh Fleet— "MacArthur's Navy"—wanted to secure the straits between New Britain and New Guinea; King had urged a direct attack on Buin in southern Bougainville; Halsey wanted no part of an attack on a Japanese island with a garrison four times the size of New Georgia's. Halsey thus countered with a proposal to establish bases on the small

Treasury Islands to the south of Bougainville and Choiseul Island to the east. Both objectives would help put the squeeze on Bougainville, yet they were still too far away to allow Allied fighters to shepherd the tactical bombers stationed in the Solomons to Rabaul. MacArthur requested that Halsey seize a position on Bougainville by early November, so his operations against western New Britain could commence in December, and that the air attack on Rabaul follow immediately thereafter.

Halsey made three decisions in the South Pacific that must rank him among the great admirals of history. The first was to send his surface forces into Ironbottom Sound during November 12–15, 1942; his victory there against uncertain odds had won the Guadalcanal campaign. The second was the Vella Lavella operation. Although in theory that operation was uncomfortably close to Japanese airpower, Halsey risked his warships and transports nonetheless; the victory destroyed Japan's position in the middle Solomons within hours at almost no cost. The third was the decision to attack Torokina beachhead (Empress Augusta Bay). There was nothing to recommend this area of Bougainville near the mouth of the Torokina River except three factors. First, the terrain was so miserable that the Japanese would not be there in force, an assumption that proved quite true. Second, Halsey and his staff had come a long way from New Georgia; they knew that a landing on Bougainville's western coast would trigger a Japanese reaction. Many of them welcomed the prospect—correctly, as events proved. Third, Halsey knew that if his Marines took the beachhead after a naval and air engagement he could hand the whole mess over to MacArthur, the Seventh Fleet, and Anzacs. Seabees and engineers, Halsey decided, could make an airstrip anywhere given a month and enough supplies. Considering the paper strengths of Japanese air and naval units the move on Empress Augusta Bay was a daring one. In fact it was excellent leadership: aggressive without being imprudent. Halsey knew his air units were numerous and good. Halsey also knew that his fleet was surpassing the ability of Japanese ships to fight at night. Halsey knew that in November 1943 the United States was launching a major new warship every week. And Halsey knew that if the occasion allowed he had aircraft carriers to put into the battle. Halsey and MacArthur during this period of World War II demonstrated leadership at its height. They probably shortened the Pacific war by at least three months and saved thousands of lives.

Taking the Torokina beachhead in Empress Augusta Bay appears in retrospect to have been a simple enough move. In practice, like all landings during that period of the war, it was based on shallow-draft landing craft like LSTs and LSIs in addition to smaller amphibious vehicles. All were vulnerable to air attack. To protect this operation and to continue sustained destruction against important targets, the Allied forces in the Solomons directed an effective and intelligent air offensive against the Bougainville bases.

In some ways Halsey's approach differed from that shown by Fifth Air Force. The mix of aircraft, regardless of geography, would have ensured a somewhat different course of events. The Marines already had a large number of tactical bombers in the Solomons. In the fall the USN temporarily released several squadrons, mostly Hellcat fighters, for land-based use because some of the carriers were not yet ready to handle full air groups. The USN was replacing the SBD Dauntless with the Curtiss Helldiver, but Marine pilots were delighted to be left behind on that adventure. In the background was Thirteenth Air Force with its B-24s, B-25s (including strafers), P-38s, P-39s, and New Zealand P-40s. On paper there were nearly 600 Allied aircraft available for use. Many never reached the front, but better than Fifth Air Force and far better than the Japanese, Allied commanders in the Solomons had a solid reserve to call upon.

The major targets in the Bougainville chain were Buin and Kahili, a few miles apart on southern Bougainville. Buka in the north of the island was a good base for bombers and helped protect Rabaul and Kavieng. Shortland Island was a well-fortified base just south of Buin. The plan devised by Halsey's airmen, until naval operations began, was simple enough: crush Buin and Kahili and damage everything else. As always it was American practice to never let a sector rest if it was within range. Large attacks alternated with smaller raids, which hopefully would bring Japanese fighters into the air where escorts could destroy them and kill the pilots.

After the New Georgia campaign there was almost no ground combat in the Solomons. (As mentioned above, the futile Japanese attacks of March 1944 at Torokina energized an Allied air arm that had little to do.) Consequently Allied bombers were attacking the Bougainville complex and Kavieng before Munda was taken. When Munda Point, Segi Point, and Vella Lavella became operational fighter havens supporting the bomber bases at Guadalcanal and the Russells, the Marines and Thirteenth Air Force enjoyed their choice of good fields. And their only major target was the Bougainville base complex. As the Allied chain of bases enlarged in the Solomons and New Guinea, the Japanese chain simultaneously decreased in size. It was still possible, as shown during the battles of November and January, for Tokyo to reinforce Rabaul, but its ability to reinforce a complex of bases began to die as the Bougainville shield collapsed.

Allied fighter pilots in the Solomons were also finding out that the Japanese were beginning to conserve their strength. Japanese fighter losses due to all causes had been so severe for the entire year that opposing every attack would have meant a rapid destruction of the force. In addition, Bougainville was well within the transport kill zone and had to be supplied by barge. Allied barge-busters helped keep Japanese forces short of important supplies. This was another cause for Japanese caution, for it lessened the ability to repair damaged planes. Sometimes fighters tried to stay hidden; sometimes they simply avoided combat; on other days they accepted battle, which always meant losses. However, nothing could hinder Japanese antiaircraft, substandard though it may be. Dangerous against medium bombers, it was more so against SBDs and Avengers. SBD pilot LeRoy Smith described a mission that went wrong:

Our briefing would be a giant map. We always took off during the dark, 4:30 A.M. or 5:00 A.M. If there was no new poop they'd let you sit in there and smoke and talk. Then some CO would waddle in and say, "This is it." Then he'd point out a gun that was giving us trouble. They'd say quiet that gun. Sometimes I'm not sure whether they cared how many dive-bombers they lost, you just had to quiet that gun because you'd keep the whole field suppressed for a while. Then the fighters can go swooping through there the whole day strafing and bombing. I can remember a day when there was a raid to Buka by Boyington's squadron, which we shared a field with. They decided to shoot up the tower. It was already on the radio. They took their F4Us and shot the hell out of the tower knowing we'd got the guns. The next day the Japs put some mounts there and they knocked down a fighter and the next day they called in the dive-bombers. It's nice to know you're wanted.

At Kavieng they had these mounts that we were told came off a damaged Japanese cruiser. They were right at the end of the runway. I think all twenty-eight of us went up. But they got us good and five of our planes didn't come back. Then two days later we had to go back after a different squad had been chopped up. Then some bright intelligence guy figures out that the Jap fire-control was on the other side of the runway—we were hitting the wrong place.

When you made your dive you wanted to get through that flak zone as soon as possible. They'd fire away before you made your run.

However, as soon as you rolled into your dive the people shooting at you usually ran for cover until the last plane got clear, then they'd be back in their revetments shooting again, but now they're shooting at your ass end. I think flak in the South Pacific was a lot less than in Europe, but it picked away at our squadrons. The losses mounted up. When we weren't bombing guns, we'd hit strips. There might be twenty-eight of us on a run, a pretty big attack. If we got those 1,000-pound bombs on the runway they couldn't fix it in a night. The 500- or 100-pound bombs could get fixed sooner. But we'd still pound away at them.

Several TBF squadrons participated in the last offensives. In the Solomons the torpedoes were left at base, and Avengers began glide-bombing airstrips. The TBF carried a good-size bomb load, so the aircraft was well suited to pounding airstrips. Like SBDs, however, they were vulnerable to Japanese flak. Harold Raney was in the turret of an Avenger and described a glide-bomb run on a Japanese airstrip:

We bombed airstrips in the Central Solomons and then moved up farther after Munda was captured. We'd come in over target about 10,000–12,000 feet and the pilots would align themselves in a straight line. The lead pilot would rock wings back and forth and then peel off into what they called a "glide." Maybe they could have picked a better name because the dive was quite steep. The TBF was a tough plane and could take a fast dive and we wanted to get rid of our bombs and get out of flak range in a hurry. I'd watch the plane behind me and I could see when the pilot released the bomb with a jerk and it would slowly separate from the plane and descend. Naturally my real job was to look for Japanese fighters. Thanks to escorts we didn't see many of them. What we did see was black puffs of smoke exploding all around us. At first they were maybe fifty feet behind us. Evidently those gunners on the ground weren't too accurate or maybe we were going faster than they thought. On succeeding trips these puffs got closer and closer. Sometimes I'd look out my escape hatch and there'd be antiaircraft puffs that seemed to be exploding maybe ten or fifteen feet away. One time I looked up at the pilot behind us, and just as the bomb separated from the bomb bay there was a black puff that I could have sworn had exploded in the bomb bay. Fortunately we all survived that one.

One day they finally hit us. I felt a great jolt: It felt like the plane stopped. My escape hatch blew out and the horizontal stabilizer on the port side disappeared. It was as though we stopped, went up, but then started to fall. It seemed like a long time but it was probably a few seconds. The pilot called on the intercom asking if everything was all right back there. Myself and the radioman said we were okay. The pilot said, "Hold on, let's see what we can do with this machine." Slowly I felt the plane begin to respond to the pilot's controls. He was trying to pull it up, out of the dive. After a bit we were flying right over the airstrip we'd bombed so many times. After we got to the end of the strip we were out over the ocean. The pilot decided to try to make it to Rendova. We felt the nose kept coming up but we continued to go down. Finally when we reached the island I looked over my gun and could see trees. I looked down and could see the ground maybe fifteen feet below us, but we were flying level. We got back or I probably wouldn't be talking right now. The landing was not the most smoothest in the world as we wobbled from side to side. We pulled over to our revetment and got out. We were very glad to feel the ground. That was the last time that plane made a mission.

Under the weight of the massed attacks the Bougainville bases began to collapse. In July 1943 Rabaul had integrated 150 aircraft from CARDIV 2 into 26th Air Flotilla and sent them to relieve the already battered units at Buin. Masatake Okumiya was at Buin during those dark hours for the empire. He watched with horror as malnutrition began to affect the eyesight of his pilots and the health of his entire unit. He described conditions in September:

The continual air battles against the savagely fighting Americans exacted a heavy and steady toll on our men. The constant fighter-plane interceptions and bombing missions meant that hardly a day passed without men dying or receiving serious wounds. The pilots and air crews did not honestly expect to survive their Buin duty tour, for the steady loss of men meant that no one could predict the time of his own passing. I could not understand the attitude of our Navy command, which treated its men with unnecessary harshness and apparent disregard. Of the one hundred and fifty air-crew members who had arrived one month ago with me at Buin, at least fifty were dead. Before another month passed we were certain that more than one half of the remaining men also would be lost. Here at Buin we suffered most heavily in the loss of our lieutenant JG [junior-grade] personnel, who formed the nucleus of the fighter pilots. Thirteen of these men had arrived in the South Pacific eighteen months ago; only one was still alive.

Okumiya was transferred back to Japan to help rebuild CARDIV 2 before he returned with it in January to participate in the last act at Rabaul. His staff at Buin, however, kept him fully informed of events. In October Buin was finished:

> By mid-October the enemy air raids against the 26th Air Flotilla at Buin had become intolerable. With its base constantly subjected to enemy bombs and strafing attacks, with living facilities reduced to the lowest possible level, and with a mounting loss of supply ships, the Navy pulled out, moving its strength directly to Rabaul. . . . The Navy could not continue to bear indefinitely the ever-increasing enemy air strength, and our position deteriorated rapidly.

This was not a move made lightly at Rabaul. Buin, along with Kahili, was the strongest imperial base at Bougainville and expected to be attacked in the near future. If Bougainville was lost, then Rabaul would be open to all-out assault. After the war American interrogators asked Captain Takashi Miyazaki, a senior staff officer of 25th Air Flotilla at Rabaul throughout most of the war, at what point the staff at Rabaul thought the Solomons campaign was lost. Miyazaki answered simply, "In October 1943 when 26th Air Flotilla withdrew their planes from Buin."

The Torokina landing took place on November 1, 1943. After the expected Japanese air attack failed to seriously damage landing operations, an American beachhead was secure within two days. Within weeks three airstrips were available on the western coast of Bougainville. The final assault on Rabaul was ready from the point of view of Allied forces in the Solomons. Courtesy of Fifth Air Force, the attack had already begun.

In early October 1943 Rabaul appeared to be set up for the kill. The number of aircraft at the base was not much more than 150, and the Bougainville shield, fielding a comparable number of aircraft, was collapsing. Halsey and his officers had planned for the landing at Torokina. MacArthur had decided to take Cape Gloucester and the Aware Islands on the western side of New Britain. Naturally the two forces promised simultaneous support; naturally nothing went as planned. Nevertheless the Japanese air garrison was in a trap in Rabaul: It could fight until destroyed, flee, or be reinforced. Following the September decision in Tokyo to defend the South Pacific to the last as a means of delaying Allied moves elsewhere, the Japanese fell into one of their worst air defeats of the war.

Fifth Air Force had long attacked Rabaul with great élan but with mixed results. In the fall Australian and American engineers developed fighter bases for P-38s on small islands southwest of Rabaul. The bombers needed no help. Bombers based at Dobodura and Moresby had a final act to play before being moved north. The first attack on Rabaul took place on October 12, 1943. Unlike earlier raids this attack was mounted during daylight and was huge. It included more than 100 B-25 strafers, forty heavy bombers, and a large escort of P-38s. It was a major success but did not live up to expectations. The men attacking Rabaul knew it was well defended. They respected this fact at a time when U.S. bombers in Europe were defying both fighters and antiaircraft. Nighttime bombing attacks on Rabaul and accurate reconnaissance gave the pilots of Fifth Air Force an excellent idea that Rabaul's antiaircraft and fighter defenses were far greater than anything attacked in New Guinea.

Rich Walker was a pilot of one of the B-25s on the first attack:

Rabaul was the hardest target without a doubt. It was heavily defended, hard to get to. After a while you begin to think like, "Well, it's just another mission." But some missions were a lot more dangerous than others and you knew that. We recently had a reunion and one pilot was talking about looking at the crews before the first raids on Rabaul and he said those crews looked scared to death. We never thought of it that way, but we wondered how we would have enough courage to get into that airplane. Everybody knew on a tough one that chances were not everyone was coming back: And in the back of your mind you'd think, "Is it going to be me?" But that was normal in our business. You can't believe what you had to fly through at Rabaul. They had four aerodromes, so there were fighters. All that naval ordnance. It was pretty exciting.

In our big Rabaul raid we only lost one plane. It's shaped like a bowl—we came in from the east to attack shipping in Simpson Harbor. I had the inside element, line-abreast of twelve aircraft. I knew if any of these guys turned into me they'd stall me out. So when I came to the turning point I turned right away; my wing went with me. The others kept on going so there were only two of us heading for the harbor. My wingman was shot down almost immediately. I put it down right on the water and told my copilot to hold his feet on the throttle. We went through there wide-open on the deck. We lined up on this freighter, the first one that was in front of us, I sure wasn't being choosy. We got to the drop point and let fly. I pulled the stick back and don't have any idea why we didn't take the ship's superstructure with us we passed so close, and right back down to the deck. As we kept flying we went right over an airfield and got greeted there, too. But we made it through and headed for home. You can see the flak vividly. It's busting all around you and the flash of the guns on the ground is very visible. Most guys aren't sightseeing: You're much better off to just focus on the target and don't think about flak.

Protected by observation posts and radar, Rabaul was difficult to attack by surprise. The October 12 attack, however, was the first, and the Japanese were not prepared. Strafer pilot Robert Larsen encountered, to his advantage, the kind of misidentification of aircraft that both sides suffered throughout the war:

On my first mission to Rabaul we got a green light from a guy in the tower. He didn't know we were enemy. He was so surprised. We had just come in over the water, popped up over this ridge, and then right in front of us was this airfield with aircraft all over. The guy in the tower probably didn't know a B-25 from a locomotive. He gave us the green light to land. We didn't land. We blew him out of his tower. We dropped parafrags and larger bombs at the same time we were shooting. Against a low-level attack there was no real defense. We destroyed many airplanes that day.

On the first day the strafers of Fifth Air Force destroyed at least forty aircraft. The small number of Japanese fighters that got in the air suffered from the escorts. Strafers and B-24s claimed a substantial number of hits against the large merchant and naval force in Simpson Bay. The Japanese later claimed that only one ship was sunk, but twenty merchantmen were damaged to one degree or another. Fifth Air Force made a number of other raids against Rabaul until the end of November. More planes were caught on the ground and more Zeros killed in the air. However, American losses mounted considerably, with fourteen aircraft lost on November 2. Admiral Halsey was not happy with this performance when he believed, correctly, that his invasion force was the major target for Japanese aircraft in the area.

Under most circumstances the early raids against Rabaul by Fifth Air Force would have been considered a great success. Kenney, however, was a MacArthur man and always willing to promise a great deal and, if the promise was not met, to claim a phantom victory. Kenney's victory claims in his memoirs were seriously inflated. Having to face a large buildup of powerful enemy forces, the Japanese had some very good fortune in October. Attacking Rabaul from Dobodura was a long stretch, and for many days the weather stopped or disrupted 5th USAAF attacks. Had the weather been good Kenney's forces would have undoubtedly applied the 5th USAAF treatment to Rabaul with considerable effect. For the tactics applied to Wewak, Hollandia, and many other bases it was necessary for the attack to be incessant. In the event, Fifth Air Force made periodic attacks throughout October and early November on Rabaul. Had there been five days of good weather, the largest air battle of the Pacific war would have taken place, and Fifth Air Force would have an excellent chance to win it. Instead, while Halsey was preparing the Torokina invasion, Japan's CARDIV 1, some 200 aircraft strong, came from Truk to Rabaul along with a large surface fleet. It is one of the great ironies of the South Pacific air war that Japanese forces reached their peak at Rabaul and nearby bases at well more than 400 planes. In addition, the pipeline of reinforcements continued and another 150 planes from CARDIV 2 would come in January. The rabbit was indeed caught in the snare.

As events played out, the aircraft of Fifth Air Force probably weakened the Rabaul garrison more by defending their own invasion fleets and fighting over landing zones in New Britain than by attacking Rabaul. (Fifth Air Force did prevent the JAAF from fighting for Rabaul. The JAAF could have added at least 400 aircraft to the defense had supplies been adequate. Fifth Air Force continued high-altitude attacks on Rabaul throughout the campaign. As discussed in earlier sections, the IJN took serious losses in New Guinea before handing the theater over to the IJA in the summer of 1943.) In late October the Japanese made one of their last major raids on Allied shipping in Oro Bay, failing to do substantial damage but adding greatly to the scores of 5th USAAF aces. In December MacArthur sent U.S. Army forces against the Arawe Islands in southwestern New Britain. The Japanese attacked the landings vigorously with planes from Rabaul and what was left at Gasmata. The Japanese ground defense was skilled but in vain: Dozens of Japanese tactical aircraft and fighters died in a useless attempt to prevent the landings. Two weeks later the Marines attacked, for the only time under MacArthur's command, Cape Gloucester on the western tip of New Britain. Even more Japanese aircraft opposed that landing, and just as many were shot down. It is likely that the Japanese lost some seventy aircraft attacking Allied shipping and trying to defend the two beachheads. They were planes that Rabaul could not afford to lose when it suffered under the brilliant and vicious assault launched by Admiral Halsey's airmen in the Solomons.

It was justice of a sort that the Marine pilots and aircrews, who flirted with strategic and personal oblivion during the Guadalcanal campaign, were primarily responsible for the final destruction of Japanese airpower at Rabaul. It was also fitting that their campaign received a tremendous boost from Thirteenth Air Force, whose original pilots had flown so intrepidly at Guadalcanal in inferior aircraft. The continued assistance of New Zealand's fighters and patrol bombers was greatly appreciated in one of World War II's most polyglot commands. There was also a symmetry in the fact that the last act at Rabaul was initiated by the worst possible occurrence from the Japanese point of view: the return of U.S. aircraft carriers to the battle.

By November 1943 both sides had constructed new carriers. The Americans, however, were launching one large carrier including escorts almost every month. Prior to January 1, 1944, the USN launched eight *Essex*-class heavy carriers and nine *Independence*-class light carriers. The new heavies were improved versions of the *Enterprise* and carried 100 aircraft. The smaller carriers, designed for speed, armament, and range, sacrificed aircraft strength and could launch fifty aircraft of any type. More of both classes entered service in 1944. Behind them were dozens of escort carriers, which were essentially converted merchantmen that carried between twenty-five and forty aircraft but were slow and could not carry the most advanced navy warplanes. To this group should be added the ancient *Saratoga*, which along with HMS *Victorious* (relieved in late summer 1943, much to the delight of its sweltering crew, from service in the South Pacific) had been Halsey's only active carrier during a tense period of battle in the summer of 1943. *Enterprise*, America's greatest warship, joined the team in early 1944 as the single carrier that specialized in night combat, the doorway through which carrier aviation had to pass to enter the postwar world.

Halsey's brilliant carrier raid was a part of a battle that never was. Relying on valid early-war experiences, Admiral Nimitz and subordinates in October 1943 sent the new carriers on raids into the Gilbert and Marshall Islands to see how the new ships and aircraft performed. During that period the Hellcat was general issue, the Helldiver dive-bomber replacing the Dauntless. The Americans were spoiling for a fight. What they did not know was that the Japanese, with new carriers and carrier groups of their own, were also searching for a battle. When the Americans withdrew from the Central Pacific, for the moment, they left behind a Japanese fleet that was in pursuit. It was one of the great missed opportunities of the war. There can be little doubt that the Americans would have crushed the Japanese and perhaps hastened war's end. For the moment, however, the USN's new weapons returned to Pearl Harbor with their very limited mission accomplished.

For the first time the great Central Pacific–versus–Southwest Pacific debate was coming to the front and center throughout the theater. Indirectly the Japanese brought matters to a head, with perhaps historic results. In late October Japanese aircraft sighted the Allied fleet that was landing New Zealand troops on the Treasury Islands. This led Admiral Minechi Koga, the commander of Combined Fleet, to send nearly 200 aircraft of CARDIV 1, the best aircraft available to the JNAF, to Rabaul. Koga also deployed a powerful force of heavy cruisers, hoping to duplicate the Battle of Savo Island off the coast of Bougainville. The battle was already in progress. Despite the misgivings of many officers, Admiral Junichi Kusaka, who was overall commander at Rabaul, sent two heavy and two light cruisers with several destroyers directly to Empress Augusta Bay on Bougainville. Awaiting him on November 3, 1943, was a U.S. task force of destroyers and "light" cruisers. (American light cruisers were classified by armament, not by weight, and the new *Cleveland*-class U.S. cruisers that fought at Augusta Bay carried twelve six-inch guns and ten five-inch guns and displaced more than 10,000 tons; a Japanese light cruiser might be an overgrown destroyer.) In a night battle, the USN soundly defeated the Japanese force. Well-aimed fire and a series of collisions brought about by USN torpedo attacks sunk one light cruiser and one destroyer and damaged another cruiser and two destroyers. The Japanese column had to return to Rabaul in complete defeat.

The defeated force entered Rabaul and met a column of eight Japanese cruisers that had arrived at dawn on November 5 and were refueling in preparation for a massive attack on the U.S. ships defending Torokina. Halsey had advance knowledge of Japanese movements and had two carriers available and another three on the way. Yet to protect Torokina he did not have the option of waiting for reinforcements. Although Halsey believed the Japanese cruiser force would be inside Rabaul Harbor, he still had to deal with nearly 400 aircraft, many with carrier training, the actions of which he could not predict. Coolly Halsey sent the veteran *Saratoga*, which possessed the best-trained air group in the Pacific, along with the new light carrier *Independence*. Launching east of Rabaul, Halsey relied on ground-based fighters for cover and sent the entire carrier force toward Rabaul. Perhaps seventy Japanese fighters were alerted by radar and in the air awaiting the strike. Realizing the priority, the U.S. fighter pilots ignored the imperial fighters and stayed with the bombers, flying with them through Japanese flak, until the critical seconds prior to attack. Confused for a moment by this unusual tactic and reluctant to enter their own flak in pursuit, the Japanese fighters could not touch the U.S. bombers as they undertook their attack runs. Ultimately the defenders downed ten U.S. aircraft, with probably equal losses, but watched the *Saratoga's* planes damage six Japanese cruisers, several severely. Defeated twice in three days, the Japanese warships withdrew to the dubious safety of Truk. Bougainville was safe.

Six days later five U.S. carriers struck Rabaul. One Japanese destroyer was sunk, one cruiser and one destroyer damaged. Considering the size of the strike, the bag was disappointing. The new task force—which included the new heavy carriers *Essex* and *Bunker Hill* along with *Independence*—had found few warships to strike and received a warm welcome from Japanese fighters. The ships soon came under attack by perhaps 100 of Rabaul's land-based aircraft, most from CARDIV 1. The Japanese counterattack taught U.S. fighter pilots some unpleasant lessons about coordination and ship defense. The first group of Japanese attack aircraft slipped through with little interference. Future ace Ted Crosby was on *Bunker Hill* that day and recalled that the air units had good weapons but were not seasoned:

> Rabaul was my first combat mission and afterward I wondered if I had got the right training. We had combat veterans on the ship, but most of us were new at the game. I just didn't have a concept of what was going on around. I was flying wing on my division leader like we were on a parade. I was too close. I was mimicking every one of his moves. So I missed what was going on because I was glued on my leader. I never did that again. I backed off to where I could see as much of what was going on as the guy I was flying with. The first thing that scared the hell out of me was when my section leader shot down a Zero. I'm right on his wing, and the first time I see the Zero he's going over us smoking. I have no idea of when my leader opened fire because I was tucked in too close on his wing. It was startling to see a burning fighter fly over you and not see what had made him burn. We knew from the radio and we could see them taking off from Rabaul. We could see 'em taking off four at a time. So I was wondering what was I doing wrong. When I backed off we joined up with retreating bombers and that kept the Japanese away from them. I was sure we had better pilots and better planes and soon I was proved right. But the first big fight was a learning experience for many of us.

The attacking airmen from the new carriers might have had some bad luck on the mission, but their commanders were sharp. Although initially badly protected because of a serious problem in vectoring fighters, the new carriers maneuvered skillfully and avoided all bombs that dropped nearby. It is no doubt fortunate they did not face the pilots who attacked *Hornet* a year before. Nevertheless after some very anxious moments all three carriers were safe; their Hellcats found the rest of the attackers and smashed them.

The carrier raid had one immediate effect: Major Japanese warships, many limping, left Rabaul. However, the retreat of Combined Fleet from Rabaul had far greater ramifications than an end to attacks on Bougainville. (A U.S. destroyer flotilla under legendary Rear Admiral Arleigh Burke finished the surface war in the theater when it attacked five Japanese destroyers attempting to evacuate Buka on November 25, 1943, sinking three without suffering a scratch.) Rabaul's commanders knew that another carrier raid was possible, that Fifth Air Force might return, and that a huge offensive was going to come from the Solomons. In December there were some fifty merchant ships of all sizes in Rabaul landing supplies of all kinds—enough to keep the 60,000-man garrison alive until war's end. However, the kill zone against merchant ships was established by definition when imperial warships left; the last merchant ship left Rabaul in March 1944. The great base was stripped of its ability to supply complex operations of any kind. Relying on extensive supplies at hand, the only thing it could do was defend its air units for a few weeks and keep its garrison ready for months. Halsey soon left the theater for greater fame, but his operations at Bougainville, followed by the carrier raids, were that of a wizard.

By December 1943 Rabaul was alone in the South Pacific. Still being hit occasionally by Fifth Air Force, it was also being bombarded by heavy and medium bombers of Thirteenth Air Force. In early December the first fighter base was operating at Bougainville. By the end of the month another fighter base was up along with a medium-bomber strip. The Solomon air command could call upon 500 combat-ready aircraft at this time within or close to Rabaul. Standing behind them were excellent reserves.

Rabaul was smashed in much the same way that Fifth Air Force had created its victims. However, the grim procedure took longer because of Rabaul's great advantage (beyond good antiaircraft): size. The major fields were many miles apart, and neutralizing one still allowed resistance from another. Yet Rabaul had another advantage: Because it was a base for so long, its garrison was able to collect a quantity of basic supplies that were much more elaborate than normal for a Japanese base. Yet the advantage was fleeting, as the garrison defending the base was so large itself. Some categories of basic supplies were used up quickly, and rations were cut back before the end of January. Nothing the Japanese did made the area safe to live in. Malaria, dengue, and jungle rot plagued the garrison, fliers included. When CARDIV 2 brought in the last group of effective fighting aircraft, all of its staff was hospitalized with malaria or dengue within three weeks. Yet as long as the Japanese were willing to reinforce the base from Truk, this base could serve as an unsinkable aircraft carrier. In December and January Marine and USAAF pilots sunk it.

By the beginning of 1944 the Allies were learning much about destroying air bases. Three lessons were basic. First, major bombing attacks should be heavily escorted by fighters. Until January a well-run attack on Rabaul would include two fighters for every single-engine bomber. Second, the attack should hit every component of the base—air and ground. Making the brutal climate of the area an ally, the attackers should make incessant physical labor a part of life. Turning good fields into swamps with heavy bombs was important. Third, there should be no respite. It was vital to make the fighters fly, the guns fire, and the bases' resources dissipate.

The Marine and USAAF attack on Rabaul brought this system to perhaps its highest peak. Often the escorts would be deadly Corsairs flown by the Black Sheep and Jolly Rogers; they might also be the lethal P-38s that covered the bombing raids of Thirteenth Air Force. Thirteenth Air Force and New Zealand P-40s and P-39s continued to soldier on into this period, even as both were being replaced by Corsairs. Because Allied fighters were so numerous and deadly, Rabaul's air officers cautioned their fighters against engaging escorts unless the situation was right. No doubt this was a sound order, but it created at Rabaul exactly the same situation faced by the P-39 "fishing fleet" of early 1942. The result was predictable: Corsairs, Lightnings, and Hellcats (there were several land-based squadrons active) would cover the flight and after the attack would strafe positions. Soon enough fighters were carrying bombs, which they could jettison in case of opposition; they were assuming they would meet none. The targets of the SBDs, TBFs, and fighter-bombers were gun emplacements, aircraft on the runway, and shipping. LeRoy Smith did not like Rabaul:

> In the early stages when we hit Rabaul, it was a real killer. It was worse than Kavieng. We would lose aircraft every mission. It had a mountain and a harbor. There was only one way for a dive-bomber to attack those fields and harbor: You had to get low. Because you couldn't get back high again to clear the next hill, they could bang away at you on

the way in and the way out. That long haul out to the open sea was a real tough run. Rabaul was terrible place.

If Japanese accounts are at all accurate, Smith was on the mark. Lieutenant General Rimpei Kato, chief of staff at Rabaul and head of the antiaircraft effort, estimated that the Japanese shot down 400 Allied aircraft during the attacks on Rabaul. He estimated that 100 fell to fighters, 300 to antiaircraft; 90 percent were SBDs and other single-engine aircraft making ground attacks. These figures are higher than those found in some U.S. sources (as usual, none are in agreement) but show the relative vulnerability of a single-engine aircraft when attacking low.

The SBD and fighter-bomber attacks were increasingly effective as the basic structure of the four major airfields was obliterated. This job was largely up to TBFs making medium-altitude bomb runs and, more importantly, on the medium and heavy bombers of Thirteenth Air Force. Because the medium-altitude attack (there were no true high-level attacks in the Pacific after 1942) seems in retrospect inappropriate for a theater without cities and factories, its importance has been badly underrated. Early-war high-level attacks on shipping and ground targets rarely succeeded because the targets were so difficult to hit and the number of planes so small. By late 1943, however, the equation had changed. A medium-level run had a great advantage over other types of attack. It was not vulnerable to low-level antiaircraft. All medium and heavy bombers attacking in daylight had fighter support, so Zero defensive attacks were rare and almost welcomed, at least by the escorts. In addition, a 1,000- or 500-pound bomb dropped from 12,000 feet penetrated deeply and made an excellent crater. And any facilities identified prior to attack were vulnerable to high-explosive bombs dropped by a good bombardier. Dismantling the fields and destroying the buildings and tents required to keep Japanese aircraft in the air thus had a devastating effect in the long run. But in the short run even a medium-level bombing mission was not something that most crewmen relished. Charles Kittell of Thirteenth Air Force was on several bombing strikes against Rabaul:

When we bombed Rabaul high we always went in at 12,000–17,000 feet for some reason. I don't know why. You'd look around and you couldn't see the other airplanes because the sky was so filled with flak. Why they didn't hit more of us I don't know. Once we got 97 percent of the bombs on the runway, or so we were told by intelligence. In this type of mission it was critical to be close because we all dropped when the leader did. So we dropped very tight. You were within three or four feet of the leader's wing tip during a bomb run—you had to be for accuracy's sake, with flak going off all the time.

Edward Brisck, like Kittell, flew a 13th USAAF B-25 against Rabaul:

When we went medium-level you had a lead plane with bombardier. We flew on his wing and dropped with him. We had some top-notch lead bombardiers. One guy was terrific. One of the worst things is to get on a long bomb run. Eighth Air Force had five-minute runs. Man, just straight ahead, kill the drift, hold the altitude, and that's deadly flying through antiaircraft. Our guy was so good he would take us on runs of less than a minute and he hit the target—that's good. I was always happy to see him on the mission. But you would get hit. Flak sounded like little pings—like hunks of metal hitting the plane. The shells would explode and you'd catch little bits of shrapnel. If you took a direct hit it was all over for your aircraft.

There's been a lot of psychological analysis since the war, but at the time stress and tension were not in vogue. You didn't do any self-analysis. You would just grit your teeth and hold your position in the formation and concentrate on your job. I'd say it was tougher on the crewmen that didn't have a job during the run like I did. When we went on medium-level missions we left our navigator behind because the lead plane did that. We lost our bombardier with the strafer modifications. But the copilot and radio operator really didn't have anything to do during the run. That had to be tense. I was very busy keeping formation and waiting for the lead plane to open bay doors and drop, and the gunners were scanning for fighters. But the movies are pretty accurate: You'd see these black puffs, and if they found your altitude you'd worry a lot more. But what the hell, you were committed, so straight ahead.

After the war Commander Okumiya, who had suffered through the collapses of both Buin and Rabaul and thus understood well how a Japanese base slowly died, discussed with American officers the relative dangers posed by different types of Allied aircraft:

B-24s were the most effective on land bases. Because our fields were few, it was the size of the bomb that did the harm. Little ones didn't do much harm. The number of crashes attempting to land on damaged fields was very great after B-24 raids. In a place like Rabaul where there were many fields, big bombs were not such a determining factor because we could land on an auxiliary field. Bombing effectiveness depends on the target. The main thing that bothered us in operation was having several fields hit at the same time, leaving nothing to be used as auxiliary. . . . There were many ships sunk by dive-bombers.

Okumiya also discussed the deadly effect that carrier raids had on the major Japanese base at Truk, pointing out that they could make multiple raids in a single day. At Rabaul the carriers launched only two raids. However, as the Torokina bases developed through December, Rabaul in essence had an aircraft carrier on its doorstep and was attacked incessantly by SBDs and TBFs. But they were not the only problem faced by the Japanese. Vice Admiral Jinichi Kusaka, the overall naval commander at Rabaul, singled out the B-25 strafers and their parafrags as the most effective weapon against planes on the ground, noting that "the low-level attacks did not give them [Japanese pilots] sufficient time to get their planes into the air and they were invariably taken by surprise."

Although a 5th USAAF trademark, the B-25 squadrons of Thirteenth Air Force were also using strafers with deadly effect. Pilot Edward Brisck described a strafer mission over Rabaul; the missed rendezvous between bombers and fighters he described was all too common. However, with the Japanese fighter strength wearing down and strafers on the loose, Brisck's unit got aggressive:

Low-level runs were risky but an extraordinary experience. You didn't want to take a hit down there but you were sure firing back. Several missions we caught them by surprise. You'd see Japanese coming out of their foxholes pulling on their pants. We caught them by complete surprise near Rabaul once. We had a briefing and a takeoff shortly after midnight. We were supposed to rendezvous with forty navy fighters. The idea was to be near Rabaul exactly at daybreak so we had enough light to see the target. We take off, look down, and see all sorts of lights circling and off we go thinking we've got a large escort. There were two squadrons of bombers, a total of twenty-four planes altogether. I was a flight leader. One of the escorts had gotten separated and was flying along and turned his landing lights on trying to read the numbers on our tail to see which way his flight was. Up toward Green Islands we had to turn all of our lights off. We had little blue lights on top of the aircraft . . . formation lights, but they are very hard to see. So we head toward Rabaul. Dawn begins to break, we look around, and we have one fighter with us. One squadron leader decided to abort with no cover. Away they went. My squad leader said, "I don't see any fighters, let's hit them." We spread out and hit Vunakanau strip. We were twelve abreast with our one fighter. There were a lot of planes on the ground, a lot of revetments. That's when you bore in. When you see something to shoot at, you do it. We dropped our bombs over revetments if possible then peeled off to make our escape over Simpson Harbor. As we broke over a cliff toward the harbor we saw a line of Japanese ships beneath us that had pulled into Simpson and they were all shooting at us. That navy fighter got right down on the deck and started strafing those ships, taking the heat off us, and got the hell out of there. When you start on the run all twelve machine guns are firing. They quit one by one due to overheating or jamming. In the last two or three seconds you've got one gun going "put-put-put." But it was extremely exciting, hard to describe. Once you start a low-level run there was really no sense in sweating. Everything was so fast and you were very busy.

Rabaul did not go quietly, but signs of breakdown were clear by mid-November. With all chance of delivering a defeat to U.S. and New Zealand forces in the Bougainville area gone, CARDIV 1 began to depart within three weeks of arrival. It had lost nearly half of its 180 aircraft and a much high percentage of valuable attack planes. As should have been obvious to Imperial High Command, the Allied air attack on Rabaul had only begun and would reach a fever pitch in the weeks to follow. That was the logic, of course, to the Torokina operation. Although Fifth Air Force was occupied on New Britain and Wewak (again), a renewed attack from that quarter could come at a moment's notice. The RAAF began a steady nighttime bombing campaign of Rabaul's installations with Beauforts, adding to the physical and psychological attrition. Combined Fleet had left Rabaul, leaving the merchant shipping in dreadful danger. Japanese intelligence realized that the Americans were preparing to strike toward the Gilbert and Marshall Islands—the open guns of the Central Pacific drive. Everything argued for withdrawal.

Instead the Japanese believed they were tying down more forces than they were spending. In the very short run this was true. However, the weeks (or days) they were gaining would later be given back in months lost. Industrial production in Japan, crippled by a miserable system of strategic distribution, could barely keep up with the losses of aircraft. To the end, at Rabaul, there were more pilots than planes. Pilot training was being cut back to man the aircraft coming off the assembly lines. Furthermore those new planes, although technically superior to their predecessors, soon began to suffer from serious problems in workmanship and cut-corners due to the lack of strategic resources.

Fuel shortages began to plague air and naval forces alike. The merchantmen and aircraft squandered at Rabaul after mid-November 1943 were second-rate in Allied terms but of reasonably sound stock in Japanese. Instead of attempting some sort of deceit (such as bogus planes combined with multiple patrols that would avoid combat whenever possible, which would have kept the Allies bombing away happily at Rabaul for weeks) the Japanese reinforced.

As always the numbers are not certain. After CARDIV 1 left the theater Rabaul still had some 140 aircraft, with a few more still on Bougainville. It is not recorded, but one might assume that an average of fifty replacement aircraft came into the theater during November; another forty joined in December. In addition, some ninety aircraft—70 percent of the fighters of CARDIV 2—joined the battle in late January. I would estimate that the Japanese threw away at least 250 airplanes, piloted by some of the best men available, for no reason whatsoever. And dozens of merchant ships were sunk and damaged while unloading at and leaving Rabaul. It is difficult to believe that the Japanese needed reconfirmation that SBDs and TBFs could sink ships, yet they found it in the waters in and near Rabaul.

Day in and day out Allied bombers struck Rabaul. When the Allied machine was rolling the numbers of attacking aircraft were staggering in South Pacific terms. In January 1944 263 sorties were flown by B-24s, 180 by B-25s, 386 by SBDs, and 227 by Avengers. Those bombers were accompanied by 1,850 fighter sorties. In the first three weeks of February the sortie numbers are just as startling: 256 Liberators, 263 Mitchells, 244 Avengers, and 573 SBDs. The total fighter sorties declined to 1,600 because Japanese interceptors were becoming more difficult to find. In other words 2,400 bombers of all types, escorted by 3,500 fighters, were over Rabaul during seven weeks. These figures are for the Thirteenth and do not include attacks made by Fifth Air Force and Anzac units.

The consequences to Japanese forces were simple enough. There were roughly 130 aircraft in 26th Air Flotilla in mid-January; knowing they were ruined as a force, Koga ordered their relief by CARDIV 2. Allied reconnaissance did not notice any decrease in Rabaul's strength in this period, so it is likely that the aircrews were flown out by air transport and the planes left for replacement pilots and to serve as a reserve for CARDIV.

When Masatake Okumiya returned to Rabaul with CARDIV 2 he was shocked by the psychological condition of the men he had left a few months before. As Okumiya recalled, "Now they [the pilots he had led at Buin] were quick tempered and harsh, their faces grimly set.

The fighting spirit which enabled us to ignore the worst of Buin was gone. The men lacked confidence; they appeared dull and apathetic." Okumiya found this decay afflicted everyone regardless of rank:

> The endless days and nights became a nightmare. The young faces became only briefly familiar, then vanished forever into a bottomless abyss created by American guns. Eventually some of our higher staff officers came to resemble living corpses, bereft of spiritual and physical strength. Neither did the Navy ever consider the problems of our base maintenance personnel, who for months worked like slaves. They lived under terrible conditions, rarely with proper food or medical treatment.

As Okumiya made clear, the men were reacting to a reality of war, not some form of panic. They believed they were losing, and they were right:

> I found on my arrival at Rabaul an astonishing conviction that the war could not possibly be won, that all we were doing at Rabaul was postponing the inevitable. Our executive personnel at Rabaul were not deluded by promises of future successes; they were experts in military aviation and had personally undergone many engagements. There existed a growing feeling of our helplessness before this rising tide of American might. Despite these convictions, they could only continue to send our pilots and air crews into combat and to their deaths. Who could blame them, then, for the mental regression into spiritual apathy and defeatism.

Okumiya made an extremely unusual command decision. Under normal circumstances when one unit relieved another it was common for the men and squadron leaders to discuss the strategic situation so those experienced in the theater could aid the new men. Okumiya was so startled by the defeatism shown by the men of 26th Air Flotilla that he dispensed with briefings and sent them to Truk immediately.

The commanders of CARDIV 2 and the other planes left at Rabaul did what they could to counter the waves of Allied aircraft. They ordered fighters not to engage a superior force. They began night attacks against Allied bases. Yet despite all precautions the force of more than 400 aircraft that had been based at Rabaul in November was down to perhaps fifty by late February. On February 17 the U.S. carriers devastated Truk with a massive raid. Combined Fleet surrendered to the inevitable and withdrew its remaining aircraft at Rabaul to Truk. Some officers talked about a counteroffensive against Rabaul, but it is unlikely that anyone but the true believers took such talk seriously. Rabaul was dead.

The death of Rabaul is clear now, but at the time it was not. The base was still in operation and possessed a tremendous garrison. The possibility that the Japanese Empire might try to reinforce Rabaul once again and renew the fight was not out of the question. So bombers of all types continued to pound the base throughout March. Significantly Allied bomber flights began to fly alone, knowing that the danger came from flak and not fighters.

The winding-up of the South Pacific air war took place quickly thereafter. MacArthur was already contemplating very long leaps in his offensive, very afraid that if he did not, Washington would shut down the Southwest Pacific Theater. (Which was exactly what Admiral King wanted to do.) He also believed that imperial forces were losing their cohesion and that a series of strikes would be extremely effective. In this estimation he was very correct. So for reasons of personal prestige and strategic flair MacArthur and Halsey—always the oddest pair of collaborators—quickly demolished what was left of the Japanese position in the South Pacific.

The first target was Kavieng, the way station for shipping coming from the Indies or Truk to Rabaul. It had a fine port, a powerful garrison, and an airfield and was one of the best-defended Japanese bases in the Pacific. But it was the shipping that both Halsey and Kenney were after. A carrier strike in early January netted little. Although busy with their frantic Saidor campaign, much of Fifth Air Force attacked the remaining airpower and shipping near Kavieng. Two ships that were sunk contained invaluable aviation ground crews being evacuated from Rabaul to Truk. At the same time, Halsey's forces seized the Green Islands southeast of Kavieng, tightening the noose around the Bismarcks.

In March 1943 MacArthur and Kenney ended the South Pacific campaign for good. North of Kavieng lay the Admiralty Islands. Their possession would do far more than cut off the Bismarcks; they would also provide future actions one of the best natural anchorages in the Pacific. Relying on an inaccurate reconnaissance report, MacArthur attacked the Admiralties on February 29 with a small force; imperial forces were large but badly placed. But U.S. troops landed in a place unexpected by the Japanese, and by the time the Japanese were ready for major counterattacks MacArthur had reinforced his expedition. Kenney sent his fighters and strafers on a withering attack against Japanese ground positions. Destroyers of Seventh Fleet stood near to shore and provided artillery support. Within a month the Admiral-

ties—Manus to many Allied seamen—were secure. Although
MacArthur's command had defied almost every convention of war it
had achieved a stunning victory with little cost.

To cap the victory Halsey dispatched a large force to the unoccupied
island of Emirau just northwest of Kavieng. By May 1 there was a
good coral airstrip in operation on Emirau, and Marine fighter
squadrons were based there. Strategically the seizure of the Admiralties and Emirau put the cork into the bottle as far as Rabaul and
Kavieng were concerned. Yet the vicious air campaign that had begun
when the Japanese struck Darwin and Moresby and had consumed
enormous blood and treasure by all involved ended with a whimper.
Anzac and U.S. aircraft continued to attack insignificant targets
throughout the area until war's end, tragically losing dozens of aircraft
in the process. Completely isolated, Japanese forces at Rabaul,
Wewak, and many other places waited in limbo for a final Allied attack, death by disease, or perhaps starvation. In the event, more than
half of the 350,000 Japanese troops bypassed in the Bismarcks, Timor,
and New Guinea lived to return to Japan. However, the air forces
these troops needed to fight an island war were long destroyed. The
defeat of Japan's air arm in the South Pacific was final and total.

CONCLUSION

It is never easy to distinguish and rate the differences among the large and small factors in military campaigns. It is even more difficult when attempting to analyze, in this case, a merciless air campaign waged for two years in the South Pacific. There were no engagements that determined the outcome of the campaign. And whereas leaders became organizers of victory, once in the air, military aviators faced a version of the infantry's squad war every day that weather allowed operations. And in theory one might simply chart the campaign by following a chronology of the line of battle, best represented by seizures and losses of air bases. Yet by definition the physical seizure of bases was done by sailors and infantrymen. Thus the airmen created the strategic preconditions for successful offense and defense, but it is not possible to pinpoint a moment when the tide of the air battle turned.

That all reflects the innumerable variables involved in the South Pacific air campaign. Technology—widely defined and especially communications and radar—and aircraft quality played crucial roles, and relative sophistication changed constantly during the first two years of the Pacific war. Both sides refined tactics in attempting to get the most from weapons, yet another important dynamic in the process. The Japanese and Allies had to cope with terrain that thwarted and physically sapped man and machine alike. Early in operations factors that proved so important on the ground were not clear, and they only grew in importance as the enemies settled in for a slugfest. The skills of the prewar pilots were exceptional on both sides, yet the quality of training and preparation of young aviators also changed, almost imperceptibly. Thus I think it valuable to sum up my views on the South Pacific air war and its place within the broader Pacific war. I would also like to offer an opinion why the Allied air arm, after a two-year struggle, gained a decisive victory over the Japanese in the South Pacific.

Given Germany's defeat in Russia, imperial Japan's great gamble—started at Pearl Harbor—was doomed to failure. No analysis of the Pacific war can start without conceding the proposition that Europe First—the Allies' fundamental World War II strategy to control first the West, then the East—was the correct one. And trying to guess how Germany and Japan might have collaborated had the Nazis won in Russia is only guesswork. When Nagumo's bombers were lurching from the imperial carriers on December 7, 1941, the Red Army had already started its stunning counterattack against the Wehrmacht outside of Moscow. From the outset of the war, then, Tokyo had very little margin for error. As Hitler's dream of empire expired, so did Japan's hope for victory. The duration of the larger conflict, however, with its immense human and political consequences, was very much determined by the course of battle in the Pacific.

Looking at the larger structure of the war, the Japanese-Allied conflicts in the Pacific took on an irregular pace. In the first six months the Japanese expanded much like a blitzkrieg, employing forces that by late-war standards would have been small. Their initial odds for success were excellent because the British, Australian, Dutch, and American opponents were disorganized and outnumbered. It is safe to say that no one in Canberra or the Pentagon, in the days prior to Pearl Harbor, expected Japan to sweep all of Southeast Asia, establish a stronghold on Rabaul, and move against the last Allied outpost on New Guinea by May 1942.

With Japan stopped from further extending its maritime line by the disaster at Midway, the Allies counterattacked sooner and more effectively than Tokyo had anticipated. Yet between June 1942 and August 1943 the battle line in the Pacific had changed little. The Allies then captured Guadalcanal and New Georgia. MacArthur and the Australians seized Lae. That was far from Tokyo, and it's no wonder that U.S. troops in the theater adopted the adage "Golden Gate in '48." Nineteen forty-eight was not so different than what was expected in Washington, and many Allied military leaders thought any Pacific war would last eighteen months longer than Europe. And many held that belief in June 1944 when the Allies successfully landed in France while the Russians were smashing the Germans in the East. The assumption that Japan would be offering formidable opposition for many months thus permeated Allied diplomacy until the conference at Yalta, even Potsdam to a degree.

However, in the year following the twin successes at Lae and New Georgia the Pacific war moved like quicksilver. The air and naval units that were operating near New Georgia and the Huon Gulf in August

1943 smashed the Japanese barrier in a year. Rabaul, Kavieng, and Wewak were pulverized or isolated by April. Much of New Guinea fell by June. At the same time, the long-expected drive from Pearl Harbor toward Tokyo was under way. The Americans took the Gilbert Islands in November 1943. In June 1944, as Eisenhower's troops were sealing Germany's doom at Normandy, the Americans crushed the Japanese army and navy at Saipan. Three months later Admiral Halsey and MacArthur were ready to fall upon the Philippines. Unlike New Georgia, Luzon was quite close to Japan and directly astride the maritime supply lines between the Indies and the Home Islands.

Considering such developments, which were catastrophic for Japan, it is surprising that Washington, London, Moscow, and Tokyo expected the Pacific war to last much longer than it did. I think the major reason for that great error lay in a mistaken appreciation of what constituted the central theater of war in the Pacific as opposed to that in Europe. Marshall and those who believed correctly in Europe First considered the Mediterranean Theater secondary. They were correct, in my opinion, and nearly two years separated the attack on Sicily from the fall of Berlin. Marshall—or any Russian general—could have testified that the bulk of Germany's ground forces had not been engaged prior to summer 1943 and that only battle against them would bring victory.

The South Pacific, in the context of the Pacific war, appeared to be akin to the Mediterranean Theater in Europe—a useful prelude to the real war. In fact, however, the South Pacific campaign was not the preliminary bout; it was the main event. Yet that is not obvious if one only counts casualties and numbers. The fact is that the systematic disasters suffered by Japan in the South Pacific dislocated the imperial military apparatus and revealed glaring weaknesses that the Allies proved quick to exploit. Failures in the Solomons and New Guinea did not equate to an El Alamein or a Sicily. No, defeat in the jungle tropics was Japan's Stalingrad.

It is hard to overemphasize the shattering consequences that the loss of Rabaul and New Guinea had on the Imperial Japanese Army. In 1943 the Japanese military had a last chance to redeploy major forces against an anticipated Allied thrust. Like the Americans the Japanese had been making war plans long before Pearl Harbor. The possibility that the Americans would advance from Pearl Harbor directly toward Japan was an obvious danger in the long run. In the weeks after Midway, however, the Japanese believed they would have considerable time to rebuild their carrier forces and prepare for another great battle with Pacific Fleet. Still confident, some firebrands in the Japanese navy continued to think of limited offensives. The army, frustrated by the Coral Sea defeat, sent a substantial force to New Guinea to attack Moresby overland.

King's brilliant but risky counterstroke at Guadalcanal was a calamity for Japan. Still, it is possible that had Yamamoto—who seemed quick to understand the potential catastrophe building in the Solomons—been willing to roll the dice the Japanese might have destroyed the Marine expedition. It is also possible that had Combined Fleet staked the war on a sustained offensive (including a close blockade of Guadalcanal), Pacific Fleet would have prevailed nonetheless, executing another Midway during fall 1942 and thereby psychologically crushing Japan's leadership. Yet considering the huge advantage in shipbuilding capacity held by the United States, and the hundreds of U.S. warships actually under construction after Pearl Harbor, 1942 was not a time for the Japanese to play it safe. If a conservative policy was deemed necessary, Yamamoto was a fool to fight for Guadalcanal. Far better to retreat to New Georgia, reinforce the horrid island, and wait for the Americans while assisting the Japanese army at Buna. The Japanese were faced with a situation fraught with peril either way. As it was, Combined Fleet and its ground-based air units allowed themselves to be trapped in a battle of attrition. They sent in forces to Guadalcanal, but never enough to make victory likely. Like so many nations in the past, Japan began to reinforce defeat. The Japanese tried to win Guadalcanal on the cheap, which was the worst possible approach to follow and ultimately the most costly. It was a turn of events so favorable to the Allied war effort that it might have been scripted in Washington.

It is ironic that a strategic move initiated by Admiral King, who loathed MacArthur, gave a flawed man but great general the opportunity to put a strategic knife in the ribs of the Japanese Empire. American historians have tended to divide the U.S. Solomons offensive (navy and Marine) and the drive through the Southwest Pacific (U.S. Army and Australians) along service lines. The imperial commanders at Rabaul and their superiors saw them as two parts of the same campaign aimed at opening the doorway to Southeast Asia. Tokyo hoped that the IJN could contain Halsey and the IJA could contain MacArthur yet saw the Allied effort as a comprehensive assault on Japan's maritime defense line. This was no small matter, as the resources of Southeast Asia were the prize Tokyo so coveted that it was willing to take on all of the Western democracies. Without oil, rubber, and rice from the Indies a modern war economy was not possible, and Tokyo understood that completely. Startling is how poorly the Imperial High Command balanced its defenses against a potential but obvious threat to the Home Islands with a more immediate danger to Southeast Asia. These calculations were not part of King's playbook. He wanted to tie down Japanese forces, prevent them from extending their perimeter, and force the Pentagon to send more resources to the Pacific. In the event, he succeeded, although not as well as had the perceived Japanese threat to northern Australia in early 1942. Throughout 1942, despite the landings in North Africa, more U.S. forces went to the Pacific than to Europe.

However, the Australian and U.S. airmen who held out while New Guinea was under siege established a strategic precedent of great consequence: The Japanese could not just walk into Moresby and grab it; it would take ground units to add that land to the empire. At Guadalcanal the same military equation applied: Once the U.S. Marines were ashore and Cactus Air Force in operation, the problem became one for the IJA to handle. It was at this moment that Japan failed to use airpower on a level that rivaled Midway (a defeat though it was). Because the Japanese operated from far-off Rabaul and were unable to extinguish Cactus, it became perilous for Combined Fleet to operate in the area, and it became hazardous and difficult to bring in Japanese troop reinforcements. This encouraged a short-sightedness, an overcaution on the part of Combined Fleet, which impeded the Japanese troop buildup on Guadalcanal.

The ground attacks made against the U.S. perimeter in October failed, and had Tokyo been smart, imperial forces would have withdrawn to New Georgia at that moment. Instead they continued to push. As important as the November naval battles were, Combined Fleet would have had to defeat the U.S. Navy on a scale dwarfing Savo Island to prevent U.S. reinforcements from reaching Guadalcanal. The Americans had learned much in three months, and a total Japanese victory was unlikely given the forces Combined Fleet allocated to the offensive. In the event, the IJN was defeated in November, which no doubt saved the lives of thousands of imperial troops scheduled to reinforce Guadalcanal to renew the struggle. U.S. troops were building up at Espíritu and Nouméa, and nothing short of a complete imperial naval blockade could have stopped them from reinforcing the garrison holding Cactus. As it was U.S. troop strength passed 40,000 in November and 50,000 in December. Additional attacks would have only been met by more U.S. firepower, more U.S. infantry, and larger Japanese defeats.

Strategically speaking, in the long run the greatest significance of the U.S. victory at Guadalcanal was that it enabled MacArthur to go over to the offensive. Most of the fighting and much of the planning in New Guinea was done by General Blamey's Australians, but there can be no doubt that the Kokoda Trail epic and the miserable battles near Buna were influenced by Guadalcanal. It seems likely that the Australians would have held Moresby regardless of the Guadalcanal campaign, because the Japanese had not committed sufficient troops to win the battle against the rapidly arriving Australian veterans. Getting Allied troops onto the northeastern shore of New Guinea was a different matter. Because the Japanese navy was deeply involved at Guadalcanal, it allowed the Americans and Australians to acquire a tenuous air superiority over the Buna area. Once cut off from supplies, the Buna-area garrison, one of the most fanatic in military history, was destroyed.

Still, the Buna campaign did not finish anything. The Japanese rushed reinforcements to Lae, but their role—despite tentative plans for a renewed attack—would be defensive. There was no leader in World War II more air-minded than MacArthur, and once Dobodura was secured—at a time when MacArthur's navy consisted of a few fishing boats, yachts, minesweepers, and barges—it became obvious to MacArthur that he could crack open New Guinea in short order. Supported by the RAAF and the Australian army and a reinforced fleet, MacArthur's forces easily seized Lae and Nadzab in September. None of this could have been achieved without fighter superiority, the ability to drop bombs on the enemy, and a large zone of air superiority within which the invaluable C-47s could operate. At the same time, Allied land-based air superiority covered a naval-amphibious campaign without carriers.

By fall 1943 it was all too clear to Tokyo that the door to Southeast Asia had been cracked open; Tokyo also knew its industrial economy would collapse if that door was kicked in. In the early part of 1943 a flood of imperial troops came to New Guinea and the Bismarcks to join a substantial garrison that began to build in late 1942 when ideas still existed about attacking Guadalcanal. These men, at least 350,000 strong, were trapped by Allied air superiority and naval mobility. The possible Australia drive from Darwin into the Indies pinned down another 100,000 Japanese troops awaiting a battle that never came. (The Australians, following a different route, made the last Allied landing in the Pacific when they hit Borneo oil fields in the summer of 1945.) Another 400,000 men were fed into the trap when Tokyo ordered major reinforcements to the Philippines.

American historians have argued for some sixty years about whether the conduct of the Pacific war was well accomplished or not. In a sense that issue cannot be resolved. The perfect battle has never been fought, as the inevitable confusion of war—Carl von Clausewitz's "friction"— makes some misstep inevitable. However, it is fact that the Japanese army, as MacArthur predicted from the beginning, put the bulk of its strength into the defense against the Southwest Pacific drive. Still, MacArthur was able to pen up some 250,000 troops in a de facto POW camp on New Guinea, another 100,000 in the Bismarcks. The garrisons at Saipan, Iwo Jima, and Okinawa would have been far larger had the Japanese army sent more of its field forces into the Central Pacific. By the time the Japanese faced debacle there, however, any attempt at reinforcement was fraught with peril, as any imperial ship had to run a gauntlet of submarines and long-range bombers. Had those reinforcements been sent months earlier, when it was still possible, the Central Pacific agony that faced American troops would have been very much worse.

To put things in perspective: There were more Japanese troops trapped on New Guinea than were deployed in the entire Central Pacific Theater; there were as many soldiers trapped on Bougainville as were faced by U.S. ground forces on Saipan and Iwo Jima; there were more regular infantry cut off on Rabaul than were defending Okinawa. MacArthur's forces paralyzed the Japanese army and forced it into a bit player's role in the Central Pacific drive aimed at Tokyo. The techniques that allowed this outcome were largely based on the accomplishments of Fifth Air Force and Allied comrades flying in the Solomons. The military techniques pioneered in the South Pacific, heavily dependent upon airpower in all aspects, helped MacArthur paralyze Japan's ground defenses at little cost.

Although the idea would no doubt have irked King immensely, the chain of events he triggered at Guadalcanal led the Allies to attack Japan from two directions. Considering the great size of the theater and the difficulty in redeploying forces, the change in Allied strategy endorsing some kind of two-armed pincers was predictable, if not inevitable. It certainly worked. By moving to threaten the Indies MacArthur ruined any chance for a concentrated imperial defense in the Central Pacific. The result for MacArthur's forces was one of the greatest victories in modern military history. (There are still historians who question the importance of MacArthur's Southwest Pacific offensive. However, the most cursory examination of the deployment of Japanese ground forces in the Pacific Theater shows that Tokyo had no doubt that MacArthur's forces threatened the existence of the empire itself. That is why they sent the bulk of the IJA reserves to meet him. When Nimitz moved, it was too late to redeploy.)

Admiral Halsey's brilliant campaign in the South Pacific was nearly as fruitful. Although painfully aware that an attack by the USN might come through the Central Pacific, Japanese forces were much too deeply involved at Rabaul to even interfere with the conquest of the Gilbert and Marshall Islands in late 1943. Although looking for a fight in October, Combined Fleet dispatched the core of its combat arm to Rabaul in November. When it returned it was desperately weakened, and Combined Fleet would have to await the U.S. attack on Saipan before offering battle. When it did the results were humiliating. Almost every Japanese officer interrogated after the war testified to the disastrous consequences that defeat in the South Pacific meant for the defense of other areas. Captain Toshikazu Ohmae saw the war from Rabaul to the catastrophe of the Philippine Sea. From a Japanese point of view it was calamity in the making:

> The specific plan to counter an American invasion of the Gilberts was as follows: Long-range aircraft from the Bismarcks would attack the U.S. invasion forces and then land in the Marshall-Gilberts. . . . Two factors changed these plans. The first was the serious damage received by several Second Fleet Cruisers at Rabaul [the November 2 carrier strike—EB]. The second factor was the intensified air war in the Solomons. Consequently, the original plans for defense of those islands [Gilberts and Marshalls] could not be carried out when American forces invaded in November, because there was insufficient surface and air strength available to make effective resistance.

Because Army and Marine air units prevented a coherent defense, the Japanese garrisons in the Solomons and New Guinea had to react to situations for which there were no instructions from headquarters. Ultimately the fortunate units in the South Pacific found a harsh haven at Rabaul, which surrendered with its dentist still providing care. On the coast of New Guinea Japanese and Australian officials helped tens of thousands of men given up for dead to return to Japan after war's end. Much of the lost army returned to help rebuild the homeland. As a military factor during hostilities, however, they were insignificant once bypassed.

At the nuts-and-bolts level the South Pacific air war tells much about the overall conflict. Japanese leaders were most aware of the empire's inferiority in terms of industrial output. They did not understand, however, Japan's inferiority in the equally important field of industrial technique. That was a lesson learned only during the heat of total war. On paper the Japanese could design a fighter that was a match for second-generation U.S. machines like the P-38 and Corsair. When it came to producing them, however, Japanese industry proved unable to create complex aviation subsystems that possessed fine tolerances for performance and reliability for operational use. The failure to make the Tony, a fully developed and well-proven design in German hands, into a reliable aircraft was the worst possible sign of Japan's inability to move beyond the Zero and the Oscar. Far too much handwork was involved in Japanese construction. And although the Zero, Oscar, and Betty had respectable serviceability rates, they were never produced in the numbers required even after it became obvious that fighter construction would dominate the air industry as the empire went over to the defensive following Guadalcanal. As a result the number of aircraft accepted into service—in dramatic contrast to other combatants—did not increase greatly during the first two years of war. As war progressed the serious decline in the quality of spare parts began to hamstring operations of planes like the Betty and Zero (which were still robust albeit beyond their time). Much the same could be said about Japanese radio communications. The Japanese had radios; they simply did not work well. As for radar design, at least, the Japanese were not far behind the Americans. Producing decent sets in large numbers, however, proved beyond the ability of Japanese industry. To make matters worse, the Japanese proved unable to master the techniques required to integrate radar with communications networks and anti-aircraft batteries.

The Japanese also showed an immature appreciation of the prosaic tasks needed to fight an extended war. It is true that Japan's war economy lacked depth, and so the empire would have to cut corners. Yet a military doctrine that stressed the utility and honor of attack led the Japanese to neglect crucial components of a war machine that lacked glamour and gave little opportunity for grand gestures and displays of bravery. The best example is Japan's poor performance in air-base construction. There was no imperial military equivalent to the U.S. Army Corps of Engineers, an entity with a long and proud history inside the U.S. Army, in Japan's military. Japanese military leaders showed little aptitude for innovation, so there were no Japanese Seabee units, either. For the cost of one cruiser the Japanese military could have deployed dozens of extra bulldozers, additional light construction equipment, and gasoline trucks. Instead, Japanese aircraft on most bases were refueled tediously using 200-gallon barrels and a hand pump. Worse yet the fields these planes operated from were constructed using much manual labor. And so it was that construction machinery was sent to the fronts in small quantities, even though it was within the capacity of Japanese industry to produce much more. It was no accident, then, that the two best Japanese bases in the Pacific—Rabaul and Clark Field near Manila—had been started by Australians and Americans, respectively. The inability to construct decent fields quickly crippled the Japanese at Guadalcanal and made General Kenney's job at Wewak far easier.

The same emphasis on combat also led Japan to neglect many fine points that could have helped logistics. Not establishing spare-parts and repair depots near the front may have made the job of Allied bombers more difficult, but it also thwarted Japanese ground mainte-nance personnel, who were always short on supplies. The lack of ade-quate numbers of good landing craft slowed off-loading from Japanese merchant ships; besides decreasing their efficiency, this often put them in peril. Shallow-draft and oceanworthy supply and assault vessels, like the Americans' LSTs and LSIs, would have been of tremendous value to the empire. But like bulldozers and small convoy escort war-ships, the construction of such vessels was secondary as Japanese ship-yards did their best to replace and repair sunken and damaged war-ships. The barges were a clever expedient but proved a feeble replacement for a decent maritime supply system. It is also unclear why Japan did so little to develop its air-transport capabilities. The Al-lies found transports of tremendous value throughout the theater, par-ticularly in New Guinea. No doubt the Japanese army could have cre-ated supply airstrips to equip men, maintain the medical apparatus, and evacuate the worst wounded. Instead supply was by parachute from bombers in insufficient quantities. The Allies often created supply strips within hours where transports could land. Considering how poorly Japanese multiengine bombers performed, it is obvious that the IJA would have been well advised to build more transports and fewer second-rate medium bombers, which Kenney's pilots downed with im-punity in New Guinea.

The same warrior spirit hindered Japan's training effort. Allied units, particularly those under Fifth Air Force, often did not receive timely rotation. Yet Japanese policy was far more draconian. Men and units did rotate, but the policy was haphazard at best. (If a unit was recalled to Japan it was probably near extinction.) Americans placed combat pilots, after their tours or perhaps between tours, in training pro-grams, helping to institutionalize the lessons of combat. A seasoned Japanese combat pilot, unless wounded, was expected to rejoin the fight. Consequently Japanese instructors were often rookie pilots who showed above-average flying skills. At the basic-training level such a policy was sound enough, and the Allies used it, too. In advance training, however, junior Japanese pilots rarely had sustained guidance from men who had been under fire. It was this factor that probably hurt the Japanese training effort initially more so than a lack of hours. There is no reason to think that in early 1943 the average green Japanese pilot had fewer hours of flight time than did Allied opponents. It is likely, however, that the advanced training a young Allied airman received was superior to that in Japan. The last stage of training received by most Allied pilots, just behind the front, was often not given to Japanese pilots at all. There were two other factors working in favor of the Allies. First, Allied aircraft would take more damage and were good at fleeing the scene if things got ugly, giving many an inexperienced pilot a second chance that Japanese rookies would never get flying flamers like the Zero and Oscar. Second, the structured Allied formations were tailor-made for introducing inexperienced pilots into a combat environment.

The sheer physical damage suffered by Japanese forces in the South Pacific Theater was staggering. Numbers concerning military losses are almost never precise. Yet I think the best were provided by Commander J. Fukamizu, who was in charge of the statistical section of the Japanese Naval Air Department (*Koko Hombru*) in charge of aircraft distribution from January 1, 1943, until war's end, when many records were burned by the Japanese military; Fukamizu re-created the numbers for American interrogators. He estimated losses by taking production totals and subtracting them from the total aircraft ready for service within a given fiscal year. His estimates of ready aircraft at the beginning of a given year appear accurate. (More recent sources confirm his production estimates almost exactly.) If the figures for total aircraft production and available aircraft are at all accurate, then Fukamizu's estimates of Japanese aircraft losses must be taken seriously. (Some researchers, perhaps correctly, believe Fukamizu's numbers are too high. If nothing else, however, they indicate the massive scale of fighting during World War II, even in a "minor" theater like the South Pacific.)

Fortunately for this study Fukamizu's figures are based on the fiscal year of April 1 to April 1. This would exclude some losses taken by the Japanese navy prior to the beginning of battle in the South Pacific and coincides almost exactly with the end of the campaign: April, 1, 1944. When evaluating these figures it is important to point out that Fukamizu was concerned only with aircraft, not with pilots. So if a plane wore out or was shot down it mattered little. Also many of the losses, both combat and operational, included aircraft that essentially wore out or needed serious repairs. Regardless, we see an air force being steadily worn down by a multitude of causes and growing increasingly ineffective.

According to Fukamizu, for the period April 1, 1942–April 1, 1943, the JNAF lost 822 fighters in combat and 768 to operational losses. During the same period the Japanese lost 631 tactical bombers to combat and 131 to operational factors. The losses of medium bombers was 291 in combat and 174 to accident and wear. During the next fiscal year (April 1, 1943–April 1, 1944) the losses went up; the percentage of operational losses also increased. These conclusions are logical, for the air war increased in tempo during this period, Japanese pilot quality declined, and the condition of Japanese fields deteriorated—all factors that would increase total losses and raise the proportion due to accidents and wear. Fukamizu claimed that between April 1, 1943, and April 1, 1944, Japanese naval fighter losses due to combat were 1,170, operational 1,673. The Japanese navy's tactical bomber force, hurt badly during this period, lost 367 aircraft to combat and 824 due to operational losses. Medium-bomber losses were 306 to combat, 663 to operational causes. (There were losses to reconnaissance and trainer aircraft that I think are unnecessary to examine. I should also caution that operational losses could have taken place anywhere in the empire. Combat losses, however, would almost certainly have taken place in the South Pacific, because it was the major theater of air war during this period.)

In raw totals, then, between April 1, 1942, and April 1, 1944, the Japanese navy lost 4,433 fighters, 1,953 tactical bombers, and 1,434 multiengine bombers. As I understand Fukamizu's figures, some of these aircraft might have been repaired and flown again, but very few aircraft in the South Pacific would have received major repairs. Those worn out were sent to the boneyard; if not, strafers would surely put them there. During this period the Japanese navy, outside of the Midway campaign, did all of its air-fighting in the South Pacific. Furthermore, if Fukamizu is correct, the JNAF lost some 40 percent of its total aircraft due to all causes in the South Pacific. Considering the pace of battle during 1944–1945 I think this is an excellent estimate. We have no similar loss breakdown for the JAAF, but it deployed at least 800 aircraft in New Guinea and got very few of them back. These losses, as was the case in the Japanese navy, slowed the increase in force levels that was essential if the air war was to be pursued.

The Allies won the war, and so there were no hostile interrogators gathering information on their operations. If 5th USAAF records are at all accurate during the same period, then Kenney's force lost 826 aircraft to combat and operational losses. Robert Sherrod, who has written the best account of the Marine air effort in World War II, claims 1,673 Marine airmen were killed (which includes combat losses, accidents, and MIAs) during the war abroad. The Marines were active in the Philippines, Okinawa, and during the Central Pacific campaign. Yet most of their fighting was conducted in the Solomons, where many Marine aircraft carried crews of two or three. Sherrod's figures would thus suggest the loss of some 400–500 aircraft in the South Pacific. The RAAF lost nearly 3,000 men killed and wounded in the war against Japan. (RAAF forces continued to fight in the South Pacific and Indies until VJ-Day.) Still, it is logical to infer that a large percentage of RAAF casualties were in the operational groups supporting Australian troops and Fifth Air Force in New Guinea. If that is the case, then the RAAF must have lost roughly 250 aircraft. About a third of New Zealand's airmen served in the Pacific. Like Australia, most of New Zealand's air casualties took place in Europe. (More than 4,000 New Zealand airmen died overall, as opposed to 6,000 soldiers, surely the highest ratio of airmen to soldiers killed during World War II.) John Lundstrom estimates USN fighter losses during the carrier battles from all causes at 108. There are no good figures for losses of Thirteenth Air Force, but because it was deeply involved in all facets of the Solomons campaign its airmen paid a stiff price. Thus we can reasonably conclude that Allied air forces lost some 2,000 aircraft to all causes in fighting the South Pacific campaign.

Yet Japan's South Pacific air defeat and the subsequent collapse of the imperial air arm go far beyond simple numbers. The early Japanese victories, aided by shock and superior forces, disguised serious errors in doctrine. There was no conceivable reason preventing the Japanese from adopting the proven finger-four formation, which was used by Germany, Britain, and the United States at the time of Pearl Harbor. The unstructured hive-of-bees formation, or the gaggle, used by Japanese squadrons played directly into Allied hands, a fact that should have been obvious early. If such unstructured formations were necessary because of bad radios, then better radios should have been provided, even if that meant a minor tactical withdrawal while Japanese industry retrofitted. It appears, however, that the radios, despite defects, existed, but many Japanese pilots refused to carry them because of added weight. Yet again the doctrine of attack triumphed over logic. If Japanese bombers had any chance of destroying Guadalcanal, indeed any Allied base, they had to attack from much lower altitudes. It was pointless to protect the bombers if the measures taken for their protection meant they would inflict little damage. Furthermore the efforts made to protect pilots were pitiful. Most of the air combat in the

Solomons occurred over Japanese territory. Why small patrol boats and floatplanes were not dedicated to the job of rescuing Japanese aircrews must remain unanswered. Perhaps the cult of death, so evident during the kamikaze campaign, was already at work.

Tactically the Allies showed an adaptability and finesse not found among Japanese forces. Allied forces fought with an aggressiveness that surprised the Japanese, who early in the war had grown accustomed to easy victories over second-rate opposition. Yet the relentless pressure applied by Allied airpower was always conditioned by what was possible and intelligent. Even when the Japanese had a significant advantage over Moresby early in the war, the Allies were able to maintain a presence and mount counterattacks. At Guadalcanal Allied tactics proved superior despite the presence of many poorly trained pilots. Every effort was made under crude circumstances to make the most of the communications network, which included Coast Watchers and radar. When units did their job they were rotated out and replaced, even if that held down the number of effective aircraft in the short term. As Allied technical superiority increased, so did the advantage in practical matters. I think that Allied leaders and airmen were far more interested in killing than dying.

I can only estimate relative mortality rates. Among imperial forces it appears that Betty crewmen suffered astronomic losses, their sacrifice followed closely by men in tactical bombers. Whether the enemy was a Corsair, lack of fuel, a bad runway, destruction on the ground, or an unexpected weather front, most Japanese fighting men deployed to the South Pacific never returned home. On the Allied side relatively few heavy and medium bombers fell to enemy fighters. However, losses to weather and antiaircraft fire, considering the size of the bomber crews, no doubt made bombing the riskiest mission facing Allied airmen. Because tactical bombers were vulnerable to fighters as well as antiaircraft, tactical bombing runs would have been terribly dangerous, perhaps worse even than medium and heavy bombing duty. Fighter pilots were at less risk, but they flew more missions. And so the airmen on both sides were more like submarine crews than infantrymen (as ground soldiers had a miserable existence and faced an excellent chance of being shot). There were, however, far more wounded than killed. Airmen, considering the theater, lived a tolerable existence and suffered fewer wounds. If something did go awry, however, death was very likely.

The loss ratio, if these figures are at all correct, would have been roughly 3:1 in favor of the Allied side. I think this is a reasonable estimate. The Allies were holding their own in fighter-to-fighter combat at the beginning, and as the months went by superior Allied tactics took advantage of an inherently superior conception of air warfare. Speed of escape, ruggedness, and firepower would trump maneuverability in the end. And so by the time the Allies deployed their second generation of fighters, they put the Zeros and Oscars in terrible straits. In addition, U.S. antiaircraft, both naval and land-based, was superior to the Japanese guns. Operational losses did favor the Japanese, but only until elite pilots began to die off and their airfields became helpless targets. And it did not help the imperial cause that hundreds of American fliers who went down were returned to duty thanks to air-sea rescue and the good auspices of native peoples. Add the fact that U.S. maintenance and field quality improved, even as the Japanese declined in these areas, and it is obvious that Japan would spiral into defeat in the South Pacific after Guadalcanal. Moreover the U.S. medical apparatus, although hampered by terrible terrain and climate, was superior in every way.

Allied airmen, outside carrier battles, sunk or helped to sink twenty-five Japanese warships. Included in this total were a battleship and a heavy cruiser, the remainder being destroyers. Even more suffered damage from Allied attack. In comparison the Allies lost a heavy cruiser and a handful of destroyers; one cruiser and several destroyers suffered some degree of damage to air attack. Those are meager losses given that the Japanese defended several landings and thus were presented many targets, often vulnerable. Beginning in late 1942 the sinking of merchant shipping by Allied aircraft, almost all in the South Pacific until the Americans assaulted the Gilberts in November 1943, began to grow large, in some months approaching the tonnage sunk by submarines. Merchant losses to air bombardment during this period would prove particularly bitter. Before late 1944 Allied aircraft could reach the sea-lanes between the Indies and Japan, but only with great difficulty. Therefore victims sent to the bottom were carrying the military supplies necessary to keep the imperial air, ground, and naval forces operating in the South Pacific. Air attacks were especially successful in January and February 1944, when Rabaul was under steady assault and the U.S. carriers made their devastating raids on Truk. We will never know how many barges and coastal merchant vessels were caught in the sights of Allied planes, but the number was high and the damage painful. As a result Japanese units were deprived of basic supplies, such as food and medicine, that these simple vessels carried.

Allied bombing killed some 10,000 Japanese servicemen at air bases. Impossible to estimate is the number of imperial soldiers killed by bombs on the various South Pacific battlefields. In any case the Allies' isolation of huge Japanese garrisons, many of which suffered hellishly from disease and starvation, did much more harm to the empire.

In terms of additional air operations the Japanese, according to their accounts and U.S. statistics, suffered the loss of a huge number of experienced pilots in the South Pacific. Because of the empire's refusal to evacuate and rotate large numbers of experienced combat pilots, the job of reconstituting new units was made that much more difficult. Worse yet hundreds of experienced ground crewmen who serviced aircraft at Buin, Kahili, and Rabaul were left behind. That came home to roost when the Japanese began to deploy complex second-generation fighters in 1944: Despite their good performance they spent too much time on the ground. Many of the best mechanics were trapped at Rabaul, working over a handful of aircraft for pointless attacks against the American juggernaut in the Admiralties.

What put the Japanese in an impossible situation was the gradual change in numerical ratios. The Allies probably gained then lost then regained modest numerical superiorities from 1942 until early 1943. However, by the end of 1943 the Allies probably achieved an operational superiority of 2:1 or more. Given the presence of superior aircraft flown by superior pilots, it is little wonder that Japanese attacks became debacles and that defending Japanese airspace bordered on suicide. Despite much talk as to the defense of Truk, it is almost certain that the simple fact that Japan's air force had been crushed caused the IJN to abandon Rabaul in February. Wewak was being pounded into oblivion as well, giving the Americans the chance to obliterate the new Japanese base at Hollandia. Whatever the exact numbers of losses, it is important to understand that actual aircraft in operation was the critical number for Japan. At no time during the South Pacific campaign did operational Japanese aircraft outnumber pilots. Analytically it might be better to view the Japanese air forces in the South Pacific as being dismantled and worn down, not simply shot out of the air.

Bloody engagements continued throughout Pacific skies even after the Japanese were driven from the South Pacific. Indeed the numbers of men killed and planes destroyed increased throughout 1944 until war's end. According to Fukamizu the numbers of aircraft in the Japanese arsenal stood at 2,980 on April 1, 1943, 6,598 a year later, and 10,429 in April 1945. This trend followed those of all the major combatants. Yet these totals include many noncombat types; they also obscure the aircraft that were receiving service, in transit, and engaging in training. Frontline strength at the point of fire was far less. And as one might expect, the Allied strength increase surpassed Japan's. By

June 1944 Fifth Air Force, which changed its accounting practices to neglect aircraft under repair, had reached 1,600 operational aircraft. Soon thereafter Thirteenth Air Force joined Kenney's force and created Far Eastern Air Force, with nearly 2,000 frontline aircraft. The RAAF continued to build its force well into the summer of 1944, as did the RNZAF. The powerful Marine air units were given bombers and a healthy reserve of aircraft of all types. When the Central Pacific drive began, Seventh Air Force, originally based in Hawaii, became a major force. After Saipan fell, Twentieth Air Force, with its dreaded B-29s, appeared, adding a new superheavy dimension to U.S. airpower. Chennault's American and Chinese airmen continued to dog the Japanese in China. And in 1944 the Royal Air Force activated a new front with a drive into Burma. Another disaster for Japan, however, was the launching of the U.S. carrier strike force. When operating at full strength it could field 1,000 aircraft, well supplied by reserves on escort carriers behind the fleet and able to operate over huge distances at great speed.

A major change took place in the Pacific air war after Japan abandoned Rabaul. The Japanese advance was stopped at Kokoda Trail and Guadalcanal in the fall of 1942. This turn of events reflected the carrier battles that brought stalemate to the South Pacific seas. Guadalcanal and Buna put Japan on the defensive. However, Japanese airpower did much physically and psychologically to impede the Allied advance to Rabaul. Slowly but inexorably Japan lost its ability to prevent Allied advances until, that is, they faced defeat at Rabaul and Wewak. It was a hard campaign for the victors, and on many days the Japanese came out on top.

After being ejected from the South Pacific the Japanese air arm, despite an increase in size, lost the ability to fight effectively. Fifth Air Force smashed JAAF units in New Guinea in June while the U.S. carriers demolished Japanese airpower near Saipan. The qualitative and quantitative advantages had shifted so far to the Allied side that every subsequent air engagement was an Allied victory or outright massacre. During the Leyte campaign, in which Japan staked everything on the ability of its air arm and the IJN to defeat the United States, imperial forces suffered total rout.

In retrospect I think it is clear that Japan's air forces had been internally shattered in the South Pacific. Because the U.S. advance was so rapid Japan never had a chance to rebuild or even catch its breath. No combatant, except for the United States, put more resources into air warfare than did Japan. Yet all of Japan's aviation technology and support apparatus proved pitifully inadequate when put to the test. In the

South Pacific Japan quickly lost its tenuous qualitative superiority and soon lost its equally tenuous quantitative superiority. Nothing Japan did could slow that process, and something resembling paralysis set in at the command level. Defensive moves were planned, yet they rarely anticipated the speed and power of the Allied pincers moving ever closer to the Indies and the Home Islands. When put to the test defensive operations were invariably disjointed, uncoordinated, and easily defeated in detail. Only the Japanese army, so badly out of position for a growing war, continued to inflict painful losses on the attackers, and then only where geography did not allow Allied maneuver. Any responsible government that cared for its population would have looked for peace. Instead Japan fought on, hoping for some incredible victory that would force some kind of compromise with an Allied coalition growing more powerful each day.

After a hard-fought victory in the South Pacific the Americans could and did treat the Japanese air forces with contempt. On some days Japanese airmen showed some of their old skills, perhaps sinking or damaging an American warship. Some of the younger imperial fighter pilots showed uncanny talent in flying their machines, making the skies dangerous for any Allied aviator who was not alert. For a few months some intrepid Japanese pilots, often flying one of the few second-generation fighters that were serviceable, made the skies over Japan dangerous for B-29 raiders. When the Superfortress attacks moved to nighttime, even that opportunity to inflict meaningful damage disappeared. For the most part, although the base numbers of aircraft increased, the quality-quantity gap between the Japanese and Allied air arms continued to widen. First-generation Allied aircraft were put to pasture, whereas Japan had to rely upon slightly improved versions of planes being flown when war started. By 1944 American carrier pilots were being graduated from a training program nearly two years long. To a lesser extent all Allied pilots arriving late in the war were trained at a level unimaginable at the time of Guadalcanal. During this same period the Japanese were throwing miserably prepared pilots into combat. Their planes were obsolescent, Japan lacked the oil to allow them adequate training hours, and the men who could have trained them effectively were for the most part dead.

What is striking about this year and a half of war is the brazen aggressiveness of Allied airpower. Halsey's task force raids on the Philippines, Formosa, and Okinawa in the fall of 1944 made a mockery of Japanese airpower. When Marine, USAAF, and Anzac fighter pilots jumped on the increasingly rare opportunity to engage Japanese fighters, they could be confident of victory. When Okinawa's airfields put the Allies in easy range of the Home Islands, lethal fighter-bombers roamed Japanese skies with impunity, attacking anything that moved, imperiled only by antiaircraft, mechanical failure, and bad weather. Army strafers and Marine tactical bombers from Luzon waged a relentless campaign on the small shipping that provided the final links between the homeland and the empire. The proud and skilled Japanese air arm ended as a strategic and tactical irrelevancy.

Japan's final act in the Pacific air war was to mount the kamikaze campaign. Even though the Americans were forewarned of many enemy moves thanks to excellent intelligence, the "special attack" campaign that first hit off Leyte came as a complete surprise. In a sense the suicidal assaults were a predictable tactic. Japanese land garrisons throughout the Pacific rarely yielded more than a handful of prisoners. These new, premeditated assaults by aircraft and pilots against ships they could not sink in any conventional manner merely plunged the Pacific war into a deeper phase of barbarism. The fact that Japan would now sacrifice all rather than yield to Allied peace demands fouled the poisoned atmosphere of global politics, already shocked as the dreadful secrets of the Third Reich came to light. The end of the Pacific war, which included the destruction of much of Japan's urban civilization, came with the U.S. deployment of the atomic bomb. Those finals acts were the tragic results of Tokyo's diplomatic obstinacy and the apparent willingness of the Japanese government and military to precipitate some sort of national suicide.

When U.S. troops and airmen occupied bases in Japan immediately after war's end they found thousands of Japanese aircraft crippled or rendered ineffective by little damage, which was done by Japanese ground crews following the surrender or by Allied attack; Japan was the Pacific war's largest boneyard. The operational units that existed at the end of the war, barring the kamikaze units, resembled those found in Germany in April 1945. A large number of aircraft existed, most of which were not truly airworthy, manned by a few veteran pilots supported by young men and who did well to land their machines in one piece. Some squadrons had three to five aircraft.

The last three months of air combat in the Pacific actually saved hundreds of Japanese airmen. The wicked old guard, like Admiral Ugaki, who supported the kamikaze effort ordered much of what remained of the Japanese air arm saved for the expected U.S. attack on Kyushu. Japanese interceptors, because of lack of fuel, constant harassment from roving U.S. fighter-bombers, and nearly certain death if they seriously engaged an American unit, also awaited the final battle. Consequently thousands of pilots trained for imperial service lived simply because they never fought.

This was not true in the South Pacific. In retrospect the Japanese air arm suffered the beginning of an irreversible downward spiral in the Solomons and New Guinea. When the Allies broke Japan's back in the air war over New Guinea and the Solomons, they demolished everything in sight. Yet we can see that Japan's qualitative and quantitative positions were better in January 1944, when Rabaul died, than they were a year later, when U.S. aircraft slaughtered the defenders of Luzon. Japan's airpower was soundly defeated in the South Pacific; during the later campaigns it was demolished with startling ease.

Thus the great sacrifices of Allied airmen in the South Pacific were repaid many times over by future triumphs that forced Japan to capitulate much earlier than Allied leadership dared hope at the beginning of 1944. Japanese airmen showed great courage and amazing tenacity. Yet it is the melancholy truth that their sacrifices were made for a cruel government bent on naked aggression, one that showed remarkable disregard for the fates of its fighting men. Perhaps there is no such thing as a good war. In rare moments in history there are necessary wars, and the Pacific war certainly was necessary. Allied airmen who fought in the South Pacific, as well as those who supported them, deserve profound recognition from free peoples.

CHRONOLOGY OF EVENTS

December 7, 1941 Japan attacks Pearl Harbor.

December 1941–April 1942 Japan seizes Southeast Asia and the Philippines.

January 14, 1942 Japan invades Rabaul and Kavieng.

March 9, 1942 Japan seizes Lae, beginning operations from New Guinea. Air offensive against Port Moresby begins soon thereafter.

May 8, 1942 Battle of the Coral Sea: Carrier battle forces Japan to cancel invasion of Port Moresby. Japanese seize Tulagi in Solomons and begin building field at Guadalcanal.

June 4, 1942 U.S. Navy wins major victory at the Battle of Midway.

July 21, 1942 Imperial Japanese Army lands at Buna and advances toward Port Moresby.

August 7, 1942 U.S. forces land at Guadalcanal; fierce Japanese air attack fails with heavy loss.

August 7, 1942 Fifth Air Force formed in New Guinea under the command of George Kenney.

August 21, 1942 Marines defeat first attack on Guadalcanal perimeter; Henderson Field receives first combat planes.

September 1, 1942 Japanese landing defeated at Milne Bay.

September 12, 1942 Marines defeat second attack at Guadalcanal in the Battle of Bloody Ridge.

September 20, 1942 Japanese army withdraws from outside Port Moresby.

October 22–25, 1942 Marines defeat main Japanese assault against Henderson Field. Japanese air offensive reaches maximum effort.

November 8, 1942 Australians defeat Japanese at Oivi-Gorari on Kokoda Trail.

November 13–15, 1942 The naval Battle of Guadalcanal; Japanese attempt to land new army fails; Cactus Air Force destroys enemy troop convoy.

November 18, 1942 Australian and U.S. troops begin siege of Japanese fortified zone at Buna-Gona-Sanananda.

December 18, 1942 U.S. forces begin offensive on Guadalcanal.

January 13, 1943 Thirteenth Air Force formed for operations in Solomons under Nathan Twining.

January 23, 1943 Australian and U.S. forces complete destruction of Japanese position at Buna.

February 1, 1943 Australians break siege of Wau.

February 8, 1943 United States declares Guadalcanal secure.

March 2, 1943 Battle of the Bismarck Sea; Allied airpower destroys Japanese troop convoy heading for New Guinea.

June 30, 1943 U.S. forces invade New Georgia in Solomons.

June 30, 1943   U.S. and Australian forces move on Salamaua north of Buna.

August 1943   Allies launch devastating air offensive against Wewak.

August 15, 1943   U.S. forces invade Vella Lavella in the Solomons.

September 4, 1943   Australians land at Lae and Finschhafen.

October 12, 1943   Fifth Air Force begins sustained Allied air assault against Rabaul. In December Marines, USN, and Thirteenth Air Force dominate offensive against Rabaul.

November 1, 1943   Americans land at Bougainville.

February 17, 1944   Japanese withdraw all active combat air units from Rabaul, effectively conceding South Pacific to Allies.

February 28, 1944   MacArthur seizes Admiralty Islands, isolating Rabaul's garrison and gaining major naval base.

March 8, 1944   Japanese launch futile attack on Torokina air base on Bougainville in the last large land battle in South Pacific.

April 22, 1944   Following fierce air offensive, Allies seize Hollandia. Wewak bypassed. Large portion of Japanese land army on New Guinea isolated and neutralized.

June 18–19, 1944   Battle of the Philippine Sea: U.S. Pacific Fleet destroys remnants of Japanese carrier strength. U.S. forces capture Saipan.

July 30, 1944   Allies complete occupation of New Guinea, trapping more than 200,000 enemy personnel.

October 20, 1944   U.S. forces land at Leyte in Philippines, triggering the naval Battle of Leyte Gulf on October 23; U.S. Pacific Fleet destroys Japanese surface fleet.

January 9, 1945   U.S. forces invade Luzon, main island in Philippines.

February 10, 1945   U.S. forces land on Iwo Jima; the island is secured on March 25 after heavy losses.

April 1, 1945   U.S. forces land on Okinawa; the most violent battle of the Pacific war ends on June 21.

July 1, 1945   Australians occupy Balikpapan on Borneo, the last large Allied operation of the Pacific war.

August 6, 1945   U.S. atomic bomb dropped on Hiroshima. Nagasaki hit on August 9.

August 15, 1945   Japan agrees to accept Allied terms, ending hostilities.

September 1, 1945   Japan signs surrender on deck of USS *Missouri* in Tokyo Bay, ending World War II.

AUTHOR'S NOTE ON TECHNICAL INFORMATION INCLUDING TABLE OF MAJOR WARPLANES IN THE SOUTH PACIFIC THEATER

The table below offers a rough comparison of capabilities for warplanes deployed in the South Pacific Theater between 1942 and early 1944. Unfortunately sources do not agree on some of the most important figures, so I have tried to rely on the sources that appeared to be the most accurate. Furthermore these figures are for aircraft flying in perfect mechanical state under ideal conditions. In the field aircraft quickly developed wear, and actual performance rarely matched theoretical performance. In addition, many key areas of performance are not so easily estimated. Rate of climb, for instance, varied greatly depending upon altitude, and a plane might be superior in a steep climb but inferior in a slow, sustained climb. The rate of roll cannot be computed easily and is not provided for some planes. A plane's structural strength cannot be easily computed. Suffice it to say that Allied aircraft were in every instance considerably stronger and more resistant to battle damage than Japanese aircraft.

Some additional remarks concerning various areas of performance are necessary. I have listed unloaded weight because extra weight (e.g., in the form of bombs or drop tanks) radically affected range. Range, as I discuss in the text, was lower in most cases than the theoretical maximum. From the sources it was not always clear whether range estimates were loaded or unloaded. Whenever possible I chose the latter, because load-carrying varied greatly and had a substantial impact on range. Range is from point to point and not to be confused with radius, which presupposes an identical takeoff and landing position. It was possible for pilots to increase range dramatically by flying at low speeds in good conditions. Both sides on occasion used this technique, although it was very hard on the crew and sometimes the aircraft. However, knowing that an attack could come from very long range did tie down defensive elements on both sides and led to a handful of very successful missions. Concerning speed, I have included, whenever possible, critical altitude (the altitude at which the aircraft was capable of its highest speed, an important consideration in weighing combat performance). However, I must also point out that aircraft reached top speeds only during combat and cruised at perhaps 75 percent of maximum. I have not included war emergency power in these figures, as it is unavailable for many models early in the war, and the data are not consistent. I use the highest horsepower ratings in normal flight; takeoff ratings, when the engine is under great stress, would be somewhat higher, as would military power used in combat.

The respective names of the aircraft (in parentheses) reflect the standard Allied designations. In some cases Anzac models of U.S. aircraft used different names. I use the Allied code-names, rather than the original Japanese designations, for imperial aircraft in order to be consistent with the text.

Last, the reader should note that the table below includes only the major aircraft employed by both sides. In practice there were smaller numbers of many other aircraft—too many to name. Furthermore each major aircraft was manufactured in several different models, performance differing significantly among them. I have tried to identify the most common models; I also list the services that deployed each airplane (the Marines flew U.S. Navy machines, and many U.S. aircraft were flown by the RAAF and RNZAF).

The data below, gleaned from several sources, should be viewed for purposes of general comparison. The most valuable sources include Francis Dean's *America's Hundred Thousand*, Douglas Gillison's *Royal Australian Air Force, 1939–1942*, Rene Francillon's *Japanese Aircraft of the Pacific War*, and finally *Jane's Fighting Aircraft of World War II*.

Japanese Fighters

Plane	Power-hp	Weight	Wingspan	Range	Speed
A6M2 Zero (Zeke)	950	4,145 lb	39'5"	1,160 miles 1,930 maximum	332 mph/15,000'
A6M3 Zero (Hamp)	1,100	4,345 lb	36'1"	1,160 miles 1,477 maximum	338 mph/19,300'
Ki-42-II (Oscar)	950	4,211 lb	37'6"	1,095 miles 1,990 maximum	329 mph/13,100'
Ki-61-I (Tony)	1,080	4,872 lb	39'4"	373 miles 684 maximum	368 mph/16,000'

Japanese Bombers

Plane	Power-hp	Weight	Wingspan	Range	Speed
G4M1 (Betty)	2 × 1,575	14,991 lb	82'	3,749 miles	266 mph/13,800'
Ki-48-II (Lily)	2 × 1,070	10,310 lb	57'3"	1,230 miles	318 mph/18,375'
D3A2 (Val)	1,200	5,666 lb	47'1"	915 miles	267 mph/20,000'
B5N2 (Kate)	970	5,024 lb	50'10"	608 miles 1,237 maximum	235 mph/11,800'

United States Fighters

Plane	Power-hp	Weight	Wingspan	Range	Speed
F4F-4 (Wildcat)	1,100	5,779 lb	38'	793 miles	328 mph/19,000'
F4U-1 (Corsair)	1,675	8,971 lb	40'12"	811 miles	390 mph/24,000'
F6F-5 (Hellcat)	1,675	9,079 lb	42'10"	1,360 miles	395 mph/20,000'
P-38G (Lightning)	2 × 1,100	12,780 lb	52'	1,222 miles	400 mph/26,500'
P-39D (Airacobra)	1,000	5,658 lb	34'	714 miles	365 mph/12,000'
P-40E (Warhawk—Kittyhawk in ANZAC service)	1,000	6,069 lb	37'3"	814 miles	358 mph/16,000'
P-47C (Thunderbolt—usually called the "Jug")	1,525	10,200 lb	40'9"	850 miles	415 mph/30,000'

United States Bombers

Plane	Power-hp	Weight	Wingspan	Range	Speed
A-20 (Havoc: Boston in ANZAC service)	2 × 1,275	14,830 lb	61'4"	825 miles	312 mph/12,000'
B-17E (Flying Fortress)	4 × 1,000	32,350 lb	103'9"	3,300 miles	318 mph/25,000'
B-24D (Liberator)	4 × 1,200	32,650 lb	110'	3,600 miles	303 mph/25,000'
B-25D (Mitchell)	2 × 1,500	20,300 lb	67'8"	1,975 miles	284 mph/15,000'
SBD-4 (Dauntless)	1,000	6,181 lb	41'6"	1,300 miles	253 mph/15,000'
TBF (Avenger)	1,700	10,080 lb	54'2"	1,215 miles	271 mph/12,000'

ANZAC Combat Aircraft

Plane	Power-hp	Weight	Wingspan	Range	Speed
Beaufighter (Mark X—optimized for low-altitude attack)	2 × 1,700	14,875 lb	57'10"	1,800 miles	320 mph/10,000'
Beaufort	2 × 1,050	14,740 lb	58'	1,600 miles	259 mph/8,900'
CA-13 (Boomerang)	1,050	5,386 lb	36'3"	930 miles	296 mph/7600'
CA-3 (Wirraway)	600	3,980 lb	43'	510 miles	220 mph/8600'
Spitfire V	1,470	5,065 lb	36'10"	459 miles	369 mph/19,500'

NOTES

Chapter 1

p. 14 *"Though a prolonged war is taken for granted . . . "* Donald Goldstein and Katherine V. Dillon, eds., *Fading Victory: The Diary of Admiral Matome Ugaki, 1941–1945* (Pittsburgh, 1991), p. 75.

16 *The center of the area was Rabaul Town . . .* See generally Lionel Wigmore, *Australia in the War of 1939–1945: Army.* Vol. 4, *The Japanese Thrust* (Canberra, 1957), p. 395.

18 *Obviously in such time the war effort . . .* United States Strategic Bombing Survey (Pacific), *Interrogations of Japanese Officials*, Vol. 1 (Washington, D.C., 1946), Interview 70.

19 *In 1936 he wrote . . .* David C. Evans and Mark Peattie, *Kaigun: Strategy, Tactics, and Technology in the Imperial Japanese Navy, 1887–1941* (Annapolis, 1997), pp. 400–401.

25 *The Australians had built small . . .* Douglas Gillison, *Australia in the War of 1939–1945: Air.* Vol. 1, *Royal Australian Air Force, 1939–1942* (Canberra, 1962), p. 396.

27 *"Military Value of British New Guinea . . . "* Japanese Demobilization Bureau Records, *Reports of General MacArthur*, Vol. 2, Part 1 (Washington, D.C., 1966), p. 24.

27 *"The strategic significance of the inaccessible . . . "* Louis Morton, *U.S. Army in World War II: Strategy and Command—The First Two Years* (Washington, D.C., 1962), pp. 198–199.

33 *"We want to invade Ceylon; . . . "* H. P. Willmott, *The Barrier and the Javelin: Japanese and Allied Pacific Strategies, February to June 1942* (Annapolis, 1983), p. 97.

33 *"In the event that the United States and Great Britain . . . "* Japanese Demobilization Bureau Records, *Reports of General MacArthur*, Vol. 2, Part 1 (Washington, D.C., 1966), p. 51.

36 *"Acquisition of air bases in the Solomons . . . "* Ibid., p. 127.

45 *The intelligence officer of . . .* James P. Gallagher, *Meatballs and Dead Birds* (Perry Hall, Md., 1972), p. 30.

46 *"Up until April 1943 . . . "* United States Strategic Bombing Survey (Pacific), *Interrogations of Japanese Officials*, Vol. 1 (Washington, D.C., 1946), Interview 24.

47   *"I can remember occasions . . . "* SBS (Pacific), *Japanese Interrogations*, Vol. 2 (Washington, D.C., 1946), Interview 94.

48   *"Our fighters were usually too outnumbered . . . "* SBS (Pacific), *The Allied Campaign Against Rabaul* (Washington, D.C., 1946), p. 61.

51   *As one War Department official put it . . .* Wesley Craven and James Cate, eds., *The Army Air Forces in World War II*. Vol. 1, *Plans and Early Operations, January 1939 to August 1942* (Chicago, 1958), p. 178.

56   *As late as Christmas Day 1941 . . .* Gillison, *Australia in the War of 1939–1945*, Vol. 1, p. 380.

56   *He further warned Brett . . .* Karl C. Dod, *The Corps of Engineers: The War Against Japan* (Washington, D.C., 1966), p. 110.

57   *"The Navy wants to take all the islands . . . "* Morton, *U.S. Army in World War II*, p. 218.

59   *Initially the fields were crude . . .* Dod, *Corps of Engineers*, p. 240.

61   *There was also Three Mile Drome . . .* Ibid., p. 143.

70   *Marine engineer Captain John K. Little . . .* Max Brand, *Fighter Squadron at Guadalcanal* (New York, 1996), p. 5.

75   *Henderson Field and the airfield complex . . .* Department of the Navy, Naval Historical Center, Washington Navy Yard, "Seabee History: Formation of the Seabees and World War II" (Naval Historical Center home page) URL: http://www.history.navy.mil/faqs/faq67-3.htm.

85   *The stay was short . . .* SBS (Pacific), *Japanese Interrogations*, Vol. 1, Interview 46.

86   *On December 7 the Japanese commander of ground forces on Guadalcanal . . .* Richard B. Frank, *Guadalcanal* (New York, 1990), p. 525.

Chapter 2

p. 104   *"On April 8 I flew . . . "* Saburo Sakai with Martin Caidin and Fred Saito, *Samurai!* (New York, 1957), p. 82.

106   *"The men had their ammo . . . "* Eric Bergerud, *Touched with Fire: The Land War in the South Pacific* (New York, 1996), p. 103.

114   *"As far as I can say . . . "* United States Strategic Bombing Survey (Pacific), *The Allied Campaign Against Rabaul* (Washington, D.C., 1946), pp. 116–117.

127   *As one might imagine . . .* Mae Mills Link and Hubert A. Coleman, *Medical Support of the Army Air Forces in World War II* (Washington, D.C., 1955), p. 795.

128   *"Medical personnel were always . . . "* Ibid., p. 732.

136   *Soon after the war . . .* SBS (Pacific), *Campaign Against Rabaul*, p. 90.

137   *"The harsh tropical environment . . . "* Henry Sakaida, *Imperial Japanese Navy Aces, 1937–1945* (London, 1998), p. 25.

140   *At about the same time Ed Stroebel's unit . . .* Garrett Middlebrook, *Air Combat at 20 Feet* (published by the author, 1989), p. 8.

141   *"Of planes sent overseas . . . "* SBS (Pacific), *Interrogations of Japanese Officials*, Vol. 2 (Washington, D.C., 1946), Interview 110.

152   *I have no doubt that many Japanese pilots . . .* Sakaida, *Japanese Navy Aces*, p. 48.

Part Two

p. 159   *In an article published in 1923 . . .*   Ronald Miller and David Sawers, *The Technical Development of Modern Aviation* (New York, 1970), p. 11.

Chapter 3

p. 196   *"Until this time . . . "* Jiro Horikoshi, *Eagles of Mitsubishi: The Story of the Zero Fighter* (Seattle, 1981), p. 25.

198   *"In those days, . . . "* Ibid., p. 23.

200   *"The Zero excited me as nothing else . . . "* Saburo Sakai with Martin Caidin and Fred Saito. *Samurai!* (New York, 1957), p. 43.

201   *Admiral Frank Fletcher, who commanded . . .* George Dyer, *The Amphibians Came to Conquer: The Story of Admiral Richmond Kelly Turner* (Quantico, Va., 1991), p. 391.

201   *"It is necessary to remember . . . "* Robert Sherrod, *History of Marine Corps Aviation in World War II* (Baltimore, 1987), p. 81.

201   *"That evening at all the night spots . . . "* Douglas Gillison, *Australia in the War of 1939–1945: Air.* Vol. 1, *Royal Australian Air Force, 1939–1942* (Canberra, 1962), p. 340.

203   *In October 1944 twelve U.S. test pilots . . .* Francis Dean, ed., *Report of Joint Fighter Conference, NAS Patuxent River, MD, 16–23 Oct. 1944* (Atglen, Pa., 1998), pp. 309–312.

207   *One might imagine how the thought . . .* Henry Sakaida, *The Siege of Rabaul* (St. Paul, 1996), p. 19.

210   *Famous ace Saburo Sakai commented . . .* Henry Sakaida, *Imperial Japanese Navy Aces, 1937–1945* (London, 1998), pp. 23–24.

211   *As Mitsubishi team leader Jiro Horikoshi later conceded . . .* Horikoshi, *Eagles of Mitsubishi*, p. 25.

214   *"The Betty had weak defensive power . . . "* United States Strategic Bombing Survey (Pacific), Military Analysis Division, Interrogation of Lieutenant Commander Ohira, Interview 157, Maxwell Documents.

214   *"The bombers looked shiny and new . . . "* James Morehead, *In My Sights: The Memoir of a P-40 Ace* (Novato, Calif., 1998), pp. 99–100.

216   *"The weather was fine, visibility good . . . "* Donald Goldstein and Katherine V. Dillon, eds., *Fading Victory: The Diary of Admiral Matome Ugaki, 1941–1945* (Pittsburgh, 1991), pp. 352–359.

219   *While flying his powerful P-38 Lightning . . .* United States Air Force Historical Research Center, Oral History Collection. Perry Dahl, recorded 1978. Maxwell Documents.

221   *Perry Dahl, so impressed . . .* Ibid.

224   *"Based on intelligence reports . . . "* James P. Gallagher, *Meatballs and Dead Birds* (Perry Hall, Md., 1972), p. 30.

Chapter 4

p. 231   *This inherent characteristic . . .* Benjamin Kelsey, *The Dragon's Teeth? The Creation of United States Air Power for World War II* (Washington, D.C., 1981), pp. 64–65.

234   *Yet bomber advocates wanted no competitors* . . . Ibid., pp. 66–67.

244   *Veteran Sammy Pierce* . . . Ernst McDowell, *49th Fighter Group* (Carrollton, Texas, 1989), p. 19.

250   *The 67th Squadron, often fielding only four planes* . . . "67th Squadron History" (1943), Maxwell Documents.

251   *In August 1942 Lieutenant Commander John Thach* . . . George Dyer, *The Amphibians Came to Conquer: The Story of Admiral Richmond Kelly Turner* (Quantico, Va., 1991), p. 392.

255   *Sakai came to the aid of his comrades* . . . Saburo Sakai with Martin Caidin and Fred Saito. *Samurai!* (New York, 1957), pp. 150–151.

256   *As Blackburn wrote in his memoirs* . . . Tom Blackburn, *The Jolly Rogers* (New York, 1989), p. 36.

257   *Boone Guyton was a lead test pilot* . . . Boone T. Guyton, *Whistling Death: The Test Pilot's Story of the F4U Corsair* (Atglen, Pa., 1994), p. 101.

258   *"As the Corsair hurtled toward earth* . . . " Ibid., p. 520.

259   *"After touchdowns with not unreasonable bounces* . . . " Blackburn, *Jolly Rogers*, p. 75.

260   *Blackburn and all concerned* . . . Ibid., p. 75.

261   *"In a short period the excellent qualities of the Corsair* . . . " Masatake Okumiya and Jiro Horikoshi with Martin Caidin, *Zero: The Inside Story of Japan's Air War in the Pacific* (New York, 1961), p. 161.

263   *However, as a scathing* . . . David W. Ostrowski, "Early P-38 Problems," in *Skyways: The Journal of the Airplane, 1920–1940* (October 1996).

265   *"The airplane was really good in the Pacific* . . . " United States Air Force Historical Research Center, Oral History Collection. Perry Dahl, recorded 1978. Maxwell Documents, p. 535.

265   *"One day I was flying and I was watching* . . . " Ibid.

268   *"Soon after their introduction to combat* . . . " Okumiya and Horikoshi, *Zero: The Inside Story*, p. 74.

270   *The P-47 was an American-style fighter* . . . Francis H. Dean, *America's Hundred Thousand: U.S. Production Fighters of World War Two* (Atglen, Pa., 1997), p. 299.

272   *"The Grummans would get on your tail* . . . " Henry Sakaida, *The Siege of Rabaul* (St. Paul, 1996), p. 9.

275   *"The fight ended up at 1,200 feet* . . . " NACI ComSoPac, "Air Battle Notes from the South Pacific No. 11," Maxwell Documents, p. 469.

283   *"In one case we got a pilot* . . . " USAAF, Office of Assistant Chief of Air Staff, Intelligence, "Interview with Major Dill Ellis, May 22, 1943," Maxwell Documents, p. 482.

290   *"The B-25 proved remarkably adaptable* . . . " Norman L. Avery, *B-25 Mitchell: The Magnificent Medium* (St. Paul, 1992), p. 100.

291   *Kenney was delighted* . . . George C. Kenney, *General Kenney Reports* (New York, 1949), p. 155.

300   *The RAAF then expanded with remarkable speed* . . . RAAF Air Power Studies Center, *The RAAF in the Southwest Pacific Area, 1942–1945* (Canberra, 1993), pp. 6–7.

Chapter 5

p. 310   *As one 5th USAAF veteran* ... Susan Sheehan, *A Missing Plane* (New York, 1986), p. 138.

312   *"In 1942 I was stationed at Fort Lewis* ... " United States Air Force Historical Research Center, Oral History Collection. Perry Dahl, recorded 1978. Maxwell Documents, p. 636.

324   *According to Sakai, his first* ... Saburo Sakai with Martin Caido and Fred Saito, *Samurai!* (New York, 1957), p. 22.

324   *Sakai believed that such training* ... Ibid., p. 24.

324   *The flying experience of the JNAF pilots at Pearl Harbor* ... United States Strategic Bombing Survey (Pacific), *Interrogations of Japanese Officials*, Vol. 1 (Washington, D.C., 1946), Interview 44.

325   *"The strength of JNAF at the beginning of the war* ... " SBS (Pacific), Military Analysis Division, Interview 479, Maxwell Documents.

325   *"JAAF had approximately 2,000 pilots* ... " Ibid., Interview 357.

326   *Fifth Air Force conducted a similar study* ... SBS (Pacific), *The Fifth Air Force in the War Against Japan* (Washington, D.C., 1947), pp. 60–61.

329   *In July, after the U.S. landings at Rendova* ... SBS (Pacific), Military Analysis Division, Interrogation of Toshikazu Ohmae, Interview 495, Maxwell Documents.

333   *Even worse than in the USN* ... John B. Lundstrom, *The First Team and the Guadalcanal Campaign: Naval Fighter Combat from August to November 1942* (Annapolis, 1994), pp. 452–457; R. J. Overy, *The Air War, 1939–1945* (Chelsea, Mich., 1981), p. 143; David C. Evans and Mark Peattie, *Kaigun: Strategy, Tactics, and Technology in the Imperial Japanese Navy, 1887–1941* (Annapolis, 1997), pp. 325–328; Philip C. Purdom, *Readings in Growth and Development of Aerospace Power.* Vol. 1. (Maxwell Air Force Base, 1970), pp. 105–115; and Wesley Craven and James Cate, eds., *The Army Air Forces in World War II.* Vol. 1, *Plans and Early Operations, January 1939 to August 1942* (Chicago, 1958), pp. 104–115.

339   *"However laboring under great pressure and in the fog of war* ... " SBS (Pacific), *The Air Campaigns of the Pacific War* (Washington, D.C., 1947), p. 63.

345   *"Nothing worse can happen to a unit* ... " James Morehead, *In My Sights: The Memoir of a P-40 Ace* (Novato, Calif., 1998), pp. 65–66.

346   *"I think that as long as we were winning* ... " SBS (Pacific), Interview 479, Maxwell Documents.

347   *"Prior to the beginning of 1943* ... " Henry Sakaida, *The Siege of Rabaul* (St. Paul, 1996), pp. 11–13.

347   *"The high losses were attributed* ... " SBS (Pacific), *Japanese Interrogations*, Vol. 2, Interview 116.

347   *In the words of Commander Nomura* ... Ibid.

349   *In May 1943 the surgeon* ... Mae Mills Link and Hubert A. Coleman, *Medical Support of the Army Air Forces in World War II.* Washington, D.C., 1955, pp. 855–856.

373   *As 5th USAAF fighter pilot Perry Dahl recalled* ... Dahl Interview, Maxwell Documents, p. 636.

Part Three

p. 415 *Those interested in pinning down the terminology should refer . . .* Rene Francillon, *Japanese Aircraft of the Pacific War* (Annapolis, 1994); Ikuhiko Hata and Yasuho Izawa, *Japanese Naval Aces and Fighter Units in World War II* (Annapolis, 1989).

418 *Recognizing correctly that Allied air efforts . . .* Douglas Gillison, *Australia in the War of 1939–1945: Air.* Vol. 1, *Royal Australian Air Force, 1939–1942* (Canberra, 1962), pp. 573–575.

426 *The results of the operation . . .* United States Strategic Bombing Survey (Pacific), Military Analysis Division (Washington, D.C., 1946), Interview 495, Maxwell Documents; and Donald Goldstein and Katherine V. Dillon, eds., *Fading Victory: The Diary of Admiral Matome Ugaki, 1941–1945* (Pittsburgh, 1991), pp. 324–331.

426 *The necessity of gutting carrier formations . . .* SBS (Pacific), Military Analysis Division, Interrogation of Toshikazu Ohmae, Interview 495, Maxwell Documents; and Hata and Izawa, *Japanese Naval Aces,* pp. 61–63.

428 *Authors John Lundstrom and Richard Frank . . .* Richard B. Frank, *Guadalcanal* (New York, 1990), pp. 609–611; and John B. Lundstrom, *The First Team and the Guadalcanal Campaign: Naval Fighter Combat from August to November 1942* (Annapolis, 1994), pp. 528, 591.

428 *Interestingly Captain H. Komoto . . .* SBS (Pacific), *Japanese Interrogations,* Vol. 2 (Washington, D.C., 1946), Interview 71.

428 *According to Vice Admiral Jinichi Kusaka . . .* SBS (Pacific), *The Allied Campaign Against Rabaul* (Washington, D.C., 1946), p. 50.

429 *Figures abound from the Allied side . . .* Richard B. Frank, *Guadalcanal* (New York, 1990), p. 611.

429 *In the classic . . .* Robert Sherrod, *History of Marine Corps Aviation in World War II* (Baltimore, 1987), p. 430.

430 *According to Miller . . .* Thomas Miller, *The Cactus Air Force* (New York, 1969), pp. 211–224.

430 *The problem of operational losses obviously afflicted . . .* XIII Fighter Command, "Combat Crew Losses, 1 July–31 October 1943," and XIII Fighter Command, "Planes Reported Lost, 1 June–1 October 1943," Maxwell Documents.

430 *As for U.S. forces the danger of accident was higher . . .* George Odgers, *Australia in the War of 1939–1945: Air.* Vol. 2, *Air War Against Japan, 1943–1945* (Canberra, 1957), pp. 7–10.

430 *U.S. figures amplify . . .* Fifth Air Force Headquarters, "5th Air Force, Order of Battle," undated, Maxwell Documents.

431 *A smaller sample fills out the picture . . .* S. W. Ferguson and William Pascalis, *Protect and Avenge: The 49th Fighter Group in World War II* (Atglen, Pa., 1996), pp. 350–352.

432 *In late 1944 a large body . . .* Francis Dean, ed., *Report of Joint Fighter Conference, NAS Patuxent River, MD, 16–23 Oct. 1944* (Atglen, Pa., 1998), pp. 309–312.

432 *In the mid-1970s . . .* Hata and Izawa, *Japanese Naval Aces,* pp. 404–425.

436 *One pilot trained in P-38s was shocked . . .* John Stanaway, *Peter Three Eight: The Pilots' Story* (Missoula, Mont., 1991), p. 9.

436   *Fifth Air Force and the RAAF* ... Odgers, Vol. 2, *Air War Against Japan*, p. 9.

436   *A study done on Fifth Air Force* ... SBS (Pacific), *The Fifth Air Force in the War Against Japan* (Washington, D.C., 1947), p. 11.

438   *The principal beneficiary* ... Ibid., pp. 12–15; and Steve Birdsall, *Flying Buccaneers: The Illustrated Story of Kenney's Fifth Air Force* (Garden City, N.Y., 1977), pp. 78–82.

439   *Kenney naturally wanted more* ... Birdsall, *Flying Buccaneers*, pp. 78–82; see also SBS (Pacific), *Fifth Air Force*.

440   *After the war U.S. records* ... SBS (Pacific), *Campaign Against Rabaul*, pp. 22–24.

443   *Therefore the Japanese 4th Air Army* ... SBS (Pacific), *Japanese Interrogations*, Vol. 2, Interview 94.

Chapter 6

p. 450   *"Concerning the P-40 and Zero* ... " U.S. Army Air Forces, Intelligence Service, "Flight Characteristics of the Japanese Zero Fighter" (December 1942), Maxwell Documents.

451   *"It was in the spring of 1941* ... " John T. Maston, ed., *The Pacific War Remembered: An Oral History Collection* (Annapolis, 1986), pp. 94–95.

452   *"The squadron consists of four flights* ... " Edward T. Maloney, ed., *Fighter Tactics of the Aces, SWPA* (Corona del Mar, Calif., 1978), p. 88.

453   *"The main reason we beat* ... " Ibid., p. 78.

455   *In a classic Thach weave* ... Maston, ed., *Pacific War Remembered*, p. 96.

459   *"My first contacts with the enemy* ... " Maloney, ed., *Fighter Tactics*, p. 9.

460   *"Lt. Shuler stated that the quality* ... " 18th Fighter Group Headquarters, "After Action Report" (August 6, 1943), Maxwell Documents.

461   *"In my judgment the Japanese lost* ... " United States Air Force Historical Research Center, Oral History Collection. Perry Dahl, recorded 1978. Maxwell Documents, p. 12.

462   *"We needed a long range high altitude fighter* ... " United States Strategic Bombing Survey (Pacific), Military Analysis Division, Interrogation of Kunio Iwashita, Interview 496, Maxwell Documents.

467   *The totals I arrived at* ... USAF Headquarters, Office of Air Force History, *USAF Credits for the Destruction of Enemy Aircraft, World War II*, USAF Historical Study No. 85 (Maxwell Air Force Base, 1978), passim; and Frank J. Olynyk, *USMC Credits for the Destruction of Enemy Aircraft in Air-to-Air Combat in World War II* (published by author, 1982), passim.

473   *"Never try to assume the offensive* ... " Maloney, ed., *Fighter Tactics*, p. 60.

478   *"I like the squadron to drop* ... " Ibid., p. 86.

478   *"When we get over target* ... " Ibid., p. 78.

479   *"The Japanese did a lot of acrobatic stuff* ... " Dahl Interview, Maxwell Documents, p. 18.

484   *"On deflection shots* ... " Maloney, ed., *Fighter Tactics*, p. 85.

490   *"Head for the main body of the enemy* ... " Ibid., p. 81.

491   *"I tripped my gun switch* ... " Charles H. Lindbergh, *Autobiography of Values* (New York, 1978), pp. 212–213.

496   *"The Zeros came in to our right . . . "* NACI ComSoPac, "Air Battle Notes from the South Pacific No. 18" (1943), Maxwell Documents.

499   *"At 1700 [hours] we received a radar contact . . . "* NACI ComSoPac, "Air Battle Notes from the South Pacific No. 20" (1943), Maxwell Documents.

503   *"Major J. L. Smith . . . "* NACI ComSoPac, "Air Battle Notes from the South Pacific No. 2" (1943), Maxwell Documents.

504   *"Radar contacted enemy flight . . . "* Ibid.

505   *"First the operator devotes less attention . . . "* Robert Shaw, *Fighter Combat: Tactics and Maneuver* (Annapolis, 1985), p. 237.

507   *"The Jap fighter planes . . . "* Maloney, ed., *Fighter Tactics*, pp. 34–35.

516   *"On reaching about three thousand feet . . . "* Bryan Cox, *Too Young to Die* (Ames, Iowa, 1989), pp. 51–53.

518   *"On July 14th at 1330 our eight Wildcats . . . "* NACI ComSoPac, "Air Battle Notes from the South Pacific No. 23" (1943), Maxwell Documents.

522   *"We always respected the Japanese . . . "* United States Air Force Oral History Program, "Interview of Major General Richard H. Carmichael" (Maxwell Air Force Base, November 1980).

523   *"Pilots generally had parachutes . . . "* SBS (Pacific), Military Analysis Division, Interrogation of Masatake Okumiya, Interview 329, Maxwell Documents.

525   *"I saw two Zeros chasing a New Zealand P-40 . . . "* NACI ComSoPac, "Air Battle Notes from the South Pacific No. 18" (1943), Maxwell Documents.

526   *"Lt. Shuler made a pass on another Zeke . . . "* 18th Fighter Group, Headquarters "After Action Report" (August 6, 1943), Maxwell Documents.

527   *"There were many pilots I knew . . . "* Edwards Park, *Nanette* (New York 1977), pp. 30–31.

Chapter 7

p. 534   *I will confine my description to bombs . . .* Department of the Army, *Ballistic Data Performance of Ammunition*, Technical Manual TM9–1907 (Washington, D.C., 1948), passim.

552   *"The 19th was a problem . . . "* United States Air Force Oral History Program, "Interview of Major General Richard H. Carmichael" (Maxwell Air Force Base, November 1980).

553   *"Sun, the great Chinese strategist . . . "* Masatake Okumiya and Jiro Horikoshi with Martin Caidin, *Zero: The Inside Story of Japan's Air War in the Pacific* (New York, 1961), pp. 158–159.

553   *"The four-engine B-17 and B-24 bombers . . . "* Ibid., p. 165.

559   *Richard Frank, who studied . . .* Richard B. Frank, *Guadalcanal* (New York, 1990), p. 610.

568   *We can get an idea of the power of U.S. . . .* United States Strategic Bombing Survey (Pacific), *Interrogations of Japanese Officials*, Vol. 2 (Washington, D.C., 1946), Interview 97.

588   *"Hell yes there were exaggerated claims . . . "* USAF Oral History Program, Carmichael Interview.

592   *"The effectiveness of enemy air strength . . . "* Okumiya and Horikoshi, *Zero: The Inside Story*, pp. 158–159.

597 *Japanese losses of small ships . . .* Mark Parillo, *The Japanese Merchant Marine in World War II* (Annapolis, 1993), pp. 190–191.

597 *After the war Fifth Air Force . . .* SBS (Pacific), *The Allied Campaign Against Rabaul* (Washington, D.C., 1946), p. 31.

598 *"With the dawn the enemy . . . "* Douglas Gillison, *Australia in the War of 1939–1945: Air.* Vol. 1, *Royal Australian Air Force, 1939–1942* (Canberra, 1962), p. 676.

603 *"Tanks and heavy artillery . . . "* Wesley Craven and James Cate, eds., *The Army Air Forces in World War II.* Vol. 4, *The Pacific: Guadalcanal to Saipan, August 1942 to July 1944* (Chicago, 1950), p. 119.

608 *"Execution of air-support missions . . . "* Robert Sherrod, *History of Marine Corps Aviation in World War II* (Baltimore, 1987), pp. 150–151.

623 *"Pilots generally had parachutes . . . "* SBS (Pacific), Military Analysis Division, Interrogation of Masatake Okumiya, Interview 329, Maxwell Documents.

623 *In his later memoirs Okumiya . . .* Okumiya and Horikoshi, *Zero: The Inside Story*, p. 229.

624 *"So heavy were the Allied air attacks . . . "* Gillison, *Australia in the War of 1939–1945*, Vol. 1, p. 669.

629 *Fifth Air Force had good reason . . .* Edward J. Drea, *MacArthur's Ultra: Codebreaking and the War Against Japan, 1942–1945* (Lawrence, Kans., 1992), pp. 78–85.

633 *"In July or August of 1943 the bulk . . . "* SBS (Pacific), *Japanese Interrogations*, Vol. 2, Interview 98.

639 *"The continual air battles . . . "* Okumiya and Horikoshi, *Zero: The Inside Story*, p. 220.

640 *"By mid-October the enemy air raids . . . "* Ibid., p. 222.

640 *After the war American interrogators asked . . .* SBS (Pacific), *Japanese Interrogations*, Vol. 2, Interview 97.

649 *If Japanese accounts are at all accurate . . .* SBS (Pacific), *The Allied Campaign Against Rabaul* (Washington, D.C., 1946), pp. 90, 103.

650 *"B-24s were the most effective . . . "* SBS (Pacific), *Japanese Interrogations*, Vol. 1 (Washington, D.C., 1946), Interview 16.

651 *". . . the low-level attacks did not give them . . . "* SBS (Pacific), *Campaign Against Rabaul*, p. 58.

653 *"Now they . . . were quick tempered . . . "* Okumiya and Horikoshi, *Zero: The Inside Story*, p. 223.

654 *"The endless days and nights became a nightmare . . . "* Ibid., p. 225.

Conclusion

p. 664 *"The specific plan to counter . . . "* United States Strategic Bombing Survey (Pacific), *Interrogations of Japanese Officials*, Vol. 1 (Washington, D.C., 1946), Interview 38.

667 *Numbers concerning military losses are almost never precise . . .* SBS (Pacific), *Japanese Interrogations*, Vols. 1–2, Interviews 50 and 86.

671 *Allied airmen, outside carrier battles . . .* Mark Parillo, *The Japanese Merchant Marine in World War II* (Annapolis, 1993), p. 206.

SOURCES AND BIBLIOGRAPHY

This book is based primarily upon the contributions of American, Australian, and New Zealand veterans of the South Pacific air war. I interviewed most of the veterans personally. Others corresponded with me or sent audiotapes, letters, and other written material describing their experiences. Without exception the men involved were candid, self-effacing, and eloquent. Although these former fighting men were describing events that occurred more than a half-century ago, their memories were crystal-clear.

In the spring of 1994 I spent several weeks at the archives at Air University, Maxwell Air Force Base, while researching a previous book. While there I photocopied hundreds of after-action reports and other contemporary documents relating to different aspects of the air war, particularly for operations in the Solomons. They were invaluable sources in themselves and served to confirm the overall validity of retrospective accounts given by the participants. In the in-text notes I refer to these documents as the "Maxwell Documents."

I also relied heavily upon the official histories commissioned by the United States and Australia. The volumes published by the U.S. Army are among the most important books written about World War II. They are cautious and objective, and display excellent scholarship throughout. Although the combat volumes were important to my research, works concerning logistics, ordnance, and the medical effort proved invaluable. Australian official histories are likewise splendid sources; although somewhat partisan in approach, they are vigorous, elegant, and accurate. American scholars should make much more use of them than is the case. All of the official histories served to corroborate the essential accuracy of testimony given to me by individual veterans. Below I also list the secondary works that were most important to my research.

I relied heavily upon the *Strategic Bombing Survey—Pacific*, compiled in the two years after the war by the United States military. I approached this source with caution because it was marked by haste and the political atmosphere created by the negotiations surrounding the Armed Forces Reorganization Act, which undoubtedly colored many of the conclusions. Yet much of the information contained in the *SBS* is unique and of tremendous value. Overall the survey remains an indispensable source for serious study of the Pacific War.

Veterans of the South Pacific

Kirkwood Adams
Norman Avery
Tony Betchik
Ted Blahnik
John Bloomer
Lloyd Boren
Edward J. Brisck
Edward H. Brown
James W. Buchanan
Harold Buell
Carl Camp
Eugene Campbell
Phil Caputo
Fred Cassidy
Frank Chadwick
Marshall Chaney
Willis Connor
Richard Cowles
Robert Croft
Bill Crooks
Ted Crosby
Cecil Cuthbert
Robert DeHaven
Bud DeVere
Thomas Dutto
Ralph Easterling
Jim Eaton
James V. Edmundson
F. C. Emberton
Frank Emmi
Victor Falk
John W. Fields
Ernest Ford
Joe Foss
Clifford Fox
Benjamin Fridge
Thomas Furlow
James P. Gallagher
John Gallagher
David Galvan
William Garing
Jim Geyton
Burt Giancola
Robert Gibson
John Glaros
Donald Gordon
Roger Haberman
Frederick C. Hargesheimer

Dan Harper
John Herbert
Lindsey P. Henderson Jr.
Fred Hitchcock
C. L. Jones
J. W. Kennedy
Charles Kittell
Frank Komperda
James Kubiak
Robert Larsen
Ray Linke
David Lister
Harold Maul
James McDowell
Garrett Middlebrook
Fred Miller
James Morehead
John Mullady
Vince Murphy
William Norris
Chuck Novak
Leonard Owczarzak
Ian Page
Joel Paris
Edwards Park
James Peters
F. B. Phillips
John Plosila
A. Polous
Thomas Powell
Robert Raney
Howard Redmond
Al Rothenberg
Robert Rutherford
Earl Sandell
Jess Scott
Clifford Smith
LeRoy Smith
Ed Strobel
J.A.O. Stub
Dean Sybrandt
Lee Tipton
David Vaughter
Richard Walker
Robert White
Jack Williamson
Robert Wyllie

Official Histories

Anderson, Robert S., and Charles M. Wiltse. *Medical Department, United States Army: Medical Supply in World War II*. Washington, D.C.: Office of the Surgeon General, Department of the Army, 1968.

Coates, James Boyd, and James C. Beyer, eds. *Medical Department, United States Army: Wound Ballistics*. Washington, D.C.: Office of the Surgeon General, Department of the Army, 1962.

Craven, Wesley, and James Cate, eds. *The Army Air Forces in World War II*. Vol. 1, *Plans and Early Operations, January 1939 to August 1942*. Chicago: University of Chicago Press, 1958.

_____. *The Army Air Forces in World War II*. Vol. 4, *The Pacific: Guadalcanal to Saipan, August 1942 to July 1944*. Chicago: University of Chicago Press, 1950.

Dexter, David. *Australia in the War of 1939–1945: Army*. Vol. 6, *The New Guinea Offensives*. Canberra: Australian War Memorial, 1959.

Dod, Karl C. *The Corps of Engineers: The War Against Japan*. Washington, D.C.: Office of the Chief of Military History, 1966.

Gillison, Douglas. *Australia in the War of 1939–1945: Air*. Vol. 1, *Royal Australian Air Force, 1939–1942*. Canberra: Australian War Memorial, 1962.

Greenfield, Kent Roberts, ed. *Command Decisions*. Washington, D.C.: Office of the Chief of Military History, 1960.

Hough, Frank, Verle Ludwig, and Henry Shaw. *History of Marine Corps Operations in World War II*. Vol. 1, *Pearl Harbor and Guadalcanal*. Washington, D.C.: Historical Division, Headquarters, U.S. Marine Corps, 1966.

Leighton, Richard M., and Robert W. Coakley. *The War Department: Global Logistics and Strategy, 1940–1943*. Washington, D.C.: Office of the Chief of Military History, 1955.

Link, Mae Mills, and Hubert A. Coleman. *The Department of the Air Force: Medical Support of the Army Air Forces in World War II*. Washington, D.C.: Office of the Surgeon General, United States Air Force, 1955.

Matloff, Maurice, and Edwin M. Snell. *The War Department: Strategic Planning for Coalition Warfare, 1941–1942*. Washington, D.C.: Office of the Chief of Military History, 1953.

_____. *The War Department: Strategic Planning for Coalition Warfare, 1943–1944*. Washington, D.C.: Office of the Chief of Military History, 1959.

Mayo, Lida. *U.S. Army in World War II, The Technical Services: The Ordnance Department—On Beachhead and Battlefront*. Washington, D.C.: Office of the Chief of Military History, 1968.

McCarthy, Dudley. *Australia in the War of 1939–1945: Army*. Vol. 5, *South-West Pacific Area—First Year, Kokoda to Wau*. Canberra: Australian War Memorial, 1959.

Miller, John. *U.S. Army in World War II: Guadalcanal—The First Offensive*. Washington, D.C.: Office of the Chief of Military History, 1949.

_____. *U.S. Army in World War II: Cartwheel—The Reduction of Rabaul*. Washington, D.C.: Office of the Chief of Military History, 1959.

Milner, Samuel. *U.S. Army in World War II: Victory in Papua*. Washington, D.C.: Office of the Chief of Military History, 1957.

Morison, Samuel Eliot. *History of United States Naval Operations in World War II: Breaking the Bismarck Barrier*. Vol. 6. Boston: Little Brown, 1950.

_____. *History of United States Naval Operations in World War II: Coral Sea, Midway, and Submarine Actions, May 1942–August 1942.* Vol. 4. Boston: Little Brown, 1967.

_____. *History of United States Naval Operations in World War II: Rising Sun in the Pacific, 1931–April 1942.* Vol. 4. Boston: Little Brown, 1974.

_____. *History of United States Naval Operations in World War II: The Struggle for Guadalcanal, August 1942–February 1943.* Vol. 5. Boston: Little Brown, 1950.

Morton, Louis. *U.S. Army in World War II: Strategy and Command—The First Two Years.* Washington, D.C.: Office of the Chief of Military History, 1962.

Mullins, William S., and Albert J. Glass, eds. *Medical Department, United States Army: Neuropsychiatry in World War II.* Vol. 2, *Overseas Theaters.* Washington, D.C.: Office of the Surgeon General, Department of the Army, 1968.

Odgers, George. *Australia in the War of 1939–1945: Air.* Vol. 2, *Air War Against Japan, 1943–1945.* Canberra: Australian War Memorial, 1957.

Rowland, Buford, and William Boyd. *U.S. Navy Bureau of Ordnance in World War II.* Washington, D.C.: U.S. Goverment Printing Office, 1955.

_____. *Japanese Demobilization Bureau Records. Reports of General MacArthur.* Vol. 2, Part 1. Washington, D.C.: U.S. Government Printing Office, 1966.

United States Strategic Bombing Survey (Pacific). *The Campaigns of the Pacific War.* Washington, D.C.: U.S. Government Printing Office, 1946.

_____. *The Air Campaigns of the Pacific War.* Washington, D.C.: U.S. Government Printing Office, 1947.

_____. *The Allied Campaign Against Rabaul.* Washington, D.C.: U.S. Government Printing Office, 1946.

_____. *The Fifth Air Force in the War Against Japan.* Washington, D.C.: U.S. Government Printing Office, 1947.

_____. *Interrogations of Japanese Officials.* Vols. 1 and 2. Washington, D.C.: U.S. Government Printing Office, 1946.

_____. *Summary Report.* Washington, D.C.: U.S. Government Printing Office, 1946.

Wigmore, Lionel. *Australia in the War of 1939–1945: Army.* Vol. 4, *The Japanese Thrust.* Canberra: Australian War Memorial, 1957.

Secondary Works

Agawa, Hiroyuki. *The Reluctant Admiral: Yamamoto and the Imperial Navy.* Tokyo: Kodansha International, 1979.

Air University. *The Development of Air Doctrine in the Army Air Arm, 1917–1941.* Maxwell Air Force Base: Extension Course Institute, Air University, 1961.

Avery, Norman L. *B-25 Mitchell: The Magnificent Medium.* St. Paul: Phalanx, 1992.

Bergerud, Eric. *Touched with Fire: The Land War in the South Pacific.* New York: Viking Press, 1996.

Birdsall, Steve. *Flying Buccaneers: The Illustrated Story of Kenney's Fifth Air Force.* Garden City, N.Y.: Doubleday, 1977.

Blackburn, Tom. *The Jolly Rogers.* New York: Orion, 1989.

Block, Geoffrey D. M. *Allied Aircraft Versus Axis Aircraft.* Old Greenwich, Conn.: We Inc., 1945.

Bradley, John H. *The West Point Military History Series: The Second World War—Asia and the Pacific.* Wayne, N.J.: Avery Publishing Group, 1984.

Brown, David. *Warship Losses of World War II.* Annapolis, Md.: Naval Institute Press, 1995.

Buell, Harold. *Dauntless Helldivers.* New York: Dell Books, 1991.

Bueschel Richard. *Kawasaki Ki–61 Hein.* Atglen, Penn.: Schiffer, 1996.

_____. *Mitsubishi/Nakajima G3M1/2/3 Rikko.* Atglen, Penn.: Schiffer, 1997.

_____. *Nakajima Ki–43 Hayabusa.* Atglen, Penn.: Schiffer, 1995.

Coletta, Paolo E., ed. *United States Navy and Marine Corps Bases, Overseas.* Westport, Conn.: Greenwood, 1985.

Cox, Bryan. *Too Young to Die.* Ames: Iowa State University Press, 1989.

Dean, Francis H. *America's Hundred Thousand: U.S. Production Fighters of World War II.* Atglen, Pa.: Schiffer, 1997.

_____, ed. *Report of Joint Fighter Conference, NAS Patuxent River, MD, 16–23 Oct. 1944.* Atglen, Pa.: Schiffer, 1998.

Dowever, John W. *War Without Mercy: Race and Power in the Pacific War.* New York: Pantheon Books, 1986.

Drea, Edward J. *MacArthur's Ultra: Codebreaking and the War Against Japan, 1942–1945.* Lawrence: University of Kansas, 1992.

Dull, Paul S. *A Battle History of the Imperial Japanese Navy, 1941–1945.* Annapolis, Md.: Naval Institute Press, 1978.

Dyer, George. *The Amphibians Came to Conquer: The Story of Admiral Richmond Kelly Turner.* Quantico, Va.: U.S. Marine Corps, 1991.

Evans, David C., and Mark Peattie. *Kaigun: Strategy, Tactics, and Technology in the Imperial Japanese Navy, 1887–1941.* Annapolis, Md.: Naval Institute Press, 1997.

Ferguson, S. W., and William Pascalis. *Protect and Avenge: The 49th Fighter Group in World War II.* Atglen, Pa.: Schiffer, 1996.

Feuer, A. B., ed. *Coast Watching in the Solomon Islands.* New York: Praeger Publishers, 1992.

Foss, Joe, with Donna Foss. *A Proud American: The Autobiography of Joe Foss.* New York: Pocket Books, 1992.

Francillon, Rene. *Japanese Aircraft of the Pacific War.* Annapolis, Md.: Naval Institute Press, 1994.

Frank, Richard B. *Guadalcanal.* New York: Random House, 1990.

Futrell, Robert. *Ideas, Concepts, Doctrine: A History of Basic Thinking in the United States Air Force, 1907–1964.* Vol. 1. Maxwell Air Force Base: Air University, 1971.

Gallagher, James P. *Meatballs and Dead Birds.* Perry Hall, Md.: Jon-Jay Publishers, 1972.

Geyton, Boone T. *Whistling Death: The Test Pilot's Story of the F4U Corsair.* Atglen, Pa.: Schiffer, 1994.

Goldstein, Donald, and Katherine V. Dillon, eds. *Fading Victory: The Diary of Admiral Matome Ugaki, 1941–1945.* Pittsburgh: University of Pittsburgh Press, 1991.

Guadalcanal Campaign Veterans. *The Guadalcanal Legacy.* Paducah, Ky.: Turner, 1987.

Guadalcanal: 50th Anniversary. Paducah, Ky.: Turner, 1992.

Harries, Meririon, and Susie Harries. *Soldiers of the Sun: The Rise and Fall of the Imperial Japanese Army.* New York: Random House, 1991.

Hata, Ikuhiko, and Yasuho Izawa. *Japanese Naval Aces and Fighter Units in World War II.* Annapolis, Md.: Naval Institute Press, 1989.

Hayashi, Saburo, and Alvin D. Cox. *Kogun: The Japanese Army in the Pacific War.* Westport, Conn.: Greenwood, 1978.

Hess, William. *Pacific Sweep: The 5th and 13th Fighter Commands in World War II.* Garden City, N.Y.: Doubleday, 1974.

Horikoshi, Jiro. *Eagles of Mitsubishi: The Story of the Zero Fighter.* Seattle: University of Washington Press, 1981.

Horn, Alex. *Wings Over the Pacific: The RNZAF in the Pacific Air War.* Auckland: Random Century, 1992.

Kelsey, Benjamin. *The Dragon's Teeth? The Creation of United States Air Power for World War II.* Washington, D.C.: Smithsonian Institution Press, 1981.

Kenney, George C. *General Kenney Reports.* New York: Duell, Sloan, and Pearce, 1949.

_____. *The Saga of Pappy Gunn.* New York: Van Rees Press, 1959.

Langewiesche, Wolfgang. *Stick and Rudder: An Explanation of the Art of Flying.* New York: McGraw-Hill, 1972.

Lindbergh, Charles H. *Autobiography of Values.* New York: Harcourt Brace Jovanovich, 1978.

_____. *The Wartime Journals of Charles A. Lindbergh.* New York: Harcourt Brace Jovanovich, 1970.

Lindstrom, Lamont, and Geoffrey M. White. *Island Encounters: Black and White Memories of the Pacific War.* Washington, D.C.: Smithsonian Institution Press, 1990.

Lundstrom, John B. *The First Team: Pacific Naval Air Combat from Pearl Harbor to Midway.* Annapolis, Md.: Naval Institute Press, 1984.

_____. *The First Team and the Guadalcanal Campaign: Naval Fighter Combat from August to November 1942.* Annapolis, Md.: Naval Institute Press, 1994.

Maloney, Edward T., ed. *Fighter Tactics of the Aces, SWPA.* Corona del Mar, Calif.: World War II Publications, 1978.

Mandeles, Mark D. *Military Revolutions During Peacetime: Organizational Innovation and Emerging Weapons Technologies.* Alexandria, Va.: J. DeBloch Group, 1995.

Maston, John T., ed. *The Pacific War Remembered: An Oral History Collection.* Annapolis, Md.: Naval Institute Press, 1986.

Mayo, Lida. *Bloody Buna.* New York: Doubleday, 1974.

McAulay, Lex. *Into the Dragon's Jaws: The Fifth Air Force Over Rabaul.* Mesa, Ariz.: Champlin Fighter Museum Press, 1986.

McDowell, Ernst. *49th Fighter Group.* Carrollton, Tex.: Squadron/Signal Publications, 1989.

McEniry, John Howard, Jr. *A Marine Dive-Bomber Pilot at Guadalcanal.* Tuscaloosa: University of Albama Press, 1987.

Middlebrook, Garrett. *Air Combat at 20 Feet.* Published by author, 1989.

Mikesh, Robert. *Zero.* Osceloa, Wis.: Motorbooks International, 1994.

Miller, Ronald, and David Sawers. *The Technical Development of Modern Aviation.* New York: Praeger Publishers, 1970.

Miller, Thomas. *The Cactus Air Force.* New York: Harper and Row, 1969.

Moore, Stephen. *The Buzzard Brigade: Torpedo Squadron Ten at War.* Missoula, Mont.: Pictorial Histories Publishing, 1996.

Morehead, James. *In My Sights: The Memoir of a P-40 Ace.* Novato, Calif.: Presidio Press, 1998.

Okumiya, Masatake, and Jiro Horikoshi with Martin Caidin. *Zero: The Inside Story of Japan's Air War in the Pacific.* New York: Ballantine Books, 1961.

Olynyk, Frank J. *USMC Credits for the Destruction of Enemy Aircraft in Air-to-Air Combat in World War II.* Published by the author, 1982.

Overy, R. J. *The Air War, 1939–1945.* Chelsea, Mich.: Scarborough House, 1981.

Parillo, Mark. *The Japanese Merchant Marine in World War II.* Annapolis, Md.: Naval Institute Press, 1993.

Park, Edwards. *Nanette.* New York: Norton Publishing, 1977.

Perret, Geoffrey. *Old Soldiers Never Die: The Life of Douglas MacArthur.* Holbrook, Mass.: Adams Media Corporation, 1996.

_____. *Winged Victory: The Army Air Forces in World War II.* New York: Random House, 1993.

Prados, John. *Combined Fleet Decoded.* New York: Random House, 1995.

Purdom, Philip C. *Readings in Growth and Development of Aerospace Power.* Vol. 1. Maxwell Air Force Base: Air University, 1970.

Royal Australian Air Force, Air Power Studies Center. *The RAAF in the Southwest Pacific Area, 1942–1945.* Canberra: Air Power Studies Center, 1993.

Rust, Ken, and Dana Bell. *Thirteenth Air Force Story.* Terre Haute, Ind.: Sunshine House, 1989.

Sakai, Saburo, with Martin Caidin and Fred Saito. *Samurai!* New York: Ballantine Books, 1957.

Sakaida, Henry. *Imperial Japanese Navy Aces, 1937–1945.* London: Osprey Publishing, 1998.

_____. *Japanese Army Air Force Aces, 1937–1945.* London: Osprey Publishing, 1997.

_____. *Pacific Air Combat WWII: Voices from the Past.* St. Paul: Phalanx, 1993.

_____. *The Siege of Rabaul.* St. Paul: Phalanx, 1996.

_____. *Winged Samurai.* Mesa, Ariz.: Champlin Fighter Museum Press, 1985.

Shaw, Robert. *Fighter Combat: Tactics and Maneuver.* Annapolis, Md.: Naval Institute Press, 1985.

Sheehan, Susan. *A Missing Plane.* New York: G. P. Putnam's Sons, 1986.

Sherrod, Robert. *History of Marine Corps Aviation in World War II.* Baltimore: Nautical and Aviation Publishing, 1987.

Smith, Herschel. *Aircraft Piston Engines, from the Manly Balzer to the Continental Tiara.* Manhattan, Kans.: Sunflower University Press, 1994.

Spector, Ronald H. *The Eagle Against the Sun: The American War with Japan.* New York: Vintage Books, 1985.

Spick, Mike. *The Ace Factor: Air Combat and the Role of Situational Awareness.* Annapolis, Md.: Naval Institute Press, 1988.

Stanaway, John. *P-38 Lightning Aces of the Pacific and CBI.* London: Osprey Publishing, 1997.

_____. *Peter Three Eight: The Pilots' Story.* Missoula, Mont.: Pictorial Histories Publishing, 1991.

Tillman, Barrett. *Wildcat Aces of World War II.* London: Osprey Publishing, 1997.

_____. *U.S. Navy Fighter Squadrons in World War II.* North Branch, Minn.: Specialty Press Publishers, 1997.

U.S. Air Force Headquarters, Office of Air Force History. *USAF Credits for the Destruction of Enemy Aircraft, World War II.* USAF Historical Study No. 85. Maxwell Air Force Base: Air University, 1978.

U.S. Army Air Force. *Pilots' Information File, 1944.* Repr. Atglen, Pa.: Schiffer, 1995 (imprint of USAAF Form No. 24).

U.S. Department of the Army. *Ballistic Data Performance of Ammunition.* Technical Manual TM9–1907. Washington, D.C.: U.S. Government Printing Office, 1948.

U.S. War Department. *Handbook on Japanese Military Forces.* Repr., with an Introduction by David Isby. Novato, Calif.: Presidio Press, 1991 (imprint of *War Department Technical Manual TM-E 30–480,* orig. publ. Washington, D.C.: U.S. Government Printing Office, 1944).

Vander Meulen, Jacob. *The Politics of Aircraft: Building an American Military Industry.* Lawrence: University of Kansas Press, 1992.

Wells, Mark. *Courage and Air Warfare: The Allied Aircrew Experience in the Second World War.* London: Frank Cass, 1995.

White, Graham. *Allied Aircraft Piston Engines of World War II.* Warrendale, Pa.: Society of Automotive Engineers, 1995.

Willmott, H. P. *Empires in the Balance: Japanese and Allied Pacific Strategies to April 1942.* Annapolis, Md.: Naval Institute Press, 1982.

_____. *The Barrier and the Javelin: Japanese and Allied Pacific Strategies, February to June 1942.* Annapolis, Md.: Naval Institute Press, 1983.

Wilson, David. *The Decisive Factor: 75 and 76 Squadrons—Port Moresby and Milne Bay, 1942.* Melbourne: Banner Books, 1991.

Winton, John. *Ultra in the Pacific.* Annapolis, Md.: Naval Institute Press, 1993.

INDEX

A–20 Havoc, 236, 287–290, 353, 586, 589, 605
A–24, 295, 418, 587
Aces, 344, 509–511, 513–516. *See also specific pilots*
Adams, Kirkwood, 544–545, 604
Admiralty Islands, 655–656, 678
Advanced Carrier Training Group (ACTG), 331
AIF. *See* Australian Independent Force
Air bases, 19, 471–472
   accumulation of wreckage, 120–121
   Allied attacks on Japanese bases, 621–656
   Allied chain across South Pacific, 52–56
   carriers vs. land bases, 41–42, 87, 90–93
   construction of, 19–20, 54–55, 59–60, 665–666
   craters on runways, 538, 543
   difficulty of destroying, 621–622
   emergency airfields, 109–110
   ground accidents on Japanese bases, 104
   Japanese seizure of, 25–26, 33–40
   location of, 1–2, 8, 10–11
   vulnerability of, 6–8
   See also specific sites
The Air Campaigns of the Pacific War (Strategic Bombing Survey), 339–340
Aircraft, Allied, 227–308
   aircraft nose art, 365
   crew pride in, 373–374
   design of. *See* Aircraft design, Allied
   development of. *See* Aircraft development, Allied
   ditching technique, 107–109, 116–117
   export of aircraft, 237–238, 288, 296, 302
   ground accidents, 102–107, 115–116, 118–119. *See also* Operational losses
   losses of, 300, 344, 428–431, 649, 668–669
   shortage of, 336–337

   trainers vs. combat machines, 333–335
   use in smuggling liquor, 401
   See also Bombers, Allied; Fighters, Allied; *specific aircraft*
Aircraft, Japanese, 79–80, 219–225
   design of. *See* Aircraft design, Japanese
   development of. *See* Aircraft development, Japanese
   losses of, 142–143, 328–330, 668, 670
   See also Bombers, Japanese; Fighters, Japanese; *specific aircraft*
Aircraft design
   airframes, 171–176
   engine design and development, 157–159, 161–164, 169–170
   original and derivative designs, 178–182
   propeller and flap improvements, 176–177, 183
   variables involved in, 185–187
Aircraft design, Allied, 163, 165–178
   bombers, 274, 276–281, 285, 288–290, 293–294, 296, 302–303, 547–548
   and compressibility problem, 257–259, 266–267
   Davis wing, 276–277
   design considerations for carrier-based aircraft, 162, 195, 251–252, 255–256, 259–260
   emergency power, 477
   engine design, 162, 170
   fighters, 160–168, 178–184, 206, 240–242, 247–248, 251, 255–257, 262–263, 266–272, 304
   See also specific aircraft
Aircraft design, Japanese
   bombers, 213, 215, 218
   engine design, 162, 165, 168
   fighters, 162, 165, 168, 181, 199–201, 204–205, 208, 210–211, 219, 221
   and maneuverability, 475–477
   See also specific aircraft

703